**Third Edition**

# Nursery Management
## Administration and Culture

### Harold Davidson

*Professor of Horticulture, Emeritus*
*Michigan State University*
*East Lansing, Michigan*

### Roy Mecklenburg

*Manager*
*Walt Disney World Nursery*
*Lake Buena Vista, Florida*

### Curtis Peterson

*Associate Professor of Horticulture*
*Michigan State University*
*East Lansing, Michigan*

Prentice Hall Career & Technology
Englewood Cliffs, New Jersey 07632

*Library of Congress Cataloging-in-Publication Data*

Davidson, Harold [date]
  Nursery management.

  Bibliography: p.
  Includes index.
  1. Nurseries (Horticulture)—Management.
2. Nurseries (Horticulture)—United States—
Management.   I. Mecklenburg, Roy.   II. Peterson,
Curtis, [date]      III. Title.
SB118.5.D38   1988         635'.068         87-2238
ISBN 0-13-617572-4

Acquisition editor: Frank Burrows
Editorial/production supervision and
    interior design: Inkwell Publishing Services
Cover design: Marianne Frasco
Manufacturing buyer: Edward O'Dougherty

© 1994 by Prentice Hall Career & Technology
Prentice-Hall, Inc.
A Paramount Communications Company
Englewood Cliffs, New Jersey 07632

Printed in the United States of America

10   9   8   7   6   5   4   3   2   1

ISBN 0-13-617572-4

PRENTICE-HALL INTERNATIONAL (UK) LIMITED, *London*
PRENTICE-HALL OF AUSTRALIA PTY. LIMITED, *Sydney*
PRENTICE-HALL CANADA INC., *Toronto*
PRENTICE-HALL HISPANOAMERICANA, S.A., *Mexico*
PRENTICE-HALL OF INDIA PRIVATE LIMITED, *New Delhi*
PRENTICE-HALL OF JAPAN, INC., *Tokyo*
PRENTICE-HALL OF SOUTHEAST ASIA PTE. LTD., *Singapore*
EDITORA PRENTICE-HALL DO BRASIL, LTDA., *Rio de Janeiro*

# Contents

## 8 WHOLESALE MARKETING OF NURSERY CROPS    *146*

## 9 NURSERY INVENTORY CONTROL    *171*

## 10 SHIPPING OF NURSERY STOCK    *186*

### PART III: CULTURE

## 11 NURSERY CROP PRODUCTION    *204*

## 12 SOIL AND NUTRITION MANAGEMENT FOR FIELD-GROWN PLANTS    *241*

## 13 MEDIA AND NUTRITION MANAGEMENT FOR CONTAINER-GROWN PLANTS    *284*

## 14 IRRIGATION OF NURSERY CROPS    *309*

## PART IV: APPENDIXES

# Preface

This book is intended as an introductory text for students and others interested either in starting or managing a plant production nursery. The stimulus for writing the book came from both students and professional nurserymen requesting guidance in various areas of nursery management. The text is divided into four areas: (1) an introduction, (2) administration, (3) culture, and (4) an appendix. The two introductory chapters, the history of the nursery industry and the current status of the industry, are included to acquaint the reader with (1) the development of the nursery industry in the United States and how it changed and will continue to change due to various forces, both internal and external to the industry. Some of the strongest forces of change have been, and will continue to be, economic, political, social, technical, and last but not least the weather; (2) the major centers of nursery production in the United States; and (3) the many types of organizations within the industry and the purpose for which they exist.

The two primary areas of the text are (1) administration and (2) culture. Within these areas the principles of business management and plant sci-ence as they pertain to nursery management have been interpreted by the authors as they viewed the state of the art in the mid-1990s. All topics have not been covered in detail, but hopefully they are presented in such a manner that the information will be useful to the reader. Where appropriate, additional readings have been suggested for those readers who may wish to pursue a subject in greater depth. The topics of plant propagation, garden center management, and landscape construction were deemed to be beyond the scope of this text. Readers are referred to Appendix A for references to these and related areas.

The fourth section of the book is the appendix. It contains lists of references, addresses of nursery organizations, nomographs, and other data that may be useful to a student of nursery management.

Since the nursery industry is very diversified, no single text can cover in detail all of the various aspects of the business. The information set forth in this text is intended to provide both general and specific information on topics related to nursery management which can be used in exercising sound management decisions. Young people would be well-advised to seek a period of "intelligent employment" within the industry prior to starting a nursery business. The production and marketing of quality plants are fascinating businesses, but both require considerable knowledge and skill if they are to be done productively and profitably.

Botanical names within the text conform to *Hortus Third*, which is an excellent dictionary of botanical nomenclature for nurserymen and others interested in the proper nomenclature for plants. The appendices contain various tables and nomographs that a nursery manager may find useful. Also included is a list of publications related to nursery management.

The authors solicit suggestions from both teachers and professional nurserymen as to how future editions can be improved in both content and manner of presentation.

## ACKNOWLEDGMENTS

The authors wish to acknowledge the many authors of the technical articles on which much of this text is based. Without published results of their research, the science information relative to nursery production would be limited. Their names, along with the journals of publication, are listed in the references following the appropriate chapters. We also wish to express our appreciation to the many nurserymen who have been our teachers and who have provided information that has proven useful in writing this text. Individuals and/or companies who provided illustrations and photographs are mentioned in the appropriate legends.

**Harold Davidson**
*East Lansing, Michigan*

**Roy Mecklenburg**
*Orlando, Florida*

**Curtis Peterson**
*East Lansing, Michigan*

Chapter **1**

# Brief History
# of the Nursery Industry

The American nursery industry undoubtedly began in Massachusetts Bay Colony, where the settlers grew young fruit trees as part of the general farm operation. As early as 1648, for example, according to a note in his journal, John Endicott traded 500 apple trees for 250 acres of land. Earlier, in a letter to Governor Winthrop in 1644, he stated:

> I humblie and heartilie thanck you for your last lettre of newes and for the trees you sent mee. . . . I haue not sent you any trees because I heard not from you, but I haue trees for you if you please to accept them whensoeuer you shall send. I thinck it is to late to sett or remoue. I could wish you to remoue in the latter end of the years your trees, and I pray you send mee what you want and I will supply what I can.

Since its early beginnings the industry has progressed steadily, although sometimes with difficulty. The short survey that follows comments on some of the historically important nurseries and nurserymen as well as modern ones (largely by regions) and discusses the major factors in the development of the industry. The chapter is summarized with a chronology of events from 1737 to

1992. For more details, the reader should consult the references and suggested readings at the end of the chapter.

## EARLY EASTERN NURSERIES

The first major commercial nursery established in the United States was the Prince Nursery, also known for many years as the Linnaean Botanic Garden, at Flushing, New York. In 1737 William Prince started by cultivating a few trees to landscape his property. His success led him to commercial production, and shortly thereafter he published a catalog listing several hundred varieties. From it were stocked nearly all of the grafted apple, cherry, and pear orchards of New York, New Jersey, Massachusetts, and Connecticut. His nursery became so outstanding for its diversity of species, particularly fruit, that in 1777, following the battle of Long Island, General Howe made it a British protectorate.

Prince Nursery continued for over a century and introduced many outstanding foreign plants to the New World. By 1827 it contained over 100 species of plants from Australia alone, including *Eucalyptus* and *Banksias*. The nursery also experimented with plant breeding and introduced a number of new selections. As a result, its catalogs during the first half of the nineteenth century were considered the best in the trade. But Prince Nursery did more than grow trees: it also trained nurserymen, including Patrick Barry, one of the founders of the famous Mount Hope Nursery.

Another early nursery was Thomas Young's on Long Island. In 1768 Young was cited by the New York Society for the Promotion of Arts for having the largest number of apple trees (over 27,000) in rows. Other well-known Long Island nurseries started prior to 1900 were James Bloodgood's (1790), Andre Parmenter's (1825), Parsons's (1838), and Hicks's (1853). Mr. Parmenter, the first practitioner of the art of landscape gardening in America, frequently visited other parts of the country to lay out gardens and pleasure grounds for gentlemen of that century. By the early 1800s nurseries flourished in New York City. Michael Flay, for example, an immigrant from England, operated nurseries at the corner of Broadway and 12th Street and in Harlem. He was noted for the introduction of several very fine camellia varieties.

With the opening of the Erie Canal in 1825 and the development of a large orchard industry in western New York, a large nursery center developed near Geneva. According to Hedrick, David Thomas was the pioneer nurseryman of western New York; by 1830 he had the most extensive collection of fruit trees west of the Hudson River. One of the first nurseries in this area was founded by Reynolds and Bateman in 1830; it consisted of 6 acres about 1 mile from the center of Rochester. In 1839 they sold it to George Ellwanger and Patrick Barry, who established the Mount Hope Nursery. It was destined to become the leading nursery of the country during the latter part of the nineteenth century.

Patrick Barry was born in Ireland, emigrated to the Untied States when he was 20 years old, and obtained a job at the Prince Nursery in Flushing. After a period of "intelligent employment," he took part of his wages in nursery stock, moved to Rochester, and established a partnership with Ellwanger. Following a visit to the nursery in 1893, George Nicholson, curator of the Royal Gardens at Kew, England, noted that the cultivation of fruit trees had reached "enormous proportions," with 400 of the 600 acres devoted to the production of fruit trees. The Mount Hope Nursery was the primary source of liners, cuttings, and scion wood for the development of many of the nurseries in the Midwest. Another famous nursery near Rochester was Asa Rowe's, the oldest and most extensive in that area in 1841 and the source of stock and scions for many of the nurseries that developed in the Michigan territory.

The first nursery in Dansville, New York, was started in 1855 by O. B. Maxwell. After he and his brother Joshua inspected the site they were convinced that the soil and climate were well adapted to growing nursery stock. They were correct; by the early 1890s, Dansville—with 1200 acres of nursery products—was on a par with the great nurseries of Geneva and Rochester. George A. Sweet, the largest grower, had 125 acres in nursery stock; he was followed by J. B. Morly and T. Kennedy & Sons, with 75 acres each.

By 1850 western New York had become the nursery center of the nation, and the number of large nurseries increased rapidly. By about 1865, besides the previously mentioned nurseries, there was the W. & T. Smith Company; T. C. Maxwell and Brothers of Geneva; A. M. Purdy of Palmyra, known the country over as a specialist in small fruit; the Maloney Brothers Nursery; and Jackson and Perkins of Newark.

Jackson and Perkins began in 1864 as market gardeners, specializing in small fruits. About 1879 they began growing a few roses and hardy ornamentals. By 1894 they were producing about 175,000 roses yearly, and by 1900 they were known not only for their roses but for their outstanding collection of clematis, peonies, and other hardy ornamental plants.

One of the finest nurseries in New England in the late 1700s and mid-1800s was John and William Kenrick's of Newton, Massachusetts. John began his horticultural work by planting peach pits. Although he was acquainted with the art of grafting, he was not acquainted with "inoculation" (budding) as a method of vegetative propagation. When he learned the art about 1794, he began a commercial fruit production nursery that became the leading business of its kind in New England. About 1797 he added ornamental trees, including the Lombardy poplar, the most salable ornamental tree in New England at that time. After John died, William continued the nursery until his own death in 1870. William also experimented in silk culture, growing thousands of mulberry trees for his silkworms.

Another outstanding New England orchardist-nurseryman was Robert Manning of Salem, Massachusetts. In 1823 he began collecting, propagating, and offering for sale fruit varieties that were hardy in New England. Through his contacts with leading horticulturists, he obtained the best varieties available from Europe. By the time of his death in 1842, he had a collection of some 2000 fruit varieties, the largest ever assembled by an American up to that time. At one of the annual exhibitions of the Massachusetts Horticultural Society, he exhibited over 160 kinds of pears.

C. M. Hovey's 36-acre nursery in Cambridge also grew a remarkable number of varieties; besides 100 varieties of forest and ornamental trees, he sold 600 varieties of pears, 200 of apples, 100 of plums, 100 of cherries, 75 of peaches, and 50 each of grapes and gooseberries, as well as varieties of currants, apricots, raspberries, and strawberries. Hovey was also the editor of *The Magazine of Horticulture* and author of *The Fruit Trees of America*, a beautifully illustrated book on native and exotic fruits. Other early nurseries of New England were Ephraim Goodale's of Arlington, Massachusetts, and Benjamin and Charles Vaughan's in Hallowell, Maine.

One of the first nurseries in New Jersey was begun about 1794 by William Coxe in partnership with Daniel Smith. Coxe was an outstanding pomologist and wrote the first book on pomology (fruit production) published (1817) in this country. He collected all the best varieties of fruits available in the United States and from many parts of Europe and was one of the first to successfully graft the better varieties of grape onto the more vigorous stocks.

John Bartram Jr. and his brother William established a nursery on the site of Bartram's Garden soon after their father's death in 1777. Their *Broadside On Stock*, published in 1783, is claimed to be the first nursery catalog published in the United States.

Philadelphia also had an extensive nursery area. Thomas Meehan & Sons was started in 1854 on 6 acres of land, and by 1908 there were 265 acres in production as well as good retail and landscape departments. Thomas Meehan popularized the planting of American trees so extensively that Nicholson refers to him as "the Nestor among American tree lovers and planters." By 1893 Meehan's nursery contained the largest collection of native American trees and shrubs to be found in any nursery in the world.

In 1897 the Conard and Jones Company of Pennsylvania pioneered the sale of seeds and plants by mail order. A few years later it became the Conard-Pyle Company, the producers of the famous "Star Roses." In 1920 Robert Pyle, who specialized in roses, introduced *Rosa hugonis* ("The Golden Rose of China") at the unheard of price of $5 per plant. Conard-Pyle is still the largest grower of roses in the eastern United States.

Bernard McMahon was another leading Pennsylvania horticulturist, with extensive plantings, nurseries, and greenhouses. McMahon received, propagated, and disseminated many of the plants collected by Lewis and Clarke on their expedition to the Northwest. The fine broad-leaved evergreen *Mahonia* now bears his name. Hoopes Brothers and Thomas, established in 1853 at West Chester, was also large, with 600 acres in production, and was widely known for its fine stock. Josiah Hoopes's *Book of Evergreens*, published in 1868, was a valuable contribution to the literature on conifers.

## EARLY MIDWESTERN NURSERIES

The famous nursery production area of Lake County, Ohio, had its initial impetus in 1853, when Jesse Storrs, a farmer-nurseryman from Cortland, New York, located on 80 acres of farm land near the village of Painsville. In 1858 Storrs offered a partnership to J. J. Harrison, a skilled propagator, because in his opinion there was not room for two nurseries in the county. By 1970, however, the county contained more than 200 nurseries, with a combined acreage of over 5000 acres. The excellent climate of Lake Erie, the wide variety of soils, and the strategic geographic location within a developing nation all contributed to Lake County's success as a major nursery center.

Storrs and Harrison soon became the largest nursery in the country—about 1400 acres. Most of the land was worked with mules, but these were gradually replaced with Percheron draft horses. The firm grew not only woody plants but also large quantities of tropical plants, greenhouse crops, and vegetable seeds. Facilities included modern greenhouses as well as storage and packing houses, one large enough to accommodate several railroad cars.

Another famous nursery of Lake County was owned and operated by Henry Kohankie. Kohankie had been foreman of the ornamental department of Storrs and Harrison Company for 15 years before starting his own nursery in 1900. The nursery developed a nationwide reputation for its wide selection of high-quality ornamental plants, and for a long time its catalog was considered the "bible" of ornamental plants by many landscape architects.

Bloomington, Illinois, also became an important nursery center, since five important railroads intersected there and the soil and climate were well suited to all types of plants. The Bloomington Nursery, later the Phoenix Nursery Company, started in 1852 by Franklin K. Phoenix, grew a general line of nursery stock, and at one time was the largest in the country. Its packing houses, cold-storage cellars, and other buildings covered more than 20 acres.

The foundation of the famous nursery industry of Missouri was laid following the War of 1812, when young James (Judge) Stark moved from his home in Bourbon County, Kentucky, to the wilderness on the west banks of the Mississippi River. He came on horseback carrying fruit tree scions in old-fashioned saddlebags. In 1816 he started a small nursery, destined to become Stark Bros. Nurseries and Orchard Company. The judge was a great believer in advertising and used it unsparingly to promote the sale of his stock.

The horse also brought the nursery industry to Shenandoah, Iowa, in 1869. D. S. Lake, an employee of a nursery at Prairie City, Illinois, traveled the Midwest on horseback selling osage orange, hedge plants, and forest tree seedlings. In 1869 he and his wife moved to the Iowa frontier and started a fruit tree nursery on a few acres of land. One hundred years later it covered some 3000 acres, with about one-third in nursery stock. Because of the fine climate and soil, Shenandoah soon became one of the major centers of the country. Its nurseries pioneered in the development of mechanized equipment for field operations, storage, packing, and shipping.

Many of the fine nurseries of Ohio, Michigan, Illinois, Missouri, Iowa, and other midwestern states that were established in the mid-1800s had direct or indirect contact with the nursery centers of New York. One of the first nurseries established in Michigan was that of Z. K. and E. D. Lay near Ypsilanti in 1833. From Asa Rowe's nursery near Rochester, New York, they brought 25,000 cultivated trees, mostly of one season's growth. One year later Timothy W. Dunham of Orleans County, New York, came to Michigan to establish a nursery and brought with him "a chest of drawers or shallow boxes filled with apple tree root grafts, about 3000 in number." Like the Lays, Dunham obtained most of his scions and plant material from Asa Rowe.

## EARLY WESTERN NURSERIES

The development of the nursery industry in Oregon began with a load of nursery stock that was transported by prairie schooner from Salem, Iowa, to Milwaukee, Oregon, in 1847. In the spring of that year Henderson Lewelling (Luelling), a nurseryman, planted about 700 small trees and shrubs in stout wagon boxes filled with a compost of soil and charcoal. In April he hitched his nursery wagon to three yoke of cattle and began the long trip to Oregon. The hazardous journey across the plains and over the Rocky Mountains took about 9 months, but the following year he joined William Meek and together they established the first orchard-nursery of grafted trees in the Northwest. Their trees, along with others obtained from the nurseries of Ellwanger and Barry and A. J. Downing, shipped via the Isthmus of Panama, formed the nucleus of the nursery-orchard industry of the Northwest. Roots from seedling apples, sprouts from wild cherry, and roots of the wild plum supplied the first understocks for grafting, and good nurseries developed rapidly. About 1850, for instance, George Settlemeir began a nursery at Oregon City, later moved it to Mt. Angel, and soon had the largest variety of fruit and ornamental trees in the Oregon territory. The nursery business expanded chiefly because of the demand for quality apples, which sold for $12–15 per bushel.

Undoubtedly the early beginning of the California nursery industry was started by Spanish missionaries. In 1769 the Franciscans left Mexico and headed north into what is now the state of California and there they established 21 missions supported by gardens and orchards. They brought with them the necessary seeds, stocks, and scions; they also brought figs, grapes, olives, and oranges. Unfortunately, according to Williamson, as a result of many unscrupulous, ignorant adventurers plunging into the production of fruit trees, the early California nurserymen (mid 1800s) were looked upon as little better than highwaymen. But once the ecological requirements of the newly introduced fruits were learned, the industry became stabilized.

The first commercial nursery of record in California was started by A. P. Smith of Sacramento in the early 1850s on land purchased from Captain John Sutter. By 1857 Smith had some 1200 roses of 200 varieties as well as many other plants. Like the nursery industry of the other states, the early California nurseries produced mainly fruit trees and grape vines to supply the heavy demands for these species.

## EARLY FLORIDA NURSERIES

In 1881, 18 year old Pliny Reasoner left his father's farm and extensive nursery in Princton, Illinois to settle in Oneco, Florida and pursued his fascination with tropical horticulture. In 1885, with his brother Egbert, he issued the first *Reasoner Brothers' Royal Palm Nursery* catalog. According to David Fairchild, Pliny was one of the first and greatest horticultural pioneers of Florida. Unfortunately, he died at the age of 25, of yellow fever. The Reasoner Brother's Nursery is the oldest continually operating nursery in Florida and is famous for the introduction of palms, pink grapefruit, loquat, mango, kumquat, avocado, lychee and many other species into Florida.

However, the earliest plantings of horticultural crops in America most likely accompanied the establishment of St. Augustine in 1565 when the Spanish introduced Mediterranean fruits (most notably, orange, pomegranate, and fig trees) to what would later become the state of Florida.

## EARLY INDUSTRY OBSERVATIONS

Most of the nurserymen of the late 1700s and the early 1800s were orchardists-nurserymen; that is, they produced fruit trees for their orchards and sold the excess. In later years nurserymen produced trees for sale and either planted or burned the excess. Initially, the primary method of propagation of fruit tree varieties was by grafting onto wild stocks; later, understocks obtained from France were used. Most of their trees were sold direct and delivered by oxcart, often over primitive roads or no roads at all. The large nurseries contained hundreds of acres—some over 1000—and catered to the wholesale trade and nursery agents.

The 1870s to the 1890s was the era of the itinerant nursery agents, many of whom were unscrupulous in their claims and careless about deliveries. Nevertheless, the results were not all evil. Traveling by horse and wagon, they sold nursery stock from farm to farm. They were responsible for the extensive plantings of elms and silver maples throughout the eastern and midwestern cities and for the familiar plantings of Norway spruce in the dooryards of most New York and midwestern farms.

Of course, not all nurserymen and agents were scalawags; most packed their goods carefully and labeled them accurately. Many nurserymen were held in high esteem, as the report of the orchard committee of the Michigan Pomological Society of 1873 testifies. When the committee evaluated the Ilgenfritz Nursery of Monroe in 1877, they stated that it had a "fine arrange-ment of packing houses and extensive cellars in which to heel-in stock. All the land upon which it is grown is thoroughly prepared and under-drained before planting is begun."

## LEGISLATION AND THE AUTOMOBILE AFFECTED DEVELOPMENT

For the nursery industry, 1912 was a significant year: the first national plant quarantine act was passed and parcel post went into effect. The Plant Quar-antine Act prohibited the importation of certain plants into the country; and Plant Quarantine No. 37, effective in 1919, created a favorable economic situa-tion for American nurserymen by severely restricting plant imports. In fact, American nurseries soon found it necessary to import skilled propagators from Europe.

Passage of the parcel post bill paved the way for various changes. First, it led to the rapid development of the mail-order business. Most of the major firms became established in the primary production areas, including: western New York; Lake County, Ohio; and Shenandoah, Iowa. This facet of the busi-ness, which relied heavily on the U.S. mail and on catalog, magazine, and news-paper advertising, prospered immediately. It is still a huge business, but when the "horseless carriage" arrived and as better roads were built and more people could afford automobiles, nurserymen also found it advantageous to develop retail outlets. Retail sales, in turn, led some of the more enterprising nurserymen to sell various types of soil amendments, garden tools and equip-ment, pesticides, garden ornaments, and outdoor furniture. This was the gene-sis of the modern garden center industry, which in 1972 accounted for more than $829 million in sales. California had the largest number of garden supply stores and recorded the greatest sales volume ($117 million); Pennsylvania, New York, Michigan, Texas, and Ohio each had sales in excess of $45 million.

## EARLY GARDEN CENTERS

Garden centers started by way of seed houses, sometimes accidentally. Some-time around 1784, David Landreth established the seed house of David Lan-dreth and Sons in Philadelphia. This was probably the first establishment of its kind in the United States. Another famous seed house was that of the Thorburns, for many years a center for horticultural interest in New York City. In 1801 its founder, Grant Thorburn, sold a rose geranium that he had placed in a pot on his grocery store counter to draw attention to the flowerpots he sold. From that insignificant beginning the establishment grew to a complete emporium of everything required in the practice of horticulture. A similar circumstance was responsible 150 years later for the formation of Frank's Nurseries of Detroit, which developed into one of the largest garden center, chain-store businesses in the country.

## CENSUS DATA ON NURSERIES

The first special census of nurseries, conducted in 1890, revealed that 4500 nurseries occupied about 173,000 acres of land and employed more than 45,000 men, 2000 women, and 14,000 animals. Two-thirds of the nurseries were small (2-25 acres) and produced a variety of materials for local demand. Another group produced either a general line of nursery stock or specialized in a few items, such as small fruit, and relied on newspaper advertising and catalogs for their orders. They delivered by mail, freight, or express. A third group, the large producers, catered to the wholesale trade by issuing trade catalogs to other nurserymen, to extensive planters, and to nursery agents. Some of these nurseries were 1000 acres or more, shipped in railroad-car lots, and in the busy season, by the trainload. A fourth group produced a general assortment of stock and sold through salesmen who canvassed from house to house and farm to farm selling millions of plants. Total nursery production in 1890 was estimated to be approximately 3.4 billion plants, primarily fruit trees and small fruit plants. Major production was centered in New York, California, Illinois, Ohio, and Pennsylvania.

In 1974 these five states were still the leaders in the production of nursery stock, according to the Census of Horticulture Specialties, but their rankings had changed. California had become the leading state, with wholesale production close to $130 million. The major production center developed in three southern California counties (Kern, Los Angeles, and Orange). In 1985 *Nursery Business* reported that California was still the leading state in the production and sale of nursery stock, with sales in excess of $435 million. It also reported that Florida was a close second with sales of $413 million. Texas, Pennsylvania, and Tennessee ranked third, fourth and fifth. New York, Oregon, New Jersey, Ohio, and Michigan ranked in the top ten nursery production states with combined sales equal to that of the two leading states. The magazine also reported total U.S. nursery production was $2.9 billion.

In 1992 *Nursery Business* reported U.S. nursery production at $5.2 billion and that the leading states were California, Florida, Virginia, and Oregon (Table 1–1). It should be noted that Virginia and Oregon have made considerable growth as major nursery production states.

**Table 1–1**  Major nursery production states, 1992 (states with sales in excess of $100 million)

| Rank | State | Production Millions of Dollars |
|------|-------|-------------------------------|
| 1 | California | 539 |
| 2 | Florida | 444 |
| 3 | Virginia | 400 |
| 4 | Oregon | 341 |
| 5 | Ohio | 328 |
| 6 | Michigan | 225 |
| 7 | New Jersey | 220 |
| 8 | North Carolina | 211 |
| 9 | Illinois | 207 |
| 10 | Connecticut | 180 |
| 11 | Pennsylvania | 163 |
| 12 | Georgia | 160 |
| 13 | Washington | 160 |
| 14 | Texas | 136 |
| 15 | Alabama | 125 |
| 16 | New York | 125 |
| 17 | Maryland | 115 |
| 18 | Tennessee | 102 |

U.S. Total in Billion $: $5,211

*Source:* 1992 Nursery Business Grower 100. This table is copyrighted material from *Nursery Business*, Brantwood Publications, Inc. No further reprinting is allowed.

## A CHANGING INDUSTRY

During the 1950s and 1960s, the total number of nurseries declined almost 50% in the 10 leading nursery states. Although the total acreage in nursery stock in seven of these states increased, three states, Florida, New York, and Texas, showed a decrease.

In addition to a change from fruit tree production to ornamental plant production (Table 1–2), the nursery industry of the United States has experienced major changes in its methods of production and transportation. Machines have gradually replaced animals and reduced the need for hand labor. The introduction of hydraulic power made possible the development of mechanical planters, tree diggers, lifting and load equipment, and high-speed packaging and potting machines.

Changes in digging and root pruning illustrate the dramatic effect of machines and hydraulic power. Earlier all plants were dug by hand, and little, if any, root pruning was done. Even with the development of the "U-blade," root pruning and digging of bare-root plants needed 6–14 teams of horses (Fig 1–1). The operation also required 6–18 people to drive the teams and operate the equipment. Beginning in the early 1900s, however, the steam engine gradually replaced horses. A large, 16-horsepower steam engine (Fig. 1–2) supplied the power for a double-barreled winch which pulled the cables

**Table 1–2**  Wholesale value of nursery products, by year (millions of dollars)

| Nursery Product | 1960 | 1970 | 1979 | 1987 |
|---|---|---|---|---|
| Ornamental plants | 125 | 233 | 760 | 957 |
| Deciduous fruit and nuts | 11 | 26 | 60 | 101 |
| Lining-out stock | 6 | 13 | 77 | NA |
| Citrus and subtropical | 7 | 6 | 20 | 16 |
| Small fruit plants | 4 | 6 | 20 | 18 |
| Foliage plants | NA | NA | NA | 449 |

*Source:* U.S. Census of Agriculture. 1959, 1969, 1979, 1988.

attached to the U-blade. Currently, the power to root prune or dig bare-root trees is supplied by a 100-horsepower twin-engine high-clearance tractor operated by one worker (Fig. 1–3). A hydraulic tree spade, also operated by one person, can dig and lift, in a matter of minutes, a 20- to 40-ft tree with a soil ball 5 ft in diameter.

The development of selective chemical weed control agents, improved pesticides, and slow- or controlled-release fertilizers also changed cultural practices significantly. But the most pronounced change in the industry was the large-scale production of container-grown plants. Although the system of

**Figure 1–1**  Root pruning shade trees in the nursery with the aid of horse power in the 1800s. (Courtesy Isaac Hicks & Son, Westbury Nurseries.)

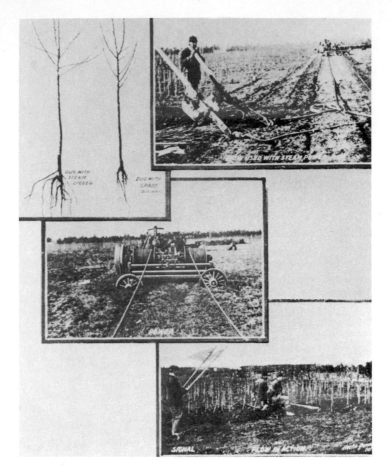

**Figure 1-2** Digging bare-root trees in a nursery with the aid of a
U-blade, double-barreled winch, and 16-hp steam engine. (From
1874 Catalog, Monroe Nursery.)

growing plants in containers was known for centuries, it was not adapted to
large-scale production of small plants until after World War II. California pioneered in its development, but it soon spread to the other parts of the nation.
The system allows nurserymen to grow, ship, and market their plants in the
same container. It lends itself to a high degree of automation and eliminates
the need to dig the crop just prior to sale.

The development of national highway systems in the mid-1950s and 1960s
brought about another major change in the shipping of nursery stock. Rapid
truck delivery permitted pick up at the site of production and delivery to the
point of sale or of planting in the landscape. This eliminated the double and
triple handling of plants shipped by railroad. Truck delivery has also contributed to greater specialization. Nurserymen now tend to produce only plants

**Figure 1-3** Digging bare-root trees in a nursery with the aid of a U-blade and high-clearance tractor. (Courtesy Bailey Nursery.)

that grow well in their area. They may specialize in shade trees, evergreens, shrubs or ground covers, or even in a limited selection of shade trees or evergreens. Nurserymen who formerly produced a wide assortment of species may concentrate on only a few species and buy the balance of their catalog needs from other sources. The relatively low cost of truck transportation and the savings from reduced handling have been responsible for this. On the other hand, a significant increase in trucking rates could change this situation.

Advances were also made in irrigation of nursery-grown plants. In the later part of the 1950s, drip irrigation was introduced into the nursery industry in the production of container-grown plants. In the 1960s fertilizer injection was introduced. Both had significant affects on the effective and efficient production of container-grown plants. In the mid-1970s trickle irrigation was introduced into field production of shade trees, which resulted in faster growth and more compact root systems.

The computer was introduced into the nursery industry in the late-1960s as an office machine to aid in the processing of orders by large nurseries. When the micro computer was developed, it was put to use in bookkeeping, word processing, inventory control, irrigation, lighting, ventilation, and temperature for more effective production of nursery-grown plants.

## SUMMARY

Some of the more significant events and developments in the brief history of the nursery industry of the United States are summarized in the following chronology.

**Chronology of Nursery Industry of the United States**

| | |
|---|---|
| 1737 | Establishment of the first commercial nursery (Prince Nursery of Flushing, N.Y.) in the United States. |
| 1847 | The "Nursery Wagon" transported container-growing plants from Iowa to Oregon. |
| 1869 | Gypsy moth brought into the United States from Europe. This voracious pest was confined primarily to the New England states. |
| 1870 | San Jose scale accidentally introduced into this country from China on ornamental plants (via San Jose, California). This serious pest was widely distributed throughout the country in the late 1800s by interstate shipment of infested nursery stock. |
| 1870 | The first large tree-moving equipment developed by the Hicks Nursery on Long Island. |
| 1873–74 | A severe freeze throughout the Midwest caused the loss of thousands of plants and the failure of many nurseries. |
| 1875 | American Association of Nurserymen founded (incorporated 1921). |
| 1881 | California law passed to prevent distribution of the grape gall louse. |
| 1890–91 | A blizzard killed millions of trees in nurseries and orchards throughout the country, causing serious financial loss to many nurserymen. |
| 1891 | *The Nursery Book* by Liberty Hyde Bailey was published. |
| 1893 | Publication of the *National Nurseryman*, a trade journal for the nursery industry. |
| 1896 | Maryland legislature passed the first law providing that all nursery stock being shipped into that state must be accompanied by a certificate, issued by an authorized official, stating that the stock was duly inspected and found to be free from indications of the presence of dangerously injurious insects and plant diseases (San Jose scale, peach yellows, rosette). Many other states soon followed this example and passed similar laws. |
| 1896–98 | A serious overproduction of nursery stock lowered prices; many nursery firms were forced out of business. |
| 1898 | Introduction of the white pine blister rust into New England. This disease was probably introduced on plants imported from Europe. |
| 1898–99 | A serious drought in the California area caused the loss of many plants, forcing a number of nurseries out of business. |
| 1904 | Discovery of chestnut blight on the grounds of the New York Zoological Park. This disease, which caused the demise of the American chestnut, was apparently introduced on plant material imported from China. |
| 1912 | Passage of the Plant Quarantine Act of 1912, the first federal plant quarantine designed to provide the necessary federal legislation to protect against the entry of dangerous insects and diseases on plants or plant products imported from foreign countries. |
| 1912 | Passage of the Parcel Post Act, which spawned the development of many mail-order nurseries. |
| 1916 | The Japanese beetle found in New Jersey was probably introduced by the importation of plants from Japan. *(continued)* |

**Chronology of Nursery Industry of the United States** *(continued)*

| | |
|---|---|
| 1919 | Plant Quarantine No. 37 enacted into law. |
| 1920 | Photoperiodism recognized as an important factor in the control of growth and flowering of certain plants. |
| 1929 | The Dutch elm disease discovered in Cleveland, Ohio. This disease and its vector were most likely introduced into the United States on elm logs imported from Europe. |
| 1930 | Passage of the Plant Patent Law. |
| 1934 | Auxins, such as indoleacetic acid, recognized as having considerable practical value in stimulating the rooting of cuttings. |
| 1936 | DDT recognized as an insecticide of major importance in the control of insects. |
| 1944 | 2,4-D first used as a selective herbicide in the removal of broadleaved weeds from lawns and for the control of selected weeds in nurseries. |
| 1946 | Development of garden center industry following World War II revolutionized the marketing of nursery stock. |
| 1949 | Container production of nursery stock developed on a large scale. |
| 1949 | Introduction of the first patented ornamental tree, "Moraine" honey locust (Plant Patent 836). |
| 1956 | Passage of Interstate and National Defense Highway Act, which led to rapid truck transport of nursery products. |
| 1956 | Introduction of hydraulic tree diggers revolutionized digging plants in nurseries. |
| 1957 | Polyethylene film used to modify environment about nursery plants. |
| 1959 | Drip irrigation used for container-grown nursery plants. |
| 1960 | Fertilizer injection introduced into the nursery industry. |
| 1965 | Federal Highway Beautification Act was enacted. |
| 1970 | Plant Variety Protection Act enacted. |
| 1975 | Trickle irrigation introduced to field production of nursery stock. |
| 1975 | Photoperiod and light intensity used to control juvenile growth of woody plants. |
| 1983 | Perennial Plant Association founded and incorporated. |
| 1983–85 | Disastrous freeze and citrus virus causes destruction of citrus groves and nursery plantings in Florida and other southern states. |
| 1984 | Root-control bags become commercially available to the nursery industry. |
| 1988 | The Garden Council established. |
| 1989 | Bar Codes started to be used by the nursery industry for retail pricing of plants. |

# REFERENCES

Anonymous. 1908. A group of pioneer nurserymen and pomologists. Natl. Nurseryman 16(6):200–203.

———. 1908. The nurseries of Pennsylvania. Natl. Nurseryman 16(6):187.

———. 1908. The Storrs and Harrison Company. Natl. Nurseryman 16(11):361–364.

Bailey, L. H. 1895. A century of American horticulture. Florist Exchange 7(17):387–394.

Barry,W. C. 1894. The nursery industry of the East. Natl. Nurseryman 2(6):70.

Coates, L. 1908. The nursery business in California. Natl. Nurseryman 16:337.

Duruz, W. P. 1941. Notes on the early history of horticulture in Oregon with special reference to fruit tree nurseries. Agric. Hist. 15(2):84–97.

Fairbanks, G. R. 1971. The History and Antiquities of the City of St. Augustine, Florida, U. of Florida Press.

Greening, C. E. 1902. Evaluation of the nursery business. Michigan State Horticultural Society, E. Lansing, Mich., p. 91.

Hale, J. H. 1891. Nurseries. Bulletin of the 11th census. Michigan State Horticultural Society, E. Lansing, Mich., pp. 470–474.

Horticultural Research Institute. 1968. Scope of the nursery industry. HRI. Washington, D.C.

Hume, H. H. 1904. Citrus Fruits and Their Culture, the H. & Drew Company, Jacksonville, Fla.

Lewis, C. E. 1953. Hicks nurseries celebrate centennial. Am. Nurseryman 98(2):20.

Manning, R. 1880. Sketch of the history of horticulture in the U.S. up to the year 1829. History of the Massachusetts Horticultural Society, 1829–1878.

Morey, R. W., and W. A. Gammel, Sr. 1984. Who are America's largest growers? Nursery Business 29(9):32–60.

———. J. Morey, and C. Morey. 1985. Nursery business 1985 Grower 100. Nursery Business 30(12):37, 39–42.

Potter, C. H. H. 1965. Lewelling's legacy—the Oregon nursery trade. Am. Nurseryman 122(2):9.

Pinardi, N. S. 1980. The Plant Pioneers, The Story of The Reasoner Family, Rainbow Press, Torrington, Conn.

Thomas, J. J. 1873. Horticulture for the people. Michigan Pomological Society, E. Lansing, Mich., pp. 489–491.

Thompson, B. F. 1843. The history of Long Island. Gould, Banks & Co., New York, Vol 2, pp. 83–87, 239.

U.S. Bureau of Census. 1967. Census of agriculture. Government Printing Office, Washington, D.C.

Williamson, R. 1893. Nursery business on the Pacific Coast. Natl. Nurseryman 1(8):95.

Wood, J. 1900. Pioneer nurserymen. Natl. Nurseryman 8(3):27.

## SUGGESTED READING

Davidson, H. 1972. History of the Michigan Nursery Industry, MAN Yearbook. Michigan Association of Nurserymen, E. Lansing, Mich., pp. I–XII.

———and D. A. Snell. 1971. Growth and development of the garden center industry in the U.S. HortScience 6(1):12–15.

Douglas, G., et al. 1947. The History of the Southern Nurserymen's Association. Southern Nurserymen's Association, Nashville, Tenn.

Fairchild, D. 1945. The World Was MY Garden. Charles Scribner's Sons, N.Y.

HEDRICK, U. P. 1950. A History of Horticulture in America. Oxford University Press, Inc., New York.

HIGGINBOTHAM, J. A. 1990. Four Centuries of Planting and Progress (A history of the U.S. nursery industry) Am. Nurseryman 171(12). Special historical issue.

HUNZIKER, H. 1984. 60 Years as a Landscape Nurseryman. Am. Nurseryman 159(8): pp. 29–76.

VAN LAAN, G. J. 1982. A Penny a Tree—the History of the Nursery Industry of California from 1850–1976. California Association of Nurserymen, Sacramento, Calif.

# Chapter **2**
# The Nursery Industry

The nursery industry of the United States has grown from its embryonic beginning on Long Island in 1737 to a multimillion-dollar, nationwide complex of businesses today. It is composed of many interrelated parts, including nurseries that produce plants, landscape firms that use plants and related materials to develop attractive and functional landscapes, garden centers that sell plant materials and garden-related items, plus maintenance firms that specialize in maintaining plants and landscaped areas.

## NURSERY CLASSIFICATION

A plant nursery is a place where hardy trees, shrubs, ground covers, vines, and herbaceous plants are propagated and grown. Nurseries in the United States are very diversified and may be classified and described according to four major criteria: (1) ownership, (2) function, (3) production system, and (4) type of plant material produced (Table 2–1).

**Table 2–1** Classification of nurseries

| | |
|---|---|
| I. Ownership | IV. Product |
|   A. Private industry |   A. General, diversified, catalog; |
|     1. Proprietorship |     offering many types of hardy |
|     2. Partnership |     plants |
|     3. Corporation |   B. Specialty, limited catalog; |
|   B. Government agencies |     specialty in one major class, |
|     1. County |     but may offer some species |
|     2. City |     from several subclasses |
|     3. State |     1. Fruit |
|     4. Federal |       a. General |
|   C. Educational institutions |       b. Tree fruits, including |
|     1. Arboretia |       nuts |
|     2. Botanical gardens |       c. Small fruits |
|     3. Universities |     2. Ornamental |
| II. Function |       a. General |
|   A. Production |       b. Shade and flowering |
|     1. Wholesale |       trees |
|     2. Retail |       c. Evergreens |
|     3. Nonprofit |         (1) Narrow-leaved |
|   B. Mail-order |         (2) Broad-leaved |
|   C. Landscape |       d. Shrubs |
|   D. Horticultural distribution centers |       e. Roses |
|     (also known as |       f. Ground covers and vines |
|     rewholesale nurseries) |       g. Herbaceous perennials |
|   E. Quarantine |       h. Indoor plants (house |
|   F. Research |       plants) |
| III. Production system |     3. Forest and conservation |
|   A. Field production |       a. Reforestation |
|     1. Bare-root |       b. Wildlife habitat |
|     2. Soil-balled |       c. Erosion control |
|     3. Pot-pot | |
|   B. Container production |     4. Liner plants |
|     1. Above ground |       a. Budded plants |
|     2. Below ground |       b. Grafted plants |
| |       c. Rooted cuttings |
| |       d. Seedlings |
| |       e. Rootstocks |
| |       f. Tissue culture |

## Ownership

Nurseries are owned and operated either by private industry or by various governmental agencies and educational institutions. Within the private sector they may be either a proprietorship, a partnership, or a corporation. The advantages and disadvantages of these legal forms are discussed in Chapter 3. Government agencies operate nurseries to supply part or all of their plant material needs, to furnish planting stock for various reforestation and conservation programs, and for quarantine purposes. Educational institutions operate nurseries to support their many and diverse programs in research, teaching, extension, and to landscape their campuses.

### Function

*Production nurseries* propagate and produce plants for a variety of purposes, including fruit production, environmental quality improvement programs, conservation projects, and research and educational programs. Production nurseries may be either profit- or nonprofit-oriented. Those that are profit-oriented are in the private sector of the industry; the nonprofit production nurseries are operated by various governmental agencies and educational institutions. Those that are profit-oriented can be subclassified as either retail or wholesale production.

*Retail production nurseries* are generally small in size, commonly 50 acres or less, and sell their production directly to the ultimate user, in most cases homeowners.

*Wholesale production nurseries* are primarily large establishments that sell their plants in wholesale units to industry-related buyers (e.g., landscape contractors, garden centers). Wholesale production nurseries may specialize in a particular type of plant material and locate in areas where climate and soil are most favorable for production. In 1975 there were over 5000 wholesale nurseries in the United States, with combined sales in excess of $900 million.

*Mail-order nurseries* deliver the products that they merchandise via the U.S. mail, the United Parcel Service, or by bus. Their contact with customers is primarily through catalogs and literature sent directly to the customer, or advertisements placed with one or more of the mass communication media. Most of the material is herbaceous perennials, small fruit, or small trees and shrubs. Potted material is grown and shipped in a lightweight medium to reduce shipping costs.

*Landscape nurseries* design and construct attractive and functional landscapes utilizing the resources available within the organization. Modern landscape firms are staffed with designers that produce the landscape plans, growers that produce the plant material, and construction specialists who carry out the plans. Landscape nurseries produce woody ornamental plants that are larger than those available from most wholesale production nurseries. However, they seldom produce all their plant material needs and usually supplement their production by purchasing smaller, readily available material from other nurseries. Some landscape nurseries subcontract parts of a landscape project to other firms. For example, it is common to subcontract lawn work to a lawn specialist, and large pools, patios, and sundecks to a building contractor. In some states a builder's license is required to do this type of construction, especially if the construction is attached to a building.

A *horticultural distribution center* (HDC) is a nursery whose primary function is to locate, purchase, and assemble in a convenient location landscape plants which, in turn, are resold to landscape nurserymen or contractors. The HDC takes title to the plant material and either holds it in a sales yard or grows it in a nursery to enhance quality prior to sale. The center may also stock for resale various items associated with planting (e.g., peat moss, tree wrap, mulch, etc.).

*Quarantine nurseries* are, as the name implies, nurseries where plants are held during a period of quarantine. They are operated by federal or state agencies charged with the responsibility of administering federal and state laws related to importation of plants.

### Production System

On the basis of production systems, nurseries may be classified as either field production or container production. Field production nurseries (Fig. 2–1) may be subclassified by the method used in digging and processing their plants; they may be either bare-root or soil-balled. Plants that are dug bare-root have the soil removed from their roots as they are harvested, whereas soil-balled plants are dug with a soil ball about their roots, which is then contained in some manner. The most common method used to contain soil-balled plants is to secure the soil ball with burlap, known in the industry as balled and burlapped (B&B). Other methods include boxing, potting, and basketing. Boxing is used for large plants, dug with large soil balls, shaped as an inverted, truncated pyramid, which is then contained with specially designed wood forms. Potting is used on small plants which are dug and lifted out of the ground with a soil ball and placed into pots. Basketing is a technique that has developed to containerize soil balls of plants that are dug with various types of tree diggers (Fig. 2–2).

**Figure 2-1** Field production of evergreens.

**Figure 2-2** Digging B&B trees in a nursery with the aid of a hydraulic digging machine. Note the wire basket lined with burlap. (Courtesy Farley Bros. Nursery.)

Growing plants in containers has been practiced for centuries, but container production of plants in the nursery is a relatively modern practice (Fig. 2-3). Since the early 1950s it has evolved into a highly scientific and successful method of nursery production. It is an excellent example of nurserymen and scientists working together in solving problems and developing a highly effective and efficient system of growing and marketing plants in containers (Table 2-2).

In the early development of container production of plants, nurserymen used tin cans, tar-paper pots, or standard clay pots as the container, and the plants were grown above ground in an area fitted for handling plants in containers. The growing medium was whatever field soil was readily available. Fertilizer and irrigation system practices were adapted from field culture. Since container production, as a large commercial venture, began in the warmer parts of the country, there were few problems with overwintering of plants. But as the practice was adopted by nurserymen in the colder parts of the country, overwintering of plants in containers became a problem that had to be solved if the practice was to be successful for northern nurseries.

**Figure 2-3** Container-grown evergreens in a production nursery. (Courtesy Monrovia Nursery Co.)

Since the 1950s major changes have been effected in the container production of plants. The containers are no longer the rusted food cans of the early years, but are designed and manufactured especially for the nursery industry. Metal containers are crimped so that they nest for shipping and storage, and are dipped in a rustproof paint so that they last for 2 or more years and make an attractive market container. Plastic containers may be obtained that serve various needs, including thin wall for inexpensive short-term crops and thick wall for long-term crops and for stacking during transport (see Fig. 2–4).

Various types and sizes of wood-fiber containers are also available. They are best used either for potting field-grown plants that will be shipped

**Table 2–2** Advantages and challenges of producing and marketing plants in containers

*Production Advantages*

1. More uniform plants. This is a result of providing optimum conditions for growth of the plants (e.g., medium, nutrition, water, light, spacing).
2. Provides a method of producing plants that are difficult to transplant.
3. Greater numbers of plants produced per unit area. Avoids need of land in rotation (cover crops) and reduces loss of plants due to cultivator injury.
4. Permits use of areas normally not usable for field production.
5. Avoids the digging operation.
6. Improves cash flow. Invested capital has a faster turnover rate.
7. Greater potential for mechanization of materials handling (e.g., potting {Fig. 2–4}, pickup, and delivery to and from production site).

*Production Challenges*

1. Total dependence upon artificial irrigation (offset by greater control of moisture levels).
2. Root development is limited by the size and shape of the container.
3. Need for repotting of plants if they are not used on schedule (potential for container-bound roots).
4. Need for winter protection.
5. Greater need to supplement and monitor levels of chemical supplements.
6. Need to leach medium periodically (to avoid excess soluble salts).
7. Need for good water drainage. On some sites it is necessary to develop wastewater disposal systems.
8. Relatively high-cost production system (offset with improved cash flow).

*Marketing Advantages*

1. Reduces transportation costs, due to lightweight medium.
2. Extends marketing season (both wholesale and retail).
3. Extends planting season.
4. Convenient prepackaged cash-and-carry item.
5. Relatively easy to maintain (water and fertilize) in sales area; no need to mulch or heel-in.
6. Better display of plants.
7. Less handling damage. Workers tend to carry plants in pots by the container rather than by their tops.

*Marketing Challenges*

1. Medium has a tendency to dry out faster, requiring greater attention to watering.
2. Plants in unsightly containers are unattractive to customers.
3. Container-bound roots, if present, limit growth and life expectancy of plants in landscape sites.
4. Overcome landscape establishment problems with container-grown plants. (This is often related to culture in growing and planting.)

and then marketed within a few weeks or for plants that will be produced and marketed the same growing season by retail production nurseries. Fiber pots are structurally weak and should not be stacked when shipping the potted plants. Also, when they become wet they deteriorate. This can be either an advantage or disadvantage, depending upon the situation. In retail produc-

**Figure 2-4** Potting machine aids in planting container-grown nursery stock. (Courtesy Cottage Gardens Nursery.)

tion it may be an advantage in that the exposed roots, which grow through the walls of the container, can be used as an indication of a good vigorous root system. These plants must be carefully handled and planted without too much delay following purchase by retail customers. However, in wholesale production rapid deterioration of containers is undesirable, since it necessitates repotting, which is an added cost of production. Other types of containers used in nursery production include tar-paper pots, wood or wire baskets, thin-walled polyethylene bags, and polyethylene-lined baskets, pots, or boxes. Since the mid-1970s nurserymen have been using square pots in an attempt to minimize the development of circling root systems, common with round pots. Also, polyethylene bags are gaining in popularity for the production of small plants, especially liners. The root system that develops in the poly bag is more fibrous, due to root-tip pruning, caused by the folds at the bottom of the bag. However, larger plants grown in poly bags do not ship as well over long distances.

The growing medium is blended to specifications. By using various ingredients, nurserymen can obtain a medium that meets their particular production and market requirements. Soil fertility regimes are carefully planned and monitored to optimize growth and quality. Various types of slow-release and soluble fertilizers have been developed to aid in maintaining fertility levels at optimum. Irrigation practices are specifically designed for the effective and efficient use of water and water-soluble fertilizers. And container-grown plants can be overwintered in northern climates with a high probability of success if certain practices are followed relative to avoiding desiccation of the foliage, cold-temperature injury of the roots, and girdling damage by rodents.

Since the early 1980s a new system of growing plants in containers has been developed in an attempt to overcome the problems of winter injury to roots, and the poor success of growing trees in containers above ground. One system, developed in Minnesota, consists of an outer watertight container buried to its top in the ground. Drainage holes are drilled into the side of the container 2–3 in. from the bottom, creating a water reservoir for water pruning of the roots. Coarse gravel is put into the bottom of the container and covered with a fiberglass mat or other type of filter. An inexpensive sleeve is inserted into the outer container and a tree is planted into a porous growing medium. After one or two growing seasons, a well-developed, easy-to-transplant tree is produced.

A second below-ground system, developed in Oklahoma, utilizes 6-oz sur-pac-filter fabric bags. The developing roots grow through the fabric but are partially girdled, which induces root initiation, resulting in the development of a more fibrous root ball. The trees are easy to transplant any time when the ground is free of frost.

### Product

Nurseries can also be classified and described on the basis of the types of plant material that they produce. Historically, the early nurseries of the nation produced fruit plants for the developing nation. Gradually, they included plants for landscaping, and as the need developed they produced seedlings of forest tree species for the forest industries and plants with special characteristics for conservation purposes and erosion control. When a nursery produces species from two or more of the foregoing categories, it is best classified as a general nursery, producing a catalog of diversified hardy plants. With the development of the railroads and especially with the advent of rapid truck transportation, large wholesale nurseries began to specialize in one or a limited number of species. Some wholesale production nurseries grow only one type of plant material, such as: shade trees, evergreens, shrubs, roses, or herbaceous perennials. Some specialize in one or two genera (e.g., *Rhododendrons* or *Taxus* and *Tsuga*). Other nurseries specialize in the production of seedlings for reforestation, conservation, and Christmas tree plantations. There are also nurseries that specialize in propagating materials for other nurseries. Their production may include dwarf rootstocks, grafted plants, rooted cuttings, seedlings, or shade-tree whips. These firms are mostly located in the major nursery production areas or on sites that provide a major climatic advantage.

## ALLIED AREAS

Within the industry there are a number of businesses that are closely allied to nursery production. They do not produce but buy, sell, and distribute plant material or provide a closely related service.

*Landscape contractors* perform the major construction operations associated with the development of large landscapes. Typical projects include shopping malls, industry-headquarters sites, industrial parks, golf courses, amusement parks, and so on. Landscape contractors purchase almost all of their plant material from nurseries that specialize in the production of large landscape plants. Arrangements for purchase and delivery of plants are often made through a nursery broker.

*Nursery brokers* are independent sales agents whose primary function is to arrange purchase-sales agreements between members of the nursery industry. They help to locate plants for the buyers and sell the products of the producers. Brokers may also arrange shipping and transportation schedules. They do not take title to the plant material but are paid a commission on sales booked with each nursery that they represent.

The *horticultural broker or distributor* is the primary supplier of the hard goods for the nursery industry. They purchase and stock for resale all types of tools, equipment, and supplies for the horticultural industries. Good horticultural brokers specialize in service to their customers by having the needed materials and supplying them when and where they are needed in the proper quantities.

The *modern garden center* is the outgrowth on the small retail nursery sales lot or fruit stand of the pre-World War II years. It is not only a retail center for plants, but it is the place where people come to purchase all their gardening supplies. Garden centers vary considerably in size, quality, and services offered. The larger, chain-operated garden centers are primarily self-service. Many operate on a low margin of profit based on a fast turnover and do a large volume of business, whereas the smaller, generally family-operated garden centers provide many special services, operate on a higher percentage markup, but do a lower volume of business. However, there are many variations between the two groups.

Sometimes the price of plants in a large garden center may be higher than those in smaller garden centers. And some fairly large garden centers offer special services to their customers. The marketing system varies with the philosophy of management and the level of competition in the market area. Most garden centers have found it necessary and profitable to broaden their product mix. Large investments in buildings, high rents for prime locations, and other high overhead costs make it necessary for garden center managers to be alert to various means of assuring sales during all months of the year, rather than being satisfied with only two peak sales periods, spring and fall, as was the situation in past years. Handicrafts, home decorations, garden furniture, pet supplies, and Christmas decorations are examples of items used to improve the cash flow at garden centers when plant sales are slow.

*Mass merchandisers and discount stores* that mass market all types of products, (including, but not limited to, groceries, clothing, furniture, hardware, and building supplies) have also a nursery department for the sale of trees, shrubs, fertilizers, bedding plants, and related items. Most of these establishments operate their "nursery or garden center" during the late winter and early spring, while others operate their plant centers through most of the gardening season. This group of merchants accounts for a large share of the market in the sale of landscape plants to the home-owner market.

*Landscape management firms*, as the name implies, specialize in maintaining the landscape plantings for individuals and businesses. Tree maintenance, as performed by the arborist, is a very specialized branch of the landscape management business. The arborist is responsible for all types of specialized activities associated with large trees, including moving, pruning, and repairing damaged trees; bracing, spraying, and fertilizing living trees; plus the removal of dead or dying trees. Specialized training is needed to perform the functions of the arborist.

Although most home lawns and landscapes are maintained by homeowners, some are maintained by professional maintenance firms; in some parts of the country there are franchised lawn-maintenance firms. Industrial and institutional landscape maintenance has become a relatively large business since the mid-1950s. There are also firms that rent and maintain plants for use in interior landscapes, including offices, malls, and public buildings.

### Combination of Functions

Within the industry can be found many combinations of the foregoing groups or classifications. Some nurseries, for example, may produce plants by both field and container culture. Also, some businesses may be made up of two or more divisions. Many mail-order nurseries commonly operate garden centers. Some large nursery businesses operate a wholesale production nursery specializing in ornamental plants, a garden center, a landscape construction department, and a landscape management department. In another situation the business may start as a small retail nursery and gradually develop over a period of years into a large wholesale production nursery with one or more allied businesses. At first it may be a proprietorship, which then becomes a partnership and finally a corporation. As a corporation it may be involved in producing evergreen seedlings for Christmas tree plantations and reforestation, ornamental evergreens and shade trees for landscape purposes (the latter produced by both field and container culture), and operating a garden center. Since the early 1980s a few of the larger corporations in the industry have also incorporated an environmental care division into their overall structure. These firms provide full service, including nursery production, landscape design, landscape construction, garden-center sales, and environmental care. The environmental care division can maintain the grounds of a small home or the property of a large industrial or university complex.

## TRADE ORGANIZATIONS*

Trade organizations that serve the nursery industry are primarily oriented about the functional aspect of the business and to some degree about the type of plant material produced. But most of the trade organizations are organized on a geographic basis.

The *American Association of Nurserymen* (AAN) was first organized in 1875 as the National Association of Nurserymen, Florists, and Seedsmen. By 1883 the seedsmen and florists had organized their own trade association. Thus, the name was changed in 1884 to the American Association of Nurserymen and was incorporated as a nonprofit corporation in 1921. The AAN is active in many types of programs, including education, promotion, and legislation that enhance the efficient and economic progress of the nursery industry. They publish a nursery trade and supply directory, special AAN summaries on topics of current interest, and a quarterly magazine, *ALI*, with in-depth articles of concern to nurserymen.

The annual meeting of the AAN held in July is a forum for the discussion of industry problems and the dissemination of information. At the first meeting four topics were discussed: costs and inequities of freight rates, grades for nursery stock, statistics on the annual production, and condition of crops and postal rates. These topics have held priority in many meetings since and will undoubtedly have high priority at future meetings.

The AAN staff in Washington, D.C., provide the management and administrative staff for each of the next five trade organizations. They are the umbrella under which these organizations are united for economy of force and unity of purpose. The AAN also offers an opportunity to its members to subscribe to a group accident insurance program and to the Dodson Savings Classification Plan for workers' compensation insurance. The AAN also publishes a wide variety of publications and audiovisuals on topics related to nursery and garden center management.

The *Horticultural Research Institute* (HRI) was organized in 1962 by a group of progressive nurserymen as a nonprofit, tax-exempt organization to plan and support research for the nursery industry. Working together with colleges/universities, governments, independent researchers, and industry firms, HRI brings research, management, and marketing data to the industry. To increase funding, the HRI Endowment Fund was created in 1975. Membership dues and contributions support the work of HRI, whose members have access

* See Appendix B for addresses.

to research findings published in the quarterly *Journal of Environmental Horticulture* and the *New Horizons* newsletter, and other technical publications.

The *National Landscape Association* (NLA) was founded in 1939 as the National Landscape Nurserymen's Association to promote better landscaping and to provide a means for the exchange of ideas and knowledge related to the profession. The association supports the publication of literature relative to landscape beautification and sponsors management clinics. In 1967 NLA came under the umbrella of the AAN for administration and promotion. Membership in NLA is open to nursery firms that do landscape work and are members of the American Association of Nurserymen.

The *Wholesale Nursery Growers of America, Inc.* (WNGA) was organized in 1964 with the major purpose of providing a forum for the exchange of ideas and information relative to the production of nursery products. The WNGA has developed a useful crop reporting system and has stimulated interest in and aided HRI in the conduct of a business analysis of the nursery industry. They are active in seeking scientific answers to problems of production and postharvest physiology of nursery crops. A quarterly newsletter contains information on technological advancements in growing and production, general business news pertaining to wholesale nurserymen, trend reports, and the latest developments in mechanization and transportation. Their meetings coincide with the annual summer meeting of the AAN and the midwinter meeting in Chicago. Membership is open to nurserymen engaged in the production of nursery stock at the wholesale level.

The *American Association of Nurserymen's Group Insurance Trust* is one of the oldest and most successful group insurance programs in existence. It is designed to provide life insurance and hospitalization with major medical insurance for the owners and full-time employees of AAN member firms. Members may select between two excellent life and health insurance plans, both featuring $100,000 major medical, double-life insurance option, and supplemental benefits to Medicare. It is composed of over 300 nursery firms and is managed by nurserymen trustees.

*Garden Centers of America* is the trade association for the garden center industry. It was organized in 1973 and operates under the AAN umbrella. It is management-oriented to give the nation's garden center retailers the management information they need to operate a profitable business. They publish a timely newsletter and conduct an annual management clinic.

## SPECIALIZED ASSOCIATIONS

The *International Plant Propagator's Society* (IPPS) was organized in 1951 to secure recognition for the plant propagator as a craftsman and to provide a forum for the dissemination of knowledge in this field. The society is divided into the eastern, western, and southern regions in North America, each division sponsoring an annual meeting. In addition, there is a region of Great Britain and Ireland, an Australian region, and a New Zealand chapter. The combined proceedings are published by the society, which also publishes *The Plant Propagator*, a quarterly magazine available to members only.

*Mail-Order Association of Nurserymen, Inc.* was founded in 1934 to promote the general interests of mail-order nurserymen by providing a forum for discussion of matters pertaining to the business. The association meets twice a year, in the summer with the AAN and in the winter at the Mid-America Trade Show.

*All-American Rose Selections* (AARS) was organized in 1938 in an attempt to bring some order out of the confusion that existed in the yearly introduction of roses. Prior to its inception, literally hundreds of inferior varieties of roses were introduced each year. Through its program of variety trials in selected test gardens, AARS has succeeded in establishing in the minds of home gardeners a high degree of confidence in its seal of quality. In 1976 All-American award winners comprised over 40% of all roses sold in the United States annually. This is a real tribute to All-American roses, since the award winners comprise less than 1% of the more than 8000 known named varieties of roses. The rose industry of the United States sells in excess of 40 million plants annually. AARS is a nonprofit organization whose sole function is to test new rose selections and to give recognition to those of merit in the form of an All-American award.

*Landscape Material Information Service* (LMIS), incorporated in January 1954 as a self-supporting, nonprofit association, was organized to act as a clearinghouse for the collection, evaluation, and dissemination of information pertinent to the interests of arborists, horticulturists, landscape contractors, nurserymen, various public agencies, and suppliers of landscape materials.

Members receive an updated plant materials availability list twice a year, a biweekly bulletin announcing contracted and planned landscape projects, and advice on the procurement of scarce plant material or other landscape supplies. Membership is centered primarily in the northeastern states.

The *Associated Landscape Contractors of America* (ALCA) was incorporated in 1961 as a nonprofit corporation (business league) to provide cohesion and coordination among industry members and to enhance the image of landscape contracting as a profession. The association publishes the monthly "ALCA Action Letter."

The *International Society of Arboriculture* was organized as the International Shade Tree Conference in 1924 (name was changed in 1975) to promote and improve the planting and preservation of trees and to assist in the beautification of the countryside. Its publications include *The Journal of Arboriculture*, the monthly *Arborists News*, and special publications and films issued on an irregular basis.

The *National Arborists Association*, founded in 1938, is an organization of commercial people engaged in arboriculture. It is interested in the business aspects of tree services and good public relations programs.

The *Nurserymen's Protective Association* provides credit information on other nurserymen (wholesale, construction, and retail) to its members.

*National Association of Plant Patent Owners* is a private trade organization whose members own one or more plant patents. The objective of the association is to keep its members informed on the rules and regulations of the Patent Office pertaining to filing for and the granting of plant patents. Its constant legislative arm is a vital force in protecting the plant patent system.

### Garden Council

The Lawn and Garden Industry established a unified marketing program in 1988 that was designed for broad consumer appeal, allowing all segments of the industry to tie into an advertising program that would increase consumer interest in gardening. The council provides merchandising programs including gardening information and camera-ready art for all seasons and all regions of the country. In addition the council sponsors national multi-media advertising including radio, television, and gardens-oriented magazines. Contact The Garden Council for full details. (See appendix C.)

The *Perennial Plant Association*, founded and incorporated in 1983, is a nonprofit organization dedicated to improving the perennial industry. Its objectives are to:

1. coordinate the interest in perennials (primarily herbaceous) into a closer relationship of mutual helpfulness to members through symposiums, conferences and correspondence,

2. educate and disseminate information on the use and care of perennials,

3. advance and promote research

4. encourage the development of curricula related to perennials

5. evaluate standards of the perennial industry.

## STATE, REGIONAL, AND LOCAL ORGANIZATIONS

In addition to the many national associations, most states have nurserymen's associations which embrace growers, contractors, landscape maintenance personnel, and garden center operators. The state associations promote and support legislation that affects the nursery industries within each state. They also conduct, in cooperation with state university extension services, educational meetings and demonstrations. Some of the larger state associations employ an executive secretary and publish a trade paper and buyer's guide.

In a few places, nurserymen within a geographic area have formed associations, either formal or informal, for the purpose of conducting seminars, sponsoring garden shows and trade shows, and supporting field demonstrations. These groups may be within the metropolitan area of a city (e.g., the Metropolitan Detroit Landscape Association), an area of the state (e.g., Long Island Nurserymen's Association), or they may involve a number of states (e.g., Southern Nurserymen's Association, a consortium of state nurserymen's associations in the South for the purpose of conducting a joint summer meeting at Atlanta, Georgia).

## CENTERS OF PRODUCTION

The centers of nursery production in the United States have changed with the development of the nation and have tended to follow the westward migration. For many years Geneva, New York, was the primary center of production. But this gradually shifted to Lake County, Ohio, which became known as the nursery capital of the country in the late 1800s and in the early twentieth century. However, other areas were gradually developing: central Illinois; Shenandoah, Iowa; and Tyler, Texas. By the mid-twentieth century, the primary center of nursery production in the United States was in southern California.

However, by 1992 Florida with total sales of $444 million was a close second to California with total sales of $539 million, Virginia was third with sales of $400 million and in fourth and fifth place was Oregon and Ohio with sales in excess of $300 million. For a current update on the leading nursery production states, plus a list of the 100 leading wholesale growers, consult the trade publication, *Nursery Business.*

### California

If one word could characterize the nursery industry of a state, "awesome" would do it for California. The growing and selling of container-grown plants has become a science with California nurserymen aided with expertise from the universities. California nurseries pioneered container-production of plants with the development and improvement of soilless media, drip irrigation, and recycling of excess water. In 1987 California lead the nation in the production of plants in containers and was the leader in the production and sale of broadleaved evergreens, fruit and nut trees, ground cover plants, roses, and citrus.

### Florida

The nursery industry of Florida is located in three distinct areas of the state as a result of its peninsular topography and its associated climatic zones. The lower-east coast nurseries (located in Dade, Broward, and Palm Beach counties) produce most of the tropical and subtropical materials used in Florida's beautiful landscapes. The central region produces the hardier sub-tropical material, citrus, and foliage plants used for indoor landscapes. Apopka, located in the center of the state, is known as the "Foliage Capital of the Nation." In the northern region, particularly in Baker County, camellias and azaleas are produced as well as many of the hardier ornamental plants associated with the gracious landscapes of the south. Although the state plant board lists some 4000 certified nurseries, most of the state's $444 million in the sale of nursery products was produced by less than 25% of the nurseries, and most of the production was container-grown foliage plants. Florida leads the nation in the production of foliage and citrus plants.

### Virginia

Virginia has experienced a very rapid flush of growth as a nursery production state; it bounded from 16th in rank in 1991 to number 3 rank in 1992 in the rankings of productions state by *Nursery Business* magazine. Production is centered primarily in the Piedmont area of the state and is mostly container-grown ornamental plants. The state produces large quantities of broad-leaved evergreens, such as azaleas, holly, laurel, and Rhododendrons along with a great variety of other ornamental species.

### Oregon

The state of Oregon has grown rapidly into one of the leading nursery production centers of the country. In the 1992 *Nursery Business* report it ranked fourth in the nation with sales in excess of $341 million. A number of large western and midwestern nurseries have established nursery farms in Oregon due to favorable climate and availability of water. It is gaining very rapidly as a major producer of container-grown plants and has been and continues to be the leader in the production of shade tree whips.

### Ohio

The nursery center of the nation, prior to 1960, was considered by many to be Lake County, Ohio. In 1854 Jesse Storrs purchased a small farm in Lake County and soon founded the nursery firm of Storrs and Harrison, which became one of the largest nurseries of the late 1800s. By 1960 some 200 nurseries were producing a wide variety of nursery stock in a narrow belt 6–10 miles in width and about 20 miles long along the southern shore of Lake Erie. Because of the moderating influence of Lake Erie, plus a deep, rich, slightly acid soil, nurserymen grow ericaceous plants, narrow-leaved evergreens, shrubs, shade trees, roses, perennials, bulbous plants, and some fruit trees and small fruit plants.

Industrialization and urbanization of this area have caused some nurseries to move to locations in other parts of the state. Southwestern and central Ohio, which are less industrialized, but have good agricultural lands and a mild climate, may become the new center for nursery production in Ohio. Many nurseries are relocating in the Ohio River valley—an interesting trend, since the first nurseries of Ohio established in 1790 were located in the Ohio River area.

### Michigan

Located in the heart of the Great Lakes area, Michigan has for over 100 years been a major producer of nursery stock. Most of the early production was directed toward supplying the rapidly expanding fruit industry with high-quality fruit trees. Although fruit trees are still produced, the major part of the production is currently in woody ornamental plants, both field- and container-grown. Michigan is also a leader in the production of evergreen seedlings for reforestation and Christmas tree plantings. The major production center is located in the western lower-half of the southern peninsula along the shore of Lake Michigan. Other centers of production are located in the southeastern and southwestern counties.

### New Jersey

The Garden State has been a major nursery area since colonial times. Major production centers are located in Middlesex and Monmouth counties, in close proximity to two major population centers, New York and Philadelphia, both important market areas for ornamental plants. In addition to a major market area, New Jersey also has a mild, maritime climate and some of the finest agricultural land in the nation, which make it a site that is ideal for the production of nursery stock. However, high land values and zoning laws unfavorable to agriculture, brought on by increased urbanization and industrialization, are limiting growth of nursery production in the central part of the state. Nursery production is almost totally directed to ornamental plants, including everything from ground covers up to 6-in.-caliper shade trees.

### North Carolina and Georgia

North Carolina and Georgia have become major nursery production states during the decade of the 1980s. A number of large northern and western nurseries have developed centers for the production of container-grown plants; many specialize in the production of broad-leaved evergreens, but a wide variety of woody, ornamental plants are produced.

### Illinois

Most of the major nurseries of Illinois are located in five counties (Cook, Lake, DuPage, Kane, and Iroquois) close to Chicago. They have the advantages of a relatively mild climate and rich loam prairie soil which favor B&B production, plus central geographical locations within the nation and many large rapidly growing urban centers within a radius of 300 miles.

Illinois nurseries, like most others that had their beginning with the opening of the West, were at first oriented toward the production of fruit plants. However, by the mid-1950s, production of ornamental plants dominated. Illinois nurseries are famous for the production of narrow-leaved evergreens, shade and flowering trees, and specimen plants for the landscape industry. The winter meeting of the Illinois State Nurserymen's Association (ISNA), held in Chicago in mid-January, gradually developed into the Mid-America Trade Show and is now jointly sponsored by ISNA, the Illinois Landscape Contractors Association, and the Wisconsin Landscape Federation.

### Pennsylvania

The history of the Pennsylvania nursery industry dates back to the times of David Landreth (1784) and Bernard McMahon (about 1800), when these men were engaged in the seed and nursery business in Philadelphia. The nurseries with the largest production are located in the counties of Indiana, Erie, Butler, and Allegheny, which are situated west of the Allegheny Mountains, where there is a good distribution of rainfall, or they are located in the southeastern counties, Chester, Montgomery, Bucks, and Lancaster, close to major market areas.

The state is known for the production of ornamental plants, including conifers, broad-leaved evergreens, shade and flowering trees, and roses. The rose production is centered in the southeastern area near West Chester. The production of broad-leaved evergreens has increased considerably over the past few years because of the increased demand for such plants. Pennsylvania nurseries are favored by a mild climate and well-drained acidic soils. A number of the Pennsylvania nurseries are known for their quality production of seedlings and liners.

### Other Centers

Many other states also produce quality-grown plants. For example, Rhode Island and Connecticut produce large quantities of narrow-leaved evergreens; Maryland has increased its nursery production considerably and produces large, landscape-sized shade trees as does New York, Illinois, and Wisconsin. Texas continues to produce roses in considerable quantity. Although lacking in quantity of state-wide production, Alabama, Arizona, Kentucky, Indiana, Minnesota, and Oklahoma do have centers of production that produce high-quality nursery products.

### SUMMARY

The nursery industry of the United States is a highly dynamic, rapidly growing industry. It is made up primarily of privately-owned, family-operated operations that are very diversified in function and in species produced. In the early development of the industry, most of the production centered about bare-root fruit trees with some woody species for landscape beautification. Currently, production is primarily on the woody-ornamental species and the production method has gradually changed from 100% field production to a combination of field growing and container growing. Also, large specimen plants are grown either in the field and then root-balled for shipping or they are grown in very large containers and sold with the containers for shipping. Large B&B plants are mostly specimen shade trees whereas large, container-grown plants are mostly palm trees. The production of herbaceous perennials has increased rapidly since 1988.

## REFERENCES

AMERICAN ASSOCIATION OF NURSERYMEN. 1977. Research summary: scope III of the nursery industry. AAN, Washington, D.C.

BOYER, C. A. 1952. Nurseries big business in Michigan. Am. Nurseryman 96(2):9.

CHADWICK, L. C. 1960. Nursery industry thrives in Ohio. Am. Nurseryman 92(1):19.

DAVIDSON, H., C. E. LEWIS, and R. A. MECKLENBURG. 1966. The Michigan nursery industry project 80. Mich. Coop. Ext. Serv. Rep. 43.

GARTNER, J., J. E. BREWER, and H. F. FLINT. 1959. The Rhode Island nursery industry. R.I. Agric Exp. Sta. Misc. Publ. 50 rev.

GORTZIG, C. F. 1969. State of the trade in the empire state. Am. Nurseryman 130(2):18.

HUDSON, A. C., and H. B. SORENSON. 1957. The Texas nursery industry. Tex. Agric Exp. Sta. MP222.

JARVESOO E. 1964. Nursery trade flourishes in Bay State. Am. Nurseryman 120(2):12.

LYLE, E. W. 1963. Roses, glamour crop of the Texas trade. Am. Nurseryman 118(2):9.

MEAHL, R. P. 1961. The Pennsylvania nursery industry. Agric. Ind. Adjustment Conf. Rep. Pa. State Univ.

MOREY, R. W. 1992. 1992 Nursery Business, Grower 100, Brantwood Publications, Inc.

PAULS, D. E., and A. H. HARRINGTON. 1960. The nursery industry of Washington. Wash. Agric. Exp. Sta. Circ. 372.

PELLETT, H. 1983. An update on the Minnesota system of container production. Am. Nurseryman 157(1):95.

POTTER, F. 1953. Nurseries play a major role in agriculture of New York state. Am. Nurseryman 98(2):9.

REIGER, R., and C. E. WHITCOMB. 1983. Grower can now confine roots to in-field containers. Am. Nurseryman 158(8):31–34.

SMITH, C. N. 1969. A fact book on the Florida wholesale woody ornamental nursery industry. Dept. Agric. Econ. Univ. Fla. Mimeo Rep. EC69–11.

SORENSON, H. B. 1963. The nursery industry of Texas. Am. Nurseryman 118(2):8.

TECH. COMMITTEE SM-33. 1969. Marketing woody ornamentals. South. Coop. Serv. Bull. 143.

WHITCOMB, C. E. 1983. Container vs. poly bags—which are better? Am. Nurseryman 157(1):101–103.

## SUGGESTED READING

HigginBotham, J. S. 1991. The State of Rewholesaling, Am. Nurseryman 174(12):48–59.

White, R. P. 1975. A century of service. American Association of Nurserymen, Washington, D.C.

Chapter **3**

# Management Applied to Nurseries

There are many definitions of management, but the one that states it best is: **Management** is the bringing together of **men (people), money,** and **materials,** in a framework of time, for an economic or sociologic purpose. Simply stated, management brings together the three primary factors of production that managers use, places them together in a framework of time, and gives them a reason or purpose for being.

How do managers manage? What are their primary responsibilities? Naturally, a manager is a person and as such is subject to all the past, present, and future forces that have molded, are molding, and will mold the person into the individual that he or she is now and will be in the future. As a result, no two managers are exactly alike, and no two managers can be expected to manage exactly alike. Each will be different as a result of his or her individual personality and past experiences. But each manager by definition will have a purpose, the factors of production, and time. How a manager uses the factors of production and time determines how successful he or she will be in accomplishing the established objectives.

A manager's primary responsibilities are basically six in number: (1) determine goals; (2) plan; (3) organize and staff; (4) direct, control, and coordinate; (5) motivate; and (6) evaluate and reward.

These six responsibilities apply to all levels of management, from foreman to president. How they are applied depends upon the purpose or objective of the organization and the level of management. They are fully applicable in the management of nurseries.

## DETERMINING GOALS

The purpose or goal is known by various names within a nursery. In the production department it is the production goal; in marketing it is the sales objective; in propagation it is the percent rooting or "take" in grafting; and to the average laborer it is the job. But to the owner or the stockholder, it is profit. In each situation, the purpose should be clearly understood. We will look at individual objectives in some detail under organization and staffing, but the overall mission of the nursery business should be clearly established and stated in such a manner that it gives direction to all units of·the organization.

To arrive at the overall objective, management must give consideration to four integral questions: (1) what products or services are needed, (2) by whom, (3) at what price and quantity, and (4) does the organization have the interest and the ability to provide the products or services? For example, assume that a person or firm is thinking of producing shade trees. They may have heard that there is a shortage of shade trees, and they have some idle land from which they would like to derive an income. Assume that the land will produce the trees and that water is available. Now a series of questions must be asked to define the objective. What is the nature of the target market? Is it homeowners in a local area, garden centers in a limited geographic area, landscape contractors in a limited area or large geographic area, or other nurseries in a local or national market area? Or is the target market some combination of these?

If the market comprises homeowners or garden centers, the demand may be for small trees that can be transported in the family car. If it is landscape contractors, the demand will be primarily for large trees processed with a ball of earth. If it is other nurseries or a combination of markets, the demand may be for a combination of sizes. What species and cultivars does the market demand, and what price will the market support? Consideration must also be given to similar products and services currently available or to be available in the market area.

Following the market study, it is necessary to formulate and state the company objective in such a manner that it will give direction to the production and marketing effort needed to accomplish the objective. For example: objective A—to produce $1^1/_2$- to 2-in.-caliper shade trees hardy in climatic zones 4 and 5 for the garden center market (Fig. 6–1). This objective limits size, geographic area, and type of market. It does not limit cultivar selection. Objective B—to produce large ($3^1/_2$- to 4-in. DBH) specimen trees for landscape projects. This objective sets the course for a long-time investment in trees of large diameter requiring powerful equipment for handling. It limits customers primarily to landscape contractors.

Either objective sets the direction for the production and marketing effort. In objective A, the production effort will be toward producing small shade trees as quickly and economically as possible. This will result in rotations of relatively short duration, relatively close spacing of trees in the nursery blocks, and a need to use practices and equipment that will meet the objective. The intended market is identified, and the merchandising program can be directed to reach the garden center market. The cash turnover is rapid, owing to the short rotations, which is an advantage when interest rates are high. In objective B, the production effort will be directed to producing large specimen trees which will require wide spacing and long rotations, and the need to develop techniques that will effectively produce high-quality trees for immediate effect in the landscape. It will require powerful equipment to move the large, heavy material. The marketing effort will be concentrated on contacting sources that have a need for large, well-developed trees, primarily landscape contractors, city park departments, golf courses, and so on. However, the cash turnover is delayed by a number of years, which is a disadvantage when interest rates are high.

Provision must also be made for modifying long-range objectives. Management must constantly evaluate the market and be responsive to trends. But all actions taken should be in keeping with the primary goal and the professional image of the nursery.

## PLANNING

Planning is for the future, but it is based on past history. It is done to accomplish an objective, with the best expenditure of resources (personnel, money, materials), in the time period specified or implied. It should be a logical process of selecting the best course of action from a number of alternatives. Unfortunately, this is easier said than done. In some organizations decisions are made by default or without sound background information. When this happens too often, objectives are seldom attained and the organization fails.

When planning, a good manager consults with advisers. He or she will try to clearly define the problem to be solved or state the objective to be attained. The manager then encourages input from the staff. Depending upon the situation, it may require the gathering and evaluating of information by staff members, followed by the development of several possible courses of action. Upon an analysis of the situation and with the best possible information available, the manager must make a decision; this is one of management's responsibilities. The manager should not avoid it by trying to get a subordinate to make it; if the manager does this, especially if it is done too often, he or she will soon become ineffective. The decision should be clear and understood by the units involved in implementing the decision.

## ORGANIZATION

The organization of a nursery business needs to be considered under three categories: (1) organization of the physical facilities, (2) the functional organization, and (3) the legal organization.

*Organization of the physical facilities* has to do with the physical relationship of production and administrative units one to the other and to the layout of propagation units and production fields for maximum efficiency. This information is discussed in Chapter 5.

*Organization for function* relates to developing the organization to maximize efficient use of people and their support systems: machines, facilities, supplies, and so on, to accomplish the various functions. It is the staffing and delegation of authority to accomplish an objective. In a group of workers, it is common that one will be more assertive than the others, and he or she becomes the leader. At that point the leader-follower organization is formed.

The leader-foreman is generally the most skilled in the particular physical skill that is being performed. He or she is expected to lead (manage) the others, and if a good working relationship exists with the followers, the job will get done. If not, there are problems and the leader will probably be replaced. This form of organization is limited by the span of control of the leader. Can he or she effectively control 3, 10, or 100 people?

The Bible (*Exodus*, 18:17–22) tells of Jethro's advice to Moses in 1450 B.C. when he was trying singlehandedly to lead the Israelites out of Egypt.

> What you are doing is not good. You and the people will wear yourselves out, you are not able to perform it alone. Listen to my counsel: You shall represent the people before God, and bring their cases to God; and you shall teach them the statutes and the decisions. . . . Choose able men from all the people, such as fear God, men who are trustworthy and who hate a bribe; and place such men over the people as rulers of thousands, of hundreds, of fifties and of tens. And let them judge the people at all times; every great matter they shall bring to you, but any small matter they shall decide themselves; so it will be easier for you, and they will bear the burden with you.

This passage from the Bible is the earliest known record of the principles of management and organization. By accepting the advice of his father-in-law, Moses created a simple, workable, line organization that accomplished the mission.

The *line organization* has been used for centuries in the functional development of organizations. It is the most common structural form found in most small- to medium-sized nurseries. When tailored to fit the needs of the nursery manager, it can be quite functional. The structure of an average, medium-sized production nursery can be represented as in Fig. 3–1. This structure illustrates the chain of responsibility for three basic functional areas: propagation, production, and sales.

Since propagation is a specialized area, it is headed by a skilled propagator who has the responsibility (goal, mission) of propagating the materials needed for field production and the implied responsibility of keeping posted on new methods of propagation related to the type of plants being produced by the nursery.

The nursery superintendent has the largest division and is charged with the responsibility of meeting the production goals. This division is organized into three subsections and staffed accordingly. The sales division is responsible for marketing the products produced.

As an organization grows in size, its functional units increase. But the ultimate size of each unit is determined by the span of control of the individual

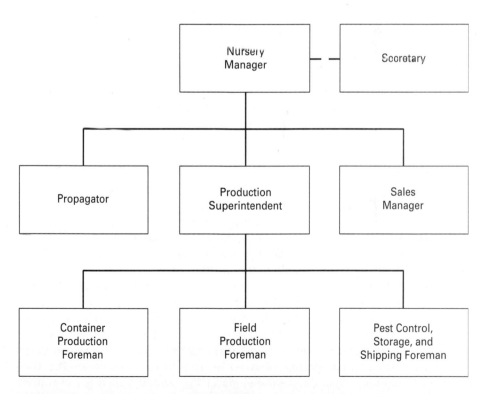

**Figure 3–1** Example of line organization for a medium-sized nursery.

leader (foreman or superintendent) in charge. At some point the business may become too large for the manager to control effectively without assistance; he or she then gradually obtains a staff, and the business is reorganized.

The *line and staff organization* (Fig. 3–2) is designed to accomplish this objective. The various staff people aid the manager in developing plans and co-ordinating the activities of the various functional units. In some situations it is desirable to add various service units that provide a service function (e.g., mechanical maintenance) to the overall organization.

The two most common staff positions are the comptroller, in charge of financial matters, and the personnel manager, in charge of labor relations. These two staff assistants aid the manager in the area of money and interior personnel management. If a customer relations director is added, his or her responsibilities should relate to exterior people relationships as opposed to interior. The position would have to do with public and government relations.

The research and development director is responsible for developing new products that the nursery might produce; testing new products that the firm might use; and developing, in cooperation with one or more of the functional units, new methods of operation. The mechanic heads the service unit and is responsible for keeping all mechanical equipment operational. It is important that the chain of command be clearly established in a line and staff organization. Basically, staff members have no command control over the functional units. They are advisory to the manager, who alone directs and controls the functional units.

Sometimes the organization becomes too large for one person to maintain effective control over the functional units, at which time the manager delegates to the staff certain specific aspects of overall authority. When this is done, the business becomes an *executive organization* in which the manager is known as president and is assisted by a group of executive vice-presidents who have authority over functional units in their specific areas of responsibility.

In organizing and staffing a nursery, it is important to keep in mind the overall goal of the organization and the span of control of individual department heads, and to develop logical groupings of functional and staff units. Also, a nursery organization must be flexible and capable of meeting the constantly changing demands for labor as influenced by season, weather conditions, and the changing demands of the marketplace.

The organizing and staffing of a large production nursery is a challenging task. The demand for labor fluctuates with the season of the year and by operations within and between divisions. For many field-production nurseries, there is a maximum need for labor in the spring and fall, with a minimum need in the winter months. In early spring the demand is greatest in the areas of digging and shipping, followed in midspring by planting (Fig. 3–3) and June budding. Then during the summer the primary need is for cultivation and pest control, in August for fall budding operations, followed in the fall months by digging and storage operations.

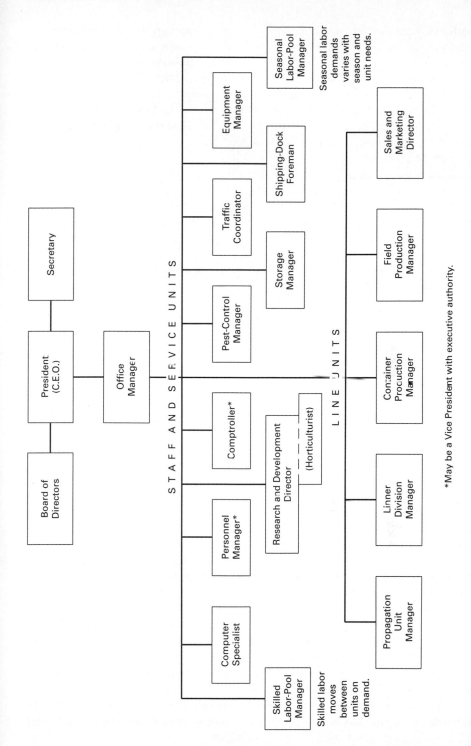

**Figure 3-2** Example of a line and staff organization for a large wholesale nursery.

Board of Directors

President (C.E.O.)

Secretary

Office Manager

STAFF AND SERVICE UNITS

Computer Specialist

Skilled Labor-Pool Manager

Skilled labor moves between units on demand.

Personnel Manager*

Research and Development Director

(Horticulturist)

Comptroller*

Pest-Control Manager

Storage Manager

Traffic Coordinator

Shipping-Dock Foreman

Equipment Manager

Seasonal Labor-Pool Manager

Seasonal labor demands varies with season and unit needs.

LINE UNITS

Propagation Unit Manager

Linner Division Manager

Container Production Manager

Field Production Manager

Sales and Marketing Director

*May be a Vice President with executive authority.

**Figure 3–3** Planting small flowering trees with the aid of a planting machine. (Courtesy Mechanical Transplanter Co.)

Nursery managers need to develop good labor management techniques, since labor often accounts for 50% or more of the cost of production. Also, federal, state, and union regulations place specific restraints upon employers rela-tive to conditions of employment and pay schedules.

The *legal form of organization* is another consideration in organizing the nursery business. The three commonly used legal forms of organization are the proprietorship, the partnership, and the corporation. Each form has advantages and disadvantages which should be evaluated prior to legally constituting the business, and periodically during the life of the organization.

The *proprietorship* is the easiest to form. Anyone who can acquire the land and wants to start a nursery can do so, as long as he or she complies with state and local laws related to zoning and taxation. In the proprietorship, responsibility is centered in one individual; there is no sharing of the profits. But the business is limited by the capabilities and limitations of the owner, and the business usually terminates upon the owner's death. This is a serious weakness of the proprietorship form of business. Many excellent small nurseries have failed to continue following the death of the owner, because no provision was made for continuation of the business.

The *partnership* is an agreement between two or more parties. It is easy to form, but at times it may be difficult to divest an undesirable partner or to market a share of a partnership. Partnerships in which the abilities of each partner complement one another are generally more successful than those in which they duplicate each other. In the nursery industry one partner may be an excellent production worker and the other a salesperson. Or one partner may be excellent in landscape design and construction, whereas the other is an excellent garden center manager. Problems sometimes develop when both partners are growers and neither is good at administration or sales.

The major weakness in the partnership form of business relates to resolving problems that arise between partners or between the spouses of partners. It can be a very precarious legal form of business and should be constituted with considerable forethought. It is well to have the articles of agreement developed by a lawyer, following careful consideration by all parties. It is possible to develop limited partnerships and open-end-agreement contracts. The limited partnership allows some partners to limit their liability while at least one partner remains fully liable for the debts of the business. Open-end partnership agreements allow for taking in new partners and for the death, retirement, or resignation of partners.

The *corporation* is another legal form of business, designed to provide for the continuity of a business and to limit the liability of a stockholder. Many nurseries that start as proprietorships convert to a corporate form as they grow and develop in size. The corporation is limited by a charter that must be obtained from the state in which the business is incorporated. Also, the business must be managed by a board of directors, hold an annual meeting of stockholders, and file an annual report, generally with the secretary of state in the state of incorporation.

There are many ways that the corporation can be constituted, including public and private. In the public corporation, the stock is for sale to the general public, whereas in the private corporation (commonly referred to as subchapter S) the stock is kept within a closed, private group (commonly within a family). Many commercial nurseries are private (subchapter S) corporations. In general, the private form of corporation meets the needs of most nursery businesses. But when there is serious disagreement within the group and a stockholder wishes to divest himself or herself of one portion of the business, it may be difficult to obtain fair market value for the stock, since there may be a charter limitation as to whom it can be sold.

In organizing a nursery business, it may be desirable to have multiple forms of legal structure to gain the advantages of each. For example, it may be more desirable for a proprietor to own the land and structures, and lease these to the nursery. The production nursery may be a private corporation engaged in agricultural production, which in turn sells its product to another corporation, a sales-oriented organization, which markets it in interstate commerce. The two corporations remain smaller than one large corporation that owns all land and capital assets; this may provide a tax advantage. It limits restrictions placed upon businesses that engage in interstate commerce to

only that corporation that is so engaged. It also reduces the size of capitaliza-
tion, which may permit young people to buy into the nursery at considerably
less equity than if the nursery owned all the land and capital assets. It also
permits the landowner to sell or will his or her lands without consent of
the corporation. This may present a problem to the production nurseries
renting land, but by long-term lease arrangements it can generally be managed in an equitable manner. In any case, when developing a corporation or a
combination of business forms, it is advisable to obtain the services of a
lawyer who is familiar with the various legal and financial requirements,
advantages, and limitations.

## CONTROL AND COORDINATION

Control and coordination involves those activities that are needed to keep an
organization headed on the course that it was assigned or that it chose to follow. Control relates to activities within a unit, whereas coordination relates to
activities between units. In a small operational unit, control is direct and is accomplished primarily by voice; there is little need for written directives or
written communication, but as an organization grows and the levels or eche-
lons of management increase and the functional units are spread over a greater
geographic area, control becomes indirect and must be accomplished by written directives or written communications, and direct control becomes minimal. One effective indirect means of obtaining control is to develop and
publish a policy manual for standard procedures and policies. It is best developed in cooperation with key employees and staff advisers. Some items that
might be covered in the manual are tabulated in Table 3–1.

Another control mechanism is to set attainable goals for each functional
unit. Depending upon the type of unit, the goals may be daily, weekly, monthly,
seasonal, or yearly. For a digging crew, daily goals are in order, whereas for a
propagator it may be $x$ thousands of cuttings per month, season, or year; for
the production and sales managers, the goal may be $x$ number of plants/
species/season; and for the general manager, the goal is dollars of profit.

Since there are objectives to be obtained, there must be some form of reporting. Records and reports are another means that managers use to gain control over their operational units. Records and reports should contain accurate,
up-to-date information if they are to be valuable to the manager. Collecting and
processing data that are not going to be used in making management decisions
is a worthless practice that should be discouraged. But collecting data that,
when processed, will be used for evaluation purposes and as a basis for future
planning and management decisions is an implied responsibility of all levels
of management.

Two excellent tools that can be used by management as a guide to labor
productivity are: the reasonable-expectancy table (Table 3–2) for individual

**Table 3–1** Suggested topics to be covered in policy manual for a nursery

| | |
|---|---|
| Administrative | Personnel |
|   Mail handling |   Affirmative action policy |
|   Private use of facilities |   Clothing and dress |
|   Workers in administration area |   Equal opportunity and discrimination |
| Equipment |   Grievances |
|   Borrowing |   Hours of work |
|   Care and servicing |   Lost and found |
|   Purchasing |   Lunchroom |
|   Returning to storage |   Parking |
|   Use |   Promotion |
| Finance |   Right to Know Law |
|   Income Tax Withholding |   Safety and injuries |
|   Insurance |   Sick leave |
|   Loans to employees |   Tardiness and absenteeism |
|   Medical benefits |   Termination |
|   Overtime pay |   Vacations |
|   Paid holidays |   Work rules |
|   Pay periods and paydays | Plants |
|   Payroll savings |   Handling and care |
|   Rainy day pay |   Sale to employees |
|   Retirement programs | Supplies |
|   Unemployment compensation |   Obtaining within the nursery |
|   Wage review |   Purchases for the nursery |
|   Worker's Compensation |   Returning to storage |

performance and the labor requirements table (Table 3–3) for crew performance. Both are developed from labor productivity records maintained by the production foremen. The data, from records kept on the various functions performed within the nursery, can be processed into meaningful information that can be used in planning labor needs, estimating future cost of production and cash flow requirements for the business, and evaluating production. Table 3–3 is an example of how raw data can be converted into a more meaningful unit; average labor-hours per 1000 trees.

Digging and planting large trees varies considerably by the size of the ball and with the type of equipment used. Therefore, average labor-hours to dig and plant shade trees have been converted to graphs (Figs. 3–4 and 3–5) which can be used to estimate labor-hour requirements when digging and planting large trees.

Record taking and reporting must be made as simple as possible. Various types of forms are available or can be designed to obtain data on individual work performance, use of equipment and supplies, expenditure of funds, and so on. The uniform chart of accounts for use in financial management developed by the Horticultural Research Institute can be a useful management tool in this area. There are charts for nursery production, landscape, and retail operations.

**Table 3–2** Reasonable expectancy for labor-hours

A. Digging evergreens by hand

| Plant Size | Production System | Plants per Labor-Hour | | |
|---|---|---|---|---|
| | | Spreading (e.g., Yews, Mugho Pine) | Compact Upright (e.g., Yews) | Large Type (e.g., Spruce, Pine) |
| 12–15 in. | B&B | 15.4 | | |
| 15–18 in. | B&B | 10.2 | 11.1 | |
| 18–24 in. | B&B | 8.3 | 9.8 | 8.3 |
| 2–2½ ft | B&B | 6.5 | 7.6 | 7.6 |
| 2½–3 ft | B&B | 4.5 | 6.2 | 5.7 |
| 3½ ft | B&B | 3.8 | 4.5 | 3.0 |
| 3½–4 ft | B&B | 2.6 | 3.8 | 2.0 |

B. Digging B&B trees by hand

| Caliper (in.) | Trees per Labor-Hour |
|---|---|
| 1–1¼ | 24 |
| 1½–2 | 14 |
| 2½–3½ | 9 |
| 4 | 3.5 |

Based on data from 6- to 10-worker digging crews. Includes carrying out and loading on pallets.

Based on data from 8-worker crew. Includes burlapping, topping, and tying tops.

*Note:* Data were obtained from a number of sources, and are not intended as a standard. Data and reasonable expectancy tables should be collected and developed for each nursery.

Each operational unit manager should establish contact with other operational units to coordinate activities, especially when an operation is highly dependent upon coordinated or sequential activities.

## EMPLOYEE MOTIVATION, EVALUATION, AND REWARDS

Motivating, evaluating, and rewarding employees are important management functions. They sometimes do not receive the attention from nursery managers that they deserve. The three functions are closely interrelated. For example, a spontaneous statement such as "Well done," "A good job," or "Excellent" made by a manager as an evaluation of employee performance is one of the most appreciated rewards and one of the best positive motivators that is available to management. But all too often, its impact and value are overlooked. The proper and timely granting of employee rewards can have a major impact upon the success or failure of the business. Every employee is entitled to have his or her performance evaluation: to receive praise and ad-

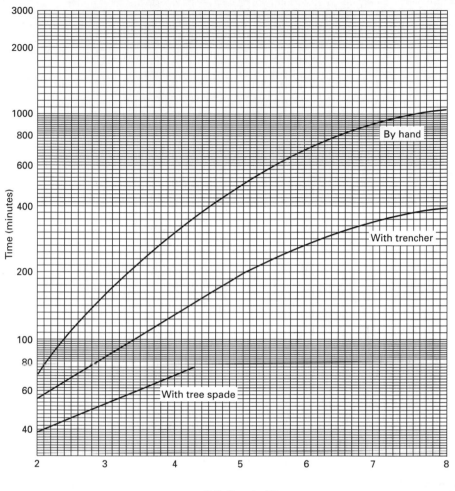

**Figure 3–4** Average time for digging B&B trees. (The data in Figures 3–4 and 3–5 were obtained from a number of sources, and are not intended as a standard. Data should be collected and developed individually for each nursery.) (From Davidson and Speakman, 1969.)

vancement for work well done, rebuke for failure, and punishment for unacceptable behavior or performance.

A good nursery manager is cognizant of the fact that the most important factor of production relates to the employees. The manager must never forget that employees are people, and that they have needs, aspirations, skills, and ideas. It is how the manager perceives employees and satisfies these needs and

**Table 3-3** Nursery labor requirements[a]

| | Average Labor-Hours/1000 |
|---|---|
| *Planting in the Nursery* | |
| Shade tree whips, $1^{1}/_{2}$-in. caliper | |
| With tractor-drawn planting machine (V-shaped plow to open trench, plus closing disks and packing wheels), 8-worker crew | |
| Planted on 8-ft centers in rows $\bar{x} = 4000/10$-hr day | 20.0 |
| Shade tree whips, $1–1^{1}/_{4}$-in. caliper | |
| Hole marking and digging $10 \times 10$ ft (cleared land, experienced crew, good weather) $\bar{x} = 2100$ holes/134 labor-hours | 64.0 |
| Preplant pruning (remove from storage rack, prune roots and top, return to rack) $\bar{x} = 16$ trees/labor-hour | 62.5 |
| Planting by hand into predug holes: fill and water $\bar{x} = 5.4$ trees/labor-hour | 185.2 |
| Evergreen transplants | |
| With tractor-drawn mechanical transplanter, Model 2000, two-row, 10-worker crew, 9–10-in., spreading, BR | |
| Long rows $\bar{x} = 10,000/10$-hr day | 10.0 |
| Short rows (< 1000 ft) $\bar{x} = 8000/10$-hr day | 12.5 |
| *Pruning or Trimming* | |
| Shade trees | |
| From the ground | |
| $1–1^{1}/_{4}$-in. $\bar{x} = 5850$ trees/148 labor-hours | 25.3 |
| $^{3}/_{4}–1^{1}/_{2}$-in. $\bar{x} = 300/10$-hr day | 34.0 |
| With pole trimmers, $1^{1}/_{2}–2^{1}/_{2}$-in. $\bar{x} = 300/10$-hr day | 34.0 |
| With step ladders, $1^{1}/_{2}–2^{1}/_{2}$-in. $\bar{x} = 200/10$-hr day | 50.0 |
| Evergreens cone-shaped 2–4-ft (i.e., Capitata yews) | |
| With long-bladed knife $\bar{x} = 10,000/10$-hr day | 1.0 |
| With power-pack hedge shears $\bar{x} = 4500/10$-hr day | 2.2 |
| With long-bladed hedge shears $\bar{x} = 2000/10$-hr day | 5.0 |

**Table 3-3** (continued)

| | Average Labor-Hours/1000 |
|---|---|
| Evergreens spreading 18–24-in. (i.e., Pfitzer juniper) | |
| With power-pack hedge shears (winter only for junipers) $\bar{x} = 7000/10$-hr day | 1.5 |
| With long-bladed hedge shears $\bar{x} = 4000/10$-hr day | 2.5 |
| *Digging* | |
| Evergreens | |
| By hand B&B | |
| 15- or 18-in. spreading, 10-in ball $\bar{x} = 10$ workers: 450/10-hr day | 220 |
| 4-ft upright 12–14-in. ball $\bar{x} = 10$ workers: 200/10-hr day | 500 |
| 5–6 ft upright, 18-in. ball $\bar{x} = 8$ workers: 130/10-hr day | 615 |
| With Jiffy balling machine | |
| 15–18-in. plants, digging and potting $\bar{x} = 8$ workers: 900/10-hr day | 88.8 |
| 15–18-in. plants, digging and B&B $\bar{x} = 12$ workers: 800/10-hr day | 100 |
| Shade trees | |
| By hand (varies with size of ball, see Figs. 3–4 and 3–5) | |
| With tree-spade digging machine (includes tying branches, digging, packaging into burlapped wire baskets, secured, trunks wrapped) 10-hr day, from barn to digging area, minimum moving from field to field and back to barn at end of day | |
| 66-in. Vermeer, truck-mounted $\bar{x} = 10$-worker crew: 25/10-hr day (2.8 labor-hr/tree) | 2800 |
| 44-in. Vermeer, on tractor $\bar{x} = 7$-worker crew: 80/10-hr day (53 min/tree) | 875 |
| 30-in Vermeer, on tractor $\bar{x} = 7$-worker crew: 150/10-hr day (28 min/tree) | 467 |
| 28-in. Caretree, on Bob Cat (skid tractor) $\bar{x} = 10$-worker crew: 230/10-hr day (26 min/tree) | 435 |

[a]Average labor productivity for selected nursery operations. Data obtained from a number of nurseries. Each nursery manager should develop tables for the particular set of conditions, methods of operation, machines, and work force (Table 3–1, 3–2 and 3–3 are for illustration only.)

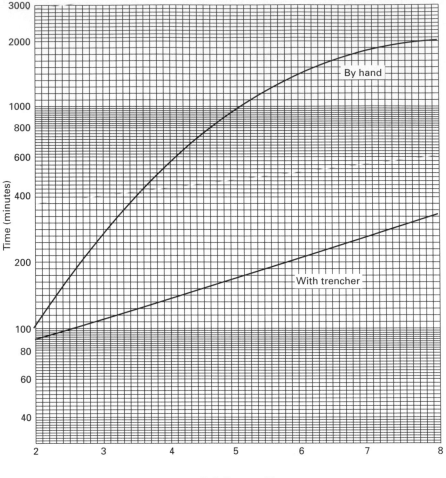

**Figure 3-5** Average time for planting B&B trees. (From Davidson and Speakman, 1969.)

skills that determines to a large degree the productivity of the employees and, ultimately, the success of the business.

Each person has a basic need for food, clothing, and shelter. And most people have a need to be with others. Human beings are social; they like to be with others of their own kind and enjoy the company of members of the opposite sex. People work to satisfy these physiological and sociological needs. However, people also have dreams and aspirations that go beyond these basic needs. They are called the ego or psychological needs: the need to be recognized as an individual and not just a statistic, the need to express and carry out ideas, and the need for praise and recognition.

When an employee is hired, he or she should be informed of his or her duties and responsibilities. The person should also be told the procedure for evaluation and reward. Communicating the job responsibilities varies with the position. For temporary, seasonal employees the communication may be verbal and rather specific. For top management the communication may be in writing, but general in nature. However, for middle management a detailed job description, in writing, may be in order, because it is necessary to clearly define the scope of the position and the limits of responsibility.

An application form should be used for most positions. The form serves a number of functions: to obtain (1) personal data on the applicant (name, address, date of birth, medical history, etc.), (2) pertinent information on the applicant relative to the position, (3) a history of previous employment, and (4) if applicable, a statement of the applicant's expectations. The form thus serves as the first step in the evaluation process. The form also screens out those applicants who do not wish to complete formal, written documents for one reason or another. A follow-up interview provides the nursery manager with a second opportunity to evaluate the potential employee. At this time the manager should also explain the unique characteristics and philosophy of the nursery and try to determine if the applicant has the desired qualifications for the position.

Once an employee has been hired, he or she should undergo training appropriate to the position and the person's background. All too often managers fail to train new employees properly. The initial period, after a person joins a nursery, is extremely important both to the person and to the nursery. New employees must learn what is expected of them and how far they can proceed on their own. Also, the employer must learn how to best motivate the new employee and how much responsibility can be delegated to the employee as he or she matures and develops as a productive part of the labor-management team.

Young people, especially those who have made a substantial investment in their education, by devoting two or more years of their lives to obtaining a college education, will need to obtain training in the work ethic. Unfortunately, people from urban areas have little opportunity to learn and practice the physical skills associated with the nursery industry. Academic institutions are not equipped to provide these, which are best learned on the job. They will need to serve a period of apprenticeship, learning the art and skills associated with the nursery industry. However, nursery managers have an obligation to these young employees, to the nursery industry, and to themselves to provide this period of internship. By doing so, they will be making an investment in a human resource that will pay substantial dividends in the future.

It has been said that a good supervisor is someone who is proactive and mission-oriented and who can motivate employees to understand and accept the mission statement of the organization (nursery) that employs them. Within each department or division of an organization there are various goals (objectives, duties) that must be met to accomplish the overall mission. These goals need to be clearly communicated to new employees as well as what rewards are to be expected for jobs well done.

Naturally, there is the contracted reward, an hour's pay for an hour's work for hourly workers, and a yearly salary for people in management. However, there are other rewards—some of them financial and others psychological—that can often be more appreciated by employees than the contracted reward. These include cash bonus, time off, fringe benefits, and a commendation such as a "thank you" for a job well done. But one of the very best incentives is participation. When people are asked for their advice they feel important, that they are a part of the team, a part of the organization. However, a manager who solicits advice must be prepared to evaluate the suggestion(s) carefully and to adopt those that contribute to accomplishing the set goals and then provide appropriate recognition (rewards) when it is deserved.

For the applicant the evaluation process commences at first contact with the employer. The applicant should be sure the contact is appropriate for the position. A letter should be neatly typed and supported by a vita sheet or completed application form. At the interview the applicant should be clean and dressed appropriately for the position.

After working for a predetermined period, the new employee should be evaluated. The evaluation should not be made too quickly or on insufficient evidence of performance, but slowly and deliberately. The employee should be commended for accomplishments and counseled in areas or skills that could be improved upon. Also, when appropriate, an increase in salary should be given, since incentive pay is an important means of rewarding good performance.

Most new employees begin as *hourly workers* whose primary function is the performance of physical skills. Although they work with materials, the skills employed require little technical knowledge. They may include such jobs as digging holes to plant trees, digging and lifting plants, packing, or making cuttings. Hourly workers can be evaluated on the basis of quantity and to some degree the quality of production. In most nurseries, standards of quality are set by management. In some establishments the quality standards are high and must not be sacrificed for quantity, whereas in other establishments, by design, the standards of quality are somewhat lower, in the interest of obtaining quantity of production. Nevertheless, the objective set for the worker is generally some type of daily goal, and the compensation is wages paid at an hourly rate. In establishments where quality of performance is appreciated, superior performance should be provided with additional rewards, such as a rate of pay greater than the average or a bonus paid at the end of a season or at some other predetermined time period. However, in addition to these standard methods of earned or contractual rewards for labor, management should also be cognizant of other methods of reward appropriate to the age level, social background, and the desires and expectations of the workers. Young people hoeing weeds in the nursery will often work better and faster if they know they will be rewarded with time off with pay. Most people will do a better job if they know that their work is appreciated and will be rewarded accordingly. Hourly workers usually move up to "skilled workers" when they have acquired a degree of technical knowledge and the appropriate skill level.

*Skilled workers* also work with materials, but the jobs are more demanding of technical knowledge and ability. Examples are budding and grafting; application of fertilizers and pesticides; and operating equipment, such as tree diggers. Skilled workers are evaluated both on the quantity and quality of their performance. Their earned rewards may include in addition to a higher wage rate such fringe benefits as days off with pay, paid vacation, and health insurance. Various supplementary rewards may be expense-paid trips to professional meetings or an opportunity to obtain additional training at company expense.

*Foremen* are the first level of management. They are charged with the responsibility of getting a job done; this is most commonly accomplished by managing people and materials. Therefore, one of the foreman's responsibilities is to motivate, evaluate, and reward the workers. However, foremen are evaluated by their superiors on how well they get the job done. Since the foreman's job is a management position it includes the responsibility of maintaining records on the use of the resources (workers and materials) over which he or she has responsibility. A simple but meaningful system is one that accounts for both the workers and machine-hours that go into each job, plus a record of the materials that were expended. In a nursery the job may either be plant-production-oriented or it may be nonproductive, such as maintenance of roads, digging a pond, and so on. Nevertheless, it is important to management to obtain data on productivity to evaluate the crews' performances. The data can also be used to develop reasonable expectancy and staffing tables, in estimating cost of production, and for cash flow analysis.

The foreman's earned rewards are similar to those of the skilled laborer: higher salary, various fringe benefits, and so on. In addition, there should be certain supplementary rewards for jobs that are well done, particularly under adverse situations: weather, time, shortage of personnel. These supplementary rewards might be a cash bonus or a gift appropriate to the person and the situation. Care must be exercised in giving a bonus on a regular basis; it can easily become an expected, earned reward. Foremen should seldom, if ever, be evaluated on a monetary productivity basis, although this is done in some nurseries or landscape construction firms. A couple of examples will illustrate the point.

In a landscape construction firm, a job is bid at a monetary value, and the foreman who is assigned to the job is sometimes evaluated on how much money was made on the job. If the job is profitable, the foreman may share in a bonus, whereas if the job lost money, the individual may be reprimanded or even be discharged. But foremen in most firms, either landscape or nursery, have control over only two factors of production—workers and materials; they should be evaluated only on their ability to use these two factors effectively. If they bid the job or have a degree of financial control, it is reasonable to evaluate them on profitability of the job.

A foreman in charge of a digging crew in a nursery is provided with a mechanical tree digger, a crew of workers, and the needed materials, such as burlap, wire baskets, pinning nails, twine, and so on. The job is to harvest a certain number of trees per day (week or season). Implied within the objective is that the trees be firmly balled and that no damage be done to the trees being dug or to the trees that remain in the block to grow on to larger sizes. If this objective is attained (assuming that it was attainable), the reward is a good monthly salary. However, if performance is above average—the trees are well balled, there is no damage to the trees, the job was done in less than average time, and the customers of the nursery are pleased with the quality of the product—the foreman should be given a supplementary reward, generally praise and possibly a bonus. The foreman, in turn, should praise the workers and share a portion of the bonus with them.

In making the evaluation of the crew's performances, various means are utilized: visual observation of the crews on the job, comments from customers on the quality of the product, and digging records of the number of trees dug and the labor-hours utilized to accomplish the job. From the digging records, the nursery superintendent or the nursery manager will obtain the data needed to arrive at average times to dig and process trees of various size classes and to estimate costs to harvest plants of various sizes. Since management has the data on wage rates and costs of supplies, equipment, and so on, they are in a position to make the necessary calculations to evaluate the economic productivity of the system and to make the appropriate rewards or effect changes in the system.

Similar types of evaluations can be made for all the divisions of the nursery if the goals or objectives are clearly defined. In propagation the goal is output of young plants, seedlings, cuttings, grafts, and so on. In the nursery it is the production of salable plants to meet a market objective, and digging crews are evaluated and rewarded on the basis of productivity and the quality of their performance.

The goal of top management is to produce a profit for the organization. Therefore, management is evaluated on the basis of profitability and is rewarded accordingly. This topic is discussed in Chapter 7.

## SUMMARY

Although the management process can be divided into and discussed as six component parts—(1) setting goals, (2) planning, (3) organizing and staffing, (4) directing, controlling, and coordinating, (5) motivating, and (6) evaluating and rewarding—it is a unified process with each part dependent upon all others. Successful managers constantly evaluate and seek ways to improve the use of their resources. Managers must keep abreast of changing demands in the marketplace and changing methods of production in order to make sound management decisions relative to the long-range goals of the organization. Changes in goals or in methods of production will of necessity affect the organizational structure, which in turn will modify methods of control, coordination, motivation, and so on. And once the new structure is developed to meet the newly developed objectives, the process starts over again. Management is a never-ending process. It is a logical process that good managers understand and practice in a successful manner. Poor managers either fail to understand the process or fail to practice one or more of the parts that make up good management.

For additional information on management, the reader should consult one or more books on the topic; a few are listed as Suggested Reading. Another source of good management information is the Small Business Management Series, published by the Small Business Administration and sold by the Superintendent of Documents, Washington, D.C. 20402.

## SUGGESTED READING

CARROLL, S. J., JR., and H. L. TOSI, JR., 1973. Management by objectives. Macmillan Publishing Co., Inc., New York.

COVEY, S. R. 1990. The 7 Habits of Highly Effective People. Simon & Schuster.

DALE, E. 1973. Management: theory and practice. McGraw-Hill Book Company, New York.

DAVIDSON, H., and T. SPEAKMAN. 1969. Time study for planting trees. Weeds, Trees, Turf. 8(8):18.

DRUCKER, P. F. 1977. An introductory view of management. Harper's College Press, New York.

PETERS, T. J., and R. H. WATERMAN, JR. 1982. In search of excellence. Warner Books, Inc., New York.

PINNEY, J. J., and R. D. PINNEY. 1985. Beginning in the nursery business. American Nurseryman Publishing Company, Chicago.

STRONG, E. P. 1965. The management of business. Harper & Row, Publishers, Inc., New York.

# Chapter 4
# Selection of a Nursery Site

The selection of a site for a nursery should be done with considerable care and thought, since location will have a major effect on the overall success of the organization. Soil, water, and environment are factors of paramount importance in the selection of a site for a production nursery, whereas for a garden center the important considerations are population density, social customs, and traffic patterns. However, each factor should be considered and evaluated for the effect it will have on the overall success of the business. The factors are grouped into four convenient categories for discussion: ecological, economic, sociological, and biological.

## ECOLOGICAL FACTORS

### Climate

For the production of nursery stock, either field-grown or container-grown, a mild climate with a long growing season and an even distribution of rainfall is most desirable. Areas with extremes in temperature, especially rapid fluctuating temperatures, or those that are subject to wind, hail, or ice storms should be avoided. Sites should be selected that afford protection from drying winds, and alternate freezing and thawing. Within a large geographic area, there are sites to be found that have a favorable microclimate for the growth of plants. Sites close to a large body of water are often temperature-moderated by the lake effect up to 2 or more miles from the shoreline.

### Topography

The land for efficient operation should be relatively level; steep slopes should be avoided, but rolling land can be terraced. Sites that are subject to flooding or are known to be frost pockets should be avoided. Areas with large outcroppings of rock and large stones are less desirable as sites for a field-production nursery than those that are free of such obstructions, which impede many operations associated with modern nursery practices.

### Soil

The media for container-grown plants are generally artificially blended (Chapter 13). Therefore, the native soil is not an important site factor for a container-production nursery. But it is an important consideration relative to drainage and trafficability. Container-production nurseries need a dependable source of supply for sand, peat moss, water, fertilizer, containers, and so on, and these materials should be available at reasonable prices.

The selection of soil type for a field-production nursery will vary with the type of nursery stock to be produced. Seedlings and bare-root plants can be produced best when grown on sandy or sandy loam soil because (1) it does not crust over following rains or irrigation, allowing better seedling emergence; (2) it exhibits less tendency to heave, minimizing injury due to lifting of the plants out of the ground when the ground thaws in the spring; (3) it can be worked earlier in the spring and sooner after rains; (4) it requires less power for cultural operations; and (5) plants can be removed from it with less damage to the roots. Plants that are marketed with a soil ball about their roots are best produced in either a silty loam or a clay loam soil.

Soils for the production of quality nursery stock must have good structure and porosity. These characteristics have a strong influence upon air-water relationships, nutrient availability, the activity of microorganisms, and ultimately upon plant growth and development. Soils with a granular or crumb structure make excellent soils for field-production nurseries. These soils have good drainage characteristics while retaining adequate moisture for plant growth. They contain a balanced supply of clay minerals and soil colloids, which function as adsorption sites for plant nutrients. And they permit digging operations even in wet seasons.

The optimum soil reaction (pH) for the production of most woody plants is between 5.0 and 7.2. Therefore, it is desirable that the proposed nursery site have a pH within or close to this range. Soils with a pH greater than 7.2 should be avoided because it is difficult and costly to lower their pH. Acid soils can be corrected fairly easily with lime.

Although it is desirable that the soil have an optimum level of fertility, it is not an absolute requirement, since the intensity and balance of most elements can be modified fairly readily with commercial fertilizers. However, soils that test high in calcium and magnesium should be avoided as sites for the production of woody species, since high levels of these two bases will induce trace element deficiencies. Soils for field-production nurseries should contain 2–5% organic matter and must be free of pests, including noxious weeds, nematodes, insects, disease organisms, and herbicide residue, which might restrict the growth or impair the quality of nursery crops.

A valuable guide in selecting a site for a field production nursery is the past agronomic history of the site. A soil that is currently producing or recently produced a productive agricultural crop is to be desired over one that has a past history of low productivity. In addition, the native vegetation of the area can be a clue to the productive potential of the site. Assistance in evaluating potential nursery sites may be obtained from the U.S. Soil Conservation Service, county agricultural agents, the state department of agriculture, and soil, insect, disease, and horticulture specialists located at the state university. The Soil Conservation Service has available, upon request, excellent soil maps that can be of considerable value in selecting sites for a nursery. They provide information about crop production potential, drainage, soil depth, slope, and so forth.

### Water

An ideal nursery site, with respect to water, would be one where there is good rainfall distribution throughout the planting and growing season, with a minimum of rain (or snow) during the digging and shipping season. Since this is almost impossible to find, it is best to locate a site where there is access to a dependable supply of quality water. The delivery capability will vary from a few hundred gallons per minute to many thousands of gallons per minute, depending on the size and type of nursery to be established (see Chapter 14).

Water can be obtained either from a municipal water system or from streams, rivers, ponds, lakes, or wells. It should be free of alkalies, excessive salts, or industrial wastes that might be detrimental to plant growth. Irrigation water for use on seedlings and young transplants should have less than 200 parts per million (ppm) of dissolved solids. Whereas, the water used on larger field-grown or container-grown plants may have from two to three times this amount. A Solu-bridge can be used to estimate this value. A reading of 0.3 millisiemens (ms) per centimeter at 25°C is equivalent to 200 ppm of dissolved solids. Irrigation water that contains calcium in excess of 500 ppm is likely to raise the pH of the soil, which in time could have an adverse effect upon the growth of the plants (see Chapters 12 and 14).

In some areas of the country, sodium and boron can cause problems in the propagation and production of young plants. The sodium absorption ratio of the irrigation water should be less than 10 and the boron content less than one-half part per million (ppm). In addition to a supply of water for the nursery stock, a source of safe drinking water must be available for employees. Prior to making the final selection of the site for a nursery, consult with the state geologist or with the state department of natural resources relative to state laws pertaining to water rights.

### Air

Air pollution is a problem to be considered in selecting a site for a nursery. Air that is polluted with sulfur dioxide ($SO_2$), fluorides (e.g., hydrogen fluoride {HF}) photochemical smog, and ozone ($O_3$) should be avoided. These phototoxic pollutants are produced primarily by industry, motor transportation, and by the generation of electricity. Therefore, it is undesirable to locate either downwind from an industrial site that could be a potential source of pollution or in a confined geological area where photochemical smog concentrates due to poor air circulation.

### Environmental Audit

Since soil, water, and air pollution have become problems in the production of nursery crops in some areas it may be desirable to obtain an environmental audit of the soil and water resources prior to the transfer of agricultural property from a seller to a buyer. The audit serves as an assurance to the buyer that the edaphic environment is free of pollutants as claimed by the seller. The audit protects the seller against claims of soil or water pollution that may have occurred sometime after the sale of the property. Environmental audits can be obtained from organizations that specialize in the testing of soil and water as they relate to the environment and to public health.

## ECONOMIC FACTORS

### Cost of Land

The initial cost of the land will often determine if a nursery establishment can be started on a given site. Generally, it is thought that a production nursery engaged in extensive production cannot afford to produce plants on high-priced land. On the other hand, nurseries engaged in intensive production, landscape nurseries, or garden centers can afford higher-priced land provided that other factors do not limit productivity or sales. In addition to land costs, the annual taxes and property assessments will affect the net return on the investment and may in some cases preclude the operation of a nursery on the site. Many fine nurseries have closed or are closing operations on certain sites as a result of increased taxes caused by higher land values, brought about by urbanization.

One solution to high land costs is for an individual to own the land and lease it to the nursery on a long-term lease. This allows an individual to capitalize on appreciation of land values but permits a nursery to program production. In some states tax advantages can be obtained if the land is committed by contract to long-term (at least 10 years) agriculture. Information on these contracts can be obtained from the Cooperative Extension Service in the various states or from real estate agents who specialize in farm properties.

### Labor

Since nurseries rely on considerable hand labor to perform much of the work associated with production and landscape construction, a supply of manual labor must be available. Field-production nurseries, because of the seasonal nature of their operations, experience periods of peak demand for labor followed by periods where there is little need for labor. This seasonal need for unskilled labor is met in part by the employment of migrant laborers. However, with the passage of labor laws, many nurseries are finding it difficult to obtain seasonal labor. Some have solved this problem by employing high-school students, off-duty firemen, retirees, homemakers, and so on, on a part-time basis, whereas others are contracting for the employment of laborers from the various territories of the United States. Still other nurserymen are either contracting out some of the production operation (e.g., digging and packaging) or they are mechanizing many of the traditional hand operations associated with the nursery industry. In addition to manual laborers, nurseries also need individuals capable of performing various skilled operations (e.g., propagators, pesticide applicators) and others who have abilities as supervisors or managers.

### Facilities

Power is needed by most nurseries; some need only one form while others may require many forms. Electric power is needed for lighting and the operation of equipment, including irrigation pumps, refrigerators, potting machines, computers, typewriters, and so on. Three-phase electric power is desirable to operate certain types of machines (e.g., soil mixing, potting, packaging, and computers). If the three-phase lines are not close to the site, it can be costly to have the power brought to the site. This cost might be avoided by careful selection of the site or by using alternative sources of power, such as diesel-powered generators.

Oil, gas, or coal is necessary for the operation of the heating plant. Since the energy crisis of the mid-1970s, it is necessary to check on the availability of a dependable, noninterrupted supply of heating fuel at a cost that the business can afford. Gasoline is needed in large quantities to power trucks, tractors, cars, and other equipment used in the nursery. This should be contracted for delivery to the nursery so that the business can take advantage of bulk rates and submit the associated charges for a federal tax credit, which is permitted for off-the-road use.

Good transportation facilities are necessary for most nurseries. A high percentage of the nursery stock shopped in the United States is transported by motor truck. However, substantial amounts are also transported by railroad, particularly from the Northwest, and some is transported by airplane. Since motor freight is the primary means of transport, nurseries should locate so that trucks carrying heavy loads may have access without restriction. This is particularly important for nurseries located in the northern parts of the country, where weight limitations are often imposed on county roads during the spring-thaw period.

A garden center located on a road or highway that affords easy access is much more desirable than one located on a superhighway or on a second-class or unpaved road, where access is difficult. In some situations a site located on the right-hand side of the road for people going home from work in large urban areas may be more desirable than one located on the left side.

### Competition

Competition should always be evaluated before starting a new business. This is particularly true when the establishment will serve a limited clientele or market in a limited geographic area. The number of similar establishments and the progressiveness of each should be carefully considered. An elementary question that should be answered prior to starting a new business is: "What can I produce (product or service) that is superior to my competition, is needed by others, and can be sold for a profit?" However, competition is not a problem in selecting a site for a production nursery that will have a large market area (e.g., many states or the nation). In fact, the presence of other nurseries in the area may be an asset. Nurserymen often cooperate with each other on the use of specialized equipment, human resources, and in shipping arrangements.

## SOCIOLOGICAL FACTORS

Many sociological factors have influenced and will continue to influence the development of the nursery industry just as they influence many other segments of the economy. Increased population, wealth, and leisure time all point to a greater demand for nursery products. But these factors vary considerably between communities, and it behooves enterprising nurserymen to know these trends. The mode of life and the ethnic background of the people may also influence the acceptance of the products and services to be offered or the manner by which they can be merchandised.

City or township clerks should be contacted relative to zoning restrictions, building codes, permits, and business licenses prior to buying land to develop a nursery or prior to improving the present facilities. Local zoning laws may prohibit or restrict the development of a nursery, landscape construction firm, or a garden center on a given site.

The availability and quality of the schools, churches, hospitals, civic associations, and cultural centers are also important considerations for all segments of the nursery industry. Communities that support these facilities are prone to support good landscapes and are therefore good sites for garden centers and landscape nurseries. The availability of these facilities will indirectly affect a wholesale nursery's ability to attract and keep good personnel.

## BIOLOGICAL FACTORS

Various biological factors should also be investigated prior to selecting a site for a nursery, including the presence of any serious insect, disease, or weed pests. In addition, in some parts of the country deer can be a serious pest, causing extensive damage to nursery stock. County agricultural agents can often provide information on the presence and seriousness of these pests in their counties. Extension specialists, located at land-grant universities, can provide information on the control and eradication of pests. The Department of Natural Resources or a related agency can provide information on deer populations (including seasonal patterns), deer management programs, fence construction, and advice on site selection.

## SUMMARY

Establishing a successful nursery, landscape operation, or garden center is not a simple matter. It requires a large investment in land and facilities, familiarity with the laws and restrictions on all levels and units of government, and the assembling of a cohesive, productive group of people to accomplish the goals of the organization. Therefore, prior to selecting the site, all factors should be considered and evaluated. Advice from specialists in the area of real estate, soil science, horticulture, entomology, pathology, water resources, and associated areas should be solicited and evaluated. Considerable assistance may be obtained from county agricultural agents, soil conservation service, and extension specialists located at land grant universities. And it is highly desirable to have worked in the industry for a number of years prior to starting a nursery business. There is no substitute for experience.

## REFERENCES

DAVIS, D. D. 1973. Air pollution damages trees. USDA Forest Service.

ENGSTROM, H. E. 1941. Nursery practice for trees and shrubs suitable for planting on the prairie plains. USDA Misc. Publ. 434.

HAMILTON, D. 1980. Consider crop, economic and environmental factors when selecting a nursery site. Am. Nurseryman 151(5):10.

McANINCH, J. B., et al. 1983. Deer damage control in N.Y. agriculture. N.Y. State Dept. Agriculture and Markets, Div. of Pl. Ind.

PETERSON, G. W., and R. S. SMITH, JR. 1975. Forest nursery division in the U.S. USDA Agric. Hand. 470.

RICHARDS, L. A. 1954. Diagnosis and improvement of saline and alkali soils. USDA Agric. Hand. 60.

STOECKELER, J. H., and G. W. JONES. 1957. Forest nursery practice in the Lake States. USDA Agric. Hand. 110.

———, and P. E. SLABAUGH. 1965. Conifer nursery practice in the prairie plains. USDA Agric. Hand. 279.

# Chapter 5

# Organization and Development of the Nursery

The organization and development of a nursery site should be done with considerable care and forethought to maximize efficiency of production and to minimize loss of time. Some thought should also be given to future expansion and ways of attaining long-range goals. A detailed planometric map (Fig. 5–1) of the site, locating all existing facilities, natural or man-made, should be developed. Then with the aid of overlays, plans can be made to develop the site, including the location of production areas, irrigation facilities, shipping-receiving-storage areas, administrative headquarters, residences, circulation and parking, windbreaks, and beautification. A separate overlay should be made diagramming the location of all underground utilities, including depths, location of valves, and so on.

## GENERAL CONSIDERATIONS

The actual size and location of the individual units within the nursery will vary with the size and type of the operation, topography, soil type, cultural practices, equipment and extent of mechanization, availability of labor, and various economic factors.

**Figure 5–1** Planometric map of production nursery illustrating physical layout, control, and expansion potential. Dashed lines indicate areas for expansion.

The *best sites* in a field-production nursery should be allocated to the production areas, since soil is one of the major production assets. When possible, irrigation facilities should be centrally located within the production area to minimize the length of main lines and laterals.

*Shipping-receiving-storage facilities* are best located at a site that will be easily accessible from a major highway. The area should include adequate parking and turnaround area, elevated docks, adequate assembly areas, and restroom facilities for employees and truck drivers.

The *administrative headquarters* should be located to provide centralized control over production, shipping, and sales. In planning the building, consideration should be given to the interrelationship and coordination required by the various departments that will be housed in the headquarters. Adequate parking and convenient access to the sales area need to be provided for customers. If residences are to be constructed on the property, they should be located away from the commercial areas but conveniently connected to them.

*Circulation and parking* are important considerations in the development of nurseries and garden centers. Access and parking for customers should be made as easy and as convenient as possible. Preferably, these facilities should be blacktopped. Roads to the shipping-receiving-storage areas should also be readily accessible, about 30 ft in width, with no sharp-angle turns. In parts of the country where snow is a problem, it is advisable to locate the facility close to a major roadway to minimize snowplowing. Also, space at the sides of roads and parking areas must be available for piling of snow. Roads within the production area can be of crushed stone or gravel. They should be between 20 and 30 ft in width, but the gravel area can be confined to a 12- to 15-ft strip in the center. Roadways within the production area often serve as turnaround areas for field-operation equipment.

*Windbreaks*, if used, are planted on the windward side of seed beds and young transplant areas to reduce the dehydrating, eroding, and abusive effects of strong winds. Unfortunately, as the plants in the windbreak grow, so do their roots, which soon compete with the nursery crops for the available water and nutrients. Windbreaks that support vegetation 6 ft or more in height can materially reduce the yield of crops immediately adjacent to and up to several feet from the windbreak. The distance is roughly proportional to the height of the windbreak. Also, plants in the windbreak can harbor insects, diseases, and mammals that could be injurious to the nursery crops. If windbreaks are planted, avoid species that are known to be an alternate or primary host to a disease or insect that is a pest of nursery crops. Two good uses of evergreen plantings in a nursery are for protecting outdoor propagation areas with sheared hedges and the screening of storage room walls from the heating rays of the sun. These plantings can also serve as a source for seed or cuttings if the appropriate species or cultivar is planted. In areas where a permanent natural windbreak is undesirable, it could be advantageous to construct a windbreak out of snow fencing or to interplant with an annual crop such as corn between every two or three seed or liner beds.

In developing the overall plan for the nursery, consideration must also be given to constructing storage areas for equipment, tools, fertilizer, pesticides, and other materials. Container production nurseries will need storage areas for the basic ingredients of their growing media (sand, peat, bark, and so on); a holding area for containers; and special storage tanks for fertilizer concentrate.

*Employee facilities*, such as parking areas, locker rooms, lunchrooms, restroom facilities, and foremen's offices, should be carefully planned and properly constructed and maintained. Clean, neat facilities for employees are important in maintaining morale, which will have a direct effect upon production efficiency.

*Public areas* of the nursery should be planned and landscaped. Mature, well-maintained specimen plants can be developed into attractive synoptic plantings, which will aid in selling smaller nursery plants.

## SPECIFIC CONSIDERATIONS

*Production areas* of nurseries include propagation greenhouses, seed beds, cold frames, liner beds, and the blocks or container yards. In most nurseries, production is centered on one farm, but in large nurseries production is often distributed over a number of farms. When a nursery offers a diverse product mix, it is desirable to organize the production effort either by method of production (field vs. container) or by plant type (herbaceous vs. woody; evergreen vs. deciduous; trees vs. shrubs vs. ground covers; etc.) When a number of farms are utilized, it is good management to concentrate compatible plant types onto one farm to gain production efficiency.

Seedbed areas are best situated on level, well-drained sandy loam or silty loam sites with a moderate level of nutrition and the pH appropriate to the crop. The beds should be oriented in an east-west direction if a lath or snow fence is to be employed for shade, so that the lath strips will be oriented in a north-south direction. This orientation produces a moving sun-shade pattern during bright sunny days, which will prevent sunscalding of the seedlings or newly rooted cuttings beneath, which could occur if the lath strips were oriented in an east-west direction.

The width of the seedbeds is generally determined by the width of equipment used in working the area. The wheels of all heavy equipment should be confined to pathways between the beds. Some commonly used widths are 36, 42, and 48 in. Prior to planting, it is highly desirable to obtain a soil analysis to determine levels of nutrients and presence or absence of nematodes. In many situations, it is also desirable to fumigate or sterilize the soil prior to planting to assure freedom from diseases, weeds, and other pests.

Liner beds are areas of the nursery where young plants are grown under intensive culture for a period of 1–2 years prior to planting, either in the field or in containers. The liner beds may be open fields exposed to the elements, or they may be protected by shade houses (Fig. 5–2). Shade houses are utilized to temper the climate to produce better-quality plants for transplanting.

Plantings in the liner area are either in beds or in long, narrowly spaced rows. The spacing between the rows is determined primarily by the equipment utilized to plant, care for, and dig the plants. Spacings of 3, 4, 5, and 6 in. between rows are common. The actual spacing in the rows is determined by species, growth rate, and desired size of the transplants. Where beds are utilized, the width is adjusted to accommodate the equipment, but a 3 1/2- or 4-ft bed with 10-in. pathways is common (Fig. 5–3). A 100-ft liner bed, 42 in. wide, planted to eight 5-in. rows with plants 4 in. in the row would support a population of 2520 plants. If the offset system of planting is utilized, that is, four rows are mechanically planted at a time followed by four additional rows interplanted between the others, the width of the pathway may have to be increased by one row width to accommodate the offset of the equipment.

Prior to planting of liner areas, the land must be properly prepared, including plowing, disking, leveling, sterilizing, or preplant weed control and subsoiling if necessary. The soil should be prepared to a depth of at least 6 in., although deeper preparation is needed for tap-rooted species. Moisture is crit-

**Figure 5–2** Young evergreens planted in liner beds, protected by a shade house. (Courtesy Zelenka Nurseries.)

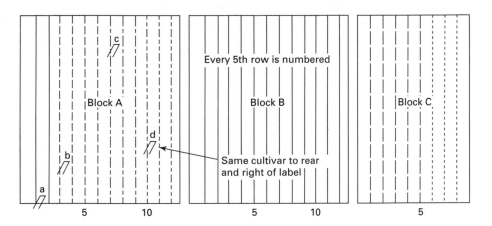

**Figure 5–3** Liner beds 52 in. on centers.

**Figure 5–4** Designation of blocks and rows in a field-production nursery.

ical to producing optimum growth in this intensive production area. Therefore, a readily available source of good quality water is an essential factor in the proper management of the area.

*Field-production areas* of large nurseries may consist of one or more farms designated by name. Each farm is subdivided into blocks and rows. For ease of management, some form of designation is assigned, generally letters for the blocks and numbers for the rows. Two standard systems are used for labeling plant material within production nurseries. In propagation beds, small field-production areas, and in container-production nurseries, the most common method of labeling is from left to right and from front to rear (Fig. 5–4). In large field-production nurseries, especially when planting is done mechanically, the labeling system conforms to the direction in which the rows were planted (Fig. 5–5).

## PLANTING DESIGNS

The organization or design of nursery production areas varies from area to area of the country and from nursery to nursery. The primary designs are the row, square, offset square, rectangle, equilateral triangle, interplanting, or a

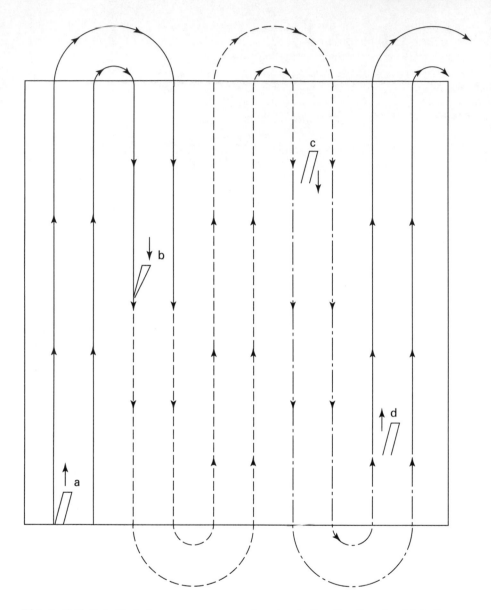

**Figure 5–5** Labeling of nursery rows, conforming to the direction in which the rows were planted in large field-production nurseries using multirow planting machines.

combination of two or more systems. The determining factor in organizing production areas should be production efficiency. When land is expensive, intensive cropping systems may be warranted. When land is relatively inexpensive, the use of wider spacing may be justified. However, a balance is desirable, particularly with the use of large equipment currently employed in planting, maintaining, and harvesting nursery stock.

The *row* is the oldest and simplest method of planting nursery stock on level terrain. However, on hilly, well-drained sites, the straight row can still be used, whereas on hilly, poorly drained sites, the row is modified to follow the contour. The row is used primarily in the production of bare-root plants such as herbaceous perennials, roses, shrubs, and small-diameter trees. The spacing between rows is determined by the width of equipment used in planting, maintaining, and harvesting the crops. The standard width between nursery rows in many field-production nurseries is 42 in., but this is modified to fit production methods. Long nursery rows can be planted, cultivated, and harvested much more efficiently than a series of short rows, since less time is spent in turning around at the end of the rows.

The *square design* (Fig. 5–6) is commonly used for the field production of B&B material such as large trees and specimen evergreens. It is also used extensively in the placement of containers within the beds of container-production nurseries. It allows for cross cultivation in the maintenance of field-production nurseries and lends itself to harvesting on the diagonal (Fig. 5–7) for thinning of the field block or container bed when harvesting a crop of small plants for early market. The spacing between plants following harvesting is the diagonal of the former square. This can be calculated by use of the Pythagorean theorem: $c = \sqrt{a^2 + b^2}$. The square design is used where land costs are relatively low because it efficiently utilizes only 78% of the land, but this disadvantage is partially compensated for by its advantages.

The *offset square* is used in some nurseries. This is where the plants in even-numbered rows are offset between the plants in the odd-numbered rows. However, this system gains little advantage over the square, since the distance between plants in the row remains the same. It also sacrifices the advantages

**Figure 5–6** Square design.

**Figure 5-7** Digging on the diagonal.

of cross cultivation and harvesting on the diagonal. It is used, sometimes, when planning a marketing program, incorporating three times of harvest. When this is done, every other row is dug, followed a year later by every other plant in the remaining row, and finally the widely spaced plants are harvested.

In the *rectangular design* (Fig. 5–8), the distance between rows is greater than the distance in the row. It is the least efficient in space utilization (less than 78%), but it is employed where land is relatively inexpensive or where larger mechanical equipment is utilized in maintaining and harvesting operations.

A modification of the rectangular design is the *rectangle-square system* (Fig. 5–9). It is used to decrease loss of space but still allows for the movement

**Figure 5-8** Rectangle design.

**Figure 5-9** Rectangle-square design.

of large digging equipment between every two double rows. Another modification is the *interplanting system* (Fig. 5–10), employed where wide spacing is used for a long-term crop. In this system, a short-term crop is interplanted to gain a quick cash return. However, it has the disadvantage of different cultural requirements, and if not properly cared for and harvested on time it can lead to problems in management. In some situations the interplanted short-term crop could be a quick cash crop (e.g., vegetables). It is desirable to integrate the cultural programs for the two crops prior to planting to assure compatibility.

A variation of the interplanting system that is used in the production of field-grown shade trees requiring large-sized digging equipment for harvest is to plant two rows of rapidly maturing plants between every two, three, or four rows of shade trees. The open alley, produced by early harvest of the interplant crop, allows easy access of the heavy digging machines for harvesting of the large shade trees.

The *equilateral triangle-hexagon design* (Fig. 5–11) should be used when it is desired to maximize the utilization of space (Table 5–1). It is most commonly used in container-production nurseries where land is expensive and maximum production per unit area is desired, but it can also be used in field-production areas where land is expensive. In this design 91% of the space is utilized when the plants reach their maximum size. The rows are offset from the square but the between the-row distance is 15% less than the spacing between plants in the row. However, plants in the ground cannot be cross-cultivated and harvesting time is critical.

A space-efficient design for shade trees, which permits easy access of equipment into the blocks, is to plant the trees in four- or five-row units, utilizing the equilateral triangle design, with a wide alley between each unit. This

**Figure 5–10**  Interplanting design.

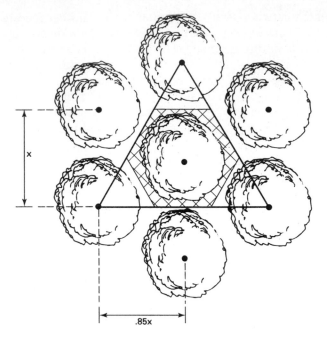

**Figure 5–11** Equilateral triangle-hexagon design.

is for access of the large equipment used in maintenance and harvesting. The alley can be seeded to a sod to allow equipment to function during periods when the soil is wet. The area in plants can either be clean-cultivated or sod strips can be established between the rows with clean cultivation in the rows. Herbicides can be used to aid in maintaining the planted areas in a weed-free condition (Fig. 5–12).

### Economic and Cultural Considerations

The physical organization of the plantings within a nursery will vary with the situation, but the following economic and cultural factors should be considered.

1. *The efficient use of land.* The equilateral triangle produces the most efficient use of space; the square-rectangle is the least efficient.
2. *The size of plant for the market objective.* If the market objective is for small plants, the spacing can be relatively close, but if the objective is to produce large, landscape-sized plants, the spacing must be wide to accommodate the crown of the plant.
3. *The cultivar.* If the cultivar has a narrow, upright habit of growth, the spacing can be close, whereas if the cultivar is widespreading or of a weeping habit, the spacing must be wider.

**Table 5–1** Plant Density for Various Spacings in the Nursery

| Spacing (ft) | Square feet/Plant, $1 \times w$ | Area/Plant, $0.7854d^2$ | Number/ 1000 ft² | Number/Acre | Number/ Equilateral Triangle[a] |
|---|---|---|---|---|---|
| 2 × 2 | 4 | 3.14 | 250 | 10,890 | 12,620 |
| 2 × 3 | 6 | 3.14 | 167 | 7,260 | |
| 2 × 4 | 8 | 3.14 | 125 | 5,445 | |
| 2.8 × 2.8[b] | 8 | 6.28 | 125 | 5,445 | |
| 3 × 3 | 9 | 7.07 | 111 | 4,840 | 5,600 |
| 3 × 4 | 12 | 7.07 | 83.3 | 3,630 | |
| 3 × 6 | 18 | 7.07 | 55.5 | 2,420 | |
| 4.2 × 4.2[b] | 18 | 14.14 | 55.5 | 2,420 | |
| 4 × 4 | 16 | 12.57 | 62.5 | 2,722 | 3,150 |
| 4 × 6 | 24 | 12.57 | 41.7 | 1,815 | |
| 4 × 8 | 32 | 12.57 | 31.3 | 1,361 | |
| 5.7 × 5.7[b] | 32 | 25.13 | 31.3 | 1,361 | |
| 5 × 5 | 25 | 19.64 | 40.0 | 1,742 | 2,018 |
| 5 × 6 | 30 | 19.64 | 33.3 | 1,452 | |
| 5 × 8 | 40 | 19.64 | 25.0 | 1,089 | |
| 5 × 10 | 50 | 19.64 | 20.0 | 871 | |
| 7.1 × 7.1[b] | 50 | 39.27 | 20.0 | 871 | |
| 6 × 6 | 36 | 28.27 | 27.8 | 1,210 | 1,400 |
| 6 × 8 | 48 | 28.27 | 20.8 | 907 | |
| 6 × 10 | 60 | 28.27 | 16.7 | 726 | |
| 8.5 × 8.5[b] | 72 | 56.55 | 14.1 | 605 | |
| 8 × 8 | 64 | 50.27 | 15.6 | 680 | 785 |
| 11.3 × 11.3[b] | 128 | 100.53 | 7.8 | 340 | |
| 10 × 10 | 100 | 78.54 | 10.0 | 435 | 500 |

[a]Distance between rows = 0.85 in-the-row distance.

[b]Spacing resulting from removing diagonal rows.

4. *Equipment use in maintaining and harvesting.* When the horse and mule were used for cultivation, the spacing between rows was fairly narrow. But with modern equipment of high horsepower, it is necessary to increase the spacing between the rows to permit entry and movement of the equipment—especially at the time of harvest.

5. *Economic return on investment.* Although many agricultural enterprises, including container-production nurseries, measure return on investment per acre of land, it is more appropriate for a field-production nursery to evaluate a total production system, including land, spacing, maintenance, and harvesting to maximize return on total investment, not only on land. Land use is one input into the system, and it should be used efficiently. But materials handling is the major cost input in the production of nursery products, and if machines make labor more effective, it may be necessary to redesign the production areas to obtain the most effective materials-handling system, even though it calls for less efficient use of land.

**Figure 5–12** Shade trees growing in a nursery with grass sod between the rows. Rows are treated with a selective herbicide. (Courtesy Manbeck Nursery.)

## CONTAINER-PRODUCTION AREAS

The design of container-production areas is strongly influenced by a number of factors, including irrigation and drainage, materials handling, cultural and maintenance requirements of the plants, size of the containers, and the costs involved. *Irrigation* is an absolute requirement in the development of container-production nursery areas, since plants in containers are totally dependent upon a supply of water. Container-grown plants should be grouped according to their water requirement to obtain maximum benefit from the irrigation system (Chapter 14).

*Drainage* is the companion factor to irrigation and must be considered in the development of the container area, since large volumes of water are applied to the plants throughout the growing season, and much of this water falls outside the containers or drains through them. It is necessary to remove this excess water from the area to assure drainage of the media within the containers, and to carry on various plant maintenance and materials-handling operations. If the site is not well drained, it will have to be graded and a drainage system developed. Excess water should seldom be allowed to drain back into a pond used for irrigation of nursery stock, since it may be high in soluble salts or contaminated with weed seeds, herbicides, or spores of various fungi, any of which have the potential of causing plant production problems. In most situations excess water is disposed of via county or municipal drainage facilities. However, in recent years, some communities have enacted ordinances prohibiting the disposal of water contaminated with excess soluble salts into these facilities.

This necessitates developing other means to dispose of the excess water. Two alternatives are to construct holding ponds or to install "French" drains at various sites within the area if the soil profile permits. The water collected in the holding ponds might possibly be reused within the nursery if it is of acceptable quality. However, in most situations it is either used to irrigate agronomic crops or is allowed to evaporate into the air. If the water can be reused, the ponds should be constructed fairly deep with a relatively small surface area, whereas if the water cannot be reused, the ponds should be constructed fairly shallow with a large surface area. French drains are simply deep holes or trenches dug through low-porosity topsoils into high-porosity subsoils. The trenches are then filled with rocks or crushed gravel. These drains allow the excess water to percolate into the soil and recharge the underground water supply. The area about the beds is graded to channel the water to the drains.

*Materials handling* is probably the most significant factor in the development of the area. Plans need to be developed and the area designed to expedite the efficient handling of materials through the various phases of production, including media preparation, potting, setting out of containers, pickup of containers for shipping or rearrangement for overwintering, and loading for shipping. A well-planned design should provide for a logical rotation of crops through the production cycles so that double handling of the containers is kept to a minimum. The design of the area must also provide for the space needs of machines, especially transport equipment, used in the operation of the nursery.

The cultural and maintenance requirements of the plants will also influence the design of the container area. Plants that have special requirements are best grown together in areas where their special needs can be met most efficiently. Also, plant maintenance requirements such as fertilizing, pest control, pruning and training, and spreading for growth increase, must be provided for, although in some situations the planted containers are spaced when set out to meet their spacial needs throughout the production cycle. This is done to minimize handling, but it sacrifices water efficiency if the plants are watered by an overhead means.

In areas of the country where it is necessary to provide winter protection for container-grown plants, overwintering structures (see Chapter 17) must be planned for in the development and organization of the site. When such facilities are to be constructed, they should be designed and located so that plant material can be moved into and out of the facility with efficiency. Also, the structure must be oriented and built in a manner to withstand the force of wind in areas where winds are a problem.

Size of containers is another parameter that affects the overall design of the container area. Containers are best grouped by size to aid in providing for the water requirements, ease of handling, and maintenance. The various areas might include small (1 and 3 gal), medium-sized (5, 7, 15 gal), and large (20 gal or larger) containers. Within each area the containers can be subgrouped into beds by species. The size and arrangement of the beds is influenced by the growth habits of the plants, the rotation program, and the size and physical limitations of the area.

For maximum utilization of space within the beds, containers are set touching one another in offset rows. As the plants grow and require additional space, the containers are spaced and rearranged, commonly utilizing the equilateral triangle-hexagon design. In some situations, the interplanting (understory) design is utilized. In this design shade-tolerant species are grown under the canopy of taller-growing plants. Where space is not a factor or where either physical requirements of the plants or the physiography of the area impose limitations, other designs are utilized.

### Blow-over

A significant problem confronting nurserymen who produce container-grown plants in windy areas is *blow-over*. The problem is caused by the wind that blows many container-grown plants over due to lack of stability. This is due in large part to the light weight of the growing medium and the size of the plants. Growers can make use of a number of options to minimize blow-over. The most commonly used technique is to mass small-sized plants pot to pot within the growing area. However, as the plants grow and need to be spaced apart the chances for blow-over are increased and one or more of the following techniques can be used to stabilize the plants and to minimize blow-over.

1. A wire frame, composed of 6 × 6 in. openings, that is 4 ft wide and of the desired length is stretched over the container bed at a height of approximately 4 to 6 in. (adjusted for height of containers). It is secured to either wood or metal supports at both ends of the bed and as needed along the length of the bed on both sides. The plant containers are placed into the openings and grown in place by standard container-production methods.

2. For growers who are situated on well-drained sites and desire to grow container-grown plants, there is the option to use the in-the-ground-support container method with a pot in pot technique. This consists of augaring holes, of appropriate depth and diameter, into the soil to accommodate the in-the-ground-support container. Into the bottom of this container is placed either a small amount of gravel or a brick on to which is set the plant container. The gravel or brick allows for good drainage from the media within the plant container. The in-the-ground pot provides for excellent stability against blow-over due to high-velocity winds.

3. Another technique employed for plants, especially trees, growing in larger containers or in production sites that do not lend themselves to the use

of the in-the-ground-support system is the use of the wire trellis and plant saddles. In this system a wire of suitable gauge is stretched the length of the row and is secured at both ends and as needed in the row. The height of the trellis is adjusted to fit the species to be supported, but should be kept as low as possible to assure good development of taper (see page 344). Tree support saddles are clamped onto the trellis as needed and the bowls (trunks) of the trees are secured to the saddles. As the trees increase in size and stem diameter it is necessary to adjust the ties to prevent girdling of the stems.

The cost of developing container-production areas should be carefully researched prior to construction. This includes the raw materials for plant production (e.g., ingredients for the medium, water, fertilizers, containers, etc.); the cost of land leveling, irrigation, drainage, and so on; and the costs of operating the facility. In some situations the initial cost of development could be a limiting factor in effecting a successful cash flow except at low interest rates (see Chapter 7), whereas in other situations the development or expansion of a container production facility may be a desirable capital investment for nurseries that are expanding, especially when reinvesting income derived from previous crops.

### Field-Grown / Container-Grown Plants

A new method of producing plants, especially trees, in nurseries is *field-grown / container-grown*. This system utilizes grow-bags for in-the-ground field production phase, followed by the use of containers during the last phase of production, just prior to sale.

In this system young plants, for example, trees (whips), are planted into grow-bags and grown under standard field production methods for a year or two depending upon species and size of the grow-bags. When this phase is completed the plants are dug, generally in the spring, and the grow-bags are removed. Removing of the bags effectively root prunes the trees without serious stress. Following planting, new roots soon emerge at the small nodule that developed on the roots where they penetrated the grow-bags. The trees are potted into containers of appropriate size and grown using standard container production methods for the second phase of production. Many of the trees are sold in the fall of that season and some in the following spring.

The system lends itself to a number of modifications that allows for versatility of production and marketing. For example, in the field production stage the trees can be planted in grow-bags all of one size and all the plants harvested at one time and planted into containers for the second phase of production. Or, the trees can be planted into grow-bags of different sizes (i.e., 14 and 18 in. or 14, 18, and 24 in.) sequentially in the same row. After a year or two of growth the plants in the smallest bags are harvested and moved into containers. A year or two later the plants in the next size bags are harvested and moved into the second phase and this is followed by the largest trees that were allowed to develop to full size prior to moving to the container phase.

Any number of combinations of bag sizes can be used or (if one desires different species with different growth rates) can be produced in the same row or in alternate rows depending upon individual production plans.

## PRODUCTION PROGRAMMING

It is extremely difficult to efficiently produce a wide range of plant material. Growing a wide variety of species, each requiring its special method of propagation and field culture, does not lend itself to production efficiency. In order to gain a greater degree of management control over production, it may be desirable to specialize either by type of plant or by method of production. Limiting production to plant groups that have similar production requirements and are compatible with production capabilities is one means of gaining production efficiency. Also, with increased mechanization of routine production operations there is greater need for standardization of techniques. Specialization and standardization permit managers to plan and control production, thus ensuring a greater chance of success in the business. But nursery managers must be careful not to become too specialized, since monoculture is very vulnerable to disaster should there be a major change in weather conditions, plant pests, or market demand. It is seldom desirable that one genus or one class of plant material make up more than 20–25% of the total production effort.

Production programming must begin with a market analysis to determine if there is a market for the product, the potential demand, in what size and form, and how many plants per year would meet the production goal. Information must be obtained on production requirements related to propagation, soil and water requirements, general culture in the nursery, and pest problems. An estimate must be made of the resources that will be needed, the production efficiency or mortality that can be expected, and the costs involved. The production requirements are summarized, in part, in Fig. 5–13.

Up-to-date technical information should be collected and summarized so that the manager, propagator, and grower will have available, in abstract form, the details needed for planning the best production system and timing of operations. This information should be updated periodically with practical, relevant experience data as they are accumulated within the production nursery.

## ESTIMATING PLANT MATERIAL REQUIREMENTS

Once a production quota has been established for the end product, it becomes necessary to calculate the quantity of cuttings to be stuck, grafts to be made, or seeds to be sown in order to produce the transplants and ultimately the liners that will either be field-planted or planted in containers in order to

Species _____ Size class _____

Sales of market                     Previous sales _____
  information
_____ Projected sales    _____
_____   Garden center _____
_____   Wholesale      _____
_____   Landscape      _____
Technical data                      Other          _____
                                    Projection for planning _____
Propagation: method and times _____
_____
Soil and water _____
_____
Plant requirements _____
_____
Pests _____
_____
_____
Expected growth performance _____
_____
_____
Additional data _____

Resources needed

Space:
  Propagation bench space _____ sq. ft.
  Liner beds          _____ sq. ft.
  Fields              _____ acres

Materials:
  Fertilizer   _____
  Pesticides _____
  Other      _____

Labor inputs _____
_____

Estmated losses:
  Through replacements _____
  Through grade-out    _____
  In-the-field         _____
  In liner beds        _____
  In propagation       _____

Equipment needs _____
_____
_____
_____

Cost estimates _____
_____
_____
Notes     _____
_____
_____
_____
_____

**Figure 5-13** Nursery production information.

meet production quotas. In each step of the operation there is a mortality that can be expected plus a loss of material at grade-out for some classes of plant material, and a factor for replacements. These data may be available from past records or an estimate can be made based on information obtained from other sources.

Estimates for subsystem quotas are obtained by working backward from the estimated production or sales figure. The calculation is made for each step in the production cycle by dividing the production quota of that phase of production by its estimated return percentage (Table 5–2). This is obtained by subtracting the percent mortality from 100%. For example, if 10,000 is the production goal, 10,000 represents 100%; if replacements are 5%, 10,530 plants must be produced to meet sales plus replacements (10,000 ÷ 0.95 = 10,530). Combining percentage loss figures to calculate the material needed to start the production cycle results in a figure less than what is actually needed.

## ESTIMATING SPACE REQUIREMENTS

Space requirements can be estimated for propagation, liner production, and either field or container production. When a perpetual production system is designed, it is necessary to know the rotation system that will be employed in addition to the planting densities that will be used in the field- or container-production areas, the liner area, and the propagation bench. This information can then be used in planning for and adjusting the space needs for the total operation.

**Table 5–2**  Estimate of Plant Material Requirements

|  |  |
|---|---|
| *Species:* | Taxus 'Hicksi' |
| *Class:* | B&B 3–4 ft |
| *Rotations:* | Field 5–1; linear 2–1 |
| *Propagation:* | Evergreen cuttings, Dec.–Apr. |

| *Estimated Goal for:* | *Plants* |
|---|---|
| Sales objective | 10,000 |
| Replacements 5%[a] | |
|   First revision | 10,530 |
| Grade-out (if applicable) | |
|   (not applicable with B&B material) | |
| Field mortality 15% | |
|   Second revision (liners needed) | 12,400 |
| Liner loss 10% | |
|   Third revision (transplants needed) | 13,770 |
| Propagation loss 25% | |
|   Fourth revision (cuttings to stick) | 18,350 |

[a]Percentages must be obtained from past experience. These are for demonstrative purposes only.

Using this information, the various department heads (propagation, field, container, storage, shipping, etc.) can plan and program their space, labor, and material requirements. For example, the propagator can assemble all the production programs for the current season and plan his or her material, space, and labor requirements.

After the individual species to be propagated have been classified by method of propagation and a priority index assigned (Table 5–3), the space and time requirements can be estimated and adjusted to fit the limitations imposed by the available bench space (Fig. 5–14). In the example here, group D has priority 1 and is plotted first, followed by groups A and C. Group C must be delayed by 5 weeks due to space limitations, but group A is programmed according to schedule. Group B, with priority 3, is split into two groups, $B_1$ stuck on time and $B_2$ delayed until week 5; the cuttings can be held in storage until space is available. Similar estimates can be made by other department heads, who coordinate their activities with each other under the overall control of the production manager.

**Table 5–3**  Propagation Space Needs and Allocation Chart

| | | Space Needed | | Adjusted | |
| Group | Priority | (ft²) | Weeks | Square Feet | Weeks |
|---|---|---|---|---|---|
| A | 2 | 500 | 45–5 | — | — |
| B | 3 | 1000 | 40–5 | $B_1$:500 | 40–5 |
| | | | | $B_2$:500 | 5–17+ |
| C | 2 | 500 | 5–15 | 500 | 10–20+ |
| D | 1 | 1500 | 42–10 | — | — |

**Figure 5–14**  Propagation space availability diagram.

## PRODUCTION LAND UTILIZATION

### Field-Grown Crops

Land used in the production of field-grown stock is generally occupied for several years. In addition, the land may be out of production, either lying fallow or in a cover crop, for a period of time that will vary from a few months to a number of years prior to replanting. One salable acre of nursery crops will require a number of non-salable acres to support the program. Table 5–4 lists estimated acreage requirements for selected classes of field-grown nursery stock.

Management practices will vary with type of nursery and production objective. Therefore, the estimated acreage requirements should be used only as a guide where individual data are not available. Another land requirement that must be added to these figures is the land needed for turnaround and service areas. It is estimated that these requirements may vary between 5 and 10% of the production requirement.

### Container-Grown Crops

Land used in the production of container-grown crops is occupied for only a few months for crops with a rapid production cycle, up to 1–2 years for species with longer production cycles. This is one of the major advantages for container production—shorter rotation time—leading to faster turnover of invested capital. The actual space requirement varies with the market objective, the climate, various cultural practices, and spatial arrangements.

If the market objective is to produce small plants in small containers on a rapid rotation, 1 acre of land may produce two to three crops per year, so that only 0.5 or 0.33 acre of space is required per area of annual sales. However, for large plants on a 2-year rotation, it may take as much as 2 acres of land or as little as 1.5 acres per acre of annual sale. Climate and various cultural operations will influence growth rates, which will affect turnover rates. Nurseries located

**Table 5–4** Estimated Acreage Requirements for Field-Grown Nursery Stock

| Class[a] | Average Age at Sale | Years in Rotation | Land Required per Acre of Annual Sale |
|---|---|---|---|
| Broad-leaved evergreens | 3.5 | 0.8 | 4.3 |
| Range | 2.6–4.5 | 0.5–1.4 | 3.5–5.0 |
| Narrow-leaved evergreens | 3.5 | 0.9 | 4.4 |
| Range | 2.4–5.3 | 0.5–1.3 | 3.3–5.8 |
| Deciduous shrubs | 2.7 | 1.3 | 4.0 |
| Range | 1.8–4.4 | 0.5–3.2 | 2.4–5.8 |
| Ornamental trees | 4.4 | 0.7 | 5.1 |
| Range | 2.1–8.2 | 0.2–1.9 | 3.3–8.8 |

[a]Range = shortest to longest period reported.

*Source*: Data from *South. Coop. Ser. Bull.* 143 (1969).

in southern latitudes have longer growing seasons and are capable of producing crops in a shorter period than nurseries located in northern climates. Also, plants that are produced under optimum cultural conditions of light, nutrition, moisture, and pest control can be produced on a shorter production cycle, which will reduce the time that each container-grown plant occupies space in the nursery. Finally, the space needs will be influenced by the spatial arrangement of the containers through the production cycle.

Container-production nurseries that are operated on a profit basis must be cognizant of utilizing space efficiently and minimizing rotation time when planning the development of a production system. By careful planning, many container-production nurseries can increase their production efficiency on both an acre basis and on invested capital.


## SUMMARY

The organization and development of the land areas within a nursery should be carefully planned prior to development. The best sites should be reserved for plant production. Each unit should be located and developed to produce optimum growth of plants and to maintain their quality following harvest but still permit efficient use of labor in each phase of the production, maintenance, and marketing effort. The time spent in carefully planning the layout and development of the nursery site is well worth the effort in the efficiency that can be gained in the use of the other factors of production.


## REFERENCES

DAMBACH, C. A. 1948. A study of the ecology and economic value of crop field borders. Graduate School Stud. Ohio State Univ. Bio. Sci. Ser. 2.

GILFORD, J. C. 1974. Some thoughts on production planning. Proceedings of the 9th Refresher Course for Nurserymen, Pershore College of Horticulture, Pershore, England, pp. 34–43.

STOECKELER, J. H. 1957. Forest nursery practice in the lake states. USDA Agric. Hand. 110.

WIANT, H. V., JR. 1973. Efficiency of regular spacing planting designs. Tree Planters Notes 24(3), p. 31.

# Chapter 6

# Laws, Regulations, and Codes

The nursery industry, like other major industries, must comply with certain laws and regulations. The laws and regulations are promulgated by government primarily for the protection of people. Federal laws and regulations, other than tax laws, that are of concern to the nursery industry include (1) Federal Social Security and Unemployment Compensation, (2) Fair Labor Standards Act of 1938 as amended, (3) Occupational Safety and Health Act of 1970, (4) Migrant and Seasonal Agricultural Worker Protection Act of 1983, (5) Plant Pest Acts and Quarantines, (6) Federal Environmental Pesticide Control Act of 1972, (7) Federal Warranty Act of 1975, (8) Federal Price and Services Act of 1936, (9) Plant Patent Act of 1930 as amended, (10) Plant Variety Protection Act (PVPA), 1970, (11) Equal Opportunities for Individuals with Disabilities (1990), (12) workers' compensation, and (13) Trade Practice Rules for the Nursery Industry. In addition, various state and local units of government have laws that affect the nursery industry.

## FEDERAL LAWS AND REGULATIONS

The following is a synopsis of federal laws and regulations as they affect the nursery industry. For specific details and up-to-date information on these laws and regulations, since they are amended periodically, the nursery manager should contact the American Association of Nurserymen or a lawyer. The AAN is in a position to provide member firms with useful information on all federal regulations and legal decisions relative to the nursery industry.

The 1935 *Federal Social Security Act* provided for federal-state cooperation in an old age assistance and unemployment insurance program. The Old Age and Survivors Insurance (OASI) program is designed to provide an income in the worker's old age and to assure some income for dependents after his or her death. The cost of the program is borne by both employers and employees. Every employer who employs one or more persons is liable for this tax. Employers pay a tax on each employee's wages up to a base amount (which changes with time). The employee pays a similar tax. However, the employee's share of the tax is deducted by the employer at the close of each pay period and forwarded to the Director of Internal Revenue. As of January 1, 1990, the wage base was $43,000 and the tax rate was 7.15%, paid equally by employer and employee. Current information on OASI and the necessary forms are available from the district director of the Internal Revenue Service.

In January 1991 all agricultural employers were required to withhold federal income taxes (and state income taxes where applicable) for any agricultural workers already subject to Social Security (FICA) withholdings. Employers should obtain copies of Federal W-4 forms "Employee's Withholding Allowance Certificates" from the Internal Revenue Service (IRS). For complete details contact an IRS office or a tax attorney.

*Federal Unemployment Compensation* became effective for agricultural workers January 1, 1978. Under the federal law the tax, paid by the employer, is 6.2% of the first $7000 of wages (percentage and base change with time. If employees are covered by a state unemployment compensation law, the employer receives a credit against the federal tax. Since the wage base and tax percentage vary with the individual states, it is suggested that nurserymen contact their state unemployment compensation agency for specific data. Most states impose substantial penalties for late payment or failure to pay unemployment compensation taxes.

The *Fair Labor Standards Act* of 1938 (referred to as the Federal Wage-Hour Law) established 25 cents as the minimum pay for 1 hr of labor. But the law was limited to firms engaged in interstate commerce, and agriculture was exempted from coverage under the law. Over the years minimum pay has increased and coverage has been extended with fewer exemptions. As of January 1977, the only agricultural exemption was for an employer who used less than 500 worker-days of agricultural labor during the preceding calendar year.

Also, overtime (not less than 1.5 times the employee's regular rate) must be paid for hours worked in any week in excess of 40.

For many years agriculture had a seasonal exemption, but as of January 1977 there was no seasonal exemption. Within a nursery organization, the only personnel exempt from the minimum pay and overtime requirements are executive, administrative, or professional employees, each of whom must meet the test for exemptions as required by the latest regulations.

Nurserymen must comply with the Federal Wage-Hour Law's equal-pay provisions. The law requires equal pay, regardless of sex, for equal work on jobs that require equal skill, effort, and responsibility, and are performed under similar conditions. Exceptions to the law are payments made because of a seniority system, a merit system, a system that measures earnings by quantity or quality of production, or a differential based on any factor other than sex.

Employers found in violation of the law can be required to pay the difference in back wages for 2 years as well as increase the pay of the employee(s) who had been paid the lesser amount. An employer cannot reduce the wage of other employees in order to come into compliance with the act.

Time and payroll records must be maintained for 3 years. The records must show daily and weekly hours worked by all nonexempt employees. Also, the records must show overtime payments separately from straight-time payment, total earnings, deductions, and net pay.

The latest amendment to the law also contains a number of new provisions and penalties to the child labor portion. The law prohibits the use of oppressive child labor in interstate commerce or in the production of goods for interstate commerce. The law limits the use of child labor by age group and type of activity.

Individuals 18 years of age or older may be employed in any occupation without regard to the time of day or the number of hours worked. But minors under 18 years of age may not be employed in occupations declared to be hazardous by the Secretary of Labor. Examples of hazardous occupations within the nursery industry are operation of a tractor of over 20 PTO horsepower; operation of power-driven posthole digger or driver; operating or assisting in operation of trencher, earth-moving machine, forklift, power-driven saws; driving a vehicle transporting passengers; working on a ladder or scaffold of over 20 feet; and handling or applying agricultural chemicals classified under the Federal Insecticide, Fungicide or Rodenticide Act as category 1 and category II.

Minors under 16 years of age may be employed in agricultural occupations, except those which have been declared to be hazardous. But their employment is not permitted during school hours. All minors must be paid minimum wage unless certificates are obtained for the employment of full-time students at 85% of the minimum.

Employers must maintain records on the employment of all individuals under 19 years of age. Such individuals should be required to furnish either an age or employment certificate (obtained from local school authorities) or a copy of their birth certificate as proof of age.

By act of congress the minimum wage was raised to $3.80 per hour as of April 1, 1990 and was increased to $4.25, as of April 1, 1991. (For current minimum wage rates contact local Social Security Office.) Also, in 1991 the penalties for violations of the *Fair Labor Standards Act* were increased from a maximum of $1000 to $10,000. A penalty may be assessed for each employee who was subject to violations. Violations of minimum wage of overtime provisions of the Act will carry the same penalty.

The Williams-Steiger *Occupational Safety and Health Act* (OSHA) of 1970 was enacted by Congress "to assure so far as possible, every working man and woman in the nation safe and healthful working conditions and to preserve our human resources." This act covers all employers with 11 or more employees.

The general duty clause of the act states: "Each employer (1) shall furnish to each of his employees a place of employment free from recognized hazards that are causing or are likely to cause death or serious physical harm to his employees; (2) shall comply with the occupational safety and health standards promulgated under this act." However, the act also places some responsibility on employees. The general duty clause also states: "Each employee shall comply with occupational safety and health standards and all rules, regulations and orders issued pursuant to this Act which are applicable to his own actions and conduct."

Landscape contractors are subject to the general construction safety and health standards, which include first-aid services, provisions for medical care and consultants, wearing of hard hats, eye and face protection, and so on.

If growing horticultural commodities is the primary activity of the establishment, it is considered agriculture; thus most safety and health standards do not apply. However, the general-duty clause is applicable to employees of the establishment. Nurserymen should obtain a copy of subpart J. Regulations 1910.141 through 1910.148, for regulations and standards that apply to nurseries.

As of September 1976, five federal standards apply to nurseries, including SMV emblem, housing in labor camps, anhydrous ammonia, tractor-rollover protection, and PTO guards. The SMV (slow-moving vehicle) emblem must be displayed on all slow-moving equipment operating on public roads. The emblem must be kept clean and be replaced when faded.

Nurserymen who operate labor camps must obtain a license, generally from the department of health in the state where the camp is located. Requirements for licensing are based on a 1968 U.S. Department of Labor standard on housing agricultural workers. The standard covers environmental aspects of temporary housing for employees, such as building construction, sanitation, water, refuse disposal, and so on.

The anhydrous ammonia standard requires that equipment used in applying anhydrous ammonia meet certain standards. Nurserymen should ask suppliers to certify in writing that their equipment meets OSHA standards.

The rollover protection standards as published by OSHA require that all tractors of more than 20 engine horsepower manufactured after October 25, 1976, must be equipped with rollover protective structures, (ROPS) and a seat belt. Employers must instruct employees on operation practices and ensure the use of seat belts when operating tractors with rollover protective structures.

Safety standards on guarding of farm equipment, effective October 25, 1976, require power-takeoff (PTO) drives to be guarded. Also, signs must be placed at prominent locations on tractors and PTO-driven equipment specifying that PTO safety shields must be kept in place.

Record-keeping requirements are very specific. They are contained in the booklet entitled "Record Keeping Requirements Under the Williams-Steiger Occupational Safety and Health Act of 1970." Every nurseryman should obtain a copy from a district office of the U.S. Department of Labor. Employers who violate the law can be assessed costly penalties.

OSHA provides that states may develop their own safety and health laws and assume most of the enforcement processes. But the state program must be at least as effective as the federal program. Most states have developed and are enforcing programs in safety and health.

To assure compliance with this far-reaching piece of legislation, nursery managers may wish to organize an OSHA committee within the nursery. The committee, chaired by a key employee, should be responsible for advising the manager on matters pertaining to safety and health, keeping informed on all state and federal requirements, and seeing that nursery employees comply with all applicable standards.

In 1987 OSHA expanded the "right to know" rules regarding hazard communication to include virtually everyone in the work place. The new standards require all employers to develop a hazard communication program including the following items.

1. Log all chemical products in the workplace.

2. Label all hazardous chemical containers.

3. Keep Material Safety Data Sheets (available from suppliers) in an area where they are immediately available in an emergency.

4. Identify and train employees who could be exposed to hazardous chemicals.

5. Develop and maintain a written program that explains how employees are informed and trained about the hazardous chemicals in the workplace.

These standards apply to all employers, therefore nurserymen would be well advised to obtain a copy of the standards and to develop a hazard communication program to be in full compliance with OSHA standards. To do otherwise could lead to financial disaster.

*The Migrant and Seasonal Agricultural Worker Protection Act of 1983* (MSAWPA) replaced the Farm Labor Contractors Registration Act (FLCRA) of 1964. The purpose of this act is to remove the restraints on commerce caused by activities detrimental to migrant and seasonal agricultural workers; to require farm labor contractors to register under this act; and to assure necessary protection for migrant and seasonal workers, agricultural associations, and agricultural employers. MSAWPA eliminated the requirement for nurserymen, or their employees, who employ migrant and seasonal agricultural workers to register as farm labor contractors and to be fingerprinted. Totally exempt from any aspects of the act are employers hiring less than 500 man-days of labor in any calendar quarter in previous year. Also exempt are those who hire or transport workers within a 25-mile radius of their permanent residence and for not more than 13 weeks a year. Family businesses owned or operated by members of same immediate family are exempt provided that a member of same family does recruiting. Nurserymen hiring migrant and seasonal agricultural workers, beyond the exempted states, must do so through a registered farm labor contractor. It is the contractor's responsibility to arrange all the details of employment and to assure compliance with MSAWPA.

The *Plant Pest Act of 1912* and the *Plant Pest Act of 1957* are the basic laws of plant quarantines in the United States. Prior to 1912, there were no laws protecting the United States from the entry of foreign pests or to prevent and control their distribution within the country. The 1912 Act, as amended by Congress, gave authority to the Secretary of Agriculture to regulate by quarantine the importation and interstate movement of nursery stock, other plants, and plant products that may be vectors of foreign plant pests.

There are three levels of quarantine that affect nurserymen, depending upon their sources of materials and the geographic distribution of their products:

1. *Foreign quarantines* affect the movement of plants and plant products between nations. But in general, few nurserymen are concerned with foreign quarantines, except as they affect shipments to and from Canada and Mexico. Nurserymen wishing to import or export plants or plant products should obtain a copy of "Foreign Quarantine Notices," Title 7, Chapter III, Part 319, from the Animal and Plant Health Inspection Service (APHIS), USDA, and obtain a special permit, which can be obtained in most states through the state department of agriculture or from APHIS. There are some plants and plant products that cannot be imported into the United States from certain foreign countries. Details are contained in "Foreign Quarantine Notices," which is updated periodically.

Canadian quarantine regulations limit shipping of all clonally produced fruit trees and ornamental stock of the genera *Malus*, *Prunus*, *Cydonia*, *Chaenomeles*, and *Vitis* to Canadian nurseries holding valid permits to import this type of plant material. Details of the regulation are available from the AAN. In addition, nonfood nursery stock must be certified Japanese beetle free for export to Canada after the following treatment: B&B, containerized, and potted nonfood plants are dipped in a dip solution containing 32 oz (2 lb) of chlorpyrifos (active ingredient) per 100 gal of water. The plants are to remain in the dip solution until bubbling ceases. Upon removal from the dip solution, plants must be allowed to drain until the soil is reasonably dry, but not less than 3 days. Plants held for more than 3 days must be protected from reinfestation. (Chlorpyrifos is produced by Dow Chemical Co. as Dursban 4E.)

2. *Interstate quarantines* are of major concern to nurserymen engaged in interstate shipment of plants. These may be federal or state quarantines. The general policy in the enforcement of interstate quarantines is to permit unrestricted movement of all plant products within the regulated area and to restrict shipments beyond the quarantined area to uninfested products and plants. Examples of domestic quarantines include golden nematode, Mexican fruit fly, citrus blackfly, pink boll-worm, imported fire ant, witchweed, and schleroderris canker. A number of states impose exterior quarantine requirements on nursery plants moving in interstate commerce. Nurserymen in states where Japanese beetles are known to exist must have their production land treated so that the plants can be certified as free of Japanese beetles when they are shipped into states imposing the quarantine. Copies of federal regulations may be obtained by writing: Plant Protection and Quarantine Program, APHIS, USDA, Federal Building No. 1, Hyattsville, MD 20782.

3. *Intrastate quarantines* or regulations are authorized by state legislation and are imposed and administered by the state agency in charge of plant pest regulation, generally a part of the state's department of agriculture. These regulations are designed to prevent the spread of specific pests within the state and as a means of preventing other states or the USDA from restricting the movement of plants and plant products from the entire state rather than from just the infested portion of the state.

A quarantined area is usually a civil boundary such as national, state, or county. In order to move regulated products out of a quarantined or restricted area, they must be inspected or subjected to some pest-destroying treatment and carry a certificate assuring their freedom from the pest upon which the quarantine is placed. All states have laws pertaining to the inspection and movement of nursery stock. Nurserymen should be familiar with these laws and comply accordingly. The AAN publishes a quarantine wall chart and maps of quarantine areas. All nurserymen shipping nursery stock interstate should have up-to-date copies of the chart and the selected maps to post in the shipping area of the nursery. But nurserymen should invite inspection, since the plant inspector can help identify plant pests and suggest control measures before they become serious problems.

A state license is required in all states of persons, partnerships, or corporations growing and/or desiring to sell nursery stock. The license is obtained from the director of agriculture, but in some states it may be available from the secretary of state. Also, all nursery stock must be inspected and found free of serious pests before it may be sold or moved from place to place. Nurserymen are required to make application for inspection and are often assessed a fee, usually on the acreage of salable stock. Nurserymen must comply with all federal and state quarantines, rules, and regulations.

Nurserymen shipping nursery stock out of state have been required to file a nursery inspection certificate with the state department of agriculture in the various states into which stock was shipped. However, since 1974 many states have accepted a current list of certified nurseries and nursery stock dealers in lieu of the individual certificates. This change was recommended and adopted by the National Plant Board in 1974. An up-to-date list of states accepting the list in lieu of certificates is generally available through the Department of Agriculture, Plant Industry Division, within each state.

The *Federal Environmental Pesticide Control Act* (FEPCA) of 1972 (amendments to Federal Insecticide, Fungicide and Rodenticide Act [FIFRA]) were enacted to protect people and the environment from the hazards of dangerous pesticides. The act classifies pesticides and pesticide applicators, and it limits the application of pesticides according to the applicator's training and certification. The act is administered by the Environmental Protection Agency (EPA).

Pesticides are classified into two categories: general use and restricted use. General-use pesticides are those which when applied in accordance with directions for use will not generally cause unreasonable adverse effects on the environment. Restricted-use pesticides are those which when applied in accordance with directions for use may cause unreasonable adverse effects on the environment, including injury to the applicator. The misuse of pesticides, including use, that is "inconsistent with label directions" is in violation of FIFRA and is subject to a fine.

The EPA is responsible for classifying and updating the classification of pesticides. Anyone can purchase and apply general-use pesticides, but since October 1977, only certified pesticide applicators can purchase and use restricted-use pesticides. The law requires that individuals who use or supervise the use of restricted-use pesticides be certified either as a private applicator or as a commercial applicator. They must keep a record of all restricted-use materials used for 3 years.

A private applicator is a person who uses or supervises the use of restricted-use pesticides for the purpose of producing an agricultural commodity on property owned or rented by the applicator or his or her employer, or on the property of another person if applied without compensation (other than trading of personal services between producers of agricultural commodities).

A commercial applicator is a person who uses or supervises the use of any pesticide that is classified for restricted use for any purpose or on any property other than as provided for by the private applicator classification.

To be certified, a person must be determined to be competent with respect to the use and handling of pesticides. States can develop their own programs for training and certifying applicators, subject to the approval of the federal EPA administrator. In most states, the state department of agriculture administers the certification and licensing of pesticide applicators. Two pesticide applicator manuals are available from the Superintendent of Documents, U.S. Government Printing Office, Washington, DC 20402: "A Guide for Private Applicators" for those applying pesticides only on their own or rented crop land, and "A Guide for Commercial Applicators" for those applying pesticides on other people's property for hire. The manuals are helpful to those who wish to become certified as pesticide applicators. For up-to-date details on classification of pesticides, procedures for certification, liabilities, and so on, nurserymen should contact their state department of agriculture or the agriculture agents of their local county Cooperative Extension Service.

The Magnuson-Moss *Warranties Act* of 1975 supplements the Uniform Commercial Code (UCC) in force in all states except Louisiana. The act requires that written warranties on all "consumer products" manufactured after July 4, 1975, and costing more than $10 must be designated either "limited" or "full" and that the warranty designation must be made clearly and conspicuously. A "consumer product" is "any tangible personal property, including nursery products, which is to be distributed in commerce and which is normally used for personal, family or household purposes."

The act, administered by the Federal Trade Commission (FTC), does not require the seller to grant warranties, but if a warrant is offered, the law is applicable. To qualify as a "full warrant" under the act, the seller (nurseryman) must warrant that he will remedy (repair, replace, or refund) without charge in a reasonable time in the event of a defect or failure of the product. A full warrant includes the cost of replanting if the plant was planted by the nurseryman. However, a nurseryman is not under obligation to fulfill a warrant if it can be shown that the plant died or was damaged as a result of storms, animals, or by the warrantee's (customer) failure to provide reasonable and necessary maintenance. Nurserymen not wishing to be obligated by the full-warranty requirements may grant a "limited warranty," in which they state the limitations of the warrant.

The FTC, through the publication of regulations, will clarify and particularize the seller's obligations under the act. The act does not regulate state laws related to contracts which also govern laws of warranty. Therefore, nurserymen offering written warranties may wish to consult an attorney familiar with the laws and regulations pertaining to warranties to ensure that their warranty complies with both state and federal laws. Current information on the latest federal regulations on warranties can be obtained by writing to one of the regional offices of the FTC or the AAN. Information on state laws can be obtained from the office of the state attorney general or from state nursery associations.

The Robinson-Patman *Price and Services Act* of 1936, an amendment to the antitrust act of 1914, prohibits a seller from discriminating between his or her business customers in price and service and prohibits a buyer from knowingly receiving illegal favors or services. The act applies to the sale of tangible goods in interstate commerce and is enforced by the FTC. In essence, the act requires that a seller treat all commercial customers equally with regard to the price of the same product and service offered. The simplest way for nurserymen to comply with the act is to sell from a price list (catalog) which is uniform for all customers competing for the product, in wholesale units.

*Americans with Disabilities Act* (ADA), Public Law 101-336, dated July 2, 1990. The preamble to the law states that the Congress of the United States finds that some 43 million Americans have one or more physical or mental disabilities and that, historically, society has tended to segregate and discriminate against individuals with disabilities. The purpose of this law, which became effective July 26, 1992, is to provide a clear and comprehensive national mandate for elimination of discrimination against individuals with disabilities, and to provide a clear, strong, consistant and enforceable standards addressing discrimination against individuals with disabilities.

This law will affect nurserymen (or their agents) who employ 25 or more employees for each working day in each of 20 or more weeks in the current or preceding calendar year following the effective date. However, two years following the effective date the minimum number of employees will drop to 15 for each working day in each of 20 or more weeks.

The law defines the term "qualified individual with a disability" to mean an individual with a disability who, with or without reasonable accommodation, can perform the essential functions of the employment position. The *essential functions* of a job should be a written description that is made available prior to advertising or interviewing applicants for the job. The job description should be considered evidence of the essential functions of the job.

The law goes on to detail many of the factors that employers can or cannot do when interviewing prospective employees; the details of which can be obtained from national or state trade associations.

The *Plant Variety Protection Act (PVPA)* in force since December 1970 provides legal protection to developers of new varieties of plants that reproduce sexually—by seed. The law states that protection may be extended to a novel variety if it meets three qualifications:

1. *Distinctness.* The variety must differ from all known varieties in one or more of the following ways—morphological (shape, color), physiological (such as disease resistance), or other characteristics (such as milling characteristics of a new variety of wheat).

2. *Uniformity.* If any variations exist in the variety, they must be describable, predictable, and commercially acceptable.

3. *Stability.* The variety, when sexually reproduced, must remain unchanged in its essential and distinctive characteristics to a degree expected of similarly developed varieties.

The owner of a new–and novel–variety who obtains a Certificate of Protection under the PVPA has control over the use of that variety for 17 years. The owner of the Certificate may bring civil action against persons infringing on his or her rights.

Application forms and detailed information for variety protection may be obtained from the Plant Variety Protection Office, Grain and Seed Division, Agricultural Marketing Service, United States Department of Agriculture, National Agriculture Library, Beltsville, MD 20705.

The Towsend-Purnell *Plant Patent Act*, an amendment to the general patent law, was passed by Congress in 1930 and amended slightly in 1954. The significant portion of the statute states, "Whoever invents or discovers and asexually reproduces any distinct and new variety of plant, including cultivated sports, mutants, hybrids and newly found seedlings, other than a tuber-propagated plant or plant found in an uncultivated state, may obtain a patent, therefore. . . ." Characteristics that may distinguish a new variety (cultivar) of a plant for patent consideration include, among others, habit of growth; color of stems, leaves, flowers, or fruit; resistance to cold, drought, heat, or disease; productivity or lack of productivity of flowers or fruit; fragrance; storage qualities; and ease of asexual propagation.

The plant patent is a grant by the federal government to the inventor (or his or her heirs or assignee) the right to exclude others from asexually propagating the plant or selling the plant so reproduced for a period of 17 years from the date of issue. Application for a plant patent may be obtained from the Commissioner of Patents, Washington, D.C. 20231. Nurserymen wishing to patent a plant may wish to discuss the topic with a current holder of a plant patent and to contact an attorney or agent registered with the patent office. A copy of "Directory of Registered Patent Attorneys and Agents" is available from the Commissioner of Patents.

*Workers' compensation insurance* (WCI) must be carried by employers who hire one or more employees that work in a hazardous occupation (listed in section 3, workers' compensation law) and by all employers who employ three or more employees. If coverage is not required by law, an employer may obtain workers' compensation insurance on a voluntary basis. The insurance may be obtained from any private insurance company authorized to transact the business of workers' compensation insurance within each state.

Rates for WCI vary according to the type of employment, the hazards involved, and the personal injury history of the company. Insurance groups working through trade associations (e.g., AAN) offer special WCI savings plans. These plans are designed to provide dividends on WCI premiums, depending upon the claim experience of policyholders within the group. Nurserymen are advised to consult their state or national trade association or Dobson Insurance Group, P. O. Box 559, Kansas City, MO 64141, for details of the plan.

*Trade practice rules for the nursery industry* as promulgated by the FTC in 1956 and amended in 1979 as *Guides for the Nursery Industry* are designed to foster and promote the maintenance of fair competitive conditions in the interest of protecting industry, trade, and the public. In general, the rules consider it an unfair trade practice to sell, offer for sale, or distribute industry products by any method, or under any circumstance or condition, which has the capacity and tendency or effect of deceiving purchasers or prospective purchasers as to quantity, size, grade, kind, species, age, maturity, condition, vigor, hardiness, number of times transplanted, growth ability, growth characteristics, rate of growth or time required before flowering or fruiting, price, origin or place where grown, or in any other material respect.

Among practices prohibited by the foregoing are direct or indirect representations: (1) that plants have been propagated by grafting or bud selection methods, when such is not the fact; (2) that industry products are healthy, will grow anywhere without the use of fertilizer, or will survive and produce without special care, when such is not the fact; (3) that plants will bloom the year round, or will bear an extraordinary number of blooms of unusual size or quality, when such is not the fact; (4) that an industry product is new variety, when in fact it is a standard variety to which the industry member has given a new name; (5) that an industry product cannot be purchased through usual retail outlets, or that there are limited stocks available, when such is not the fact; (6) that industry products offered for sale will be delivered in time for the next (or any specified) seasonal planting when the industry member is aware of factors that make such delivery improbable; (7) that the appearance of an industry product as to size, color, contour, foliage, bloom, fruit, or other physical characteristic is normal or usual when the appearance so represented is in fact abnormal or unusual; (8) that the root system of any plant is larger in depth or diameter than that which actually exists, whether accomplished by excessive packing material, or excessive balling, or other deceptive or misleading practice; (9) that bulblets are bulbs; and (10) that an industry product is a rare or unusual item, when such is not the fact.

All commercial nurseries should have a copy and be familiar with the trade practice rules for the nursery industry. Copies of the rules may be obtained from the FTC.

## STATE AND LOCAL LAWS

*Most states have laws* related to (1) environmental pesticides; (2) labor standards; (3) liens; (4) licenses; (5) occupational safety; (6) pest control, including diseases, insects, and vertebrates (deer, rodents, birds, etc.); and (7) sales taxes.

In some states wholesale nurserymen are required to collect a sales tax on gross in-state sales unless they are presented with a copy of a resale certificate, a farmer's exemption certificate, an exempt use certificate, an exempt organization certification, a direct payment permit, or identification of the purchaser as a government agency. Out-of-state customers are exempt from the tax except when the plants are delivered to a point in or picked up in the state of sale.

*Municipal laws* affecting nurserymen generally relate to licenses, property zoning, and road limitations. Information on these laws and regulations can be obtained from state nurserymen's associations, the state department of agriculture, and various units of local government, especially the city or township clerk.

## METRIC EQUIVALENTS*

The United States is the only major nation in the world that has neither adopted the metric system nor established a time schedule for conversion. Nevertheless, nurserymen who do business with foreign countries need a conversion table to convert U.S. units to metric units or metric units to U.S. units. Table 6-1, listing approximate metric units, is suggested for use in grading nursery stock either by caliper, height, spread, or size classes.

## CODES

Various codes, including numbers, colors, letters, and bar codes are used in the nursery and landscape for many purposes.

*Numbers* are used by many nurseries that use electronic data processing equipment to code the plant material by species, cultivar, and grade, to expedite processing. The order forms of some firms are specially designed to simplify ordering and to speed processing. Prepunched IBM cards can be rapidly assembled into an "order deck" to rapidly and accurately prepare the necessary documents to process the order.

Climatic zones within the United States and Canada are designed by number. These zone numbers are used by nurserymen to designate areas of the country where their plants are expected to be hardy and where the plants will make optimum growth. However, these zones of hardiness do not apply to plants growing in containers since the root systems are exposed to ambient air temperatures which can at time be greater than or lower than cardinal temperature that results in death of root tissue. The zones are also used in planning shipping schedules for spring and fall deliveries.

*See Appendix E for metric conversions.

**Table 6–1** Metric Conversions for Nursery Stock Graded by Caliper, Height, Spread, and Size Class

| U.S. Units | Metric | Approx. Metric | Nursery Stock Size Classes — U.S. Units | Approx. Metric |
|---|---|---|---|---|
| *Inches* | *Centimeters* | *Centimeters* | *Inches* | *Centimeters* |
| 0.5 | 1.27 | 1.5 | 3–6 | 8–15 |
| 1 | 2.54 | 2.5 | 6–9 | 15–25 |
| 1.5 | 3.81 | 4.0 | 9–12 | 25–30 |
| 2 | 5.08 | 5.0 | 12–15 | 30–40 |
| 2.5 | 6.35 | 6.0 | 12–18 | 30–50 |
| 3 | 7.62 | 8.0 | 15–18 | 40–50 |
| 3.5 | 8.89 | 9.0 | 18–24 | 50–60 |
| 4 | 10.16 | 10.0 | | |
| 4.5 | 11.43 | 11.0 | *Feet* | |
| 5 | 12.70 | 13.0 | 2–2½ | 60–80 |
| 5.5 | 13.97 | 14.0 | 2–3 | 60–90 |
| 6 | 15.24 | 15.0 | 2½–3 | 80–90 |
| 6.5 | 16.51 | 16.0 | 3–3½ | 90–100 |
| 7 | 17.78 | 18.0 | | |
| 8 | 20.32 | 20.0 | | *Meters* |
| 10 | 25.40 | 25.0 | 3½–4 | 1.00–1.25 |
| 12 | 30.48 | 30.0 | 4–5 | 1.25–1.50 |
| 15 | 38.10 | 40.0 | 5–6 | 1.50–1.75 |
| 18 | 45.72 | 50.0 | 6–8 | 1.75–2.50 |
| *Feet* | | | 8–10 | 2.50–3.00 |
| 2 | 60.98 | 60.0 | 10–12 | 3.00–3.50 |
| 2.5 | 76.20 | 80.0 | 12–14 | 3.50–4.00 |
| 3.0 | 91.44 | 90.0 | 14–16 | 4.00–5.00 |
| | | | 16–18 | 5.00–5.50 |
| *Meters* | *Meters* | *Meters* | 18–20 | 5.50–6.00 |
| 3.5 | 1.07 | 1.00 | | |
| 4 | 1.22 | 1.25 | | |
| 5 | 1.52 | 1.50 | | |
| 6 | 1.82 | 1.75 | | |
| 7 | 2.13 | 2.00 | | |
| 8 | 2.44 | 2.50 | | |
| 9 | 2.94 | 2.75 | | |
| 10 | 3.05 | 3.00 | | |
| 12 | 3.66 | 3.50 | | |
| 14 | 4.27 | 4.00 | | |
| 16 | 4.88 | 5.00 | | |
| 18 | 5.48 | 5.50 | | |
| 20 | 6.09 | 6.00 | | |

Zip-code numbers are used by mail-order nurserymen when processing their mailings to gain financial advantages by bulk mailing.

Numbers are also used to identify or code orders, estimates, employees, equipment, and prices. Where orders are identified by number, a convenient practice is to combine the order number and the date received or processed into a date-order number by year, month, day, order (e.g., 87-07-20-333). This not only provides immediate identification of the order but provides a rapid means by which sales or purchases can be analyzed by any desired time period.

Prices can be coded by numbers to fit the needs of the nursery. One effective method is to designate that the last digit of a number series be the number (of dimes and all previous digits indicate the number) of dollars. For example, a price code 176 means that the wholesale price is $17.60, and the code 100 means that the wholesale price is $10. Various modifications can be made to this system.

Seedlings and transplants are commonly coded by number to indicate the number of years in a seed or transplant bed (e.g., 2-1 indicates 2 years in seedbed, 1 year in transplant bed; 2-0 indicates 2-year seedling).

*Color* is used to aid in the rapid identification of items. Colored tapes or flagging are used to identify specific plants in the nursery that have been selected by or for a customer. It is a good practice to reserve one color tape (e.g., red-striped) for use in identifying plants that are to be rogued from the nursery or a landscape planting. This specific tape should never be used for any other purpose. Colored tape is used to identify female plants of a dioecious species (e.g., holly). This aids in identifying female plants when they are not in flower or fruit.

Colored labels can be used to identify size classes to expedite the assembling of orders by inexperienced help. They have also been used by bedding plant growers to identify plants of a certain price. For example, plants priced at $2.50 per flat may have a blue label, whereas plants priced at $3.00 per flat may have a red label, and so on.

Another use for color coding is for the identification of clones, particularly of deciduous species during the dormant period. Color codes can be used to excellent advantage in coding scion wood and understocks, especially when a number of different clones are involved, as in the grafting or budding of fruit tree varieties on clonal understocks. Color-coded fruit trees are appreciated by orchardists, who must make large plantings with inexperienced help. The color codes are best applied with spray paint.

Some nurseries, particularly landscape nurseries, use distinctive colors to identify their tools and equipment to avoid loss while working on jobs with other contractors. Distinctive colors are also used to identify special equipment that should be used for only certain jobs, such as sprayers to apply 2,4-D-type herbicides.

Colored forms or tabs can be used to expedite the processing of orders or messages within the office. Many nurseries use specifically designed color-

# USDA Plant Hardiness Zone Map

| RANGE OF AVERAGE ANNUAL MINIMUM TEMPERATURES FOR EACH ZONE | |
| --- | --- |
| ZONE 1 | BELOW -50°F |
| ZONE 2 | -50° TO -40° |
| ZONE 3 | -40° TO -30° |
| ZONE 4 | -30° TO -20° |
| ZONE 5 | -20° TO -10° |
| ZONE 6 | -10° TO 0° |
| ZONE 7 | 0° TO 10° |
| ZONE 8 | 10° TO 20° |
| ZONE 9 | 20° TO 30° |
| ZONE 10 | 30° TO 40° |
| ZONE 11 | ABOVE 40° |

The zones of plant hardiness in the United States—This map is an adaptation of the color map on the reverse side. It lacks many fine details of the color map but may be useful for small-scale reproduction in books, magazines, and nursery catalogs.

**Figure 6–1** The Plant Hardiness Zone Map illustrates the expected minimum temperatures of most of the horticulturally important areas of the United States (excluding Alaska and Hawaii) and Canada. It shows 10 different zones, each of which represents an area of winter hardiness for certain ornamental plants. (From USDA Agric. Res. Serv. Misc. Publ. 814.)

coded order forms for this purpose. The various colored sheets within a set of forms aid in identifying the action to be taken. For example, a wholesale nursery may use a yellow form for the shipping and the receiving copy, a white form for the office copy, pink for order acknowledgment, and green for use by the shipping department. A landscape firm can use various colored forms to control and coordinate landscape sales (e.g., white—sales record, orange—nursery division, green—construction division, pink—record division, etc.)

Certain *abbreviations* are used as standard practice in the nursery industry, although there is some variation between nurseries. Some of the more common abbreviations are:

| | |
|---|---|
| B | Budded |
| B&B | Balled-and-burlapped |
| B&P | Balled-and-potted |
| BR | Bare-root |
| C | Cutting |
| CAL | Caliper |
| CG | Container-grown |
| COLL | Collected plants from native stands |
| DBH | Diameter Breast Height |
| FP | Field-potted |
| FR | Field row or field run |
| G | Grafted |
| HT | Hybrid tea |
| RC | Rooted cutting |
| TC | Tissue culture |
| PB | Peat-balled |
| RP | Rose pot or root-pruned |
| S | Seedling |
| SPEC | Specimen |
| Std | Standard |
| T,TT | One for each time transplanted |
| X,XX,XXX | Used to designate degree of heavy grades; some nurseries use this symbol to indicate number of times transplanted. |

An example: *Picea pungens* Moerheim, G, 10-12, 4 yr, TT. This is a Moerheim blue spruce that was grafted, transplanted twice, is now 4 years old, and averages 10-12 in. in height.

### Bar Codes

Bar Codes, along with Universal Product Codes (UPC) and scanners, first began to make their appearance into the nursery industry in the late 1980s and in the early 1990s. They were primarily used for identification, sizing, and pricing of plants sold in garden centers by mass merchandisers who purchased large quantities of plants from a single supplier. The grower tagged the plants, generally with a picture tag and a bar code. The picture tag displayed a color photograph of the plant, the common name in large print, and the botanical name in smaller size print. The UPC and bar code is programmed to print out, when scanned, the botanical and common names as well as the size and price of the plants.

The Universal Product Code is a series of 12 digits which, when integrated with a computer to interpret the code, will print out the information at the time of sale as well as process the information into management information. Growers should contact the Uniform Code Council* in Dayton, Ohio to obtain details of this valuable management tool.

UPC and bar codes, along with scanners and the computer, can also be utilized in tracking product inventory and product movement, shipping and receiving, billing, and accounts payable. Each of these functions can increase the efficiency and profitability of large wholesale nurseries by improving accuracy, timeliness, and expenses.

## SUMMARY

Nurserymen must comply with a number of federal, state, and local laws and regulations. These have been summarized briefly within this chapter. Since laws and regulations are subject to modification with time, it is desirable that nursery managers keep informed of changes that will affect their nurseries. This is best accomplished by maintaining membership in the AAN as well as in various state and local nursery associations. Codes, including numbers, colors, and abbreviations, are used within the industry for many reasons. Where standard codes exist, they should be utilized.

## REFERENCES

AMERICAN ASSOCIATION OF NURSERYMEN. 1975. The Federal Warranty Act. ALI 2(4):4.

———. 1975. Buyers and sellers beware. ALI 2(4):16.

———. 1979. Guides for the nursery industry. Federal Register 44(40):11,177-11,179.

HICKS, A. H. 1991. UPC: Harness the Power of the Computer. Am. Nurseryman 174(12):106.

FLEMING, W. E. 1972. Preventing Japanese beetle dispersion by farm products and nursery stock. Agric. Res. Serv. USDA Tech. Bull. 1441.

*Uniform Code Council 8163 Old Yankee Rd. Dayton, OH 45458

LEVERETT, E. J., JR., and J. H. PADGETT, 1972. Complying with the occupational safety and health act. Am. Nurseryman 135(11):10.

MOREFIELD, K. R. 1972. OSHA and nurseries. Am. Nurseryman 136(4):28.

———. 1974. Wage hour laws. ALI(1):5.

PUBLIC LAWS 1912. An act to regulate the importation of nursery stock. U.S. Statutes at Large. 62nd Congress. Vol. 31, part I, pp. 315-319.

PUBLIC LAWS 1930. Plant Patents Act. U.S. Statutes at Large. Vol. 46, part I, Chapter 312, p. 376.

PUBLIC LAWS 1935. Social Security Act. U.S. Statutes at Large. 74th Congress. Vol. 49, part I, pp. 620-648.

PUBLIC LAWS 1938. Fair Labor Standards Act. U.S. Statutes at Large. 75th Congress, 3rd Session. Vol. 52, pp. 1060-1069.

PUBLIC LAWS 775. 1954. Plant Patents. U.S. Statutes at Large. Vol. 68, part I, Chapter 1259, p. 1190.

PUBLIC LAW 85-36. 1957. Federal Plant Pest Act. U.S. Statutes at Large. 85th Congress. Vol. 71, pp. 31-35.

PUBLIC LAW 91-596. 1970. Occupational Safety and Health Act. U.S. Statutes at Large. 91st Congress. Vol. 84, pp. 1590-1620.

PUBLIC LAW 91-577. 1970. Plant Variety Protection Act. U. S. Statutes at Large. Vol. 84, part II pp. 1542-1559.

PUBLIC LAW 92-516. 1972. Federal Environmental Pesticide Control Act. U.S. Statutes at Large, 92nd Congress. Vol. 86, pp. 973-999.

PUBLIC LAW 97-470. 1983. Migrant and Seasonal Agricultural Worker Protection Act. U.S. Statutes at Large, Vol. 96, pp. 2583-2600.

PUBLIC LAW 101-336. 1990. Americans with Disabilities Act. Congressional Quarterly Almanac. Vol. 46, pp. 452-459.

SIMPSON, R. C. 1973. Understanding quarantine effects. (Reported by H. G. Tilson.) Am. Nurseryman 137(10):74.

U.S. DEPARTMENT OF COMMERCE. 1970. Plant patents. Superintendent of Documents, Washington, D.C.

## SUGGESTED READING

MANWELL, J. P. 1984. Warranties. Part 1. What you should know about. ALI 11(3).

——— 1984. Warranties. Part 2. ALI 11(4).

Federal and State Quarantine Summaries. A.A.N. 1250 I St. N.W., Suite 500, Wash. D.C. 20005.

# Chapter 7
# Financial Management

Proper management of money and the effective evaluation of sources of money are a major part of the long-range development and operating plan of a nursery and are essential to the life of any business. The growth of a nursery results in increasingly complex financial management. It is as essential for the manager to understand financial management as it is for the manager to understand production techniques, marketing, and all the other factors of the business. To develop and manage the financial aspects of a nursery business properly, nursery managers should have the services of a lawyer and an accountant and understand the appropriate management use of the information provided by these professionals. They only advise. The manager makes decisions and, therefore, must understand financial management.

## FUNCTION OF FINANCIAL RECORDS

The importance of financial management cannot be overemphasized. Money is used to purchase labor, materials, and in some cases the management and technical expertise necessary to start and operate a nursery. Financial statements and records are used (1) to evaluate the current financial health and past accomplishments of the nursery firm, (2) to determine the appropriate income tax liability, and (3) to assist in securing the additional financial support needed for a growing business. They may also be used to help predict the growth potential of the nursery and to help identify those divisions of the nursery with the greatest potential for profit. Financial records are one of the major sources of information needed in the management of a nursery, but not the only source. Financial records are not to be used as a substitute for good judgment and experience in nursery production, marketing, and personnel management.

## FINANCING A NURSERY BUSINESS

Money is needed to finance the purchase of equipment, land, structures, supplies, and labor necessary to begin to produce nursery crops. A nursery manager usually has three potential sources of funds needed to establish and operate a nursery business (Fig. 7–1):

1. *The owner's personal savings.* The owner's investment of personal savings, cash value of insurance policies and funds generated by mortgaging personal property demonstrate his or her commitment to the business and ability to earn and save, both of which are important in developing the proper personal and business credit ratings needed to obtain future financing.

2. *Funds generated in the nursery through profit and depreciation accounts.* The sale of products and services in a business produces money needed for general payment of taxes, cost of bad debts, interest and loan

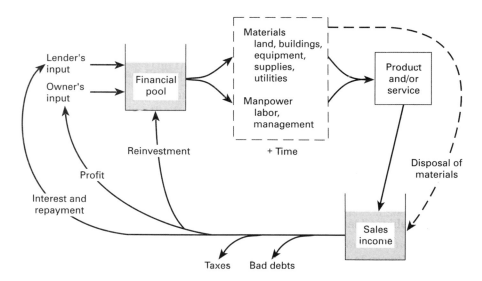

**Figure 7–1** Business cash-flow cycle.

repayment, profit, and depreciation. Depreciation allowances are charged against sales income each year to purchase and replace the equipment, buildings, and facilities when they are no longer functional. In rapidly expanding and profitable nurseries, capital needs may frequently rise more rapidly each year than can be provided by profits and depreciation allowances from the nursery.

3. *Borrowed funds.* Borrowed funds are used both to initiate and, in most cases, to operate a nursery. There are a variety of sources of borrowed financing available to the nursery manager, including partnerships, contract growing, and loans from a variety of financial institutions.

### Partnerships

Partnerships can be developed for the purpose of obtaining additional funds for capital investments. This normally involves sharing management decisions and profits with all full partners. A successful business partnership usually requires that the partners have separate and well-defined management responsibilities. A partner supplying only financial resources may become less desirable when at a later date these financial resources are no longer needed. This problem is alleviated by developing limited partnerships for a specific investment in a crop. Limited partnerships permit the principal partner to retain almost complete management control at all times. Limited partners may invest in a specific crop which the nursery plants, maintains, harvests, and markets for the partnership. The terms of the partnership agreement should specify the yearly investments required of the limited partner, the services provided by the nursery, the terms of marketing, and the distribution of profits. Limited partnerships are easiest to develop for an established firm, because the investor considering a limited partnership is usually relying on the principal partner's demonstrated nursery management ability, as well as detailed production cost analyses, as partial security for the investment. Certain income tax advantages can be provided to the limited partner, which may make this type of investment appealing to the investor. Limited partnerships may also be developed to allow key employees or individuals with valuable technical expertise to become involved in the financing and management of a division of the firm. In this case the primary purpose of the partnership may be to obtain expertise or to retain and motivate a valuable employee rather than to obtain financing, even though the employee invests funds in the firm and shares in the profits derived from the limited partnership.

### Contract Growing

Another source of funds, called *contract growing*, involves using capital obtained from other firms which are involved in marketing nursery stock. A manager may contract to produce a specific crop at a specified price for another firm in return for receiving the financing necessary to produce the crop. In some cases the marketing firm may provide the plants, supplies, and equipment needed to produce the crop. The firm loaning the money receives the benefit of having the entire crop at a specified price (a hedge against inflation) to complete the range of nursery products in markets, whereas the nursery receives the benefit of the financing and a guaranteed market for the crop. Contract growing agreements generally require that the nursery manager producing the crop share some of his management control in return for capital financing.

### Borrowing from Financial Institutions

A nursery manager may also borrow money from a number of traditional financial institutions. Borrowing from a financial institution involves obtaining capital to be repaid with interest on a specified schedule in an agreement or note signed by the nursery manager and the creditor. One of the advantages of borrowed funds is that the nursery manager does not share management control with creditors as is usually the case with contract growing or partnerships.

In most cases, buildings, land, nursery stock, equipment, or other assets which are owned either by the nursery or by the owner of the nursery are placed as security or collateral for the loan. If the loan is not repaid as agreed, the ownership of these assets or property is transferred to the financial institution and can be sold to repay the loan. The value of the assets or property identified as collateral must be such that the loan can be repaid even if the assets are under an unfavorable forced-sale condition. Since creditors have a prior claim on the income and assets of the nursery, they will usually accept a relatively lower rate of interest in comparison to contract growing agreements. The identification of the amount, duration, and purpose of the loan (Table 7–1) plus a knowledge of the nursery's ability to repay the loan allows for a better understanding and evaluation of the credit status by both the owner and the lender.

## EVALUATION OF ALTERNATIVE INVESTMENTS

The nursery manager must determine the best expenditure for the limited capital available before approaching financial institutions or any other source of funds. Not all of the potential capital investments that can be outlined by a nursery manager can or should be financed. Capital investments must be thoroughly evaluated by the manager to ensure the sound financial management of the nursery. The evaluation procedure has a number of logical steps, each of which is essential if the proper management decisions are to be made.

The initial step is a thorough search within the nursery operation and the markets it serves for all possible profitable investments for the available capital. A nursery manager can identify alternative crops to produce requiring different types of production and harvesting equipment, storage and packaging

**Table 7-1** Classification of Business Loans

I.  Time
    A.  Short-term loans (up to 1 year): used to finance working capital during short periods of high expense and low income. Bankers will generally lend up to 80% of accounts receivable.
    B.  Intermediate loans (1-5 years): used to finance equipment. Bankers may supply up to 90% of the value of the equipment being purchased.
    C.  Long-term loans (5 years or more): used to finance land, buildings, and other capital improvement or expansion. Bankers may supply up to 60-70% of the assessed value (not market value) of property and real estate.
II.  Security provided
    A.  Real estate
    B.  Crop
    C.  Stocks and bonds
    D.  Equipment
III.  Type of lender
    A.  Banks
    B.  Government agencies
    C.  Finance companies
    D.  Private individuals
    E.  Private businesses
IV.  Purpose of loan
    A.  Purchase real estate, such as additional land, greenhouses, storage facilities, lath or shade facilities, install drainage for production field, and so on
    B.  Purchase lining out stock, fertilizer spray materials, equipment, and so on
    C.  Pay labor and management

*Source:* Murray and Nelson (1960).

facilities, marketing techniques, and labor requirements. These alternative investments must be described in detail. The total capital required and the added earnings expected (cash flow) should be forecast for each alternative investment. Once this information is available, a realistic estimate can be made of the economic benefit of each investment. Profit may not be the only factor considered; the impact of income taxes and other taxes, as well as the potential for future growth and ability to provide a stable future income, may also play a major role in the selection of an investment. The actual decision must be based, at least in part, on the economic forecast for each potential investment in a crop, type of equipment, or facility.

There are a number of methods for measuring or comparing the potential economic benefit for alternative nursery investments. These methods of analysis vary considerably in their complexity and reliability. It should be kept in mind, however, that detailed methods of comparison are no substitute for realistic estimates of potential earnings, costs, and a complete consideration of all the alternatives. No decision can be any better than the reliability of the data used in making that decision.

### Urgency Analysis of Alternative Investments

Some nursery managers, particularly in the early stages of the growth of the firm, tend to evaluate a potential investment in a crop or type of equipment only when presented with a crisis deadline. For example, a nursery manager may discover that as a result of overproduction, rooted juniper cuttings must either be sold substantially below cost, planted in the nursery's own production fields, or destroyed. The decision must be made within a few weeks or the marketing and planting season will be past and the plants will be worthless. The urgency of the decision and the impact on current sales and planting activities frequently precludes consideration of long-term management goals. The decision to plant the rooted cuttings is frequently made even though the manager is aware that they may well be beyond his or her current and projected ability to profitably market them.

Not all investment decisions based on how urgently the investment is needed are unprofitable, nor are they necessarily less profitable than decisions that may be made with other criteria. Some decisions must be faced without taking the time to consider alternatives. For example, if a tree-digging machine breaks down during the digging season and requires extensive repair, a replacement must be purchased immediately to allow harvesting to proceed. Making an investment based on urgency may be necessary, but may be inappropriate for long-term investments and is an inappropriate substitute for good financial management.

### Payback-Period Analysis of Alternative Investments

A second method of capital investment analysis involves the determination of the payback period for alternative investments. The *payback period* is the time it takes for earnings from the investment to pay back the entire initial investment. For example, a nurseryman might have the opportunity to produce and market 4 1/2-in. caliper shade trees. The manager could either buy 2- to 2 1/2-in. caliper trees or buy 6- to 8-ft whips, to begin to produce the trees. Purchasing 6- to 8-ft whips might require a 10-year production period with additional investments each year in cultural care and land cost. The 2 1/2-in. caliper trees might require only a 5- to 6-year production period, with yearly investments for cultural care for only the 5- or 6-year period. Since no earnings are received until the trees are sold, the planting of 2 1/2-in. caliper trees has the shortest payback period (5 or 6 years versus 10 years). Payback period, however, may be unrelated to the potential profit that could be earned with the alternative investment proposals. Tree whips might be purchased for $5.00 each, while the 2 1/2-in.-caliper size might cost $27.50 each. Not only are the 6- to 8-ft tree whips substantially cheaper to purchase, they would cost less to ship and plant and might have a higher survival rate after planting. The 6- to 8-ft whips could produce a greater profit even though they require a longer investment period.

The payback period method measures how quickly an investment can be converted to cash and is, therefore, a measure of the firm's liquidity (the relative ability to convert assets into cash) or financial flexibility rather than profit. There may be management advantages in having increased flexibility provided by shorter-term investments as compared to long-term investments, but this advantage should not be confused with the profitability of a potential investment. It is also more difficult to forecast the marketability of a nursery crop many years in the future for a long-term crop investment, increasing the risk involved.

### Simple-Rate-of-Return Analysis
### of Alternative Investments

A third method for analyzing alternative investment opportunities is to compare the *simple rate of return* on an average yearly basis. Consider the following investments. An investment in tree-digging machine A of $25,000 will produce additional earnings (savings in labor) of $7500 per year. The depreciation is $5000 per year over an expected machine life of 5 years. The simple rate of return for machine A is:

$$\frac{\text{additional earnings} - \text{annual investment}}{\text{total investment}} = \text{percentage annual rate of return}$$

$$\frac{\$7500 - 5000}{\$25,000} \times 100 = 10\% \text{ rate of return}$$

Ten percent is the average annual rate of return for this particular investment. An alternative investment could be made in a more efficient machine, B, which could only be leased. This machine would cost $6400 per year and provide a savings of $8000 in labor per year. The simple rate of return would be

$$\frac{\$8000 - 6400}{\$6400} \times 100 \text{ or } 25\%$$

Therefore, even though machine B would produce only $500 more per year in earnings than machine A, its simple rate of return on invested money would be 25%, as compared to 10% for machine A. The simple rate of return indicates which investment would provide the largest added earnings on a yearly basis.

The simple rate-of-return analysis, however, is not really comparable to interest rates on borrowed funds, because the total investment is not made for the life of the machine. The entire $25,000 investment in Machine A is not utilized for the full 5-year period. In fact, during the last (or fifth) year of use, the remaining investment is only $5000 and the additional earnings are $7500.

### Discounted-Cash-Flow Analysis
### of Alternative Investments

A *discounted-cash-flow analysis* (DCF) accounts for the size of investments, their length, and the date they are made, as well as the amount and date that income occurs. The profit from a potential investment in the nursery is compared by DCF analysis to the profit that could be derived by investing the same sum at a fixed rate of interest in a bank or elsewhere.

DCF analysis allows for the direct comparison of two nursery investments that have different investment schedules, differing rates, and dates of earning income. For example, a $1000 income at the end of 5 years is not comparable to a $200 income per year for 5 years, even though they both provide $1000 in income for a 5-year investment. Incomes and investments can be directly compared only if they can be adjusted in value to the present time. For example, the present value of a $1000 income to be earned 5 years from now can be viewed as the amount of money that must be invested now in order to grow to $1000 at a compound interest rate (using the current rate of interest offered by banks). The amount of money that must be invested to obtain a specific income in 5 years can be obtained by multiplying the income by a discount factor for compound interest rates. (Discount factors are available in table form for a variety of interest rates and years; see Appendix K and Aplin and Casler [1973].) The discount factor for 7.5% interest for 5 years is $1/(1+0.075)^5$, or 0.6966. Multiplying the 5-year 7.5% interest discounting factor of 0.6966 times $1000 produces a present value of $696.60.

$$Pv = \$1000 \times 0.6966 = \$696.60$$

Another way of saying the same thing is that a present investment of $696.60 at an annual 7.5% interest will produce $1000 in 5 years.

An income of $200 per year for 5 years can be assigned a present value in a similar manner. Each $200 annual income is adjusted to present value by multiplying times the appropriate discounting factor (current interest rate and years). These present values are added to determine the present values of the $200 per year for 5 years (Table 7-2). Thus, the present value (Pv) of an income of $200/year for 5 years is worth $809.17; as calculated by DCF analysis.

**Table 7–2** Discounted-Cash-Flow Analysis of the Present Value of $200 Income per Year for 5 Years

| Year | Income | Discounting Factor | Present Value |
|------|--------|--------------------|---------------|
| 1 | $200 | 0.9302 | $186.04 |
| 2 | 200 | 0.8653 | 173.06 |
| 3 | 200 | 0.8050 | 161.00 |
| 4 | 200 | 0.7488 | 149.75 |
| 5 | 200 | 0.6966 | 139.32 |
| | | | Total: $809.17 |

The same answer can be obtained by using the formula for present value of an annuity:

$$Pv = \frac{a \left[1 - (1 + i)^N\right]}{i}$$

$$Pv = \$200 \times 4.04588 = \$809.18$$

where

Pv = present value
$a$ = periodic investment
$i$ = current interest rate
$N$ = years

This results in the same answer (1 cent variation due to rounding) as the previous calculation.

### Break-Even-Point Analysis

Investment analysis may also be used to answer the question: What is the most efficient rate of production? A *break-even analysis* is based on the fact that in each nursery operation there are fixed costs which do not change (within certain limits) as the volume of production either increases or decreases. These costs might include the cost of capital invested in equipment, buildings, and land. Variable costs, on the other hand, are directly tied to the volume of production and sales, increasing and decreasing in direct proportion to increases or decreases in volume.

The assignment of a nursery selling cost as either fixed or variable is to some degree the result of management judgment.

A break-even analysis requires the graphic display of fixed costs, cost of goods sold, variable costs, and net sales at two different volumes or rates of operation. Figure 7-2 shows a break-even analysis of a nursery having the following financial data at two different rates of production:

| | | |
|---|---|---|
| Total sales | $30,000 | $95,000 |
| Fixed costs | −15,000 | −15,000 |
| Variable costs | −23,000 | −70,000 |
| Net profit | $−8,000 | $+10,000 |

The break-even point (intersection of total sales and total costs lines in Fig. 7–2) of these two programs is gross sales of $56,000, which occurs at a production of 2750 units.

Sound financial management requires (1) a thorough search for alternative profitable investment opportunities, (2) an accurate forecast of investments required and potential economic benefit, and (3) the use of an appropriate investment analysis method. The final decision should be based on the investment analysis, as well as the manager's experience in production,

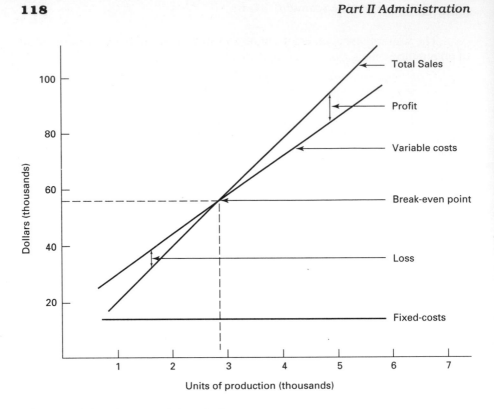

**Figure 7-2** Break-even-point analysis.

marketing, personnel management, estimate of the potential growth in the demand for nursery stock, and good judgment.

## NEGOTIATING A LOAN

Successful financial management usually requires the borrowing of funds
from a variety of potential lending institutions. Most lenders will want financial data from the nursery, audited by a certified public accountant, as well as
information concerning the ownership and management and the objectives of
the proposed financing. The extent of information required will, in part, depend on the size and nature of the financial commitments.

Lending institutions are interested in the nature of the business organization (e.g., incorporation documents, corporate or business by-laws, lease
agreement, and long-term contracts) and the history of the business requesting financing. They will also want to know as much as possible about the man-

agement of the firm; their personal and family backgrounds; biographical data, including relevant training and experience; evidence of personal character; and the financial status of owners and management. They will be interested in the possible replacement of key management personnel with other employees should they become incapacitated. The lending institution may be interested in the type of accounting system used, a current balance sheet (Table 7–3), a profit and loss statement (Table 7–4), the relevant financial ratio analysis comparisons (Table 7–7), and the long- and short-range financial outlook of the entire nursery industry. They may also wish to see an audit of the accounts and past financial records of the firm.

The lenders will be interested in the objectives of the loan; the payback schedule, the projected budget (how the money will be used), and the resulting schedule of the investment. It may be beneficial to indicate alternative payback options that might be available as a result of changing the schedule of production, harvest, and sale of the nursery crop. The proposed budget should indicate the payback options of all other financial commitments in addition to the one being negotiated. The lenders will also be interested in the nature of proposed collateral, particularly an estimate of its forced liquidation value as well as the liquidity of all the assets of the nursery business. Other assets would include the volume and history of accounts receivable, owner's personal assets, and the value of equipment, vehicles, land, and buildings. The use of nursery stock as security or collateral for a loan requires that the nursery stock in the field be given an estimated forced-liquidation value. The forced-liquidation value can be very low if the rate of construction of new homes, for example, drops dramatically and, therefore, very conservative estimates should be used.

## ASSESSING VALUE TO A NURSERY CROP IN THE FIELD

There are at least three ways to assign value to a nursery crop in the field. One system begins with the wholesale price of nursery stock of a similar size and grade, then subtracting a harvesting and selling cost to arrive at an "in-the-field" value. A manager might estimate that harvesting and marketing a particular nursery crop contributes 25% to the total cost of the crop. The in-the-field value of the crop would be 75% of the wholesale price. This method will include profit in the value assigned to the crop. A second method, based on costs of production, totals all production expenses, including labor, equipment, supplies, cost of land, taxes, and plants involved in developing the nursery crop to its present stage. This method will overestimate the value of the nursery crop when it is very young because the planting and cultural care may be substantial for the first 1 or 2 years, during which relatively little

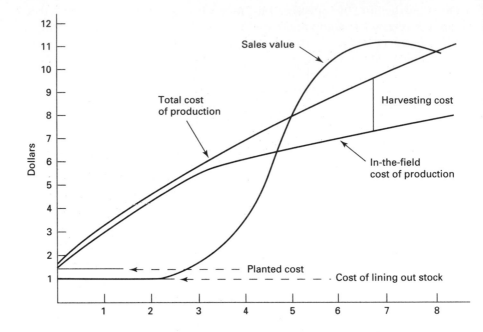

**Figure 7–3** Cost of production versus sales value for field-grown nursery crops.

growth occurs (Fig. 7–3). Just before harvest, the crop is growing at a maximum rate and the cultural care tends to be at a minimum, making its sale value greater than production costs. However, if harvest is substantially delayed, the sale value of the crop may not continue to increase, because of reduced growth and quality resulting from crowding. An estimating method based on costs of production does not include profit in the estimated value of the nursery crop in the field, and could be very erroneous for recently planted crops.

A third method for assigning value to a nursery crop uses an outside consultant to provide a professional appraisal of what the specific nursery crop would sell for in a forced auction sale. The value would be reduced by the auction sale expenses to develop an in-the-field value for the crop.

A reduction of the estimated value of a nursery crop by any of the foregoing methods may be taken to provide a conservative estimate of what the crop might be worth as a result of a forced sale. Nursery crops or any other item of collateral should be precisely defined, since the nursery would be turning over control of that crop to the lending institution if and when the terms of the loan were not met. Each block of nursery stock to be assigned as collateral should be inventoried and the block described by a surveyed description.

## INFORMATION NEEDED ABOUT
## THE LENDING INSTITUTION

The successful negotiation of a loan also requires that nurserymen know as much as possible about the lending institution. In many cases, the refusal of a loan has little to do with the quality of the firm and management requesting the loan, but is the result of regulations and limits set by the lending institution. A business manager requesting substantial financing should know the lending institution's loan limits (the maximum loan that can be made to one customer and the maximum length of time it will be loaned). Financial needs exceeding the institution's loan limit or time limit may require that the lender collaborate with other lending institutions.

The board of directors of the lending institution determines the broad guidelines and nature of the loans it will make. Each lending institution has more information about and greater confidence in specific types of businesses and is more inclined to make loans to these types of businesses than to others. The preparation of information and negotiation of loans is a time-consuming process, particularly for large, long-term, nursery-business loans. It would be desirable to work with a stable lending institution which does not frequently change its loan guidelines and has remained interested in loans to agricultural businesses for a long period of time. Those lending institutions having strong ties with agricultural industries will quite likely be more confident in making nursery-business loans.

It will save time and effort if the nursery manager knows the limits of the loan authority given to the individual representing the lending institution. Lending institutions usually have a loan committee that limits the amounts and length of time of loans granted by its employees. Potential loans beyond the limits, both in time and dollar amount, must be reviewed and authorized by the loan committee. The nursery manager will want to know how frequently the loan committee meets in order to estimate the time necessary to obtain financing.

In negotiating a loan, it is usually most productive for the business manager to present the general purpose and nature of the financing needed and the supporting business information and documents. The specific terms of the loan should be negotiated rather than requesting the lending institution to accept or reject a single specific proposal.

As in any business transaction, it is well to compare the financial services of competing lending institutions. The effective interest cost of the loan, the amount of collateral required, as well as other conditions should be compared to the conditions offered by other financial institutions. Lending institutions vary considerably in their willingness to lend money to a specific type of business, and it is well worth the time spent in finding the institution most favorable to your business.

## COMPUTING THE FUTURE COST
## OF A NURSERY CROP

A number of simple formulas can be used to calculate the return of a nursery crop investment. For example, 5000 *Taxus media* 'Hicks' are to be grown for 5 years. Assume that the transplants will cost 75 cents each and that it costs $250 to plant them. The annual cost of caring for these plants will be $750 for labor, $100 for materials, and $750 for overhead. All costs will be financed at 8.5% per year.*

$$5000 \text{ plants} \times 75 \text{ cents} = \$3750$$
$$\text{planting cost} \qquad = \underline{\quad 250}$$
$$\$4000$$

The future value (in 5 years) of this investment at 8.5% interest can be calculated using the formula for *future value of invested capital:*

$$Cn = Co(1 + i)^n$$

where

$Cn$ = value of the invested capital at year $n$
$Co$ = invested capital at year 0 (beginning of investment)
$n$ = number of years of investment
$i$ = interest rate per year

$$Cn = \$4000 (1 + 0.085)^5 = \$4000 (1.5037) = \$6014.80$$

The investment in caring for these plants is: labor, $750/year; materials, $100/year; and overhead, $750/year; or $1600/year for 5 years.

$$\$9481.41 = \frac{\$1600[(1 + 0.085)^5 - 1]}{0.085}$$

The maintenance costs equal $9481.41. The total investment in the plants after 5 years is $6014.80 + $9481.41 = $15,496.21 or $3.10 per plant.

There is usually little reason to assign all assets of the nursery to the lending institution, even if the loan is substantial. The ratio of assets to loan value should be negotiated to allow for future financial flexibility. As the value of assets changes, increasing as in the case of growing nursery stock, it should be part of the loan agreement that some of the assets can be removed from the loan security.

At certain times of the year, a nursery may have the opportunity to invest with the bank for relatively short periods of time when a positive cash flow condition exists. These investment opportunities could be part of the overall loan arrangements with the financial institution.

---

*Rates used are for illustrative purposes only. Actual rates may vary with time and circumstance.

## USING FINANCIAL INFORMATION
## TO EVALUATE MANAGEMENT

Evaluating the financial management of most nurseries is a very difficult task because of the complexity of nursery operation. In the United States there are relatively few production nurseries that produce one product by a single system and sell that product to a single type of buyer. Therefore, it is extremely difficult to compare and evaluate the actual cost of production. Management is evaluated on how effectively they have managed all three factors of production and primarily on how much profit is generated. Two of the most valuable financial documents for evaluating management are a balance sheet and a profit-and-loss statement.

### Balance Sheet

Sound financial management of a nursery requires the periodic evaluation of the financial well being or status of the firm. The operation of a nursery results in a constant change in the firm's assets, liabilities, and net worth (the difference between assets and liabilities). A *balance sheet*, prepared periodically by an accountant, is a statement of the financial status of the nursery on the date the balance sheet was prepared. By itself, it does not indicate the rate of change or even the direction of change of any of the assets or liabilities of the firm. Balance sheets are usually issued on a regular basis—monthly, quarterly, or annually—and are of greater significance when compared to similar reports for the same period of previous years.

The assets and liabilities recorded on the balance sheet are divided into current and long-term entries. If the item can be converted into cash within 1 year, it is considered current. This distinction helps to predict the current year's financial position as distinct from the long-range financial position of the firm. An example of the accounts that might be included in a production nursery business balance sheet are shown in Table 7–3. The Horticultural Research Institute (HRI) has developed a uniform chart of accounts which is suggested for use by the entire nursery industry. The widespread use of a uniform chart of accounts would make the comparison of industry-wide financial ratio analysis (discussed later in the chapter) more reliable and efficient.

### Profit-and-Loss Statement

One of the prime concerns of a nursery manager—the potential profit from the operation of the nursery—is not displayed on a balance sheet. An *income statement* or *profit-and-loss statement* combines the total sales over a period of time (month, quarter, or year) and subtracts the total expenses for the same period of time showing the profit or loss developed by the firm (Table 7-4). This is one of the most important statements provided by an accountant. If the nursery is to survive for any length of time, it must show a

**Table 7–3** Balance Sheet Items

| Assets | Liabilities |
|---|---|
| Cash assets | Current liabilities |
|   Checking and savings balances |   Accounts and notes payable |
| Receivable assets | Accrued liabilities |
|   Accounts receivable |   Interest payable |
|   Reserve for bad debts |   Federal income and other taxes |
| Inventory assets |   Royalties owed |
|   Plants | Long-term liabilities |
|   Hard goods |   Mortgages and loans |
| Prepaid expense assets | Equity liabilities |
|   Expenses paid prior to due date |   Total received for common and |
| Equipment and facilities asset |     preferred stock |
|   Land and improvement to land |   Undistributed profits |
|   Equipment, furniture, and fixtures |   Total owed owners |
|   Production, shipping, and warehousing facilities | |
|   Sales and administration facilities and equipment | |
| Depreciation allowance assets | |
|   Improvement to land | |
|   Equipment, furniture, and fixtures | |
|   Production, shipping, and warehousing facilities | |

profit. Management decisions to expand or change production, as well as the ability to obtain financing, will be influenced substantially by a profit-and-loss statement. To a creditor, the profit-and-loss statement will indicate the potential ability to pay back existing liabilities as well as additional loans.

Since profit, the reward for the risk of operating a commercial enterprise, is a measure by which a commercial nursery is evaluated, it is important to have an understanding of the various concepts of profit. The concept of what constitutes a profit varies with the accounting system, the age of the business, the age of the owner(s), and the legal type of organization of the business.

The interpretation of a profit-and-loss statement as well as other financial statements depends upon the type of accounting system used by the firm. Most production nursery accounting systems are on a cash basis. Some of the larger production nurseries may be on an accrual basis in order to more effectively be managed as part of a much larger corporation. Expenses in a cash-basis accounting system are recorded at the time payment is made, and income is recorded at the time of receipt. The nursery production cycle (the length of time between the initial planting of a crop and the date of harvest) is usually much longer than the accounting period of a balance sheet or profit-and-loss statement. The accounting period may be quarterly, or more commonly 1 year, whereas the production cycle may range from a few weeks to

**Table 7–4** Items Normally Included in a Profit-and-Loss Statement

| | |
|---|---|
| Income | Operations |
|   Income from production operations |   Contract labor |
|     Sale of green goods—plants |   Royalties |
|     Sale of hard goods |   Travel |
|     Sale of services offered |   Utilities |
|     Service charges |     Gas and electricity |
|   Other income |     Water and sewer |
|     Gain on sale of fixed assets |     Telephone |
|     Rental income |     Heat |
| | Shipping and warehousing expense |
| Expenses |   Employees |
|   Production expenses |     Wages |
|     Cost of goods |     Fringe benefits |
|     Cost of plants used in production |     Insurance |
|     Cost of plants purchased for resale |     Taxes |
|     Cost of materials used in production |     Supervisory salaries |
|     Insurance expenses |   Equipment, furniture, and fixtures |
|     Taxes |     Cost to purchase or rent |
|   Employees |     Cost to maintain |
|     Wages |     Insurance |
|     Fringe benefits |     Taxes |
|     Taxes |     Depreciation |
|     Supervisory salaries |   Facilities |
|   Equipment, furniture, and fixtures |     Cost to purchase or rent |
|     Cost to purchase or rent |     Cost to maintain |
|     Cost to maintain |     Insurance |
|     Insurance |     Taxes |
|     Taxes |     Depreciation |
|     Depreciation |   Operations |
|   Facilities |     Shipping supplies and materials |
|     Cost of greenhouses, overwintering, |     Automations costs |
|       and shade houses |   Utilites |
|     Depreciation |     Gas and electricity |
|     Insurance |     Water and sewer |
|     Maintenance and repair |     Telephone |
|     Taxes |     Heat |

6 years. The cash basis system of accounting is misleading if the nursery is changing rapidly by expanding or contracting the volume of nursery crops planted each year. The cash expenses involved in buying the lining-out stock and caring for an increasing volume of nursery stock in the ground could very well be greater than the income from the sale of the relatively small volume of mature harvested nursery stock. In a cash basis accounting system, the inventory of nursery crops in the ground is not assigned a value until it is sold, so the profit-and-loss statement will show little, if any, profit, since income has been used to increase nursery crop inventory. However, this has been a common accounting practice in the nursery industry.

An accrual-basis accounting system will include the value of unsold inventory and plants under production. This provides a more realistic indication of the potential health of the business and reflects an increase or decrease in production volume. However, an accrual-basis accounting system may present a misleading financial picture because it will overvalue crops under production that have become unmarketable due to weather conditions, insects, disease, economy, or a drop in market demand.

## DISCRETIONARY SPENDING

Net receipts in a nursery operation will also vary considerably with discretionary spending. By what amount will expenditures for capital assets (land, buildings) be increased as the nursery grows? What amount will be invested into new plant production inventory? What will be invested in new equipment? These decisions will dramatically affect the net profit of a business.

When a nursery business is young, and particularly if the management is young, there is a strong tendency to reinvest profits into land, plant production inventory, and related facilities to expand the business. Under the cash system of accounting, the value of an expanding field inventory is not adequately reflected in the standard financial records that are maintained by most nurseries. An expanding nursery will appear to be unprofitable under a cash accounting system. As the owners of the nursery grow older and, to some extent, as the business ages, there is a desire to maximize personal income. This can be done in a number of ways that will affect net profit. The most common are a reduced rate of expansion, increased salary, and fringe benefit programs. Another is improved office facilities and modes of transportation. They are all rewards for financial success. None of these rewards, however, necessarily reflects a true evaluation of the nursery business. Much of the financial success of many older nurseries may be due to an economic increase in land value due to urbanization or potential recreational use.

The 1976 Tax Reform Act requires corporate farms to use accrual accounting and to assign values to unsold nursery stock inventories. However, it contains the following exemption: "This section shall not apply to the trade or business of operating a nursery." In an accrual basis of accounting, "changes in resources and obligations including those resulting from the generation of revenues and the occurrence of expense are recorded as they occur (or nearly so)" (Edwards et al., 1974). The inventory of unsold nursery stock in the field or in containers would be assigned a value in an accrual basis of accounting. The increase in value of unsold plants each year would be considered as income in accrual accounting. Production costs including harvesting would be considered expenses only in the year they occur. This dramatically changes potential tax liability. In March 1979 the IRS advised that accrual-basis accounting can be changed to cash bases and the nurseries continuing to use accrual-basis accounting need not maintain inventories.

## DETERMINING PROFIT

One of the ways to evaluate the success of an investment in nursery stock is by determining the costs of the various factors of production in a realistic manner and determining the true profit when these costs are deducted from the sales income. True profit is calculated as the effective rate of interest returned on the investment made in the production of the crop or crops during the production period.

When planning the production system for a nursery, after it has been determined what species of plants are going to be produced, it becomes necessary to determine the specific inputs that will be required, some of which are (1) how many plants must be grown to meet a specific market objective; (2) how long the production cycle is and how much land is needed; (3) how much manpower and skill will be required to carry out the various physical operations required in the production cycle; (4) what facilities, equipment, materials, and supplies will be required; (5) how much money will be invested during the production cycle; and (6) how the various factors (labor, machines, land, and other facilities) can be synchronized to produce the best production system. Once this has been done and the production goal is clearly defined, it will be feasible to evaluate whether that goal has been accomplished.

## COST OF PRODUCTION

Since plants are the marketable product of the nursery which are sold to produce income, a system must be developed to determine the money inputs that are invested to produce the plants. However, most production nurseries produce many species of plants to make up the salable product mix. Each species has its own special input requirements in the way of material and labor skills, so that it becomes almost impossible to accurately determine the dollar inputs into their production. However, if the species are grouped into larger categories, such as shade trees, flowering shrubs, and so on, it does become possible to determine average costs of production for these groups.

It is impossible to place a true value on plant material growing in a nursery. This is because the plants gain a true sales value only when a buyer consummates an offer to buy. Up to that point plants in a nursery have only a potential or an estimated value in-the-ground which could be substantially reduced by various economic, biological, or climatic factors. A slowdown in the national economy, or periods of high interest rates which reduce the rate of housing construction, can be quickly reflected in the public demand for plant material; this was dramatically seen in the great depression of the late 1920s and early 1930s and the period of high interest rates in the 1980s and 1990s.

In the winter of 1873-1874 a severe freeze throughout the Midwest caused the loss of thousands of plants and the failure of many nurseries; and the blizzard of 1890-1891 caused serious financial loss to many nurserymen. A beautiful block of shade trees that might have a potential value of many thousands of dollars could be reduced to a worthless jungle by a brief but devastating hail or sleet storm. Also, a severe drought, such as the one that affected the midwestern United States in the mid-1930s and the one that devastated parts of Europe in 1976, can seriously reduce any potential value that nursery stock might have. But nursery stock either in the ground or in containers does have potential value. Certainly, the nurseryman who owns the stock must place a value on the plants, a value for which he would be willing to sell the plants at a profit, and a forced-sale value which might be the dollar value that he would be willing to accept for the plants, in situ, if he were forced to sell. The forced-sale value most likely would be close to the actual dollar costs that he has invested in the production of the plants, but would not reflect a profit. Therefore, cost-of-production information is needed to determine how much is invested in the plant material in order to estimate an in-the-ground value. Cost-of-production information is helpful in providing nurserymen with factual information to make better management decisions relative to production scheduling and pricing. It is also valuable in evaluating changes in cultural methods and productivity of labor. Without production records, including costs, the nursery manager cannot fully evaluate production efficiency. It is very likely that without production cost records, plant material could be priced at a level below the actual total cost of production and be sold at a net loss without the manager being aware of it.

The first step is to determine what data are to be collected, how they are to be collated and processed into usable information, and how much time and money will be budgeted to accomplish the goal. It is pointless to collect data if there are no plans to use the data, and a waste of time and money if there are no predetermined objectives for the use of the information that is generated upon processing the data.

Nurseries that produce relatively few species or types of plant material or that specialize in a limited product mix can develop and operate relatively simple systems for obtaining production cost data. Nurseries that produce a wide selection of species or a diverse product mix, on the other hand, will need more elaborate systems. However, they need not be complex, and it may be more practical to begin obtaining cost-of-production data within broad plant categories such as outlined in Table 9–1, and later by individual varieties or cultivars.

### Systems for Estimating the Cost of Production

Two systems are available for estimating the long-term costs of producing nursery stock. The first system involves obtaining direct costs (obtained from daily time sheets and material records) on labor and material inputs, whereas the second system involves estimating inputs of labor from staffing tables developed over a period of years. In both systems a method is suggested for estimating costs of land, facilities, various overhead expenses, and interest charges. For management purposes it might be desirable to calculate an in-the-ground cost of production based on field data including direct labor and material inputs only, whereas a price-list cost of production would also include overhead and interest charges. The in-the-ground cost would represent the average total cost of production (investment) up to a given point in the production cycle.

Nurseries that have a computer can collect cost data as it is generated on a daily basis from other programs such as purchased materials, labor, and overhead costs. This data can then be processed to determine cost of production for each crop produced by the nursery. The Zelenka QIC (Quality Inventory Control) System accomplishes this by summarizing direct and indirect labor cost from the Production Control System; cost of materials and supplies, directly related to crop production, are obtained from the Supply Inventory/Usage System. Also, provision is made to spread overhead costs equitably over each crop. The intent of the Accounting Module is to provide management with the necessary information for profit margin analysis and for establishing pricing structures.

### Planting, Maintaining, and Harvesting Costs

One convenient and meaningful system for production nurseries is to collect and process the data within three categories: planting, maintaining, and harvesting, the three primary functions in the production cycle. Figure 7-4 illustrates the system. The dollar values used in the example are for illustrative purposes only. Each manager must collect and process his or her individual data. In year zero, 4000 young shade trees were purchased. Cost includes plants and transportation. The average cost was $6.73/plant. The direct labor and material costs (obtained from daily time sheets and material records) for planting and maintaining the first year were $3720 and $1840, respectively. Unit values can be calculated for comparative analysis if desired. This information is tabulated for both the in-the-ground value and the price-list cost.

### Overhead Costs

*Overhead* is the total of all costs of production that cannot be charged directly to the blocks of plant materials, including such things as rent for use of land and facilities, administrative and management salaries, taxes, and so on. There are various ways of determining overhead and equating it to the various factors of production. One method commonly employed in nurseries is to equate total overhead to total direct labor (DL) and to calculate a percentage factor. Overhead is applied as a function of labor cost because many overhead costs are related to labor more directly than to other functions of production costs. This value may vary from a low of 50% of DL to a high of 150% of DL. In the example, 100% of DL was used throughout. Nurserymen are cautioned to calculate the value of their own management services and to include all indirect costs of production.

| | Year 0 | | | Year 0+1 | | | |
|---|---|---|---|---|---|---|---|
| | Units | Cost/units | In-the-ground cost | Price list cost | Units | Cost/units | In-the-ground costs |
| Cost of plants | 4000 | $6.73 | $26,920 | $26,920 | 3950 | | 32,480 |
| Labor: planting | | .42 | 1,680 | | | | |
| : maintaining | | .51 | 2,040 | 3720 | | .24 | 960 |
| Materials: planting | | .36 | 1,452 | | | | |
| : maintaining | | .10 | 388 | 1,840 | | .13 | 525 |
| | | | W 32,480 | W 32,480 | | | W 33,965 |
| Overhead (100%DL) | | | | 3720 | | | |
| Interest (7.0%) | | | | 2534 | | | |
| Total | | | W 32,480 | W 38,734 | | | |
| Plants lost | -50 | | | 9.81 | -39 | | |
| | 3950 | | \|x̄\| = 822 | | 3911 | | \|x̄\| = 8.69 |
| Plants sold | | | | | | | |
| Labor: harvesting | | | | | | | |
| Materials: harvesting | | | | | | | |
| Overhead: Harvesting | | | | | | | |
| Plants remaining / costs outstanding | | | | | | | |

**Figure 7–4** Example of cost-of-production schedule for field-grown shade trees.

**Figure 7-4** (continued)

Year O+4

| Units | Cost/units | In-the-ground costs | Price list cost |
|---|---|---|---|
| 3353 | | 32,439 | 49,118 |
| | .45 | 1500 | 1500 |
| | .20 | 650 | 650 |
| -6 | | | 52,768 |
| 3347 | | 34,589 | 3694 |
| 2150 | | | 56,462 |
| | 1.04 | = 10.33 | 16.87 |
| | .64 | - 22,210 | - 36,271 |
| | | | 2236 |
| | | | 1378 |
| | | | 2236 |
| | | | 42,121 |
| | | | |×| = 19,59 |
| 1197 | | 12,379 | 20,194 |
| | | 10.34 | 16.87 |

Year O+5

| Units | Cost/units | In-the-ground costs | Price list cost |
|---|---|---|---|
| 1197 | | 12,379 | 20,194 |
| | 1.00 | 1200 | 1200 |
| | .38 | 450 | 450 |
| | | 14,029 | 1200 |
| | | | 23,044 |
| | | | 1613 |
| | | | 24,657 |
| -4 | | |×| = 11.76 | 20.67 |
| 1193 | | - 11,854 | - 20,835 |
| 1008 | 1.23 | | 1240 |
| | | | 736 |
| | .73 | | 1240 |
| | | | 24,051 |
| | | | |×| = 23,86 |
| 185 | | 2175 | 3822 |
| | | 11.76 | 20.67 |

Figure 7-4 (continued)

*Interest* on invested capital is another factor that should be included, since money invested in plants could have been placed into a bank or other interest earning investment. This interest is potential income foregone in order to invest in the crop and is, therefore, a cost of the production of that crop.

A 7.0% interest charge is used in the example. The rate will vary with years, but a fair value prevailing within the community should be used. Note the significant increase in cost of production when overhead and interest on invested capital are included. Maintenance data are collected and processed in a similar manner for the ensuing years, and the average cost of production is calculated. At the end of each year an actual inventory count is taken of the plants within the block, and an average cost-of-production value is calculated.

When plants are sold, harvesting data are collected and processed. All these data are tabulated under price-list cost, since the plants are being removed from the site. No interest is charged to cost of production. However, it may be charged in the sales division if the sale is on credit. Once the plants are sold, their average value must be removed from the ledger. The sale and removal of some of the plants in a block will result in a much higher unit cost for maintenance, and a lower total value of plants remaining on the site, with a higher individual unit value per plant. At some point the resulting higher individual unit value of plants may exceed the average obtainable selling price, necessitating a decision by management as to the prudence of maintaining the few remaining plants. By keeping up-to-date, accurate records, the decision to remove all plants from a block can be made before the cost of maintaining them exceeds their potential selling price.

### Determining Profitability with a Cost-Sales Analysis

From the estimated cost of production records and from the records for sales, a cost-sales analysis can be prepared to fully evaluate the profitability of having grown the 4000 trees for a period of time extending over 7 years. One method of evaluation is to determine the future value of all inputs and income through the production cycle and to determine if there was a positive cash flow (Fig. 7–5). In the example, with 7% interest rate, a 100% direct overhead, and estimating sales costs at 10% of the selling price, there was a positive cash flow of $15,607.

A somewhat better tool to employ for this evaluation is discounted-cash-flow analysis, equating all finances back to year zero and determining an interest rate that results in a zero (or close to zero) net cash flow. All of the yearly financial inputs, less interest, and all yearly net sales are tabulated and the net cash flow determined by years (Table 7–5). These values are then discounted to year zero by using various interest rates (Table 7–6). This can be done fairly rapidly with the aid of a computer and in a few minutes with the aid of a desk calculator. A partial set of interest rates is tabulated in Appendix K. For more detailed rates, consult interest tables contained in a handbook related to mathematics.

|  | Yr | Production inputs | 1 — Current value | 2 | 3 — 7.0% Interest factor | 4 — Future value 0+6 yrs. |
|---|---|---|---|---|---|---|
| 1 | 0 | Plant costs | 2 6 9 2 0 | | 1.5007 | $ 4 0 4 0 0 |
| 2 | | | | | | |
| 3 | | Labor, direct costs | | | | |
| 4 | 0 | | 3 7 2 0 | | 1.5007 | 5 5 8 3 |
| 5 | 1 | | 9 6 0 | | 1.4026 | 1 3 4 7 |
| 6 | 2 | | 1 1 1 8 | | 1.3108 | 1 4 6 5 |
| 7 | 3 | | 1 5 2 1 | | 1.2250 | 1 8 6 3 |
| 8 | 4 | | 3 7 3 8 | | 1.1449 | 4 2 7 9 |
| 9 | 5 | | 2 2 0 9 | | 1.0700 | 2 3 6 4 |
| 10 | 6 | | 1 0 0 0 | | 0 | 1 0 0 0 |
| 11 | | | | | Σ | 1 7 9 0 0 |
| 12 | | | | | | |
| 13 | | Material costs | | | | |
| 14 | 0 | | 1 8 4 0 | | 1.5007 | 2 7 6 1 |
| 15 | 1 | | 5 2 5 | | 1.4026 | 7 3 6 |
| 16 | 2 | | 8 3 2 | | 1.3108 | 1 0 9 0 |
| 17 | 3 | | 9 9 6 | | 1.2250 | 1 2 2 0 |
| 18 | 4 | | 2 0 2 8 | | 1.1449 | 2 3 2 2 |
| 19 | 5 | | 1 1 8 7 | | 1.0700 | 1 2 7 0 |
| 20 | 6 | | 7 0 0 | | 0 | 7 0 0 |
| 21 | | | | | Σ | 1 0 1 0 0 |
| 22 | | Overhead costs | | | | |
| 23 | | (100% direct labor) | | | | 1 7 9 0 0 |
| 24 | | | | | Σ Σ | 8 6 3 0 0 |
| 25 | | | | | | |
| 26 | | Sales income | | Selling costs | | |
| 27 | 0 | | | (est. 10%) | | |
| 28 | 1 | | | | | |
| 29 | 2 | 100 @ $18.00 | 1 8 0 0 | - 1 8 0   x | 1.3108 | 2 1 2 3 |
| 30 | 3 | 450 @ 21.00 | 9 4 5 0 | - 9 4 5 | 1.2250 | 1 0 4 1 8 |
| 31 | 4 | 2150 @ 25.00 | 5 3 7 6 0 | - 5 3 7 5 | 1.1449 | 5 5 3 8 5 |
| 32 | 5 | 1008 @ 30.00 | 3 0 2 4 0 | - 3 0 2 4 | 1.0700 | 2 9 1 2 1 |
| 33 | 6 | 180 @ 30.00 | 5 4 0 0 | 5 4 0 | 0 | 4 8 6 0 |
| 34 | | | | | | |
| 35 | | | | | Σ | 1 0 1 9 0 7 |
| 36 | | | | | | |
| 37 | | | | | | |
| 38 | | Profit = | 1 0 1, 9 0 7 | - 8 6 3 0 0 | = | $ 1 5, 6 0 7 |
| 39 | | | | | | |
| 40 | | | | | | |

**Figure 7–5** Plant materials cost-income analysis.

When evaluated at an interest rate of 15%, the example project generated a negative cash flow, but at 12% the cash flow was positive, in excess of $1700, indicating that the project earned a profit in excess of 12% but less than 15%. If outside sources of funding were used to finance the project, it would be necessary to subtract the effective rate of interest from the profit percentage to

**Table 7-5** Net Cash Flow

| Year | Input | Net Sales | Net Cash Flow |
|------|-------|-----------|---------------|
| 0 | −36,200 | 0 | −36,200 |
| 1 | − 2,445 | 0 | − 2,445 |
| 2 | − 3,068 | + 1,620 | − 1,448 |
| 3 | − 4,038 | + 8,505 | + 4,467 |
| 4 | − 9,504 | +48,385 | +38,881 |
| 5 | − 5,605 | +27,216 | +21,611 |
| 6 | − 2,700 | + 4,860 | + 2,160 |
| | | Total Net | +27,026 |

determine the percentage of net profit in order to truly evaluate management for organizing and directing the enterprise.

Discount analysis of the project points out an important point relative to cash flow. When the discount rate is high, a faster turnover of cash flow is much more desirable, since the present value of long-term future income declines rapidly. Note the rapid drop in discount factors for 15% compared to 12%. Also, depending upon the amount of return on investment that is desired and the rate of turnover in cash flow, the value of the last remaining plants in a block of nursery stock may become a significant factor. In the example, if 15% were desired, it becomes important to sell the last 112 plants, whereas if 12% is a satisfactory rate of return the last 112 trees could be sacrificed without significantly affecting the rate of return on the investment. Naturally, other factors must be considered, namely, land cost and the projected sales income from alternative uses of the land. In the example, the projected income was relatively low. Also, in the total financial evaluation of the business, the sale of the last remaining plants may become a source of supplementary income rather than direct income from the project, provided that the land cannot be programmed for some more productive use. In many production nurseries, the last remaining plants may not be salable or must be sold at less than full market value.

**Table 7-6** Discounted-Cash-Flow Analysis

| Year | Net Cash Flow | 12% | | 15% | |
|------|---------------|--------|-------|--------|-------|
| | | Factor | Value | Factor | Value |
| 0 | −36,200 | 1.0000 | −36,200 | 1.0000 | −36,200 |
| 1 | − 2,445 | 0.8929 | − 2,183 | 0.8696 | − 2,126 |
| 2 | − 1,448 | 0.7972 | − 1,154 | 0.7561 | − 1,095 |
| 3 | + 4,467 | 0.7179 | + 3,207 | 0.6575 | + 2,937 |
| 4 | +38.871 | 0.6355 | +24,702 | 0.5718 | +22,226 |
| 5 | +21,611 | 0.5674 | +12,262 | 0.4972 | +10,745 |
| 6 | + 2,160 | 0.5066 | + 1,094 | 0.4323 | + 934 |
| | | Total Net | + 1,728 | Total Net | − 2,579 |

### Another System for Estimating Cost of Production

Another system for estimating the cost of production is a method proportioning the various financial inputs by land, capital assets, direct materials, estimated labor inputs, and overhead expenses. Many of the financial inputs to start a nursery are for land and capital assets, such as propagation structures, storage facilities, and so on. It is difficult to equate a fair cost of the use of these facilities to plant production cost, since they are not direct costs. Nevertheless, they are costs of production and must be included.

One method is to own and develop these facilities under a proprietorship, which then rents them to the nursery, which may be a corporation or a partnership. For example, it may require 10 acres of land at $100 per acre for 7 years to produce 4000 trees. Land costs for the production of the trees would be $1000 per year for 7 years. This would be posted to cost of production as noted in Table 7–7. Similar estimates can be made for the use of other capital assets. Materials that go directly into the production of the plants can be fairly accurately estimated either on an acre basis (e.g., fertilizer, pesticides, etc.) or on an individual plant or per 1000 plant basis, whichever is most desirable. The data are then converted to the number of plants being costed (in the example, 4000 trees).

Supplies to develop the land and facilities are charged to the owners and are reflected in the rent charges. Equipment charges may either be rent, if owned by a proprietor and leased to the nursery, or they may be calculated as an overhead cost, depending upon which is the most equitable approach to the problem. Over a period of time management should develop production tables that reflect the average productivity for the equipment or for the labor-machine combination used to accomplish the various jobs in the nursery (e.g., digging, planting, packaging, etc.: Figs. 3–3 and 3–4).

Labor skills that are directly related to the production of the plants should be charged accordingly. This is best done on a unit basis (generally per 1000); but for large balled and burlapped shade trees the costs may be equated to a single tree. For some labor skills the actual production may be determined on the number of units produced per hour. Labor skills not directly related to plant production and those that span many categories (supervisors, administrative staff, and management) are best equated as an overhead cost. All overhead costs, those that are not directly related to plant production, can be equated to either direct labor or material costs. In most nurseries, they are applied as a percentage of direct labor, as noted in the previous example.

It requires money to pay for the materials, the labor skills, and the rent for land and facilities. The money may be obtained from outside sources or from within the nursery organization. But regardless of where it comes from, it should earn a fair rate of interest. This must be reflected in the discount rate as well as the profit due management for the risk involved in producing the nursery stock. If management could put the finances available into low-risk bonds that earn 7.5%, this might be the interest rate that should be charged for

**Table 7-7** Estimated Cost-of-Production Schedule and Cash-Flow Analysis for 4000 Trees

*A. Production Costs and Cash Flow*

| Year | Rent ($100/acre) | Storage Facilities ($50/1000 ft³) | Materials, Estimated to Nearest $100 | Direct Labor Estimated to Nearest $100 | Overhead, 50% of DL | Total Yearly Investment | Net Sales Income[a] | Net Cash Flow |
|---|---|---|---|---|---|---|---|---|
| 0 | $1,000 | — | $28,800 | 3,000 | 1,500 | −34,300 | 0 | −34,300 |
| 1 | 1,000 | — | 500 | 1,000 | 500 | − 3,000 | 0 | − 3,000 |
| 2 | 1,000 | 50 | 800 | 1,500 | 750 | − 4,100 | + 1,620 | − 2,480 |
| 3 | 1,000 | 150 | 1,000 | 1,500 | 750 | − 4,400 | + 8,500 | + 4,100 |
| 4 | 1,000 | 100 | 2,000 | 4,000 | 2,000 | − 9,100 | +47,250 | +38,150 |
| 5 | 1,000 | 50 | 1,500 | 2,000 | 1,000 | − 5,550 | +27,000 | +21,450 |
| 6 | 1,000 | 50 | 800 | 1,000 | 500 | − 3,350 | + 5,000 | + 1,650 |

*B. Sales Income*

| Year | Plants | Price | Income | Sales Expense | Net Sales Income |
|---|---|---|---|---|---|
| 0 | 0 | | 0 | | 0 |
| 1 | 0 | | 0 | | 0 |
| 2 | 100 | 18 | 1,800 | 180 | 1,620 |
| 3 | 450 | 21 | 9,450 | 945 | 8,500 |
| 4 | 2100 | 25 | 52,500 | 5,250 | 47,250 |
| 5 | 1000 | 30 | 30,000 | 3,000 | 27,000 |
| 6 | 200 | 30 | 6,000 | 600 | 5,400 |

*C. Discounted-Cash-Flow Analysis*

| Year | Net Cash Flow | 12% | | 15% | |
|---|---|---|---|---|---|
| | | Factor | Value | Factor | Value |
| 0 | −34,300 | 1.0000 | −34,300 | 1.0000 | −34,300 |
| 1 | − 3,000 | 0.8929 | − 2,679 | 0.8696 | − 2,609 |
| 2 | − 2,480 | 0.7972 | − 1,977 | 0.7561 | − 1,875 |
| 3 | + 4,100 | 0.7179 | + 2,943 | 0.6575 | + 2,696 |
| 4 | +38,150 | 0.6355 | +24,244 | 0.5718 | +21,814 |
| 5 | +21,450 | 0.5674 | +12,170 | 0.4972 | +10,665 |
| 6 | + 1,650 | 0.5066 | + 836 | 0.4323 | + 713 |
| | | Total Net | + 1,237 | Total Net | − 2,896 |

[a]From Table B.

the use of the financial input. If management desires an additional 7.5% as compensation for the additional risk of investing in the nursery as compared with investing in low-risk bonds, the suggested discount rate might be 15%. In the example, it can be seen (Table 7–7C) that the potential net cash flow earns a positive cash flow at 12%, but a negative cash flow at 15%, making the venture questionable from the start. At the desired 15% discount rate, either the income from sales is delayed too long or is not great enough, or the amount invested the first year is too great. A reevaluation of the production system and nursery crop is warranted.

## ACCOUNTS RECEIVABLE

Accounts receivable are the uncollected bills the nursery has on its financial records for nursery stock it has sold. This is probably the most difficult area of financial management for most nurseries. The credit policy established by a nursery for its customers must reflect the cost of borrowing money, the credit policies of competing nurseries, and the individual customer's current credit rating. Wholesale nurseries in a common market area will frequently establish informal exchanges of credit information on their customers who have unpaid bills. This practice tends to limit the total debt a customer can develop in a market area and encourages customers to pay up long-standing bills.

## TOTAL NURSERY PROFITS

Profitability of the nursery must be measured by the cost involved and the sales income generated by the total product mix. An evaluation must be made to determine if the various production systems within the nursery are in balance to maximize productivity of the business. Once the basic assets (land, buildings, equipment, permanent labor force) are assembled, it becomes obligatory that management utilize the assets to the best advantage. Certain fundamental questions must be answered and reevaluated on a continuing, periodic basis: Is the product mix the best for the potential sales market? Are the production facilities being used to optimum capacity? Are the various labor skills being employed most effectively? What changes can be made in the production system to maximize returns on investment?

The product mix is the combination of plants that are being or could be produced by the nursery. Over a number of decades, nursery production has gradually shifted from emphasis on the production of fruit trees to the production of woody ornamental plants. Even within nurseries, there has been a shifting to the production of those species that grow well within a given climate. Once a production nurseryman has determined the primary species of plants to grow and has developed the facilities and assembled the labor skills to accomplish the production goals, he or she needs to determine if nursery income could be supplemented by producing selected supplementary species with the facilities and labor skills available. It may be that the current production systems are not fully utilizing the existing facilities, or that at certain times of the year the full-time labor force is not fully productive. All too often the propagation and storage facilities of large production nurseries are empty when they might be used in a supplementary manner. It might be possible to modify current production practices in order to maximize the effective and efficient use of expensive greenhouse space and plant storage facilities. In some situations the production of supplementary species may require additional labor. However, the relatively small added labor input, coupled with the essentially "free" use of existing facilities, may be well worth the investment. Management is evaluated and rewarded on the productive utilization of all three factors of production (materials, personnel, and money). Thus, management must be constantly evaluating all factors of production and trying to put together the most productive and profitable system.

Nursery managers are in a position to use computers to evaluate their production systems. By programming a computer with data relative to cultural practices, labor productivity, and cost information, the manager will be able to simulate various types of nursery production systems and cycles and test their potential worth by discount analysis. Nursery managers have a very powerful tool at their disposal; it awaits their use.

Taylor et al. (1986a,b) have developed a cost model for both a small container nursery and a field nursery which would be appropriate for plant hardiness zones 5 and 6. The model is based on the Columbus, Ohio, area using cost data from nurseries in the north central United States during 1984–1985, and assumes that both of these operations were new installations and that all supplies, land, and so on, had to be accounted for in the cost analyses. Both the field and container nursery cost analyses indicate that a comparison of the cost of producing plants with the income from the sale of plants at wholesale catalog prices produce a loss in most cases. Selling costs are not included. These analyses indicate that starting a new, profitable nursery in the north central United States would be very difficult. Existing nurseries can remain competitive because they have purchased land, buildings, and equipment at lower prices and because they may share buildings, equipment, and management with other enterprises. Both of these studies dramatically demonstrate the necessity for accurate cost analysis for both existing and proposed nursery production operations.

## CASH-FLOW ANALYSIS

One of the financial problems common to all types of nursery businesses is the highly seasonal nature of the annual sales cycle. It is not uncommon to find production nurseries that develop 50% of their annual sales during one quarter of the year. Cash-flow problems result because expenditures precede sales and do not occur in a similar annual cycle. In many cases the major labor input in harvesting nursery stock (which requires substantial cash) occurs almost completely before the nursery stock is paid for by the consumer. Table 7–8 illustrates a typical monthly sales distribution for wholesale nursery growers in the north central United States. A few nursery firms have been partially successful in their efforts to develop other products or services that provide income and productively use labor during the periods of the year when nursery income and labor needs are minimal.

The fluctuation in income and expenses during the year requires short-term financing during the periods of the year when expenses exceed income. A projected cash-flow budget should be prepared based on past cash-flow data and the future payment and income projections. The cash-flow analysis should be prepared at least once a year in monthly increments, and might be required more frequently in cases where projections are altered by dramatic shifts in marketing or production. The total cash expenses and the total income from all sources are tabulated on a monthly basis, and positive or negative cash flow for each month is recorded (Table 7–9). A cumulative positive or negative cash flow developed for each month will indicate the necessity for short-term loans well in advance, allowing for proper financing. A cash-flow budget also indicates opportunities for short-term investment of surplus funds for some periods of the year.

## RATIO ANALYSIS

Ratio analysis allows a manager to compare the annual financial performance of a nursery as it changes with time and to compare it with other businesses, possibly with other nurseries. Financial ratios from two different businesses and ratios developed for different years within the same business are useful only if the basis for each financial ratio is understood. Each ratio relates to a specific financial performance area of the business and as a result provides a different perspective of the financial performance of the business. It is important to understand how your nursery business might logically be expected to differ from other types of businesses, and even other nurseries serving the same market segment. An understanding of these differences will help you to understand differences in ratios. A number of financial ratios can be used to evaluate and diagnose profitability, efficiency of production, and management, and to highlight opportunities available to the manager to

**Table 7–8** Percentage of Annual Sales by Month

| Dec. | 3.4 | Mar. | 12.1 | June | 7.2 | Sept. | 5.0 |
|------|-----|------|------|------|-----|-------|-----|
| Jan. | 2.5 | Apr. | 18.7 | July | 4.9 | Oct. | 6.8 |
| Feb. | 3.2 | May | 13.8 | Aug. | 3.8 | Nov. | 5.6 |
| | 9.1 | | 44.6 | | 15.9 | | 17.4 |

*Source:* HRI operating cost study, 12th edition, 1988.

improve his operation. Figure 7–6 illustrates the relationship between a number of basic financial ratios. These ratios can be used to compare the nursery to businesses in general as well as to other nurseries. The data for creating these ratios will come from the nursery's balance sheet and/or income statement.

***Margin management.*** The net profit margin shown in the lower right hand of Figure 7–6, indicates how well the net revenue (sales) is being used to cover the cost of operating the nursery. The net profit margin ratio does not indicate how to increase net profit, only that improvement could or should be made. This ratio frequently indicates that further financial and management analysis is needed to improve the net profit produced by the assets currently invested in the nursery. A large nursery may develop distinct divisions, such as field production, container production, retail and wholesale divisions and so on, and may develop a net profit margin ratio for each division. These ratios would indicate which divisions might have financial problems or demonstrate where opportunities to improve profitability exist.

***Capital management.*** The asset turnover ratio (in the lower left hand of Figure 7–6) consists of net revenue (sales) divided by total assets which indicate how efficiently the nursery uses capital. It documents the number of dollars in revenue generated by each dollar invested in the business. Capital management ratios can be expected to change with time as the production of a young nursery expands to take advantage of new markets.

***Financial management.*** This section of Figure 7–6 utilizes two financial ratios: a return on assets ratio (net profit divided by total assets), and a leverage ratio (total assets divided by net worth).

**Figure 7–6** The Strategic Profit Model. *Source:* George Koziarz, 1988.

**Table 7-9** Cash-Flow Statement

| | From January 1 to December 31[a] | | | | |
|---|---|---|---|---|---|
| | Jan. | Feb. | Mar. | Apr. | May |
| Cash balance first of month | $2,000 | $2,000 | $1,000 | $2,400 | $6,900 |
| Funds provided: | | | | | |
| Receipts from customers | $5,000 | $1,000 | — | $15,000 | $20,000 |
| Bank operating loan | | $5,000 | $10,000 | | |
| Total funds provided | $5,000 | $6,000 | $10,000 | $15,000 | $20,000 |
| Total funds to be accounted for | $7,000 | $8,000 | $11,000 | $17,400 | $26,900 |
| Funds applied | | | | | |
| Salaries | $1,400 | $1,400 | $1,500 | $1,500 | $1,400 |
| Hourly payroll | 1,000 | 1,000 | 4,000 | 6,000 | 4,000 |
| Commissions | | | | | 1,000 |
| Installment payments | 250 | 250 | 250 | 250 | 250 |
| Purchases for resale | | | | | |
| Freight out | | | | | 500 |
| Packaging supplies | | 2,000 | 1,000 | | 2,500 |
| Purchases of liners | | | | | |
| Manure, peat, and fertilizer | | | | | 1,000 |
| Rent expense | | | | | |
| Advertising and promotion | | | 500 | 500 | 500 |
| Other operating expenses | 2,350 | 2,350 | 1,350 | 2,250 | 1,850 |
| Bank operating loan repayment | | | | | 5,000 |
| Distribution of profit | | | | | |
| Total funds applied | $5,000 | $7,000 | $8,600 | $10,500 | $18,000 |
| Cash balance end of month | $2,000 | $1,000 | $2,400 | $6,900 | $8,900 |

[a]Figures are taken from the cash receipts journal and the cash disbursements journal.

*Source:* Smith et al. (1970).

The return on assets ratio can be calculated by multiplying the asset turnover ratio by the net profit margin ratio, cancelling out net revenue in both ratios, and leaving net profit over total assets. This ratio is an indication of the earning power of the nursery's assets. Earning power can be improved by increasing revenue, by increasing prices, or by increasing the volume of production through improved management of assets such as labor, materials, inventory, overhead expenses, and facilities.

The leverage ratio indicates the degree of solvency (the degree the nursery relies on borrowed funds) of the nursery business. Since borrowed funds or capital have a fixed interest and principle payment schedule, a low leverage ratio (a modest amount of borrowed funds) indicates an ability to survive periods of reduced business and income because the fixed interest and principle payments are relatively small. A high leverage ratio indicates a high level of borrowing and a willingness to take risks in return for an increased rate growth.

**Table 7–9** (*continued*)

| | | From January 1 to December 31[a] | | | | | |
|---|---|---|---|---|---|---|---|
| June | July | Aug. | Sept. | Oct. | Nov. | Dec. | Total |
| $ 8,900 | $ 5,900 | $4,900 | $ 1,900 | $ 3,900 | $ 8,900 | $10,000 | |
| $21,000 | $ 5,000 | $3,000 | $10,000 | $15,000 | $10,000 | $ 5,000 | $110,000 |
| | | | | | | | $ 15,000 |
| $21,000 | $ 5,000 | $3,000 | $10,000 | $15,000 | $10,000 | $ 5,000 | $125,000 |
| $29,900 | $10,900 | $7,900 | $11,900 | $18,900 | $18,900 | $15,900 | $127,000 |
| $ 1,400 | $ 1,400 | $1,400 | $ 1,400 | $ 1,400 | $ 1,400 | $ 1,400 | $ 17,000 |
| 3,000 | 2,000 | 2,000 | 3,000 | 2,000 | 2,000 | 1,000 | 31,000 |
| 1,000 | | | | | | | 2,000 |
| 250 | 250 | 250 | 250 | 250 | 250 | 250 | 3,000 |
| 3,000 | | | | 2,000 | | | 5,000 |
| 1,500 | | | | 1,000 | | | 3,000 |
| | | | | 500 | 1,000 | | 7,000 |
| 2,000 | | | | | | | 2,000 |
| | | | | | 1,000 | | 2,000 |
| 500 | | | | | | 500 | 1,000 |
| | | | 500 | | | | 2,000 |
| 1,350 | 2,350 | 2,350 | 2,850 | 2,850 | 2,350 | 1,850 | 26,100 |
| 10,000 | | | | | | | 15,000 |
| | | | | | | 7,000 | 7,000 |
| $24,000 | $ 6,000 | $6,000 | $ 8,000 | $10,000 | $ 8,000 | $12,000 | $123,100 |
| $ 5,900 | $ 4,900 | $1,900 | $ 3,900 | $ 8,900 | $10,900 | $ 3,900 | $ 3,900 |

**High yield management.** The return on investment ratio is the best indication of profitability of the nursery. It can be calculated by multiplying the previous two ratios (leverage ratio $\times$ return on assets ratio), cancelling out total assets in both ratios leaving net profit over net worth. The return on investment ratio indicates the relative success of the nursery in creating a satisfactory return on investment for the owner or owners. A low ratio may indicate an inefficient production, marketing, sales, or financial management system. A difficult business climate or losses resulting from natural disasters such as flood or frost can also be detected. The use of the ratios in the strategic profit model highlights the nursery's primary financial goal—earning an appropriate rate of return on net worth—and at the same time indicates to management those areas to investigate to improve the return on investment or net worth.

**Nursery industry ratios.** The annual operating cost study for members of the Horticulture Research Institute provides an opportunity to compare average data on production, marketing, sales, and management activities within a specific nursery to other similar nursery businesses. This comparison may indicate with precision where to begin to focus on developing greater efficiency and profitability.

The use of any ratio analysis is limited to comparisons with similar firms and with ratios of past years' financial data for the same firm. Ratios and operating-cost data, even those most specifically related to the nursery industry, serve only to identify areas where a firm differs. Ratios do not indicate whether these differences are healthy or unhealthy. The median ratios of the nursery industry are not absolute standards that must be approximated. The goals of the firm (growth, profit, quality of product, stability, etc.) should not include the creation of financial ratios that approximate the median for the industry.

## SUMMARY

Financial management makes use of financial records to document the growth potential, profitability, and the value of the assets of a nursery to obtain capital for operation and expansion of the firm. These records can also be used to help decide what kinds of expansion, production, purchases, and so on, will be most beneficial. The cost of production can be documented by financial records indicating the profitability of various types of nursery products and practices. Financial records and proper financial management are essential to start, manage, and evaluate the success of the nursery. Financial management is the core of the nursery business, and all aspects of the business are affected by it.

## REFERENCES

AMERICAN ASSOCIATION OF NURSERYMEN. 1979. Update, a report of the Allied Landscape Industry. AAN. Washington, D.C.

AMERICAN NURSERYMAN. 1976. Tax Bill Exemption. Vol. 144, No. 8, pp. 110–111. Am. Nurseryman Publishing Company, Chicago.

APLIN, R. D., and G. L. CASLER. 1973. Capital investment analysis: using discounted cash flows. Grid Publishing, Inc., Columbus, Ohio.

EDWARDS, J. D., R. H. HERMANSON, and R. F. SALMANSON. 1974. Accounting I, 3rd ed. Richard D. Irwin, Inc., Homewood, Ill.

HORTICULTURAL RESEARCH INSTITUTE. 1971. Uniform chart of accounts for nursery production, landscape, and retail operations. HRI, Washington, D.C.

HORTICULTURAL RESEARCH INSTITUTE, Inc. 1988. Operating cost study. HRI, Washington, D.C. (studies for 1965 through 1982 are also available.)

KOZIARZ, G. 1988. A Rational Look at Ratios. Am. Nurseryman, September.

MURRAY, W. G., and A. G. NELSON. 1960. Agricultural finance. Iowa St. Univ. Press, Ames, Iowa.

PERKINS, G. S. 1973. The economics of ornamental nursery management. Fla. Agric. Exp. Sta. Univ. Fla. J. Ser. 5180, pp. 411–415.

SMITH, E. M., G. C. HIMES, and H. HOLLAR. 1970. A method of utilizing accounting for nurseries producing field grown stock. Coop. Ext. Serv. Ohio St. Univ. Bull. 520.

TAYLOR, R. D., H. H. KNEEN, D. E. HAHN, and E. M. SMITH, JR. 1986a. Calculating the bottom line for a small container nursery. Am. Nurseryman, February.

———. H. H. KNEEN, D. E. HAHN, E. M. SMITH, JR. and S. UCHIDA. 1986b. Calculating field nursery costs. Am. Nurseryman, February.

TOWER, R. B. 1962. A handbook of small business finance. Small Business Management Series 15 (Small Business Administration). Superintendent of Documents, Washington, D.C.

# Chapter 8
# Wholesale Marketing of Nursery Crops

The wholesale marketing of nursery crops can be discussed from a number of viewpoints, depending on how one views the marketing process. The retail garden center manager, the mass merchandiser, landscape architect-designer, landscape contractor, wholesale salesman, production nurseryman, and so on, are all involved in wholesale marketing, and each has very personal requirements and interests in the process. Each of these individuals will define the marketing of nursery crops differently. Each will also positively or negatively evaluate the current nursery crop marketing process in relation to how well it satisfies his or her own needs. Marketing, as defined by Kohls, is "the performance of all business activities involved in the flow of goods (in this case nursery crops) and services from the point of initial agricultural production until they are in the hands of the ultimate consumer." Owing to a lack of space in this text, only the wholesale marketing of nursery crops in relation to retailers such as garden centers, landscapers, and mail-order nurserymen will be considered.

The flow of nursery crops from the producer to the retailer is quite complex, in part because of the vast variety of nursery crops, the rapid expansion of the nursery industry, and, in many cases, the long distances that nursery crops are shipped from producer to consumer. A study of the nursery industry in Michigan revealed that approximately 75% of the nursery stock sold at the retail level was produced out of the state. Nursery crops were shipped into Michigan from a majority of the states in the continental United States. At the same time, many wholesale production nurseries in Michigan sell 75% or more of their crops out of the state. A 1990 survey indicated wholesale nurseries in some states sell an even higher percentage out of state, (Alabama 93.8%, Oregon 87.2%) whereas other states' nurseries sell predominately in state (Florida 77.2%, Georgia 70.9%, Illinois 82.3%, and California 83.5%).

A similar marketing pattern would be expected in most of the major nursery market areas in the United States.

## SPECIALIZATION IN PRODUCTION NURSERIES

There are a variety of reasons for the long-distance shipments of nursery stock in the United States. A specific nursery crop may be more economically produced in one section of the country because of a more optimal climate and soil, lower land and labor costs, greater availability of technically trained employees, lower-energy requirements, longer growing season, and possibly more progressive nursery management. Many production nurseries also specialize in the type of consumer they serve as well as in the nursery crops they produce, and therefore serve a broader geographic area. The same species and cultivar of shade tree, for example, will be grown, pruned, harvested, packaged, and labeled quite differently, depending upon whether the tree will be merchandised through a garden center in early spring as a packaged plant, or through a landscape contractor as a balled and burlapped plant in late summer. The production nursery manager frequently makes irreversible cultural, harvesting, and packaging decisions which commit the nursery crop to a specific type of marketing channel and consumer. The same plant will be needed by each retail market in specific quantities and stages of growth, with specific delivery schedules, labeling and reorder potentials. State laws in some states may dictate some of the requirements.

Most production nurseries, to obtain the benefits of specialization, have directed their nursery crop production to serving a relatively narrow segment of the market. In this way the management of a nursery can more efficiently provide the nursery crop and the necessary services needed by a specific type of retail marketing firm. Developing a successful, profitable wholesale marketing program for a nursery crop begins with an understanding of the needs and nature of the customer. Too often a marketing program begins with a specific product that must be sold. A marketing program should not be a crisis-solving activity. It is an essential part of the nursery management process and must be considered as the first step in the planning and organization of a production nursery.

## TYPE OF NURSERY CROPS NEEDED
## BY LANDSCAPERS

A landscape nurseryman has specific plant needs and will usually want larger plants than will retail garden centers. The nursery stock will usually be B&B, boxed, or container-grown, with very limited quantities purchased as bare-root plants. This in part reflects the reduced maintenance and extended transplanting and sales season, as well as improved transplantability of B&B, boxed, or container-grown plants compared to bare-root plants. If the landscaper is buying plants for a landscape project, specific plants and sizes may be called for by the architect, which in some cases may be produced by a limited number of nurseries or, at times, may be unavailable. Therefore landscape architects are a source of information for the nursery grower in determining the types of plants to be produced and the production system to be used.

### Timing Deliveries for Landscapers

The landscape planting season has gradually expanded into the summer and winter seasons as a result of cultural and technical innovations. Landscape planting can now be carried out most of the year with some exceptions. However, the ability of workers and equipment to function properly under existing weather conditions will reduce efficiency during the winter season in the northern United States. A landscaper therefore has a more constant need for plants throughout the year than do garden centers, which have pronounced spring and fall seasons.

The landscaper may want to schedule the delivery of plants to a landscape site on a specific day or in some cases at a specific hour of the day to improve efficiency of costly planting equipment and labor and to eliminate the damage to plants resulting from reloading and excessive handling.

Landscapers may frequently purchase rather large quantities of the more commonly used nursery stock which they plan to hold in their own lath, shade area, or temporarily plant in their own fields until needed in a future landscape project. This provides a convenient, inexpensive, immediately available source of landscape plants. Some will produce larger trees which are expensive to ship long distances and unusual specimen plants which are difficult to find in production nurseries. Other landscapers will purchase only those plants needed on a current landscape project.

### Price Quotations for Bidding

Landscape projects may be bid months or even years before the landscape project begins. The production nursery may need to guarantee a price, 1, 2, or even 3 years before delivery in order for the landscaper to submit a bid. Wholesale nursery catalog prices are usually valid for only part of the year and, therefore, the wholesale nursery manager must be able to anticipate the market in order to make price quotations for a future date. Large production nurseries supplying quotations will usually want to know the name of the project the landscaper is bidding, particularly if the landscape project is large enough to approach exhausting the regional supply of one size or variety of landscape plant. A number of landscape contractors obtaining prices and guaranteed delivery for the same project will create the illusion of a shortage, which drives prices up and prevents other landscapers from preparing a competitive bid. A production nursery can supply price quotations and guarantee delivery to many landscapers if they are bidding the same landscape project. This keeps the prices down for the landscapers and increases the chances of the production nursery supplying the plants for the project. Production nurseries also may offer volume discounts for the opportunity to supply all the plant needs for the project, providing a more efficient shipment to the site.

### Services Provided by the Nursery Broker

In the larger market areas, an independent broker may buy in large quantities and maintain nursery stock on a sales lot in order to wholesale it to retailers. The nursery broker may also provide the service of finding and procuring unusual specimen plants needed by the landscape contractor. Other nursery stock brokers may not handle or store landscape plants, but in effect serve as sales representatives for a number of production nurseries. This type of broker may be asked by the landscaper to obtain prices for all plant needs, saving considerable time and expense for the landscaper. The broker may arrange for the digging and specific delivery schedules if needed. Because of the volume handled by a broker and knowledge of the availability of nursery stock and the availability of transportation, the broker may be able to arrange efficient, combined order shipments with a reliable trucker, realizing substantial savings in the cost of plants and transportation for the landscaper.

## TYPE OF NURSERY CROPS NEEDED BY GARDEN CENTERS

In contrast to landscapers, retail garden center managers are usually interested in large quantities of commonly used landscape plants for short, high-volume seasonal sales periods. A large northern chain of retail garden centers, Frank's Nursery Sales, Inc., reported 11.3% of their sales in the first quarter of the year, 39.1% in the second, 20% in the third, and 29.4% in the fourth quarter of the year. The fourth-quarter sales (October, November, and December) are primarily Christmas-related items. The dominance of the second quarter (April, May, and June) spring plant sales in retail garden centers is a serious challenge for garden center managers. Well over half of the plant sales in most garden centers will occur during the second quarter of the year. Garden centers in mild climates will have more uniform sales throughout the year as a result of a longer growing season.

A garden center's merchandising program often begins in winter with the sale of indoor plants, bird seed, pet supplies, and crafts. Spring sales begin with the display of fertilizers, grass, vegetable and flower seeds, dormant packaged bare-root perennials, deciduous plants such as roses and fruit trees, and flowering shrubs. In the northern United States, the sales season begins with the first comfortable spring days. Dormant plant sales will be followed by B&B or containerized plants and bedding plants. Peak sale opportunity for landscape plants such as flowering shrubs and trees may be only the week or two that the plant is in bloom in the community. The garden center manager will usually develop an advertising program which is fixed weeks or even months in advance of the sales period. This program will be timed to promote those types of plants that attract the interest of the consumer. Advertising programs might also feature items priced at or below cost called *loss leaders*, specifically chosen to increase traffic in the store.

### Timing Deliveries for Garden Centers

The timing of nursery stock deliveries for retail garden centers is one of the most important challenges for the production nursery specializing in serving garden centers. Many garden center managers will buy only from those production nurseries that demonstrate the ability to deliver their products consistently when requested. Consumers are interested in purchasing nursery stock the first few warm days in spring, particularly if they occur on a weekend. This does not allow sufficient good weather for a local nursery to harvest plants from the field, package, and deliver nursery stock to the garden center in time for early spring sales. Southern nurseries have a distinct advantage in providing early deliveries for northern garden centers. Many northern nurseries utilize a variety of different storage facilities to hold nursery stock harvested and packaged during the preceding fall and winter (see Chapter 17). This allows the northern production nursery to ship fall harvested nursery stock in early spring before the local climate would permit field harvesting.

The sale of nursery stock in garden centers is highly dependent upon the weekend weather. A rainy cold weekend will almost stop sales, whereas a warm sunny weekend will substantially stimulate sales. A production nursery specializing in providing nursery stock for garden centers must be able to respond to a good-weather weekend by accelerating deliveries. The production nursery must also be able to deliver nursery stock according to the retailer's scheduled advertising program. A garden center loses not only the potential sale but customer confidence when an advertised plant is not available as a result of limited supplies. The short duration of garden center sales requires that every available display space be filled with plants, and that every effort be made to restock immediately after sales.

## TYPE OF NURSERY CROPS NEEDED FOR MAIL-ORDER NURSERIES

The mail-order nursery uses a sales catalog as well as other forms of advertising to sell nursery stock that will be delivered for the most part via parcel post or a parcel service. Mail-order catalogs are usually mailed in mid- to late winter, but early fall catalogs specializing in fall planted bulbs are also common. This industry is particularly sensitive to parcel post rates and makes every effort to reduce the bulk and weight of its nursery products, packaging, and catalogs. Most mail-order items are either bare-root dormant plants or are grown in small containers and lightweight soil. Nursery stock is usually dug in the fall, processed during the winter, packaged, and shipped in early spring. Bare-root dormant plants are usually moistened and wrapped in moisture-proof material, frequently sealed in polyethylene bags, and packed in cardboard containers. The mail-order catalog has been the single most important public source of information and sales motivation for the entire nursery industry, including garden center sales and landscape plantings.

### Timing Deliveries for Mail-Order Nurseries

The scheduled shipment of mail-order nursery stock is usually based on the estimated time of optimal planting weather for the particular area to which it is being shipped. Shipments may also be limited by the chances for freezing damage to plants during delivery. The entire marketing area (frequently a major segment of the continental United States) will be divided into zones having the same optimal planting dates. A mail-order nursery frequently limits shipping season to only a few months to allow the consumer to plant nursery stock at the best time of year for plant survival.

## WHOLESALE NURSERY SALES ORGANIZATIONS

A variety of different types of nursery sales organizations and agreements with nursery salespersons can be found in the industry. Some production nurseries will hire their own staff who work on a salary and/or commission to sell the nursery's products. The nursery's market area might be divided into districts so that each is the exclusive area for one salesperson. The sales actually booked by the salesperson as well as orders made directly by customers that were originally contacted by the salesperson are his or her accounts and contribute to sales commissions. The sales staff frequently spends a great deal of time personally visiting each customer in the district, providing marketing and management information. It usually takes a number of years of travel before the salesperson can develop the maximum sales potential in the district.

Some nurseries have a separate sales division which markets the nursery's products and, as mentioned earlier, may market plants and related items not produced by the parent nursery. This provides a more complete line of products and services and makes for a more efficient sales organization. Nursery brokers sometimes called representatives or "reps" operate their own independent sales organizations, selling on commission products from a number of production nurseries. Nurseries more frequently use a rep for out of state sales. These individuals will only book orders. The shipments will originate from the production nursery. A rep will, in most cases, be able to provide a complete line of nursery crops and related products as well as arrange for special shipment, delivery, and other services. The rep receives a commission on all orders personally booked and all orders direct to the production nursery from customers the broker originally contacted. A rep can sell a more complete line than most salespersons representing a single nursery (and the rep usually will write larger orders in a smaller territory than will most salespersons). Both brokers and salespersons will frequently provide assistance in developing advertising programs, display patterns, delivery timing, loss-leader sales, and so on, for retail garden center managers. They may provide data on the previous years' orders, delivery dates, and reorders to assist the buyer in developing this year's purchasing decisions. They are also excellent sources of nursery industry information as a result of their travel and experience with the industry.

Selling nursery stock to discount or department stores with garden center sections usually involves dealing with a head buyer in the home office before the salesman has the opportunity to contact the manager of each store. The buyers for some discount chains may know little about the nursery business but a great deal about merchandising. Frequently, the time, quantity, and nature of the initial shipment is established by the buyer in the home office, and subsequent reorders originate with the store manager. The nursery sales force may have to contact each of the individual store managers as well as the head buyer. Many discount or department stores and some garden center managers want large color tags with the botanical and common names and a picture to help identify and sell the plant and some will want the nursery stock prepriced.

Buyers may also directly contact production nurseries in order to gain more information on the price, quality, and availability of nursery crops. Many buyers for mail-order, garden center, and landscape firms will periodically visit production nurseries searching for new sources of plants as well as new types of plants. Buyer trips to production nurseries are one of the best ways to evaluate the quality and availability of common as well as unusual types of landscape plants, and are encouraged by production nurseries. Some production nurseries will host open houses or field days for landscape architects, municipal arborists, and landscape contractors. Many landscape architects will make extensive searches for unusual, high-quality plant material to add variety and interest to their landscape designs.

## STANDARDS

*American Standards for Nursery Stock*, sponsored by the AAN, and approved by the American National Standards Institute, is the recognized standard for nursery stock in the United States. It is designed to facilitate the commerce of nursery stock by standard grades for deciduous shade and flowering trees, deciduous shrubs, coniferous and broad leaved evergreens, roses, vines, and ground covers, fruit trees, small fruits, lining-out stock, seedlings, bulbs, corms, and tubers. The standards apply to harvesting of field-grown plants by all three methods—ball and burlap, ball and potted, and bare root—and to box and container-grown plants. In addition, they set standards for the minimum size of root systems for ornamental plants of all types. The standards are used by most buyers and sellers of nursery stock and are the commonly expected minimum acceptable size and quality of plants. These standards do not preclude anyone from producing, marketing, or using plants and procedures which do not conform to the standards. It is advisable to indicate in the nursery catalog where a plant product or procedure does not conform by being either below or above the AAN standards.

Where minimum-maximum size ranges are stated, an average size is required. That is, when one hundred 6- to 8-ft trees are ordered, the plants should average about 7 ft, not just make grade at 6 ft. Since it is almost impossible to establish standards for quality of living products, it is necessary to rely on the integrity of the individual nurseryman, and where this is not forthcoming, to seek other sources of supply.

The standards are reviewed and updated periodically to meet the requirements of the American National Standards Institute. The latest edition may be obtained from the AAN office in Washington, D.C.

### Deciduous Trees

Caliper of the trunk shall be the determining measurement in grading deciduous shade and flowering trees. The measurement is made 6 in. above ground level for trees up to and including those 4 in. in diameter. Above this size the measurement is to be made 12 in. above the ground (Fig. 8–1). Caliper is stated in ¼-in. units up to 2-in. size, in ½ in. units up to 4-in. size, and in 1-in. units above 4 in. (e.g., 1¼–1½ in., 2–2½ in., 5–6 in.). The standard recognizes four major types (standard shade trees, slow-growth shade trees, small upright trees, and small spreading trees) and suggests optimum and maximum heights and minimum root spread for trees of various caliper within each type. Height is quoted in single-foot units up to 6 ft and in double-foot units over 6 ft (e.g., 5–6 ft, 6–8 ft).

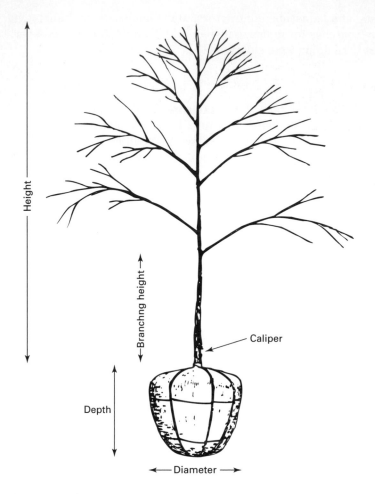

**Figure 8–1** Caliper measured 6 in. above ground level if 4 in. or less: if more than 4 in. measure at 12 in.; caliper determines size of rootball (see Table 8–1). (From American Association of Nurserymen.)

### Deciduous Shrubs

Deciduous shrubs are divided into seven types and graded by height and number of canes or stems (Fig. 8–2). The height classes for dwarf and semi-dwarf shrubs is stated in inches up to 24 in. (3-in. units up to 18 in., 6-in. units between 18 and 24 in.), and ½-ft units over 6 ft (e.g., 12–15 in., 18–24 in., and 2–2½ ft). Height classes for strong-growing shrubs is stated in 6-in. series up to 24 in., single-foot units between 2 and 6 ft, and in double-foot units above 6 ft (e.g., 12–18 in., 4–5 ft, and 6–8 ft). The standards suggest a minimum root

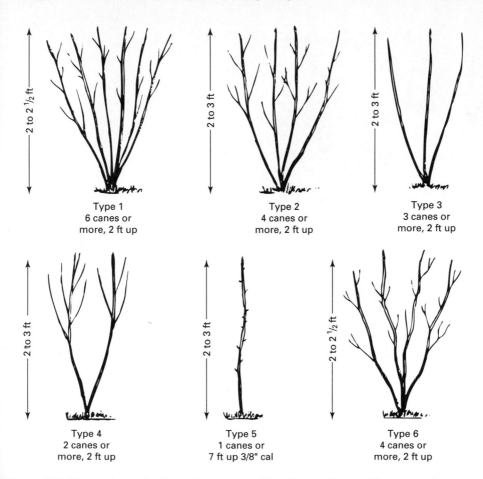

**Figure 8–2** Comparisons in the various types of deciduous shrubs. (From American Association of Nurserymen, 1990.)

spread and indicate that the average height of a grade is close to the mean of the height class (e.g., size of plant, 4–5 ft; minimum root spread, 14 in., and average height, 4½ ft).

### Evergreens

Evergreens (Fig. 8–3) are divided into narrow-leaved and broad-leaved plants, and each group is subdivided into types based on habit of growth. The types include:

1. Conifer (Narrow-leaved plants)
   a. Creeping or prostrate

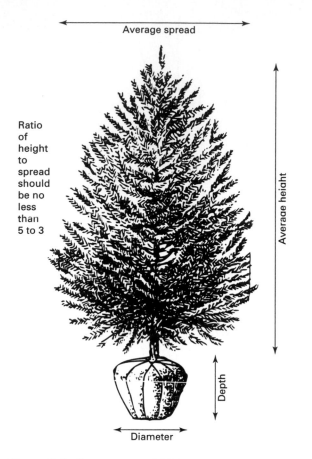

Average spread

Ratio
of
height
to
spread
should
be no
less
than
5 to 3

Average height

Depth

Diameter

**Figure 8–3** Cone or pyramidal-type evergreen.
(From American Association of Nurserymen, 1990.)

    b. Semispreading
    c. Broad spreading, globe, and upright
    d. Cone (pyramidal)
    e. Broad upright
    f. Columnar
2. Broad-leaved plants
    a. Spreading
    b. Semispreading
    c. Globe and dwarf
    d. Broad upright
    e. Cone

The height or spread in each group is stated using 3-in., 6-in., 1-ft, and 2-ft intervals. The interval varies with type, but the following intervals are fairly standard.

| | |
|---|---|
| 3-in. intervals up to 18 in. | 12–15 in. |
| 6-in. intervals between 18 in. and 4 ft | 2½–3 ft |
| 1-ft intervals from 4 ft up | 5–6 ft |

Measurement of height begins at ground level and stops where the main part of the plant ends, not at the tip of a shoot.

### Christmas Trees

Nurserymen interested in standards for Christmas trees should write to the Fresh Products Branch, Fruit and Vegetable Quality Division, Food Safety and Quality Service, U.S. Dept. of Agriculture, Washington, DC 20250, and request a copy of "United States Standards for Grades of Christmas Trees."

### Rose Grades

Rose standards apply only to field-grown roses when sold either bare-root or individually wrapped and packaged or in cartons. Roses are graded by number, and caliper of canes. Consideration is also given to weight of canes, depending upon grade and variety. The basic rose grades are No. 1, No. 1½, and No. 2. Each grade must have a minimum number of strong canes, generally 3, or a certain length and in each case branched not higher than 3 in. above the bud union (Fig. 8–4). Roses that do not meet these standards are called culls.

### Fruit Tree Grades

Caliper is the basic standard for fruit trees and is taken 2 in. above the collar or bud. It is generally stated in sixteenths of an inch; classes being stated in the odd-number series (e.g., 5/16 to 7/16, 9/16 to 11/16). In the three West Coast states, 1-year-old standard fruit tree stocks are commonly graded in intervals of ⅛ in. Trees should have reasonably straight stems, and all grades 5/16 and larger (except 1-year sweet cherries) should be branched and well rooted.

Citrus trees are graded in ⅛ in. increments and caliper is to be taken ½ in. above the bud union.

### Balling and Burlapping

Balling and burlapping (B&B) or boxing of trees and shrubs is one means of packaging plants for market. It is a practice associated with large trees and

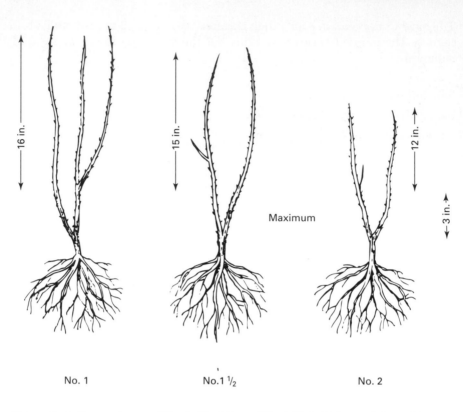

16 in.

15 in.

Maximum

12 in.

3 in.

No. 1

No.1 ½

No. 2

**Figure 8–4** Comparisons of No. 1, No. 1½, and No. 2 Hybrid Tea and Grandiflora roses. (From American Association of Nurserymen, 1990.)

with evergreens of various sizes. Although some plants can be successfully transplanted without a large ball of earth, it has become an accepted practice to transplant large trees B&B or boxed.

American Standards for Nursery Stock recommends minimum sizes of balls for five general plant types (Table 8–1). Although the recommendations are for plants that have been field-grown under favorable conditions, it is recognized that the root system of plants varies with species, soil conditions, and cultural practices, and that the ultimate size of the ball depends largely upon the integrity of the nurseryman. However, ball sizes should always be of a diameter and depth large enough to obtain the fibrous roots necessary to assure successful transplanting. The depth of the ball may vary with tree species, soil type, and the area of the country where the tree grows. The diameter/depth ratios in Figure 8–5 can be used as a guide in balling plants.

Ball depth ratios reflect root distribution which will vary with different tree varieties, the region of the country where they are grown, and the soil

**Table 8-1** Recommended Balling and Burlapping Specifications for Four General Types of Plants

| Spreading Conifer and Broad-leaved Evergreens | | Cone and Broad Upright Conifers and Broad-leaved Evergreens | | Columnar Evergreens | | Standard Shade Trees | |
|---|---|---|---|---|---|---|---|
| Spread (ft) | Diam. (in.) | Height (ft) | Diam. (in.) | Height (ft) | Diam. (in.) | Caliper (in.) | Diam. (in.) |
| 1½ | 10 | 1½ | 10 | 1½ | 10 | 1¼ | 18 |
| 2 | 12 | 2 | 12 | 2 | 12 | 1⅓ | 20 |
| 2½ | 14 | 3 | 14 | 3 | 13 | 1¾ | 22 |
| 3½ | 18 | 5 | 20 | 4 | 14 | 2 | 24 |
| 4 | 21 | 6 | 22 | 5 | 16 | 2½ | 28 |
| 5 | 24 | 7 | 24 | 6 | 18 | 3 | 32 |
| 6 | 28 | 8 | 27 | 7 | 20 | 3½ | 38 |
| 7 | 32 | 9 | 30 | 8 | 22 | 4 | 42 |
| 8 | 36 | 10 | 34 | 9 | 24 | 4½ | 48 |
| | | 12 | 38 | 10 | 27 | 5 | 54 |
| | | 14 | 42 | 12 | 30 | 6 | 60 |
| | | 16 | 46 | 14 | 33 | 7 | 70 |
| | | 18 | 50 | 16 | 36 | 8 | 80 |
| | | | | 18 | 40 | | |

Source: American Association of Nurserymen, 1990.

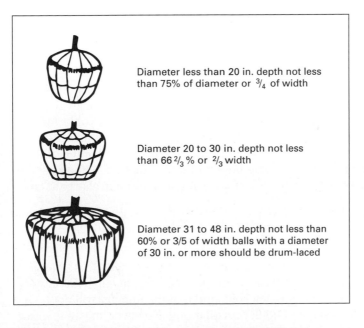

Diameter less than 20 in. depth not less than 75% of diameter or ³/₄ of width

Diameter 20 to 30 in. depth not less than 66 ²/₃ % or ²/₃ width

Diameter 31 to 48 in. depth not less than 60% or 3/5 of width balls with a diameter of 30 in. or more should be drum-laced

**Figure 8-5** Ball Diameter/Depth Ratios for B&B Plants (Courtesy of American Association of Nurserymen, 1990.)

type. Most palm trees are transplanted with a minimal root system and no soil ball.

## STANDARD UNITS OF NURSERY STOCK

Wholesale nursery stock is usually priced in no more than four or five of the following units: 1, 10, 25, 30, 50, 100, 250, 500, and 1000. The unit price may reflect the savings resulting from not having to break bundles or pallets in storage and the savings involved in processing a few large orders as compared to many small orders. The pricing by unit discounts may also be as much the result of traditional practice as it is a reflection of current actual costs. Some nurseries give a discount on total sale rather than numbers of plants. Some wholesale catalogs may indicate that different plants in unit quantities may be combined as one order to receive an even better unit price. In some cases no unit price under 10 or 25 is listed or accepted, or an additional charge may be made for units of less than 10 or 25 of one item. Prices for orders substantially in excess of the 1000 rate are usually negotiated. A wholesale buyer such as a landscape designer or contractor may want to personally select the plants in the production field in order to obtain a specific shape or form. Some nurseries will indicate that this is possible only with an additional 20% charge for the special service to cover the additional paper work and the additional cost of digging a specific plant within a row.

## SHIPPING AGREEMENTS

All wholesale prices are listed in the catalog as FOB (free on board) the production nursery. The buyer bears the shipping cost. In some cases the production nursery will operate its own trucks and is fully responsible for any damage during shipment. In most cases nurseries arrange shipment for the buyer, but the sale is still under the standard FOB terms (see Chapter 10). Additional boxing, packaging, or bailing beyond that normal for harvesting the crop is usually done by the production nursery for an additional charge at cost.

## WARRANTY

In many cases a wholesale catalog contains the statement that no warranty is expressed or implied as to the description, productivity, quality, viability, or any other matter of the nursery stock sold, and that the nursery will not be responsible for the result secured upon transplanting. However, most nurseries warrant their plants to be true to name and in a healthy condition when shipped. The survival of nursery stock, as well as the subsequent growth and production of flowers, fruit, and so on, is to a large degree the result of the care the plant receives during storage and after transplanting. It is not reasonable for the production nursery to be responsible for the performance of the plant. Wholesale catalogs may also indicate that the production nursery accepts no responsibility for the warranty the buyer may give to his customers, including any governmental department or agency.

## NURSERY CROP MARKETING CHANNELS

Nursery marketing channels, as mentioned earlier, reflect the nature and location of the consumer, the optimal production environment, and to some degree the existence of management expertise and availability of labor. The marketing channels for nursery stock sold by retailers in the northeastern United States were documented by E. Jarvesoo many years ago and the data are supported by *Trade Flows and Marketing Practices Within the United States Nursery Industry* (The University of Tennessee, Agricultural Experiment Station, 1990). It is very probable that some of the plant materials in these surveys were purchased from a specific area but not grown there. Materials are often purchased from the other production nurseries and wholesaled again in order to provide a more complete line of nursery stock. As shown in Fig. 8–6, over one-half (51%) of the shade trees sold in the northeast were shipped in, Tennessee (34%), Oregon (8%), and Ohio (6%) being the largest suppliers. Approximately one-third (35%) of the deciduous ornamental trees (flowering trees) were shipped into the northeast, with the majority coming from Oregon (18%), Ohio (7%), and Tennessee (4%). It is interesting to note the change in rank of Oregon and Tennessee when comparing shade trees and flowering trees.

In contrast, evergreen trees, narrow-leaved evergreen shrubs, and broad-leaved evergreen shrubs were predominantly purchased in the northeast. This could be expected because the northeastern states are a major production area of evergreen trees and narrow-leaved and broad-leaved evergreen shrubs for the states east of the Mississippi River. Approximately one-fifth (19%) of the deciduous shrubs and one-half (40%) of the roses retailed in the northeast were shipped in (Figs. 8–7 and 8–8).

Surveys in other major market areas would be expected to yield similar relationships reflecting the production advantages available in various areas of the continent. The growth of housing and commercial construction in the sun belt has stimulated an east-to-west movement of landscape plants. As a general rule, production areas will supply nursery crops to market areas and garden centers having a more severe climate and a later spring than the area of production. This is usually a north-south relationship, but might also reflect the climatic protection provided by the lake effect, such as the Great Lakes or maritime climates along the coasts. The warmer-to-colder climate shipment of

**Figure 8–6** Sources of supply and main destinations of deciduous shade trees, northeast, 1963.

**Figure 8–7** Sources of supply and main destinations of deciduous shrubs, northeast, 1963.

**Figure 8–8** Sources of supply and main destinations of deciduous roses, northeast, 1963.

Scale of miles

0   200   400   600   800   1000

nursery crops reflects the advantages offered by longer growing season, reduced winter injury and overwintering costs, as well as the ability to spring-harvest field-grown nursery stock and deliver it to a retail outlet for the first spring sales. In some cases the development of spring growth and flowers can be delayed in cold storage in order to time flowering for maximum sales in northern retail market areas.

### Selling Southern Grown Nursery Stock in Northern Markets

There appear to be limits to how much milder or warmer the production climate may be in relation to the consumer's climate. Most of the northeastern retail outlets surveyed by Jarvesoo did not report the purchase of woody nursery crops (with the exception of roses) in 1963 from zones 8, 9, and 10 (Figs. 8–6, 8–7, and 8–8). It would seem apparent that many outdoor nursery crops moving from warmer to cooler climatic zones (Fig. 8–6) are rarely shipped to a climatic zone more than 20°F colder (mean annual minimum temperature). Exceptions to this relationship include roses and some juniper and arborvitae species. A number of reasons for the limitation in movement of nursery crops to colder climates can be proposed. The distances involved may make freight costs prohibitive. However, as shown in Figs. 8–6 through 8–8, substantial quantities of nursery crops are shipped from the west to the east coast of the United States. Plants grown more than two climatic zones warmer may be in full growth during early spring shipment and be vulnerable to frost damage. The cost of delaying growth and flowering by cold storage to avoid frost damage may be prohibitive. Many nursery crops adapted to northern climates have specific cold-exposure requirements for breaking dormancy and specific day-length requirements for vegetative growth, flowering, and the development of low-temperature hardiness. Plants best adapted to cooler northern climates may be unable to adapt to the high summer temperatures and humidities in some southern climates. These requirements of plants adapted to northern climates may preclude their efficient growth in production climates more than two climatic zones warmer.

A number of nursery crops, such as *Cornus florida* and *Cercis canadensis*, can be found growing in native stands over a range of four climatic zones. However, these native stands have developed into ecotypes that are adapted to a specific habitat and are not necessarily capable of surviving over the entire range for the species. This has been found true with almost every species of native woody plant that has been studied. If a specific plant variety is genetically adapted to the climate of a northern market, the fact that it has been grown for a number of years in a much milder climate will not alter that genetic potential. It will be able to develop its full genetic potential for low-temperature hardiness when grown for one growing season in the northern climate to which it is genetically adapted. This is also true for plants having the genetic potential for high temperature and/or high humidity tolerance and produced in cooler or dryer climates. Many nursery crops are reproduced vegetatively as new varieties and little information is available concerning their climatic limitations. If information is lacking concerning the climatic limitations of a new variety, it might be advisable to purchase these nursery crops from production nurseries in a similar climatic zone. The flow of nursery crops from the site of production to the ultimate consumer is quite complex and is changing with the development of new technology, new nursery crops, and the changing costs of transportation versus production.

### Obtaining Marketing Information

The degree of specialization in marketing channels results in a considerable challenge for both the buyer and seller of nursery crops. The American Association of Nurserymen publishes several directories (Production Nursery, Garden Center and Landscape Contractor Members, Forestry Tree Nurseries, State Trade Associations) and a guide to plant locators (see Appendix A). Plant locator references are published by trade associations, plant societies, botanical gardens, universities, and by a number of publishing companies. Plant locators are also available which include nurseries in Canada, England, Germany, France, and Switzerland. A relatively new service now available provides computerized regional information about nurseries throughout the United States. Some computerized plant locator services are updated daily.

Many state nursery trade associations provide listings of the production nurseries in that state producing various categories of crops, such as shade trees, deciduous shrubs, fruit trees, indoor foliage plants, ground covers, and so on. Additional information for the buyer is available in both the classified and unclassified advertising in nursery trade journals and trade association publications such as the *American Nurseryman, Nursery Business, Home and Garden Supply, Southern Florist and Nurserymen, Pacific Coast Nurserymen, The Voice of MAN*, and others (Appendix C). In many cases the production nursery's advertisement in a trade journal is very brief providing only the name, address, telephone number, and the type of crops produced. The wholesale buyer may obtain the production nursery's current catalog by contacting the nursery. The wholesale nursery catalogs provided by production nurseries are the most detailed and accurate source of information concerning the availability of nursery crops.

### Marketing at Nursery Association Meetings

Trade association meetings provide an additional opportunity for buyers to contact production nursery salespersons and to become aware of the availability of various types of nursery crops. These contacts may be informal discussions between buyers and salesperson or may be the result of an exhibit in a formal trade show. Most state, regional, and national nursery trade association meetings are partially financed by fees charged for exhibit space in the trade show rooms and are a major attraction for the meeting. A 1990 survey of wholesale nurseries in 23 states indicated that nurseries spent, on the average, as much of their advertising budget on trade shows (22%) as they did on their catalog (21%). A broad range of plants as well as pesticides, fertilizers, specialized landscape construction equipment, supplies, tools, and production nursery equipment are on display at most nursery trade shows. The trade fair is certainly one of the most effective opportunities for production nurserymen and wholesale buyers to meet.

The actual sales booked at the trade exhibit are commonly less important than the subsequent sales made as a result of contacts made during the trade show. A recent extensive survey demonstrated that only 7% of annual sales were made at trade shows while 40% were telephone sales, 44% were made person to person and the remaining were mail orders. A high percentage of sales made by established nurseries are made to repeat customers (ranging from 63% in Arizona to 94% in Delaware), and this handicaps newer growers as they attempt to "break in" to the market. Trade shows allow them to exhibit their products, to make important contacts and to ultimately make sales.

### Booking Wholesale Nurseries' Crop Orders

There has been a gradual change in the purchasing practices for nursery crops. A number of years ago most orders were booked 3–5 months before spring delivery, and the traditional state and regional annual trade meetings, held during the winter season, provided an ideal time for ordering plants. Orders for nursery crops, particularly from garden centers, are currently placed well before the winter season. A number of regional trade exhibit meetings are scheduled in summer or early fall, allowing orders to be booked 6–9 months before spring delivery. The dates for state and regional meetings are usually consistent from year to year to eliminate conflict between meetings.

A number of regional trade shows have become major promotional events for the industry: the Western Association of Nurserymen, Trade Show and Meeting, Kansas City, Missouri; the Garden Living Industries of the Eastern United States, Kiamesha Lake, New York; Mid-America Trade Show, Rosemont, Illinois; Mid-Atlantic Nurserymen's Trade Show, Cockeysville, Maryland; Southern Nurserymen's Association Trade Show, Atlanta, Georgia; TAN-MissLark Regional Convention, Nursery and Garden Supply Show, Houston, Texas; Pacific Horticulture Trade Show, San Diego, California; and others. In many cases the regional trade shows have an educational program in addition to the trade exhibit.

Almost every state having a substantial market for nursery crops has a state nurserymen's association meeting with a trade fair. This places a substantial burden on the wholesale nursery marketing to 8–10 states, particularly if it is expected that the nursery exhibit and, thereby, support the association in each state. The state meetings, in many cases, have strong educational programs in conjunction with the Cooperative Extension Service and their land-grant university. Members of the state nurserymen's association are encouraged to buy from those nurseries exhibiting in the trade show, and by doing so, support the association. These meetings are important because they deal with the issues and challenges facing the nursery industry, including relations with state legislature and various regulatory agencies.

### Pricing Nursery Stock

The pricing of nursery stock is primarily controlled by supply and demand. Setting prices is limited by production costs, plant quality, and the service, and reliability of that service provided at delivery. Price changes for nursery stock will not occur simultaneously for all types of plants to be sold.

Three methods are commonly used to establish current prices. A production nurseryman may look to the current wholesale catalogs from other nurseries serving the same marketing area as a guide for altering prices. Another method is based on an evaluation of the future supply and demand relationship for that particular nursery crop. And, obviously, the cost of production will provide the lower limits of wholesale prices, particularly if that crop is going to continue to be produced. Although having current competitive pricing is important, it is not unusual for a nursery to sell a substantial portion of its product at a negotiated rather than a listed price. The sales organization, commission salespersons, and brokers are a valuable source of information concerning the supply and demand anticipated for specific nursery crops and marketing channels.

### Projecting Future Sales

Changes in the supply and demand for a specific plant will reflect adverse growing conditions such as winter damage or drought in a particular production area, changes in consumer demand, and the national economy. The garden center industry tends to expand, at a somewhat greater rate, increasing demand for garden-center-type plants during periods of general economic recession. Apparently, when consumer earnings decrease, the consumer spends more time and effort on "do it yourself" gardening and landscape projects. The demand for plants used in landscape construction, on the other hand, is influenced by the construction of highways, housing, public buildings, educational and medical facilities, shopping centers, and major industrial complexes. Changes in the volume of landscape construction commonly occur 2–3 years after changes in the volume of building construction making the nursery industry slow to recover from economic recession.

The relative demand for plants used in landscape construction such as shade trees and sod can be estimated by noting changes in construction starts and allowing sufficient time for the delay between construction starts and landscape planting. Unfortunately, a 3- to 6-year or longer crop cycle from propagation to harvest of shade trees is, for example, too long in most cases to take full advantage of reliable economic predictions and changes in the construction industry.

A future demand for nursery stock can be enhanced by a number of other procedures. The development of a patented landscape plant allows the production nursery to control production and therefore the supply of that plant to the consumer. The number of patented landscape plants has grown dramatically for a variety of reasons. Advertising patented plants to both wholesale and retail consumers is more obviously rewarding to the nursery owning the patent because it develops demand only for those specific nursery crops produced by the nursery. The ability to create demand through advertising and to control supply has stimulated the investment in breeding and selection programs for patented landscape plants. The demand for the entire spectrum of nursery crops could be stimulated by the growth of a coordinated national advertising program such as the nursery industries' Garden Council (see Chapter 2). A well-coordinated cooperative advertising program of sufficient size could have a major impact on the nationwide demand for nursery crops and the growth of the entire nursery industry.

A nursery marketing-research program exists in Ohio to advertise and promote the sale of nursery stock in Ohio and to conduct research on the production and sale of nursery stock. Anyone who sells nursery stock, including growers, retailers, landscapers, and mass merchandisers, with plant sales of over $10,000 is required to contribute 0.0025% of gross receipts to the Ohio Nursery Stock Marketing Program (ONSMP). The program is administered by a committee from the nursery industry. ONSMP supports a 60 minute weekly radio call-in show carried on 18 Ohio stations, a weekly newspaper column distributed to 94 daily newspapers in Ohio and 10 "media tours" by "the Ohio nurserymen" visiting flower/garden shows which are covered by TV and radio broadcasts and by newspapers.

### Developing a Marketing Program

The development of a wholesale marketing program for a production nursery begins with an analysis of the needs of the customers: garden center buyers, landscape contractors, city foresters, and other nurserymen. These needs reflect, in part, the needs of the ultimate customers. The market analysis is followed by a production study of species to be produced, cultural requirements, production methods, rotations, costs, and so on. These data are then evaluated against an estimate of potential income from future sales and against product competition to determine an estimate of probability for success of the program. A 1990 survey indicated that nurseries budgeted an average of 2.8% of sales for advertising. In states with a newly established nursery industry the percentage was higher.

A successful marketing program for nursery products requires the input of as much factual production and marketing data that are available, matched with the best estimates of future demands, price structure, and potential product competition. Management must integrate all of this information and continually modify production and marketing programs to remain economically sound in a constantly changing business environment.

## SUMMARY

Wholesale marketing of nursery crops is rapidly changing as a result of many factors, especially changes in market demands, production technology, and modes of transportation. In recent years, the marketing phase has quite possibly changed more than any other aspect of nursery management. The nursery industry of the United States continues to expand, creating many new opportunities for profitable marketing. Because of its relatively small size as compared with other industries, it is difficult for nursery managers to obtain good market information. Currently, the best information is obtained through various trade associations, trade journals, and from attendance at trade shows and meetings. Hopefully, the Nursery Marketing Council, established in 1977, will serve as the major source of market information for the industry.

The growers' ability to anticipate market demands is a limiting factor in the growth of the nursery industry and poses one of the most significant marketing challenges for the nursery industry of the future.

## REFERENCES

AMERICAN ASSOCIATION OF NURSERYMEN. 1990. American standard for nursery stock. AAN, Washington, D.C.

———. 1979. Partners for profit. Nursery Industry Cooperative Advertising Program. AAN, Washington, D.C.

———. 1973–74. Sources of plants and related supplies, an Allied Landscape Industry Service. AAN, Washington, D.C.

BENDER, F., and V. BENSEN. 1968. Marketing channels of floricultural products and ornamentals in Maryland. Agric. Exp. Sta. Univ. Md. Misc. Publ. 642.

BROOKER, J., and S. C. TURNER. 1990. Trade flows and marketing practices within the United States nursery industry. Agr. Expt. Sta. Univ. of Tenn. Southern Coop. Services Bulletin 358.

FRANK'S NURSERY SALES, INC. 1975. Ann. Rep. 6399 E. Nevada, Detroit, Mich. 48234.

JARVESOO, E. 1969. Procurement and sales practices of retail outlets for ornamental nursery products. N.J. Agric. Exp. Sta. Rutgers Univ. Bull. 824.

U.S. DEPARTMENT OF AGRICULTURE. 1990. Plant hardiness zone map. USDA Agric. Res. Serv. Misc. Publ. 1475.

# Chapter 9
# Nursery Inventory Control

An inventory or stock control system is needed in all phases of nursery production and merchandising in order to maintain control of plant materials, equipment, tools, and supplies. Numerous systems are available, from the very simple to the complex. The following systems can be used effectively to maintain control of materials within nurseries.

## PLANT MATERIAL INVENTORY

A plant inventory system is designed to provide management with data that can be used for making management decisions. An inventory of plants is needed to plan a sales campaign and project future trends. By maintaining an up-to-date sales inventory, management can minimize overselling or leaving plants unsold, thus assuring a higher percentage of satisfied customers. A knowledge of the plant inventory can be the basis of planning work schedules, labor needs, storage requirements, and land use. Inventory data are needed when planning production programs, calculating production costs, and making pricing decisions. Plant inventory control systems can also provide information to evaluate cultural practices. To accomplish these ends a nurseryman must know how many plants of each variety (cultivar) are available, in each size, within the nursery. The actual system of plant inventory control will vary with the size and type of nursery and with the degree of sophistication desired by the nurseryman. Plant inventory systems vary from a daily update available from a computer to little, if any, control. For a small nursery or a large nursery specializing in one genera, such as rhododendrons, or one type of plant material, such as selected shade trees, the system can be relatively simple. But for a large, general nursery growing a wide selection of plants, the system can be rather complex. A common technique is to inventory and obtain cost of production data by plant groups (Table 9–1).

Taking of the physical inventory is facilitated by an integrated layout of the nursery using planting blocks and standard labeling of rows (see Chapter 5). The count is made by trained individuals using calipers and measuring sticks (Fig. 9–1) to obtain diameters of trees and heights or spread of shrubs. Another handy device is a template tree grader, designed to caliper trees up to 3 in., by sizes, as recommended by *American Standards for Nursery Stock.* An aid in measuring height and spread of shrubs is a stick marked in size classes. For tabulating the actual count in the field, a clipboard equipped with a series of mechanical counters is most commonly used.

Automatic recording of tree caliper measurements is possible through the use of a Polycorder and a Fowler caliper (Fig. 9–1). Measurements can be taken over a range of 0–8 in. (0–200 mm) with an accuracy of 0.001 in. (0–0.3 mm). The components of this system include the Polycorder (a portable, electronic notebook), a Fowler Max-Cal electronic caliper, and Omnidata's model 565F interface cable. With the use of an electronic notebook the problems commonly associated with data collection are eliminated. The Polycorder is programmable and the data can be transferred directly to a computer.

Another electronic device, similar to the Polycorder, that lends itself to speeding up inventory is the *Psion Organizer.* It is a "pocket diary" into which plant inventory data can be taken in the field and then transfered electronically to the computer, where it can be processed as needed for sales and planning. The Psion is manufactured in England and is currently used for taking inventory at Princeton Nurseries in New Jersey.

Other measurements, in addition to caliper, can also be made and recorded in the Polycorder, including soil moisture readings from soil moisture blocks, weights from an electronic balance, and tree and shrub heights and diameters with the aid of electronic measuring tapes.

**Table 9–1**  Grouping of Plants for Inventory and Production Cost Analysis

| | |
|---|---|
| 1. Shade trees | 6. Fruit trees |
| 2. Small or flowering trees | 7. Small fruits |
| 3. Large evergreens | 8. Container stock |
| 4. Small evergreens | 9. Bed material |
| 5. Deciduous shrubs | 10. Propagation |

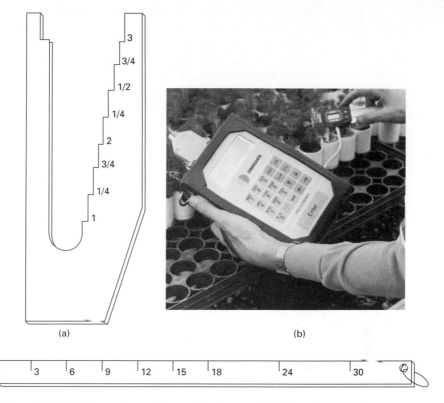

**Figure 9–1** Equipment used for grading trees and shrubs in nurseries. (a) Template-type tree grader; (b) Polycorder; and (c) measuring stick shrub grader.

Nurserymen generally count and measure all trees and specimen plants, whereas representative samples—portions or rows, or small plots—are used to estimate the inventory of seedlings, small evergreens, deciduous shrubs, roses, and so on. A complete inventory is taken in most field-production nurseries at the end of the growing season and periodic inventories are made as needed. In large container-production nurseries the inventory is updated daily, weekly, or monthly. The data are recorded onto the *field inventory data collection form* (Fig. 9–2). In some nurseries this may be the extent of the plant inventory, but in others these field data are processed into more meaningful information for use by management.

In some larger nurseries the field inventory data are posted to an *inventory flow sheet* (Fig. 9–3) together with new planting and sales data. By proper posting of the flow sheets, it is possible to determine fairly accurately the status of the plant material within the nursery by type and location. If accurate data are collected, it is possible to determine plant losses and to estimate growth rates. This information can also be used to pinpoint problem areas and

| Block ___17___ | | | | | | | | | |
|---|---|---|---|---|---|---|---|---|---|
| Rows of parts of rows | Species | Size | Date_____ | | Date_____ | | Date_____ | |
| | | | REG | PG | REG | PG | REG | PG |
| 30-31 ↑ N | Acer reburn 'Red Sunset' | NS | 2 | 1 | | | | |
| | | 2-2 $\frac{1}{2}$ | 54 | 0 | | | | |
| | | 2 $\frac{1}{2}$-3 | 107 | 5 | | | | |
| | | 3-3 $\frac{1}{2}$ | 16 | 1 | | | | |
| | | 3 $\frac{1}{2}$-4 | 3 | 1 | | | | |
| | | 4-4 $\frac{1}{2}$ | 1 | 0 | | | | |
| | | 4 $\frac{1}{2}$-5 | – | – | | | | |
| | | | | | | | | |
| 31-32 | Acer rubrum 'October Glory' | NS | 14 | 1 | | | | |
| | | 1 $\frac{3}{4}$-2 | 73 | – | | | | |
| | | 2-2 $\frac{1}{2}$ | 115 | 3 | | | | |
| | | 2 $\frac{1}{2}$-3 | 76 | – | | | | |
| | | 3-3 $\frac{1}{2}$ | 14 | 1 | | | | |
| | | | | | | | | |
| | | | | | | | | |
| | | | | | | | | |
| | | | | | | | | |
| | | | | | | | | |
| | | | | | | | | |
| | | | | | | | | |
| | | | | | | | | |
| | | | | | | | | |
| | | | | | | | | |
| | | | | | | | | |
| | | | | | | | | |
| | | | | | | | | |

REG = Regular Grade     Initials:     ___HD___ _____ _____
PG = Park Grade (less than standard quality)
NS = Not Saleable

**Figure 9–2** Example of a field inventory data collection form.

to check on cultural practices. The inventory flow sheets should be designed to fit the needs of the nursery manager. Figure 9–3 is an example of a form designed for a nursery specializing in the production of shade trees. The columns headed "Est. unit sales" and "Est. end. inv." are for the manager's best estimate of sales and final inventory. If they are not needed by management, they can be omitted from the form.

## Acer rubrum 'Red Sunset'

**Var. Year — N**

| Pg. | | N Units sold | N End inv. | N Est. units sales | N Est. end inv. | N+1 Units sold | N+1 End inv. | N+1 Est. units sales | N+1 Est. end inv. | N+2 Units sold | N+2 End inv. | N+2 Est. units sales | N+2 Est. end inv. | N+3 Units sold | N+3 End inv. | N+3 Est. units sales | N+3 Est. end inv. |
|---|---|---|---|---|---|---|---|---|---|---|---|---|---|---|---|---|---|
| planting year | NP | | (100) | | | NP | | | | NP | | | | NP | | | |
| | NS | | 100 | | | | 97 | | | | 19 | | | | | | |
| | 1½ or 4" | | | | | | | | | | | | | | | | |
| N | 1½" | | | | | | | | | | 45 | | | | 15 | | |
| | 1¾" | | | | | | | | | | 29 | | | | 38 | | |
| | 1" | | | | | | | | | | | | | | 25 | | |
| | 2½" | | | | | | | | | | | | | 10 | 5 | | |
| | 3" | | | | | | | | | | | | | | | | |
| | 3½" | | | | | | | | | | | | | | | | |
| | Total | | 100 | | | | 97 | | | | 93 | | | 10 | 83 | | |
| Loss | U % %B | U | % %B | | | 3 U | 3 % %B | | | 0 U | 0 % 7 %B | | | 0 U | 0 % 7 %B | U | % |

**Var. — N+1** (N column crossed out)

| Pg. | | N | N+1 Units sold | N+1 End inv. | N+1 Est. units sales | N+1 Est. end inv. | N+2 Units sold | N+2 End inv. | N+2 Est. units sales | N+2 Est. end inv. | N+3 Units sold | N+3 End inv. | N+3 Est. units sales | N+3 Est. end inv. |
|---|---|---|---|---|---|---|---|---|---|---|---|---|---|---|
| planting year | NP | | NP | (60) | | | NP | | | | NP | | | |
| | NS | | | 60 | | | | 45 | | | | 16 | | |
| | 1½ or 4" | | | | | | | | | | | | | |
| N+1 | 1½" | | | | | | | 13 | | | | 20 | | |
| | 1¾" | | | | | | | | | | | 13 | | |
| | 1" | | | | | | | | | | | 9 | | |
| | 2½" | | | | | | | | | | | | | |
| | 3" | | | | | | | | | | | | | |
| | 3½" | | | | | | | | | | | | | |
| | Total | | | 60 | | | | 58 | | | | 58 | | |
| Loss | U % %B | | 0 U | 0 % %B | | | 2 U | 33 % 33 %B | | | 0 U | 0 % 33 %B | U | % |

**Var. — N+2** (N and N+1 columns crossed out)

| Pg. | | N | N+1 | N+2 Units sold | N+2 End inv. | N+2 Est. units sales | N+2 Est. end inv. | N+3 Units sold | N+3 End inv. | N+3 Est. units sales | N+3 Est. end inv. |
|---|---|---|---|---|---|---|---|---|---|---|---|
| planting year | NP | | NP | NP | (100) | | | NP | | | |
| | NS | | | | 100 | | | | 36 | | |
| | 1½ or 4" | | | | | | | | | | |
| N+2 | 1½" | | | | | | | | 58 | | |
| | 1¾" | | | | | | | | | | |
| | 1" | | | | | | | | | | |
| | 2½" | | | | | | | | | | |
| | 3" | | | | | | | | | | |
| | 3½" | | | | | | | | | | |
| | Total | | | | 94 | | | | 94 | | |
| Loss | U % %B | | | 4 U | 4 % 4 %B | | | 2 U | 2 % 6 %B | U | % |

| | N | N+1 | N+2 | N+3 |
|---|---|---|---|---|
| Page totals (Sub total) | 100 | 157 | 247 | 235 |
| Sub total loss | U % %B | 3 U | 10 U 4 % 4 %B | 2 U 2 % %B |
| Total | | | | |
| Total loss | U % %B U % | U % %B U % | U % %B U % | U % %B U % |

Use for 2 or more pages

**ABBREVIATIONS**
NP = number planted
NS = not saleable
U = units
%B = percent of base planted

**NOTES**
Units sold: obtain from sales records
End inventory: obtain from field inventory
Est. unit sales: manager's best estimate
Est. end. inventory: estimated and inventory

**Figure 9–3** Growing inventory flow sheet. (Courtesy Studebaker Nurseries, Inc.)

Data from the flow sheets or from the field inventory forms are used to post the *sales inventory*. This is generally done at the end of the growing season but prior to the sales period for field-production nurseries. However, for container-production nurseries the sales inventory is posted with new data (plants for sale) on a daily, weekly, or monthly basis. The sales inventory, maintained by the sales department, can be posted either to a *sales inventory card* (Figs. 9–4 and 9–5) or it can be entered into the inventory file of a computer. Sales data must be posted promptly if the system is to be effective. Notation is made of the buyer and the sales posted by use of the sales inventory fraction, the numerator being the number of trees removed from inventory and the denominator the number of plants remaining. The summary column provides quick reference as to the total balance remaining within the size class. At the time of posting the sales inventory cards, the block number where the plants are to be dug can also be noted. The production manager can precode the cards if he or she desires that the blocks be cleared on a priority basis. The data are filed alphabetically either by botanical names or by common names within plant groups (Table 9–1). The sales inventory can also be posted with current price information as an aid in quoting prices to customers during the selling season.

Each nursery manager must adjust the plant inventory system to the situation and develop it to provide the control and information necessary to make sound management decisions. Electronic computers (Fig. 9–6), particularly those equipped with video readout screens, are ideal for the rapid and efficient processing of production and sales inventories within large nurseries. They can be used to provide an immediate update of both production and sales

| Species: Acer rubrum | | | Cultivar: 'Red Sunset' | | | | | | | | | | | | |
|---|---|---|---|---|---|---|---|---|---|---|---|---|---|---|---|
| Sales inventory card | Size | | 2" | | | 165 / 350 | | | | 2 ½" | | | 500* | | |
| | Blocks | 10 | 17 | 96 | | 10 ** | 17 | Σ | | | | | | | Σ |
| | No. | 4 | 20 | 5 | | 1 | 1 | 31 | | | | | | | |
| 1/10 | Cot Gard | 10 | | | 10/10 | | | 21 | | | | | | | |
| 3/11 | D&L Land | 15 | | | 10/10 | 5/0 | | 6 | | | | | | | |
| 3/16 | Lan. P.D. | 2 | | | | 1/0 | 1/0 | 4 | | | | | | | |

*Price code: Last digit is number of dimes; previous digits are dollars: e.g. = $16.50, 550 = $55.00.
**Underlined numbers are park grade classification.

**Figure 9–4** Example of a sales inventory card.

Species: <u>Ilex crenata</u>
<u>"Green Thumb"</u>

| Size | 1 Gallon | | | 5 Gallon | | | ___ Gallon | | |
|---|---|---|---|---|---|---|---|---|---|
| Stage | I | II | III | I | II | III | I | II | III |
| Date | | | | | | | | | |
| 1/4 | A-1 77/001 1000 | A-1 76/391 500 | A-2 76/411 755 | | | | B-3 75/531 355 | | |
| 1/10 | | | | | | | B-3 255 | | |
| 2/7 | 77/215 500 | | | | | | | | |
| 2/12 | | A-1 955 | A-2 1255 | | | | B-3 200 | | |
| 2/20 | | | A-2 1055 | | | | | | |
| 2/25 | | | A-2 705 | | | | | | |
| 3/7 | | | A-2 205 | B-1 500 | | | | | |
| 3/15 | | | | | | | B-3 100 | | |
| 3/20 | | | | B-1 500 | | | | | |
| | Stage I: Newly planted | | | | | | | | |
| | II: Actively growing | | | | | | | | |
| | III: Saleable plants | | | | | | | | |

Annotations: Accession number → 75/531; Quantity → 355; Location → B-3

**Figure 9–5** Example of an inventory form for a small or medium-sized container-production nursery.

inventories. They can also be programmed to provide an analysis of sales, by variety, customer, geographic area, and by salesperson. In addition, the computer can be used to update sales books, prepare price schedules, and with the input of field inventory data, can be programmed to estimate potential sales inventory.

Modern computers with the aid of highly sophisticated software can now provide nursery managers with timely and accurate data related to inventory (Fig. 9–7) which can be used to develop long-term plans for crop production and marketing and to evaluate the production efficiency of subunits within the nursery and the effectiveness of sales programs. To develop a quality inventory control program it is first necessary to determine what one desires to control and evaluate. Some managers may wish to develop a program that inventories only plants and materials. Whereas, other managers may wish to develop a fully integrated program that provides timely, accurate information on all phases and aspects of the business. To accomplish the fully integrated program it is suggested that the following units be considered.

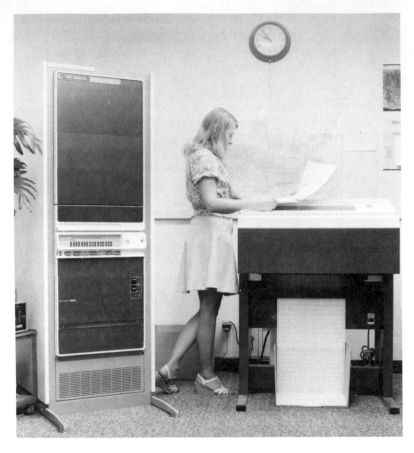

**Figure 9–6** Computer used for inventory control and for other business records. (Courtesy Monrovia Nursery Co.)

Marketing plans (long and short range)

Physical inventory of all plants in production, storage, staging, and shipping facilities.

Production plan

Propagation inventory and disbursements

Purchased materials

Cost accounting

Selected Subsystems

*The market plans* future sales forecast for nursery stock has always been a challenge for nursery managers. Not only is it necessary to forecast next year's sales but also what the demands might be for nursery stock some years in the

# QIC INVENTORY REPORT

08/10/92     PAGE 1

| PIC NUMBER | DEPARTMENT # | TOWNSHIP DESCRIPTION | EMPLOYEE # | SECT | ZONE | SUBS | PIC DESCRIPTION | QIC REVIEW |
|---|---|---|---|---|---|---|---|---|
| agq62 | 4600 | | 186 | | | | AG Space Age House G62 | ☐ YES ☐ NO |

| COUNT DATE | START TIME | END TIME | SPECIAL NOTATIONS | | | | REPLACE PIC SIGN | PIC SIGN |
|---|---|---|---|---|---|---|---|---|
| 8-11-92 | 9:30 | 10:00 | EA | | | | ☐ YES ☐ NO | ☐ YES ☐ NO |

| ITEM # | DESCRIPTION | | CROP SUFFIX | | PLANTING DATES | |
|---|---|---|---|---|---|---|
| IMMEDIATE SALEABLE | FUTURE SALEABLE | FUTURE DATE | UNSALEABLE | REASON | | TOTAL |
| amasbftz 57 | Ash Green Marshall Seedless 6/8" | | 3 | | **/**/**-02/21/92 | 57 |
| asum01cz 29 | Ash Green Summit 1" | | 3 | 902 ↓ | **/**/**-02/21/92 | 29 |
| aaut6ftz 4 | Ash White Autumn Purple 6/8' | | 3 | | **/**/**-02/21/92 | 4 |
| phtu06fz 20 | Plum Thundercloud Purple Lf 6/7' | | 3 | | **/**/**-02/21/92 | 20 |
| asum01cp 14 0 | Ash Green Summit 1" | | 1 | | 01/01/01-05/20/92 | 14-0 |
| prds5ftc 178 152 | Pear Cal Redspire Wht 5/6' | | 1 | | 01/01/01-05/20/92 | 104 152 |
| pthu06fp 175 0 | Plum Thundercloud Purple Lf 6/7' | | 1 | | 01/01/01-05/20/92 | 175 0 |
| amas6ftc 200 | Ash Green Marshall Seedless 6/8' | | 1 | | 01/01/01-05/20/92 | 200 |
| asum6ftc 76 72 | Ash Green Summit 6/8' | | 1 | | 01/01/01-05/20/92 | 76 72 |
| asum01cc 30 38 / 20 0 | Ash Green Summit 1" | 09/14/92 | 1 | | 01/01/01-05/20/92 | 50 38 |

*CONTINUED*

**Figure 9-7** Sample of QIC Inventory Report. Computer generated data indicating current inventory in Space Age House G62 as of 08/10/92. Pencil changes indicates actual counts; computer data will be updated. (Courtesy of Zelenka Evergreen Nursery.)

future. It is this forecast that is the beginning of the production cycle, with propagation, of plants that can take 5 to 10 years before they attain saleable size. Therefore, it becomes prudent to production planning to have an effective method to measure the current market and at the same time a process that provides input into future market trends.

The market plans are developed by feeding into the computer all orders for nursery stock. Those for delivery within a year or a shipping season will become a part of the current sales inventory and the current market plan. Orders to be delivered one or more years in the future will become a part of the projected sales along with other raw data collected by salespeople from customers of the nursery and trend information that is gleaned from articles in trade journals, horticulture magazines, and contacts with knowledgeable plant people.

As this information is collected, tabulated, and evaluated against past sales records and long-term trends it is used to set production quotas for the crops to be produced and to provide benchmark data to determine facility needs to meet long-term production quotas and future budget requirements.

*Production plans*, as predicated by the market plan, are then developed for all species and cultivars to be produced. Determinations are made of the number of cuttings that must be stuck, buds set, or grafts made; facility, space and material requirements are estimated, and production schedules are developed for each species or cultivar. And, in some cases two or more production schedules are developed for individual species or cultivars depending on the market objectives. All this information is fed into the computer and serves as the base for the long-term production control plan.

The *production control* (PC) subsystem monitors *all* production activities, including labor, materials, equipment used in planting, maintaining, and harvesting of all plant material. Production control is used for updating perpetual inventory at each production site. It also accumulates cost data that is used to monitor and determine the cost of production of each plant. Many reports can be generated summarizing production activities by type of work done, specific crew, time period, location, variety or cultivar, and by a specific item. In addition the PC subsystem allows comparison of efficiency of production crews to preestablished standards.

To accomplish all of this requires careful planning by management and the computer department supported by accurate and timely data reported and recorded by each production crew leader on a daily basis. These data plus data from other subsystems are recorded and processed on Multiplan spreadsheets.

The *physical inventory* (PI) of plants subsystem monitors previous and current inventory counts by crop (species, variety, cultivar, or other in-house designations). The system allows the use of formulas which will determine when spot counts will be made at various locations. The inventory figures are updated by the production control subsystem, both of which process the data with the aid of Multiplan spreadsheets. To accomplish this all production and storage areas are assigned alpha-numeric codes which in turn are keyed to the alpha-numeric columns and lines on the spreadsheets. All inventory figures are verified through planned periodic physical inventories.

The *propagation inventory and disbursements* (PID) subsystem monitors current and future crops in their early stages of production, and those in propagation prior to being disbursed to field or container production or sold as liners. PID also monitors commitments made by suppliers of liners as well as future in-house propagation to assure that future production needs are met. By the integrated use of PID, PC, and PI it is possible to monitor survival, growth, and progress against the organizational plans for production and marketing.

The *purchased materials* subsystem tracks purchase orders and related receipts of plant stock and supplies from vendors. The system provides summary displays and reports which show open purchase orders by vendor, by item, and anticipated delivery date. All receipts of goods are also maintained and summarized within the system. Provision is made for quantitative and qualitative verification of materials received.

## EQUIPMENT INVENTORY

A considerable financial investment is made in equipping and maintaining a production nursery. Equipment needed for the many and varied operations within a modern nursery includes cars, trucks, tractors, and wagons; tillage, planting, and potting machines; fertilizer spreaders; pumps; injectors and irrigation equipment; sprayers; digging machines; and storage equipment. Besides the large equipment, many types of hand tools, such as axes, digging spades, shovels, pruning equipment, knives, sharpening stones, towing chains, drafting equipment, and so on, are also needed. Some form of management control must be maintained over the equipment if the organization is to function efficiently. The primary means of gaining control of equipment is to maintain a physical inventory of all equipment and to develop plans for security, proper use, and maintenance.

When major pieces of equipment are purchased by the nursery, they should be given an inventory number. A code number combining year of purchase, functional unit, and purchase can be used. For example, if the 34th purchase of the year was a tractor purchased in 1987 for use primarily by the production division (Division A), it would be identified as 87A34. This number should be painted or stamped onto the equipment and then entered into the inventory and maintenance records. The equipment inventory, either a card file or a computer file, is kept in the business office as a record of purchase with name of supplier, purchase price, depreciation schedule, and other related information. The maintenance card, with proper identification number, name, year, and model, is sent to the mechanic to record all maintenance and repair data. Equipment purchases should be limited to as few manufacturers as is feasible to reduce the inventory of parts that need to be maintained by the mechanic. Knowing which parts are stocked by a local supplier can reduce the nursery's spare parts inventory.

Some nurseries find it desirable to maintain a "use log" on some equipment (tractors, trucks, diggers, etc.) to determine the efficiency of the equipment. For efficient use and security, all equipment should be assigned to responsible individuals and the individuals properly instructed in its use and maintenance. Company policy pertaining to use and maintenance of equipment should also be clearly stated in a policy manual of the nursery. Painting equipment, especially small items and hand tools, in a distinctive color can aid immeasurably in preventing loss. The use of distinctive markings can also minimize the mixup of equipment among divisions of a nursery or among crews in a landscape company.

Valuable equipment should be stored in a locked facility that also provides protection from the weather. Company policy should provide the necessary guidelines for the cleaning and storing of equipment. By establishing and maintaining a good equipment inventory and management system, it is possible to gain a high degree of control over the equipment, and at the same time assure its effective and efficient use.

## SUPPLIES

Nurseries also have large financial investments in supplies. Management can gain control over the use and expenditure of supplies by maintaining an inventory control system, providing appropriate areas for storage, and by establishing security methods. Table 9–2 is an example of a supply inventory system for a production nursery. The items are classified by phases of production (propagation, planting, harvesting), equipment maintenance, and physical-plant supplies. Each stocked item is described along with the common unit of purchase. In addition, it is desirable to list sources of supply, price per unit, and pertinent comments. These data, commonly kept on file cards, can also be put into a computer for rapid video display of supply information as well as an electronic means of supply inventory control.

Supplies for the divisions of the nursery should be purchased primarily by the business office. But provisions should be made for a responsible employee to make purchases for the nursery in an emergency or in the best interests of the business. Supplies should be stored in proper facilities and when appropriate under proper security. Packaged supplies such as fertilizer and peat moss should be stored in covered sheds to minimize destruction by wind and rain, whereas inorganic materials such as brick or stone may be left exposed. All chemicals should be stored in their original containers and marked with the year of purchase and used in order of purchase date.

**Table 9–2** Partial Inventory of Supplies for a Production Nursery[a]

| Class | Item | Units |
|---|---|---|
| Propagation | | |
| Budding and grafting | Strips, 0.016 gauge, $1/4 \times 5$ in., 1200/lb | lb |
| | Ties, no. 4 fruit | M |
| | Tape, $1/2$ in. wide | roll |
| | Wax | lb |
| Containers | Pot, peat | |
| | 2$1/2$ in. | ea. |
| | 3 in. | ea. |
| | 4 in. | ea. |
| Labels | Pot, wooden, painted | |
| | 3$1/2 \times 5/8$ in. | M |
| | 10 $\times 5/8$ in. | M |
| | Plant, plastic, | M |
| | 5$1/2 \times 1/2$ in. | |
| Media | Sand | yd$^3$ |
| | Peat moss | bale |
| | Perlite, ft$^3$ | bag |
| Rooting | Hormone, IBA, 0.2% | lb |
| Planting and maintenance | | |
| Containers | Fiber, $6 \times 6$ | ea. |
| | Poly, 2 qt. 600 per | case |
| | Zarn | |
| | 6 qt. 160 per | case |
| | 3 gal, 100 per | case |
| Fertilizers | 18–9–9, 50 lb per | bag |
| | 10–6–4, 40 lb per | bag |
| | 0–20–0, 50 lb per | bag |
| Fungicides | Captan, 50 wp, 5 lb per | bag |
| | Karathane, 25 wp, 3 lb per | bag |
| | Truban, 25 EC | qt |
| Herbicides | Casoron, 4 G, 5 lb per | bag |
| | Princep, 80 wp, 5 lb per | bag |
| | Roundup, 5 gal per | cont. |
| Insecticides | Guthione, 50 wp, 2 1/2 lb per | bag |
| | Sevin, 5 dust, 50 lb per | bag |
| Media | Sand | yd$^3$ |
| | Bark, hardwood | yd$^3$ |
| Polyethylene film | Std. | |
| | Clear 4 ml, $40 \times 100$ | roll |
| | White, 4 ml | 1000 ft$^2$ |
| Shade cloth | Saran, 63% shade | 1000 ft$^2$ |
| Soil fumigants | Dowfume, six 1$1/2$-lb cans per | carton |
| Harvesting | | |
| Baskets | Wire | |
| | $24 \times 20$ in., 100 per | ea. |
| | $30 \times 24$ in., 100 per | ea. |
| Burlap | Untreated, $36 \times 36$ in., 500 per | bale |
| | Treated, $36 \times 36$ in., 500 per | bale |

*(continued)*

**Table 9-2** (*continued*)

| Class | Item | Units |
|---|---|---|
| Containers | Fiber, 10 × 10 in. | ea. |
| Nails | Pinning | |
| | 6D oval head | |
| | 350 per lb, 45 lb per | carton |
| Tape | Plastic tagging, ⅝ in., 12 rolls per | box |
| Tree wrap | 4-in. width, 50 yd/roll, 12 rolls per | carton |
| Twine | Sisal, 3-ply, 6 balls per | bale |
| | Jute, 4-ply, 10 lb per | ball |
| Storage and shipping | | |
| Containers | Shipping, cardboard | ea. |
| Media, packing | Peat moss | bale |
| Tarps | Shade, poly, 15 × 20 ft | ea. |
| Equipment maintenance | | |
| Antifreeze | Prestone | gal |
| Fuels | Gas | |
| | Unleaded | gal |
| Lubricants | Slip grease | lb |
| Oils | 10-W-40, 9 qt per | case |
| Physical plant | | |
| Heating | Oil | gal |
| Paper | Stationery, 500 sheets per | box |
| | Hand towel, 16 rolls per | box |
| | Toilet, 100 rolls per | box |

<sup>a</sup>Example of selected items, not a complete list.

Poisonous chemicals should be stored in a specially marked storage cabinet and flammable materials kept in fire-resistant containers. Only usable quantities of supplies should be kept in work areas with the balance in a locked supply-storage facility.

A periodic inventory (monthly, quarterly) of supplies should be taken to determine use rates and to prepare orders for bidding. In some nurseries, considerable quantities of material (gas, oil, containers, plastic, soil, peat, etc.) are used, and competitive bids from three or more suppliers are worthy of consideration. If the use rate exceeds the normal rate as determined by past history or by logical estimates of use, the manager should review the situation with his key supervisors and determine if corrective measures are needed.

## SUMMARY

Inventory data on plants, equipment, and supplies must be collected and processed in a meaningful manner if the nursery is to attain its objective. However, it should be remembered that few people like to collect data and to keep records. All forms should be as simple as possible, and methods of recording data should be carefully worked out to make certain that it can be done expeditiously and correctly. Steps should be taken to explain the need for record keeping to everyone involved and to make the process as painless as possible. Recording, filing, and analyzing data requires time and is expensive. Do not record too many data; this can be as bad as recording too few; record only what can and will be used. A well-planned and carefully monitored system of inventory control can provide management with an effective tool for maintaining control over materials.

## REFERENCES

BROOKHOUSE, S. 1990. Quality Inventory Control, Inhouse publication, Zelenka Evergreen Nursery.

RITTER, B. R. 1988. Put Inventory Control in the Palm of Your Hand. Am. Nursery 168(5): 57–60.

# Chapter 10
# Shipping of Nursery Stock

The shipping of nursery stock is the operation in the nursery-to-market chain that is most vulnerable to loss of plant quality; control of the plant material usually passes from the seller to the buyer via a third party, the carrier (Fig. 10–1). Considerable forethought, planning, cooperation, and coordination by all three parties are needed to prevent losses. Each of the parties has a vested interest in the operation and should take the necessary positive actions to ensure that the products ordered are delivered in the best possible condition, in the right quantities, grades, varieties, and at the right time.

## PLANT MATERIAL

Nursery stock is a perishable product. Because it is living material, it has moisture and temperature requirements that must be provided for during shipping. The variety of plant material shipped by nurseries ranges from dormant seedlings to large shade trees in full leaf weighing many tons. This necessitates considerable variations in the methods of packaging and means of transportation. Most small plants are dug bare-root during the dormant season and are shipped in packages or in large nursery boxes; the roots must be kept damp

**Figure 10–1** Staging area for loading and shipping of nursery stock. (Courtesy Monrovia Nursery Co.)

and the plants maintained in a dormant condition. Damp, aged shingletow, or similar material spread about the roots during packaging provide the needed moisture. The optimal temperatures for nursery stock while in transit will vary slightly with the type of plant material and the time in transit (Table 10–1). Plants that are dormant should be maintained at a temperature close to 35–40°F; whereas, nondormant plants, such as container-grown plants should be maintained at a temperature close to 55°F. If delivery can be effected in 5 days or less, the temperature can range between 30 and 65°F without serious injury to the plants. However, either a long delay enroute or exposure to a temperature below freezing or above 80°F could result in injury to the plants.

Large plants are typically dug B&B with plain, treated, or plastic burlap about the soil ball. Some nurserymen support B&B stock within wire baskets. In some parts of the country, the root ball is contained within a wooden box. In the past, most large trees were transplanted during the dormant season, but with the development and proper use of mechanical tree diggers, they can now be moved in full leaf. The plants should be taken from the field immediately after digging and placed in a cool, humid area and the root balls and foliage watered to minimize water stress.

Plants in full leaf must be shipped at a temperature above freezing but as low as practical to reduce transpiration. Shade trees in full leaf, nondormant evergreens, and container plants transported in open trucks should be protected with a strong, Saran tarpaulin during shipping. The Saran tarpaulin (90% shade) provides a barrier to the sun's rays and excessive wind damage but allows heat to escape. Spraying deciduous plants in full leaf with antitranspirants is a beneficial practice when the RH of the ambient atmosphere is above 85%. The film remains effective for several weeks. However, at low RH the antitranspirant film cracks and peels from the surface of the leaf within 2–3 days following treatment; its long-term effectiveness is minimal. When transporting large trees on open carriers, the trees and tarpaulins must be tied down securely to avoid wind whip and possible physical damage when the vehicle passes through a tunnel or under a low bridge. Some of the positive actions that can be taken to help ensure the viability of plant material during shipping are summarized in Table 10–1.

Desiccation during shipment can be minimized by watering the plants prior to digging and utilizing rapid methods of transport. When delays in transport happen, the plants are subject to drying out. When possible, keep the plants in a cool, humid area; ventilate if in a closed van, and water balled or containerized stock. Plants that arrive in a wilted condition should be placed in shade and watered immediately. If the critical wilting point has not been reached, the plants can be saved. Balled and burlapped plants should be misted or watered with the aid of a root feeder. Dormant bare-root plants will benefit either by being immersed into a tank of cool water or by being buried in a moist medium (sawdust, wood chips, soil) for several days to allow the buds to absorb water.

Freezing damage can be avoided by selecting rapid methods of transportation and avoiding shipment when low temperatures are predicted for the proposed route or by using carriers with heated trucks. The greatest cause of cold temperature injury to nursery stock during shipping is delays with railroad cars during winter months. Plant material that arrives with frost on the foliage may not be injured, provided that the low, critical temperature for the species was not reached (Table 17–1). Frosted shipments should be placed in a cool area (35–40°F) and allowed to thaw gradually prior to handling.

## BUYER'S RESPONSIBILITIES

The buyer of nursery stock initiates the transaction by completing a purchase order which lists varieties, size, quantity, and price per unit. It is also the buyer's responsibility to specify shipping instructions, including shipping dates, means of transportation, and any special handling procedures. Orders should be placed as early as possible, and a confirmation of the order obtained

**Table 10–1** Suggested Moisture Control, Temperature, and Other Actions to Ensure Successful Shipping of Plant Material

| Class of Plant Material | Moisture Control | Temperature (°F) | Notes |
|---|---|---|---|
| **Dormant** | | | |
| Bare root (roses, shrubs, fruit trees, shade trees, and small fruit trees) | Damp, aged shingletow about roots or poly liner within container | 35–40 | Shipped in nursery boxes |
| Packaged (roses, shrubs, fruit trees, and small fruit) | Damp medium in package about roots | 35–40 | Individually packaged; shipped in nursery boxes |
| Perennials (flowering, strawberry plants) | Poly liner within container | 28–35 | Shipped in nursery boxes |
| **Balled and burlapped** | | | |
| Shade trees | | | |
| Dormant | | 30–40 | Tipped and tied |
| In leaf | Water[a] prior to digging; store in cool area with high humidity | 40–60 | Tipped and tied |
| **Evergreens** | | | |
| Dormant | | 30–50 | Stacked on balls; tarp if in open truck |
| Nondormant | Moisten soil[a] prior to shipping | 40–60 | Stacked on balls; tarp if in open truck |
| **Containerized** | | | |
| Small sizes (1–5 gal) | Watered and drained[a] prior to shipping | 50–55 | Decked or stacked 3–5 high on cans |
| Large sizes (barrels) | Watered and drained[a] prior to shipping | 40–60 | Tipped and tied Saran tarp if in open truck |

[a]Water adds considerable shipping weight, 8.34 lb/gal. Root ball should be damp, never dry, and seldom wet to field or container capacity.

from the seller to assure a contractual obligation. Dates of delivery should be stated so that plant material will arrive on time. Avoid the use of "will advise" for time of shipment. The seller will hold such orders in the inactive shipping file until advised to ship by the buyer. It is better to supply the seller with a delivery schedule that allows the grower some flexibility in his or her digging and shipping program, but assures timely delivery of quality stock. When time of delivery is important to meet a deadline in a planting program or material is being advertised in a garden center merchandising program, this information must be communicated to the seller so that he or she can take the necessary steps to assure timely delivery. A lead time of 2 weeks is usually the minimum required to process a large order.

In addition to the shipping date, the buyer should clearly indicate where to ship the plants, particularly if the plant material is to be shipped to a place other than to his or her place of business. This is especially true for plant material being shipped to a landscape construction site. In some cases the hour of delivery may be important. Landscape contractors may want to specify the hour of delivery to assure that workers and equipment will be available to unload large B&B trees.

If a specific means of transportation is desired, this information should be provided to the seller, or the buyer must arrange for the necessary transportation. When shipping instructions are not provided, it is left to the best judgment of the shipper who acts as an agent for the buyer, since most purchases are FOB the seller's nursery. If the buyer sends a truck to pick up the plant material, he or she should have some concept of the size and weight of the load (see Appendix I) and supply a vehicle that will accommodate it. It is also his or her responsibility to provide the necessary tarps, ropes, and materials to protect the plants and to secure the load.

The buyer should become acquainted with the seller. A visit to the nursery will help to determine the quality of the plant material and to become acquainted with the total production and shipping operation. Details of the purchase agreement should be discussed and agreed upon. Many large wholesale production nurseries have a minimum total order in dollars that will be accepted, and in some cases a minimum quantity within a size class (e.g., 10 BR shrubs, 5 B&B trees, 20 1-gal containers, or 5 5-gal containers). Handling procedures should be discussed and agreed upon to assure a maximum degree of quality control. The buyer should make the necessary financial arrangements with the seller and provide a number of credit references if he or she is a new customer.

Unloading and servicing of the plant material upon delivery is the buyer's responsibility. An appropriate area should be available to receive, store, and protect the plants. In most situations the plants will need water, and if bare root, the material will have to be heeled-in to protect the root system from desiccation or exposure to freezing temperatures. One-year-old wood chips make an excellent mulch for this purpose.

Special equipment is needed for unloading large B&B trees. The practice of rolling B&B plants off the truck-bed can break the balls and result in premature death of the plants. A forklift, a tractor equipped with a front-end loader, or a small crane is much more effective and less damaging to the plant material.

The plant material should be inspected and counted immediately upon arrival and any discrepancies from the order as booked should be brought to the attention of both the seller and the carrier. The buyer has the right to open damaged cartons and examine the contents prior to signing the delivery receipt. A detailed description of damage, if any, should be noted on the delivery receipt, dated, and endorsed by consignee and carrier. This information should be sent to the seller within a 10-day period of receipt of the order. Failure to do so is tacit acceptance of the order as delivered. Plants that arrive in a frozen, dried, or pest-infested condition should be called to the attention of the state plant inspector to obtain a professional judgment on the quality of the nursery stock.

### Uniform Commercial Code

Buyers and sellers should familiarize themselves with the Uniform Commercial Code (UCC) to avoid legal problems resulting from lost or damaged plant material or supplies. The UCC is accepted as law in all states except Louisiana. Also, nurserymen should be clear as to when title for the plant material or other supplies passes from the buyer to the seller. This requires an understanding of the standard abbreviation in almost all sales contracts: FOB—meaning *free of board*.

When FOB is used it means the seller agrees to put the buyer's merchandise on a truck and the buyer takes title to the merchandise and is responsible to pay the transportation charges. This is the term of common usage in the nursery industry.

FOB (place of destination) means the title passes to the buyer when the seller *properly* delivers the merchandise to the location specified by the buyer. Under these terms the seller pays the shipping costs.

FOB (place of shipment) means the title passes from the seller to the buyer when the merchandise is delivered to a common carrier. The seller pays the transportation to the carrier.

FAS (free along side vessel) means the title passes from the buyer to the seller when the merchandise is delivered to the dock along side the vessel or air port terminal.

## SELLER'S RESPONSIBILITIES

The seller has the responsibility of digging, assembling, packing, and shipping the order. All stock shipped shall be of the size, grade, quantity, and quality specified in the order and should conform to the latest edition of *American Standard for Nursery Stock*. The seller's responsibility begins upon receipt of the order.

One of the first decisions that the seller must make is to accept or reject the order. First, is the plant material available for sale, and second, does he wish to make a contractual obligation with the buyer? If the customer is new to the nursery, he or she should check credit references and discuss financial arrangements. The stock records should be checked for inventory count by variety and size to either confirm the order or to communicate the necessary adjustments to book the order. Upon acceptance, the appropriate quantities are deducted from inventory for sale. The invoice (Fig. 10–2) is typed and copies

# 03/09/92    PACKING SLIP    ORDER # - 4450    PAGE 1

5131481    CUSTOMER    Nursery

0    SHIP TO    Nursery

SPECIAL ORDER INST

SPECIAL CUST INST

Wayne Kaiser    615-446-4434    Wayne Kaiser    615-446-4434

| REQUEST SHIP | SHIP WEEK | AD DTE | SLSM | CUST PO | TERMS | FOOTAGE: | FREIGHT#: |
|---|---|---|---|---|---|---|---|
| 03/09/92 | 03/09/92 | **/**/** | 3/88 | | NET 30 | | TRUCK: jhent |

CONTACTED:         DATE/TIME DEL:         LOADER:         ATL:
                                          AMT REC'D:

| ITEM # ITEM DESCRIPTION | ORDER PIC | QTY PIC | QTY SHIP | BO | SUB | SUB DESC/ITM# |
|---|---|---|---|---|---|---|
| Potted | | | | | | |
| yden10i Yew Spd T Densiformis 10/12" | 150 agd10 | 150 | | | | |
| yden12i Yew Spd T Densiformis 12/15" | 50 agj15 | 50 | | | | |
| yden15i Yew Spd T Densiformis 15/18" | 75 agg34 | 75 | | | | |
| ycap18i Yew Pry T Capitata 18/24" | 20 agg13 | 20 | | | | |
| Container Grown | | | | | | |
| jol01pc Jun Spd Pf Old Gold #1 Pot | 80 agg02 | 80 | | | | |
| jchi0lpc Jun LoSpd Blue Chip #1 Pot | 75 agg18 | 75 | | | | |
| jstr0lpc Jun LoSpd Blue Star #1 Pot | 25 agg20 | 25 | | | | |
| jtan0lpc Jun LoSpd Tam New Blue #1 Pot | 20 agg28 | 20 | | | | |
| yadn0lpc Yucca Adams Ndl (filament) #1 Pot | 40 agj47 | 40 | | | | |
| bcrp0lpc Barberry Crimson Pygmy Red #1 Pot | 25 agj17 | 25 | | | | |
| brog0lpc Barberry Rose Glow Var #1 Pot | 20 agg40 | 20 | | | | |
| spes0lpc Spirea Peppermint Stick #1 Pot | 30 agf26 | 30 | | | | |
| sald1pbc Spruce Alberta Dwarf #1p-10/12" | 25 age10 | 25 | | | | |
| jstr2pcc Jund LoSpd Blue Star #2P-12/15" | 10 SHIPSUB | 10 | | | | |
| mjre2pdc Maple Jap Red #2p-15/18" | 30 age24 | 30 | | | | |
| pmug3pcc Pine Mugho #3P-12/15" | 60 agk49 | 24 | agk45 | 36 | | |
| sald3pfc Spruce Alberta Dwarf #3P-24/30" | | | | | | |

**Figure 10-2** Invoice Packing Slip.

sent to appropriate individuals for action, with a copy to the buyer, which confirms the order. In small to medium-sized nurseries, most of this paperwork is accomplished by a staff of trained clerks employing standard forms and following standard operating procedures. Larger firms accomplish much of the paperwork for booking, invoicing, and inventory control by the use of computers (Fig. 9–6).

The process of assembling, packing, and shipping of the order requires considerable coordination within the nursery and with the carrier. Nurseries that operate on a seasonal basis with a peak shipping season in the spring generally designate a key employee as shipping clerk, whereas larger nurseries that are shipping 10–12 months of the year employ or contract for a traffic coordinator and utilize a computer along with a software system, such as ORBIT (Order, Billing, and Inventory Transaction) that coordinates and controls plant inventory from the time of sale through shipping, billing, and accounting. The ORBIT system was developed specifically for the nursery industry. With a UNIX Operating System and a UNIFY Relational Database Management System the user can obtain immediate and accurate information about any area relating to the ORBIT system.

UNIX is a portable, universal, interactive multi-user operating system developed and trademarked by AT&T Bell Laboratories. Portable means that the system can be adapted for use on different makes of computers. Universal indicates that the operating system was not designed for a specific application. Multi-user means that the system will support several users at the same time (simultaneously) on the same computer.

The UNIFY Database Management System, as developed by the UNIFY Corporation, allows the development of applications on one machine that easily port to other machines. It runs on over 150 different computer systems, from micro to mini to mainframe. The system is easy to learn and information retrieval is fast.

The ORBIT system is divided into five multiple modules, including:

1. *Order entry* is the process of entering, modifying, or deleting any order entry transaction (i.e., new orders, credit memos, debit memos, and revision or cancellation orders). To be able to input these types of transactions, the inventory and customer master file must be previously set-up. Within the order entry module, acknowledgment, substitution and revision letters are printed. Also, open and closed ORBIT master files are developed. *Open* files are files that have not been invoiced, whereas, *Closed* files are those that have been invoiced and shipping is in progress.

2. The *shipping* module schedules orders for shipping, reduces inventory as orders are shipped, maintains and updates a "dock" inventory, calculates freight charges, and prepares transactions to be invoiced.

3. The purpose of the *invoicing* module is to print invoices, print invoice registers and to post invoiced open ORBIT transactions to the closed ORBIT files and to the Accounts Receivable system.

4. The purpose of the *accounts receivable* module is to give the accounting and credit departments direct control of the input into the accounts receivable master file and obtain immediate and accurate information about any area relating to accounts receivable. Invoicing will post invoices to the accounts receivable system, therefore eliminating user input for those transactions.

5. The *reports* module produces a hard copy of a requested report and allows the user to view many of the reports on a CRT. Some of the reports included in the ORBIT system are in the areas of Customer Masters, Inventory Worksheets, Open Order Reports, and Sales Summaries. With the UNIFY database the user has endless capabilities for retrieving data, and with very little technical knowledge can create their own special reports.

The traffic coordinator or shipping clerk is responsible for arranging the most dependable, rapid, and economical means of transportation. He also coordinates assembling and packing of the order. Upon receipt of the order in the shipping department, it should be keyed to a shipping date. Orders that must arrive at the buyer's site on a specific day or hour of the day should be noted on the shipping schedule to assure timely delivery.

The traffic coordinator can select from a number of means of transportation, each with advantages and disadvantages. Air freight is fast but expensive and is generally utilized for lightweight shipments needed in a hurry. Bus freight and United Parcel Service (UPS) are used for small, lightweight shipments (less than 50 lb/package) that can be delivered within a 2- to 5-day period. Both of these require that the shipper bring the material to the terminal and the buyer pick it up at a terminal, although UPS will deliver. Railroad boxcar, a common method of shipping nursery stock in the past, is now used only on a limited basis. The railroad boxcar takes from 6 to 10 days for direct shipment from coast to coast, but at times delays of 3 weeks or more are encountered. The charge is based on 100-lb units/mile, with a minimum shipping charge that is often two or three times the 100-lb rate. Although most wholesale nurseries that ship via railroad boxcar are equipped with a railroad loading dock, few buyers have railroad siding and docking facilities, necessitating double handling at the receiving end.

Motor freight is the most common means of shipping nursery stock. Direct motor freight can pick up plant material at the production site and deliver directly to the seller, avoiding multiple handling and delays often experienced when material moves by common carrier and passes through various terminals enroute.

When it is necessary to ship less than a truckload (LTL), the traffic coordinator can arrange a pooled or split load if two or more orders are to be delivered in the same geographic area of the country. Pooled loads require more coordination to assemble and are more costly, since a stopover charge is added to each order. But pooled loads are less expensive and are generally delivered faster than LTL shipments. Motor freight is charged on a mileage basis per trailer. Thus, it is advantageous to obtain a full load or to split-load rather than employ LTL shipments.

Bare-root plants are normally packaged in the storage area and delivered to the loading dock. Containers for shipping nursery stock should be sturdy; preferably only those that can withstand a 250-lb test should be used. This is to prevent breakage during shipping and crushing of containers that are on the lower layer. Overwatering plant material prior to boxing for shipment in fiberboard-type containers soaks and weakens the container, contributing to breakage and damage to plant material.

Containerized and B&B material are picked up at the growing or storage sites and delivered to the loading dock. Many forms of mechanical equipment are utilized in packaging and loading. Automatic bundling, tying, and strapping machines (Fig. 10–3) aid in packaging bare-root orders. Forklift trucks lift and transport heavy loads about the nursery and into the carrier (Fig. 10–4). Some nurseries employ self-tracking lowboy trailers or electric carts to transport container material. Where possible, pallets of various types and endless belt units are employed to expedite the movement of plant material in the loading process.

Plant material loaded into railroad cars or motor freight trailers must be carefully stacked to avoid damage to the plants, and shifting of the load during transport. At the same time, maximum advantage of the total space available can be taken. Small B&B plants and those in metal containers are generally stacked three to four tiers high, whereas plants in nonmetal containers are generally shelved to avoid breakage of the containers. B&B trees in wire baskets require that the trunks be protected with some form of padding to avoid injury during loading and transport. Split loads shipped in closed vans can be divided with a barrier to aid in unloading and to minimize loss of plant material destined for the next stop enroute.

Since trucking is very expensive it is recommended that only fully-loaded trucks should be dispatched. The crew foreman should estimate space requirements in advance for each load and check with the sales department to coordinate shipping to customers who are located in close proximity to each other. With good coordination between the loading foreman and the sales shipping clerk it is possible to fully utilize the total space within a trailer as well as to keep within weight limitations. Currently, 80,000 pounds is the legal limit for commercial vehicles nation wide.

Accurate records must be maintained. A careful count of plants and packages must be made at the time of loading to assure that the buyer receives what was ordered and that the seller bills the customer for the material shipped. The seller is under obligation to conform to the most current issue of *American Standard for Nursery Stock*. All stock must be correctly labeled; in some states plants must be tagged with their botanical name. Following loading, the seller must provide the carrier with a copy of the invoice and other appropriate information. In split loads, it is advisable to place the

**Figure 10–3** Automatic nursery stock tying machine. (Courtesy Saxmayer Corporation.)

invoices in separate envelopes and to mark them with information that the driver will need to expedite delivery. This information generally includes buyer's name, place of delivery with any special directions, time of delivery if applicable, and telephone numbers of people to contact in the event of a delay. At the time of departure, the shipping clerk should notify the buyer, either by fax or by telephone, of the expected time of arrival and the name of the carrier.

**Figure 10–4**  Forklift aids in loading nursery stock. (Courtesy C. E. Lewis.)

In addition to shipping records, it is desirable that the party who arranges for the shipping maintain an up-to-date file on each carrier hired to haul plant material. The file should contain copies of the carrier's certificate of insurance and permits to operate a motor vehicle in the various states enroute. The certificate of insurance is needed to assure fiscal responsibility in the event of an accident, and up-to-date permits assure transit within the various states. Also, some shippers will enclose a sealed temperature recorder within the trailer to obtain an accurate record of the temperature that the plants were exposed to during transit. This data can be very valuable should there be a question of plant viability at the time of or following delivery to the buyer.

It is desirable for the seller to obtain cargo insurance when arranging shipments by exempted carriers not booked through a trucking broker. The seller holds title to the plant material until it is delivered either to the buyer or to a common carrier. Nurserymen who hire trucking firms are advised to contract their trucking needs through a reliable trucking broker or a trucking company known for their reliability in handling plant material, who will arrange the necessary details and carry the appropriate cargo insurance.

Most traffic controllers maintain an order board, updated twice daily, so that sales and administrative staff can quickly respond to inquiries relative to shipping of orders.

## CARRIER'S RESPONSIBILITIES

The carrier is responsible for transporting the plant material from the seller to the buyer. In most situations the carrier (railroad, motor carrier, bus, UPS, or U.S. mail) is a third party, but in some situations the buyer may send a truck to pick up the plant materials or the seller may deliver in one of his or her own trucks. Nevertheless, it is necessary for the carrier to comply with local, state, and federal laws pertaining to the operation and maintenance of motor carriers. The Interstate Commerce Commission (ICC) is the agency of the federal government that regulates motor carrier transportation interstate and across international boundaries. The ICC regulates motor transport by various economic regulations, which apply only to commercial carriers who do hauling for hire; nurserymen who do their own trucking, under a farm license, are exempt from the economic regulations. However, truck safety regulations, administered by the U.S. Department of Transportation (DOT) apply to all owners of trucks operating in interstate commerce. These regulations are contained in *Federal Motor Carrier Safety Regulations* published by the DOT, available from the Superintendent of Documents in Washington, D.C. Topics contained in the regulations are qualification of drivers, driving of motor vehicles, parts and accessories necessary for safe operation, notification, reporting and recording of accidents, hours of service of drivers, inspection and maintenance, and driving and parking rules. Every employee who does interstate trucking should be provided with a copy of the regulation, be required to read and understand the regulations, keep an updated driver's log, and turn it in for inspection on a regular basis.

Although nurserymen are exempt from the economic regulations of the ICC, they are subject to the federal highway use tax. This tax is imposed on all motor vehicles or vehicle-trailer combinations having a taxable gross weight of more than 26,000 lb. The Internal Revenue Service (IRS) publishes a schedule showing taxable gross weight for various motor vehicles and vehicle-trailer combinations. The tax must be reported and paid to the District Director of the IRS.

In addition to the federal regulations, many states and local communities have laws or regulations pertaining to the operation of motor vehicles. Nurserymen who transport nursery stock into other states should be acquainted with the applicable laws and regulations. A book that covers laws and regulations that drivers need to know is *Professional Truck Drivers Handbook*. Order copies from Private Truck Council of America, 2022 P Street, NW, Washington, DC 20036.

Interstate truckers are subject to the economic regulations of the ICC under the Federal Motor Carrier Act. They must obtain a license from the commission, which also regulates rates, territories, routes, insurance coverage, and so on. However, Congress has exempted agricultural and horticultural commodities from the act, thus allowing truckers who haul plant material for nurserymen greater flexibility in service and rates. The exemption holds only

**Table 10-2** Partial List of Horticultural Commodities Exempted from Coverage under the Federal Motor Carrier Act.

---

Bark
Bulbs
Christmas trees
Containers, crates, boxes (used to move exempted commodities or being returned for reuse)
Flowers, cut or growing
Grass seed
Greenery
Humus
Leaves
Manure, natural or dried
Nursery stock
Peat moss, dried, shredded, baled
Plants: flower and vegetable
Roots, asparagus, mint, rhubarb, etc.
Seeds
Trees
Wreaths (natural with small amounts of foundations or decorative material)

---

if exempted commodities are carried in the truck or trailer combination at any one time. If a trucking firm transports a mixed load of exempt and nonexempt material, it is subject to the economic regulations. Table 10–2 lists some of the exempted horticultural commodities. As a result of this special exemption, many for-hire truckers devote a major portion of their effort to servicing nurseries and other agricultural industries.

Since drivers are primarily responsible for the operation of their vehicles and loads, they should supervise loading and tie-down to assure proper weight distribution and securing of loads (Fig. 10–5). To avoid economic penalties for overweight, a weight estimate of the load should be made at the time of loading (Appendix I).

Most truckers can estimate the weight of the load by the pull on the engine as they leave the loading dock. To obtain an accurate weight, the trucker can have the load weighed at a local business (grain elevator, foundry, etc.) that is equipped with the necessary scales.

## REGULATED CARRIERS

Some nursery stock, primarily boxed and packaged material, is shipped via regulated motor carriers. They charge rates regulated by the ICC and can transport only within the geographic area specified in their certificate of operating authority. Long-distance shipments can pass through a number of terminals and be transported by a number of carriers enroute to the consignee, which can result in delays and possible injury to the plant material. To avoid delays, buyers can request "through routing" from the carrier that will make

**Figure 10–5** Shade trees loaded and tied for shipping. (Courtesy Studebaker Nurseries, Inc.).

the final delivery. This information should then be communicated to the seller, who will make the necessary arrangements. If the buyer cannot obtain through routing, he or she should request the shipper to select the best routing available. However, many shippers select "open routing," which passes the responsibility to the carrier to route the shipment; this often results in delays.

Regulated carriers must issue a bill of lading for each shipment received for transport. The bill of lading provides a description of the product (contents, number, weight, size, etc.). The product should be described in wording that conforms to the motor carrier's classification requirements. To do otherwise can result in higher rates. For example, a shipment of bare-root shrubs boxed and marked "dormant nursery stocks" or "perishable nursery stocks" would cost more to ship than the same shipment boxed and marked "shrubs, other than balled in earth, tops tied and roots wrapped." The latter wording conforms to the motor carrier's classification. Also, some carriers refuse to handle perishable shipments. To avoid this possibility, nurserymen should avoid the use of "Perishable" but mark the bill of lading "Do Not Delay! Early delivery requested." When possible, labels on containers should be in large, easy-to-read print and placed on the front and back of the container rather than being typed and placed on top of the container. Only the name and destination of the buyer need to be on the outside of the container. The bill of lading contains all other necessary information.

Upon delivery the regulated carrier must present a freight bill covering the shipment, listing rates assessed; total charges to be collected; special charges (with details); and the route, including name of carriers that participated in the shipment and terminals through which the shipment moved. This information is needed in the event a claim or lawsuit should be filed against a carrier for damages to the plants suffered while in transit.

If it should become necessary to file a claim for damages or overcharges against a carrier, nurserymen should engage a traffic service agency. The traffic service agency will also audit freight bills for overcharges and provide assistance in tracing and expediting shipments that are lost or delayed in transit.

### Freight Charges

Freight charges are based on a rate per mile for truck and trailer of a given size. Many nurseries, especially those that produce container-grown plants, provide a schedule of shipping charges. These charges are established for zones of delivery, at various distances from the production site. The charges are stated either as truckload or LTL-zone rates (Table 10–3).

Pooled deliveries are also booked on a rate per mile plus a stopover charge for each partial loading. If all customers are in the same geographic area, the charge per customer can be proportioned either by weight or space. However, where there is considerable difference in mileage between stops, a more equitable basis for proportioning charges is the adjusted LTL charge. This charge can be obtained by first calculating a LTL reduction factor, which

**Table 10–3** Example of Shipping Charges from Container-Production Nursery to 10 Delivery Zones[a]

| A. Truckload rates [Maximum load: 6500 1-gal containers or equivalent (1 5-gal = 2 3-gal = 4 1-gal)] | |
| --- | --- |
| *Zone* | *Price* |
| 1 | $200 |
| 2 | 250 |
| 3 | 300 |
| - | - |
| - | - |
| - | - |
| 10 | 1500 |

| B. Less-than-truckload rates | | | |
| --- | --- | --- | --- |
| | *Price* | | |
| *Zone* | *1 gal* | *5 gal* | *3 gal* |
| 1 | $0.05 | $0.25 | Double 1-gal rate |
| 2 | 0.10 | 0.50 | |
| 3 | 0.14 | 0.60 | |
| - | - | - | |
| - | - | - | |
| - | - | - | |
| 10 | 0.25 | 1.40 | |

[a]Each distal zone increases by a radius of approximately 100 miles.

is applied against the LTL charge for each customer. The LTL reduction factor is obtained by dividing the total freight charges for a pooled load by the total charges for LTL delivery to each customer. The factor is then used to adjust the LTL charge to each customer. For example, LTL charges to three customers are $400, $600, $800, whereas the total pooled cost is $1400. The LTL reduction factor is 0.78 and the adjusted charges are $310, $470, and $620. With the aid of a simple desk calculator, these calculations can be made rapidly and accurately.

The traffic coordinator or shipping clerk can estimate cost of shipments with the aid of official state highway maps, a Rand McNally road atlas, or a mileage guide for major cities available from the Household Goods Carrier's Bureau.

Many individual truckers give allowances to nurserymen who load or unload LTL shipments aggregating 10,000 lb or more in one calendar day. Firms that load or unload LTL shipments totaling 10,000 lb or more should negotiate with truckers for the "Loading/Unloading Allowances." Although the allowance may be only a few cents per 100 lb, in the course of a year the amount can be sizable, particularly to heavy-volume shippers or receivers.

Shippers should consider executing a "no-recourse clause" on bills of lading on collect shipments. Failure to do so leaves the shipper liable to pay any uncollected freight charges that the carrier is unable to collect from consignee. Executing the no-recourse clause could save the shipper from having to pay uncollected charges if the consignee should happen to go bankrupt.

Also, in 1990 the Supreme Court ruled that shippers became liable when a trucker fails to maintain an accurate file at the Interstate Commerce Commission. Truckers must provide the ICC with tariff files outlining their rates. If a trucking company negotiates a lower rate with a shipper, but does not alter its file to reflect the rate, the shipper becomes liable for the difference between the negotiated rate and the rate on file. Nurserymen should scrutinize every negotiated shipping contract for compliance with ICC regulations.

A package express service, known as XpressPAX, is available through the Greyhound Bus Company. For a nominal fee the bus company provides an appropriate-sized shipping container, packing materials, and assistance in packing shipments. It can frequently provide same-day service to points up to 300 miles.

## SUMMARY

Shipping of nursery stock is an operation of considerable importance to nurserymen. Individual nurserymen and nurserymen's organizations have spent and will continue to spend considerable time and energy trying to assure delivery of quality plants to the customer. At the first meeting of the American Association of Nurserymen in 1876, transportation of nursery stock was a topic that received major attention. Delays in shipment and high transportation rates were the primary complaints of the day. However, with positive action on the part of all parties—shipper, carrier, and buyer—directed toward maintaining plant quality during the postharvest preplanting period, it is possible to deliver the product to the ultimate customer in a condition that is a credit to the grower and to the activities of the carrier. "Green survival—it depends on you," the motto of the AAN, is most appropriate when applied to the operation of shipping of nursery stock.

## REFERENCES

AMERICAN ASSOCIATION OF NURSERYMEN. 1963. Transportation summary. AAN Newsletter 580:1–19.

BROOKHOUSE, S. 1990. Introduction to the ORBIT System, Inhouse Publication, Zelenka Evergreen Nursery.

HALL, G. C., and C. E. WHITCOMB. 1976. Antitranspirants: an investment or an unnecessary expense? Am. Nurseryman 144(2):14.

OSSIAN, W. 1973. Shipping nursery stock today. Am. Nurseryman 138(1):20; 138(2):14.

U.S. DEPARTMENT OF TRANSPORTATION. 1975. Federal motor carrier safety regulations. Title 49. Transportation, p. 123.

## SUGGESTED READING

*Guide to Maximizing Recovery of Loss and Damage Claims.* 1978. AAN Transportation Consultants-Bohman Industrial Traffic Consultants, 335 East Broadway, Gardner, Mass.

BARRETT C. 1983. Practical handbook on private trucking. Traffic Services Corp., Washington, D.C.

Chapter **11**

# Nursery Crop Production

In this chapter we trace the basic information needed for starting and operating a field or container production nursery. A nursery business can be a profitable enterprise, but it requires a sizable investment of money for labor and equipment, plus a considerable amount of management time. The part-time nursery owner often becomes dissatisfied with the unforeseen and exacting conditions under which a successful nursery must be operated. Therefore, it is not usually managed part-time, and is not considered an easy money maker or income supplement.

The purpose of this chapter is to provide a schedule of operations from plant selection to harvest for field or container production (Fig. 11–1). Portions of this chapter were adapted from extension publications listed in the reference section. These references as well as the others contain additional information on nursery practices. Many cultural recommendations and methods of production will be given as examples, however, the authors realize that local conditions and specific technologies may not be applicable to your situation. To satisfy your special needs, you should consult with Cooperative Extension Specialists at your state university.

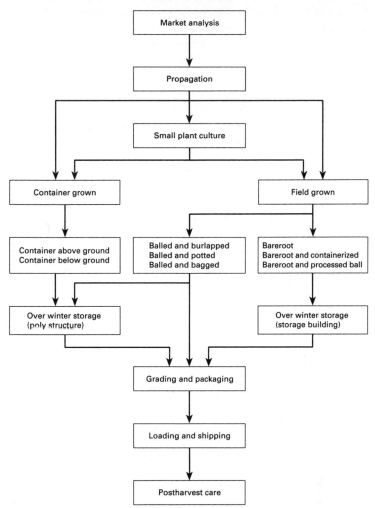

**Figure 11-1** Flowchart of nursery crop production. (Adapted from Stinson et al., 1971.)

## PLANNING THE OPERATION

Deciding on what trees and shrubs to grow is an important first step and a most perplexing question for the grower. Consider growing those trees and shrubs for which there is a potential market, that are well suited to your site, and that fit your expertise. Of course, there are many tree and shrub species that satisfy this criteria. Nursery catalogs and standard textbooks may be consulted for detailed information. Observing what is popularly grown in the market area and consulting with other growers will also give valuable clues to help you decide on species and quantities. A conservative approach might be to choose a few of the good sellers that are easy to grow and gradually increase inventories to meet market demand.

There are several genera of trees and shrubs that are common to many ornamental landscapes and will probably remain so for many future years. The tree genera are *Acer, Cornus, Gleditsia, Magnolia, Malus, Abies, Picea, Pinus, Prunus,* and *Quercus,* while the shrub genera include *Berberis, Cotoneaster, Buxus, Forsythia, Ilex, Juniperus, Rhododendron, Rosa, Taxus,* and *Viburnum.* Selected and improved cultivars are available for most of these commonly accepted plants. Avoid plants that are losing their popularity or seem to be going out of style. Many older crabapple (*Malus*) cultivars that are susceptible to disease are being replaced by resistant selections. A grower should always determine the preferred sizes, foliage and flower colors, textures, densities, or formal and informal plant forms to successfully meet market demands.

How will the plants be harvested? This management decision influences production practices as well as handling procedures. For example, plants may be marketed bareroot, bareroot and containerized, bareroot with processed balls, balled and burlapped, balled and potted, or container grown. Some of the harvesting and marketing characteristics are given in Table 11–1.

Should a grower produce or buy liners? A beginning nursery grower may find it more convenient and profitable to purchase plants for lining-out than to produce them. Liner production requires expert attention to many details, as well as special propagation facilities and small plant culture production areas. If liners are purchased for the first few years, a new grower can concentrate on growing quality plants at a profit and avoid the risks involved in propagation. After concentrating on growing practices and establishing the business, the new grower might consider improving profits by producing lining-out stock.

## LINER PRODUCTION FROM SEED

Desirable and quality tree and shrub seedlings are much more likely to be obtained when the seed source or parentage is known. Seed should be from sources that are well adapted to the nursery's market areas. Local seed collection is best because it provides for identification of parentage and allows harvest at the correct maturity. However, there may be just a few species in a range and a limited amount of seed present in the local area. Also, local seed collection involves labor costs and handling knowledge.

If possible, a nursery should have its own seed orchard for the propagator to collect from known and acceptable plants. Many of our ornamental

**Table 11-1** Marketing Alternatives for Field-Production or Container-Production Systems

| Methods | Characteristics | Marketing Period | Plant Types |
|---|---|---|---|
| Bareroot | Dormant digging; soil removed from roots; storage facilities needed; less shipping weight | Dormant season | Deciduous |
| Bareroot and containerized | Same as bareroot, except roots reestablished in container growing mix | Dormant season | Deciduous |
| Bareroot and processed ball | Same as bareroot, except roots enclosed in burlap and pack in growing mix | Dormant season | Deciduous |
| Balled and burlapped | Ball of soil remains; expanded digging season; improved postharvest life | Spring or fall season with proper conditions | Evergreens, deciduous |
| Balled and potted | Same as balled and burlapped, except less precision on digging; roots protected in sturdy containers | Same as balled and burlapped | Evergreens, deciduous |
| Balled and bagged | Same as balled and burlapped, except less time and effort in digging; more roots retained; sandy soils may be used | Spring, summer, or fall seasons | Evergreens, deciduous |
| Container above ground | Less handling damage; extends market season; more uniformity; reduces shipping weight | Spring, summer, or fall seasons | Evergreens, deciduous |
| Container below ground | Same as container above ground, except protection of roots in winter; plant stability in wind; no circling roots in bottom of container | Spring, summer, or fall seasons | Evergreens, deciduous |

*Source:* Adapted from Ponder et al. (1983).

landscape plants, such as red maple, redbud, dogwood, sugar maple, and oaks, have broad geographic distribution. These native species usually adapt and grow much better than introduced ornamentals. Research with redbuds and dogwoods has shown that plants produced from southern seed will winter kill in the north, while plants from northern seed sources grow slower in the south than do plants from southern seed sources. Regardless of whether seed are collected locally or purchased, growers should be aware of prior collection and handling conditions. Commercial firms will usually cooperate in defining seed origin and identifying parentage if this information is known.

Some seed may be sown shortly after collection. Seeds of some tree and shrub species will germinate and grow immediately, while others will require an overwintering process to satisfy dormancy requirements. Seed from some species will require special treatments to meet germination requirements. This specific information and more can be found in several standard texts. U.S.D.A. Handbook No. 450 and *Plant Propagation-Principles and Practices* by Hartmann, Kester and Davies are considered by many horticulturists to be valuable information resources for plant propagators and growers of ornamental landscape plants.

## LINER PRODUCTION FROM VEGETATIVE METHODS

Vegetative or asexual propagation has become an established means of producing plants by using roots, stems, or leaves of stock plants that have the desired ornamental landscape traits. Asexual propagation is popular because it produces an identical clone with the same genetic make-up as the original stock plant. Asexual propagation is accomplished by several methods, such as cuttage, graftage, layerage, division, and tissue culture. Specific techniques on each of these methods for ornamentals is thoroughly covered in other publications (see Appendix B).

## SMALL PLANT CULTURE

Seedlings or rooted cuttings may be transplanted from the propagation bed or flats into well prepared ground beds, small containers or directly into field production rows. When plants are kept in small plant culture the objective is to provide protection and optimum conditions for rapid vigorous growth by allowing sufficient space between plants, by giving adequate water and fertilizer, and by eliminating competition from weeds and pests.

Certain types of nursery plants, such as narrow-leaved and broad-leaved evergreens, are usually transplanted into liner beds or coldframes for growing one or two years rather than directly into fields (Fig. 11–2). Table 11–2 gives recommended spacing in transplant beds, coldframes, and fields for different types of plants. Vigorously growing seedlings, well-rooted cuttings or properly knitted grafts should be transplanted, while unhealthy and poorly developed plants from propagation should be rogued out and discarded. Only those plants of the best quality should be allowed to occupy valuable production space. For additional information on production quota estimates, space requirements, planting designs, labeling blocks or rows, programming, and record keeping, review Chapter 5.

**Figure 11-2** Young nursery plants lined-out in beds for growing 1 or 2 years.

**Table 11-2** Suggested Spacing for Young Nursery Stock in Small-Plant Culture When Transplanted into Transplant Beds, Cold Frames, or Fields

| Type of Plant | Propagated by: | Being Transplanted into: | Recommended Spacing Between Rows | Recommended Spacing In the Row |
|---|---|---|---|---|
| Narrow-leaved evergreens | Seed | Beds | 6–10 in. | 3–6 in. |
| | | Fields | 3½–4 ft | 4–5 ft |
| | Cuttings | Frames | 6 in. | 3 in. |
| | | Fields | 3½–4 ft | 2–3 ft |
| | Grafts | Frames | 8 in. | 4–6 in. |
| | | Fields | 3½–4 ft | 2–3 ft |
| Deciduous | Seed | Beds | 8–12 in. | 4–6 in. |
| | | Fields | 3½–4 ft | 2–3 ft |
| | Cuttings and grafts | Fields | 3½–4 ft | 2–3 ft |
| Broad-leaved evergreens | Seed | Beds | 4–10 in. | 4–10 in. |
| | Cuttings and grafts | Frames | 4–10 in. | 4–10 in. |
| | Seed, cuttings, and grafts | Fields | 3½–4 ft | 2½–3 ft |

*Source:* Adapted from Stinson et al. (1971).

### Fertilization Programs for Liners

Suggested fertilizer programs for nitrogen in small plant culture include selecting from 1 or 2 of the following.

1. *Ground Beds.* Apply annually to deciduous trees and shrubs 5–6 lbs.; narrow-leaved evergreens 4–5 lbs.; and broad-leaved evergreens 2–3 lbs. of nitrogen/1000 sq. ft. A well-drained, medium-textured loam soil with a pH of 6.0 to 6.5 is preferred for most nursery plants.

2. *Containers (pots or flats)*. Supplemental fertilizer during the growing season is necessary for optimum growth of most container-grown crops. Limited volume and nutrient reserve of containers, low cation exchange capacities of most commonly used soilless media, and rapid leaching of nutrients from frequent irrigations all contribute to the need for supplemental fertilization. A choice of three fertilizer programs includes: a complete slow-release fertilizer at manufacturer's recommended rate; or a slow-release fertilizer applied in combination with soluble fertilizer at 150 ppm N (weekly); or when no other form of nitrogen is applied in slow-release or granular form then soluble N at 250-300 ppm N (weekly) is suggested. The key to proper management of micronutrients and container media is to have the pH between 5.0 and 6.0. Once the pH rises above 7.0, most micronutrients become tied up in the medium and are unavailable.

These recommendations may vary with species, stages of plant growth, environmental conditions and the concentration of other essential elements. These recommendations are intended to be general guidelines only. While it is difficult to determine the exact nutrient levels to apply for each species, broad ranges of plants can be grown under similar fertility levels. For example, if growers will group their plants (*Taxus* together, *Ilex* together, etc.) fertilization within a genus usually varies less than between genera. Satisfactory growth can be obtained by fertilizing at a specific concentration within a genus. Further groupings according to plant size within a species enhances more efficient fertilization, watering, pruning, and other cultural practices. For further information on nutrition management refer to Chapter 12 for field-grown plants and Chapter 13 for container-grown plants.

### Handling Softwood Cuttings

Softwood cuttings that are well rooted in flats have traditionally been moved from the propagation area to outdoor frames where they are usually shaded for several days before exposure to full sunlight. Many progressive growers have started using the same structure for propagation and small plant culture to eliminate the need for moving at this stage. The structure conforms to the hardening-off needs of the tender young plants, the growing-on requirements and over-wintering protection (Fig. 11–3). Some growers prefer ground beds instead of flats, however, the fact that the flats can be moved directly to the place where the plants will be planted is a great convenience. If adequate space and cutting material is available, many growers in warmer climates (U.S.D.A. hardiness zones 9 and 10) direct-stick three cuttings in one or two gallon containers placed outdoors with a pot to pot arrangement for mist propagation. This is a more efficient procedure that saves time, materials and labor but requires more land. Traditionally many tree species have been propagated by budding. In recent years, graft incom-

**Figure 11-3** Quonset-style house used during propagation, growing, and storage for small plant culture. (Also see 18–2.)

patibility problems have developed on 5- to 10-year-old plants, such as red maple. Softwood cuttings have started to replace budded trees and provide improvements in production.

### Handling Hardwood Cuttings and Grafts

Hardwood cuttings of narrow-leaved evergreens and dormant deciduous plants, which root and develop shoots at the same time, are usually carried over in the propagation greenhouse at reduced temperatures. If slower growing narrow-leaved evergreens require shaded beds for several years before being lined out in the field, then they are moved to beds or frames in early spring after rooting. Hardwood cuttings of vigorous deciduous plants, such as forsythia and privet, may be collected in early winter, held in cold storage to form callus and then lined out in early spring. These cuttings should form roots in a few weeks, followed by shoot growth. If shoots elongate before these stored cuttings are planted, death occurs in the field. Grafted stock of dormant deciduous trees are often handled in the same way as dormant callused and unrooted cuttings. If plants are grafted dormant and placed in storage for knitting (callusing), they are usually lined out in early spring. Grafting understock for evergreens is usually started in pots and managed in the greenhouse until the scion is fully callused and growing well.

### Handling Seedlings

Many types of fast-growing seedlings are direct seeded in field rows or ground beds and grown to a marketable size. Some of these plants are used as understock for budding. Budding is nearly always performed on well established field-grown plants. Seedlings of broad-leaved and narrow-leaved evergreens and deciduous plants may be started and grown in seed beds for one or two years under shade if needed, before being lined out in the field. Seeds may be sown in early spring to prevent overwintering losses from birds, rodents, erosion, and so on. Narrow-leaved evergreen seedlings to be dug and potted to serve as grafting understock, to be lined out in the field or to be container-grown plants are usually transplanted in early spring.

## FIELD-GROWN CROPS

Producing nursery plants in the field for garden centers or landscape contractors may take from 2–7 years from the date of propagation, depending upon the type of plant grown, until the plants are sold. Determining the most efficient field design, crop rotation schedule, soil management, transplanting, fertilization, irrigation, pruning, pest control, winter protection, and harvesting are important to the success of a field nursery operation. The main goal for a nursery business is to produce quality plants at a profit.

### Field Planting Design

Spacing plants in the field should make efficient use of land, facilitate traffic flow and ease of access. Distance between rows should depend on final market size and on the width of equipment to perform field operations, such as planting, maintaining, and harvesting crops. Table 11–3 gives the recommended spacing and the numbers of years to reach marketable size for different types of nursery plants. When large equipment will be used in a field and the between-row spacing is greater than the in-row spacing, then there should be two tree rows and multiple shrub rows for every aisle row. This wide row design provides for better space utilization. Stock marketed bare root is normally planted closer in-row, with less between-row space. Selective harvesting of young plants may be used to obtain desired spacing in-row and to improve cash flow.

Whichever field design is chosen (see Chapter 5), it is important to be able to get into the field throughout the year. Grass sod established in aisles with a weed-free strip in rows allows for maximum accessibility to the field (Fig. 5–12). Established sod aisles will support heavy equipment movement when the soil is wet, reduce soil compaction, erosion, and decrease the area to be kept weed free. Maintenance mowing or growth retardant applications will be required on sod aisles.

**Table 11-3** Spacing and Average Production Time Required for Different Types of Field-Grown Nursery Crops in Hardiness Zones 9 or 8 and 7 or 6

| Type of Plant | Spacing | | Production Time in Years by Hardiness Zone | |
| --- | --- | --- | --- | --- |
| | Between Rows | In Rows | 9 or 8 | 7 or 6 |
| Large deciduous trees | 3½–5 ft | 18 in. | 1 | 2 |
| | 3½–5 ft | 36–48 in. | 4 | 5 |
| | 8–14 ft | 3½–6 ft | 6 | 7 |
| Small deciduous trees | 3½–4 ft | 18 in. | 2 | 2–3 |
| | 3½–4 ft | 36–48 in. | 3–5 | 4–6 |
| Evergreen trees | 4 ft | 2–2½ ft | 4 | 6 |
| Deciduous shrubs | 3½–4 ft | 12–24 in. | 2–3 | 3–4 |
| Evergreen shrubs | 3½–4 ft | 2–3 ft | 3 | 5 |

*Source:* Adapted from Stinson et al. (1971).

## Crop Rotation Plans and Soil Management

The rotation of field-grown nursery crops requires more planning than rotations for farm crops because some nursery crops require 2 years to reach marketable size, while other types require 7 or more years (Fig. 11–4). If a nursery wishes to have an annual supply of standard deciduous trees, a crop, such as red maple, must be planted each year so that red maples will be ready for marketing 7 years later. For example, if the nursery is to market 1000 red maples each year, it must plant 1000 trees each year. Actually, 1053 might need to be planted to allow for 5% losses in the field from numerous causes (see Table 5–2). In any one year, an established nursery could be growing 7371 red maples. In addition, extra fields will be planted to a green manure crop for 1 or 2 years for soil improvement. Similar crop rotation plantings must be done for each type of plant grown in the nursery. Some nurseries will review past sales trends for each species and use an adjustment factor (i.e., 10%) to increase or decrease future plantings to meet market demands.

Good soil conservation procedures denotes correct soil management and certain supporting practices, such as contouring, terracing and diversion ditching. In some nurseries these supporting practices are essential but in all nurseries, good soil management is paramount. Important soil management practices include attention to crop rotation which aids in the maintenance of organic matter thus improving soil structure and tilth, drainage and fertility.

Organic matter is confined largely to the surface soil. The removal of a block of balled evergreens removes a large amount of the surface soil, leaving the subsoil which is low in organic matter. The percentage of top soil removed depends upon planting distances and size of ball dug. Figuring spacing at 42 in. rows and 36 in. in the row and the balls dug at 15 in. depths the following approximate percentages of soil to the 15 in. depth are removed: 15 in. balls remove 10%; 18 in. balls remove 15%; 24 in. balls remove 25%; and 30 in. balls

**Figure 11-4** Nursery planting and rotation plan for field-grown stock. (Adapted from Stinson et al., 1971.)

| TYPE OF PLANT | SPACING BETWEEN ROWS | IN ROWS | BLOCKS | | | | | | | LENGTH OF ROTATION |
|---|---|---|---|---|---|---|---|---|---|---|
| LARGE DECIDUOUS TREES (A) | 5' | 18" | A-1: PLANT '93, THIN '96, HARVEST '98, COVER CR. '99, REPLANT 2000 | A-2: PLANT '94, THIN '97, HARVEST '99, COVER CR. 2000, REPLANT '01 | A-3: PLANT 1995, REPLANT 2002 | A-4: PLANT 1996, REPLANT 2003 | A-5: PLANT 1997, REPLANT 2004 | A-6: PLANT 1998, REPLANT 2005 | A-7: PLANT 1999, REPLANT 2006 | 7 YEARS |
| SMALL DECIDUOUS TREES (B) | 4' | 18" | B-1: PLANT '93, THIN '96, HARVEST '97, COVER CR. '98, REPLANT '99 | B-2: PLANT '94, THIN '97, HARVEST '98, COVER CR. '99, REPLANT 2000 | B-3: PLANT 1995, REPLANT 2001 | B-4: PLANT 1996, REPLANT 2002 | B-5: PLANT 1997, REPLANT 2003 | B-6: PLANT 1998, REPLANT 2004 | | 6 YEARS |
| EVERGREEN TREES (C) | 4' | 2' | C-1: PLANT '93, HARVEST '97, COVER CR. '98, REPLANT '99 | C-2: PLANT '94, HARVEST '98, COVER CR. '99, REPLANT 2000 | C-3: PLANT 1995, REPLANT 2001 | C-4: PLANT 1996, REPLANT 2002 | C-5: PLANT 1997, REPLANT 2003 | C-6: PLANT 1998, REPLANT 2004 | | 6 YEARS |
| EVERGREEN SHRUBS (D) | 4' | 2' | D-1: PLANT '93, HARVEST '96, COVER CR. '97, REPLANT '98 | D-2: PLANT '94, HARVEST '97, COVER CR. '98, REPLANT '99 | D-3: PLANT 1995, HARVEST '98, COVER CR. '99, REPLANT 2000 | D-4: PLANT 1996, HARVEST '99, COVER CR. 2000, REPLANT '01 | D-5: PLANT 1997, HARVEST 2000, COVER CR. '01, REPLANT '02 | | | 5 YEARS |
| LARGE DECIDUOUS SHRUBS (E) | 4' | 1' | E-1: PLANT 1993, HARVEST '95, COVER CR. '96, REPLANT '97 | E-2: PLANT 1994, HARVEST '96, COVER CR. '97, REPLANT '98 | E-3: PLANT 1995, HARVEST '97, COVER CR. '98, REPLANT '99 | E-4: PLANT 1996, HARVEST '98, COVER CR. '99, REPLANT 2000 | | | | 4 YEARS |
| MEDIUM DECIDUOUS SHRUBS (F) | 4' | 1' | F-1: PLANT 1993, HARVEST '94, COVER CR. '95, REPLANT '96 | F-2: PLANT 1994, HARVEST '95, COVER CR. '96, REPLANT '97 | F-3: PLANT 1995, HARVEST '96, COVER CR. '97, REPLANT '98 | | | | | 3 YEARS |
| SMALL DECIDUOUS SHRUBS (G) | 4' | 1' | G-1: PLANT 1993, HARVEST '94, COVER CR. '95, REPLANT '96 | G-2: PLANT 1994, HARVEST '95, COVER CR. '96, REPLANT '97 | G-3: PLANT 1995, HARVEST '96, COVER CR. '97, REPLANT '98 | | | | | 3 YEARS |
| VINES AND GROUND COVERS (H) | 4' | 1' | H-1: PLANT 1993, HARVEST '94, COVER CR. '95, REPLANT '96 | H-2: PLANT 1994, HARVEST '95, COVER CR. '96, REPLANT '97 | H-3: PLANT 1995, HARVEST '96, COVER CR. '97, REPLANT '98 | | | | | 3 YEARS |

remove 40%. This is a heavy loss of top soil each time a block of evergreens is removed with a ball of soil, and this condition must be corrected before the soil is again in good condition to produce crops.

The problems of good soil management within the field nursery are much the same as those existing in general farm crop production. Crop rotation has long been considered an essential practice in the successful production of farm crops. A well developed crop rotation plan for a nursery includes the use of sod, green manure, fall cover, winter cover, and companion crops alternated with or accompanying the nursery crops. It is difficult to build up organic matter in a depleted soil. One of the best methods is the use of sod crops. Experimental evidence would seem to indicate that even with the extensive use of green manure crops, it is barely possible to maintain the organic content of the soil.

While there is little precedent to follow, nurseries may be able to obtain the desired results by having the land in sod or green manure crops 30–40% of the time. The length of time that it takes to produce a salable crop of nursery stock and the method followed in digging the crop are factors influencing the rotation adopted. The objective of effective soil building practices is to maintain a favorable productivity balance. The following rotations are suggested, however they can be modified to fit the practices followed in individual nurseries. *NC* with 1–6 represents nursery crop and 1–6 years in field. *SG* means small grain seeded to grass and legumes. *GMWC* represents green manure and winter cover crops and *S* means sod crop.

1. Perennials or liners to mature in 1 year and dug from the field bareroot.
   *Rotation plan:* Repeat 4 or 5 years with nursery crop followed by sod crop (grass and legumes) for 2 years..
   NC–1, NC–1, (NC–1), SG, S

2. Shrubs to mature in 2 years and dug bareroot.
   *Rotation plan:* Repeat at 4 years with nursery crop for 2 years and sod crop (grass and legumes) for 2 years.
   NC–1, NC–2, SG, S–1

   *Rotation plan:* repeat at 7 years with nursery crop for 2 years, green manure and winter cover crops for 1 year, with nursery crop for 2 years and sod crop (grass and legumes) for 2 years.
   NC–1, NC–2, GMWC, NC–1, NC–2, SG, S–1

3. Shrubs or small trees in 3 years and dug bareroot.
   *Rotation plan:* Repeat at 5 years with nursery crop for 3 years and sod crop (grass and legumes) for 2 years.
   NC–1, NC–2, NC–3, SG, S–1

4. Small trees, large shrubs or small evergreens in 4 years and dug bareroot or with a ball.

*Rotation plan:* Repeat at 6 or 7 years with nursery crop for 4 years and sod crop (grass and legumes) for 2 or 3 years.
NC–1, NC–2, NC–3, NC–4, SG, S–1, (S–2)

5. Evergreens or trees in 5 years and dug with a ball.
   *Rotation plan:* Repeat at 8 years with nursery crop for 5 years and sod crop (grass and legumes) for 3 years.
   NC–1, NC–2, NC–3, NC–4, NC–5, SG, S–1, S–2

6. Evergreens or trees in 6 years and dug with a ball.
   *Rotation plan:* Repeat at 9 years with nursery crop for 6 years and sod crop (grass and legumes) for 3 years.
   NC–1, NC–2, NC–3, NC–4, NC–5, NC–6, SG, S–1, S–2

With the use of sod traveled aisles, it may be possible to keep a field in production for longer periods of time with consecutive nursery crops. After a crop has been harvested, the sod aisle would be plowed and planted and the old crop row would become the aisle planted to sod. This plan could be continued for an extended time period. The idea might not work if very heavy equipment were moved down the aisle rows too often. The heavy equipment could cause soil compaction and subsequently reduce crop growth. At this time, it is not known whether enough soil compaction would occur for this to be a real concern.

For some field operations, fall plowing may be more of an advantage than winter cover crop. With fall plowing the physical condition of the soil is improved with alternative freezing and thawing of the soil and allows for exposure of pests, earlier spring planting, and a lighter spring work load. Although many nurseries use the moldboard plow, some have found that the chisel plow gives better results. A chisel plow mixes the field debris or green manure crops all through the soil instead of depositing it in a layer at the bottom of the plowed layer. It is not recommended if the cover crop has long branches, because they may become tangled in the plow blades. For best results the plow should be pulled across the field a second time with the furrows at right angles to those of the first pass. A crawler tractor is recommended to avoid soil compaction. Final soil preparation should consist of disking or harrowing twice before planting. For additional information on soil management see Chapter 12.

### Fertilization

It is more convenient to apply fertilizer to planting sites well ahead of planting crops. Ideally, the needed mineral elements should be applied to cover crops either one or two years before planting crops. The result is a more uniform and desirable soil fertility at planting time. Any needed lime should be applied at least six months before planting crops. Fertilizer and lime needs for phosphorus, potassium, magnesium and calcium should be determined through soil test recommendations. Representative samples for each field should be collected and sent to a soil testing lab before planting and at least every other year. Regular soil testing and foliar analysis often detects nutritional problems before they become serious.

Unless requested, soil test procedures do not routinely analyze for nitrogen which is generally the most critical nutrient. Nitrogen fertilizers must be applied each year due to leaching and crop use. Generally, annual nitrogen rates per acre for field-grown crops should be: 200 to 250 lb for deciduous trees and shrubs, 150 to 200 lb for narrow-leaved evergreens, and 100 to 150 lb for broad-leaved evergreens. Higher rates are for lighter soils and lower rates used on heavier soils. The total amount of nitrogen applied should be divided into two or three applications annually. With two applications, early spring and late fall are recommended times of treatment, with approximately half the nitrogen per acre applied on each date. If three nitrogen applications are made, the third application would best be applied in early summer, with approximately one-third the total nitrogen per acre applied on each date. Weather conditions may modify timing and amounts of applications each year. Higher rates of nitrogen fertilization on newly planted crops may cause damage to plants during periods of drought stress.

To compute how much fertilizer to apply per acre, divide the pounds of nitrogen per acre needed by the percent analysis of the desired nutrient. For example, if you want to apply 100 lb of nitrogen per acre and you use ammonium nitrate, a 33–0–0 fertilizer formulation, divide 100 by 0.33, which gives you an application rate of about 300 lb. To adjust levels of phosphorus and potassium for woody ornamentals, the suggested rates in Tables 12–13 and 12–15 should be satisfactory.

Most field production nurseries broadcast inorganic, granular fertilizers using hopper drop or rotary type spreaders. However, in-row banded-fertilizer treatments are becoming more popular because of the increasing cost of fertilizer and the advantage of directing root growth. When band placement is utilized, application rates may be reduced to two-thirds with narrow row spacing and to half with wider rows. Banding of fertilizer is more practical during the first two years of growth for many nursery crops. Some growers employ the combination of fertilizer bands, in-row weed control, trickle irrigation, and sod aisles since it encourages more root development in the soil mass close to the plant's main stem that will be moved when the plant is dug.

### Transplanting Liners

The objective for field-grown crops is to provide optimum conditions for rapid vigorous growth by allowing sufficient space between plants, by providing adequate water and nutrition, and by preventing excessive competition from pests and weeds. Information on pest control strategies in propagation, small plant culture and production is discussed in Chapter 16. After the small plant culture stage, liners are ready to be moved into production fields in either fall or spring. Fall planting is preferred by many growers because some root growth will take place before ground temperatures drop below 45°F and because there is usually ample soil moisture for the liners to become established before spring shoot growth. A minimum of six weeks should be allowed for root development before the ground freezes. Fall transplants are better able to withstand the stresses of the hot and sunny summer days. For spring planting, liners should be transplanted after the ground thaws and as soon as the soil is workable. Be sure young liners are well established before the first critical summer; this cannot be overemphasized. If the transplant survives the first summer with a good root system, then the chances of the plant living to salable size are excellent. Only the best liners should be transplanted for field production. Field irrigation, if location permits, should be considered insurance against drought stress and poor growth instead of an added production expense.

Planting when the ground is too wet causes soil compaction and undesirable clods to form in clay soils, with subsequent poor root growth and development. A good way to get an indication of soil moisture is to pick up a handful and roll the soil out into a ribbon with your thumb and index finger. If the ribbon breaks into sections about an eighth to a fourth of an inch in length, then the soil is suitable for working. Loose, gritty or sandy soils can often be worked satisfactorily when slightly wet with no harmful effects.

Most nursery transplanters (Fig. 3–3) are modifications of the tobacco or potato transplanters and use the same basic principle of operation. Transplanters are designed to be pulled by a tractor to plant one or more rows at a time. The basic components are a plow which opens up the furrow, seats mounted behind and on either side of the plow, a table top mounted in front of the seats to hold the liners and V-shaped blades behind the plow to close the soil around the liner. To set a uniform distance between the liners, some planters use dripping water as gauge. The drip rate of the water is controlled by an adjustable value on the water tank. By adjusting the drip rate, the distance between the plants can be changed.

Puddling liners before transplanting them into the field prevents the roots of liners from drying out before they are planted. The procedure is as follows:

1. Dig a hole 3 ft across and 2 ft deep.
2. Fill the hole half full with water.
3. Add clay soil to the water until a slurry is formed, about the consistency of buttermilk. If disease control or root promoting chemicals are added to the bath a barrel should be used instead of the hole to prevent soil contamination.
4. Quick dip the root systems of the liners in the slurry.

5. Protect the roots with moist packing material, such as sphagnum moss and wrap with burlap or plastic.

Liners should be puddled just before they are to be transported to the field. Container-grown (flats or pots) liners should have the growing medium removed by dipping in water before puddling. This procedure allows the roots to be placed in direct contact with the field soil. If the growing medium is not removed, it will dry out faster than the surrounding soil. Water is not able to move by capillary pressure from the field soil into the growing medium, because of differences in texture and pore space. During planting it is important not to drag the liner on the bottom of the furrow, or an undesirable J-shaped root system will develop (Fig. 15–3). If a heavy soil is too wet during planting, the sides of the furrow may become glazed by the plow blade and inhibit root growth away from the furrow.

### Irrigation

Portable irrigation systems were once popular, however there use is limited because of the labor involved in moving the pipes from field to field. These overhead systems require high-capacity pumps to apply large volumes of water. Based on available evidence, trickle irrigation appears to be the system of the future for field production. There are many advantages, such as it is less expensive to install, and is a durable product that does not require constant movement and it requires less water than an overhead system. A major advantage of trickle is that plants can be dug during dry spells simply by running the system before digging. Trickle irrigation prevents drought stress rather than correcting it, by daily application of small amounts of water directly to the root zone in the row, and not wasting water between rows. Crops can also be fertilized through a trickle system by injecting fertilizer into the main line near the pump. The injection can be done either with a positive pressure injector or by using a by-pass method. This allows the grower to fertilize as needed by the crop with less labor.

Trickle irrigation is a simple system to install and can be easily performed by the grower. The water source can be a pond, stream, or well, however a well is preferable since it usually provides a cleaner supply of water. A 2-in. well with a 2-horsepower pump is adequate; whereas for conventional irrigation systems water flow is measured in gallons per minute, trickle irrigation is measured in gallons per hour. The main line that comes from the pump to the field is usually 2-in. black polyethylene or PVC pipe (Fig. 14–2). A time clock connected to a solenoid valve allows the system to run a specified length of time each day. To strain out any particles that might plug the irrigation system, a 100-mesh in-line screen filter should be connected on the pump side of the solenoid valve. The interval of irrigation time may be adjusted to satisfy the needs of different crops during the growing season. For large acreages, several solenoid valves attached to a zonal time clock will allow several fields to be run from the same pump in sequential order. For example, if there are 6 fields to run off one pump, the system could be run for 2 hours in the first field, then the zonal time clock would switch off the water on the first field and turn on the water to the second field for 2 hours, and so on. The 2-in. main line runs underground from the pump to the field and then runs along perpendicular to the crop rows. Risers are attached to the main line at each crop row and a one-half in. black polyethylene pipe runs from the riser down each row. One emitter or water outlet is placed by each plant.

There are several types of emitters that may be used. The least expensive is the microtube (Fig. 14–3) which is a very small piece of polyethylene pipe (0.025 in., 0.035 in. or 0.045 in. in diameter) that is inserted into the one-half in. line. The flow rate of the water is determined by the inside diameter of the microtube and by its length. Either one or two gallons per hour is desirable. With the microtube system, the length of tube must be varied as the one-half in. line changes grade (shortened uphill and lengthened downhill) to provide a uniform flow rate. Pressure compensating emitters are also available at a slightly higher cost but their installation eliminates the labor required in adjusting microtube lengths (Fig. 14–5). These emitters automatically adjust to changes in line pressure caused by grade changes and give a uniform flow rate throughout the field. The small diameter microtubes are more susceptible to rabbit chewing, disconnections from deer passing through the area, and clogging from algae growth.

### Root Pruning

The root systems of most tree and shrub crops growing under field production may spread 3 to 9 ft from the base of the plant. Since most bareroot or soil balls are dug from 12 to 24 in. in diameter, unless something is done to confine the root system, a considerable portion of the roots will be lost when the plant is dug. If root growth is not modified, the loss of the roots can have a severe shock upon the plants, which may even be fatal. Root pruning as practiced in nurseries is the cutting off of the distal parts of roots to stimulate lateral root formation closer to the main stem of the plant. It is not practical to individually root prune each plant in a nursery row. Therefore, growers will effect the same results by disking or plowing in the aisle row close to the plants. Root pruning is done in some nurseries with a U-shaped blade that is drawn under the plants in the row by a tractor (Fig. 1–3). This prunes basal roots and those that extend into the aisle, but not those in the row. Root pruning should be done in late summer or fall, at a time when top growth has ceased or is declining. The roots will continue to grow actively until the soil temperature drops below 45°F. Therefore, the root system can be pruned and new roots formed without the plant being stressed by top growth. New spring top growth can then adjust to the slightly restricted water intake capability of the pruned

**Figure 11–5** Trickle irrigation with in-line emitters.

root system. Root pruning is often done during the second year for rapidly growing shrubs, every 2–3 years for trees, and sometimes the summer before stock is to be dug.

There are two other methods being used to restrict root growth. Some growers are using the combination of fertilizer bands, in-row weed control, trickle irrigation and sod aisles to encourage more in-row root growth. Another approach being tested is the use of a root-control bag that is placed in the transplant hole and back filled with the field soil to plant the liner. There are advantages and disadvantages of this root control bag with a final verdict still to be made. The advantages include: less time and labor in digging; higher proportion of roots retained in the ball; forms a ball in sandy soils; and a longer postharvest life on retail lots without rewrapping. A few disadvantages are: the cost of the bag plus poly sheet for the bottom of the hole; more time required with planting; trickle irrigation may be needed in dry summers, because of limited soil volume for roots; and the bag must be removed when planted in the landscape. Further research and grower evaluations on more species, transplant establishment and survival, and growing methods are necessary to determine situations in which the root control bag may be used during production.

### Culture for Specific Types of Crops

Although all nursery crops require regular attention as far as moisture, nutrition, and pest control are concerned, each type has slightly different cultural requirements from the others. Transplanting requirements, spacing, appropriate pruning, soil type, pH needs, and length of time to reach marketable size are matters that must be managed for optimum growth.

Deciduous shade trees are usually lined out in the field as 1 or 2-year-old plants (seedlings, grafts, or cuttings) at an 18 in. spacing. About the third year the trees are dug bare root for market or replanted for growing on at a wider spacing. For those that will be grown on, final tree size and intermediate harvest are the primary considerations for in-row spacing. A general rule is to plant the trees 3 ft apart for each inch of anticipated trunk diameter. For example, trees to be sold at 2-in. diameter should be planted 6 ft apart in-row with about a 10-ft row spacing, depending on harvesting equipment. Generally, for 2-in. caliper trees sold balled and burlapped, in-row spacing is 5–6 ft, with 9–12 ft between rows. Trees to be harvested as bareroot stock are normally planted closer together, with less between–row space. After the first year, the leader should add about 18–24 in. or more of new growth each year for the faster growing deciduous shade trees, while slow growers will average 12–18 in. of new growth annually.

Some growers cut back tree liners in late winter to a 2-in. stub in order to force a straight trunk from vigorous sprout growth that flushes out. If some cut backs produce an excess of sucker growth, the dominant sprout should be kept for training and the excess suckers removed in late spring. This is a useful practice on species where it is difficult to obtain a straight trunk, such as oaks. Grafted or budded cultivars with stems that have a tendency to bend over from excessive top growth are tied to individual stakes to protect the bud sprout, to prevent wind breakage, and to assure straight trunks. Stakes should be confined to the lower portion of the stem, allowing the upper portion to sway in the wind. The stakes are driven into the soil on the prevailing wind side of the small trees so that the wind will not rub the tree against the stake and damage the bark. The support should be removed as soon as the tree has developed sufficient caliper to support the crown (Fig. 15–1). The supports are usually removed at the end of the second growing season.

The first dormant (late winter) pruning should include tying up crooked leaders, trimming very bent leaders back to upright buds, and shortening long side branches back to 10–12 in. The second winter pruning should induce symmetry in the plants by heading back long side branches to about 12–15 in. to produce a narrow, pyramidal crown with a central leader. Two-year transplants should not be too severely pruned in winter or the new flush can result in production of excessively long and soft tender shoots that will be susceptible to wind breakage and drought stress in summer. Two-year trees should also be limbed up about 12–18 in. above the ground. In late spring after bud break, soft trunk sprouts can be rubbed off easily in seconds. Low sprouts on the trunks provide two useful purposes and should not be removed too high on young trees. The low sprouts shade the trunk to reduce the chance of summer sunscald and the leaves manufacture food to increase trunk diameter.

Nursery pruning to direct the growth of young trees and to correct any structural weakness is very important if mature trees are to function as expected in the landscape. As the trees develop, excess side branches are removed so that those that are left are spaced about 12–18 in. apart. Branches selected for permanent scaffolds must have wide angles of attachment with the trunk for greatest strength. Radial branch distribution should allow five to seven main scaffolds to fill the circle of space around the trunk. With radial spacing, branches radiate from the trunk like spokes on a wheel. Because no one limb is directly over another they do not compete for light.

Dormant (late winter) pruning produces a more natural growth pattern, in contrast to summer pruning. Trees pruned in late winter make vigorous flushes of growth in spring that harden off before the insects that damage terminals have built up to summer population levels. A basic rule to follow in pruning young trees, is to concentrate heavy removal in winter and as light as possible in summer. Summer pruning may have a dwarfing effect by removing leaves that manufacture necessary food for growth in height and trunk caliper. Therefore, except for light shaping to shorten any disproportionately long branches, and of course to remove broken, injured or diseased wood, summer pruning should not be practiced. Deciduous shade trees such as birch, maples, and elms have a tendency to lose sap profusely if they are pruned in late winter. Pruning bleeders earlier in winter permits the fresh cuts to dry out and the ends of the sap ducts to shrivel before sap movement in spring.

The culture of deciduous flowering trees (cherry, crabapple, hawthorn, dogwood, redbud, *magnolia*, etc.) is similar to that of deciduous shade trees. Liners are field planted as 1- or 2-year-old seedlings, cuttings, or grafts. They are usually grown to marketable sizes at a spacing of 18 in. in the row and dug bareroot. Most upright (excurrent) types are pruned to a single leader, while spreading (decurrent) trees are allowed to develop as multi-stem specimens with several leaders. Branches within 3–4 ft of the ground on marketable size plants are removed early in the summer to allow wound healing before spring sale. Deciduous flowering trees are usually ready to market in 6 years or sooner.

Deciduous shrubs are lined out at 12–24 in. spacings as 1- or 2-year-old seedlings or cuttings. Many deciduous shrubs will produce much bushier growth with more canes and branching from the base, if they are pruned several times during field culture. Plants used for hedging, especially, need to be well branched at the base with a dense form. Shrub liners should be headed back about half their height during the first winter pruning. Fall transplants should be allowed to develop a root system before forcing vigorous spring growth. Further dormant trimming of laterals during the second and third year will benefit the appearance of many shrub types. The roots are pruned either in second or third year depending on plant type. Small to medium growing cultivars are usually ready to be harvested after three years in the field, while large growing cultivars are ready after four years (Table 11–3). Most deciduous shrubs are dug bareroot.

Narrow-leaved evergreen shrubs that are started as rooted cuttings, such as juniper, arborvitae, *Taxus* and *Chamaecyparis* are usually lined out on 2 or 3 ft spacings. Upright types may be pruned to maintain one leader, and laterals are often sheared several times to give dense, symmetrical growth. Crops are root pruned in the second and fourth years, and are dug either balled and burlapped or balled and potted after five years in the field. Spreaders are handled in a similar manner as upright narrow-leaved evergreen shrubs, except that they are not pruned to one leader. The pruning procedure for spreaders is to cut back some each year to produce a tight shape and to prevent spindly growth. To maintain healthy growth of lower branches cut back the longer branches that develop on the top so the lower branches will be exposed to light. Spreaders are root pruned in the third year and are dug either balled and burlapped or balled and potted after four or five years in the field.

Narrow-leaved evergreen trees, such as pine, spruce, and fir are usually lined out at 2–3 ft spacing as 2 or 3-year-old seedlings or grafts. Many species make only one rapid flush of growth in late spring. The first pruning occurs when new growth or elongated candles have almost reached their maximum length and the needles are still short, the tip of all candles (including the central leader) should be removed. This technique causes many new buds to form in the axils of the needles. The following spring's growth will be much more densely branched, bushy, and symmetrical. If you shorten the candles by more than a fourth, it merely reduces the tree size without producing any more lateral branching. Tip pruning is usually done until the plants reach 5–6 ft in height, then fertilizer rates are reduced to prevent excessively long internodes and unreachable branches. Narrow-leaved evergreens are grown in a protected area from winter winds that may cause browning of foliage. Evergreens also require a well-drained soil for optimum growth as well as a loam that contains sufficient clay to hold a soil ball at the time of harvest.

Broad-leaved evergreen shrubs (azalea, *Rhododendron*, holly, boxwood, *Pieris*, etc.) are usually lined out at 18–24 in. in the row as 1- or 2-year-old cuttings depending on species. Many broad-leaved evergreen shrubs develop a shallow, dense root system and prefer moisture retaining organic soils or mulching. These shrubs are grown in the same manner as narrow-leaved evergreen shrubs, except for the species that require an acid soil (see Table 12–1). This plant type is particularly susceptible to winter injury and must be grown with good windbreak protection. Shrubs are pruned to encourage dense growth, thus a careful shaping in late winter is usually sufficient. If flower buds remain on young plants and flowers are allowed to set seed, this will reduce vegetative growth. Therefore, pruning flowering species should include cutting off the flower buds on small plants to be reserved for future growth. If thinning of the crop is planned, with some plants to be sold and others to be grown on, pruning the reserve shrubs will direct digging to the salable plants. Broad-leaved evergreen shrubs are balled and usually marketed after 4–5 years in the field.

## CONTAINER-GROWN CROPS

In the nursery trade there is a distinction made between potted stock, container-grown stock, and containerized stock. *Potted stock* refers to seedlings, rooted cuttings, or recently grafted plants that are grown for a period of time in small pots before they are planted in containers or lined out in the field. *Container-grown stock* is grown in the container from a seedling, rooted cutting, or graft to salable size in a relatively small volume of growth medium. *Containerized stock* is a field-grown plant that is dug and put in a container to be sold.

### Plant Types for Container Culture

Many woody species of plants are successfully grown in nurseries, in containers, and possibly in the future nearly all woody species will be container-grown. Today it is estimated that 80–90% of the woody ornamental plants produced in warmer climates, like California, Florida, and Texas, are grown in containers, and this trend keeps increasing. The reasons for this success include: extension of sales and planting seasons; development of more attractive sales packages; easier transportability for the producer and consumer; greater control of environmental and cultural production factors; and more efficient use of production and sales areas. Other advantages as well as challenges are listed in Table 2–2.

Ideal plants for container culture are those with poorly developed root systems, which can be easily handled in containers, do not require expensive and extensive winter protection and can be produced to salable size in a minimum length of time. Generally any shallow-rooted plant, whether deciduous or evergreen, is best grown in containers. Many plants which can be grown in one part of the country cannot be grown in other places because they grow poorly in some environments. Plants should also be selected with the modified environment of the container in mind. Good quality yews are very difficult to produce as container-grown stock, so they are seldom attempted. Deciduous plants have not been found to be a problem. Growth forms are similar to field-grown plants if the containers are adequately spaced to allow for rapid growth. However, from a business point of view, it is not practical to grow deciduous plants in containers since they can be grown much more cheaply in the field. Certain types of plants respond well to container culture and they are more profitable to produce when grown in containers: broad-leaved evergreen shrubs, such as azalea, many *Rhododendron* cultivars, holly, boxwood, *Euonymus*, *Pyracantha*, and many tropical foliage species; and narrow-leaved evergreen shrubs, such as spreading and dwarf forms of juniper, pine, *Chamaecyparis*, spruce, fir, and hemlock.

### Production Schedule for Container-Grown Plants

The primary objective of a production schedule for container-grown plants is to grow high-quality plants for the most profit. A grower may lose sight of the profit motive in attempting to produce the best quality plants. Since container-grown plants represent a greater capital investment to produce than field-grown plants it becomes essential to reduce costs by producing the plant in as short a time period as possible. A grower should start with good-sized vigorous plants. While it is not good practice to stuff extra large field-grown plants into containers it is also not wise to put a 2-in. seedling or cutting into a five-gallon container. Nursery crops should be programmed so that the plants are of appropriate size and are vigorous when they are transplanted to the container. Stock to be container-grown is usually planted in early spring although recently some retail nurseries have begun planting large liners in early fall to guarantee a supply for early spring sales.

Generally, most types of nursery stock in one-gallon containers are grown for a period of two years, although some stock reaches marketable size in one year, depending on environmental influences. A few slow-growing

**Table 11–4** Average Production Time and Sizes of Container-Grown Nursery Crops for Different Plant Types Growing in Hardiness Zones 9 or 8 and 7 or 6

| Type of Plant | Plant Size | Container Size (gal)[a] | Production Time in Years by Hardiness Zone | |
|---|---|---|---|---|
| | | | 9 or 8 | 7 or 6 |
| Shade and flowering trees | Height:<br>12–15 in. | 1 | 1 | 1 |
| | 15–18 in. | 1 | 1 | 1 |
| | 18–24 in. | 1 | 1 | 1 |
| | 2–3 ft | 2 | 1.5 | 2 |
| | 3–4 ft | 2 | 2 | 3 |
| | 4–5 ft | 5 | 2.5 | 3 |
| | 5–6 ft | 5 | 3 | 4 |
| Small-growing deciduous shrubs | Height:<br>9–12 in. | 1 | 1 | 1 |
| | 12–15 in. | 1 | 1 | 2 |
| | 15–18 in. | 1 | 1 | 2 |
| | 18–24 in. | 2 | 2 | 3 |
| Medium-growing deciduous shrubs | Height:<br>12–15 in. | 2 | 1 | 2 |
| | 15–18 in. | 2 | 1 | 2 |
| | 18–24 in. | 2 | 1.5 | 2 |
| | 24–30 in. | 5 | 2 | 3 |
| Spreading narrow-leaved evergreen shrubs | Width:<br>6–9 in. | 1 | 0.5 | 1 |
| | 9–12 in. | 1 | 1 | 1 |
| | 12–15 in. | 2 | 1 | 2 |
| | 15–18 in. | 2 | 1.5 | 2 |
| | 18–24 in. | 5 | 2 | 3 |
| Dwarf or globe narrow-leaved evergreen shrubs | Height:<br>6–9 in. | 1 | | 1 |
| | 9–12 in. | 1 | 1 | 1 |
| | 12–15 in. | 2 | 1.5 | 2 |
| | 15–18 in. | 2 | 2 | 3 |
| | 18–24 in. | 5 | 3 | 4 |
| Narrow-leaved evergreen trees | Height:<br>12–15 in. | 1 | 1 | 2 |
| | 15–18 in. | 2 | 1 | 2 |
| | 18–24 in. | 2 | 1.5 | 3 |
| | 24–30 in. | 5 | 2 | 4 |
| | 30–36 in. | 5 | 2 | 4 |

(*continued*)

**Table 11–4** *(continued)*

| Type of Plant | Plant Size | Container Size (gal)[a] | Production Time in Years by Hardiness Zone | |
|---|---|---|---|---|
| | | | 9 or 8 | 7 or 6 |
| | Width: | | | |
| Spreading broad- | 9–12 in. | 1 | 1 | 1 |
| leaved evergreen shrubs | 12–15 in. | 2 | 1.5 | 2 |
| | 15–18 in. | 2 | 2 | 3 |
| | 18–24 in. | 5 | 2.5 | 3 |
| | Height: | | | |
| Dwarf or Globe | 9–12 in. | 1 | 1 | 1 |
| broad-leaved | 12–15 in. | 2 | 1 | 2 |
| evergreen shrubs | 15–18 in. | 2 | 1.5 | 3 |
| | 18–24 in. | 5 | 2 | 3 |
| | Height: | | | |
| Large-growing broad- | 12–15 in. | 1 | 1 | 1 |
| leaved evergreen | 15–18 in. | 2 | 1 | 2 |
| shrubs or small | 18–24 in. | 2 | 1.5 | 3 |
| trees | 24–30 in. | 5 | 2 | 3 |
| | 30–36 in. | 5 | 2 | 4 |

[a]American Association of Nurserymen trade designations and container specifications are as follows: 1 gal equals minimum of 5.5 in. across top and height of 6 in. or equivalent volume; 2 gal equals minimum of 7 in. across top and height of 7.5 in. or equivalent volume; 5 gal equals minimum of 9 in. across top and height of 10 in. or equivalent volume.

*Source:* Adapted from Stinson et al. (1971).

dwarf types may be grown for three or four years. Table 11–4 indicates the approximate years for production of different types of container-grown nursery crops in several container sizes.

The rule for proper spacing of container-grown plants is that the leaf tips of adjacent plants should just be touching. This spacing procedure results in compact growth of good quality as well as an efficient use of production space. Spacing too closely results in spindly growth and loss of the lower foliage. If you apply this spacing rule, most spring transplants can be placed pot tight or rim-to-rim for the first year of growth. This production technique shades and protects newly establishing roots in pots from hot summer rays of the sun until the top growth develops a canopy over the pot rim. At the beginning of the second year they are usually spaced as far apart as the crown diameter of the plants. This spacing may require three times the original space at the start of the second year. Many growers in cold climates provide for this expansion space by having extra wide aisles between the over wintering structures.

In planning the production of container-grown crops the following should be considered: a planting schedule, including kinds of plants, numbers needed, container sizes, and planting dates; total area required for each crop and all-weather surfaces for access to the plants; types and quantity of growing media and fertilizer program (see Chapter 13); building space, equipment, tools, irrigation system (see Chapter 14), and winter protection structures required (see Chapter 17); and labor for planting, moving, and cultural practices. The crop succession if fairly simple for one year crops, because each year one crop replaces another. Crops requiring two years will need about three times as much growing space the second year as they did the first year. Crops requiring three or four years usually remain at the second year spacing. A crop succession plan, with the space requirements drawn to scale should be worked out in advance of planting so that costly errors (under-or overestimates) will not be made.

### Site Preparation and Growing Surfaces

Site preparation should include provisions for adequate drainage, an efficient layout, freedom from weeds, year-round use and a suitable base. A good site for growing nursery crops in containers should be well drained in order to carry off large amounts of water in a short time during rainstorms or by overhead summer irrigation. Careful site planning can reduce costs. It should include an efficient layout of growing areas and roadways for maximum use of machinery. Roadways should be constructed to carry heavily loaded trailer trucks with sufficient area allowed at all turns for the trucks to be maneuvered easily. Where container stock is being handled in large quantities with pallets and forklifts or wagons and tractors, it has been found worthwhile to pave those high-traffic areas with asphalt.

The base or growing surface should be relatively inexpensive to install and maintain. The site should be free from weeds and should be one which permits working year-round. Several kinds of materials have been used for bases for container plants in different parts of the country. The best kind for a particular location usually depends upon cost and availability. Those most commonly used include black plastic, fabric weed barrier, crushed stone or asphalt. The least expensive solution is to spread black polyethylene sheets over a well-drained surface. Before black plastic is laid down in the nursery, the area should be carefully graded, smoothed, and firmed so the center of the bed is raised with a 2% crown above the edges for beds 100 ft wide (see Fig. 14–4). This grading will prevent puddling of water around containers and aid in rapid movement of water from the container bed. Loss of plants may result from water standing in low places on the plastic if the bed is not graded properly for good drainage. Some containers are manufactured with drainage holes in the bottom or very close to the bottom. These smooth bottom pots may cause problems on a plastic surface or gravel base. This is particularly true for plants susceptible to root rot. An herbicide, such as dichlobenil (Casoron), may be applied to the soil before the film is put in place. When the containers are placed on the film, weeds will not grow under the plastic, roots stay in the pots and mud is eliminated. Black plastic will disintegrate and must be replaced af-

**Figure 11-6** Container site with crushed stone over the fabric weed barrier.

ter each crop. Another, but more expensive solution is to put down 6 in. of crushed stone (one-half to three-quarters in. diameter) over the black plastic or fabric weed barrier and place the containers on the stone (Fig. 11-6). This scheme has all of the advantages of film, plus the additional benefit of being more permanent. The material is more expensive than sheets of black plastic, but it is more durable and allows for better drainage.

### Containerizing Nursery Crops

Nursery stock can be planted in one to five-gallon containers by labor and machines using rooted cuttings, one-year-old seedlings, dormant unrooted cuttings, dormant grafts or plants previously grown in smaller pots. Some nurseries propagate their own plants, while others prefer to purchase liners. Planting is usually done in the late winter or spring as soon as shipments begin to open up areas for the newly potted plants. The plants should be placed in the center of the container, at the depth at which they originally grew (usually the root collar) and the growing medium placed around the roots to assure good contact. The container is filled to within one-half to one in. (depending on pot size) of the rim to leave a space for water accumulation during irrigation. Most nurseries (small or large) devise an assembly line system with machines and labor so that the planting operation can be done efficiently. Usually there are separate crews or individuals responsible for supplying plants and pots, filling pots, placing plants in pots, loading the planted plants, and moving them to the growing area where they are set in place. A crew of five workers is usually able to plant, place and hand water at the rate of 7000 to 12,000 per day provided the procedure is well planned by management. The same crew can do up to 20,000 per day with a semi-automatic potting machine once they become familiar with the procedures. A plan that works well in small nursery operations is to place the filled containers on a flatbed truck or wagon, have two workers punching holes, two workers planting and placing the plants into the beds while one worker waters. The worker that is watering will need to stop periodically and move the truck or wagon down the aisle between two beds. A modification of this procedure would be to have the containers already filled and properly spaced in the growing area. This procedure is used for larger container sizes. Each worker performing physically demanding jobs should be rotated frequently for the comfort of the worker and maximum efficiency of the operation.

### Pruning Container–Grown Plants

Pruning and shearing practices are the same for both a finished plant in a container and field-grown crops. Because of their usually faster growth rate when container grown, all of the various types of plants should be sheared and formed more frequently in container culture. It is normally necessary to cut back leaders three or four times each growing season. If prostrate forms are not spaced adequately and pruned regularly, they will have a tendency to grow with a more upright habit and detract from the salable form.

There are several objectives of pruning container-grown nursery stock. One objective is to get as large a plant as possible, as quickly as possible, and at the same time, obtain a healthy plant with a form or shape that will be marketable. Usually this means a plant that is dense, compact, symmetrical, healthy, and vigorous, and a plant which is produced and sold at a profit. Another important objective of pruning is to produce a plant that transplants successfully, whether planted by a landscape contractor or homeowner. A good balance between root and shoot growth in container culture is vital to the successful establishment of a plant when it is planted in the landscape.

Definite rules for pruning ornamental plants in a nursery are difficult to give because plants vary widely in habit of growth. Pruning is both a dwarfing (in summer) and an invigorating (in winter) cultural practice, depending on how and when the heading-back or thinning-out pruning is done. Usually a larger plant can be produced faster with minimum pruning, as severe pruning produces a smaller but more dense plant. The natural growth habit of a plant indicates the pruning needed to shape the plant. Rounding off (primary sides and tops without regard to natural form) is a poor method of pruning. The commercial grower should use a combination system of pruning, which includes both heading-back terminals and thinning-out branches.

This consists of heading back to increase density of thin plants, thinning areas of an otherwise dense plant, and thinning of dense growth to produce a plant that is taller and wider than it should be for its container size. Thinning may be used to increase size of flowers and fruit by reducing the number of flowering branches after buds have developed. This is accomplished by increasing the amount of water and nutrients available for flower buds left on the plant. Heading-back plants before flower buds are set increases the number of branches and flowers, but will usually reduce flower and fruit size.

Effective pruning of nursery plants begins with selection of the cuttings as well as pruning practiced early in the life of plants propagated from cuttings or seedlings. A compact container-grown plant can be produced more easily from large 4–6 in. cuttings than from smaller 2–3 in. cuttings. Smaller cuttings sometimes root faster, but take longer to produce plants to the size where heading back is done to increase density of the potted plants. However, a 4–6 in. cutting usually has enough leaves to produce good rooting, and because of this will reach the stage sooner where pruning is begun to produce well branched plants. When transplanting rooted cuttings, excessively long roots should be cut back. This will encourage branching and growth of new roots, and reduce development of kinked, circling, and girdling roots. Cuttings and seedlings of species trained as shrubs should be pruned early in small plant culture and frequently to produce many breaks (lateral branches) low on the main stem to encourage a good production and distribution of canes for scaffold branches.

The grower should carefully manage the pruning procedures because they are labor intensive and expensive. Much less time is required to prune small plants than larger ones. The main scaffold branches should be formed early so later growth will be well distributed over the plant and more easily controlled. Young plants should be pruned as often as needed to produce the branching necessary for the best quality plant. The number of times pruning will be required from first potting until plants are sold will vary depending on several factors: natural habit of plant species or cultivar; fertilization level; time in nursery production; size of container in balance with top growth; local conditions as it affects length of growing season; and time of year plants are potted. A combination of heading back and thinning should be practiced on older plants to produce compact growth in the natural shape of the plant rather than to indiscriminately shear plants regardless of growth habit, density, or size.

## HARVESTING METHODS

Usually nursery crop schedules are planned to produce marketable-size plants for late winter shipments to meet the demand for early spring sales. Traditionally, the selling of nursery stock in the fall has been minimal. However in recent years, fall nursery stock sales have increased due in part to the efforts of the Garden Council with their national marketing campaigns and the landscape industry's desire to improve fall sales. If more nursery stock could be sold in the fall season, fewer plants would need to be held in winter storage.

### Bareroot Digging and Handling

Deciduous trees and shrubs are dug in the fall when top growth slows and leaves drop, indicating the first signs of dormancy. If deciduous plants are dug before reaching this dormant stage, they may grow very poorly when replanted the same fall or the following spring. A tractor-drawn U-blade is used for undercutting and lifting the plants from the row. Some nurseries use a modified potato digger for digging smaller sizes, such as rose bushes. Once the plants are dug they may be trimmed, graded, and bunched in the field or stacked in covered wagons with roots protected from drying out and transported to cold or common storage facilities. More often, the plants are quickly moved to storage to prevent drying; and the trimming, grading, labeling, and packaging to fill orders is done during the winter months when little outdoor work can be done. Trimming is done to remove dead, diseased, and broken roots and branches. Also, those trees and shrubs to be marketed as containerized stock can be potted using a container-growing medium.

Cold or common storage of bareroot nursery stock has several advantages for the nursery operation. Fall digging helps to spread the work load of preparing stock for sale over the winter months. It is more convenient for labor to label, grade, and bundle plants for rapid handling in the busy spring shipping season. Cold storage extends the period in the spring when nursery stock can be safely kept bareroot, thus extending the sales period. In the northern and midwestern United States, the spring season is short and it is important that nurseries shipping into those regions have dormant plant materials to ship when planting time arrives. Cold storage also results in minimum losses from winter weather and animals, plus less digging in the wet, early spring conditions.

Several types of storage are used for overwintering of bareroot nursery stock (see Chapter 17). The preferred modern method of storing bareroot stock is refrigerated storage with temperatures maintained between 32 and 38°F. An advantage of this system is that the low temperatures enable a grower to better control growth of parasitic and saprophytic fungi. Many of the damaging fungi will grow well at temperatures below those at which woody plants break dormancy. Treating plants with fungicides will also help to control fungi. A constant concern with overwinter storage is drying out of the root system. Buildings should be moisture tight with the roots packed in a moist packing material. Shingletow is a commonly used packing material for roots. Artificial humidification devices designed to maintain humidity near 95% within the entire storage area provide automated environmental control.

Once a building is filled with nursery stock, the mass of the plants affects the distribution of the air, so that some areas are colder or damper than others. These variations can be checked by placing high/low thermometers at several levels and locations in the building. Sensitive plants should be placed in the best spots (more constant temperature and humidity), and those which are easily stored can be placed in the poorer locations. In any case, walkways must be arranged to allow both for easy access to the stock and for good air circulation. Plants with very dense and fibrous root systems are especially susceptible to decay in storage. These types should be put in spots with better air flow and semi-evergreen types should be located where they can be easily and routinely inspected. When bareroot plants are sold, moist packing material should be provided around the roots and then the roots should be wrapped with a moist-retaining material, such as plastic. Those trees and shrubs to be marketed as bareroot and processed ball have the roots packed with an organic planting medium and secured firmly with burlap, just before delivery.

### Digging and Handling Balled Stock

Generally the larger sizes of deciduous types and all evergreen types of field-grown nursery stock are dug as a balled and burlapped, balled and potted, or balled and bagged. Many people assume that all trees are now dug with mechanical diggers, which is not true. It is still often more efficient and desirable to dig large orders of small trees bareroot or small quantities balled and burlapped by hand. Most large shade trees of 3 in. caliper and above are dug mechanically.

Use of mechanical diggers increases the number of plants that can be dug in a day. Some growers use wire baskets with a burlap lining to drop the root balls in once the plants are dug. The wire baskets can be ordered in many sizes and can be tightened around the ball with hooks. The use of wire baskets has caused some concerns about root girdling in the landscape. Research evidence seems to indicate that removing wire baskets at planting time is not necessary to assure growth and survival of large tree roots. However, it is recommended that you should remove any rope across the top of the ball, and bend back or remove the basket loops. There are, of course, many other types of containers available that can be used in conjunction with mechanical diggers, such as the balled and bagged system that was previously mentioned. It is important to dig the proper size ball for a particular size plant. The American Association of Nurserymen (AAN) has designated certain minimum specifications (see Chapter 8).

A relatively new method of handling field-grown nursery stock that has become popular in the last few years is balled and potted digging. This means digging plants with a ball of earth and then potting the plants immediately into a container. This technique allows plants to be dug practically year round, giving the flexibility of root balls without the precise digging and wrapping involved with balling and burlapping. These plants are usually dug in early spring, potted and sold as soon as the roots become established in the container; or they may be dug in August and September after the top growth has ceased but while the roots are still actively growing (soil temperature above 45°F). Balled and potted plants usually adjust to their container in four to six weeks and are ready to be sold, or held over in polyethylene structures for an early spring market. Field potting is also feasible during the hot summer months after plants have made their initial flush of growth. These plants should be dug early in the morning, potted, and moved to a holding area quickly so that the root system does not dry out. The holding area should be shady and have an overhead sprinkler irrigation system. The plants should be held in this area until sufficient root regeneration occurs and leaves remain in a turgid condition.

### Handling Container-Grown Stock

Container-grown nursery stock is ready to be sold when it has reached an appropriate size for the container. Table 11–4 indicates the usual time it takes to grow different types of stock to salable size. Sorting the stock into groups by grade is a time consuming operation. Each plant must be examined and labeled. A limitation on container-grown stock is that it cannot be carried through an additional year in the same container. If plants are held too long in the same container, the root system will become pot bound (will have developed into a heavy tight spiral around the inside wall and bottom of the container). When the plants are finally sold and planted, the root growth into the soil surrounding that spiral mass will be very slow to develop if at all.

The *Minnesota-in-ground container production system* was developed in 1981 to overcome three serious problems associated with traditional container-growing methods: root circling in the container; plant stability in the wind; and winter injury of roots. The system was designed for tree production and has some unique features. A sturdy plastic container is buried in the ground to its top. Drainage holes 2 in. from the bottom create a reservoir for water pruning the roots by lack of oxygen. A 3 in. layer of gravel is placed in the bottom of the container to support the growing medium above the standing water. A fiber mat is placed on top of the gravel to prevent the growing medium from settling into the water-saturated gravel bed. An open-bottom liner is placed inside the buried container to hold the growing medium and to plant the tree liner. Trickle irrigation may be used to supply and manage the water needs of the tree. Field test results are limited, but the potential merits of this in-ground container system continue to be encouraging.

During the past few years, growers and researchers have developed several other possible solutions to the problems associated with container tree production. The *Environmentally Friendly Container* (EFC) features an unconventional placement of drain holes. The EFC plastic containers have holes a few inches up the side rather than at the bottom, which creates a water reservoir at the base. The reported benefits include increased growth; reduced blow-over from increased weight; reduced watering and runoff; elimination of rooting out through drain holes; less maintenance of interior plants; and indications of controlling waterborne pathogens. The EFC containers have been used both in-ground and above-ground as well as the pot-in-pot concept to increase the water reservoir and reduce heat stress. The pot-in-pot technique involves sinking a permanent container into the ground and then placing another container, which holds the tree, inside the buried one. The double-container system provides insulation from temperature extremes, prevents blow-over and simplifies harvesting. The pot-in-pot method has gained a strong following by many growers (Fig. 11–7). Another alternative to the conventional plastic container is the *Soil Sock*. A wire basket supports a foam rubber liner with a plastic bottom which then sits on top of the ground. This approach which is a substitute for burlap insulates the root system from high temperatures in addition to air-pruning. The *Poly Jacket* is another innovative, unconventional container which is available in two versions: the Water Saver and the Insulator. Each consists of an inverted and truncated plastic cone that fastens into one of two bases. The outer Insulator cone elevates the inner container above the base, providing some protection from extreme temperatures. The Water Saver allows the inner container to sit in an inch of standing water in the base. The reported benefits of this cone-shaped container insert system include insulation, water conservation and stability. The price which is associated with any container system is a primary concern of growers. Of course, all container prices will have to be measured against the advantages before growers can gain an accurate figure of how much these and other innovative containers actually cost.

Most container-grown nursery plants are sold in early spring. Actually, both container-grown and balled stock can be successfully planted from early spring to late fall, but most customers prefer to plant in the spring. This planting tradition came about because deciduous field stock is usually transplanted at these times.

### Postharvest Care of Nursery Plants

Considerable effort by nursery operations is given in production, as previously mentioned, and in the postharvest storage and shipping practices (see Chapters 10 and 17) to provide the best possible care for nursery stock. Many times this special handling is negated by insufficient care in the garden center or improper planting in the landscape. Growers should inform retailers and customers about proper care and landscape management practices. Many growers are using care tags on every plant species offered for sale. Cooperative Extension Service bulletins are available for retailers to provide their customers with instructions on planting, watering, fertilizing, pruning, and pest control. This service costs little, and the potential benefits are great for our industry.

**Figure 11-7** Container plants using the pot-in-pot method.

## SUMMARY

Nursery crop schedules begin with a market analysis to determine production quotas for different types of ornamental landscape plants. Once a production quota has been established to meet market demands, propagation by seed, cuttage, and/or graftage starts the systemic production practices for liners in small plant culture that will be planted either as field-grown crops or container-grown crops in order to meet production quotas. Nursery growers must satisfy the cultural requirements of each crop for optimum growth of quality plants, which is the overall objective of the nursery.

## REFERENCES

BEESON, R. C. 1991. Scheduling woody plants for production and harvest. HortTechnology 1(1):30–36.

BEESON, R. C. and E. F. GILMAN. 1992. Water Stress and Osmotic adjustment during post-digging acclimatization of Quercus virginiana produced in fabric containers. Journal of Environmental Horticulture 10(4):208–214.

CHADWICK, L. C. 1953. Soils, sod, green manure, winter cover and companion crops and fertilizers for nursery stock production. Ohio Nursery Notes 22(5&6).

CHAPMAN, D. J. 1983. Cutting propagation for shade tree cultivars encourages development of regional plants. Am Nurseryman 158(4):39–44.

CHONG, C., G. P. LUMIS and R. A. CLINE. 1991. Shade tree growth and nutritional status as influenced by fabric container and trickle fertigation. Journal of Environmental Horticulture 9(4):187–191.

CHONG, G., G. P. LUMIS and R. A. CLINE. 1989. Effects of fabric containers. Am. Nurseryman 170(11):51–55.

COOK, T. and J. L. GREEN. 1985. Many grasses available for nursery aisles and plant protection. Am. Nurseryman 161(1):89–96.

DICKEY, R. D., E. W. MCELWEE, C. A. CONOVER, and J. N. JOINER. 1978. Container growing of woody ornamental nursery plants in Florida. Florida AES Bulletin 793.

FEUCHT, J. R. 1986. Wire baskets can be slow killers of trees. Am. Nurseryman 163(6):156–159.

FLEMER, W. F., III. 1981. How and when to prune nursery stock. Am. Nurseryman 153(8):11–132.

GILLIAM, C. H. and E. M. SMITH. 1980. Fertilization of container-grown nursery stock. Ohio CES Bulletin 658.

GILMAN, E. F. and R. C. BEESON. 1990. Producing and transplanting trees in fabric containers. Nursery Digest 24(9):21–22.

HENDERSON-COLE and D. L. HENSLEY. 1992. Influence of field-grown fabric containers and various soil amendments on the growth of green ash. Journal of Environmental Horticulture 10(4):218–221.

INGRAM, D. L., U. YADAV and C. A. NEAL. 1987. Do fabric containers restrict root growth in the deep south? Am. Nurseryman 166(6):91–96.

KENNEDY, L. W. and E. M. SMITH. 1981. Care of nursery stock in retail outlets. Ohio CES Bulletins 562.

LUMIS, G. P. 1990. Wire baskets: a further look. Am. Nurseryman 172(4):128–131.

MARTIN, C. W. and D. J. CHAPMAN. 1985. Softwood cuttage can be an easy and useful propagation method. Am. Nurseryman 161(11): 37–39.

MCGUIRE, J. J. 1972. Growing ornamental plants in containers: a handbook for the nurseryman. Rhode Island CES Bulletin 197.

MOLLER, G. M. 1985. How one Oregon grower produces trees from softwood cuttings. Am. Nurseryman 16(5):68–69.

PELLET, H. 1983. An update on the Minnesota System of container production. Am. Nurseryman 157(1):95–101.

PETERSON, C. and R. HEATLEY. 1989. Crabapples—a selection guide. Michigan CES Bulletin E-2177.

PETERSON, C. and R. HEATLEY. 1986. Planting and care of ornamental landscape plants. Michigan CES Bulletin E-1947.

PETERSON, C. and R. HEATLEY. 1986. Selecting ornamental plants. Michigan CES Bulletin E-1936.

PETERSON, C., R. HEATLEY, G. ADAMS, D. SMITLEY, and D. ROBERTS. 1987. Diagnosing problems of ornamental landscape plants. Michigan CES Bulletin E-2024.

PONDER, H., C. GILLIAM and R. L. SHUMACK. 1983. Starting and operating a field shade tree nursery. Alabama CES Circular ANR-235.

REIGER, K. 1988. The bag way. Am. Nurseryman 168(10):117–118.

REIGER, K. 1988. Taking off the bag. Am. Nurseryman 167(3):99–101.

REIGER, R. and C. E. WHITCOMB. 1983. Growers can now confine roots to in-field containers. Am. Nurseryman 158(8):31–34.

SMEAL, P. L. and J. S. COARTNEY. 1985. Starting a nursery business in Virginia. Virginia CES Publication 430-015.

SMITH, E. M. 1986. Fertilizing landscape and field-grown nursery crops. Ohio CES Bulletin 650.

STINSON, R. F., D. R. MCCLAY, and G. Z. STEVENS. 1971. Nursery production—a teacher's manual. Pennsylvania AES Teacher Education Series, 12(45).

TILT, K. 1992. Growing solutions. Am. Nurseryman 176(11):62–65.

YAWNEY, H. W. 1984. How to root and overwinter sugar maple cuttings. Am. Nurseryman 160(8):95–102.

## SUGGESTED READING

BLUHN, W. L. and J. L. GREEN. 1979. Growing nursery stock—is it for me? Oregon CES Manual 5.

DIRR, M. A. and C. W. HEUSER Jr. 1987. The reference manual of woody plant propagation. Varsity Press, Inc., Athens, Georgia.

DURYEA, M. L. and T. D. LANDIS. 1984. Forest nursery manual: production of bareroot seedlings. Martinus Nijhoff/Dr. W. Junk Publishers, Hingham, Massachusetts.

HARTMANN, H. T., D. E. KESTER, and F. T. DAVIES. 1990. 5th ed. Plant Propagation Principles and Practices. Prentice-Hall, Inc. Englewood Cliffs, N.J.

HEUSER, C. W., Jr. and R. F. STINSON. 1989. Nursery production. Pennsylvania State University, PA.

INGRAM, D. L., J. T. MIDCAP, and D. L. GUNTER. 1980. Starting a wholesale nursery business. Florida CES Circular 409A.

MACDONALD, B. 1986. Practical woody plant propagation for nursery growers. Timber Press, Portland, Oregon.

SCHOPMEYER, C. S. 1974. Seeds of woody plants in the United States. USDA Agricultural Handbook 450. Superintendent of Documents, Washington, D.C.

STANLEY, J. and A. TOOGOOD. 1981. The modern nurseryman. Faber and Faber Ltd., London.

WELCH, W. C. 1974. Entering the nursery or greenhouse business. Texas CES Bulletin L-1221.

WHITCOMB, C. E. 1989. Production of landscape plants. Lacebark Publications, Stillwater, Oklahoma.

WHITCOMB, C. E. 1989. Plant production in containers. Lacebark Publications, Stillwater, Oklahoma.

# Chapter 12
# Soil and Nutrition Management for Field-Grown Plants

Soil is the field-production nurseryman's number one asset, since it is from the soil that the essential mineral elements and water are obtained for plant growth and development. The soil also provides a medium of support for the plants and is the home for billions of microorganisms that play a vital role in changing the chemical and physical properties of the soil into an ecosystem capable of supporting plant growth. Therefore, it is imperative for a nurseryman to have an appreciation and understanding of this complex system since his livelihood is dependent upon it.

A nurseryman should know (1) the essential mineral elements—how they affect plant growth, their deficiency symptoms, and methods for preventing or correcting deficiencies; (2) the role that soil reaction (pH) plays in the availability of the various mineral elements and ultimately in the growth of plants; (3) the concept of nutrient-element balance and how nutrient-element balance affects the growth of plants; (4) how soils and plants are tested for the various elements; and (5) how to interpret the results of the tests as they relate to the particular situation. To fertilize effectively, a nurseryman should also have a knowledge of cation-exchange capacity, fertilizers, soluble salts, the importance of maintaining soil structure, and the organic matter content of soils.

Although there is no unanimity in defining soil, it is commonly thought of as that portion of the earth's surface which has been derived from rock and in some cases organic remains and with which living organisms are usually associated. Rocks that have weathered are broken down by the processes of disintegration and decomposition into smaller particles having a changed physical and chemical state capable of supporting the growth of plants when supplied with water in the proper ambient atmosphere. Soil is the product of the rocks from which it was derived, but is also dependent upon the length of time and the intensity of the chemical, physical, and biological forces that have acted upon it. The soil, in turn, is the source of the essential mineral elements for plant growth.

## ESSENTIAL ELEMENTS

The essential mineral elements, often referred to as plant nutrients, may be divided into two groups. The major or *macronutrients* include the elements nitrogen, phosphorus, potassium, calcium, magnesium, and sulfur. Nitrogen or potassium are most commonly deficient in soils of low fertility and commonly need to be added to nursery soils. Under normal conditions, phosphorus, calcium, magnesium, and sulfur are in ample supply in most agricultural soils and therefore seldom limit the growth of woody species.

The second group is called the *micronutrients*, since they are needed in very small quantities. They are also known as the trace or minor elements. They include boron, copper, iron, manganese, molybdenum, zinc, and chlorine. It should be pointed out that although they are needed in only trace or micro quantities, they each perform an essential function in plant growth and development which is not minor.

The function of each of these elements in plant growth and its deficiency symptoms are discussed briefly. For more detailed information, reference should be made to a modern textbook on plant physiology.

### Macroelements

*Nitrogen* (N), as a constituent of protein, is involved in all the physiological processes taking place in plants. A deficiency of nitrogen is expressed in woody plants as a decrease in vigor and a light green to a yellowing of the foliage; the older leaves express the symptoms first. Under a prolonged deficiency, the leaves scorch and drop off. An excess of nitrogen can result in excessive growth and a decreased flowering and fruiting. An excess of nitrogen may also predispose plants to various pathological and physiological disorders, such as fireblight and soft, weak growth.

*Phosphorus* (P) is needed for root development, flowering, and fruit formation. It is found in large quantities in meristematic tissue and is essential for cell division. A phosphorus deficiency ultimately results in stunted plants. Early indications of inadequate phosphorus within many species of plants are the development of a bronze or purple coloration of the petioles on the underside of the leaves, followed by a yellowing of the leaves, particularly at the time of flowering and fruiting. However, phosphorus deficiency is seldom observed in woody perennial plants growing in a field-production nursery or in the landscape. Apparently, the roots, which penetrate throughout a vast volume of soil, are able to absorb enough phosphorus to supply the plant's need.

*Potassium* (K), although not an integral part of the plant tissue, is important for plants. It modifies the absorption of other nutrient elements, influences the carbohydrate-nitrogen relationship, and is thought to influence the absorption and utilization of water, which in turn affects the drought and possibly the cold-temperature resistance of plants. A lack of potassium in broad-leaved plants is first expressed by a marginal yellowing of the older leaves, followed by scorching and leaf drop. In needle-leaved plants, an apical brown tip is separated from a green basal portion by a yellow band. There is also a decrease in the number of years that the needles persist on needled-evergreen plants.

*Calcium* (Ca) is one of the primary elements in the development of woody plants. It is a constituent of the cell walls; it modifies the permeability of membranes and is important for development of roots. Since calcium is relatively immobile within the plant, deficiency symptoms are exhibited first in the apical portions. Although a deficiency is not too common in woody plants, it is manifested by death of the terminal portions, yellowing and necrosis of the adjacent young leaves, plus severe distortion; margins are ragged and often rolled. This is more commonly associated with seedlings than with mature plants.

*Magnesium* (Mg) is an integral part of chlorophyll—the green pigment in plants—making it essential for photosynthesis. Also, certain enzyme systems, and respiration, do not function properly at low magnesium levels. Some form of chlorosis in older leaves is associated with a magnesium deficiency, but the expression varies considerably with the species. It is reported that dead areas developing suddenly between the veins are an indication of an inadequate supply of magnesium. In advanced stages of magnesium deficiency, shoots defoliate and become devoid of leaves except for a few at the tip.

*Sulfur* (S) is a constituent of protein and various volatile compounds. When sulfur is deficient, plants are stunted and the leaves are light green or yellow, starting with the young leaves and progressing to the older leaves. Growth is restricted and stems are thin but remain erect. However, sulfur deficiency has not been a problem in the production of nursery crops. Perhaps this is due to its presence in most complete fertilizers as a contaminant and in various forms of nitrogen, phosphorus, and potassium salts that are used in the production of nursery crops. It is also an air pollutant in industrial areas.

### Microelements

*Iron* (Fe) is a catalyst in chlorophyll formation and for oxidation-reduction reactions. Its availability in the soil decreases with high pH, high phosphates, or in high concentrations of heavy metals or carbonates. Young leaves exhibit an interveinal chlorosis with the veins remaining green. Woody perennials exhibit dieback of branches if exposed to iron deficiency for extended periods of time.

*Manganese* (Mn) is needed for assimilation of carbon dioxide in nitrogen metabolism and for the formation of organic acids and carotene. It may be deficient in soils of high pH or if large quantities of calcareous material have been used as a soil amendment. The deficiency symptoms are similar to those for iron. Manganese deficiency has been reported for red, sugar, and Norway maple, and it probably occurs on other woody species. Manganese toxicity has been observed in some woody species (apple, holly). Early symptoms of Mn toxicity are chlorotic leaves, premature defoliation, and suppressed growth with smooth, raised pimples (measles) underlain by small dark-brown spots in the young bark of some species. Later the pimples develop sunken areas and the bark begins to crack. In advanced stages, the bark becomes very rough, cracked, and scaly. Manganese toxicity appears to be cultivar-specific and is associated with acid soils, anaerobic conditions, and with some steam-sterilized soils.

*Zinc* (Zn) functions in cell elongation and in seed development. Zinc deficiency, although not too common in woody ornamentals, is manifested by older leaves having a yellow to bronze color. The leaves are relatively narrow with a wavy margin and rosetted due to reduced internodes. Dieback of shoots can occur where the deficiency is acute.

*Boron* (B) aids in proper root development, flowering, and fruiting and is necessary for nitrogen and carbohydrate metabolism. The application of excess lime may induce boron deficiency, which is more common in sandy soils than in clays. Death of the growing points, brittleness and dieback of the stems, combined with scorched, curled, and often rosetted leaves are symptoms sometimes associated with boron deficiency in field-production nurseries.

*Copper* (Cu) is a catalyst in respiration and is needed for carbohydrate and protein metabolism and in seed formation. Although copper deficiency is not too common in woody perennials, it has been reported in young fruit trees and in azalea plants growing for prolonged periods in containers. In fruit trees, the deficiency is expressed by a withering and death of young shoots in the late spring or early summer. In azaleas the new leaves are smaller than normal and soon become scorched; the early symptoms resemble potassium deficiency or frost damage.

*Molybdenum* (Mo) is needed for protein synthesis, but is needed in such minute quantities that it seldom limits growth of woody plants.

## SOIL REACTION

The reaction of a soil (pH) is an indication or a measure of the degree of acidity or alkalinity of a soil. Soil reaction can be stated or measured in a number of ways. It is common to speak of a soil as being slightly acid, moderately acid, or very acid; or in other cases, as being slightly alkaline. A more accurate method of expressing soil reaction is to express it in terms of the hydrogen-ion concentration. Therefore, soil reaction is expressed as the logarithm of the reciprocal of the hydrogen-ion concentration, and a pH scale of 0 to 14 is employed with 7 as the neutral point. The "p" indicates a logarithm and the "H" indicates hydrogen-ion concentration. Each pH unit is divided into tenths. It should be remembered that the scale is logarithmic, and with each increase or decrease of one pH unit the change in hydrogen-ion concentration is 10 times as great. Since the values are logarithms, they do not lend themselves to averages.

The soil reaction (pH) can be determined by the use of a pH meter or by the use of dyes and special pH test papers. Test papers, available in handy dispensers, are color-sensitive and practical for making quick tests. Soils should be mixed with buffers of solutions for maximum accuracy when determining the soil reaction. The operator should be familiar with the limitations of each technique and check his results periodically with known standards. A pH meter should be carefully protected and calibrated prior to use.

The soil reaction has a strong influence upon the availability of the various mineral elements needed for plant growth (Fig. 12–1). Also, plants grow better when grown in soil at the optimum pH range for the particular species. The primary and secondary nutrients are readily available within a pH range of 6.0–8.0. But the availability of these elements declines rapidly as the soil reaction becomes more acid. Iron and manganese are readily available at low pH values, but as the pH of the soil solution increases their availability declines. The lack of iron or manganese, due to high pH of the soil, can become a limiting factor in the production of certain woody species.

The most favorable soil reaction for the growth of most woody plants is between a pH of 5.5 and 7.5. Within this range, the essential mineral elements are readily available, the microorganisms of the soil carry on their beneficial functions, and fortunately, toxicity due to aluminum is minimized. However, some species of plants grow best under acid conditions (e.g., blueberries and rhododendrons) whereas others under more alkaline conditions. Nurserymen should be familiar with the optimum pH range for their crops and select sites accordingly for their production. For example, pin oak and red oak grow best in soil with a pH range of 4.5–6.0. They tolerate a pH between 6.0 and 6.8, but in soils with a pH greater than 6.8, they are often chlorotic and grow poorly. The soil reaction (pH) preferences for selected plant species are listed in Table 12–1.

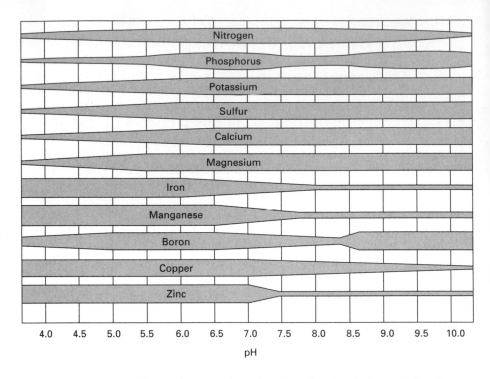

**Figure 12-1** Availability of plant nutrients in mineral soil as influenced by pH: the wider the bar, the more available the nutrient is. (Modified from Truog, 1947).

## MODIFYING SOIL REACTION

Where the soil reaction is too acid for optimum plant growth, it can be modified by the application of limestone. However, the amount of limestone that needs to be applied will vary with the degree of change that is desired, the soil texture, the content of organic matter, and the form of limestone to be used. Where the soil reaction is too alkaline, it can be acidified by the application of sulfur. The amount to be applied will depend upon the soil type and the number of pH units that the soil reaction is to be modified. The best recommendations for the amount of limestone or sulfur to apply are based on soil tests performed by persons trained in the analysis of soils. Production nurserymen should consult with their county agricultural agents or soils specialist for advice on management practices that are best for their soils and environment.

Effecting a pH change of nursery soils is best done when the land is not in crop production and well in advance of planting the nursery crop. The material should be spread evenly over the soil and thoroughly disked into the soil prior to plowing. In some situations it may be desirable to make split or multiple applications. Tables 12–2, and 12–3 can be used as a guide for the amount

**Table 12-1  Soil Reaction (pH) Preferences for Selected Plants**

| Common Name | Botanical Name | pH Preference 4 | 5 | 6 | 7 | 8 |
|---|---|---|---|---|---|---|
| **Shade and Flowering Trees** | | | | | | |
| Almond, flowering | *Prunus triloba* | | | X | X | X |
| Ash, American mountain | *Sorbus americana* | | X | | | |
| Ash, European mountain | *Sorbus aucuparia* | | | X | X | |
| Ash, white | *Fracinus americana* | | | | X | |
| Beech, American | *Fagus grandifolia* | | X | X | | |
| Birch, American white | *Betula alba* | | X | X | | |
| Birch, cherry | *Betula lenta* | | X | X | | |
| Cherry, dwarf flowering | *Prunus glandulosa* | | | X | X | |
| Crabapple, plum-leaved | *Malus prunifolia* | | | X | X | |
| Crabapple, showy | *Malus floribunda* | | X | X | | |
| Dogwood, flowering | *Cornus florida* | | X | X | | |
| Elm, American | *Ulmus americana* | | | X | X | |
| Hawthorn | *Crataegus biltmoreana* | | | X | X | |
| Hawthorn, English | *Crataegus laevigata* | | | X | | |
| Hickory, shagbark | *Carya ovata* | | | X | | |
| Holly, American | *Ilex opaca* | | X | | | |
| Holly, English | *Ilex aquifolium* | X | X | | | |
| Honey locust | *Gleditsia triacanthos* | | | X | X | X |
| Kentucky coffee tree | *Gymnocladus dioica* | | | X | X | X |
| Magnolia, saucer | *Magnolia soulangiana* | | X | | | |
| Magnolia, southern | *Magnolia grandiflora* | | X | | | |
| Magnolia, star | *Magnolia stellata* | | X | | | |
| Maidenhair tree | *Ginkgo biloba* | | | X | X | |
| Maple, sugar | *Acer saccharum* | | | X | X | |
| Oak, black | *Quercus velutina* | | | X | | |
| Oak, English | *Quercus robur* | | | X | | |
| Oak, pin | *Quercus palustris* | | X | X | X | X |

(continued)

**Table 12–1** Soil Reaction (pH) Preferences for Selected Plants (*continued*)

| Common Name | Botanical Name | pH Preference (4 – 8) |
|---|---|---|
| Oak, bur | *Quercus macrocarpa* | ~8 |
| Oak, red | *Quercus rubra* | ~5 – 5.5 |
| Oak, southern live | *Quercus virginiana* | ~5 – 5.5; ~6 – 7 |
| Oak, white | *Quercus alba* | ~6 – 7.5 |
| Pecan | *Carya illinoinensis* | ~6 |
| Sour gum | *Nyssa sylvatica* | ~5.5 – 6 |
| Sourwood | *Oxydendrum arboreum* | ~6 – 6.5 |
| Sweet gum | *Liquidambar styraciflua* | ~6 – 7 |
| Sycamore, American | *Platanus occidentalis* | ~6 – 7 |
| Tulip tree | *Liriodendron tulipifera* | ~6 |
| Willow, weeping | *Salix babylonica* | ~5.5 |
| Witch hazel | *Hammamelis virginiana* | ~6 |
| **Ornamental Shrubs** | | |
| Azalea, hiryu | *Rhododendrum obtusum* | ~4.5 – 5.5 |
| Azalea, pink | *R. periclymenoides* | ~4.5 – 5 |
| Barberry, Japanese | *Berberis thunbergii* | ~6 – 7 |
| Bayberry | *Myrica pennsylvanica* | ~5 – 5.5 |
| Beautybush | *Kolkwitzia amabilis* | ~6 – 6.5 |
| Boxwood, common | *Buxus sempervirens* | ~6 – 6.5 |
| Butterfly bush | *Buddleia davidii* | ~6 |
| Buttonbush | *Cephalanthus occidentalis* | ~6 – 7.5 |
| Chokeberry, black | *Aronia melanocarpa* | ~5 – 6 |
| Chokeberry, red | *Aronia arbutifolia* | ~5 – 6 |
| Cotoneaster | *Cotoneaster tomentosus* | ~6 – 7.5 |
| Cotoneaster, rock | *Cotoneaster horizontalis* | ~6 – 6.5 |
| Daphne, February | *Daphne mezereum* | ~6 |
| Daphne, rose | *Daphne cneorum* | ~6 – 6.5 |

| Common name | Scientific name | | | | |
|---|---|---|---|---|---|
| Deutzia | *Deutzia gracilis* | | | xxxxxxxxxx | |
| Deutzia, Lemoine | *Deutzia lemoinei* | | | xxxxxxxxxxx | xxxxxxxx |
| Dogwood, goldentwig | *C. sericea Flaviramea* | | | xxxxxxxxx | |
| Euonymus, winged | *Euonymus alata* | | xxxxxxxxx | xxxxxxxx | |
| Fire thorn | *Pyracantha coccinea* | xxxxxxxxxx | xxxxxxxx | | xxxxxxxx |
| Fringe tree, white | *Chionanthus virginicus* | | | | |
| Hackberry, nettle tree | *Celtis occidentalis* | xxxxxxxxxxx | xxxxxxxxxx | xxxxxxxxxx | xxxxxxxx |
| Heather, Scotch | *Calluna vulgaris* | | | | |
| Hibiscus, Chinese | *Hibiscus rose-sinensis* | | xxxxxxxxx | xxxxxxxxxxxx | |
| Holly, Japanese | *Ilex crenata* | | xxxxxxxxx | xxxxxxxxx | |
| Hollygrape, Oregon | *Mahonia aquifolium* | | | xxxxxxxxxxxxxxx | |
| Honeysuckle, Tatarian | *Lonicera tatarica* | | xxxxxxxxx | xxxxxxxxxxxx | xxxxxxxxx |
| Hydrangea, Peegee | *Hydrangea paniculata Grandiflora* | | | | |
| Lilac, common | *Syringa vulgaris* | | | xxxxxxxxx | |
| Lilac, Persian | *Syringa persica* | | | xxxxxxxxxx | |
| Mock orange | *Philadelphus coronarius* | | | xxxxxxxxxxx | |
| Mountain laurel | *Kalmia latifolia* | | xxxxxxxxx | xxxxxxxxx | |
| Oleander | *Nerium oleander* | | xxxxxxxxx | xxxxxxxxx | |
| Rhododendron | *R. maeronulatum* | | | | |
| Rhododendron, alpine | *R. hirsutum* | | xxxxxxxxxx | xxxxxxxxxx | xxxxxxxxx |
| Rhododendron, Carolina | *R. carolinianum* | xxxxxxxxxxxxxxxxx | | | |
| Rose, hybrid tea | *Rose sp.* | | xxxxxxxxx | xxxxxxxx | |
| Rose, Japanese | *Rosa rugosa* | | | | |
| Rose, memorial | *Rosa wichuriana* | | xxxxxxxxx | xxxxxxxxx | |
| Rosebay, mountain | *Rhododendron catawbiense* | | xxxxxxxxx | | |
| Rose of sharon | *Hibiscus syriacus* | | xxxxxxxxxx | xxxxxxxxx | |
| Serviceberry | *Amelanchier canadensis* | | | | |
| Spirea | *Spirea vanhouttei* | | xxxxxxxxx | xxxxxxxx | |
| Sumac, smooth | *Rhus glabra* | | xxxxxxxx | xxxxxxxx | |
| Sumac, staghorn | *Rhus typhina* | xxxxxxxx | | | |
| Viburnum, double-file | *Viburnum plicatum Tomentosum* | | | xxxxxxxxxx | xxxxxxxxxx |
| Viburnum, maple-leaved | *Viburnum acerifolium* | | | | |
| Wayfaring tree | *Viburnum lantana* | xxxxxxxxxxx | xxxxxxxxxx | xxxxxxxxxx | |

*(continued)*

**Table 12-1** Soil Reaction (pH) Preferences for Selected Plants *(continued)*

pH Preference

| Common Name | Botanical Name | pH Range (approx.) |
|---|---|---|
| **Evergreens** | | |
| Arborvitae, American | *Thuja occidentalis* | 6.0–7.5 |
| Fir, balsam | *Abies balsamea* | 4.8–5.3 |
| Fir, Douglas | *Pseudotsuga menziesii* | 6.0–6.5 |
| Fir, Fraser | *Abies fraseri* | 4.5–5.0 |
| Hemlock, Canada | *Tsuga canadensis* | 5.0–5.5 |
| Hemlock, Carolina | *Tsuga caroliniana* | 5.0–5.5 |
| Juniper, creeping | *Juniperus horizontalis* | 5.0–6.0 |
| Pine, mugho | *Pinus mugo* | 5.0–6.0 |
| Pine, red | *Pinus resinosa* | 5.0–5.5 |
| Pine, Scots | *Pinus sylvestris* | 5.0–5.5 |
| Pine, white | *Pinus strobus* | 4.5–6.0 |
| Spruce, Colorado | *Picea pungens* | 6.0–6.5 |
| Spruce, Norway | *Picea abies* | 5.0–5.5 |
| Spruce, white | *Picea glauca* | 5.0–5.5 |
| Yew, Japanese | *Taxus cuspidata* | 5.0–6.0 |
| **Vines** | | |
| Bittersweet, American | *Celastrus scandens* | 4.5–5.3 |
| Clematis, Jackman's | *Clematis jackmanii* | 5.5–6.0 |
| Dutchman's pipe | *Aristolochia durior* | 6.5–8.0 |
| Honeysuckle, trumpet | *Lonicera sempervirens* | 6.5–8.0 |
| Ivy, Boston | *Parthenocissus tricuspidata* | 6.5–8.0 |
| Ivy, English | *Hedera helix* | 6.5–8.0 |
| Virgin's bower | *Clematis paniculata* | 6.5–7.3 |
| Wisteria, Japanese | *Wisteria floribunda* | 6.5–8.0 |

Fruit Plants

| Common name | Scientific name |
|---|---|
| Apple, common | *Malus pumila* |
| Apricot | *Prunus armeniaca* |
| Blueberry, high bush | *Vaccinium corymbosum* |
| Cherry, sweet | *Prunus avium* |
| Grapefruit | *Citrus paradisi* |
| Orange, sweet | *Citrus sinensis* |
| Peach | *Prunus persica* |
| Pear, common | *Pyrus communis* |
| Plum, American | *Prunus americana* |
| Raspberry, black | *Rubus occidentalis* |
| Raspberry, red | *Rubus idaeus* |

Grass

| Common name | Scientific name |
|---|---|
| Bluegrass, annual | *Poa annua* |
| Bluegrass, Canada | *Poa compressa* |
| Bluegrass, Kentucky | *Poa pratensis* |
| Fescue, chewing | *Festuca rubra var. commutata* |
| Fescue, red | *Festuca rubra* |

Ground Covers

| Common name | Scientific name |
|---|---|
| Bearberry, common | *Arctostaphylos uva-ursi* |
| Bugleweed, carpet | *Ajuga reptans* |

*Source:* Spurway (1944).

**Table 12-2** Materials and Rate to Decrease the Soil pH by 1 Unit below pH 6.0

| | Rate (lb/100 ft²) | | |
|---|---|---|---|
| Material | Sandy Loam | Loam | Clay Loam or Peat |
| Aluminum sulfate | 2.5 | 5 | 7 |
| Iron sulfate | 2.5 | 5 | 7 |
| Sulfur | 0.5 | 1 | 1.5 |

**Table 12-3** Recommended Tons of Limestone per Acre,[a] Estimated from Soil pH and Texture, to Raise the pH of a 6⅔-in. Plow Layer of Different Soils to pH 6.5

| Texture of Plow Layer | pH Range | | | |
|---|---|---|---|---|
| | 4.5–4.9 | 5.0–5.4 | 5.5–5.9 | 6.0–6.4 |
| Clay and silty clay | 6 | 5 | 4 | 2½ |
| Clay loams or loams | 5 | 4 | 3 | 2 |
| Sandy loams | 4 | 3 | 2½ | 1½[b] |
| Loamy sands | 3 | 2½ | 2 | 1[b] |
| Sands | 2½ | 2 | 1½[b] | ½[b] |

[a]Lime recommendations based on a liming material having 25% passing through a 100-mesh sieve and having a neutralizing value of 90%.

[b]It is preferable to recommend 2 tons/acre so as to obtain uniform application and to justify the expense of application.

of sulfur or limestone to use in affecting a pH change. However, these tables are only estimates and do not account for variations in potential acidity, especially exchangeable aluminum. A lime requirement test, known as the SMP or Ohio lime requirement method, is used in a number of states; it measures both the active and the potential acidity. This gives a more precise determination of lime requirement than an estimate from soil pH and soil texture. A comparison of this measurement (Lime Index) and the lime requirement are given in Table 12–4.

The maximum amount of lime that should be applied in any season is 5 tons/acre. Nursery soils should be retested for additional lime needs prior to preparation of the land for a cover crop.

Various forms of limestone have varying abilities to modify the acidity of soils. This difference in ability is referred to as the "neutralizing value" and is equated on the basis of pure calcium carbonate. Pure calcium carbonate has a molecular weight of 100, and soil scientists use it as the basis to equate the neutralizing value of other forms of limestone. For example, the molecular weight of pure calcium hydrate is 74. By dividing 100 by 74, the percent value is 135. This indicates that 1 lb of calcium hydroxide is equal to 1.35 lb of calcium carbonate, or when equated on the basis of 1 ton of pure calcium carbonate, 1480 lb of calcium hydroxide is equally effective. The relative neutralizing value of several liming materials is tabulated in Table 12–5. Most

**Table12–4** Tons of Limestone Needed to Raise Soil pH of Mineral Soils to pH 6.0, 6.5,or 6.8, as Determined by the Lime Index Method

| | *Tons Lime per Acre (9-in. Plow Depth)*[a] | | |
|---|---|---|---|
| *Lime Index* | *To pH 6.0* | *To pH 6.5* | *To pH 6.8* |
| 7.0 | — | — | 0.5 |
| 6.9 | — | 0.5 | 1.0 |
| 6.8 | 1.1 | 1.5 | 1.8 |
| 6.7 | 1.9 | 2.4 | 2.6 |
| 6.6 | 2.7 | 3.3 | 3.6 |
| 6.5 | 3.5 | 4.3 | 4.7 |
| 6.4 | 4.3 | 5.3[b] | 5.7[b] |
| 6.3 | 5.1[b] | 6.2 | 6.7 |
| 6.2 | 5.8 | 7.2 | 7.8 |
| 6.1 | 6.6 | 8.1 | 8.9 |
| 6.0 | 7.4 | 9.1 | 10.0 |

[a]To convert lime recommendations to depth of plowing other than 9 in., divide above rates by 9 and multiply by the depth of plowing.

[b]The maximum lime recommendation for one season is 5 tons. Retest soil in 2 years for additional lime needs.

*Source:* Coop. Ext. Serv. Mich. State. Univ. Ext. Bull. E-550 (1976).

**Table 12–5** Neutralizing Value (Percent Calcium Carbonate Equivalent) of Various Liming Materials

| *Material* | *Neutralizing Value* |
|---|---|
| Calcium carbonate (pure) | 100 |
| Magnesium carbonate (pure) | 119 |
| Calcium hydrate (pure) | 135 |
| Magnesium hydrate (pure) | 172 |
| Calcic limestone | <100 |
| Dolomitic limestone | <108 |
| Calcic hydrated lime | <135 |
| Dolomitic hydrated lime | <170 |

*Source:* Coop. Ext. Serv. Mich. State Univ. Ext. Bull. 471.

limestone quarries can supply an analysis of the calcium carbonate equivalent of their product. This is required by law in some states.

The lime recommendations given in Table 12–4 are for limestone with a neutralizing value of 90. If the material to be used has a neutralizing value significantly different from 90, the amount should be adjusted. Figure 12–2 can be used for this purpose. For example, a material with a neutralizing value of 135 would require 0.65 ton to equal 1 ton of the 90% material. The values in Table 12–4 are multiplied by the factor, in this case 0.65. Liming materials react at different rates because of their chemical composition, coarseness, and hardness. The finer a limestone is ground, the more quickly it will react. Also, the more porous calcite materials will react more quickly than harder dolomitic materials.

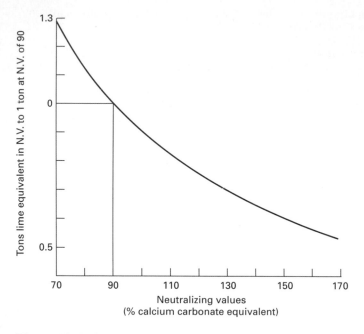

**Figure 12–2** Conversion chart to determine amounts of limestone of various neutralizing values (N.V.) that are equivalent to 1 ton of lime with an N.V. of 90. (From Coop. Ext. Serv. Mich. State Univ. Ext. Bull. 471.)

## CATION EXCHANGE CAPACITY

One of the interesting phenomena of nature is the ability of soil to adsorb various mineral nutrients when applied as fertilizers and then to release them to be absorbed by plants for use in their metabolism. The ability of the soil to hold certain minerals is known as cation exchange capacity (CEC). The exchange capacity of soil developed as a result of the weathering of rocks into small clay particles which possess negatively charged crystal surfaces. The negative charge is due to the dissociation of hydrogen from the exposed hydroxyl ($OH^-$) radical leaving the attached oxygen with the charge and from charges in the structure of the clay upon weathering. Clay particles adsorb thousands of hydrogen ions ($H^+$) and other exchangeable cations, such as $Ca^{2+}$, $Mg^{2+}$, $K^+$, and $Na^+$, upon their surfaces. The force with which these ions are attracted to the clay particles also influences the ease by which they may be exchanged. It is dependent upon the nature of the exchange complex, the size of the ions, the number of valence electrons, the degree of hydration, and the concentration of salts. The smaller the ion and the greater the charge per unit of mass, the tighter it will be held and accordingly the more difficult to replace. On the other hand, ions that are highly hydrated are more easily replaced. The common soil cations $Na^+$, $K^+$, $Mg^{2+}$, $Ca^{2+}$, and $H^+$ are listed in order of decreasing hydration. This explains, in part, why hydrogen ions play such an important role in soil, why calcium is the predominant mineral ion in most inorganic soils, and why potassium might be expected to be replaced and leached from a soil by improper fertilizer practices.

Anions, such as $H_2PO_4^-$, $NO_3^-$, and $SO_4^-$ are absorbed primarily in the organic matter within the soil. They are made available to plants through the decomposition of the organic matter by various microorganisms within the soil. The anions then become part of the soil solution and can be absorbed by the roots of plants.

Cation exchange takes place when a plant root makes contact with a clay particle. The root exchanges one or more hydrogen ions for an exchangeable cation which is absorbed by the plant and used in its metabolism (Fig. 12–3). A knowledge of CEC can be of value to a nurseryman planning a soil management program.

Most plants grow best on a specific soil type and under a specific set of environmental conditions. But it is impractical to provide all the ecological conditions required of plants in any one nursery. Therefore, it is desirable to

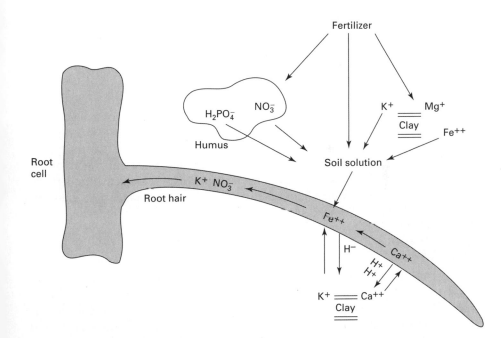

**Figure 12–3** Diagrammatic representation of an ion absorption from clay particle, humus particle, and the soil solution.

classify the soils of a field-production nursery into soil management groups on the basis of their CEC or pH, to develop a soil management program for each group, and to grow within each group those plants that lend themselves to the program (see Table 12–8).

A knowledge of CEC and levels of fertility are also valuable in developing fertilizer programs for nurseries and landscape plantings. Soils of low CEC should be fertilized more frequently at relatively low rates, since they do not have the physiochemical ability to hold large quantities of nutrient on their exchange complex. Thus, to ensure an adequate supply of nutrients for optimum plant growth, the fertilizer should be applied more often. On sites with a high CEC, the fertilizer may be applied less often and at a higher rate if needed. However, all fertilizer applications should be made on the basis of need, as indicated by a soil test.

## NUTRIENT-ELEMENT BALANCE IN PLANTS

Nutrient-element balance is a fundamental concept in plant nutrition. The concept is that plant growth is a function of two variables of nutrition: intensity and balance. The intensity and balance are reflected in the chemical composition of the leaves when the plants are in the same stage of growth or development, all other factors being constant. Maximum growth and yield occur only upon the coincidence of optimum intensity and balance. An imbalance of elements can result in toxicity or deficiency which can limit growth. For example, boron toxicity can be induced by a high ratio of (Ca + K)/Mg or (Ca + Mg)/K but not by a high ratio of (K + Mg)/Ca. A ratio of less than four for (Ca + Mg)/K is desirable for optimum growth of apples and less than three and one-half for alfalfa and corn. Calculations are based on milliequivalents per 100 g. A deficiency of manganese can be induced by a high accumulation of one or all three major bases (Ca, Mg, K) in proportion to manganese. There may be little or no response to increases in nitrogen fertility unless phosphorus levels are in balance with nitrogen. Heavy phosphorus fertilization of soils can induce deficiencies of iron, copper, manganese, and zinc.

## LEAF ANALYSIS

The chemical composition of leaves can be determined by chemical analysis. This analysis, made with the aid of a spectrograph and other supporting equipment, provides valuable data on the mineral composition of the plant. But like a financial statement that reflects the financial status of a business as of a particular day, leaf analysis reflects the nutritional status of the plant as of the day the samples were collected.

The nutritional status of plants changes constantly throughout the growing season. For most plants, growing under optimal levels of nutrition, the concentrations of nitrogen and potassium decrease with time: calcium, magnesium, iron, and manganese increase, while phosphorus, boron, and copper remain relatively unchanged. Therefore, to interpret leaf analysis data intelligently, it is necessary to establish a standard method, including when to sample, the part of the plant to sample, and standards to compare the data. Since the nutrition of leaves is fairly well stabilized by the end of the growing season, this is the time that is recommended that samples be collected; with evergreens they may be collected through the end of December. The portion of the plant to be sampled varies with the plant type. For deciduous species and evergreens such as pine, the middle foliage from the current year's growth is suggested; for evergreens such as juniper and arborvitae, the current year's growth is sampled. Leaves or shoots should be collected at random and combined into a composite sample for analysis. The data can then be compared with standard values to determine the relative nutritional status. Table 12–6 lists some suggested standards for deciduous and evergreen species; more exact values are available at laboratories that conduct chemical analysis of plants. Table 12–7 lists nutrient-element standards for diagnosis of nutrient problems in sugar and red maple trees. It may be necessary in some situations to supply the laboratory with healthy foliage for a reference standard since standards have not been established for all woody species. Although exact fertilizer recommendations cannot be made based solely on leaf analysis data, a trained horticulturist with knowledge of the crop and the site where the plants are growing, plus a current soil test, supplemented with information on past fertilizer and cultural practices can usually suggest a cultural program that will improve the quality of growth.

## SOIL TESTS

A good soil testing program is desirable to serve as a basis for nurserymen to make sound soil management decisions for maintaining adequate pH levels and a reasonable balance of nutrients to ensure good plant growth. However, it is important to know what testing procedures were used in order to make a meaningful interpretation of the data. Since different extraction techniques are used by soil testing laboratories, it is not always possible to compare test results between laboratories. Soil samples must be taken with care to ensure that the results of the test and the fertilizer recommendations developed from them are meaningful. Soil tests are performed on a very small sample of the greater mass, and if the sample is not representative of the whole, the results are not meaningful. Samples taken from the upper 6–8 in. of soil, which may be satisfactory for annual crops, have only limited value for deep-rooted perennial crops, since they do not reflect the true nutrient status of the soil-root zone from which the plant is absorbing its nutrients. Soil samples (cores 12–18 in. deep) should be taken at a number of locations in each field to be planted to develop fertilizer recommendations for long-term nursery crops.

**Table 12–6** Suggested Foliar, Nutrient-Element Standards for Deciduous and Evergreen Plants (Fall Analysis)

| Element | Deciduous | Evergreen |
|---|---|---|
| | Percent Dry Weight | |
| Nitrogen | 1.50–3.00 | 2.00–2.35 |
| Phosphorus | 0.15–0.26 | 0.25–0.40 |
| Potassium | 0.80–1.60 | 1.00–1.20 |
| Calcium | 1.40–3.00 | 0.50–1.25 |
| Magnesium | 0.30–0.45 | 0.20–0.35 |
| | Parts per Million | |
| Iron | 150–300 | 200–300 |
| Copper | 25–35 | 25–40 |
| Manganese | 50–200 | 25–50 |
| Boron | 25–50 | 25–50 |
| Zinc | 25–50 | 25–50 |
| Molybdenum | 1–5 | 1–5 |

**Table 12–7** Nutrient-Element Standards for diagnosis of Nutrient Problems of Sugar and Red Maple Trees

| Nutrient | Sugar Maple SDP | Sugar Maple STP | Red Maple SDP | Red Maple STP |
|---|---|---|---|---|
| | | Percent | | |
| Nitrogen | 0.62 | 3.10 | 0.90 | 2.70 |
| Phosphorus | 0.06 | 0.33 | 0.07 | 0.38 |
| Potassium | 0.39 | 3.30 | 0.35 | 3.70 |
| Calcium | 0.59 | 2.50 | 0.90 | 1.60 |
| Magnesium | 0.09 | 0.86 | 0.12 | 0.89 |
| | | ppm | | |
| Boron | 14 | 336 | 3.8 | 522 |
| Iron | 37 | 311 | 32 | 478 |
| Manganese | 23 | 805 | 32 | 758 |
| Zinc | 7.4 | 132 | 14 | 96 |

If a tree has symptoms and nutrient concentrations near the symptomatic deficiency point (SDP) deficiency problems should be suspected. If a tree has symptoms and nutrient concentrations near the symptomatic toxicity point (STP) a toxicity problem should be expected. (Table adapted from Smiley et al.)

Most soil testing centers provide information on the cation exchange capacity or the soil group, soil reaction (pH), the availability of the macroelements except nitrogen and sulfur, and when requested, the availability of selected microelements, total nitrogen, organic matter content, and soluble salts. For many years phosphorus and potassium were reported as oxides, $P_2O_5$ and $K_2O$, respectively, since this is the form that they are found in fertilizer. Currently, most soil testing laboratories report P and K on the elemental basis. P and K are normally in pounds per acre, Ca and Mg are reported either as milliequivalents per 100 grams or in pounds per acre, and the microelements are expressed as parts per million (ppm). To convert P and K to the oxide form, multiply by 2.3 and 1.2, respectively. To convert $P_2O_5$ and $K_2O$ to the elemental form, multiply by 0.44 and 0.83, respectively.

Very little information is available on soil fertility standards for ornamental plants. The data in Table 12–8 are provided as suggested standards until more definitive data are available.

## TYPES OF FERTILIZERS

Nurserymen have a vast array of fertilizer materials from which to select in order to meet their individual requirements and preferences. There are many ways to classify fertilizers, but one way is to classify them according to their chemical and physical properties (Table 12–9).

**Table 12–8**  Suggested Standards of Soil Fertility for Growing Woody Perennials in Field-Production Nurseries

| | | Available (lb/acre)[a] | | Exchangeable (mEq/100 g)[b] | |
|---|---|---|---|---|---|
| *Group* | *CEC* | *P* | *K* | *Ca* | *Mg* |
| Silt loam to loam | 12–16 | 35–70 | 150–200 | 5.0–10.0 | 2 |
| Sandy loam | 5–10 | 25–35 | 100–150 | 2.5–4.0 | 1 |
| Loamy sand to sand | 2–4 | 15–25 | 60–100 | 1.5–2.0 | 0.5 |

[a] $P \times 2.3 = P_2O_5$; $K \times 1.2 = K_2O$.

[b] 1 mEq/100 g Ca = 400 lb/acre; 1 mEq/100 g Mg = 240 lb/acre.

**Table 12–9**  Chemical and Physical Properties of Fertilizers

| *Chemical Properties* | *Physical Properties* |
|---|---|
| I.  State | I.  State |
|    A. Organic |    A. Dry |
|      1. Natural |      1. Pulverized |
|      2. Synthetic |      2. Granular (prills) |
|    B. Inorganic |      3. Tablet |
|      1. Natural |      4. Packet |
|      2. Synthetic |      5. Encapsulated |
| II.  Element |    B. Liquid |
|    A. Single |      1. Water-soluble |
|    B. Double |      2. Suspension |
|    C. Triple (complete) | II.  Release rate |
|    D. Multi |    A. Rapid |
| III.  Long-term effect on soil pH |    B. Slow (controlled) |
|    A. Acidic (lowers pH) | |
|    B. Neutral | |
|    C. Basic (raises pH) | |

*Organic fertilizers* are carbonaceous compounds which are either natural (Table 12–10) or synthetic. Most of the natural organic materials are multi-element compounds, but the essential elements are present in small quantities, necessitating high application rates to obtain significant amounts of the needed nutrients. They are slowly soluble and can be used with a high degree of safety. The *synthetic organic fertilizers* are manufactured products. Urea, for example, is produced under high pressure from carbon dioxide ($CO_2$) and ammonia ($NH_3$), and urea-formaldehyde (UF) is a reaction product of urea and formaldehyde. Urea is highly soluble and must be used with caution, whereas UF is slowly soluble. IBDU is a reaction product between isobutylidene and urea producing a slow-release nitrogenous fertilizer.

*Inorganic materials* provide the most available source of supply for the essential elements. They are either natural compounds that have been mined and processed into fertilizer, or they are reaction products synthesized for a specific purpose. They are available in dry or liquid formulations and vary greatly in chemical composition and solubility (Table 12–11).

Since the mid-1950s, a number of slow- or controlled-release products have been introduced as fertilizers. Magamp is an improved formulation of magnesium ammonium phosphate with the addition of nitrogen and potassium. It is a granular formulation which releases nitrogen slowly due to its solubility in water.

Osmocote is a controlled-release fertilizer. It is a homogeneous prill of water-soluble fertilizer covered with a plastic resin. The prills do not dissolve in water, but become hydrated and release the nutrients as a result of osmotic pressure. The process is moisture- and temperature-dependent. Therefore, the nutrients are not readily available when soils are dry or cold.

Slow- or controlled-release fertilizers are best utilized in the production of container-grown plants. They are relatively more expensive, per unit of plant food, than the natural inorganic fertilizers, but because of their release rate, they have a number of advantages. They can be applied at the time of planting and supply the needed nutrients for a full growing season, thus eliminating the need for additional applications of fertilizer. This can result in a considerable saving in labor. They can supply nutrients at a fairly uniform rate; thus plant growth is not limited by excess soluble salts or by leaching. Their use can reduce the loss of soluble materials through leaching and runoff, resulting in a substantial savings, and at the same time minimize contamination of the environment.

When fertilizer is manufactured and packaged for sale, the product label will indicate the chemical analysis. It is industry practice to list fertilizer analysis in the order of the three primary elements, as % elemental N, % $P_2O_5$, and % $K_2O$. Fertilizers that contain nitrogen, phosphorus, and potassium are known as complete fertilizers. However, it should be noted that a complete fertilizer does not contain all the essential elements, although some calcium, magnesium, sulfur, and microelements are commonly present in the product as carriers or as contaminants.

Fertilizers may have an acid, alkaline, or neutral reaction, depending upon the materials contained in the product. Complete fertilizers, as blended, are neutral but many will produce an acid reaction upon the soil following chemical breakdown. The reaction of various fertilizers is listed in Table 12–11.

## SOLUBLE SALTS

Another characteristic of fertilizers is their solubility. When fertilizer is applied to soil, it comes in contact with water, which causes the material to solubilize. The degree of solubility is a function of the fertilizer carrier (Table 12–11).

Soluble salts when present in the soil solution in excess quantities limits the availability of water to the plant or can reach excessive levels in plant tissue, which restricts growth and can result in death of the plant when the concentration reaches the toxic level for the species. Excess soluble salts are a potential problem to all plantsmen who use highly soluble fertilizers. When a soluble salts problem is suspected, a soil salinity test should be made with the aid of a Solu-bridge. A sample of soil is mixed with distilled water, and the solution is tested for its ability to conduct electricity. Some laboratories use the saturated paste technique, while others use a 2:1 or 5:1 distilled water/soil dilution method. The former has the advantage of being more accurate, especially with sandy soils or with soils to which gypsum or aluminum sulfate has been added. However, the latter is more rapid and less expensive, and if total accuracy is not important, the results can be of practical diagnostic value.

Soluble salts dissociate into ions which have the ability to conduct an electric current. As the concentration of soluble salts increases in the solution, conductance increases. This conductance of electricity can be measured by a Solu-bridge which has been calibrated in units called mhos. The decimal units are converted to whole numbers by employing negative exponents. For example, 0.00300 mho converts to $300 \times 10^{-5}$ mhos. This is sometimes stated as 3 millimhos or 3000 micromhos. (Most laboratories report conductance in millisiemens/cm (ms/cm).) Table 12–12 provides some guidelines for levels of soluble salts and anticipated plant responses for plants growing in field-production nursery or in a landscape.

Although there is little information available on the tolerance of ornamental plants to soluble salts, there are enough data to indicate that a reading of 3.0 ms/cm (saturated paste extract) or slightly less should be satisfactory for most plants. Some plants, such as arborvitae, juniper, and bottle bush, are very salt-tolerant and can withstand a salt concentration as high as

**Table 12–10** Natural Organic Fertilizers

| Fertilizer | Approximate Analysis | | | Rate (lb/100 ft²) | Comments |
|---|---|---|---|---|---|
| | N | P₂O₅ | K₂O | | |
| Blood, dried | 12 | 1.5 | 0.5 | 3–4 | Rapidly available source of nitrogen |
| Guano | | | | | |
| Bat | 6 | 9 | 3 | 3–4 | Partially decomposed bat manure from caves in southwest United States |
| Bird | 13 | 11 | 2 | 2–3 | Partially decomposed bird manure from islands off coast of South America |
| Kelp or seaweed | 1 | 0.5 | 9 | 5 | Good source of K |
| Manure | | | | | Manures are generally low in nutrients, but when used in larger amounts, |
| Cattle | 0.5 | 0.3 | 0.5 | | as a soil conditioner, they do add fertilizer; avoid use of fresh manure |
| Chicken | 1.0 | 0.5 | 0.8 | | or use too soon after steaming; nutrient content variable, particularly |
| Horse | 0.6 | 0.3 | 0.6 | | with bedding materials used; uncomposted animal manure often |
| Mushroom, spent | 1.0 | 1.0 | 1.0 | | contains weed seed |
| Sheep | 0.9 | 0.5 | 0.8 | | |
| Swine | 0.6 | 0.5 | 1.0 | | |
| Meal | | | | | |
| Bone, raw | 4 | 20 | 0 | 5 | Phosphorus very slowly soluble |
| Bone, steamed | 2 | 27 | 0 | 5 | Phosphorus is soluble, some nitrogen lost by steaming |
| Cotton seed | 6 | 2.5 | 2.0 | 3–4 | Acid in reaction, good for azaleas, rhododendrons, blueberries |
| Hoof and horn | 14 | 0 | 0 | 2 | Good source of organic nitrogen |
| Peanut hulls | 1 | 0 | 1 | 5 | Low in nutrients |
| Sludge | | | | | |
| Sewage | 2.0 | 1.0 | 0.5 | 5 | Variable; check source; avoid those possibly contaminated with heavy metals |
| Activated | 6.0 | 3.0 | 0.5 | 3–4 | Microorganisms added |
| Tobacco stems | 1.5 | 1.0 | 6.0 | 5 | Good source of K₂O, alkaline reaction |
| Wood ashes | 0 | 2.0 | 6.0 | 5 | Source of K₂O, very alkaline |

**Table 12–11** Inorganic and Synthetic Fertilizers, Nutrient Content, Reaction, and Solubility

| Sources | N | NO | PO | KO | Ca | S | Reaction | Solubility |
|---|---|---|---|---|---|---|---|---|
| Nitrogen | | | | | | | | |
| Ammonium nitrate | 33 | 17 | | | | | Acid | High |
| Ammonium sulfate | 26 | | | | | 24 | Very Acid | Medium |
| Calcium nitrate | 15 | 15 | | | 20 | | Basic | High |
| Nitrogen solutions | 21–49 | | | | | | | High |
| Sodium nitrate | 16 | 16 | | | | | Basic | High |
| Sulfur-coated urea | 35 | | | | | 21 | Very acid | Variable |
| Urea | 46 | | | | | | | Very |
| Ureaform | 38 | | | | | | | Variable |
| Phosphorus | | | | | | | | |
| Monoammonium phosphate | 11 | | 48 | | | | Acid | Medium |
| Diammonium phosphate | 16–21 | | 48–53 | | | | Acid | Medium |
| Phosphoric acid | | | | | | | Acid | Very |
| Superphosphoric acid | | | 69–76 | | | | Acid | Very |
| Superphosphate | | | | | | | | |
| Normal | | | 20 | | 20 | 12 | | Low |
| Concentrated | | | 40–50 | | 13 | | | Low |
| Magnesium | | | | | | | | |
| Magnesium ammonium phosphate | 6 | | 29 | | Mg16 | | Acid | Low |
| Magnesium sulfate | | | | | Mg10 | | | High |
| Potassium | | | | | | | | |
| Potassium chloride | | | | 48–62 | | | | High |
| Potassium sulfate | | | | 48 | | 18 | | Medium |

**Table 12-12** Interpretation of Solu-Bridge Data as Related to Field-Grown Plants.

| Saturated Paste Extract | Conductivity, millisiemens/cm (ms/cm)[a] | | Interpretation |
| | 2:1 | 5:1 | |
|---|---|---|---|
| | <0.15 | <0.08–0.30 | Satisfactory for seed experimentation, but too low for good plant growth. Soil needs fertilizer |
| <2.00 | 0.15–0.50 | | Satisfactory if soil is high in organic matter |
| 2.0–3.0 | 0.50–1.80 | 0.30–0.80 | Satisfactory for established plants: upper range too high for seedlings and salt-intolerant species |
| 4.0–8.0 | 1.80–2.25 | 0.80–1.00 | Toxic levels, reduced growth: do not fertilize |
| 8.0–15.0 | 2.25–3.40 | 1.00–1.50 | Many species will be stunted: suggest leaching if possible |
| >16.0 | >3.40 | >1.50 | Too high for most species of plants |

[a]ms = millisiemen, replacing millimho (mmho) as the preferred unit for expressing conductivity (soluble salt) measurements. The value remains the same—only the name changes. To convert this value to ppm multiply by 700.

8–10 ms/cm, while others, such as roses and viburnums, will be killed if the salt level is greater than 3 ms/cm.

## FERTILIZER RECOMMENDATIONS

Fertilizer recommendations for woody plants, and for ornamental species in particular, vary considerably. Most recommendations for fertilizing woody species growing in the ground have been developed from a limited number of studies utilizing mature trees. Some of the recommendations come from fertilizer studies conducted on plants growing in nurseries. Most of the studies were concerned with the three primary elements: nitrogen, phosphorus, and potassium, and with the trace element iron. The studies centered around rates and methods of application. From the results of these fertilizer studies, there is total agreement that the greatest growth response of trees was due to the addition of nitrogen to the soil. Only a few of the studies reported significant increases in growth due to the application of phosphorus or potassium. Chlorosis of oak, maple, white pine, plus a few other species, is commonly associated with lack of either iron or manganese.

### Nitrogen

Current fertilizer recommendations for woody species growing in the ground indicate that surface application is most desirable for nitrogen. Rates of application vary with tree size and with the type of fertilizer. The most common practice is to state the rate in pounds of fertilizer or pounds of nitrogen per 1000 ft². A second is to equate the rate of application to the size of the tree: pounds of fertilizer or pounds of nitrogen contained in the fertilizer per inch of trunk diameter. Fertilizer recommendations for trees based on trunk diameter can result in considerable variation in concentration of nitrogen applied per 1000 ft² and per plant. Since the greatest growth response in woody species is related to nitrogen, the best recommendation for rate of application is to base the rate on pounds of nitrogen per 1000 ft². Then regardless of the size of the tree or the fertilizer analysis, the soil will be enriched with nitrogen at a uniform concentration. The actual rate of application will vary with the amount available in the soil, the soil environment and type of fertilizer, the species to be fertilized, and the objective of the nursery manager.

The amount of nitrogen in the soil available for plant growth is a function of a number of interacting factors. Nitrogen is made available from organic materials by the activity of various microorganisms within the soil, by biological fixation of atmospheric nitrogen, and by decomposition of organic matter. It is removed from the soil by cropping and leaching and is made unavailable to plants by the activities of various soil organisms. The actual level of available nitrogen in the soil is the net result of the positive and negative forces acting at any given moment in time.

Soil microorganisms are most active during periods of warm temperature and least active when the soil is cold or is either very wet or very dry. Leaching takes place during periods of heavy rain and as a result of excessive irrigation. Nitrogen is made unavailable following application of low-N organic matter, such as sawdust. Therefore, tests for available nitrogen must be interpreted with these considerations in mind, since the actual level of available nitrogen is influenced by all these factors.

Since there are many forms of nitrogenous fertilizer available for use by nurserymen, it is important to understand the advantages and disadvantages of the most commonly used nitrogenous fertilizers. Inorganic fertilizers contain either nitrate nitrogen or ammonium nitrogen. Both the ammonium ion ($NH_4^+$) and the nitrate ion ($NO_3^-$) can be absorbed and utilized by plants. However, most plants exhibit a preference for the nitrate form.

These two forms of nitrogen react differently in the soil, since $NH_4^+$ is a cation and the other $NO_3^-$ is an anion. Because nitrate fertilizers are highly soluble and readily absorbed by plant roots, they are the most desirable for use on cold or wet soils. But because of its solubility, it can also be readily leached from soils. On the other hand, the positively charged ammonium ion becomes adsorbed to negatively charged clay or organic colloids, and leaching is retarded. The ammonium ion is converted to nitrate nitrogen by microorganisms under the conditions of warm temperature, available moisture, and good aeration.

Organic forms of nitrogen, with the exception of urea, are generally unavailable for use by plants and must be converted either to ammonium or nitrate nitrogen before they are available for absorption by plants. Urea, however, is water-soluble and can be used directly by plants or can be rapidly converted to $NO_3$ in warm moist soils. Slow- or controlled-release fertilizers, discussed previously, are also a source of nitrogen for the production of nursery crops.

Although rates of fertilizer application should be set primarily on the basis of a soil test (Table 12–12) or foliage analysis, they should be modified on the basis of plant growth and species response. Plants that have good foliage color and are making good growth may not require additional fertilizer for a year or two, whereas plants that are chlorotic and making poor growth may need an application of fertilizer. In previous studies, deciduous trees have responded with a significant increase in diameter growth when fertilized at a rate of 6 lb nitrogen/1000 $ft^2$, whereas in another study, field-grown evergreens (yews) produced their best growth at a rate of 3 lb nitrogen/1000 $ft^2$. Rates in excess of 4 lb nitrogen/1000 $ft^2$ resulted in a decline in growth.

Nurserymen wishing to accelerate growth should maintain fairly high levels of available nitrogen in the soil, whereas those desiring to slow down growth should withhold nitrogen. It is possible to deprive the nursery crop of part of its nitrogen source by leaching the soil or by sowing a cover crop. The data in Table 12–13 provide a guide to nitrogen application for the production of woody plants in field-production nurseries on mineral soils.

### Phosphorus

The application of phosphate fertilizers is seldom necessary on field-production nursery soils. When it has been determined that phosphorus in the soil is below some "critical" level (Table 12–8), it is best to apply the fertilizer to a sod or green manure crop grown prior to planting of the nursery crop. This practice ensures better distribution of the phosphorus throughout the soil. Either superphosphate (0–20–0) or triple superphosphate (0–46–0) can be used effectively (Table 12–14). In field-production areas where sod or green manure crops are not employed in the rotation with the nursery crop, phos-

**Table 12–13** Nitrogen Fertilizer Guide for Woody Plants in Field-Production Nurseries on Mineral Soils

| *Previous Crop or Manure Application* | *Nitrogen (lb/acre)[a]* |
|---|---|
| Legume and manure, 10 tons/acre | 25 |
| Legume | 50 |
| Manure, 10 tons/acre | 60 |
| No legume, no manure | 100 |

[a]If the season is cool and wet or the field is poorly drained, additional quantities of nitrate nitrogen may be necessary. Plantings on wide spacing may be fertilized by banding nitrogen at lower rates.

**Table 12–14** Phosphate-Phosphorus Fertilizer Guide for Woody Plants in Field-Production Nurseries on Mineral Soils[a]

| Available Phosphorus (lb/acre) | Pounds per Acre[b] | |
|---|---|---|
| | $P_2O_5$ | P |
| 0–19 | 100 | 44 |
| 20–39 | 75 | 33 |
| 40–59 | 50 | 22 |
| 60–79 | 25 | 11 |
| 80+ | 0 | 0 |

[a]Data based on the Bray $P_1$ (absorbed) method.

[b]Applied to sod or green manure crop prior to planting nursery crop.

phate fertilizers can be applied by banding or by the use of a pelletized fertilizer thoroughly incorporated into the soil prior to planting.

### Potassium

Potassium ions on the surface of the exchange complex are available for plant growth. Those in the interior of the soil complex, colloidal clay particles, sometimes known as the stored form, are capable of being released slowly to replace the adsorbed ions. Potassium deficiency is not a common problem on most nursery soils, although it can be in sandy soils. Nurserymen who suspect that their soil might be deficient in potassium should have it tested, and if potassium is needed, apply it to the soil prior to planting (Table 12–15). Potassium fertilizers should be worked into the soil to be most effective.

The two common forms of potassium fertilizers are the chloride form, called muriate of potash, and the sulfate form. Muriate of potash contains approximately 60% $K_2O$, is the least expensive, and is the most commonly used form. The sulfate form contains 48% $K_2O$ and is used on those crops sensi-

**Table 12–15** Potash-Potassium Fertilizer Guide for Woody Ornamental Plants in Field-Production Nurseries on Mineral Soils[a]

| Available Soil Potassium (lb/acre) | | Pounds per Acre[b] | |
|---|---|---|---|
| Sandy Loams and Loamy Sands | Loams and Clay Loams | $K_2O$ | K |
| | 0–59 | 200 | 166 |
| | 60–119 | 150 | 125 |
| 0–59 | 120–159 | 100 | 83 |
| 60–119 | 160–179 | 75 | 62 |
| 120–169 | 180–199 | 50 | 42 |
| 170–209 | 200–239 | 25 | 21 |
| 210+ | 240+ | 0 | 0 |

[a]Data based on 1.0 N neutral ammonium acetate extraction method.

[b]Applied to sod or green manure prior to planting nursery crop.

tive to chlorides or in places where large quantities of chlorides are present in irrigation water.

Potassium nitrate ($KNO_3$), which contains 44% $K_2O$, also contains about 13% nitrates and has a medium salt index (Table 12–12) per unit of plant food. This material is used extensively in fertilizing container-grown plants. It can be used as a foliar spray (5–10 lb/100 gal water), applied with a spreader-sticker as a transitory means of correcting a potassium deficiency on a nursery crop. This should be followed by a good soil development program prior to planting another nursery crop.

### Calcium

Although most soils contain adequate amounts of calcium to support plant growth, nurserymen should be aware that they are removing relatively large amounts with the sale of their product. Liming and fertilizing of soils to maintain optimum pH and nutrient levels adds large quantities of calcium and may be sufficient to make up for the loss. It should also be noted that calcium plays an important role in the aggregation of soil particles. Soils with adequate calcium are well aggregated, permitting adequate aeration and drainage, which aid in the production of quality plants. Excess calcium in a soil can produce an imbalance of the cations and could induce either a potassium, iron, or manganese deficiency, especially on soils low in these elements.

### Magnesium

Magnesium is not commonly deficient in most soils. But a magnesium deficiency can be induced by applying high rates of potassium. The ratio of exchangeable potassium to exchangeable magnesium should not be greater than 3:1 for most crops. Magnesium fertilizer should not be added if the soil magnesium exceeds 3% of the total bases, or when the soil test indicates a level greater than 75 lb/acre.

A quick, temporary source of magnesium for growing plants is to spray the foliage with a solution of magnesium sulfate when plant stress is low, early in the morning or evening (Epsom salt 20 lb/100 gal water). Dolomitic limestone applied at the rate of ½ ton/acre where the soil pH is below 5.5 will supply adequate amounts of magnesium for most nursery crops.

### Microelements

*Iron deficiency* is commonly associated with iron-sensitive species (oaks, holly, rhododendron) when they are grown on alkaline soils. It can also occur when plants are growing in compacted or waterlogged soils. Aeration or drainage of the soils will improve air porosity and iron availability. In addition, large amounts of phosphorus or heavy metals can limit the uptake of iron. Amending the soils with organic matter will improve the chelating action on the iron, preventing it from becoming "fixed" or precipitated out of the soil solution. Iron deficiency is relatively difficult to correct in plants growing in the ground. The best corrective measure for woody plants has been soil injections of iron chelate just prior to spring growth, although trunk implants of encapsulated iron are also effective on shade trees. Foliar sprays of iron have only a transitory effect on woody plants.

*Manganese deficiency* may be corrected by acidification of the soil to pH 6.0. The use of water-soluble manganese sulfate (5 lb/100 gal water) or a chelated manganese foliar spray, with a spreader-sticker, can be used to correct the deficiency. However, they must be applied annually or even twice a year to assure satisfactory results. Trees exhibiting chlorosis should be carefully diagnosed prior to treating, since an application of iron to effect a cure of a manganese deficiency would further upset the Fe-Mn balance in the soil and within the plant. Also, it has been reported that Mn chlorosis is related to high levels of P and K in the leaves of red maples and that by altering the Mn/P + K balance by subsoil acidification ($H_2SO_4$ + $MnSO_4$) it was possible to correct the chlorosis problem. It is desirable to have both a soil test and a foliar analysis to determine the fertilizer requirements needed to effect a positive change in the balance of nutrients. On alkaline soils consideration should be given to using ammonium sulfate (21–0–0) to minimize the increase of phosphorus and potassium which may contribute to the chlorosis problem.

*Boron deficiency* can be corrected by borax (1.5 to 2 lb/acre) applied to the soil or as foliar spray of Solubar (0.1–0.3 lb/acre). Excess levels of boron can create serious toxicity conditions for plants. Be sure that boron is deficient and apply at proper concentration to avoid toxicity problems.

*Copper deficiency* can be corrected readily. Bordeaux mixture applied to the foliage will alleviate the problem. Copper sulfate spray applied at 3–6 oz/100 gal water can also correct the problem.

## METHOD OF APPLICATION

Nutrient elements can enter plants through the roots, the foliage, and in some cases through the bark. When fertilizers are applied to the foliage, they must be in liquid form and be applied in dilute solutions. When applied to the soil to be absorbed by the roots, fertilizer can be in either the liquid or dry state and can be a surface application or injected into the root zone. When applied through the bark, they can be in the dry or liquid state, but most often they are encapsulated and implanted into the trunks of trees. When selecting the method to apply fertilizers to nursery crops, nurserymen should consider the nutrients, their ability to be effectively absorbed, the effect of the soil or the environment, equipment availability, the relative cost, and the effects of fertilizer salts on application equipment and the environment.

### Surface Application

Band placement along the rows is most commonly used by nurserymen. It is an effective and efficient method for the application of nitrogen, since nitrogenous fertilizers move into the root zone with the downward movement of water. However, direct surface application is not suggested for applying phosphorus, potassium, and other nutrients that become fixed on the exchange complex. These are better applied by incorporation into nursery soils prior to planting.

Fertilizers can be applied to the soil surface with the aid of various types of spreaders. Band application on either side of the row is a satisfactory means, although the fertilizer can be spread evenly over the entire area. Where large acreages arc to be fertilized, an airplane can be economically employed.

Fertilizer spreaders should be calibrated to ensure accurate and uniform distribution of the material. Calibration should be done for each fertilizer, field condition, and each individual spreader. Fertilizers vary in their chemical and physical properties; therefore, one calibration of a spreader does not apply to all fertilizers. Also, fields vary from site to site, which has an effect upon rate of travel and distribution rate. The equipment should be recalibrated whenever there is a significant change in surface conditions. Also, rate of application will vary between spreaders and the individual spreader as a result of use. It is a good practice to recalibrate spreaders and to check the rate of distribution periodically to avoid overapplication of fertilizer.

In some situations it may be more economical to contract fertilizer application to a company that specializes in application of fertilizers and pesticides to agricultural crops.

*Surface application rates* are stated in pounds per acre (lb/acre) or pounds per thousand square feet (lb/1000 ft$^2$). The two nomographs of Appendixes E and F will accomplish the conversion of lb/acre to lb/1000 ft$^2$ or lb/1000 ft$^2$ to lb/acre without calculations.

### Subsurface Incorporation

Incorporation into the soil by subsurface application is the most effective means of applying nutrients that become fixed on the exchange complex or are slow to move into the soil solution. Nurserymen can best incorporate these materials into the soil prior to planting the nursery crop. Also, when affecting a pH change, the lime or sulfur should be thoroughly incorporated into the soil. When a few trees in a block of nursery stock require the addition of potassium or one of the trace elements, these can be injected into the root zone with the aid of a punch bar or soil auger. If anhydrous ammonia is used as a source of nitrogen, this has to be chiseled into the soil.

### Foliage Application

Fertilizers can be applied to the leaves of plants, since leaves can effectively absorb the applied nutrients. The actual mechanism of foliar absorption is not fully understood. The nutrient ions apparently penetrate the cuticle either directly or through thin permeable areas associated with guard cells and tricome bases. The process is most active when the leaves are warm, and the leaf surfaces remain wet for fairly long periods. Wetting of the leaf surface is enhanced by the addition of a wetting agent to the spray solution. Nitrogen is absorbed very rapidly, within a few hours, when applied to the foliage. Potassium, calcium, magnesium, manganese, and zinc are absorbed fairly rapidly, in less than 24 hr, whereas it can take days for sulfur, iron, and molybdenum to be absorbed. Urea sprays are a convenient means for correcting nitrogen deficiency in nursery plantings during periods when the soil is cold and wet. It is generally not economical as a regular nursery practice. Calcium, magnesium, manganese, and zinc deficiency can be readily corrected with one or two sprays during the growing season.

Copper, boron, and molybdenum deficiencies can be corrected very easily by adding small amounts of these minor element fertilizers to spray solution. Copper deficiency is uncommon in nurseries that use Bordeaux mixture in the spray program.

The leaves of most plants will respond to foliar sprays of iron, but the new growth that develops after spraying will remain chlorotic. This is due to the lack of translocation of the iron within the plant. Therefore, if foliage sprays are used to correct iron deficiency, repeat applications will be necessary. Problems with iron deficiency in a nursery should be avoided by proper site selection. Correction of a deficiency might better be accomplished through the use of iron chelates injected into the soil or encapsulated iron implanted into the trunk of trees where this is practical.

### Bark Application

Applying fertilizer solutions to the bark of trees has not proven to be too effective as a means of fertilizing trees in nurseries.

## TIME OF APPLICATION

The question of when is the best time to apply fertilizer has been discussed for years. Various authorities on the topic of nutrition have recommended fall feeding of trees and others have indicated that spring applications of nitrogen are more effective than summer or fall applications. In a 7–year study on the growth of pin oaks, the variation of the individual growing season was reported to be the most important factor affecting tree growth. Also, it is important that ample moisture be available and favorable temperature conditions prevail following the application of fertilizer.

For nursery crops the best time to apply fertilizer, other than nitrogenous materials, is prior to planting, since these materials should be incorporated into the soil. Nitrogenous materials should be applied annually for best results and at a time when growth will be favorably affected. Nitrogenous fertilizer should not be applied when there is a strong possibility of producing growth that will be injured due to either environmental conditions or cultural practices. There are reports in horticultural journals which attribute some forms of winter injury to late application of nitrogenous fertilizer, whereas other reports indicate that plants that receive a fall application of nitrogen survive exposure to cold better than do nonfertilized plants. There are also reports of plants failing to respond with increased growth following fertilizer application, while other reports indicate excellent response.

To explain and justify all these different responses, it is important for nurserymen to understand growth patterns of woody plants and the ecological factors that affect growth. All plants do not respond the same to light, temperature, and moisture. Some plants grow better under long days than others (Table 15–3). Some stop growth and go dormant under short days. Some plants prefer warm temperature, whereas others grow better at lower temperatures. The same is true for moisture. The plant's growth pattern is a response to many factors, interacting simultaneously.

Woody plants can be classified by growth pattern into two types: (1) heterophyllus (indeterminate growth) types develop two types of leaves during the growing season, those preformed within the bud and those initiated during the current season of growth (e.g., birch, juniper, willow); and (2) homophyllus (determinate growth) types develop one type of leaf during the growing season, preformed within the shoot (e.g., pine, rhododendron, oak).

Heterophyllus plants respond quickly to an application of fertilizer. They continue to grow late into the season as long as the ecological conditions are favorable. However, homophyllus plants do not respond immediately by increased growth, but rather the plant builds up its nutrient reserves and expresses it in a massive growth response the following spring. Under certain artificially produced conditions (long days and warm temperature), these plants can express a growth response during the season shortly after fertilizer application. Therefore, species that are of the heterophyllus type respond best to spring and early summer applications of fertilizer. They might, however, be subject to winter injury if ecological conditions were right and the plants were given a late summer application of fertilizer. Species of the homophyllus type may not exhibit an immediate response to a late spring application of fertilizer, but will build up nutrient reserves from fertilizer applied one year for massive growth response the following year. Plants will absorb and translocate nutrients as long as soil temperatures remain favorable. Fall applications of fertilizer to homophyllus species could result in a significant increase in growth the following spring, whereas fall applications of fertilizer to hetero-phyllus species may be less effective.

## ORGANIC MATTER

The maintenance of organic matter in field soils is an important soil management consideration for field-production nurserymen committed to a sustained yield program. With the removal of top soil with many nursery products and with the use of clean cultivation practices, particularly the use of herbicides, the organic-matter content in many nurseries is gradually being depleted. This reduction in organic-matter content will ultimately result in soils of poor tilth, leading to poor plant quality and increased production costs.

Organic matter is of value because it directly influences the physical and biological properties of the soil and because some forms of organic matter serve as a source of nutrients. Organic matter that has been converted to humus improves tilth and soil structure. It reduces the tendency of clay soils to become sticky when wet or to "bake and cake" when dry.

Organic matter also improves aeration, water penetration rates in clay soils, and the water- and nutrient-holding capacity in sandy soils, all of which improve root distribution patterns and plant quality. Organic matter serves as a source of energy for microorganisms that are responsible for the conversion of mineral elements into forms available for plant growth. Organic matter may be either grown as a sod or green manure and plowed under, or it may be added by application of either animal manures or various plant products.

### Animal Manures

Animal manures have long been used as a source of organic matter and plant nutrients. Although manures contain relatively low concentrations of plant nutrients on a percentage basis, 0.5–1.5% N, 0.1–0.4% P, and 0.35–1.0% K, they supply appreciable quantities when applied at relatively high rates per acre. The actual composition of manure varies considerably (Table 12–16).

Stable manure may be applied at rates as high as 30 tons/acre, although more frequent smaller applications (5–10 tons/acre) are more effective (Table 12–10). The manure can best be applied in late winter when the soil is still frozen and cultivated into the soil as soon as it can be worked in the spring. Poultry manure contains two to three times as much nitrogen as other manures and decays rapidly, releasing ammonia, which can cause plant injury. If the poultry manure is thoroughly mixed with soil or sawdust, it is less likely to cause injury. The primary objections to the use of animal manures is the weed problem that follows application and the cost of handling. The weed problem can be minimized either by using manure obtained from confinement feeding operations or by composting the manure prior to use. Handling cost is

**Table 12–16** Average Nutrient Composition of Manure from Selected Farm Animals

| Type of Manure | Percent Water | Pounds per Ton of Manure | | | | | | | | | |
|---|---|---|---|---|---|---|---|---|---|---|---|
| | | N | P | K | Ca | Mg | S | Cu | Fe | Mn | Mo |
| Chicken | 55 | 31.2 | 8.0 | 7.0 | 74.0 | 5.8 | 6.2 | 0.03 | 0.93 | 0.18 | 0.011 |
| Dairy cattle | 80 | 11.2 | 2.0 | 10.0 | 5.6 | 2.2 | 1.0 | 0.01 | 0.08 | 0.02 | 0.002 |
| Hog | 75 | 10.0 | 2.8 | 7.6 | 11.4 | 1.6 | 2.7 | 0.01 | 0.56 | 0.04 | 0.002 |
| Horse | 65 | 13.8 | 2.0 | 12.0 | 15.7 | 2.8 | 1.4 | 0.01 | 0.27 | 0.02 | 0.002 |
| Sheep | 65 | 28.0 | 4.2 | 20.0 | 11.7 | 3.7 | 1.8 | 0.01 | 0.32 | 0.02 | 0.002 |

offset by improved growth. Animal manure is an excellent organic source of slow-release nutrients. They can be used to good advantage on soils that have been subjected to poor management or have been disturbed as a result of some type of landforming operation.

### Sod and Green Manure

Sod and green manure crops are grown in rotation with nursery crops to improve soil structure and add organic matter. Grasses in combination with legumes are excellent crops for improving nursery soils. Grasses supply organic matter, especially by their dense root system, while taprooted legumes (e.g., alfalfa) improve the internal drainage. For maximum production of organic matter, sods should be grown for 2 years. In situations where a sod crop cannot be used in rotation with nursery crops, green manure crops can often be used to advantage. They are grown for less than a growing season and are plowed under while in a succulent state and before they set seed. Tall-growing crops are usually chopped to aid incorporation. Some crops that are used as green manure include (1) annual ryegrass, (2) alfalfa, (3) field corn, (4) foxtail millet, (5) soybeans, (6) sorghum, (7) sudan grass, (8) sudan-sorghum hybrids, and (9) in some areas wheat overseeded in the spring with clover.

Sudan grass and sudan-sorghum hybrids produce organic matter yields at rates equal to or greater than thickly planted corn. They are more drought-resistant than corn and can be worked into the soil with greater ease. In the cooler parts of the country (climatic zones 3 and 4), foxtail or pearl millet may be preferred, since they grow better under cooler growing conditions (Fig. 6–1). Sudan grass, sudan-sorghum hybrids, and millet can be mowed when they start to head out, causing them to grow more thickly. Several cycles of growth and mowing can be repeated during the year, greatly increasing yield. Fertilizing green manure and cover crops is an excellent way to improve soil fertility, soil structure, and to reduce weed populations.

### Cover Crops

Cover crops are grown to protect the soil against the forces of erosion, and aid in maintaining the organic matter content of the soil. It is a common practice in production nurseries located in the northern part of the country (climatic zones 3, 4, and 5) to sow a crop of oats (*Avena sativa*) or buckwheat (*Fagopyrum esculentum*) between the nursery rows in late August or early September to help harden-off the nursery stock for winter by taking up nitrogen. When the ground freezes, the plants die, but a mulch is left to protect the soil over winter and in the early spring. The light mulch also aids in retaining moisture in the spring, enhancing digging operations. In those areas of the nursery where nursery stock has recently been removed or where it is too late to sow a green manure crop, it may be desirable to sow a winter annual such as winter rye (*Secale cereale*) or ryegrass (*Lolium* spp.) in the late summer or early fall. The crop is plowed under in the spring before it goes to seed. However, where land costs are high, a cash crop such as wheat or field corn may be grown. The grain provides a financial return from the land and at the same time the stubble adds organic matter to the soil, improving the tilth for the next nursery crop. Table 12–17 provides some guidelines for the seeding of green manure or cover crops for nursery plantings.

### Companion Plantings

In extensive plantings, where trees are planted on wide spacings, nurserymen should consider using grass aisles as companion or complementary plantings (see Fig. 5–12). Grasses, such as perennial rye grass, hard fescues, and bluegrass, make an excellent sod cover that can be used as access routes for heavy equipment, especially when the soil is wet. In addition, the sod will control erosion, modify the soil environment, add organic matter when plowed under, reduce the quantity of herbicide application, and reduce time requirements for harvesting the plants and performing various cultural practices related to the growth and development of the trees.

Grass selection will vary between geographical areas of the country, the soil type, and various management practices of the nursery. Advice on species selection, seeding rates, and cultural practices may be obtained from the county agricultural agent or a crop specialist located at a land-grant university.

Mowing of the turf will be necessary during the growing season. This should be done on a regular, periodic basis (7–10 days). However, growth control of sod is also possible with a growth-regulator chemical. Embark, applied

**Table 12–17**  Suggested Seeding Rates, Planting Depth, and Planting Dates for Selected Green Manures and Cover Crops[a]

| Crop | Seeding Rate (lb/acre) | Planting Depth (in.) | Planting Date |
|---|---|---|---|
| Alfalfa | 6–10 | ½ | Spring or summer |
| Buckwheat | 40–60 | 1–2 | Late spring |
| Corn (field) | 1–2 bushels | 2 | Spring |
| Kentucky bluegrass | 15–30 | ½ | Late summer, very early spring |
| Millet | 10–15 | ½–1 | Late spring |
| Oats | 60–80 | 1–2 | Late summer |
| Ryegrass | 10 | ½ | Fall |
| Sorghum | 5–8 | ½ | Late spring |
| Sorghum-sudan hybrids | 40 | 1 | Late spring |

[a]See county agricultural agent for local recommendations.

*Source:* After Hildebrand and Copeland (1977).

according to the manufacturer's instructions, will provide up to 6 weeks of growth suppression.

### Organic Amendments

Bark and sawdust have been found to be economical soil amendments in some situations when supplemented with nitrogen. When bark or sawdust or other similar materials are applied to or mixed with soil in which plants are growing, nitrogen deficiency can and often does develop. Microorganisms, which multiply due to the presence of the carbonaceous substrate, require nitrogen for growth. They compete more successfully for available nitrogen than do the economic crops resulting in nitrogen deficiency. However, a supplemental application of approximately 2% available nitrogen per unit weight of sawdust will minimize this problem. A C/N ratio of 20:1 or less is needed to avoid the necessity of adding supplemental nitrogen (Table 12–18). In some soils, low in available $P_2O_5$, supplemental applications of superphosphate may be needed to avoid phosphorus deficiency. Sawdust has a tendency to lower the pH of soils slightly. Where crops requiring an alkaline soil reaction are to be grown, it may be necessary to apply lime to modify this effect.

Peat moss is used to improve many types of landscape soils, but because of its high cost, it is used only in limited ways in the field production of nursery stock. It is used as a medium in container production of plants, as a propagation medium for some species, and as a packaging material.

In preparing land to be planted with a long-term nursery crop, it is highly desirable to incorporate a liberal quantity of organic matter to replace that removed with the previous crop and ensure a long-range supply, since additional application of organic matter is seldom made while the crop is on the land. The land should be plowed to a depth of 8 in. or more to incorporate and distribute the organic matter into the root zone. Following plowing, the land should be disked and, if necessary, smoothed with a harrow.

## SOIL CONSERVATION

Soil conservation is another area in a field-production nursery to which management must direct its attention if the nursery is to remain productive. Soil conservation is managing the soil so that its productivity can be optimized for

**Table 12–18**　Percent of Dry Weight of Carbon and Nitrogen and the C/N Ratio of Selected Organic Materials

| Material | % C | % N | C/N |
|---|---|---|---|
| Alfalfa | 39 | 3.0 | 13:1 |
| Legume-grass hay | 40 | 1.6 | 80:1 |
| Oat straw | 40 | 0.5 | 80:1 |
| Sawdust | 50 | 0.2 | 250:1 |

both current and future plantings. Unfortunately, many nursery practices contribute to loss of soil productivity; these include (1) loss of soil by digging operations and erosion, (2) long periods of clean cultivation, and (3) performing nursery operations when the soil is wet.

The *loss of soil by digging* B&B or balled and potted nursery stock is considerable. Digging an acre of 5-year B&B evergreens removes about 165 tons of soil, representing an average loss of 33 tons per year. Digging shade trees with a 44-in.-diameter ball removes 1.3 tons of soil, or about 470 tons of soil per acre. This is an average of 67 tons per year for a 7-year rotation. In addition to "mining" of soil, with the sale of plants, nurserymen can also lose a substantial amount by erosion. Under conditions of clean tillage, the loss of soil by erosion varies from 19 to 69 tons/acre/year, depending upon slope, soil type, and environmental conditions. When the average annual "mining" loss of soil for shade tree production is combined with the average annual loss of soil by erosion (44 tons/acre), the amount averages 100 tons of soil per year. At this rate, there would be a loss of 4.2 in. of top soil every 7 years.

*Clean cultivation of field-grown nursery stock* is commonly practiced since growth is usually best; however, it contributes to the loss of soil by erosion and to degradation of soil structure. Allowing the soil surface to remain "naked" following plowing, disking, and cultivating exposes it to erosion. Also, the extensive use of herbicides removes the protective cover of weeds, leaving soil in a prime condition for erosion. The effect of raindrops or sprinkler irrigation water hitting the soil (splash erosion) is the first step in water erosion. Splash erosion breaks down the natural structure of the soil. This breakdown of the soil aggregates results in crusting of the surface and reduced soil porosity. These, in turn, reduce water infiltration, causing more runoff, and increasing the potential for more serious forms of erosion, especially on nonlevel sites. However, as stated previously, clean cultivation of nursery crops often results in the best growth. Nursery managers should use soil management practices that not only maximizes growth of current crops but also increases the growth of crops over longer periods of time.

*Performing field operation when the soil is wet* is often necessary in field-production nurseries, especially in the spring. This practice will compact the soil and reduce its porosity. The overall effect is to reduce its production potential and add to the cost of production. If the soil can be rolled into a "ball" or a "snake," it is too wet for field operations.

## SOIL CONSERVATION PRACTICES

Little can be done to prevent the loss of nursery soil that is sold as part of the product, other than to change to a container-production system or to produce bare-root plants. However, much can be done to minimize the loss of nursery soils by erosion and to maintain or improve soil structure.

*Protecting the soil surface* with a canopy of vegetation or with mulches will reduce the effect of rain or irrigation water. Anything that can be done to promote the rapid establishment of the nursery crop is likely to reduce the amount of erosion. Planting a sod crop between the rows (Fig. 5–12) is a desirable conservation practice, where it is a viable option. The planting of green manure or cover crops, discussed previously, is also a desirable soil conservation practice as well as a means of increasing organic matter and improving soil structure. The application of mulches, such as bark or animal manure, to the soil or allowing crop residues to remain on the soil following harvest can also protect the soil surface from splash and wind erosion.

*The use of heavy equipment on the land,* particularly when the soil is wet, should be minimized. Where feasible, "minimum tillage" should be practiced to reduce the frequency that heavy equipment is upon the land. Prior to tilling the soil, consideration should be given to using a chisel plow in place of the standard mold-board plow. The chisel plow leaves crop residue on the surface, which aids in reducing erosion. Also, when possible, fall plowing should be avoided or confined to level fields, since fall plowing leaves soils exposed to erosion for extended periods. *Subsoiling and tilling* can be used to improve the drainage and percolation of water in soils that have become compacted.

*Across-the-slope tillage* or planting nursery rows on the contour will produce small dams that will slow the flow of water and minimize gully erosion on hilly sites. In areas where the terrain is composed of short, irregular slopes, this type of tillage may not be possible.

*Strip-cropping* uses the concept of growing clean-cultivated crops in alternate strips with close growing or sod crops. Strip-cropping is most effective in areas where the slopes are too steep to control water erosion by contour tillage alone, but not steep enough to require the construction of terraces. Strip-cropping is useful for nurseries situated on long sloping sites, since it permits a rotation to be developed between nursery crops and sod.

*Various water disposal systems* can be developed in nurseries to minimize soil losses by erosion, including the construction of terraces, grass waterways, and subsurface drainage systems. Terraces are earth ridges, constructed on the contour, to form a damlike channel for the interception of water, which is then slowly conducted from the field by a grassed waterway or underground drains. The shape, width, and length of waterways will vary with size of the watershed area. The driving of cars and trucks should never be permitted on terraces and waterways if they are to remain functional for the purpose for which they were designed.

The success of conservation practices depends upon good design, construction, proper use, and maintenance. Assistance in design and construction can be obtained at little or no cost, from local Soil Conservation District engineers and from the USDA Soil Conservation Service. Proper use and maintenance of soil conservation systems is the responsibility of management.

## SUMMARY

Field production is a major method for the production of nursery stock. If fields are to be productive for current and future generations, they must be well managed. By developing and practicing good soil-management methods, it is possible to maintain nursery soil productivity at relatively high levels.

## REFERENCES

ALLISON, F. E., and M. S. ANDERSON. 1951. The use of sawdust for mulches and soil improvement. USDA Circ. 891.

AMERICAN ASSOCIATION OF NURSERYMEN. 1948. Your nursery and soil conservation. AAN, Washington, D.C.

BENJAMIN, L. P., L. C. CHADWICK, and K. W. REISCH. 1964. The effectiveness of urea-formaldehyde as a source of nitrogen for container-grown woody ornamental plants. Proc. Am. Soc. Hort. Sci. 84:636–647.

BERG, A., G. CLULO, and C. R. ORTON. 1958. Internal bark necrosis of apple resulting from manganese toxicity. W. Va. Agric. Exp. Sta. Bull. 414T.

BERNSTEIN, L. 1964. Reducing salt injury to ornamental shrubs in the West. USDA Home Garden Bull. 95.

———. 1965. Salt tolerance of fruit crops. USDA Inf. Bull. 292.

BOONSTRA, R., A. L. KENWORTHY, and D. P. WATSON. 1957. Nutritional status of selected plantings of *Taxus media* "Hicksi." Proc. Am. Soc. Hor. Sci. 70:432–436.

BOWER, C. A. 1963. Diagnosing soil salinity. USDA Agric. Inf. Bull. 279.

BRADLEY, G. A., and D. SMITTLE. 1965. Media pH and extractable Fe, Al and Mn in relation to growth of ericaeous plants. Proc. Am. Soc. Hort. Sci. 87:486–493.

CANNON, T. F., L. C. CHADWICK, and K. W. REISCH. 1960. Nitrogen and potassium nutritional studies of *Gleditisia triacanthos Inermis* "Moraine." Proc. Am. Soc. Hort. Sci. 75:693–699.

———, L. C. CHADWICK, and K. W. REISCH. 1960. Nutrient element status of some ornamental trees. Proc. Am. Soc. Hort. Sci. 76:661–666.

CHADWICK, L. C. 1934. The fertilization of shade trees in the nursery. Proc. Am. Soc. Hort. Sci. 32:357–360.

COOK, T., and J. L. GREEN. 1985. Many grasses available for nursery aisles and plant protection. Am. Nurseryman 161(1): 89–96.

DAVIDSON, H. 1960. Nutrient-element composition of leaves from selected species of woody ornamental plants. Proc. Am. Soc. Hort. Sci. 76:667–672.

———, and W. BARRICK. 1975. Fertilizer practices and vegetation control on highway landscape plantings. Agric. Exp. Sta. Mich. State Univ. Res. Rep. 262.

———, and W. McCALL. 1959. Fertilizer studies on *Taxus.* Quar. Bull. Mich. Agric. Exp. Sta. 42(2):317–322.

DICKEY, R. D. 1968. Identification and correction of copper deficiency. Am. Nurseryman 128(October 15):10.

DUNHAM, C. W., and D. V. TATNALL. 1961. Mineral composition of leaves of three holly species grown in nutrient sand cultures. Proc. Am. Soc. Hort. Sci. 78:564–571.

FENN, P., and R. D. DURBIN. 1974. A nutritional disorder of red oak seedlings. HortScience 9(3):240–241.

FURUTA, T., and W. C. MARTIN. 1961. Effect of fertilizer application rate and method on plant growth. Proc. Am. Soc. Hort. Sci. 77:637–642.

GILLIAM, C. H., J. T. EASON, and C. E. EVANS. 1985. Effects of pH on Four Field-Grown Nursery Crops. J. Environ. Hort. 3(3):136–139.

GOOD, G. L., and H. B. TUKEY, JR. 1969. Root growth and nutrient uptake by dormant *Ligustrum ibolium* and *Euonymus atatus* "Compactus." J. Am. Soc. Hort. Sci. 94(3): 324–326.

GOUIN, F. R., and C. B. LINK. 1966. The effects of various levels of nitrogen, phosphorus and potassium on the growth and chemical composition of *Taxus media* "Hatfieldi." Proc. Am. Soc. Hort. Sci. 89:702–705.

HAMILTON, C. L. Terraced outlets and form drainways. USDA Farmers' Bull. 1814, July 1939.

HILDEBRAND, S. C., and L. O. COPELAND. 1977. Coop. Ext. Serv. Mich. State Univ. Ext. Bull. E–489.

HIMELICH, E. B., D. NEELY, and W. R. CROWLER, JR. 1965. Experimental field studies on shade tree fertilization. Ill. Nat. Hist. Surv. Biol. Notes 53.

JACOBSON, P., and W. WEISS. Farming terraced land, USDA Soil Conserv. Serv. Leaflet 335, November 1952.

KELLEY, J. D. 1972. Nitrogen and potassium rate effects on growth, leaf nitrogen and winter hardiness of *Pyracantha coccinia* "Lalandi" and *Ilex crenata* "Rotundifolia." J. Am. Soc. Hort. Sci. 97(4):446–448.

———, and R. W. SHIER. 1965. Seasonal changes in the macronutrient composition of the leaves and stems of *Taxus media*. Proc. Am. Soc. Hort. Sci. 86:800–814.

———, and R. W. SHIER. 1965. Seasonal changes in the micronutrient composition of the leaves and stems of *Taxus media*. Proc. Am. Soc. Hort. Sci. 87:545–550.

KIELBASO, J. J., and K. OTTMAN. 1976. Manganese deficiency contributory to maple decline. J. Arboriculture:27–32.

LUNT, H. A., A. M. KOFRANEK, and J. J. OERTLI. 1961. Coated fertilizers: general description and applications. Calif. Agric. 15(12):2–3.

———, and J. J. OERTLI. 1962. Controlled release of fertilizer minerals by incapsulating membranes: II. Efficiency of recovery influence of soil moisture, mode of application and other considerations related to use. Soil Sci. Soc. Am. Proc. 26(6):584–587.

MESSENGER, A. S., and B. A. HRUBY. 1990. Response of Interveinally Chlorotic Red Maple Trees Treated with Medicaps or by Soil Acidification, J. Environ. Hort. 8(1):5–9.

MEYER, M. M., JR. 1969. External and internal nutrition and spring growth of woody ornamental plants. Proc. Int. Plant Propag. Soc. 19:300–305.

———. 1971. Phosphorus utilization from internal and external sources in the growth of woody ornamental plants. J. Am. Soc. Hort. Sci. 96(2):209–212.

————, and H. B. Tukey, Jr. 1965. Nitrogen, phosphorus and potassium plant reserves and spring growth of *Taxus* and *Forsythia*. Proc. Am. Soc. Hort. Sci. 87:537–544.

————, and H. B. Tukey, Jr. 1967. Influence of root temperature and nutrient applications on root growth and mineral content of *Taxus* and *Forsythia* plants during the dormant season. Proc. Am. Soc. Hort. Sci. 90:440–446.

Miller, R. O., D. C. Kiplinger, and H. K. Tayama. 1967. Soluble salts. Florists Rev., November 2, p. 49.

Neely, D., E. B. Himelick, and W. R. Crowley, Jr. 1970. Ill. Nat. Hist. Surv. Bull. 30, Art. 4, pp. 235–266.

Oertli, J., and O. R. Lunt. 1962. Controlled release of fertilizer minerals by incapsulating membranes. I. Factors influencing the rate of release. Soil Sci. Am. Proc. 26(6):579–583.

Rader, L. F., L. M. White, and C. W. Whittaker. 1943. The salt index—a measure of the effect of fertilizers on the concentration of the soil solution. Soil Sci. 55:201–218.

Robertson, L. S., D. L. Mokma, and D. L. Quinsenberry. 1977. Soil erosion by water. Coop. Ext. Serv. Mich. State Univ. Ext. Bull. E–1169.

Rogers, B. L., A. H. Thompson, and L. E. Scott. 1965. Internal bark necrosis (measles) on Delicious apple trees under field conditions. Proc. Am. Soc. Hort. Sci. 86:46–54.

Schoeneweiss, D. F. 1973. Correction of lime-induced chlorosis of pin oak by liquid soil injection. HortScience 8(4):333–334.

Shear, C. B., H. L. Crane, and A. T. Myers. 1946. Nutrient element balance: a fundamental concept in plant nutrition. Proc. Am. Soc. Hort. Sci. 47:239–248.

————, H. L. Crane, and A. T. Myers. 1950. Nutrient element balance: application of the concept to the interpretation of foliar analysis. Proc. Am. Soc. Hort. Sci. 51:319–326.

Smiley, E. T., J. B. Hart, Jr., and J. J. Kielbaso. 1985. Foliar Nutrient Diagnosis of Urban Sugar and Red Maples in the Great Lakes Region. J. Environ. Hort. 3(3):104–107.

Smith, E. M. 1975. Fertilizing field-grown evergreens and shrubs. Am. Nurseryman 142(10):10.

————. 1975. Growth response of fertilized trees. Am. Nurseryman 143(1):11.

Spurway, C. H. 1944. Soil reaction (pH) preferences of plants. Mich. State Col., Agric. Exp. Sta. Special Bul. 306.

————, and K. Lawton. 1949. Soil testing, a practical system of fertility diagnosis. Mich. State Univ. Agric. Exp. Sta. Tech. Bull. 132 (4th revision).

Tatnall, D. V., and C. W. Dunham. 1961. Nutrient deficiency symptoms in American, Japanese and Chinese hollies. Proc. Am. Soc. Hort. Sci. 78:560–563.

Truog, E. 1947. USDA yearbook of agriculture, 1943–47. Superintendent of Documents, Washington, D.C.

Wikle, J. 1963. Some comments and questions on soil improvement and fertilization for shade trees. Arborist News:61–69.

Wilde, S. A. 1938. Soil fertility standards for growing northern conifers in forest nurseries. J. Agric. Res. 57:945–952.

————. 1946. Soil fertility standards for game food plants. J. Wildl. Manage. 10:77–81.

————, and W. E. PATZER. 1940. Soil fertility standards for growing northern hardwoods in forest nurseries. J. Agric. Res. 61:215–221.

WITTWER, S. H. 1963. Foliar application of fertilizer. New Horizons in the Fertilizer World. Tennessee Valley Authority.

YOUNGBERG, C. T., and R. C. AUSTIN. 1954. Fertility standards for raising Douglas fir in forest nurseries. J. For. 52:4–6.

————, and R. C. AUSTIN. 1958. The uptake of nutrients by western conifers in forest nurseries. J. For. 56(5):337–340.

ZIMMERMAN, R. H. 1959. Visual symptoms of plant nutrient deficiencies. Proc. Int. Plant Propag. Soc. 9:131–135.

## SUGGESTED READING

AMERICAN SOCIETY OF AGRONOMY. 1965. Methods of soil analysis, Parts 1 and 2. Madison, Wisc.

DIRR, M. A. 1975. Plant nutrition and woody ornamental growth and quality. HortScience 10(1):43–45.

DONAHUE, R. L., R. W. MILLER, and J. C. SHICKLUNA. 1977. Soils: an introduction to soils and plant growth. Prentice-Hall, Inc., Englewood Cliffs, NJ.

MENGEL, K., and E. A. KIRKBY. 1978. Principles of plant nutrition. International Potash Institute, Worblaufen-Bern, Switzerland.

SWANSON, B. T. et al. 1986. Soil Testing and Fertilizer Applications for Nursery Management and Production. AG-BU-2030, Ag. Ext. Serv. Univ. of Minnesota. St. Paul, MN.

U.S. DEPARTMENT OF AGRICULTURE. 1957. Soil, the yearbook of agriculture. Superintendent of Documents, Washington, D.C.

Chapter **13**

# Media and Nutrition Management for Container-Grown Plants

Producing plants in containers has become a permanent part of the nursery industry and in some parts of the country the practice has replaced field culture as the primary method of production. In contrast to field culture, the volume of medium available per plant is greatly reduced. Also, the root environment is significantly affected by the physical and chemical composition of the medium, the size and shape of the container, the surface upon which it is placed to grow, and the ambient atmosphere surrounding the containers. Therefore, good container-media management is basic to the production of quality container-grown plants. It is necessary to (1) understand the primary functions and establish some basic criteria for container media, (2) be familiar with the physical and chemical properties of some of the more commonly used ingredients and mixes, (3) understand the need for chemical supplements and method of testing and controlling their availability, and (4) understand the need for and methods of media sterilization.

## FUNCTIONS AND CRITERIA

In developing a medium for the production of container-grown plants, the functions of the medium in plant growth and development must be understood and criteria determined to produce the most functional medium for the climate and for the nursery objective. The two basic functions of the medium are (1) to serve as a means of anchorage and support for the plant and (2) to serve as a reservoir for water and the mineral nutrients for plant growth and development. In addition, the medium must have a pH conducive to plant growth, a structure that will permit gaseous exchange to provide aeration for the roots and permit water infiltration and movement.

### Anchorage and Support

The roots of plants serve to anchor them to the soil, which in turn serves to support the plant. In field production this works, since the roots can grow unrestricted. However, in container culture the roots are restricted to the confines of the container. Therefore, a medium for container production of plants in a nursery must be heavy enough to provide ballast for the species of plant it will support, unless other forms of artificial support are provided, particularly for larger trees and shrubs. Small plants produced in 1- to 5-gal containers and spaced pot to pot can be grown in a medium of low bulk density (BD)—weight per unit volume—whereas larger plants grown on wider spacings require a medium of higher BD. Where the plants are large and the BD of the medium is low, some other form of support is necessary, such as staking or tying to a wire.

### Nutrients

Plants produced in containers require the same essential elements as plants produced in field culture. The total supply of minerals available for plant growth is limited by the size of the container. This makes it desirable that the medium used for container production have a relatively high cation exchange capacity (CEC) to serve as a reservoir for mineral elements other than nitrogen or those that will be supplied by other means. Most of the organic ingredients provide this even though at a low level. The CEC for medium mixtures used in container production of plants should be reported on a volume basis, which is expressed as milliequivalents per 100 cubic centimeters (e.g., sand approximately 1 mEq/100 cc, bark approximately 11–13 mEq/100 cc). Maintaining optimum levels of nitrogen during the growing season may be done through the use of slow-release fertilizers (Table 11–9) or by the use of soluble fertilizers applied through the irrigation system (Table 11–10).

### Soil (Medium) Reaction (pH)

The optimum pH for organic mixes (Fig. 13–1) tends to be 1–1.5 units lower than those generally considered to be desirable for mineral soils

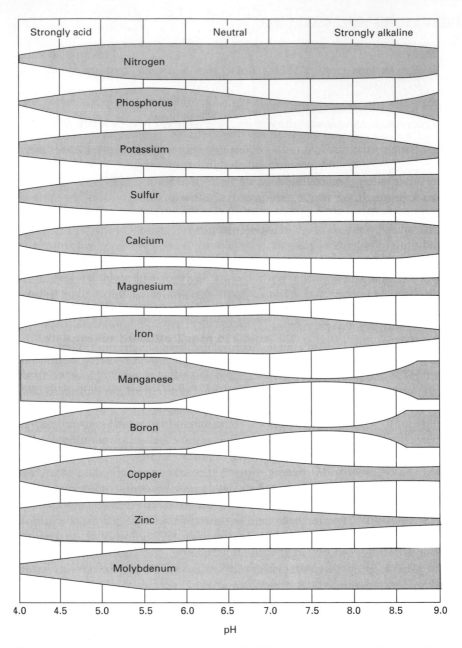

**Figure 13–1** Influence of reaction on availability of plant nutrients in organic soils. Widest part of bar indicates maximum availability. (From Lucas and Davis, 1961.)

(Fig. 12–1). Liming organic soils with a pH above 5.8 is undesirable because of the reduced availability of P, Mn, B, Cu, and Zn.

### Moisture-Holding Capacity and Porosity

Growing plants require large quantities of water for metabolic purposes and to replace that which is lost by transpiration. Therefore, one of the important functions of a good container medium is to store and supply the moisture needed for plant growth. However, for the moisture to be available to the plants requires that the roots must have a supply of oxygen, necessitating that the container medium have good aeration porosity so that the roots can carry on respiration and allow for the removal of the carbon dioxide ($CO_2$) that is generated in the process. This presents somewhat of a problem with containers, since they are relatively shallow and develop a perched water table at the bottom of the container. The shallower the container and the finer the texture, the greater the moisture-holding capacity but the poorer the aeration porosity. On the other hand, deep containers and coarse-textured materials improve the aeration porosity but reduce the moisture-holding capacity.

The effect of shallowness can be partially avoided by incorporating coarse-textured ingredients (sand, bark, perlite) into the container medium. However, sufficient coarse material must be blended into an ingredient of fine texture so that the threshold proportion is exceeded. This is the blend or mix at which pore space is minimized; as the proportion of the coarse texture ingredient is increased beyond the threshold proportion, porosity is increased (Fig. 13–2). Improvement of the porosity of a fine-textured medium requires a substantial addition (80–90% of the total bulk volume) of the coarse-texture ingredient. A medium for the production of container-grown plants should be blended to produce a mix that has good water-holding capacity and also good porosity. This is dependent upon the texture of the various ingredients and the relative proportions within the mix.

Porosity determines the volume of the container, when filled with a medium, that is potentially available for water, air, and for root growth. Pore size determines the actual volume of water and air that remains in a container medium following irrigation and drainage; the small pores function as water-retention pores, whereas large pores function as aeration pores (aeration porosity).

Aeration porosity and water retention of a container medium are also influenced by the depth of the container. A medium in a shallower container will hold a greater volume of water than the same volume of medium in a deeper container. Therefore, when characterizing water retention and aeration porosity of a container medium, it is necessary to consider container depth (see Table 13–1).

**Figure 13–2** Modifying aeration and water-holding capacity of container soil. Starting with100% soil, additions of perlite up to about 70% (critical proportion) reduce total pore space without increasing the number of larger pores. Starting with 100% perlite, additions of soil up to about 30% reduce total pore space by filling in the larger pores. The critical proportion of amendment to soil varies with the type of amendment and the type of soil. (From Spomer, 1973).

## INGREDIENTS

The two most commonly used ingredients in the production of media for container growing of woody plants have been sand and peat moss. However, soil is used in some mixes and various wood-waste products are being used to replace peat moss. Composted hardwood bark is used fairly extensively in the Midwest, pine and Douglas fir bark is used where it is readily available, and redwood sawdust is used in California.

The following information briefly summarizes some of the properties of the most commonly used ingredients as they pertain to the production of container-grown plants.

Sand consists of weathered mineral particles between 0.05 and 2.0 mm in diameter. But for container-soil mixes, the size range should be between 0.05 and 1.0 mm with less than 10% of the sand in the coarse-sized classification, between 0.5 and 1.0 mm. The mineral composition of the sand is related to the rocks from which it was formed, but for horticultural purposes sand contains few, if any, mineral elements, and has no significant buffering or cation exchange capacity. Sand may or may not be sterile, depending upon the source. The pH of sand varies with source, but most sands have a high pH and may require the addition of an acidifying agent prior to use as a medium for the production of plants.

**Table 13–1** Estimation of Porosity

Nurserymen can estimate the total porosity, aeration porosity, and water-retention porosity of a container medium by a simple technique. The only necessary equipment includes the container, a plug for the drainage hole at the bottom of the container, and a graduated cylinder or some other method for measuring water volume.

1. Plug the drain hole and fill the container with water. Measure the volume of water it contains ( = container volume).

2. Empty the container and fill it with dry soil mix. Very slowly and very thoroughly saturate the mix in the container by carefully pouring water onto the surface at one edge of the container. Keep track of the volume of water you are adding ( = pore volume).

3. Unplug the drain and catch the water that drains out of the container and measure its volume ( = aeration pore volume).

4. Porosity is obtained by dividing pore volume (step 2) by container volume (step 1) and multiplying by 100%.

5. Aeration porosity is obtained by dividing aeration pore volume (step 3) by container volume (step 1) and multiplying by 100%.

6. Water retention porosity is obtained by subtracting aeration porosity (step 5) from porosity (step 4).

In summary:

$$\text{Porosity} = \frac{\text{container mix pore volume}}{\text{container volume}} \times 100\%$$

$$\text{Aeration porosity} = \frac{\text{aeration pore volume}}{\text{container volume}} \times 100\%$$

$$\text{Water-retention porosity} = \text{porosity} - \text{aeration porosity}$$

*Source:* Spomer (1977).

*Peats* used in media for the production of container-grown plants are commonly classified into three types: moss peat, reed-sedge peat, and peat humus.

*Moss peat* is composed principally of sphagnum, hypnum, and other mosses. Sphagnum is the least decomposed of the three types. It is light tan to dark brown in color, lightweight, high in moisture-holding capacity, and high in acidity. Moss peat will hold 10 times its dry weight in moisture, and because of its high acidity it is slow to decompose. Moss peat should not be confused with sphagnum moss, which is the live portion or the young, nondecomposed residue of sphagnum. Sphagnum moss is used by nurserymen in packaging and shipping of tender plants and as a propagation medium.

*Reed-sedge peat* is formed principally of reeds, sedges, marsh grasses, and other swamp plants. It varies considerably in its degree of decomposition and acidity. The partially decomposed reed-sedge peats are brown to reddish brown in color, whereas the more decomposed types are almost black. They have a pH between 4.5 and 7.0 and a medium water-holding capacity.

*Peat humus* is derived from either reed-sedge or hypnum moss peat in an advanced stage of decomposition. It is dark brown to black in color, has a low water-holding capacity, but is more resistant to decomposition than is moss or reed-sedge peat.

*Wood products* of various types, including sawdust, wood chips, shredded bark, and wood shavings, are an excellent source of organic material for soil mixtures in the production of container-grown plants. For many years nurserymen declined to use wood products as a soil amendment because it was thought they contained materials that were toxic to plant growth. However, present evidence indicates that sawdust and most other woodwaste products contain relatively few compounds that are toxic to plant growth.

The reason for the "toxic" effect, a stunting and chlorosis of the plant, is related to the carbon-nitrogen ratio of the sawdust and its effect upon the soil-plant nitrogen relationship. When undecomposed wood products, such as sawdust or wood chips, are mixed with soil under favorable conditions of warm temperature and available moisture, they start to decompose. The decomposition is aided by various forms of microflora. These microorganisms require a source of energy carbon, which is supplied by the wood, and a source of nitrogen, which the wood does not supply except in trace quantities. Therefore, the microflora obtain the needed nitrogen from the only other available source, the soil. If there are plants present, the microorganisms compete with them for the available nitrogen, and unless there is enough for both, the plants will exhibit nitrogen deficiency. This problem can be avoided by the addition of nitrogen to the sawdust-soil mixture. If the nitrogen content of the mixture, on a weight basis, is about 1.2–1.5% and optimum conditions for biological activity are present, decomposition will proceed without depleting the supply of available nitrogen to the growing crop. Since sawdust contains about 0.2% nitrogen, the addition of 25–30 lb nitrogen/ton of sawdust is required.

*Aged sawdust* makes an excellent ingredient for container production of nursery stock. It is lightweight, has good water-holding capacity, and good aeration porosity. It does not require the addition of large quantities of nitrogen to support microbial development, and it is relatively sterile.

*Hardwood bark* is a lightweight, woodwaste product which when supplemented with nitrogen makes an excellent organic ingredient for the production of container-grown plants. It may be used alone or in combination with sand. It is lightweight, easy to handle, and the CEC exceeds that of peat. Bark contains all the trace elements and significant amounts of the major elements. Some hardwood barks may contain phytotoxic substances that are harmful to plant growth. But by composting for a period of at least 30 days, most of these compounds are eliminated. The material is readily available in many parts of the country and is relatively inexpensive.

*Pine and Douglas fir bark* is an excellent medium for the production of plants that prefer an acid root environment such as rhododendrons. It is also used either alone or in combination with sand, after the pH has been adjusted, for the production of all types of container-grown plants. Softwood bark has a low bulk density and a fairly good CEC (11–13 mEq/100 cc). It is somewhat difficult to wet (use of a wetting agent is suggested) but upon wetting it possesses a good water-holding capacity, together with good aeration. Some barks, such as Douglas fir, contain sharp slivers, which necessitates the use of leather gloves when handling the material.

*Perlite* is a lightweight, granular material obtained by heat-treating crushed lava. It weighs less than 8 lb/ft$^3$. It is sterile, has a pH close to neutral, and a water-holding capacity, on the surface of the particles, equal to three to four times its weight. The material is without either buffering or cation exchange capacity. Perlite is a good propagation medium or an amendment to decrease weight and improve aeration of container mixes.

*Vermiculite* is a very lightweight, platelike material obtained by heat-treating mica. It weighs about the same as perlite, 6–10 lb/ft$^3$, depending upon the grade; has a good water-holding capacity, equal to three to four times its weight; and a good CEC. Since the material is produced by a heat treatment, it is sterile. Vermiculite makes an excellent propagation medium and a media amendment for producing small container-grown plants. It must be handled with care when wet to avoid compressing the particles. Compressed vermiculite is an undesirable media amendment, since it results in poor drainage and poor aeration porosity.

*Turface* is a calcined clay that is excellent for improving the aeration porosity of soils or container mixes. Its bulk density is greater than perlite or vermiculite, but it has good internal capacity for holding nutrients and water.

## CONTAINER MEDIA

A good container medium must possess the criteria and perform the various functions discussed previously. In addition, it should be: (1) readily available; (2) relatively inexpensive; (3) light enough to be handled conveniently within the nursery and to be transported economically to market; (4) free of pests (weed seeds, disease organisms, insects, nematodes, herbicide residue, etc.) or be capable of being sterilized without the production of toxic substances (e.g., soluble salts, ammonia, biuret, or other phytoxins); (5) economically blended into a uniform, relatively stable medium; and (6) capable of being stored for short periods of time without significant changes in the physical and chemical properties.

### Mixes

The early container mixes, prior to 1940, incorporated a loam soil; a clean, sharp sand; and peat in various proportions. This was supplemented with lime, superphosphate, and various fertilizers, which generally included an organic source of nitrogen. But these mixes were not satisfactory because they lacked uniformity and plant performance was highly variable. Soil and sand have a high bulk density (100 lbs/ft$^3$), making them difficult to handle and costly to transport to market.

### The U.C.-Type Soil Mixes

The U.C. system for producing healthy container-grown plants was developed at the University of California, Los Angeles, in the 1940s and early 1950s. The primary objective of the system was to reduce cost of production by reducing plant losses and by lowering labor costs through mechanization. One part of the system was the development of the U.C.-type soil mixes, which have the qualities of reproducibility and reliability. The physical and chemical properties can be reproduced with a high degree of consistency, and the various mixes will function in a consistent manner under similar production programs.

The basic ingredients for the mixes are fine sand (0.5–0.05 mm) and peat moss of the sphagnum type. However, redwood shavings, sawdust, or rice hulls can substitute for all or part of the peat moss. If rice hulls are used, they should be sterilized to avoid having rice as a weed problem. The ingredients are blended on a percent by volume basis, producing five basic mixes when blended in 25% increments of fine sand to peat moss. The two most commonly used mixes were 75% fine sand plus 25% peat moss, and 50% fine sand plus 50% peat moss.

The U.C. mixes are fortified with various fertilizers to provide an available supply of the major nutrients: N, P, K, Ca, and Mg. The peat moss and fine sand contain a sufficient supply of the microelements to meet the needs of most container-grown plants. However, some acid-requiring plants (e.g., rhododendron, blueberry) and plants grown in containers for long periods of time may require a supplemental application of iron chelate or a minor element fertilizer which contains a mixture of the microelements.

The type of fertilizer to be added varies with the medium, the storage requirement prior to planting, soil salinity problems, and the supplemental fertilizer practices to be followed after planting. Six fertilizer programs are suggested for each of the five mixes, producing a total of 30 container-production media programs.

Prior to mixing the various ingredients, the peat moss should be thoroughly moistened to ensure uniform mixing. The fertilizer materials must be carefully weighed and mixed together, preferably in a small quantity of sand, prior to mixing with the various ingredients of the mix. This will aid in obtaining uniform distribution of the chemical materials throughout the mix and ensure that every cubic yard of mix is the same, both physically and chemically. The U.C. mixes can be sterilized, after blending, with a high degree of assurance that there will be no salinity problems and no detrimental effects upon plants due to soil salinity.

### Cornell Peat-Lite Mixes

The Cornell Peat-Lite mixes were developed at Cornell University in the 1960s primarily for seed propagation and production of spring annuals and bedding plants. The basic ingredients of the Peat-Lite mix are sphagnum moss and either vermiculite or perlite, to which is added specific quantities of dolomitic limestone, superphosphate, and a complete fertilizer with a ratio of 1:2:1. To make a cubic yard of these mixes, the ingredients are blended as follows:

*Peat-Lite Mix A*

| 11 bushels | Sphagnum peat moss |
| 11 bushels | Horticultural grade 2 or 4 vermiculite |
| 5 lb | Dolomitic lime |
| 1 lb | Single superphosphate (fine) |
| 2–12 lb | 5-10-5 fertilizer; 12 lb will supply the nutrient needs of annual plants for about 6 weeks. If less than 12 lb is used, a supplemental fertilizer program is necessary. |

*Peat-Lite Mix B.* Substitute horticultural-grade perlite for the vermiculite.

The Peat-Lite mixes have several advantages for growers of bedding plants: they are light in weight, and the ingredients are uniform, readily available, and sterile. But they have limited use in nursery production, since the medium provides no ballast to support the relatively heavy crowns of woody plants. They are used most successfully for starting seedlings and in the potting of roses and small shrubs for short periods of time (i.e., potting roses in late winter and growing for 1–2 months for spring sale). When they are used for larger plants, it is necessary to provide some artificial means of plant support, such as staking or tying to a wire trellis. Peat-Lite mixes must be thoroughly moistened prior to use and firmly compacted about the roots of plants to assure satisfactory results.

### Hardwood Bark

Hardwood bark, a woodwaste by-product from various forest industries throughout the United States, especially in the Midwest and eastern states, is an excellent material, either alone or in combination with sand for use as a medium for the production of container-grown plants. It is desirable to hammermill and essential to compost the bark prior to use as a plant-growth medium. The optimum particle size is between $1/8$ and $1/32$ in. Approximately 35% of the particles should be smaller than $1/32$ in. and approximately 10% should be larger than $1/8$ in. to assure good drainage and aeration.

Hardwood bark has a C/N ratio of 150:1, whereas a ratio of 20:1 is most desirable when it is used as a medium for plant growth. To reduce the C/N ratio, the bark is composted with 2 lb of actual nitrogen (6 lb of ammonium nitrate) per cubic yard. Freshly harvested bark has a pH close to 5.2, but this increases as it ages. To keep the pH in the desirable range for good plant growth, 1 lb each of elemental sulfur and iron sulfate is added per cubic yard of bark at the time of composting. It is not necessary to add calcium or magnesium, since there is an adequate supply of these elements in the bark. Phosphorus (2.5 lb of treble superphosphate per cubic yard) is also added at the time of composting. Potassium (2 lbs $K_2O/yd^3$) should be added at time of composting if it is omitted from the fertilizer program during the production phase. All the chemical supplements must be uniformly mixed with the bark prior to composting.

The compost pile should be constructed on a well-drained site to assure good drainage. After thorough wetting, the ingredients are formed into a pile 6–8 ft high, 6–8 ft wide, but of any convenient length, to assure that heating and composting will take place. During composting the temperature within the pile will reach 140°F, plus or minus a few degrees. After the temperature reaches its peak within 30–60 days and cools by 10–15°F, the pile should be remixed and piled for another period of composting. After the temperature in the pile reaches its second maximum and declines, the material is ready for use as a medium for container-grown plants. The bottom 1 ft of compost should be mixed with some of the upper portions to minimize injury from soluble salts. The postcomposting fertilizer program for plants growing in hardwood bark is dependent upon how the compost is prepared, the amount used in the container mix, and the market objective.

Composted hardwood bark is reported to suppress nematode populations and some parasitic diseases of plants. But it can contain high levels of manganese, which may be toxic to some plants; levels as high as 992–1125 ppm were associated with chlorotic, stunted Japanese holly plants grown in composted hardwood bark.

### Softwood Bark

Pine and Douglas fir bark, alone or blended with fine sand, peat moss, and perlite, is used in many parts of the country in the production of container-grown plants. It has a low pH (3.4–4.0) and is an excellent medium for growing plants. It should be hammermilled to pass through a $1/2$-in. mesh screen prior to use as a medium. Bark that has been aged for a couple of years is more desirable than is freshly milled bark. Because of the lack of uniformity of the bark from one geographic area to another, it is desirable to have a chemical and physical analysis made on the material as it is obtained from the mill and to adjust the physical and chemical properties accordingly.

Some recent studies have shown that it may not be necessary to supplement a pine bark medium with limestone and superphosphate. There seem to be adequate supplies of calcium, magnesium, and phosphorus in the bark and in irrigation water to support plant growth for at least one and possibly two growing seasons. However, since bark has a high C/N ratio (about 300:1) it must be supplemented with nitrogen. Also, it is necessary to amend the medium with potassium and the microelements. Suggested levels that should be in the "soil" (container) solution for optimum growth of plants are: nitrogen, 75 ppm; phosphorus, 10 ppm; potassium, 25 ppm; calcium 30 ppm; and magnesium, 15 ppm.

Note that these levels are in the "soil" (container) solution and are not based on a soil-water extract method. They are provided as a guide; the exact levels for any container medium will vary with the actual ingredients, the element content of irrigation water, and the frequency of natural rainfall. Plants that respond best to a higher pH level may need to have the pine bark supplemented with peat moss or fine sand and amended with limestone and superphosphate. Since pine bark dries out fairly rapidly, growers frequently supplement with peat moss or fine sand to reduce frequency of irrigation.

### Municipal Compost

Municipal compost has also been used as the organic ingredient in soil mixes for the production of container-grown plants. It consists of garbage or leaf mold that has been ground in a hammermill, sprayed with sewage, and composted in windrows for 12–16 weeks. A mixture of soil-perlite-municipal compost on a 1:1:1 volume basis has produced quality plants when fertilized with a water-soluble, inorganic fertilizer used as either a constant or biweekly liquid feed. If municipal compost or sewage is to be used as a container medium, it should be subjected to a chemical analysis, especially for heavy metals which can produce undesirable effects upon plant growth. Also, in some communities there may be laws that prohibit its use because of various environmental concerns.

### Other Materials

A great diversity of other materials, such as stones, ground corncobs, spent hops, Cocobean hulls, rice hulls, and the husks of macadamia nuts have been used as media amendments. However, prior to use they should be checked for their chemical and physical properties and tested on a trial basis prior to extensive use. There are also prepared ready-to-use mixes that can be purchased commercially. These, too, should be tested prior to use and monitored periodically during the growing season to minimize potential problems and assure optimum growth.

## CHEMICAL SUPPLEMENTS

Most media manufactured for the production of container-grown plants will require some form of chemical supplement to adjust the pH and to augment the available nutrients. A chemical analysis of the medium and its components should be obtained, unless this information is known.

Peat moss and softwood bark tend to be acidic and may require the addition of limestone to raise the pH if it is below 5.8. Finely ground pulverized limestone has been found to be the most effective material to increase the pH of container media, either by incorporation or by surface application. However, liming organic soils with a pH above 5.8 is undesirable because of reduced availability of a number of the essential elements. Some sources of peat and hardwood bark are alkaline, and sulfur or iron sulfate should be added to lower the pH. Table 13–2 suggests the pounds of limestone or sulfur needed per cubic yard of peat to affect the desired pH change.

Some of the ingredients used for producing artificial soil mixes are low in available P, Ca, Mg, Fe, and various microelements. Therefore, it is necessary to supplement the medium with an available supply of these nutrients either during composting or just prior to planting. Peat is naturally low in microelements. Manganese may be needed for naturally well-limed reed-sedge peat, whereas copper, molybdenum, and iron are needed for sphagnum moss peat and fibrous acid sedge peat. If plant deficiency problems appear, the micronutrient mixture in Table 13–3 is suggested for each cubic yard of peat in the mixture. Use only powdered or fine crystalline materials and mix gradually as the mix is blended.

Additional amounts of fertilizer may be needed, depending upon the mix and the length of time that the plants are to be grown in the container. Plants growing in mixes other than the John Innes* and the U.C. mixes will require supplemental nitrogen and potassium shortly after planting. This can be ac-

*John Innes mix—used in England.

**Table 13–2**  Pounds of Dolomitic Limestone[a] or Sulfur Needed per Cubic Yard of Peat

| *Original pH of Peat* | *Desired pH of Peat* | |
|---|---|---|
| | *pH 4.5–5.2[b]* | *pH 5.3–6.2[c]* |
| 3.4–3.9 | 8 lb limestone | 14 lb limestone |
| 4.0–4.4 | 4 lb limestone | 10 lb limestone |
| 4.5–5.2 | None | 5 lb limestone |
| 5.3–6.2 | 2 lb sulfur | None |
| 6.3–7.0 | 4 lb sulfur | 2 lb sulfur |

[a]If obtainable, a mixture of equal parts of dolomitic and calcic limestone is preferred to all-dolomitic limestone.

[b]Desirable pH for rhododendrons, many conifers, and tropical plants.

[c]Desirable pH for most bedding plants and tree nurseries.

*Source:* Lucas et al. (1971).

**Table 13–3** Suggested Micronutrient Mixtures for 1 Cubic Yard of Peat

| Compound | Weight Needed | |
|---|---|---|
| Iron chelate or ferrous sulfate | 50 | 2 |
| Manganese sulfate | 30 | 1 |
| Copper sulfate | 10 | 0.3 |
| Zinc sulfate | 6 | 0.2 |
| Sodium borate (borax) | 3 | 0.1 |
| Sodium molybdate | 1 | 0.03 |
| Total mix | 100 | 3.6 |

*Source:* Lucas et al. (1971).

complished, most satisfactorily, by the addition of one of the slow- or controlled-release fertilizers at the time of planting. The rate of application will vary with the mix and the fertility program of the nursery. If a 1:1 sand/peat medium is used, a rate of application that supplies nitrogen at 300 ppm is satisfactory to supply the nutrient requirements of the plants for about 4 months.

Plants that are to be grown for extended periods of time will require further applications of nitrogen and possibly potassium. This can be applied either as a dry surface application or as a water-soluble fertilizer. The latter can be done most effectively by proportioning a water-soluble fertilizer concentrate solution into the irrigation system (see Chapter 14). A commercial water-soluble fertilizer can be used or a mixture of equal parts of ammonium nitrate and potassium nitrate (23-0-22). An application rate that supplies nitrogen at 100–150 ppm at each watering is used for most media. But a rate of 200–300 ppm N is suggested for hardwood bark, except when the bark has been supplemented with a slow-release fertilizer prior to planting.

If a dry, surface application of fertilizer is used it is suggested that a slow-release form be used since research has demonstrated that container-grown plants not only produce better growth in a single growing season, but also have a better survival percentage than do plants fertilized in the same manner with soluble fertilizers.

Growers need to adjust their fertilizer programs to fit their specific needs and environmental constraints. Adjustments to the fertilizer program must be made periodically to increase or decrease growth to attain various cultural or marketing objectives. At the same time those adjustments are made to the fertilizer program it may be necessary to make adjustments to other cultural practices, such as irrigation, pruning, spacing, and so on, to maximize the desired results.

## TESTING AND MODIFYING

To assure uniformity of production, the media should be tested periodically to assure proper blending prior to planting and that optimum levels of nutrition are maintained during the growing season. Media samples should be tested by a reputable soil testing service for pH, soluble salts, and total available N, P,

K, Ca, and Mg. If the blending is being done correctly and the raw materials are uniformly consistent, the values for the various parameters should remain relatively constant. If there is a significant change in any of the values, measures can be taken to correct the situation before it becomes a serious problem.

Growing medium testing procedures vary considerably among laboratories. However, efforts are being made to standardize methods, and at some future date one set of standards may apply. Until that time two standards are provided; one as a guide to growers who use or subscribe to a service that employs the saturated-soil-extract method (Table 13–4) and the other as a guide to those who use a soil-water ratio method (Table 13–6) of soil testing.

### Saturated-Soil-Extract Method

*Nitrate-nitrogen* levels will vary with the age and species of the crop. Seedlings and newly propagated plants function better at lower levels than do more mature plants. Values above 200 ppm are unnecessarily high, and above 300 ppm may cause nutritional problems. Nitrogen fertilizer should be applied when the level in the saturated extract approaches the lower level. The rates given in Table 13–5 will increase soil nitrate tests about 10 ppm in the soil saturation extract.

*Phosphate* fertilizers can be applied at liberal rates to a container mix without serious problems from excess soluble salts. Generally, superphosphate (0-20-0) is preferred for container mixes because it contains calcium and sulfur. Two pounds of 0-20-0 fertilizer per cubic yard will raise the saturated soil extract test approximately 5 ppm. For most mixes testing low in phosphorus, 2–3 lb of 0-20-0 per cubic yard will provide an adequate level for the growth of most plants without causing other nutritional problems.

**Table 13–4** Suggested Nutrient Levels in Saturated Extracts for Container Medium

| | Concentration | | |
|---|---|---|---|
| | *Acceptable*[a] | *Optimum* | *High* |
| | ppm in Saturated Extract | | |
| Nitrate-N ($NO_3$-N) | 40–79 | 80–139 | 140–199 |
| Phosphorus (P) | 3–5 | 6–10 | 11–18 |
| Potassium (K) | 50–109 | 110–179 | 180–256 |
| Calcium (Ca) | 70–139 | 140–219 | 220–324 |
| Magnesium (Mg) | 30–59 | 60–99 | 100–149 |
| | mS/cm[b] | | |
| Soluble salts | .75–1.49 | 1.50–2.24 | 2.25–3.49 |

[a]Acceptable for most plants when optimal growth is not a primary concern.

[b]mS = millisiemen, replacing millimho (mmho) as the preferred unit for expressing conductivity (soluble salt) measurements. The value remains the same—only the name changes. To convert this value to ppm, multiply by 700.

*Source:* Warncke (1983).

**Table 13–5** Nitrogen Fertilizer Needed to Increase Soil Saturation Extract Test by Approximately 10 ppm

| Percent N in Fertilizer | Ounces of Nitrogen Fertilizer Per Cubic Yard of Soil |
|---|---|
| 10 | 4.0 |
| 16 | 2.4 |
| 20 | 2.0 |
| 33 | 1.2 |
| 45 | 0.8 |

*Potassium* is commonly deficient in sand, peats, and perlite. It must be added to mixes composed of these materials. Most potassium fertilizers have a high salt index (see Table 12–10); therefore, care must be used in applying them. Carriers such as potassium nitrate, potassium sulfate, or potassium phosphate are preferred for container mixes. The level of potassium in the soil mix, as indexed by the saturated-soil extract test, should be relatively low for young plants and seedlings compared to more mature plants. The levels listed in Table 13–4 are suggested levels until exact levels are established for a specific crop in a specific stage of production. Values in excess of 180 ppm are unnecessarily high and may induce nutritional problems, especially if Ca and/or Mg levels test low. The K level in the soil extract can be increased approximately 50 ppm by mixing 2 oz of 60% $K_2O$ fertilizer into a cubic yard of mix.

*Calcium* is generally adequate in container mixes with a pH of 5.5 or above. Values above 325 ppm are very high and can result in nutritional problems if Mg and/or K test low. The balance of the cations Ca, K, Mg, and to some degree ammonium and sodium is more important than the actual level. Calcium should represent about 15% of the total salts.

*Magnesium* in the saturated-soil extract should be less than one-half that for calcium, but should exceed one-half that for potassium. A minimum test regardless of the Ca and K levels is about 25 ppm Mg. Finely ground dolomitic limestone is a good source of Mg for container-soil mixes; 2 lb/yd$^3$ of mix will normally supply ample magnesium. Magnesium sulfate can also be used.

### Soil-Water Ratio Method

*Nitrate* nitrogen will vary considerably, since nitrate availability is a function of temperature and moisture. (See Table 13–6). Also, nitrates can be readily leached. If the recommended range for nitrates for a specific crop is 20–60 ppm in the soil, nitrogen should be applied when the test drops below 20 ppm. On the other end, as the test approaches 100 ppm, growth may be adversely affected; thus, the medium should be leached.

*Phosphorus* levels are seldom too low or too high to be dangerous. However, levels below 20 ppm are approaching a deficient level and may limit nitrogen metabolism in some species. And levels in excess of 200 ppm may limit the availability of micronutrients.

**Table 13–6** Suggested Nutrient Standards for Soil Mixes Having Different Soil
Densities and Extracted at Different Ratios

| Soil density (g/ml): | 0.8–1.3 (Mineral Soil) | 0.5–0.8 | 0.2–0.5 (Organic Soil) |
|---|---|---|---|
| Soil extractant ratio: | 1:8 | 1:12 | 1:24 |
| | | Parts per Million in Soil | |
| Nutrient | | | |
| Nitrate-nitrogen (NO$_3$-N)[a] | 15–40 | 20–60 | 40–120 |
| Phosphorus (P)[b] | 20–60 | 30–90 | 60–180 |
| Potassium (K)[c] | 180–300 | 270–450 | 540–900 |
| Calcium (Ca)[c] | >500 | >750 | >1500 |
| Magnesium (Mg)[c] | >60 | >90 | >180 |
| | | mS/cm | |
| Soluble salts | <0.8 | <1.00 | <1.25 |

[a]Water-soluble extract.

[b]Extracted with 0.018 $N$ acetic acid (Spurway active).

[c]Extracted with neutral, normal ammonium acetate.

*Potassium* tests over 300 ppm may indicate a soluble-salts problem when chloride carriers are being used. If soluble salts are low, a medium may test up to 1000 ppm K without difficulty, depending upon the crop and soil density. On very sandy or porous media (except those containing vermiculite in the mix), more frequent potassium application is desirable. Where chlorides are a problem, the sulfate form is suggested.

*Calcium* content is closely associated with the pH of the medium. If the pH is above 5.5, calcium will be adequate in most container mixes. However, if the ratio of Ca/Mg exceeds 5:1 or Ca/K exceeds 20:1 (percent base saturation), magnesium- or potassium-induced deficiency can result. Additional Mg and K will be needed to correct the imbalance.

*Magnesium* availability is closely associated with calcium but at a lower magnitude. The ratio of potassium to magnesium should not exceed 3:1 or a magnesium deficiency could be induced.

### Virginia Tech Extraction Method

The nutrients in the medium solution for container-grown plants can be extracted for testing by a simple field method developed by Virginia Tech. The method involves a simple three step procedure.

1. The container-grown plant is placed onto a collecting dish, with the container slightly elevated to insure good drainage. The moisture level in the container should be close to water-retention porosity.

2. Add sufficient distilled water (or tap water low in soluble salts) to the surface of the medium so that about 50 ml of water is accumulated in the

collecting dish. (Application rates will vary with the size and volume of the container). Randomly test 3 to 5 containers to obtain a good representative sampling of a block of plants.

3. The leachate is then poured into a suitable container and is ready for testing.

Research at Virginia Tech has shown that a wide range of container-grown plants can be produced if the nutrient levels and the soluble salts are maintained close to the levels listed in Table 13–7.

### Micronutrients

Since micronutrients are found in trace amounts, soil tests are not too reliable or are too expensive for routine soil testing. Plant analysis is commonly used to detect deficiency or excess levels. Chlorosis is probably the most common physiological problem related to microelement nutrition and is commonly related to iron deficiency or manganese toxicity. Conditions favoring deficiency include high soil pH, very high phosphorus levels, or excess moisture.

*Boron deficiency* can be induced by excess applications of lime, nitrogen, or potassium. It has also been associated with acid media that are being leached of boron by overwatering. *Boron toxicity* has been reported in some nurseries producing container-grown plants. The early symptoms of boron toxicity are characterized by leaf-tip yellowing and marginal chlorosis, followed by tip burning and premature leaf drop. In advanced stages terminal growth is rosetted and twig dieback occurs. The toxicity is caused by over-fertilizing with fertilizers high in boron.

*Copper deficiency*, commonly associated with highly organic media, can be prevented by supplementing the media with a micronutrient mixture containing copper (see Table 13–3).

*Iron deficiency* can be induced in plants by a number of factors other than the lack of iron in the medium. Low iron availability is associated with high pH of the medium, high levels of copper, manganese, or zinc; high phosphates or calcium carbonate, low medium temperature, or excess moisture.

**Table 13–7** Virginia Tech Extraction–Method Standards for vigorous container-grown plants (Pine bark medium)

| Element | PPM in leachate |
|---|---|
| N | 50–100 |
| P | 10–15 |
| K | 30–50 |
| Ca | 10–30 |
| Mg | 10–30 |

Soluble salts 0.5–2.0 mS/cm.

*Manganese deficiency* is most commonly expressed on plants growing in a highly organic medium with a pH of 6.8 or higher. The condition is aggravated by low temperature and excess moisture.

*Zinc deficiency* is not too common, but can be caused by cool, wet weather that reduces the availability of zinc.

### Soluble Salts

During the growing season the container medium should be tested monthly for soluble salts. The reading should be in the desirable range for the test method (Table 13–8). Readings below optimum indicate low levels of nutrition, which will result in reduced plant growth. A more complete medium test may be needed to determine the proper fertilizer to apply. This can often be determined by checking fertilizer records or by questioning those responsible for the fertilizer program.

## MEDIA STERILIZATION

Another important factor in the successful production of container-grown plants is that the medium be free of organisms harmful to plant growth. Newly mined sand is relatively free of harmful organisms and can be used without sterilization. However, most soil and some sand and peat moss that have become contaminated will contain harmful organisms, such as bacteria, fungi, insects, and weed seeds. These organisms can cause serious problems if they are not eliminated from the medium prior to planting.

Various species of fungi, especially *Rhizoctonia* and *Pythium*, have caused the needless loss of thousands of plants in nurseries as a result of root

**Table 13–8**  Readings and Interpretation of Soluble-Salt Data for Container-Grown Plants

| Conductivity,[a] *(millisiemens/cm)* | | | |
|---|---|---|---|
| *5:1 Organic Soils* | *2:1 Mineral Soils* | *Saturated Paste Extract, All Soils* | *Interpretation* |
| <0.350 | <0.5 | <2.0 | Low nutrient status for growing plants |
| 0.35–.65 | 0.500–1.0 | 1.50–2.24 | Desirable range for most growing plants; upper range may be high for some species |
| 0.65–0.90 | 1.0–1.5 | 2.25–5.00 | Higher than desirable for most species |
| >0.90 | >1.5 | >5.00 | Excess soluble salts, wilting or death of plants |

[a]To convert mS/cm to parts per million (approx.), multiply by 700.

*Source:* Modified slightly from Coop. Ext. Serv. Mich. State Univ. Ext. Bull. 1736 (1983).

rots. Grubs of insects chewing upon the roots have resulted in many plants being dwarfed, malformed, or destroyed. And weeds competing for available nutrients, moisture, and light reduce growth rates as well as decrease customer acceptance of the product. All of these problems and others can be minimized or eliminated by composting, sterilizing, pasteurizing, or fumigating. Composting was discussed previously under the heading Hardwood Bark.

### Heat Treatment

Although plantsmen use the term "sterilization" in reference to heat treatment of soil to rid it of harmful organisms, a more correct term is "pasteurization," since the temperatures used (140–180°F) destroy only certain of the harmful organisms. Various means of heat treatment can be employed, but it is desirable to obtain a soil temperature of 140–150°F and to maintain the temperature for at least 10 min but no more than 30 min to destroy most plant pathogenic fungi and bacteria (Fig. 13–3). This temperature regime will allow certain beneficial organisms to survive, especially nitrifying bacteria, which

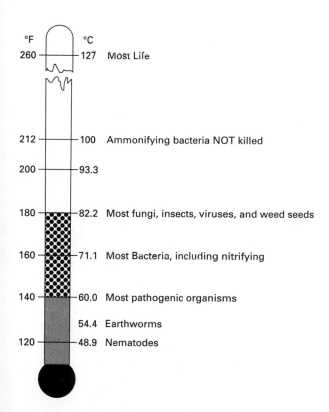

**Figure 13–3** Temperatures maintained for 15 minutes will destroy most organisms listed.

aid in the nitrification of ammonia. The lower temperature also minimizes the problem of excess ammonia release encountered with temperatures above 160°F. Aerated steam has been used effectively to obtain the 140°F temperature. The necessary equipment can be obtained from agricultural engineering firms specializing in soil sterilization. The heat treatment of nursery soils is thoroughly discussed in the "U.C. System for Producing Healthy Container-Grown Plants."

### Fumigation

Chemicals can also be used to rid soil of harmful organisms. In general, they are less destructive of the physical properties of the soil, but they are more costly. Also, many chemicals are very specific as to the organisms that they will control. Therefore, chemicals for treating soil must be carefully selected and applied at the proper concentration to a soil mass that is in the proper physical condition.

The optimum media temperature for best results is close to 70°F. When media are cold, wet, and poorly aerated, chemical treatments are ineffective. Following treatment, the media should be aerated for a period of from 2 days to 2 weeks to allow the chemical to dissipate prior to planting. Warm, sandy media need less time to aerate than do damp media. A number of fumigants, available to nurserymen, will effectively sterilize media, including methyl bromide, formaldehyde, vapam, and chloropicrin.

*Methylbromide** is the most commonly used all-purpose nursery soil fumigant. It will destroy most of the common fungi that cause plant disease problems, except verticillium wilt. It is effective against most weed seeds and nematodes. It is easy to use and has a short treatment and post-treatment aeration-time requirement. *However, the material is very toxic to people and animals and must be used with caution.* If it is handled with reasonable care, it can be a very effective tool for nurserymen in the preplanting control of harmful organisms.

Media and other material to be fumigated must be enclosed in a gasproof chamber, and the methylbromide gas injected into the chamber at a concentration at 2 lb/100 ft$^3$ for nematode and weed control and at 4 lb/100 ft$^3$ for fungus control. A treatment period of from 24 to 48 hr is desirable followed by an aeration period of 48 hr.

A polyethylene tarp free of holes makes an excellent gasproof enclosure. However, the tarp must cover the material to be fumigated in such a way as to ensure free distribution of the gas within and at the same time prevent the gas from escaping, either through holes or cracks along the edges. A special dispenser is provided for injecting the gas into the chamber.

*Methylbromide is a restricted-use pesticide.

*Formaldehyde* is an excellent fungicide that has been used by plantsmen for many years, both as fumigant for inorganic soils and as a surface sterilant for propagation benches and storage facilities. It is very water-soluble and will penetrate a soil mass to the depth of wetting, where it volatilizes and becomes an effective media fumigant. Treated media should be covered for at least 24 hours with a gasproof cover. This must be followed by an aeration period of from 10 to 14 days to permit the gas an opportunity to fully dissipate. Any residual gas can be harmful to young plants. Formaldehyde is very irritating to the eyes and nasal passages and is toxic to plants; it must be used with caution.

*Vapam* (sodium *N*-methyl dithiocarbamate dihydrate) is also an effective media fumigant. It can be used to control most fungi, insects, nematodes, and weeds. It is water-soluble and can be applied in water either to the medium surface or by injection into the media. The chemical should be sealed into the media with an additional application of water. Vapam is most effective when the medium is at a temperature of 60–70°F. The media should be aerated either by cultivation or turning it in a pile 5–7 days following treatment. The media may be safely planted about 2 weeks following treatment provided that there was adequate aeration to rid the soil of chemical residue.

*Chloropicrin*, commonly known as tear gas, is another excellent media fumigant. The medium must be treated in an airtight chamber, as the material is very volatile. It should be slightly damp but well aerated and at a temperature of 65–70°F for best results. The exposure period should last for at least 24 hr, preferably for 48 hr or more if the medium is not well aerated. Plantings may be made when there is no longer any trace of gas, approximately 7 days.

*Chloropicrin* is a very effective fumigant and herbicide. But it is also a potent tear gas and is corrosive of most metals; therefore, it must be used with caution. Small quantities are added to methyl-bromide as a warning agent. It should not be used in areas where people will be exposed to its irritating property. The treatment area should be free of valuable plants and metal objects. Any metal that is exposed to the gas should be washed with kerosene to prevent corrosion.

## POST-TREATMENT

Following treatment, sterilized or pasteurized media should be placed into clean, sterile containers for use or stored in an area that has also been thoroughly sterilized. It is a poor plantsman who would go to considerable effort to rid media of harmful organisms and then expose them immediately to reinoculation by handling it with contaminated equipment or by placing it into contaminated containers or storage bins. Media sterilization is only a part of a total program of good plant culture. All people in the production cycle must be cognizant of maintaining sanitary conditions in plant propagation facilities, growing areas, storage facilities, and in the packaging and shipping areas.

## SUMMARY

Producing and marketing of quality plants in containers requires careful planning and constant monitoring of each phase of production to assure attainment of production objectives. Blending of the media mixture and maintaining nutrients at the proper intensity and balance is one part of the total production effort. However, it has been the weakest link in the production cycle at many container-production nurseries. By practicing good sanitation and maintaining suggested nutritional standards, growers can grow quality plants and obtain a good economic return on their investment.

## REFERENCES

Boddy, R. M. 1976. Container-grown rhododendrons. Proc. Int. Plant Propag. Soc. 26:87–93.

Boodley, J. W., and R. Sheldrake, Jr. 1972. Cornell Peat-Lite mixes for commercial plant growing. N.Y. State Coll. Agric. Cornell Univ. Inf. Bull. 43.

Bosley, R. W. 1967. Ground bark—a container growing medium. Proc. Int. Plant Propag. Soc. 17:366–370.

Brown, E. F., and F. A. Pokorny. 1975. Physical and chemical properties of media composed of milled pine bark and sand. J. Am. Soc. Hort. Sci. 100(2):119–121.

Davidson, H., and W. McCall. 1964. Metal ammonium phosphate fertilizers for container-grown plants. Quart. Bull. Mich. Agric. Exp. Sta. 46(3):416–419.

Dewerth, A. F. 1961. Horticultural Perlite for Texas gardens. Tex. Agric. Prog. 7(6):3–6.

Flint, H. L., and J. G. McGuire. 1961. Effects of different soil levels of nitrogen and potassium on growth of *Forsythia intermedia* and *Viburnum plicatum tomentosum* in containers. Proc. Am. Soc. Hort. Sci. 78:553–559.

———, and J. G. McGuire. 1962. Nitrogen range for optimum growth of some woody ornamental species grown in containers. Proc. Am. Soc. Hort. Sci. 80:622–624.

Gartner, J. B., D. C. Saupe, J. E. Klett, and T. R. Yocom. 1970. Hardwood bark as a medium for container growing. Am. Nurseryman 13(8):11.

———, T. D. Hughes, and J. E. Klett, 1972. Using hardwood bark in container-grown woody ornamentals to slow-release fertilizers. Am. Nurseryman 135(12):10.

———, S. M. Still, and J. E. Klett. 1973. The use of hardwood bark as a growth medium. Proc. Int. Plant Propag. Soc. 23:222–231.

Gillian, C. H., and E. M. Smith. 1980. Sources and symptoms of boron toxicity in container-grown woody ornamentals. J. Arboricult. 6(8):209–212.

Gouin, F. R., and C. B. Link. 1973. Growth responses of container-grown woody ornamentals to slow-release fertilizers. HortScience 8(3):208–209.

Kelley, J. D. 1962. Response of container-grown woody ornamentals to fertilization with urea-formaldehyde and potassium frit. Proc. Am. Soc. Hort. Sci. 81:544–551.

KLETT, J. E., J. B. GARTNER, and T. D. HUGHES. 1972. Utilization of hardwood bark media for growing woody ornamental plants in containers. J. Am. Soc. Hort. Sci. 97(4):448–450.

LEDA, C. E., and R. D. WRIGHT. 1991. Dolomitic Lime Particle Size and Container Media pH. J. Environ. Hort. 9(4):226–227.

LUCAS, R. E., and J. K. DAVIS. 1961. Relationships between pH values of organic soils and availabilities of 12 plant nutrients. Soil Sci. 92:177–182.

———, P. E. RIEKE, and R. S. FARNHAM. 1971. Peats for soil improvement and soil mixes. Farm Sci. Ser. Coop. Ext. Serv. Mich. State Univ. Ext. Bull 516.

MALIEKE, R. B., and J. B. GARTNER. 1975. Hardwood bark as a soil amendment for suppression of plant parasitic nematodes on container-grown plants. HortScience 10(1):33–34.

MATKIN, O. A. 1971. Soil mixes today. Proc. Int. Plant Propag. Soc. 21:162–164.

———, and P. A. CHANDLER. 1957. The U.C. type soil mixes. In U.S. system for producing healthy container-grown plants, Sec. 5, Agric. Exp. Sta., Univ. Calif. Manual 23.

MCVEY, G. R. 1977. How soil chemistry can work for you. Proc. Int. Plant Propag. Soc. 27:227–284.

MONTANO, J. M., J. T. FISHER, and D. J. COTTER. 1977. Sawdust for growing containerized forest tree seedlings. Tree Planter's Notes 28(2):6–9.

MORRIS, W. C., and D. C. MILBOCKER. 1972. Repressed growth and leaf chlorosis of Japanese holly grown in hardwood bark. HortScience 7(5):486–487.

RICHARDSON, T. 1976. Rhododendron production. Proc. Int. Plant Propag. Soc. 26:301–303.

RIEKE, P. E., and R. E. LUCAS. 1968. Greenhouse soil notes. Soil Science Dept., Mich. State Univ.

RIGBY, F. A. 1963. Ground bark as a growing medium for container nursery stock. Proc. Int. Plant Propag. Soc. 13:288–291.

SANDERSON, K. C., and W. C. MARTIN, JR. 1974. Performance of woody ornamentals in municipal compost medium under nine fertilizer regimes. HortScience 9(3):242–243.

SPOMER, L. A. 1973. Soils in plant containers: soil amendment, air and water relationships. Ill. Res. 15(3):16–17.

———. 1975. Principles of nursery container soil amendment. Am. Nurseryman 142(3):12.

———. 1977. How much total water retention and aeration porosity in my container mix? Ill. State Florists Assoc. Bull. 369:13–15.

STILL, S. M., M. A. DIRR, and J. B. GARTNER. 1976. Phytotoxic effects of several bark extracts on mung bean and cucumber growth. J. Am. Soc. HortSci. 101(1):34–37.

SWANSON, B. T. et al. 1986. Soil Testing and Fertilizer Applications for Nursery Management and Production. AG-BU-2030, Ag. Ext. Serv., Univ. of Minnesota. St. Paul, Minn.

SWANSON, B. T. et al. 1989. Container Fertilizers, Amer. Nur. 169(7):39–49.

WARNCKE, D. D., and D. M. KRAUSKOPF. 1983. Greenhouse growth media: Testing and Nutrition guidelines, Ext. Bul. E-1736. Coop. Ext. Serv., Michigan State University, East Lansing, Mich.

————, R. E. LUCAS, P. E. RIEKE, and W. H. CARLSON. 1973. Interpreting saturated paste soil tests for flowers, bedding plants and greenhouse vegetables. Mimeograph, Dept. of Crop and Soil Sciences, Mich. State Univ.

WHITE, J. W., and J. W. MASTALERZ. 1966. Soil moisture as related to "container capacity." Proc. Am. Soc. Hort. Sci. 89:758–765.

WRIGHT, R. D. 1983. Study indicates need for changes in nutrition programs for plants in containers. Am. Nurseryman 157(1):109–111.

WRIGHT, R. D. 1987. The Virginia Tech Liquid Fertilizer System for Container-Grown Plants, Col. of Ag. and Life Sci. Info. Series 86–5.

YEAGER, T. H., and R. D. WRIGHT. 1983. Phosphorus in pine bark media—what is a suitable level for good plant growth? Am. Nurseryman 157(1):48.

————, and R. D. WRIGHT. 1983. Phosphorus in pine bark media—is incorporating superphosphate best? Am. Nurseryman 157(1):49.

## SUGGESTED READING

BAKER, F., ed. 1957. The U.C. system for producing healthy container-grown plants. Agric. Exp. Sta. Univ. Calif. Manual 23.

BUNT, A. C. 1976. Modern potting composts. The Pennsylvania State University Press, University Park, Pa.

GILLIAM, C. H., and E. M. SMITH. 1980. Fertilization of container-grown nursery stock, Bull. 658, Coop. Ext. Serv., Ohio State Univ.

JUDD JR., R. W. 1983. Soilless Mixes for Nursery Production. J. Environ. Hort. 1(4):106–109.

LAWRENCE, W. J. C., and J. NEWELL. 1962. Seed and potting composts, 5th ed. George Allen & Unwin (Publisher) Ltd., London.

PATTERSON, J. M. 1975. Container growing. American Nurseryman Publishing Company, Chicago.

# Chapter 14
# Irrigation of
# Nursery Crops

Nursery crops, like other agricultural crops, require water if they are to develop into healthy, salable plants. Water is an important nutrient required by all plants. It functions in plants as a solvent, a heat regulator, and as a biochemical reagent in photosynthesis. It is a major modifier of growth; its availability or nonavailability during certain phases of growth can seriously affect survival, growth rate, and the ultimate size of the plants. Properly irrigated stock will be larger and more vigorous. Therefore, an understanding of irrigation practices is essential to nurserymen, particularly those who produce plants in containers.

Nurserymen who produce plants by field culture require or use water for two primary reasons: either to assure a higher survival rate following transplanting or to increase growth, whereas nurserymen committed to container culture require water not only to increase survival rates following potting and to increase growth, but they have an absolute requirement for water, almost on a daily basis. Container-grown plants have limited soil-moisture reservoirs, defined by container size and the moisture-holding capacity of the medium, which must be resupplied at short, periodic intervals to assure continued survival. The method of growing is the basis for determining the amount of water, type of equipment, and labor that is needed to meet the irrigation requirements within nurseries.

In addition to providing moisture for survival and growth of the nursery crops, the irrigation system can also be used to apply water-soluble fertilizers, to protect some crops from damage due to late spring frost, to moisten the soil to aid digging and transplanting operations during dry periods, and to seal in volatile soil sterilants and herbicides.

## SOURCES OF WATER

A reliable source of clean water is a fundamental requirement for irrigation. Rivers, streams, drainage ditches, lakes, ponds, reservoirs, and wells are the common sources of water. Nurserymen who plan to use water from rivers, streams, drainage ditches, lakes, and ponds that have a multiple or public ownership should be familiar with the state and local riparian (water rights) laws, as they may face possible injunctions prohibiting or limiting their use of public water. States located in arid or semiarid areas of the country have strict laws pertaining to water rights. In other parts of the country, riparian laws are not as well defined. A new irrigator upstream can seriously reduce the amount of water available downstream, as can another irrigator drawing from the same lake or reservoir. Complete ownership of the water rights or purchase of water from a dependable supply is usually preferable. Should it become necessary to sink wells for a source of water, it is suggested that information on underground water be obtained from the state geologist and that a reliable well driller, who is familiar with the area, be employed to do the drilling, develop the well, and conduct a pumping test. Nurserymen producing container-grown nursery stock should have, if possible, an alternative source of water to assure a reserve supply in the event of an emergency.

## WATER QUALITY

In addition to sources of supply, water quality should also be investigated. Water high in soluble salts or contaminated with industrial wastes, particularly heavy metals or polluted with herbicides, must be avoided. Most nursery plants will not tolerate saline conditions, and some are injured by high levels of sodium, boron, or chlorides found in some water.

Water quality (levels of salinity) is characterized by electrical conductivity (EC). Since the unit of measurement is very small for most natural water samples, it is commonly expressed as millisiemens/cm (mS/cm). Water for irrigation purposes should have an EC value of less than 0.25 mS/cm (Table 14–1). Water that has an EC in excess of 0.75 mS/cm is high in soluble salts and should be used with caution. Water used on container-grown plants can have

**Table 14–1** Classification of Water for Irrigation

| mS/cm[a] | Salinity Level | Irrigation Value |
|---|---|---|
| <0.25 | Low | Excellent for irrigation on most soils; normal leaching suggested |
| 0.25–0.75 | Moderate | Satisfactory for irrigation; moderate leaching suggested |
| 0.75–2.25 | High | Avoid use on soil with poor drainage; plant salt-tolerant crops; leaching necessary |
| >2.26 | Very high | Not recommended for irrigation purposes; a few salt-tolerant crops can be grown under special salinity culture |

*Source:* Wilcox (1955).

[a]mS = millisiemen, replacing millimho (mmho) as the preferred unit for expressing conductivity (soluble salt) measurements. The value remains the same—only the name changes. To convert this value to ppm, multiply by 700.

levels somewhat higher than average, but it is desirable to apply a sufficient quantity at each irrigation to leach the soil.

High levels of sodium (Na) in irrigation water can also be detrimental to some plants. However, its relationship to the cations calcium (Ca) and magnesium (Mg) is important in determining its toxic effects. This is known as the sodium-absorption ratio (SAR) and can be calculated from the formula

$$SAR = \frac{Na}{\sqrt{\dfrac{Ca^{2+} + Mg^{2+}}{2}}}$$

The concentration of each element is expressed in milliequivalents per liter. An SAR value of 10 or less is considered safe for most nursery situations. But levels in excess of 10 could present problems on soils with a high cation exchange capacity (fine-textured soils).

Boron, a constituent of all natural waters, is found in toxic concentrations in irrigation water in limited areas of the United States, primarily in the Southwest. Since plants vary in their tolerance to boron in the soil solutions, no exact value can be stated. Nevertheless, relatively low concentrations, in the order of 0.03–0.05 ppm, are needed for normal growth, and relatively high levels (0.5 ppm or greater) should be avoided.

Water containing more than 2.5 mEq/liter of residual sodium carbonate (RSC) is not suitable for irrigation. Water that contains less than 1.25 mEq/liter RSC is probably safe, and those with levels in between are considered marginal.

Appraising water quality for use in irrigation of nursery stock need not be complex. With an understanding of some general chemistry, making a few chemical determinations and some calculations, it is possible to avoid the hazards associated with using poor-quality water. Some states have either private, state, or municipal laboratories where these tests are made for a fee. Details on the analysis of irrigation water are contained in USDA Agricultural Handbook 60.

In areas where high-soluble salts are a problem, it is desirable to construct large, shallow settling ponds to allow the alkali salts to settle out prior to using the water for irrigation or misting. In some situations distilling or even deionizing the water may be desirable prior to using it on sensitive, high-value crops (e.g., azaleas). Sediment and organic debris, harmful to pumps and sprinkler heads, should be screened out. If it is not, the irrigation equipment can be expected to malfunction; nozzle orifices can become plugged or changed in size, but even more serious, the pump may malfunction, which could result in damage to either equipment or to the plant material.

In addition to water quality and pH, nurserymen would be well advised to obtain tests for the calcium and magnesium content of their water supply in order to make better decisions related to fertilizer management, especially when producing plants in containers. Water that contains 40 ppm of calcium can supply most, if not all, the plant's needs for calcium; thus avoiding the need to augment the medium with dolomite prior to planting. It is also desirable to maintain a calcium-magnesium balance of 2 to 1 to assure optimum growth. An excess of calcium in the medium solution would upset this balance, producing a magnesium deficiency. Should this deficiency develop it can be quickly corrected with a foliar spray of magnesium sulfate (1 lb/100 gal of water).

## SOIL MOISTURE DETERMINATION

Crops should be irrigated when the soil moisture in the root zone drops to a predetermined level. Soil moisture levels can be determined by feel of the soil, by calculation, or by the use of various types of soil moisture meters. Experienced plantsmen estimate the appropriate time to irrigate nursery stock by knowing the stress symptoms of plants, by the feel of the soil or by the length of time since the last rain or irrigation. To estimate soil moisture by the feel of the soil, samples are collected from various depths in the root zone and the moisture level is estimated by feel (Table 14–2). To calculate soil moisture, a soil sample collected from a depth of 8–12 in. is placed in a tight container, weighed, dried in an oven (12–24 hours at 100°C), and reweighed. Total moisture (TM) in percent is calculated by the formula

$$TM\% = \frac{(\text{original wt of soil}) - (\text{dry wt of soil}) \times 100}{\text{dry wt of soil}}$$

Available moisture is then estimated by subtracting the wilting coefficient of the soil (data available from soils reference manual or county agriculture agent) from the percent TM.

**Table 14–2**  Soil Feel Chart

| Percentage of Remaining Available Water | Feel or Appearance of Soil | | |
|---|---|---|---|
| | Coarse Textured | Medium Textured | Fine or Very Fine Textured |
| 0% (dry) | Dry, loose, flows through fingers | Powder-dry; sometimes slightly crusted but easily breaks down into powdery condition | Hard, baked, cracked; sometimes has loose crumbs on surface |
| 50% or less (low) | Still appears to be dry; will not form a ball with pressure | Somewhat crumbly, but will hold together with pressure | Somewhat pliable, will ball under pressure |
| 50–100% (good to excellent) | Forms weak ball, breaks easily, will not stick | Forms a ball and is very pliable; sticks readily if relatively high in clay | Easily ribbons out between fingers; has a slick feeling |
| Above field capacity (over-irrigated) | Free water will be released with kneading | Can squeeze out free water | Puddles and free water forms on surface |

*Source:* Irrigating small acreages. Coop. Ext. Serv. Mich. State Univ. Ext. Bull. 320.

For sandy soils low in organic matter (<11%), a quick technique is to place the soil sample, about 20–25 g, in a screen-bottom metal container set in a metal cap and obtain the weight. Gradually, pour a small quantity (25 cc) of methyl alcohol over the soil and ignite to drive off the moisture. The sample is reweighed and the available moisture calculated by the previous formula.

Various instruments have been developed to provide a measure of soil moisture. The soil moisture meter is well adapted for use in most field-production nurseries. It consists of special plaster of paris blocks that are buried in the soil at the desired depth and location, and then electrical resistance is measured with a moisture meter. The dial of the meter reads in relative soil moisture, 100 representing a fully saturated soil and 50 or less indicating a need for irrigation. A large variety of soil moisture tensiometers are available. Also, with the advent of low-cost computers and related software, it is now possible to develop digital computer control systems as an aid in irrigation management. A number of computer-controlled systems are currently in use in both nurseries and greenhouse establishments. The advantages gained by the use of computer-controlled irrigation include: 20–30% reduction in the use of water; 10–12% reduction in labor for irrigation-related activities; improved scheduling of irrigation; and other work-related activities. Computer software for use in the operation of an irrigation system and for making calculations pertaining to the dilution of fertilizer solutions can be obtained from most Cooperative Extension offices associated with Land Grant Universities.

Leaf temperature has been used to a limited extent to determine when to irrigate ornamental plants in the landscape. Since leaf temperature is generally higher for plants exhibiting moisture stress, it is possible to relate leaf temperature to the need to irrigate. Leaf temperatures can be quickly estimated with the aid of a portable infrared radiometer. It could possibly be used to determine irrigation needs in a nursery.

## WATER-ABSORBING HYDROGELS

*Water-absorbing polymers* (hydrogels) are a group of compounds capable of absorbing many times their weight in water. Many of these compounds have been suggested for use in the production of container-grown plants. Some research has shown hydrogels to reduce watering requirements of container-grown plants. However, other research has demonstrated no significant growth increases or other positive cost-effective gains to warrant their use in the production of container-grown plants.

### Estimating Water Requirements

Irrigating field-grown nursery crops is based primarily upon experience, but it does vary with the size of the area to be irrigated, the size of the plant material, and the level of moisture in the soil. Since acreages vary, it is desirable to discuss water requirements on an acre basis and adjust total requirements accordingly. To apply 1 acre-in. of water requires 27,154 gal of water. It is a common practice in many nurseries to apply ½ in., 1 in., or 2 in. of water at a time. This would require between 13,600 and 54,300 gal of water, whereas in other nurseries water for growth is applied when the soil moisture drops to some predetermined level. For example, a soil with a 30% moisture-holding capacity is to be irrigated when the soil moisture in the upper 9 in. has dropped to 50% of field capacity. Since only 30% of the 9-in. depth is moisture, it may be estimated that this equals 2.7 in. of water. Fifty percent of this value equals 1.35 in. or a requirement of 37,000 gal of water to restore the soil to field capacity. If the irrigation system is 75% effective (allowing for evaporation and drift), it would require approximately 50,000 gal of water or 1.85 acre-in.

The water should be applied at a rate not to exceed the infiltration and percolation rates of the soil, and under some conditions the rate of application may be further limited by work schedules. At a percolation rate of ½ acre-in./hr, it would take 3 hr and 40 min to apply the needed water, in the previous example. If applied at a faster rate, the net result would be either a puddling of the soil or erosion of the soil, plus the extra expense of pumping more water than necessary.

　　A source of supply and a pump with a capacity of 13,600 gal/hr (230 gal/min) per acre would be needed. Nurserymen can, by making similar calculations, estimate their water needs on a per acre basis and then with a knowledge of water availability, work schedules, and costs involved, estimate the size of the irrigation system that will be required for a specific situation.

## PUMPS AND POWER

After it has been determined that an adequate source of good quality water is available, the next decision is what type of system will be used to distribute the water; this includes pump(s), power source, water distribution system, and sprinkler units. At this point it is advisable to seek the services of an irrigation specialist who can provide the detailed information. But it is desirable for nurserymen to have a basic understanding of the various systems.

　　Although there are many types of pumps to select from, the horizontal centrifugal and deep-well turbine pumps are fairly standard for irrigation purposes. The horizontal centrifugal pump is easy to operate, is highly efficient, but is limited to a suction lift of about 22 ft or less and must be primed. Turbine pumps, although more costly than centrifugal pumps and generally more difficult to inspect and repair, are not limited to the 22 ft depth and do not require priming.

　　The actual selection will depend upon (1) the volume of water to be pumped during the peak use period and (2) the total head in feet* (dynamic pumping head), which is the sum of:

1. The total rise in feet from the pumping level to the elevation of the highest point in the irrigation system

2. The friction head in feet for the main line plus the longest lateral (information available from manufacturer)

3. The average sprinkler operating pressure, expressed as friction head in feet (information available from manufacturer)

4. Various miscellaneous friction losses (valves, fittings, etc.) estimated to be 10% of the total head in feet

Power to operate the pump is generally supplied by gasoline, propane, or diesel engines, or by electric motors. If an electric motor is to be employed as a power source, the power company should be contacted prior to purchase to determine availability and cost of electric power and to coordinate installation activities.

---

　　*The total head in feet may be converted to pounds per square inch (psi) by dividing by 2.31, which is the height in feet of a column of water 1 square inch in area that weighs 1 pound.

Energy is expressed in horsepower; 1 horsepower is equivalent to 33,000 foot-pounds per minute, or 0.746 kilowatt. The horsepower rating of an engine or motor is the amount of power that the engine or motor will develop when operated at full load for short periods of time. Brake horsepower is the effective horsepower that the machine is capable of producing over extended periods at the power shaft. The brake horsepower (BHP) requirement can be calculated by the formula (1 gal water = 8.35 lb):

$$\text{BHP} = \frac{\text{GPM} \times 8.35 \times \text{total head (in feet)}}{33,000 \times \text{pump efficiency}}$$

For example, the brake horsepower needed for a pump required to deliver 300 GPM against a total head of 200 ft with a pump efficiency of 75% would be 20:

$$\text{BHP} = \frac{300 \times 8.35 \times 200}{33,000 \times 0.75} = 20$$

For most portable irrigation systems, a gasoline engine may be the best choice. An electric motor or diesel engine is more desirable for permanent systems. When using gasoline or diesel engines, it is desirable to increase the BHP requirement by 25–30%, since the engine is not as efficient over extended periods of use as it is for brief periods of operation under ideal conditions. Also, if the engine were designed to operate on a moving vehicle, the cooling system might have to be modified (e.g., larger radiator and possibly a shroud around the fan) or irrigation water can be run through the radiator. The pump and power sources used in portable systems can be mounted as a unit on a skid, a wheeled trailer, or a truck-bed. An estimate of fuel consumption may be made if one assumes that a well-tuned gasoline engine used for pumping consumes 0.1 gal (U.S.)/hp/hr and for a diesel engine 0.07–0.08 gal (U.S.)/hp/hr.

Tractor power can be used to provide the necessary horsepower to drive power-take-off-driven pumps. But when tractors are used for this purpose, nurserymen should check with the farm equipment dealer as to the maximum continuous dependable power that the tractor engine should deliver at the PTO shaft to drive the pump. In addition, when such units are employed, care must be taken to properly connect and align the PTO shaft. Improper connection or alignment results in excessive wearing of parts and could result in breakage.

Stationary units should be located close to the water source and mounted on a level, solid foundation. Since engines used to power irrigation pumps are often left running unattended for long periods, it is desirable to provide certain safety devices to shut off the engine in the event of a mechanical failure and to prevent bodily injury. Three common failures are: (1) the pump overheats, (2) it loses oil pressure, and (3) it loses prime. If possible, the power unit should be enclosed in a locked building or a fenced area. In addition, container-production nurseries should have both an auxiliary source of power and a pump to substitute in the event the primary source fails.

A few points to consider that may aid in the proper functioning of the pump are: (1) the pipe or hose on the suction side of the pump should be one size larger than the discharge side in order to reduce friction and improve efficiency of the pump; (2) the intake should be placed low enough into the water to assure that an air swirl does not develop over the intake screen, allowing air to be drawn into the system causing a loss of suction; (3) it should also be placed a few inches above the bottom to reduce the intake of sediment; and (4) where a surface source of water is used, a strainer should be used to prevent various forms of debris from being drawn into the pump and causing trouble. In some water sources, a debris barrier may need to be constructed in addition to the strainer to prevent plugging of the intake.

Centrifugal pumps must be primed. There are a number of devices that can be connected to the pump to accomplish this, but a simple method is to keep a barrel or tank of water close by, which is used to fill the suction pipe and pump chamber.

## DISTRIBUTION SYSTEMS

Distribution systems for irrigation may be classified by the method of conveying water or by the degree of permanence of the system. Surface irrigation methods are adapted to relatively flat areas with medium- to heavy-textured soils. Subsurface irrigation is best adapted to peat, muck, and sandy soils, whereas overhead irrigation is adaptable to a wide variety of areas. It is especially well adapted for use in most nurseries. Water can be applied fairly uniformly over uneven topography, and the system is highly adaptable to the many variable situations found in nurseries.

In a permanent installation, the pump, the power source, the main lines and laterals, and in some cases the sprinkler heads, are in fixed positions. The pump and power source are enclosed in a building. The pipes used in the permanent system may be reinforced concrete, asbestos cement, or poly(vinyl chloride) (PVC). All are satisfactory and will withstand the operating pressure of the system if the proper pressure-rated pipe has been selected. The lines should be of a diameter large enough to permit delivery of water without excessive friction loss. Since most of the pipes in a stationary system are below ground, they must be set deep enough to permit cultivation, and in cold climates deep enough to prevent freezing or be installed on a slight gradient to permit draining prior to the onset of freezing temperatures. The permanent system, although relatively more expensive, requires less labor to operate. They are used primarily in high-value, intensive-production areas (e.g., propagation, seed beds, liner, and container production).

In a semiportable system, the pump, power source, and main distribution lines are permanent, but the lateral lines and application equipment are portable. In a fully portable system, everything can be moved from place to place. The pipe used in portable systems is mostly manufactured from either lightweight aluminum or PVC and is equipped with various types of quick-coupling devices. For efficiency it is suggested that all irrigation pipe and couplers in a system be of the same brand. The portable system, although the least expensive to install, requires considerable labor to operate. It is used most commonly in field-production areas.

Sprinkler heads are available in a wide selection of types. Nurserymen should select the type best adapted to their needs and to the soil's ability to absorb water. Water should be applied at a rate equal to but no faster than the soil's absorptive capacity or water is lost to evaporation and soil erosion occurs, especially on hilly terrain. Rotating sprinklers used in nurseries are commonly spaced 50–60 ft apart, operate at a pressure of 50–60 psi, and deliver 5–20 GPM. The spacing between heads and lateral lines, on an average, should not exceed 65–70% of the diameter of the spray pattern of the sprinkler head.

Some nurserymen use traveling, gun-type sprinklers (Fig. 14–1) that discharge about 500 GPM at 80–90 psi pressure. They cover large areas and save labor but require more power to operate and may deliver water too fast for the soil's absorptive capacity.

**Figure 14–1** Traveling gun-type irrigation sprinkler in a field-production nursery.

# WATERING FIELD-GROWN CROPS

Since field-grown nursery crops are watered to increase survival rate following transplanting or to increase growth, and since they may be produced on either close or wide spacing, depending upon the type of plant material and the market objective, it is desirable to discuss irrigation of these crops accordingly.

### To Increase Survival Rates

Following transplanting, the plants must be watered immediately. This can be accomplished with some type of irrigation system or with the aid of a water wagon. In intensive areas, a permanent overhead system may be most appropriate, but as the spacing is increased, a semiportable system may be the most economical approach. In areas where the density of plants per unit area is low, the most economical approach may be the use of a water wagon. However, in situations where the crop is of high value (e.g., larger-caliper shade trees), it may be more desirable to use trickle irrigation.

### To Increase Growth

Most field-production nurseries are located in areas where the natural rainfall throughout the growing season is sufficient, at least in most years, to supply the water necessary for growth. Therefore, they seldom install irrigation systems to increase growth. However, production nurseries located in drier climates and nurseries that produce high-value crops find it financially advantageous to invest in some form of supplemental irrigation to increase growth rates. In some situations, the system may be used only once every 5–6 years, whereas in other situations it may be used yearly. In nurseries where the stock is grown fairly intensively, a semiportable system can be most effective and efficient. But in nurseries where the plants are grown on fairly wide spacing, the use of trickle irrigation may be more efficient.

*Trickle irrigation* is gaining in acceptance by nurserymen for the production of large shade trees (Fig. 14–2). It is based on the concept that best plant performance is obtained by maintaining a favorable soil moisture condition in the root zone. With trickle irrigation it is possible to produce a salable tree more rapidly and with a more compact root system. This has been shown to be especially true for nurseries located in the southeast where spring planting is often delayed by periods of wet weather in March and April combined with spring shipping. Trickle irrigation increased the survival rate and the growth of high-value nursery crops and at the same time used a limited water resource more efficiently. Water is applied under low pressure (less than 15 psi) and at a slow rate (1–2 GPH) for a time period sufficient to maintain the soil in which the roots are developing at or close to field capacity. Since only a portion of the soil area (10–20%) is irrigated, less water is used (Fig. 14–3).

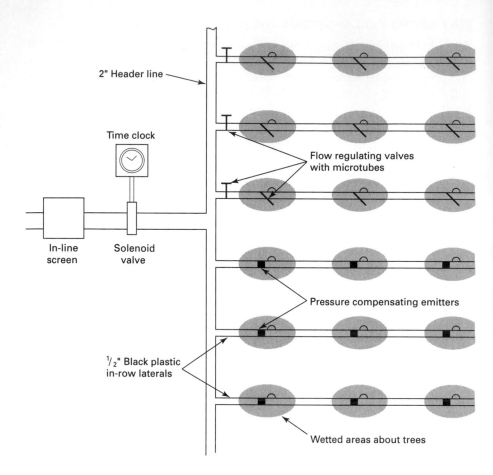

**Figure 14–2** Trickle irrigation in a nursery. Upper half of the diagram illustrates the use of flow regulating valves and microtubes; lower half of the diagram illustrates use of pressure-compensating emitters.

A time clock and solenoid valve can be installed into the line to activate the system for a predetermined time period each day when in use.

Water is delivered to each tree by means of either a microtube or a pressure-compensating emitter. When microtubes are used, it is necessary to control the water delivery rate. This is best accomplished by inserting a flow regulating valve in each lateral and adjusting the number and size or length of the microtubes so that the system is balanced. For example, using a 1.0-GPM flow valve will require using either 30 microtubes at 2.0 GPH, or 60 microtubes at 1.0 GPH, or 120 microtubes at 0.5 GPH. The use of pressure-compensating emitters, although more expensive, negates the need for balancing of the sys-

**Figure 14–3** Trickle irrigation.

tem. Emitters are available in various flow rates, permitting flexibility in designing a system to meet the production plan of the nursery.

## WATERING CONTAINER-GROWN PLANTS

Container-grown plants are watered with the aid of an irrigation system modified to meet the needs of the situation. In parts of the country where water is costly or availability is limited, the system should be both effective and efficient. In areas where water is inexpensive, readily available, and where runoff is not a problem, the system need only be effective. To be effective, water must be applied to the containers when it is needed and in an amount necessary to maintain quality growth. To be efficient, the water must be applied to the interior of the containers.

Enough water must be applied to each container to replace that which is lost by evapotranspiration, to provide for growth, and to assure control of salinity within the medium. The daily loss due to evapotranspiration is a function of environment (temperature, humidity, wind, etc.) and the size and species of the plants. Experienced plantsmen estimate this loss on a daily basis by the appearance of their plants. Also, a correlation can be developed with the loss of water, by evaporation, from a pan of water located in the close proximity to the plants.

Salinity control in container-grown plants requires that the entire soil mass become wetted and that some water leach through the container and drain away from the root zone. In some studies, as little as 0.14 quart of water per day was needed to irrigate plants growing in 1-gal containers, whereas 2 gal water/day were needed to water larger plants growing in 15-gal containers. The actual water regimen for a nursery growing container-grown plants will have to be developed by experience. There are a number of systems available to supply water to container-grown plants; each has its advantages and limitations. A system or systems that will accomplish the job most effectively with minimum degradation of the environment should be employed.

*Overhead sprinkler irrigation* is the most common system used to water small container-grown plants. It applies the water over the tops of the plants at a fairly rapid rate. It is relatively inexpensive to install and operate. But it can be relatively inefficient in the use of water, depending upon placement and size of containers; as much as 80% of the water can be lost between the containers. It is most efficient when watering 1- to 5-gal containers, spaced close together. It is least efficient when watering containers on wide spacing. With a greater public demand for maintaining high water quality standards and control of water runoff from agricultural lands, Congress amended in 1972 the Federal Water Pollution Control Act (originally drafted in 1956). This Act gave the U.S. Environmental Protection Agency the responsibility of setting water standards, which has been deligated to regional boards. Nurserymen should become acquainted with their region's standards and augment programs to recycle water, reduce runoff and protect the environment by reducing pollution. A number of methods to accomplish these goals is offered within the following sections of this chapter.

The actual design of a permanent system for a large container nursery will vary with the size of the area and the capacity of the pump. But the input and output should be in balance, and the design must provide for overlap of distribution patterns to assure fairly even distribution of water. A modular design adapted to meet the needs of various situations is effective for many container-production areas. The output of water is balanced with the input and the area modified accordingly. For example, using a pump that delivers 1600 gallons per minute (GPM) would permit the use of 100 sprinkler heads with a discharge of 16 GPM or the use of 200 heads with discharge of 8 GPM. Since it is desirable to have as even a water distribution pattern as possible, it is more advantageous to use the larger number of heads at low GPM but at the higher suggested operating pressure.

If a container area is designed as shown in Fig. 14–4, it is possible to develop a modular design for the irrigation system. One approach would be to arrange the water distribution by beds, using full-circle (360°) sprinkler heads in the center, half-circle (180°) heads on the sides, and quarter-circle (90°) heads on the corners. If the beds are designed to be 100 ft wide and the sprinkler heads were distributed on a GPM equivalent basis over eight beds, it

**Figure 14-4** Container production area overhead irrigation system.

would require 11 full-circle heads at 8.35 GPM with a radius of 41 ft, 24 half-circle heads at 4.40 GPM with a radius of 40 ft, and 4 quarter-circles at 2.86 GPM with a radius of 35 ft per bed, and the beds would be 600 ft long. The eight beds, totaling 480,000 ft², a little over 11 acres, would require approximately 3 hr to irrigate with 1 in. of water. This would amount to approximately 0.7 in. of water falling on the container-bed area if 30% was lost to evaporation and drift. Total water efficiency would depend upon spacing of the containers. When spaced pot to pot in the equilateral triangle design, the water efficiency would be close to 63%.

Small to medium-sized areas can be watered effectively by using self-propelled rotating sprinklers. Each container, within the radius of discharge, receives an equal volume of water as the sprinklers propel themselves forward.

The advantages of this system are: (1) uniform water distribution, (2) highly portable, and (3) relatively inexpensive. However, it does require more labor to operate.

*Pulse irrigation* is a modification of overhead irrigation where a given quantity of water is applied in a series of short pulses rather than the same quantity in one time period. For example, if an irrigation system is programed to apply water to four areas sequentially and each area is to be irrigated for 60 minutes, the total time period is four hours. However, if the water is applied sequentially in 15 minute units of time and the process is repeated twice for a total irrigation time of 3 hours, there is a reduction of 25% in water usage.

To use the pulse method of irrigation it is necessary to have an automated irrigation system plus a dual programmable irrigation controller with a minimum of three independent starts on each program. By adjusting the system to fit individual needs of the crops, the climate, and the work schedules, it is possible to reduce water consumption and runoff, and reduce pollution by a more effective and efficient liquid fertilizer program.

*Subsurface irrigation* (also known as capillary irrigation or ebb and flow irrigation) is used to water plants in greenhouses, and by nurserymen in Europe, but has not been widely used by nurserymen in the United States until recently. With this system, the container-grown plants are set into a watertight tray and subirrigated with or without a fertilizer solution. After a period of time (for soaking of the medium), the water or fertilizer solution is allowed to drain by gravity into a holding tank where it is monitored for soluble salts and adjusted with fresh water or fertilizer as needed. For this system to operate effectively it is necessary to have a level area and a medium with good capillary conductivity. The water level in the tray(s) can be controlled effectively with a float valve and a microswitch connected to a time clock to control the ingress and egress of the water (Fig. 14–5).

The ebb and flow method of irrigation has been adapted for use in nurseries producing large quantities of container-grown plants utilizing overhead irrigation where runoff and water pollution are a problem. In this situation water recycling is the solution. The entire container production area becomes the tray or drainage basin. The area needs to be graded to provide a 2–3% slope for drainage and the excess water or fertilizer solution is allowed to drain by gravity through drainage tiles or ditches into appropriate settling and/or collecting ponds. After a period of settling, the water solution needs to be tested for its chemical and biological properties, including: soluble salts (see page 264) and levels of nitrogen and potassium; pesticide contamination, the presence of weed seeds and undesirable pathogens (see page 394). After the water has been decontaminated of undesirable pathogens by chlorination or bromination and the weed seeds filtered out it can be chemically adjusted by either the addition of fresh water and/or supplemented with the lacking nutrients, should this be necessary, prior to recycling.

**Figure 14-5** Ebb & flow irrigation bed.

*Surface irrigation* applies water to the surface of the medium within the container and is a most efficient means for watering large containers. It requires an extensive system of pipes and tubes, which gives rise to its more commonly used name, "spaghetti" system. This system must be designed to meet the water requirements of the plants and the cultural operations of the nursery. In general, the system utilizes 1-in. plastic pipe as a secondary supply line to which are attached a number of 3- to 5-ft distribution tubes to which are attached a number of small diameter tubes to carry the water to each container (Fig. 14–6). Depending upon the texture of the soil and the size of the container, it may be necessary to spread the water in some way so that the entire surface is wetted rather than just a small area beneath the emitter.

A few problem areas that have been encountered with the use of plastic tubing are: (1) plugging with dirt and mineral deposits; (2) displacement of the tubes by workers or animals; (3) rodents biting the tubes, causing them to leak; (4) algae developing in clear tubing; and (5) water freezing in the tubes, causing splitting. The rodent problem can be minimized by the use of rodenticides, and the algae problem can be minimized by using black tubing. To avoid having water freeze in the tubes, the system is drained or blown out prior to freezing temperatures. Blowing out the system with an air compressor is the most effective way to assure that it is free of water.

Poly(vinyl chloride) (PVC) pipes can be used to overcome many of the problems associated with the more flexible tubing. By using nozzles of the same material and with the aid of solvents, it is possible to put together a system that is extremely functional. The main lines and laterals can be buried below ground, eliminating the problem of exposed laterals; and not being exposed to the sun also increases the useful life of the system. Many types of nozzles, emitters, and spitters are available to apply water directly to the containers at controlled flow rates which increase the effective and economic use of water and soluble fertilizers. Sand traps or filters should be installed to prevent plugging of the nozzles. Also, with the addition of electronic control units it is possible to regulate irrigation periods for time intervals of a few seconds to many minutes. Electronic controls provide a high degree of flexibility to the system. It can be expanded very easily by the simple addition of a few extra subunit controls and low-voltage solenoid valves.

### Estimating Water Requirements for Container-Grown Plants

The amount of water required to water container-grown plants varies with a number of factors, including the type and size of the plant material, the container capacity for holding water, climatic conditions (temperature, humidity, wind), and the type of irrigation system (sub or overhead). Some species of plants transpire moisture at a faster rate than do others. Also, large

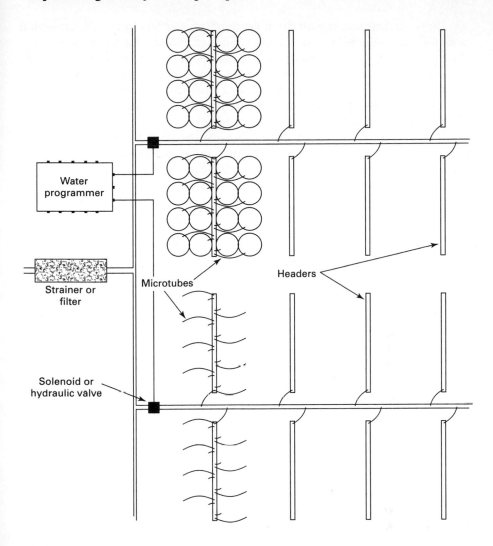

**Figure 14–6** Container irrigation automated microtube system.

plants, contained in a pot of similar size and conformation, use water at a more rapid rate than do smaller plants of the same species.

The *capacity of the containers* to hold moisture varies with each type of medium and with the depth and conformation of the container. Materials such as peat moss and composted bark have a much higher moisture-holding capacity than does material such as sand or milled bark. Therefore, plants growing in a medium with a low container capacity for moisture must be watered more frequently than those growing in a medium with a high container capacity. However, this varies with the volume of the medium in the container and with the height/diameter ratio of the container. Plants growing in wide, shallow or tall, narrow containers require watering more frequently than do plants growing in containers that have a height/diameter ratio that is close to 1.0. Wide, shallow containers lose substantial amounts of water by evaporation; whereas tall, narrow containers do not hold as much available water, owing to the downward force of the longer water column.

*Climatic conditions* strongly influence the need for water. Transpiration rates are rapid during periods of warm temperature and low relative humidity, as are evaporation rates from soil surfaces, requiring more frequent watering of container-grown plants. Transpiration loss is greatest during periods of bright sunshine, when leaf temperatures can be 20–30°F higher than air temperature. During such periods a high vapor-pressure deficit develops between the plant and the ambient air (see Chapter 17), resulting in a rapid loss of moisture from the plants.

The water requirement of container-grown plants is influenced by each of these factors and must be considered when planning the irrigation program. When small containers are placed close together in beds, the most effective way to water the plants is by overhead irrigation, even though some of the water will fall between the containers and upon paths and roadways. The actual amount will vary with the size of the container and the watering practice of the nursery. However, 1-gal containers, which have an actual volume of close to 100 fluid ounces (3 liters) would have a water requirement of 7.6 fluid ounces when the upper half of the medium reached 50% water-holding capacity (assuming that the medium has a moisture-holding capacity of 30%). This would require 0.7 acre-in. of water or approximately 20,000 gal/acre per irrigation. It is fairly common practice to apply ½–1 in. of water at each irrigation and to vary the frequency of application as influenced by the need for water. During periods of cool, cloudy weather the plants may need to be irrigated only once in 3–6 days, whereas during hot, dry periods they may require water every day and for some species even twice a day. Overhead irrigation is best accomplished in the late afternoon or early evening, to minimize loss of moisture due to evaporation. However, for plants that are subject to diseases (e.g., botrytis and mildew) it is best to apply the water early in the morning or to use surface irrigation.

When using overhead or surface irrigation, the plants should be grouped according to the size of the container and a large enough volume of water should be applied so that some flows out the drainage holes. The actual water requirement will vary with the factors previously discussed, but about 2 gal of water is needed per irrigation for containers described as the 15-gal size.

### Excess Water

In some parts of the country disposing of the excess water following the irrigation of container-grown plants can be a problem. Prior to 1975, excess water that did not percolate into the soil was channeled into drainage ditches and discharged either into county drainage systems or municipal storm sewers. Since the mid-1970s, many municipalities have enacted laws prohibiting the discharge of water high in soluble salts into storm sewers. Therefore, this excess water must be disposed of by other means.

One step in solving the problem is to use irrigation water more efficiently, reducing the volume of wastewater that is generated by container production. The wastewater can be disposed of in some manner or it can be impounded or reused for irrigation. If the site conditions and local laws permit, the wastewater can be disposed of through a leach-field system. The runoff from the beds can be channeled into a series of settling tanks (e.g., 30-in. cement culverts placed on end), where the particulate matter is allowed to settle out before the water flows into the leach field. The county drain commissioner or appropriate water management authority should be consulted prior to constructing the system. A permit may be required, and the authority may be in a position to offer constructive suggestions relative to the construction and operation of the system. If the wastewater cannot be disposed of via a leach field or if it is desired to reuse the water, it will be necessary to construct a collecting pond. Information pertaining to the construction of collecting ponds can be obtained from the U.S. Soil Conservation Service.

Waste irrigation water impounded in a collecting pond is generally high in soluble salts (Table 14–1) and could be polluted with herbicides or disease organisms. Therefore, it should not be reused for watering of nursery stock without proper testing. If the water is free of pollutants and the soluble salt level is low, it can be used to irrigate container-grown plants. Where the level of soluble salts is too high for use on nursery stock, it might be possible to use the water to irrigate a salt-tolerant agricultural crop. If this is not a feasible option, the wastewater will either have to be desalted to remove part or all of the soluble salts prior to reuse or be diluted with water low in soluble salts. This can be accomplished with the aid of a proportioner. The resulting mixture has a salt concentration acceptable for irrigating container-grown plants.

By developing a fully integrated system of production that (1) makes use of slow-release fertilizers, including split applications, to maintain optimum nutrient levels, especially for nitrogen and potassium; (2) minimizes the use of soluble fertilizers; and (3) maximizes efficient use of water by employing trickle or drip irrigation methods, it is possible to solve the excess water problem and the pollution of underground water sources in a manner that it becomes an asset rather than a liability to the nursery.

### Fertilizing by Means of an Irrigation System

Sprinkler irrigation can be used to apply fertilizers. Most water-soluble fertilizers can be applied through the irrigation system, but because of economic considerations and various chemical and biological reactions that take place within the soil, it is generally not practical to apply all these materials through the irrigation system. Application should be restricted to those that can be economically applied through the irrigation system and which do not form complex chemical compounds in the soil that render them unavailable for plant growth.

Fertilizing through the irrigation system saves labor and permits greater control over levels of nutrition. Many growers apply small quantities of fertilizer (especially nitrogen) at each watering. When a constant fertilizer program is employed, it is necessary to soil-test on a regular basis, keep accurate, meaningful records, and adjust the fertilizer program to the condition of the crop and the environment. Various agencies, including the Cooperative Extension Service, fertilizer companies, and private horticultural consulting firms, are available to develop fertilizer programs for the crops to be grown in a given environment. Some agencies also publish bulletins that are helpful in developing and understanding fertilizer programs for crop production.

***Nitrogen.*** Most forms of nitrogen, except those that contain free ammonia, can be applied successfully through the irrigation system. Sources containing free ammonia can damage the leaves of plants, and much of the ammonia would be lost by volatilization. Three common nitrogen salts— ammonium nitrate, ammonium sulfate, and potassium nitrate—can be used when applied at recommended rates.

***Potassium.*** The common potassium salts—potassium chloride, potassium sulfate, potassium nitrate, and potassium carbonate—are all soluble in water and can be applied through the irrigation system if necessary, particularly with container-grown plants.

***Phosphorus.*** Most of the common fertilizer salts of phosphorus are relatively insoluble and if introduced into the irrigation system may clog the smaller sprinkler heads. The soluble form may be economically used for container production, but it is not suggested for field culture because of its high cost.

***Other nutrient elements.*** Most of the other nutrient elements can be applied through the irrigation system if necessary. However, most agricultural soils have a sufficient supply for field-grown nursery stock, and for container-grown plants they should be added to the medium at the time of soil preparation.

Fertilizer amendments can be easily introduced into the irrigation system by a number of means. One simple method is to pour the dissolved fertilizer into the water source and to allow the pump to draw the solution into the system. However, this is not a very accurate method. Most accurate and dependable methods require that the nutrient solutions be injected or proportioned into the distribution system.

For centrifugal pumping systems, the suction pipe can be tapped close to the pump and fitted with the necessary pipe or hoses to connect the nutrient supply to the irrigation system. The pump will draw the solution into the system when the valve is opened. With turbine pumps the nutrient solution must be injected into the system under a pressure greater than that of the irrigation system.

Soluble fertilizers can be injected into the irrigation system by means of various types of proportioners or injectors. These mechanical devices are designed and constructed to combine specific amounts of concentrated stock solution and water in various predetermined ratios. When 1 unit of stock solution is combined with 99 units of water, forming a total of 100 units, the proportioner is listed as having a dilution ratio of 1:100, whereas when the combination is 1 unit to 11 units, making a total of 12, the proportion is listed as 1:12.

*Proportioners*, currently available, utilize either Bernoulli's principle or positive displacement. In the first type, a venturi is constructed in the water main, and the line supplying the liquid concentrate is connected at the low pressure point in the venturi. This system is subject to variation in dilution ratios as a result of differences in flow rate or in line pressure. However, these limitations can be modified with the aid of pressure regulators and adjustable valves.

*Positive displacement units* inject a measured quantity of stock solution into a measured volume of water with the aid of pistons of varied stroke length and cylinders of known diameters and lengths. Such units are designed to give relatively consistent dilution ratios over rather wide variations in water pressure. When selecting a proportioner (injector) for a container-production nursery, consideration should be given to the capacity of the system, the dilution ratios available, desired mobility, and maintenance of the unit.

The major advantages to be gained by nurserymen utilizing proportioners are: (1) fertilizer can be applied uniformly at a known concentration, (2) the fertilizer may be applied at the optimum concentration for the species and for the prevailing climatic condition, (3) the fertilizer is applied at the same time that the plants are watered thus saving labor, and (4) the loss of plants due to excess soluble salts is minimized.

Many, very sophisticated proportioners are available for use for fertilization of nursery crops growing either in containers or in the field. Prior to purchase, growers should know the advantages and limitations of the various proportioners and then match nursery objectives to the equipment. Also, keep in mind the flow rate of the irrigation system, size of inlet and outlet pipes, and maintenance requirements. In addition, if the system is to be connected to a source of drinking water it will be necessary to install a backflow valve.

Fertilizer concentration may be stated by any one of a number of methods, but one of the best for constant feeding is to state the concentration in part per million (ppm). The most common concentrations used for fertilizing container-grown plants are 50, 100, or 200 ppm. To obtain a specific concentration with the aid of a proportioner, it is necessary to formulate a concentrated stock solution of known concentration. To accomplish this, it is necessary to know the dilution ratio of the proportioner and the percentage availability of the nutrient element to be applied. If, for example, it is desired

to apply nitrogen at a concentration of 100 ppm with the aid of a 1:100 proportioner and the fertilizer analysis is 33-0-0, the stock solution should contain
4.05 oz/gal.

$$\text{wt/gal of water} = \frac{\text{ppm} \times \text{weight of water} \times \text{proportioner ratio}}{\% \text{ nutrient in fertilizer}}$$

$$\text{oz/gal of water} = \frac{\dfrac{100}{1,000,000} \times 8.34 \text{ lb/gal} \times 16 \text{ oz/lb} \times 100}{0.33}$$

$$= \frac{1 \times 10^{-4} \times 1.33 \times 10^2 \text{ oz/gal} \times 1 \times 10^2}{0.33} = \frac{1.33}{0.33} = 4.05$$

This information for various types of proportioners and fertilizers is tabulated in tables available from many suppliers of water-soluble fertilizers,
or it can be readily estimated from the fertilizer proportioner nomograph
(Appendix H).

   *Hydraulic displacement* of fertilizer solutions from a tank is an efficient,
inexpensive, nonelectrical injection system adaptable to trickle irrigation systems. The tank(s) must be air- and water-tight. The flow through the tank can
be controlled by placing a pressure regulator in the line.

   The prevailing climatic condition will influence the metabolism of plants
and their need for moisture and fertilizer. During periods of high temperature and high light intensities, most plants grow faster requiring more water
and nutrients. During periods of low temperature and low light intensities, plants grow at a slower rate and utilize less water and nutrients. Constant
feeding automatically adjusts to these conditions, since fertilizer is applied
simultaneously.

### Acidifying Water

   At times it may be advantageous to acidify irrigation water. This is particularly true for nurseries that grow their crops in containers or benches and
use water that has an alkaline reaction. Water used to irrigate nursery and
greenhouse crops nearly always contain calcium and magnesium carbonate.
The concentrations will vary with geographic areas and the depth of water
supply, but carbonates cause the water to have an alkaline reaction. The constant use of alkaline water tends to increase the alkalinity of the soil. Since
many species of plants do not grow well in alkaline soils, it is desirable, in
some situations, to acidify the water. This can be accomplished by neutralizing the alkalinity of the water with the aid of acid.

   A high grade of phosphoric acid has been used to neutralize the alkalinity of greenhouse water for many years, and more recently the process has
been used in the production of container-grown plants in nurseries. The advantages of acidification are:

1. Avoids a gradual increase in the soil reaction (pH) from carbonate accumulation
2. Permits injection of one or more of the anions essential for plant growth with minimum modification of salt concentration
3. Minimizes plugging of small-diameter irrigation equipment
4. Reduces sodium uptake by foliage in areas where sodium is a problem salt

When acid is mixed with concentrated fertilizer solutions, the resulting mixture will contain acids of the salts present in the fertilizer. These mixtures have a high corrosive potential to the irrigation equipment that is exposed to the concentrated solutions prior to dilution. Thus, separate injectors are advisable when employing both acid treatment of irrigation water and concentrated fertilizer solutions.

Acidified water used in irrigation of nursery stock should have a pH between 5.8 to 6.5, which is considered optimum for use on most plants. To estimate the quantity of acid required, determine the milliequivalents per liter of carbonates in the water and multiply by the acid factor (Table 14–3). For example, water analysis reports 2.5 mEq/liter of carbonates. The acid injector has a ratio of 1:200 and a 50-gal acid stock solution tank is available. Two hundred × 50 equals 10,000 gal of water to be neutralized (ten 1000-gal units). To neutralize with 75% phosphoric acid requires 175 fluid ounces (10 × 7.0 × 2.5) be mixed with the 50 gal of water for acid injection. The treated water as it is delivered from the nozzle should be tested and the acid solution adjusted accordingly to obtain the desired pH. The solution should be monitored on a regular basis to assure uniformity of water quality.

Acids can be very dangerous materials and should be used with great caution. They are available in various strengths and degrees of purity. Sulfuric acid is commonly available at 66° Baumé grade, which is highly concentrated. When added to water, considerable heat is generated. Therefore, it should be

**Table 14–3** Percent Grade or Degree Baumé, Acid Factor, and Comments on Three Acids Used to Acidify Irrigation Water in Nurseries and Greenhouses

| Acid | Percent Grade or Degree Baumé | Acid Factor (oz/1000 gal) | Notes |
|---|---|---|---|
| Phosphoric | 75% | 7.0 | Most commonly used; contains 52% $P_2O_5$; use food grade; avoid by-product acids—contain harmful heavy metals |
| Sulfuric | 66°Be (98%) | 3.2 | Dangerous to handle; an explosion can occur if water is added to the acid |
| Nitric | 42°Be (67%) | 10.5 | Contains 15% N; avoid mixing with organic materials; dangerous to handle |

*Source:* Adapted from Matkin and Petersen (1971).

added slowly in small quantities, preferably with rapid stirring. Water should not be added to the acid, as an explosion can occur.

## PURIFICATION OF RECYCLED WATER

Water that is being recycled, following the irrigation of nursery stock, will often contain various undesirable contaminants, such as herbicide residues, nematodes, and various plant pathogens that can be redistributed to healthy plants causing serious disease problems. Therefore, the recycled water needs to be purified prior to recirculation. Three materials used to accomplish this are chlorine, bromine, and ozone, with chlorine being used more extensively than bromine or ozone.

*Chlorine* gas, one of the four halogens (bromine, chlorine, fluorine, and iodine), is a poisonous, yellow-green gas. When it is mixed with water it hydrolyzes to form hydrochloric and hypochlorous acids. These, in turn, break down into their respective ions, which are known collectively as free available chlorine (FAC). It is these ions that react with the organic matter, fertilizer, and colloidal materials in the water. The chlorine demand is the difference between the amount of chlorine added to a given quantity of water and the amount of FAC remaining at the end of a given contact time. Since the water recycling requirements differ from nursery to nursery and since chlorine is a deadly poison it is therefore highly recommended that an irrigation engineer be engaged to design and install the chlorination system.

The equipment needed for chlorination of recycled irrigation water, include: cylinders of chlorine (150 lbs), 1 vacuum pressure regulator, that is attached to the cylinders of Cl, a series V500-remote vacuum chlorinator, an injector, and a chlorine testing kit. Most of these materials are available through industrial gas supply firms located in most major cities.

Since chlorine gas is a poisonous gas it is important to follow a few safety guidelines:

1. Secure Cl tanks in an upright position.
2. Never change tanks alone.
3. Have available a full-face respirator with the Cl canister or have an independent air supply.
4. Always use new lead gaskets when connecting tanks.
5. Check all connections with concentrated NH solution. Household NH is not strong enough. A leak will look like cigarette smoke.
6. Have protective caps in place when moving tanks.

*Brominization* of recycled irrigation water has been practiced on a limited basis in some nurseries since 1989 when it was reported in the literature to be an effective germicide with a broader spectrum of activity on plant pathogens than chlorine. All that is required is to maintain a free bromine level of 5–10 ppm in the irrigation water. This is accomplished by injecting a strong solution of bromine, from its holding tank, into the irrigation system. The concentrated bromine solution is created by dissolving a number of Agribrom tablets into a known quantity of water. This method of water purification holds considerable potential for use in the nursery industry.

*Ozone*, another form of oxygen, has been used for more than a century for the sterilization of municipal water. It is currently being tested, in western nurseries, for the sterilization of recycled water. Ozone ($O_3$) reacts with a variety of organic compounds, including plant pathogens, deactivating them by the process of oxidation. With the use of ozone generators it is possible to sterilize large quantities of recycled water faster and safer than with either chlorine or bromine. If current tests, in the western nurseries, prove to be successful in that there are no serious phytotoxic effects on the plants and if the process is economically balanced with the production cost/profit margin it is likely that ozone generators will be used to sterilize recycled water in the nursery industry within the next few years.

## FROST PROTECTION

Sprinkler irrigation systems can also be used to protect some nursery crops from cold-temperature injury. Southern nurseries are periodically exposed to temperatures below freezing during the winter months, and northern nurseries are periodically exposed to cold injury due to radiation frost in the spring following dehardening of plant tissue. Also, the roots of balled and burlapped plants, and container-grown plants can be damaged if exposed for extended periods to low killing temperatures (see page 411). Some of this cold-temperature injury can be minimized by timely and appropriate application of water to the plants just prior to and during the period of cold-temperature exposure.

Some protection of plant roots can be obtained by irrigating container-grown and B&B plants just prior to the onset of a predicted cold period. The media when exposed to the cold temperatures will take longer to freeze and will remain at the freezing point longer than if the media were dry. Also, irrigating the media shortly after the freeze will hasten the thawing and prevent desiccation injury.

Protection of the stems and foliage of plants can be obtained by spraying with water during the danger period. This is accomplished with the use of sprinkler irrigation equipment. The applied water will freeze and release heat, known as *latent heat of water*. This liberated heat will protect the stems and foliage of plants down to about 15°F depending upon the volume of water applied and the wind speed. On a clear night with little wind, 0.10 in. of water per hour (IW/H) will protect plants down to 27°F, but it will require close to 0.25 in. of water per hour to protect plants down to 15°F. This is referred to as a radiation frost. If wind is blowing at 7–8 miles per hour it will take up to 0.8–0.9 in. of water per hour to protect plants down to 15°F.

Also, timing and rate of application is very important. If the atmospheric conditions are dry the irrigation system should be turned on at a higher temperature, for example, 39°F. Under damp conditions the sprinklers can be turned on at 34°F. Water must be applied continuously throughout the danger period. Sprinklers should rotate at close to 1 revolution per minute. It is imperative the water be applied at the rate that it freezes on the foliage to gain the advantage of the latent heat. To assure protection, the irrigation system must be in good working condition and be activated when the temperature approaches the critical low temperature and continue until the temperature warms to 32°F and the ice is melting from the plants. A reliable temperature alarm system should also be installed to warn that the frost protection system should be activated. Also, close communication with the local weather service is desirable during frost-sensitive periods.

Certain types of plants, unfortunately, are much too brittle to withstand the ice load that builds up during such a situation and they should not be treated. The damage due to breakage could be far greater than the protection offered against radiation frost. Freezing of water is not too effective in protecting plants against strong windborne freezes, since the wind removes the liberated heat too rapidly to be effective. This situation is similar to evaporative cooling which reduces plant temperatures to below air temperature.

Nurserymen who plan to use sprinkler irrigation systems for frost protection should contact both the Cooperative Extension Service and their irrigation company to obtain information and system designs for their individual needs.

## EXCESS SOIL MOISTURE

Although plants require water for growth, too much water about their roots for too long a period of time can cause problems. The problem results from oxygen restriction to the growing roots. The roots have a continual need for oxygen to carry on the process of respiration, which in turn produces energy needed for growth. When plants suffer from excess moisture, they often exhibit one or more of the following symptoms: wilting of the foliage and succulent shoots, chlorosis of the foliage, reduced vigor, necrosis of the foliage and tender shoots, and death. The degree of expression of the symptoms is dependent upon the plant species and the duration of the flooded condition.

Plants that have been growing well, as a result of good culture, will often exhibit a sudden wilting of new leaves and shoots when their roots are inundated with water, especially if the water remains for more than a few hours.

Plants that have been exposed to flood conditions for a number of days may completely dehydrate some weeks after the flood. This is due to injury that was done to the roots during the flood period. Plants that are classified as drought-tolerant have a greater tendency to exhibit this type of injury. However, most plants will dehydrate if the excess water remains in the soil long enough to damage their root hairs.

Excess moisture in a propagation bench or liner bed will often result in wilting and death of new shoots. Examination of the cuttings will reveal dead bark on the basal portion of the cutting and a discoloration of the pith. In advanced stages the basal area of the cutting will exhibit rot. However, similar symptoms can be produced by an application of root-inducing hormone at too high a concentration.

Trees and shrubs planted into areas with poor drainage will soon exhibit chlorosis of the foliage and lack of vigor. Where the poor drainage situation is compounded by excessive water, the plants may fail to leaf out in the spring and will die.

The reasons for excess water in the root zone of plants are many and varied. However, they can be reduced to two primary causes: poor drainage and excessive or too frequent applications of water. Poor drainage may be due to soils of medium to low porosity or to artificially created situations that impede drainage. If plants must be planted in poorly drained sites, some thought should be given to selecting species that are adapted to such a site, or to artificially draining the areas.

When planting in pots, containers, benches, or in disturbed-soil areas, attention must be given to providing for adequate drainage. All too often pots and containers have no drainage holes or the holes have become plugged, and disturbed sites have had the soil structure destroyed so that the planting site functions as a sealed basin. The practice of mulching to reduce weed growth and evaporation from the soil surface can sometimes accentuate an excess-moisture problem in the soil. This is particularly true on clay sites during periods of abundant rainfall.

For a plant to grow it must have water, but too much water can be detrimental. Good drainage is one of the cardinal points in growing healthy plants. Never plant into containers without drainage holes, and check the percolation rate of clay and disturbed soils prior to planting. If it is found to be lacking, some type of artificial drainage should be installed prior to planting.

## SUMMARY

Water is a biochemical reagent for photosynthesis and as such is a major modifier of plant growth. Knowledge of water's response to changes in the ambient temperature is essential in utilizing water to effectively moderate soil and medium temperatures during plant production (this is especially true for container production). Due to water's unique properties, maintaining water content at or near field of container capacity during periods of temperature extremes reduces temperature fluctuations in the soil or growth medium and lessens temperature extremes, thus reducing the potential for root injury in container-grown plants and dessication of the foilage in both field or container-grown plants. Periodic (also known as *pulse*) irrigation during hot midday periods in summer will cool the foliage and aid in the reduction of vapor pressure deficit and at the same time cool down the soil or medium environment. Also, water can be used to protect plants from frost damage in late spring and early fall and minimize damage to stems and roots of container-grown plants, due to cold temperatures, that are overwintering in various types of enclosed structures.

## REFERENCES

AUSTIN, B. 1989. Brominization vs. Chlorination, Proc. Inter. Plant Prop. Soc. Vol. 39:310–311.

BIR, R. E. 1989. Spray Water of Let It Drip? Am. Nurseryman 169(3) 80–87.

BOODLEY, J. W., C. F. GORTZIG, R. W. LANGHANS, and J. W. LAYER. 1966. Fertilizer proportioners for floriculture and nursery crop production management. N.Y. State Coll. Agric. Cornell Ext. Bull. 1175.

BOOKER, L. J. 1967. Irrigating container-plants. Am. Nurseryman 126(7):71.

———, and N. W. STICE. 1964. Mechanized irrigation for nurseries. Proc. Int. Plant Propag. Soc. 14:336.

BOSLEY, R. W. 1966. A fertilizer injection system. Proc. Int. Propag. Soc. 16:311–314.

BOUYOUCUS, G. J. 1937. Evaporating the water with burning alcohol as a rapid means of determining moisture content of soils. Soil Sci. 44:337–383.

———. 1950. A practical soil moisture meter as a scientific guide to irrigation practices. Agron. J. 42:104–107.

COSTELLO, L., and J. L. PAUL. 1975. Moisture relations in transplanted container-plants. HortScience 10(4):371–372.

CORR, B. E. 1989. Proportioner Practicality. Amer. Nurseryman 170(9):61–71.

DAUGHTRY, B. 1983. Chlorination of Irrigation Water. Proc. Inter. Plant Prop. Soc. 33:596–599.

DAUGHTRY, B. 1988. Control of Phytophthora and Pythium by Chlorination of Irrigation Water. Proc. Inter Plant Prop. Soc. 38:420–422.

DAUGHTRY, B. 1990. Conservation of Water and Fertilizer Using Pulse Irrigation. Proc. Inter. Plant Prop. Soc. 40:390–393.

DAVIS, J. R., and R. L. COOK. 1954. Fertilizing through irrigation water. Mich. State Univ. Ext. Bull. 324.

———, and R. L. COOK. 1955. Frost protection with sprinkler irrigation. Mich. State Univ. Ext. Bull. 327.

EAKES, D. J. et al. 1985. Influence of Trickle Irrigation on Six Field-Grown Woody Landscape Species Based on Net Evaporation. J. Environ. Hort. 3(3):139–142.

FURUTA, T. 1973. Studies of plant subsystems in container production. Am. Nurseryman 138(12):8.

———. 1974. Irrigation of ornamentals. Proc. Int. Plant Propag. Soc. 24:99–104.

KEEVER, G. J. et al. 1989. Effect of Hydrophylic Polymer Amendment on Growth of Container-Grown Landscape Plants. J. Environ. Hort. 7(2):52–56.

KENWORTHY, A. L. 1974. Trickle irrigation, simplified guidelines for orchard installation and use. Farm Sci. Mich. State Univ. Agric. Exp. Sta. Res Rep. 248.

KIDDER, E. H., and R. Z. WHEATON. 1958. Supplemental irrigation. Mich. State Univ. Ext. Bull. 309.

MATKIN, O. A., and F. H. PETERSEN. 1971. Why and how to acidify irrigation water. Am. Nurseryman 133(12):14.

MONK, R. 1962. Tolerance of some trees and shrubs to saline conditions. Proc. Am. Soc. Hort. Sci. 81:556–561.

OKI, G. 1964. B-1-F fertilizer metering system proceedings. Proc. Int. Plant Propag. Soc. 14:335.

PATEL, S. I., and H. H. TINGA. 1973. Growth of subirrigated Japanese holly as affected by soil type and depth. HortScience 8(1):27–28.

PONDER, H. G., and A. L. KENWORTHY. 1975. Hydraulic displacement of tank fertilizer solution(s) into a trickle irrigation system. HortScience 10(3):261–262.

———, and A. L. KENWORTHY 1976. Trickle irrigation of shade trees growing in the nursery. I. Influence on growth. J. Am. Soc. Hort. Sci. 101(2):100–103.

RATHIER, T. M. and C. R. FRINK. 1989. Nitrate in Runoff Water from Container-Grown Juniper and Albert Spruce Under Different Irrigation and N Fertilization Regimes. J. Environ. Hort. 7(1)32–35.

REGAN, R. 1988. Sprinkler Salvation. Am. Nurseryman 168(5)70–77.

RICHARDS, L. A. 1954. Saline and alkali soils. USDA Agric. Handb. 60.

ROBERTS, B. 1972. The role of water in shade tree growth. Am. Nurseryman 135(3):12.

ROHWER, C., and M. R. LEWIS. 1940. Small irrigation pumping plants. USDA Farmer's Bull. 1857.

SACHS, R. M., T. KRETCHUM, and T. MOCH. 1975. Minimum irrigation requirements for landscape plants. J. Am. Soc. Hort. Sci. 100(5):499–502.

SPURWAY, C. H., and C. E. WILDON. 1938. Water conditioning for greenhouses. Mich. Agric. Exp. Sta. Circ. Bul. 166:3–10.

STAEBNER, F. E. 1940. Supplemental irrigation. USDA Farmer's Bull. 1846.

STOECKELER, J. H., and E. AAMODT. 1940. Use of tensiometers in regulating watering in forest nurseries. Plant Physiol. 15:589–607.

TOMLINSON, W. M. 1964. Automatic one-gallon container irrigation. Proc. Int. Plant Propag. Soc. 14:308–312.

WALLIS, M. T. 1971. Capillary watering. Proceedings of the Refresher Course for Nurserymen. Pershore College of Horticulture, Pershore, England, pp. 32–33.

Whitcomb, C. F. 1985. Water Quality and Plant Production in Containers. Proc. Inter. Plant Prop. Soc. 35:672–677.

White, R. G., and E H. Kidder. Tractor power take-off driver pumps. Mich. State Univ. Coop. Ext. Serv. Misc. Ser. Circ. E–23.

Wilcox, L. V. 1955. Classification and use of irrigation waters. USDA Circ. 969.

Zazueta, F. S. and A. G. Smajstrla. 1987. Computer Control of Irrigation Systems, Proc. Inter. Plant Prop. Soc. 37:518–522.

## SUGGESTED READINGS

Chu, P. 1985. Your Irrigation Water Sample, Proc. Inter. Plant Prop. Soc. 35:682–684.

Gonzalez, R. A. 1992. A Computer-Controlled Drip Irrigation System for Container Plant Production. Hort. Technology 2(3):402–407.

Johnson, M. 1972. Irrigation, nursery container production. Coop. Ext. Serv. Univ. Mass. Publ. 73, pp. 23–25.

McDonald, S. E. and S. W. Runninh. 1979. Monitoring irrigation in western forest tree nurseries. USDA. Forest Service, Rocky Mtn. Forest and Range Exp. Sta. Gen Tech. Rpt. Rm-61.

Pain, C. H., W. W. Hinz, C. Ried, and K. R. Frost. 1975. Sprinkler irrigation. Sprinkler Irrigation Association, Silver Springs, Md.

Rubey, H. 1954. Supplemental irrigation for eastern United States. The Interstate Printers and Publishers, Inc., Danville, Ill.

Skimina, C. A. 1987. A 17-Year Case History of Research and Implementation of Water Recycling on Container Nursery Stock. Proc. Inter. Plant Prop. Soc. 37:82–87.

Skimina, C. A. 1992. Recycling Water, Nutrients, and Waste in the Nursery Industry. Hort. Sci. 17(9):968–971.

Wells, R. 1989. Water Recycling at Monrovia Nursery Company, Azusa, California, and Dayton, Oregon—An Overview, Proc. Inter. Plant Prop. Soc. 38:475–479.

Whitcomb, C. 1990. Recycling Irrigation Water, Proc. Inter. Plant Prop. Soc. 40:444–448.

Weiser, C. J. 1985. Principles of Plant Freezing Resistance and Injury, Proc. Inter. Plant Prop. Soc. 35:229–236.

# Chapter 15
# Modifying Plant Growth and Development in the Nursery

Plants, like any other biological organism, are the product of heredity and environment. Trees growing in a natural environment develop a form and structure related to the multiplicity of stresses to which they are exposed over a period of time. A tree that develops in a dense stand within a forest will have a narrow crown and a tall, lean stem due to crowding and limited light within the stand, whereas a tree that develops in an open area will have a broader, fuller crown with a stem of greater caliper and more taper. Trees growing in a nursery also develop a form and structure related to the stresses imposed upon them by nature and modifiers—climate, moisture, soil, nutrients, and light—plants in a nursery can also be modified in their development by various cultural modifiers, such as spacing, staking, pruning, spraying of chemicals, planting, digging, and by a host of biological modifiers, such as diseases, insects, vertebrates, weeds, and human beings (Table 15–1). Unfortunately, too little attention has been given to the effects of the various cultural modifiers (practices) on the development of plants in nurseries, whereas considerable information is available on the major environmental and biological modifiers.

**Table 15–1** Summary of Primary and Cultural Modifiers of Various Plant Characteristics or Plant Qualities

| Plant Part | Quality or Characteristic | Primary Modifiers | Cultural Modifiers |
|---|---|---|---|
| Stem (trunk) | Diameter (caliper) | Site, moisture, light, wind | Spacing, shoot pruning, fertilizing, spacing, shoot pruning, staking |
| | Taper | Same as for diameter | |
| | Height | Light, moisture | Fertilizing, pruning, space, day length, root pruning, cultivation, chemicals |
| Branches | Length and compactness | Species selection, moisture, light | Same as for stem height |
| | Branch angle | Species or cultivar selection | Pruning, branch spreading, cytokinin |
| Foliage | Color and size | Light, moisture, species selection | Fertilizing, root pruning, irrigation, shade |
| | Sheen of needles | Cultivar selection | Dormant oil on some species |
| | Defoliation | Cold temperature, short days | Chemical defoliants, root pruning |
| Roots | Depth | Site, species selection, soil aeration | Root pruning, copper screening |
| | Branching | Species or cultivar selection | Root pruning, preparation of planting site |
| | Compactness | Drainage | Trickle irrigation, fertilizer placement, organic matter |
| | Malformation (Curl, kink & encircling) (J or bilateral) | Container | Improper planting Method of planting |
| Flowers | Induction | Maturity | Photoperiod, chemicals, C/N ratio, pruning, root pruning, ringing, bending |
| | Inhibition | Juvenility | Chemicals, C/N ratio, pruning |
| Fruit | Set | Pistillate (female) flowers | Pollinizers, hormone sprays, fertilizer (N) |
| | Prevention | Male plants of dioecious species, double-flowered forms | Hormone sprays, removing flower buds |
| Plant | Cold acclimation | Low-temperature, short-photoperiods, ecotype | Root pruning, withholding water |

## SHOOT MODIFICATION

Spacing was discussed in Chapter 5 from the point of view of organization of the nursery for land utilization and various management practices. However, spacing also has an effect upon the growth and development of plants in the nursery. Plants, either in the field or in containers, that are to be sold as specimens must be spaced far enough apart so that they can grow in an unrestricted manner. If they are spaced too closely, or allowed to remain too long in high-density plantings, their branches touch, they become malformed, and their sales appeal decreases. With sapling trees, whether grown in the field or in containers, there is a tendency to overlook the importance of spacing and to grow them too close. At close spacing, saplings tend to grow taller, but the lower foliage is shaded and tends to drop off. At wider spacing, which allows a greater volume of space per plant, they develop more caliper, better taper, and better appearance. Where possible, nursery rows for saplings should be oriented in a north-south direction to maximize exposure of the lower branches of young trees to sunlight.

The density of seeding also affects the growth and development of seedlings. Most buyers prefer seedlings of good caliper ($\frac{3}{16}$–$\frac{1}{4}$ in. or $\frac{1}{4}$ in. and up) with appropriate height and appearance, plus a well-developed root system. However, too low a density in the seedbed results in fewer seedlings that are too large for profitable management. The optimum density should be determined for each species to be grown. Information on seeds and seedling culture is contained in USDA Agricultural Handbook 450, *Seeds of Woody Plants in the United States*, and in *Plant Propagation Principles and Practices* (see Appendix A).

### Staking and Pruning

*Staking and pruning* are strong modifiers of plant form and structure. Since they are closely related and interact with wind, they will be discussed together. Pruning the stem (trunk, bole) of young trees induces a preferential distribution of the photosynthates toward the upper portion of the stems, whereas the action of wind induces a preferential distribution of the photosynthates toward the lower portion of the stem. Staking young trees has a tendency to promote growth of the upper portion of the stem to the detriment of the basal portion. In experiments where the stems of young trees were staked for a number of years, it was found that the stems became unstable and could not support their crowns when the stakes were removed and subjected to the stress of crown weight and wind action. Unstaked trees exposed to the stress of moderate, multidirectional wind produced stems that supported their crowns under the stress of normal wind conditions. Staked trees grew taller but produced stems of less caliper and less taper. Unstaked trees, exposed to moderate multidirectional winds, produced stem growth that was uniformly distributed around the circumference of the stem and was of normal cell structure, whereas trees exposed to a unilateral wind force tended to increase the growth of the stem in the area of maximum stress. This can be seen on trees along an ocean front and on trees improperly staked (Fig. 15–1). Removing the lower branches from the stem contributed to a decrease in caliper and taper of some but not all species of trees.

The development of stems of trees is related to the amount of photosynthate available and its distribution within the tree. There is a strong tendency for the photosynthate (carbohydrates) to accumulate and be utilized in growth processes in the upper portions of a tree. But, owing to physical stresses that are produced in free-swaying stems, there may be an increase in the level of auxin which causes the food materials to be distributed to the stress areas, resulting in greater caliper and improved taper of the stem.

*Taper* is the gradual decrease in diameter of the trunk in an apical direction. Taper can be calculated between two points on the stem by dividing the diameter difference between the two points by the diameter of the basal point (Fig. 15–1). Since diameter of the apical measurement is usually smaller,

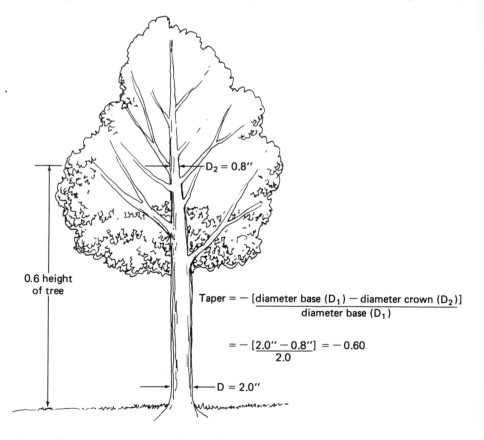

$D_2 = 0.8''$

0.6 height
of tree

$$\text{Taper} = -\frac{[\text{diameter base } (D_1) - \text{diameter crown } (D_2)]}{\text{diameter base } (D_1)}$$

$$= -\frac{[2.0'' - 0.8'']}{2.0} = -0.60$$

$D = 2.0''$

**Figure 15–1** Determination of taper for a young tree.

the taper value is negative. It has been determined experimentally that the taper parameter for sapling trees, where the wind load occurs at a point about 0.6 of the height of the tree, should be close to –0.60. A taper of this magnitude produces a tree in which stress is distributed uniformly in the region of the trunk where wood development is most advanced and decreases rapidly in the region toward the top, where the wood is least developed.

One objective in producing shade trees in a nursery is to develop a straight, strong leader. For most species, this can be accomplished by allowing the saplings to sway in the wind. But with some species and with budded clones, especially when growing on sites where the wind is strong or primarily from one direction, it may be necessary to support the sapling temporarily by staking. If staking is done, it should be confined to the lower portion of the stem, allowing the upper portion to sway in the wind. The support should be removed as soon as the tree has developed sufficient caliper to support the crown.

*Pruning practices* vary with cultivar, market objective, and the personal preference of nurserymen. All pruning in the nursery should be done to enhance the natural form and beauty of the plants. The market objective will also influence the type and amount of pruning that can be done. A market objective that calls for small plants at low price does not permit much pruning, whereas a market objective that is to supply specimen shade trees requires considerable pruning.

Pruning is both an art and a science. It is a practice often abused by the uneducated. Good pruning practices and proper timing can enhance the beauty of nursery plants. Poor pruning and improper timing can seriously reduce their value.

A good nursery pruning program commences with the planting of the liners. Spreading evergreens and some shrubs should be cut back to induce branching and compactness of growth. Trees that normally grow with a central leader should have multiple leaders reduced to one—the straightest. Trunk pruning of shade trees may or may not be done, depending upon the market objective and preference of the nurseryman. Some nurserymen prefer to retain lateral branches and branchlets as long as possible to aid in the development of the trunk, whereas others prefer to strip the buds and branchlets from the trunk to aid in developing smooth bark. Small branchlets can easily be removed by running a gloved hand along the trunk. If branchlets are left on, they can be headed back to permit cultural operations within the blocks. When the desired caliper and taper are established, the lower laterals can be removed to produce a tree with the desired form.

In addition to developing good stem structure for trees, pruning young plants in the nursery is done to improve the crown structure. Thinning the crown will reduce the weight and wind resistance during the early life of young trees, thus aiding in stem development. Excurrent tree species should be limited to a single leader. Double or multiple leaders often are subtended by narrow branch angles which are generally weak and tend to break during storms in later life. Also, branches that join the stem at acute angles should be removed if they are not absolutely necessary for the overall form of the tree. They, too, are weak structurally and can be easily damaged as they grow larger. Branches selected for the main scaffolds should form wide angles (30–60°) to assure that they will withstand stress when they are older. As the trees grows and matures in the nursery, branches that grow inward or that cross and rub other more desirable branches should be removed. In more vigorous species, it may be necessary to headback branches that grow more rapidly than others to keep the crown in balance. Should it become necessary to headback a leader, owing to excessive growth, the cut should be made directly above a bud. If the tree has two or more buds per node, a desirable practice is to remove all but one of these buds. This encourages the development of a single leader and avoids the problem of multiple leaders. To minimize the development of a crook at the point where the new leader develops, support the bud with a small piece of masking tape wrapped about the bud's stem. This practice aids in the development of straight, upright growth of the new developing leader.

Evergreens are pruned or sheared either to enhance their natural form or to correct malformations in growth. Most large evergreens require little pruning; a double or multiple leader may need to be removed periodically. Rapidly growing pines are best pruned during a flush of growth (candle stage) to ensure the development of terminal buds; to delay until the flush of growth has terminated results in poorly shaped trees. Evergreen shrubs (e.g., junipers and yews) will often benefit by two shearings during the growing season, developing into dense plants.

**Time of pruning.** Deciduous shade trees growing in nurseries are best pruned in winter. Priority should be given to those species that have a propensity for copious sap flow in the spring. Beech, birch, maples, and yellow wood should be pruned in December or early January to permit time for the wounds to dry and thereby reduce the amount of sap flow in the spring. Species such as ginkgo and oak can be delayed until late winter, as they produce little or no sap flow from pruning wounds.

Spring pruning of plants in nurseries should be kept to a minimum since this is the time of most active growth for most plants. It is also the time of maximum spore release, with the greatest potential for infection of plants through wounds. Pruning of shade trees in spring should be limited to new plantings and those trees that may require some corrective maintenance. Other activities in the nursery often have a greater priority in the spring, including harvesting, shipping, and planting.

Late spring or early summer, depending on the season, is the time to prune evergreens, such as pines, spruce, and Douglas fir: just before their spring flush of growth.

Summer pruning in nurseries is confined primarily to vigorously growing shrubs and to those indeterminate types of trees, such as ash, honey locust,
pin oak, and zelkova, that grow too rapidly in relationship to trunk development. Pruning is needed to keep the crown of the tree in balance with taper
development of the trunk and to improve branching. Avoid pruning determinate types of trees in late spring or early summer, to avoid stimulating a second flush of growth that could be subject to attack by borers or leafhoppers
that otherwise could have been avoided.

Late summer and fall is another peak season for digging and shipping for
many nurseries; therefore, pruning is delayed until late fall or early winter. It
is also a poor time to prune plants in most parts of the country since the new
growth that results may not harden in time for the onset of winter.

*Clean tools* must be used when pruning in the nursery. It is a good practice to clean and sterilize pruning equipment at the end of each row and especially after pruning a tree or shrub that was or is suspected of being infected
with a disease. All open wounds are potential sites for disease infection. Clo-
sure of pruning wounds can be hastened by keeping the plants in a healthy,
vigorous condition by maintaining adequate levels of moisture and nutrition.
The application of tree paint to wounds is of minimal value and is seldom used
in nurseries.

### Water Modifiers

The growth of plants in the nursery is greatly influenced by the availability of water. Trees suffering from moisture stress produce significantly
less growth than trees growing under optimum levels of soil moisture. Trickle-
irrigated trees growing in nursery rows exhibited greater trunk diameter increase than do nonirrigated trees. Plants growing in containers can also be
modified by availability of water. The trunk caliper, a primary criterion in determining shade tree price, increases as irrigation rates increase for container-
grown trees. Increased irrigation rates also produced a larger root system.
(Use trickle or drip irrigation to avoid excess water problems, see page 336).
Maximum growth of forsythia plants was achieved when the media were
irrigated after 0.1 atm but before 1.0 atm of moisture stress was attained
(Table 15–2). Significant growth reduction resulted when soils were allowed
to dry to a point where 5 or more atmospheres of moisture stress had developed. Maintaining medium soil moisture at high levels is unnecessary after
growth has stopped due to limitations by other climatic modifiers, such as low
temperature or short day lengths.

### Chemical Modifiers

Shoot growth of some species can be modified by chemical means.
Various chemicals are effective in reducing growth of shoots, while others
are effective in accelerating shoot growth. Still other materials can be used
as chemical pruning agents and for control of sprouting.

**Table 15-2**  Influence of Five Moisture Regimes on Growth of *Forsythia intermedia* Grown in Containers

| Moisture Regime | Oven Dry Weight (g) | |
|---|---|---|
| | Mean Shoot Growth | Mean Root Growth |
| Irregular below 0.1-atm stress | 3.69 | 5.06 |
| Irregular at 0.1-atm stress | 5.28 | 6.65 |
| Irregular at 1-atm stress | 5.26 | 5.81 |
| Irregular at 5-atm stress | 3.99 | 4.81 |
| Irregular at 15-atm stress | 2.19 | 3.26 |
| L.S.D. | | |
| 0.05 | 1.37 | 0.31 |
| 0.01 | 1.86 | 0.42 |

*Source:* Wikle et al. (1961).

Maleic hydrazide (MH-40), succinic acid (commonly known as aminozide), abscissic acid (ABA), ancymidol, and other chemical growth regulators have been used to restrict the growth of woody plants. Gibberellic acid accelerates the growth of some species of woody plants. Selected fatty acids (e.g., Off-Shoot-O) can be used as chemical pruning agents, whereas the ethyl ester of napthaleneacetic acid has been used to inhibit sprouting following pruning, and from the base of some grafted or budded plants (e.g., crabapples). However, most of the chemical modifiers are still in the developmental stage and should be used with caution. Only products that are registered for a specific use should be used, and they should be applied according to the product label.

The effectiveness of chemical growth regulators varies with species, stage of growth, climatic conditions, and method of application. As a general rule, plants that have hairy leaves and distinct internodes respond better to foliar sprays than do plants that have waxy leaves or enclosed growing points. Also, plants in the early stages of vegetative growth respond better than those that are dormant, in flower, or in a late stage of growth. Foliar applications should be made when the temperature is between 60 and 80°F and the relative humidity is high (50% or greater). At low temperatures the chemical fails to penetrate, and at high temperature with low relative humidities the materials evaporate prior to penetration. The chemicals should remain on the foliage for at least 1 hr to assure effective penetration. The effectiveness of treatment is also influenced by formulation of the chemical. Some materials are emulsions and must be carefully mixed with water to produce a stable mixture. Emulsions should be applied as a fine mist uniformly over the entire plant. Excessive applications should be avoided, since large accumulations of the emulsion can girdle stems of tender plants. Chemical pruning agents selectively kill the meristematic growing point of a shoot without affecting the subsequent growth of lateral buds; therefore, timing and method of application are extremely important. The best response on woody species has been when the chemical was applied as a fine mist when the plants were in the early stages of a flush of growth and the new shoots were 2–4 in. in length. Sprays applied prior to bud break, in the spring, have not been effective, and later applications have resulted in phytotoxicity.

Sprouting, which commonly develops at the base of grafts, can be successfully inhibited in nursery stock by a single spray application of naphthaleneacetic acid ethyl ester (NAA-ethyl ester), when applied at a concentration of either 0.25 or 0.50% to the base of the trees just prior to bud swell in the spring.[1]

Chemical growth regulators have also been used to modify the angle of branching on young trees. Although the technique has not been tested extensively, applying cytokinins at a concentration of 0.02% on the lateral buds of young apple trees resulted in crotch angles of 60° versus 36° for nontreated buds.

### Modification by Light

The growth of stems can be influenced by light. The juvenile growth and development of seedlings of many woody species can be modified by light intensity and photoperiod. Long photoperiods, produced by extending the natural day length to approximately 16 hr by supplementary low-intensity light (100 foot-candles {ft-c}) or by breaking the night period with a short period of light (Fig. 15–2), will cause many species of the plants to remain vegetative (Table 15–3). Species such as rhododendron and white oak grow in flushes. By control of light intensity or photoperiod, where possible, growth of many species of plants can be accelerated. However, all other modifiers (temperature, moisture, nutrition) must be maintained at optimal levels. The plants must also be conditioned for low-temperature survival prior to planting outdoors if the plants are to be grown in areas exposed to low temperature.

Blue spruce seedlings grown in a greenhouse for 20 weeks under continuous light at 900 ft-c made six times the growth of similar seedlings grown under short days. They also made twice the growth of seedlings grown under a light regime that provided 12 hr of light at 900 ft-c or a 2-hr light break (100 ft-c) in the middle of the dark period. Seedlings of hardwood species responded in a similar manner.

In another experiment, 1-year-old nursery-grown seedlings of 20 hardwood species were grown for 20 weeks with supplemental light at night. VHO fluorescent lamps supplied 700–800 ft-c of light to the seedlings. Control plants were grown both in a greenhouse without light and in a nursery adjacent to the greenhouse. At the end of the experiment, 18 of the 20 species had responded to supplemental light by increased height growth. Smoke trees under supple-

[1]See prior page.

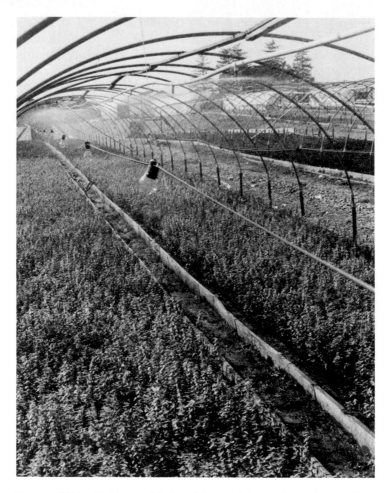

**Figure 15-2** Lights used to break the night period: photoperiodic responsive plants remain vegetative. (Courtesy Conard-Pyle Co.)

mental light made nine times more growth than similar seedlings grown in the nursery. Most hardwood species doubled or quadrupled their growth rates when given supplemental light at night. It is highly probable that most species of woody plants, in their juvenile state, are amenable to increased growth by the use of extended photoperiods.

It is also possible to increase growth of some species by shading. For example, it is reported that Red-Osier dogwood made their best growth when grown under 75% natural light. Also, *Viburnum opulus* 'Nanum' grew best when placed under 30–47% shade than those placed in 65% shade or in full sun. Similar findings have been observed for other species. Container-grown *Euonymus japonica* 'Aureo-marginata' plants made their best growth and had

**Table 15-3** Partial List of Woody Species Vegetatively Responsive to Long Days

| Botanical Name | Common Name |
|---|---|
| Acer negundo | Boxelder |
| Acer palmatum | Japanese maple |
| Acer rubrum | Red maple |
| Acer saccharum[a] | Sugar maple |
| Aesculus hippocastanum[a] | Common horsechestnut |
| Betula pendula | European white birch |
| Betula platyphylla | Asian white birch |
| Catalpa bigononiodies | Common catalpa |
| Catalpa speciosa | Western catalpa |
| Cercis canadensis | American redbud |
| Cornus florida | Flowering dogwood |
| Cornus kousa | Japanese dogwood |
| Cornus nutallii | Mountain dogwood |
| Fagus grandifolia | American beech |
| Fagus sylvatica[a] | European beech |
| Hibiscus syricus | Rose-of-sharon |
| Juniperus horizontalis | Creeping juniper |
| Kolkwitzia amabilis | Beautybush |
| Larix decidua | European larch |
| Larix sibirica | Siberian larch |
| Liquidambar styraciflua[a] | American sweet gum |
| Liriodendron tulipifera[a] | Tulip tree |
| Magnolia soulageana | Saucer magnolia |
| Paulownia tomentosa[a] | Princess tree |
| Phellodendrom amurense | Cork tree |
| Picea abies[a] | Norway spruce |
| Pinus banksiana[a] | Jack pine |
| Pinus caribaea | Cuban pine |
| Pinus echinata | Shortleaf pine |
| Pinus resinosa | Red pine |
| Pinus sylvestris | Scots pine |
| Pinus taeda | Loblolly pine |
| Platanus occidentalis | Eastern sycamore |
| Populus alba | White poplar |
| Populus balsamifera | Balsam poplar |
| Populus deltoides | Eastern cottonwood |
| Quercus alba[a] | White oak |
| Quercus robur | English oak |
| Quercus rubra[a] | Red oak |
| Rhododendron catawbiense[a] | Mountain rosebay |
| Robina pseudoacacia | Black locust |
| Salix babylonica | Weeping willow |
| Tsuga canadensis | Canada hemlock |
| Ulmus americana | American elm |
| Viburnum carlesii | Korean spice viburnum |
| Viburnum opulus | Cranberry bush |
| Weigela florida | European flowering weigela |

[a]Growth in flushes.

the highest quality when grown under shade and trickle irrigated once daily. Apparently, light saturation for some species is less than full natural light; growing these species in partial shade results in improved growth. The majority of species responding to shade are those found naturally growing as understory plants in forests.


## ROOT MODIFICATION

*Root pruning* as practiced in nurseries is done to reduce vegetative growth, develop more compact root systems, aid in the hardening of plants for digging prior to placing them in storage or shipping to market, modify the root system to fit a given container, and encourage a radial root distribution. Root modification in the nursery is generally accomplished by various methods of root pruning. Root pruning in the field is generally accomplished with a "U-blade." The blade is attached to a high-powered tractor (Fig. 1–3) and either pushed or pulled at the appropriate soil depth to prune the roots. But roots can also be modified by planting method, fertilizer placement, trickle irrigation, the use of barriers, such as: air, water, and copper screens, and with container-grown plants by the container.

Plants that are becoming too large for the space available in a field nursery or are growing too rapidly can be modified in growth by root pruning, which will reduce the rate of vegetative growth and help control size. To ensure greater success in transplanting, nurserymen root prune plants that develop sparse root systems or taproots (e.g., *Sophora japonica, Pinus sylvestris*). Root pruning for these purposes is best done when the plants are young, either before planting in the field or 1–2 years after planting. Root pruning in the field should be done after the plants have completed a flush of growth and when there is an adequate supply of soil moisture. Root pruning should not be done during a flush of growth, during drought periods, or just prior to an anticipated drought. Immediately following root pruning, the area should be watered to settle the soil about the roots, to establish soil to root contact, and to assure a supply of water for the plants' metabolic requirements. If no irrigation is available, delay root pruning until there is a high probability of rain.

The method of planting can dramatically modify the root system of nursery-grown trees. At the time of planting, it is essential that the roots of bare root plants be carefully positioned to assure uniform, radial distribution. When bare root trees and shrubs are hand-planted, the roots are generally well distributed. But with mechanical planters there is a great chance of roots being poorly distributed. Some machines open a narrow trench into which the roots are inserted. This often results in a bilateral root system, especially in heavy soils. In other situations, if the roots are dragged in planting, the plants develop a unilateral root system (Fig. 15–3). Trees with either a uni- or bilat-

**Figure 15-3** Unilateral root system, the results of roots that were dragged when planted as a liner.

eral root system do not develop good anchorage in the soil and blow over fairly easily in wind storms. They are restricted to a limited moisture supply and are prone to dehydrate more rapidly during the periods of drought than plants with well-distributed, radial root systems.

### Aeration

Root systems can be modified by aeration and the addition of various soil amendments. Aerating compacted soils will often result in improved root growth. Incorporating organic matter and slow-release fertilizers into the soil about the roots can greatly influence their development. This technique can be used when preparing large trees for transplanting. A trench is dug around the tree in the area where maximum root growth is desired. It is then backfilled with a loam soil enriched with organic matter and a slow-release form of fertilizer. In a few months the trench will be filled with a mass of fibrous roots that aid in successful transplanting.

### Trickle Irrigation

*Trickle irrigation* is effective in modifying the root system of plants growing in field-production nurseries. An examination of the roots of a number of species of trees grown under trickle irrigation showed that sugar maples produced more fibrous roots, whereas honey locust produced larger roots than did nonirrigated trees. Pin oaks produced both more fibrous roots and larger roots. Trickle irrigation did not affect the depth of root penetration but did increase the mass of the root system contained within the root ball.

### Container Effects

Root systems of container-grown plants can be modified by the size, depth, and shape of the container, as well as by various root pruning techniques. Root development of container-grown plants is proportional to the volume of medium in the container in which the plant is growing, which in turn is a function of the diameter and the depth of the container. The shape of the container is also a significant root modifier. In round containers with smooth interior surfaces, plants that remain for too long a period of time develop encircling roots, whereas in square containers or in round containers with vertical ridges on the sides, the roots have a tendency to grow to the corner or to the ridge and then grow down rather than develop in a circular manner. Nurserymen producing seedlings in containers to be used as field liners which in turn will be harvested as B&B plants should avoid small-volume containers, especially those with a low diameter-to-depth ratio. Square containers with a depth of 4–6 in. have been found to be most satisfactory in producing plants with a well-developed root system. Liners produced in deeper containers fail to develop good fibrous roots in the upper portion of the containers, and when grown in narrow pots tend to develop a spiral root system. The roots of container-grown plants can also be effectively root-pruned by growing the plants either on a wire bench or on a copper screen. When grown on the wire bench, the roots are air-pruned, whereas when grown on a copper screen, they are pruned by the toxic effect of the copper.

### Fabric Containers

In the mid-1980s a method of growing plants in the ground in fabric containers was introduced to the nursery industry. These containers are cylindrical with sides of strong, non-woven, black geotextile polypropylene fabric through which water and nutrients filter freely. The base of the container is constructed of a clear, low-density polyethylene that prevents downward root growth. Early research with these fabric containers indicated that the trees produce a more compact fibrous root system. Following transplanting, in full leaf, the trees did not wilt and established new roots faster than trees produced and harvested by standard nursery techniques.

However, over the ensuing years nurserymen and researchers have reported mixed results from the use of fabric in the ground bags. Some have reported no significant difference in top growth whereas others have reported that top growth was less than comparable field-grown trees. When carbohydrate levels in the roots was tested the levels were always higher on those trees that had been produced in the fabric containers. This may be an advantage for bag-grown trees following transplanting. The fabric bags should be removed at the time of transplanting to prevent malformations and girdling of roots which would result in poor growth and death of the trees. (See page 83 for another way to use fabric containers to produce plants in a nursery).

### Wire Baskets

Nurserymen that produce large-sized shade trees often use wire baskets to contain the soil balls. Some questions have been raised as to the affect of the wires on the tree roots as they increased in diameter. Some thought there would be a girdling of the roots. However, research has shown that the roots, as they increase in diameter, grow around the basket wires forming a complete union of root tissue that is fully functional. The roots are not permanently girdled.

## TEMPERATURE RESPONSES

The temperature of the root medium can also modify the growth of roots, especially those plants growing in containers. For most plants, the optimum temperature range for root growth is 60–80°F. But low and high temperatures can result in injury or death of roots. Plants growing in metal or high-density polyethylene containers and exposed to direct solar radiation will often have medium temperatures in the range of 100–125°F (38–52°C) resulting in death of roots or heat stress. Heat stress of the root system can result in reduced growth rates, leaf chlorosis and wilting, abnormal branching habit, and reduced flower number and quality. The economic ramifications of heat stress to container-grown nursery crops include, in addition to death of plants, reduced plant quality resulting in a lower selling price, and a longer production time resulting in increased production costs; all of which result in less profit.

These high-temperature effects* can be reduced to some degree by using fiber or papier-mache-type containers which are poor conductors of heat, or by using light-colored containers (white, yellow) which will reflect some of

*See Chapter 17 for low-temperature effects.

the solar energy. Sun screens can be sited to shield containers from solar radiation and midday irrigation, to reduce media temperature, and can be effective in reducing heat stress of roots.

## FLOWERING AND FRUITING

Modifying flowering and fruiting varies with the objective of nurserymen. Nurserymen often want plants to produce flowers or fruits, because they are more marketable. At other times they may want to prevent flowering or fruiting, since fruiting usually causes a reduction in growth.

They may also desire to keep plants in a juvenile condition, since cuttings from juvenile plants initiate roots more readily than do cuttings from mature plants. Flowering plants that are heavily set with flower buds or are in flower will not only sell much more readily than similar-sized plants without buds or flowers, but the plants will command a higher price in the marketplace. There is also a sales advantage to having fruit on plants such as English and American holly, fire thorn, mountain ash, and others, since this is what the customers desire.

The physiology of flowering and fruiting is very complex and is thoroughly discussed in other books and scientific reviews (see Suggested Readings). But the basic information developed by plant scientists can be used by nurserymen to modify the flowering and fruiting of plants in the nursery. For years nurserymen have attempted to induce the plants to flower by stem pruning, root pruning, ringing of stems, bending of branches, bark inversion, and withholding water and nitrogen. They have maintained plants in a juvenile condition by heavy pruning and by applying high levels of nitrogen. Since the mid-1950s, plant scientists have learned to control the growth and flowering of a number of woody plants by modifying the photoperiod, and since the 1960s they have been able to modify, to a certain degree, the flowering response of woody species with the aid of chemical growth regulators.

Early spring pruning of young vigorous apple trees helps to stimulate growth but discourages the formation of flower buds, whereas pruning similar trees at the time of flower bud differentiation can stimulate flower bud formation but retard vegetative growth. The same response has been reported for the application of nitrogen fertilizer to young apple trees. For many years it was thought that applying nitrogen to plants would keep them in a vegetative condition, while withholding nitrogen would cause them to differentiate flower buds. It has been demonstrated, on young apple trees, that applying nitrogen in the late fall or early spring prior to growth will, in fact, induce more vegetative growth. But once extension growth has ceased, an application of nitrogen can stimulate floral differentiation in those buds still undifferentiated. Timing is the important factor.

*Root pruning* or digging plants such as flowering dogwood a year in advance of sale is done by some nurserymen to stimulate the initiation and development of floral primordia. Root pruning is basically a growth-retarding process, but if performed at the right time in the growth cycle it can be effective in stimulating flower bud development on some species (e.g., wisteria). The pruning should be done when the foliage is fully developed and just prior to bud initiation for the species.

The *practice of ringing* (girdling) or scoring and bark inversion are used by orchardists to induce a "tardy" fruit tree into bearing, and it has been and is used, to a limited degree, to promote flowering. Ringing is the practice of removing a strip of bark from a branch or the trunk of a tree, whereas scoring is cutting through the bark of a tree into the wood without removing any bark. Bark inversion involves removing a ring of bark from the trunk of the tree and replacing it in an inverted position. The operation is best performed in the spring of the year when the bark is slipping; this will leave the cambium in place to heal the wound. It is recommended that the exposed area be protected from the sun to prevent drying. The injury disrupts the downward movement of elaborated carbohydrates and organic substances, thus reducing root growth. The net effect is to decrease vegetative growth and to induce flower bud initiation. Ringing should not be practiced on stone fruits, since it usually results in death of the tree.

The *effect of photoperiod* on the flowering of plants has been known since 1920 when the length of the day was found to be the controlling factor in the flowering of tobacco. Since that time photoperiodism has been thoroughly researched and is known to control many other responses in plants, including germination of some seeds, shoot elongation, rhizome formation, sex expression, winter hardening, and others. Commercial flower growers soon took advantage of the knowledge that chrysanthemums and poinsettias could be induced to flower by short days. They used long days to keep plants vegetative and induced them into bloom by putting them under short days. This is commonly done by pulling black cloth over the plants in the late afternoon or by interrupting the night period by a half-hour of low-intensity light. Unfortunately, there are only a few reports relating the influence of photoperiod to flower initiation and expression in woody plants (Table 15–4).

Flower bud formation in *Rhododendron catawbiense* is enhanced by growing the plants on long days (16 hours) until the flush of growth is about one-half complete (10–14 days), at which time they should be transferred to short days. Maintaining the plants under long days results in malformed flower buds with leaflike bracts and petal-like stamens.

Flower development and expression in *Abelia grandiflora* and *Hibiscus syriacus* occur under long days on the current season's growth. However, flowering in weigela is more typical of other wood species in which initiation of flower buds occurs one season and flowering the next season after certain physiological requirements are satisfied. Weigela can be induced to flower the

**Table 15–4** Classification of Woody Species with Respect to Day-Length Requirement for Flowering

| *Botanical Name* | *Common Name* |
|---|---|
| Long-Day Species | |
| *Abelia grandiflora* | Glossy abelia |
| *Caryopteris incana* | Blue spiraea |
| *Hibiscus syriacus* | Rose-of-sharon |
| *Ribes rubrum* | Red currant |
| Short-Day Species | |
| *Bougainvillea glabra* | Paper flower |
| *Coffea arabica* | Coffee |
| Long-Day/Short-Day Species | |
| *Cestrum nocturnum* | Night jessamine |
| *Rhododendron catawbiense* | Mountain rosebay |
| Day-Neutral Species | |
| *Buddleia davidii* | Summer lilac |
| *Calluna vulgaris* | Scotch heather |
| *Cornus florida* | Flowering dogwood |
| *Hydrangea macrophylla* | French hydrangea |
| *Malvaviscus arboreus mexicanus* | Turk's cap |
| *Pinus* sp. | Pine |
| *Salix repens* | Creeping willow |
| *Syringa vulgaris* | Common lilac |
| *Viburnum* sp. | Viburnum |

*Source:* Davidson and Hamner (1957).

same season by growing the plants on long days for a period of 6–8 weeks, exposing the plants to short days for 6–8 weeks, followed by defoliation and a return to long days. Within 7–8 weeks following return to long days, the plants will be in full bloom. There are some cultivars of weigela that produce flower buds and bloom on current season's wood when exposed to long days. Weigela fails to bloom when exposed to short days.

Chemical growth regulators can also be used to modify the flowering response in some woody ornamental plants. In weigela, spraying plants growing under long days with maleic hydrazide (MH) 2500 ppm is as effective as subjecting the plants to short days for 6–8 weeks. Plants sprayed with MH will bloom about 7–8 weeks following treatment.

Flower bud development in rhododendron can be enhanced by soil or foliage application of growth regulators. Soil applications of Phosfon (2,4-dichlorobenzyl-tributal phosphonium chloride) 0.4 g/gal container or foliar applications of succinic acid (0.25–1.0%) enhanced the development of flower buds on young plants. Azalea plants can also be induced by short days or by the use of growth retardants. The growth regulator should be applied to elongating shoots at the time that shoot elongation is about one-third to one-half complete, since this is the time that the meristem is most precocious. Flowering and fruiting of holly can be enhanced by the use of growth retardants. Phosfon applied as a soil drench to young holly plants in a vegetative condition resulted in flowering and an abundance of fruit.

*Fruiting of trees* for use in orchard plantings is an essential requirement and is generally considered to be a desirable attribute in most ornamental trees, but not in all. Under some situations the development of fruit on plants can be less than desirable. Most people like to see fruit on holly, yews, mountain ash, and crabapples, but wish to avoid fruit set on ginkgo, mulberry, maple, and elm. Others would like to prevent the fruiting of crabapples, apples, cherries, and so on. Thus, nurserymen must be able to meet the demands of all groups relative to fruiting. To assure fruiting, it is necessary to plant those that have the ability to produce fruit, that is plant species that have perfect or monoecious flowers or female plants of dioecious species.

*Perfect flowers* are those that have both anthers and pistils in the same flower. In most species they will produce fruit by self-pollination, but other species may require cross pollination to set fruit. It is important to know if cross pollination is required for fruit production in fruit tree species. Most of the following fruit trees are self-fruitful: apricots, citrus, European-type plums (fruitfulness aided by planting two varieties), figs (except Smyrna types), peaches (except J. H. Hale and a few other varieties), quince, and sour cherries. A number of apples, pears, sweet cherries, and American-Japanese-type plums are self-unfruitful. To ensure fruit set, plant at least two and sometimes three varieties near each other. Some fruit tree varieties produce little or no pollen, or their pollen fails to fertilize the ovules. Therefore, at least two varieties should be planted in the same vicinity: *apples:* Baldwin, Gravenstein, Turley, Rhode Island Greening, Stamen, and Winesap; *pears:* Bartlett and Seckel; *sweet cherry:* Bing, Lambert, Napoleon. When planning an orchard, it is advisable to check the planting plan with a fruit specialist to assure proper plant selections and fruitfulness of all trees.

In *monoecious species* the reproductive structures are in separate flowers but on the same plant (e.g., pine, spruce), but only the female flowers or strobile produces fruit. In dioecious species the reproductive structures are on separate plants. The word "dioecious" is derived from the Greek words *di* (two) and *oikos* (house): thus, two households. The fruit is borne by the female plants, but a pollinizer (a male plant) must be located in the vicinity to ensure fertilization. A number of valuable fruit and ornamental plants are dioecious (Table 15–5).

Over the years plants have been selected and grown either for their outstanding fruiting characteristics (e.g., holly, pyracantha, yew) or for the lack of fruiting (e.g., ginkgo, mulberry, yew). When propagated by vegetative means, these selections become established as either male or female clones. For example, in *Taxus* the clones 'Densiformis,' 'Nigra,' and 'Wellsley' are male, whereas 'Kelsey,' 'Vermeulen,' and 'Jeffrey' are female. But 'Brown,'

**Table 15-5**  Partial List of Genera with One or More Dioecious Species

| Genera | Common Name |
|---|---|
| Acer | Maple |
| Actinidia | Actinidia |
| Ailanthus | Tree of heaven |
| Aucuba | Aucuba |
| Baccharis | Saltbush |
| Celastrus | Bittersweet |
| Cephalotaxus | Plum-yew |
| Chionanthus | Fringe tree |
| Cotinus | Smoke tree |
| Diospyros | Persimmon |
| Fraxinus | Ash |
| Ginkgo | Maidenhair tree |
| Glymnocladus | Kentucky coffee tree |
| Helwingia | Helwingia |
| Hippophae | Sea buckthorn |
| Ilex | Holly |
| Juniperus | Juniper |
| Lindera | Spice bush |
| Maclura | Osage orange |
| Morus | Mulberry |
| Myrica | Bog myrtle |
| Nemopanthus | Mountain holly |
| Orixa | Orixa |
| Phellodendron | Cork tree |
| Populus | Poplar |
| Rhus | Sumac |
| Ribes | Currant |
| Salix | Willow |
| Schisandra | Magnolia vine |
| Shepherdia | Buffalo berry |
| Skimmia | Skimmia |
| Smilax | Greenbrier |
| Taxus | Yew |
| Vitis | Grape |
| Zanthoxylum | Prickly ash |

'Hatfield,' and 'Hicks' have both male and female plants being sold within the clone. In the case of 'Hicks,' there were apparently two selections made, one male and the other female. They should have separate clonal names. Brown was introduced as a male clone, but at some point there was a mixup in propagation, or sex reversion took place and went unnoticed. In order to conform to standards of nomenclature, a clone must maintain the characteristics for which it was selected. Thus, considerable care must be exercised in propagation and production to assure trueness to name.

*Fruiting can be avoided,* at least in some species, by planting either the male form of dioecious species or by planting double-flowered forms (e.g., horsechestnut, cherries, Paul's scarlet hawthorn). Many of the double-flowering forms are unfruitful because of the morphology of their floral structures.

Fruit set can be influenced by temperature and to some degree by day length. Fruit set in Burford holly, for example, was enhanced by growing the plants under short days (9-hr day length) and low-temperature regimes (18°/14°C day/night temperature). Plants grown under long days and higher day/night temperature made more vegetative growth but set less fruit.

Fruiting can also be prevented, at least in some species, by the use of chemical sprays (e.g., naphthyleneacetic acid [NAA], maleic hydrazide [MH-30], caustic agents, and emulsifiable polyethylene films). Various caustic agents such as dinitro compounds can be used to prevent fruiting, but some foliage burn can be expected. Sprays of emulsifiable polyethylene applied to *Thuja* at full bloom completely prevented cone formation, but the material was of little value in preventing fruiting on other species. NAA has been the most versatile hormone spray for preventing fruiting of trees.

Before applying chemical sprays to prevent fruit set or to remove unwanted fruit, nurserymen should be familiar with a number of limitations in their use.

1. All chemicals have registered uses. By law, a chemical must be registered with the Environmental Protection Agency (EPA) before it can be used. Unfortunately, many of the chemicals have been cleared for use only on fruit crops.
2. Concentration is critical. At low concentration, hormone sprays cause the set of fruit; at high concentrations they can cause phytotoxic effects on the flowers and growing shoots.
3. The time of application and weather conditions can modify the response. If applied at the wrong stage of flower or fruit development, the response can be different from that which was anticipated. If applied prior to a rain or a cold period, the results may be negative. If hormone sprays are to be used to prevent the development of fruit, they should be applied at the proper time for a given species and at the recommended concentration. If a dinitro is used, it should be applied in such a manner as to avoid contact with the foliage of evergreens, since it may cause them to drop their needles.

## WINTER SURVIVAL

The winter survival of plants is important to nurserymen everywhere, but especially to those located in the colder climates. Nurserymen have a sizable investment in plant material, which if injured, could result in a serious economic loss. They are, therefore, concerned with the causes of winter injury and measures that can be taken to prevent or minimize the extent of damage. Winter injury to plants can be caused by desiccation, low temperature, or by various physical and biological agents.

Winter desiccation injury is most commonly associated with evergreens, both narrow- and broad-leaved, and semievergreens. During the late winter months when the soil in the root zone is frozen and the foliage is exposed to radiation from the sun, the leaves lose moisture which the plant cannot replace. This results in desiccation of the leaves and sometimes of the stems of sensitive species. The response varies with species and even with cultivars within the species. For example, *Pinus strobus* is more sensitive to winter burn injury than is *Pinus nigra*. This is also true for *Taxus baccata* compared to *Taxus cuspidata* or *Taxus media*. With *T. cuspidata* the cultivars most sensitive to desiccation in the Midwest are 'Aurescens' and 'Thayesae.' In the *T. media* group the most sensitive are 'Brownii' and 'Green Mountain.' This may be due to the degree of water deficiency that the plants can endure. It can be prevented by shielding tender species from the direct rays of the sun and from wind during the winter months. The application of antidesiccants (transpiration inhibitors) to minimize desiccation injury has not been fully successful. Some success has been reported when the antidesiccant is applied in two applications during the winter, especially covering the lower surface of the leaves.

Low-temperature injury can be classified into three areas: (1) early fall or late spring frosts, (2) extremely cold temperature, and (3) rapid change from warm to cold. Early fall or late spring frosts, at temperatures slightly below freezing, will often injure plants that would normally withstand temperatures some 30–40° lower if the plants had been fully acclimated for winter. These frosts are the unseasonably low temperatures that occur every 5–10 years. When it occurs in the fall of the year, the injury is manifested by the splitting of stems in plants like azaleas, holly, and rhododendrons. The same type of injury can take place in the late winter if there is a period (3–5 days) of warm temperature (40–50°F) followed by a rapid drop in temperature across the freezing point. A condition like this occurred in the Midwest in 1973 and in 1984, causing extensive injury to young evergreen transplants. However, when the frost takes place in late spring, the drop in temperature may not be as great, and the injury is primarily the freezing of the tender new shoots. Although the injury may appear to be rather extensive, the plant will soon recover and in 3 months to a year the aesthetic damage will be remedied, but the nursery may have sustained an economic loss. Extremely low temperatures, which normally occur in midwinter, can result in injury to flower buds, roots, shoot buds, branches, or stems, and at times if the temperature is low enough, in death of the plant.

Plants that survive cold periods have the unique ability to acclimate themselves prior to the onset of cold temperatures. The actual mechanism of cold acclimation is not fully understood.* But it appears that decreasing day length and/or gradually decreasing temperatures in the fall of the year aids in increasing cold acclimation of woody plants in northern latitudes. Exposing weigela, rhododendron, and hibiscus to short days prior to the onset of low temperatures was effective in inducing cold hardiness, whereas exposing the plants to long days prior to the onset of low temperature resulted in considerable winter injury.

Exposure to short days and low temperatures prior to the onset of freezing temperatures aided in developing cold hardiness in yews and Red-Osier dogwood, whereas only declining air temperature was associated with increased cold acclimation of 'Hetzi' juniper and other conifers. Woody plants respond to the short days and/or low temperature by a significant reduction in the water content of their stems. In Red-Osier dogwood, it was noted that there was a decrease in water permeability of root cells which acted as a barrier to water uptake. Thus, it appears that cold acclimation is related in part to moisture relationships and tenderness of growth. High soil moisture and high levels of fertility do not appear to bear a direct relationship on winter hardiness. However, species that do not harden in response to short days may be predisposed to low-temperature injury by maintaining high levels of moisture and nutrition during a warm fall.

To aid in hardening plant material for winter, avoid cultural practices that predispose the plants to injury.

1. Do not expose plants to long days or high temperatures prior to the onset of winter. Plants that were growing under lights or in warm places (greenhouse) should be gradually conditioned for winter either by 2–3 weeks' exposure to low temperature or short days.

2. Avoid late (time varies with area of the country) pruning, cultivating, fertilizing, and field irrigation of plants susceptible to winter injury.

3. Dig tender plants (e.g., althea, buddleia, deutzia) prior to onset of low temperature and place them into winter storage, where temperature control is possible.

4. Avoid growing plants that are not cold-hardy.

*Various physical and biological agents*, including frost, ice and snow, snowmobiles, rabbits, mice, and deer, can also be the cause of winter injury to plants in the nursery. Frost heaving is primarily associated with young

---

*Readers wishing to study this area in detail are referred to the articles listed under Suggested Reading.

plants transplanted into clay or clay loam soils in the fall. As the ground freezes and thaws, the young plants which have not established firm root contact with the soil are heaved out of the ground and eventually dehydrate and die unless they are replanted prior to dehydration. This type of injury can be avoided by planting fall transplants onto well-drained sites or by delaying the planting onto clay sites until spring.

Damage due to ice and snow is a physical injury sustained by plants due to the weight of the materials. In most cases the injury is immediately visible, but with some plants (e.g., boxwood) the injury may not be apparent for a year or two following the ice or snow storm. The plant appears to recover from the physical crushing of the snow or ice, grows well the following summer, but begins to die the following year. The delayed appearance of damage is because only the lower bark was injured. The plant is able to obtain water and nutrients from the soil for about a year, but eventually the roots die as a result of the injury to the bark, which in effect girdled the stem. This type of injury can be avoided by providing support to the plants prior to the onset of winter. This may be a wire or wire fencing stretched along both sides of a row of boxwood or similar plants.

With the advent of the recreational use of snowmobiles, some nurserymen, in northern areas of the country, have experienced injury to plants due to snowmobiles. This injury has been confined mostly to the loss of leaders from young evergreens, such as pine, spruce, and fir. The leaders are broken by the vehicle as the driver speeds across the snow-covered landscape unaware of the damage being done to the plants below. The only protection from this type of injury is to fence or post the property against trespass, which may or may not be effective.

Rabbits, mice, and deer can do considerable damage to nursery stock during the winter months. Rabbits will either chew the bark off the stems and larger branches of deciduous trees or they will bite off the tops and side branches of smaller transplants. All types of young fruit trees, crabapples, flowering dogwood, and sweetgum are subject to their depredation. Rabbits can be kept out of limited areas of the nursery by various types of exclosures. But the most satisfactory method in extensive plantings is to reduce their population by shooting (permit may be necessary). The use of repellents to keep them away from valuable plants is of limited value.

Mice depredate nursery stock mostly by girdling plants at the ground line (Fig. 15–4). Occasionally, when the snow level is high, their activity is extended up onto the trunk and lateral branches. Mice have a special fondness for crabapples, arborvitae, junipers, and yews but will also work on pines and deciduous trees, if their preferred food source is not available, although they seldom chew on any trees within the stone fruit classification (e.g., peach, cherry). Removal of their natural shelter, such as weeds and sod, will aid in minimizing their depredations, but it is not a guarantee. Various types of poison baits can be used to reduce mice populations, but nurserymen must

**Figure 15–4** Girdling of trees by mice in a nursery.

be cautious in their use, since they are toxic to fish, birds, and warm-blooded animals. Where possible, encouraging or stocking an area with natural predators may be one of the best methods of reducing rodent populations in nurseries located in rural areas.

Deer can cause extensive damage to nursery stock by chewing buds and tender branches (i.e., arborvitae, birch, yew), rubbing the trunks of young trees when developing their antlers, and trampling small plants when they are in large herds. Injury due to deer activity can be minimized by the use of repellents and fences but shooting (by permit) may be necessary if the herd is large and known to have its winter feeding area in the vicinity of the nursery.

## DEER CONTROL FENCING

Deer can also be excluded from nursery stock by the use of electrified-visual-grazing tape. The fence acts as a psychological barrier since the deer do not like being zapped by the electricity. The tape is a yellow polyethylene ribbon with strands of stainless steel through it that carries 3–7000 volts. It is supported about 3½–4 ft above the ground by ⅜ in. fiberglass rods. The fence should be baited every two weeks with peanut butter to attract the deer to the tape and the voltage should be checked every 2–3 days to be sure the voltage is at the correct level. The power is supplied by a deep cycle marine battery. Two batteries are needed—one on line and one on the charger. (To obtain more information contact K Fence Company, RR 1, Box 195, Zumbro Falls, MN 55991.)

### Diversion Feeding Station

Another method of deer control that has proven to be effective for some nurserymen is the use of diversion-feeding stations. The stations, well stocked with shelled corn, are set up around the perimeter of the area to be protected, preferably in a wooded area or open meadow. By checking and restocking the stations every 2–3 days, deer damage to nursery stock can be kept to a minimum.

Nurserymen must take steps to minimize the depredations of deer and rodents prior to critical damage periods. One of the best methods to avoid deer damage is to locate the nursery away from the cover of woods that shelter deer populations. Another alternative is not to plant those species of trees and shrubs that deer prefer for browsing, such as *Thuja spp.*, *Taxus*, *Juniperus spp.*, *Euonymus spp.*, and *Forsythia*, close to wooded areas. Baits should be in place before snow covers the ground, and repellents must be applied while it is still warm. Inspection of the nursery should be made weekly during the winter months to check for deer or rodent activity. If deer or rodents are found to be active, appropriate action can be taken to reduce their population and minimize damage to valuable plants. Table 15–6 is a partial list of animal repellents. They should be used according to label instructions. Tobasco sauce (also Louisiana hot sauce) 1 tablespoonful/gal has been used fairly successfully as a repellent to protect plants from injury due to the activities of deer, mice, and rabbits. Plants to be protected should be sprayed biweekly. A small amount of spreader-sticker (tablespoon/gal) added to the mixture will improve its effectiveness. Additional information on repellents and bait for the control of birds, deer, mice, and rabbits in the nursery may be obtained from the local county agricultural agent or the U.S. Fisheries and Wildlife Service. In many states it is unlawful to gas, poison, shoot, trap, or otherwise harm wild animals or wild birds without special permits. Nurserymen should check with the law enforcement divisions of their Department of Natural Resources and obtain the necessary permits prior to instituting a vertebrate control program that invokes harming wildlife.

## SUMMARY

Plants growing in a nursery can be modified in their growth by various environmental, cultural, and biological modifiers. These modifiers may have either a positive or negative effect upon the plants. By good ecological management,

**Table 15-6**  Partial List of Animal Repellents

| Material | Repellent for: |
|---|---|
| Alkylpyridines | Dogs |
| Aluminum powder | Seed deterrent for birds |
| Bloodmeal | Rabbits |
| Bone tar oils | Deer, dogs, and rabbits |
| Copper naphthenate | Porcupine and squirrels |
| Lemon grass, oil of | Dogs |
| Mustard, oil of | Dogs, rats, and raccoons |
| Nicotine sulfate | Many animals |
| Rosin | Deer and rabbits |
| Sodium pentachlorophonate | Mice and rats |
| Sulfur | Rodents |
| Tobasco sauce | Deer and rabbits |
| Thiram (tetramethylthiuramdisulfide) | Animals and birds |
| TNB-A | |
|   (trinitrobenzene-aniline complex) | Rabbits |
| ZAC | |
|   (zinc dimethyldithiocarbamatecyclohexylamine) | Deer and rodents |

it is possible for nurserymen to produce high-quality plants while reducing the negative effects of pests.

## REFERENCES

ADAMS, D. G., and A. N. ROBERTS, 1968. Time of flower initiation in *Rhododendron* 'Roseum Elegans' as related to shoot and leaf elongation. HortScience 3(4):278–279.

BAILEY, R. 1992. Deer Control Fencing. Unnumbered Information Sheet, Bailey Nurseries, St. Paul, Minn.

BEATTIE, D. J. and H. L. FLINT, 1973. Effect of K level on frost hardiness of stems of *Forsythia intermedia* Zab. 'Lynwood'. J. Am. Soc. Hort. Sci. 98(6):539–541.

CATHEY, H. M. 1965. Initiation and flowering of rhododendron on following regulation by light and growth retardants. Proc. Am. Soc. Hort. Sci. 86:753–760.

———. 1968. Response of some ornamental plants to synthetic abscissic acid. Proc. Am. Soc. Hort. Sci. 93:693–698.

———. 1970. Chemical pruning of plants. Am. Nurseryman 131(9):8.

CHADWICK, L. C. 1962. Use of growth regulators to prevent fruiting. Am. Nurseryman 115(6):96.

CHEN, P., P. H. LI, and C. J. WEISER. 1975. Induction of frost hardiness in red-osier dogwood stems by water stress. HortScience 10(4):372–374.

COLLINS, W. C. 1962. Hardening plant materials for winter. Proc. Int. Plant Propag. Soc. 12:86–88.

CRILEY, R. A. 1969. Effect of short photoperiods, cyocel and gibberellic acid upon flower bud initiation and development in azalea 'Hexe'. J. Am. Soc. Hort. Sci. 94(4):392–396.

# 368

Part III Culture

DAVIDSON, H., M. J. BUKOVAC, and D. C. MACLEAN. 1963. Photoperiodic and chemical control of vegetative growth and flowering in weigela. Proc. Am. Soc. Hort. Sci. 82:589–595.

———, and C. L. HAMNER. 1957. Photoperiodic responses of selected woody ornamental shrubs. Quart. Bull. Mich. Agric. Exp. Sta. Mich. State Univ. 40(2):327–343.

———, and A. OLNEY. 1964. Clonal and sexual differences in the propagation of Taxus. Proc. Int. Plant Propag. Soc. 17:156–161.

———, and D. P. WATSON. 1959. Teratological effects of photoperiod on *Rhododendron catawbiense* Mich. Proc. Am. Soc. Hort. Sci. 73:490–494.

DAVIS, R. E. and C. E. WHITCOMB. 1977. Effects of propagation container size on development of high quality seedlings. Proc. Int. Plant Propag. Soc. 25:448–453.

DEWILDE, R. 1962. Hardening of plant materials for winter. Proc. Int. Plant Propag. Soc. 12:84–85.

DRINKARD, A. W., Jr. 1915. Some effects of pruning, rootpruning, ringing and stripping on the formation of fruit buds on dwarf apple trees. Va. Agric. Exp. Sta. Tech. Bull. 5:96–120.

FLEMER, W. III. 1981. How and when to prune nursery stock. Am. Nurseryman 153(8):11, 126–132.

FLETZ, T. A. 1973. Soil temperature influences. Am. Nurseryman 137(1):16.

FUCHIGAMI, L. H., C. J. WEISER, and D. R. RICHARDSON. 1973. The influence of sugars on growth and cold acclimation of excised stems of red-osier dogwood. J. Am. Soc. Hort. Sci. 98(5):444–447.

FURUTA, T., W. C. STONE, W. HUMPHREY, and T. MOCK. 1973. Chemical control of root growth in containers. Am. Nurseryman 137(8):9.

GARNER, W. W., and H. A. ALLARD. 1920. Effect of the relative length of day and night and other factors of the environment on growth and reproduction in plants. J. Agric. Res. 18:553–606.

GOUIN, F. R. 1977. Hot news for rodents and deer. HortScience 12(1):10.

GOURLEY, J. H., and F. S. HOWLETT. 1972. Ringing applied to the commercial orchard. Ohio Agric. Exp. Sta. Bull. 410.

HANOVER, J. W., and D. A. REICOSKY. 1972. Accelerated growth for early testing of spruce seedlings. For. Sci. 181(1):92–94.

———, E. YOUNG, W. A. LEMMIEN, and M. VAN SLOOTEN. 1976. Accelerated-optimal-growth: a new concept in tree production. Mich. State Univ. Agric. Exp. Sta. Res. Rep. 317.

HARRIS, R. W. 1969. Staking and pruning young *Myoporum laetum* trees. J. Am. Soc. Hort. Sci. 94(1):359–361.

———, W. B. DAVIS, N. W. STICE, and D. LONG. 1971. Root pruning improves nursery tree quality. J. Am. Soc. Hort. Sci. 96(1):105–108.

———, W. B. DAVIS, N. W. STICE, and D. LONG. 1971. Influence of transplanting time in nursery production. J. Am. Soc. Hort. Sci. 96(1):109–111.

————, et al. 1972. Spacing of container-grown trees in the nursery. J. Am. Soc. Hort. Sci. 97(4):503–506.

HASKELL, T. 1953. Practical blossom control for the arborist. Proc. Nat. Shade Tree Conf. 29:4–17.

HAVIS, J. R. 1964. Freezing of rhododendron leaves. Proc. Am. Soc. Hort. Sci. 84:570–574.

————. 1965. Desiccation as a factor in winter injury of rhododendron. Proc. Am. Soc. Hort. Sci. 86:764–769.

————. 1973. High summer temperatures of containers in New England. Am. Nurseryman 137(2):7.

————, R. D. FITZGERALD, and D. N. MAYNARD. 1972. Cold-hardness response of *Ilex crenata* Thumb. 'Hetzi' roots to nitrogen source and potassium. HortScience 7(2)/fj195–196.

HENINGER, R. L., and D. P. WHITE. 1974. Tree seedling growth at different soil temperatures. For. Sci. 20:363–367.

HOWE, G. H. 1914. Ringing fruit trees. N.Y. (Geneva) Agric. Exp. Sta. Bull, 391.

INGRAM, D. L., C. MARTIN, and J. RUTER. 1989. Effect of Heat Stress on Container-Grown Plants, Proc. Inter. Plant Prop. Soc. 39:348–353.

KELLEY, J. D. 1972. Nitrogen and potassium rate effect on growth, leaf nitrogen and winter hardiness of *Pyracantha coccinea* 'Lalandi' and *Ilex crenata* 'Rotundifolia'. J. Am. Soc. Hort. Sci. 97(4):446–448.

KLINGAMAN, L., and J. H. KING. 1983. What size and shape container are best for growing seedlings? Am. Nurseryman 157(1):87–93.

KOZEL, P. C., and K. W. REISCH. 1972. Guidelines for chemical pruning. Am. Nurseryman 135(2):13.

KRIZEK, D. T., and R. H. ZIMMERMAN. 1973. Comparative growth of birch seedlings grown in the greenhouse and growth chambers. J. Am. Soc. Hort. Sci. 98(4):370–373.

KUHNS, L. J., and T. D. SNYDER. 1975. Phytotoxicity of copper-treated burlap on balled and burlapped *Cotoneaster divaricata*. HortScience 10(6):613–614.

LARSON, P. R. 1965. Stem form of young *Larix* as influenced by wind and pruning. For. Sci. 11(4):412–424.

LEISER, A. T., and J. D. KEMPER. 1968. A theoretical analysis of a critical height of staking landscape trees. Proc. Am. Soc. Hort. Sci. 92:713–720.

————, and J. D. KEMPER. 1973. Analysis of stress distribution in the sapling tree trunk. J. Am. Soc. Hort. Sci. 98(2):164–170.

————, et al. 1972. Staking and pruning influence trunk development of young trees. J. Am. Soc. Hort. Sci. 97(4):498–502.

LUMIS, G. P., and H. DAVIDSON. 1967. Preventing fruit formation on landscape trees. HortScience 2(2):61–62.

————, R. A. MECKLENBURG, and K. C. SINK. 1972. Factors influencing winter hardiness of flower buds and stems of evergreen azaleas. J. Am. Soc. Hort. Sci. 97(1):124–127.

Lumis, G. P. 1990. Wire Baskets: A Further Look, Am. Nurseryman, 172(4):128–131.

Marth, P. C. 1963. Effect of growth retardants on flowering fruiting and vegetative growth of holly (*Ilex*). Proc. Am. Soc. Hort. Sci. 83:777–781.

Martin, C. A., et al. 1989. Effects of Irrigation Rate and Media on Growth of Acer rubrum L. in Large Containers. J. Environ. Hort. 7(1):38–40.

Mcguire, J. J. and H. L. Flint. 1962. Effects of temperature and light on frost hardiness of conifers. Proc. Am. Soc. Hort. Sci. 80:630–635.

———, J. T. Kitchin, and R. Davidson. 1965. The effect of different growth retardants on growth and flowering of *Rhododendron obtusum* 'Hinodegri'. Proc. Am. Soc. Hort. Sci. 86:761–763.

McKenzie, J. S., C. J. Weiser, and P. H. Li. 1974. Changes in water relations of *Cornus stolonifera* during cold acclimation. J. Am. Soc. Hort. Sci. 99(3): 223–228.

Meier, K. 1972. Pruning: the key to salable plants. Am. Nurseryman 136(6):112.

Mityga, H. G., and F. O. Lanphear. 1971. Factors influencing the cold hardiness of *Taxus cuspidata* roots. J. Am. Soc. Hort. Sci. 96(1):83–86.

Myers, S. P. , and P. C. Kozel. 1972. Practical procedures for increasing flower bud initiation of rhododendron. Am. Nurseryman 135(3):13.

Newman, S. E., and M. W. Follett. 1988. Irrigation Frequency and Shading Influences on Water Relations and Growth of Container-Grown *Wuonymus japonica* 'Aureomarginata'. J. Environ. Hort. 6(3):96–100.

Robinson, J. T., and D. Hamilton. 1983. Effects of light levels on Viburnum growth, nutrient uptake and hardiness. Am. Nurseryman 157(3):93–95.

Vaartaja, O. 1954. Photoperiodic ecotype of trees. Can. J. Bot. 32:392–399.

Weigle, J. L., and A. R. Beck. 1971. Flowering characteristics of weigela and their relationship to progeny age at first bloom. J. Am. Soc. Hort. Sci. 96:685–686.

Whitcomb, C. E. 1981. Growing tree seedlings in containers. Bull. 755, Agric. Exp. Sta. Okla. State Univ.

White, W. C., and C. J. Weiser. 1964. The relations of tissue desiccation, extreme cold and rapid temperature fluctuations to winter injury of American arborvitae. Proc. Am. Soc. Hort. Sci. 85:554–563.

Wikle, J. S., H. Davidson, and E. A. Erickson. 1961. Soil moisture studies with container-grown plants. Quart. Bull. Mich. Agric. Exp. Sta., Mich. State Univ. 44(1)/fj125–128.

Williams, D. J., and B. C. Moser. 1974. Response of woody ornamentals to a fatty acid pinching agent. HortScience 9(4):349–350.

Williams, M. W., and H. D. Billingsley. 1970. Increasing the number and crotch angles of primary branches of apple trees with cytokinins and gibberellic acid. J. Am. Soc. Hort. Sci. 95(5):649–651.

Williams, R. R., and R. W. Rennison. 1963. Summer nitrogen: a new method of bringing apple trees into bearing. Exp. Hort. 9:34–38.

Wong, T. L., R. W. Harris, and R. E. Fissell. 1971. Influence of high soil temperatures on fine woody plant species. J. Am. Hort. Sci. 96(1):80–82.

WRIGHT, R. D. 1976. Influorescence development and fruit set in *Ilex cornuta* Lindl. et Paxt. cv. "Burfordii" as influenced by temperature and photoperiod. J. Am. Soc. Hort. Sci. 101(2):182–184.

ZEHNDER, L. R., and F. O. LANPHEAR. 1966. The influence of temperature and light on the cold hardiness of *Taxus cuspidata*. Proc. Am. Soc. Hort. Sci. 89:706–713.

## SUGGESTED READING

BORLAND, J. 1988. Maping Flaws, (Average Low Killing Temperatures For Plant Parts) Am. Nurseryman, 168(8):46–56.

CATHEY, H. M. 1975. Comparative plant growth retarding activities of ancymidal with ACPC, Phosfan, Chlormequat and SADH on ornamental plant species. HortScience 10(3):204–216.

GEISLER, D., and D. C. FERREE. 1984. Responses of plants to root pruning. Horticult. Rev. (6):155–188.

GILMAN, E. F. 1990. Tree Root Growth and Development I. Form, Spread, Depth, and Periodicity. J. Environ. Hort. 8(4):215–220.

GILMAN, E. F. 1990. Tree Root Growth and Development II. Response to Culture, Management, and Planting. J. Environ. Hort. 8(4)220–227.

LEVITT, J. 1956. The hardiness of plants. Academic Press, Inc., New York.

NEWMAN S. E., and F. T. DAVIS, Jr., 1087. High Soil Temperature and Water Relations of Endomycorrhizal Nursery Crops. J. Environ. Hort. 5(2):93–96.

PERRY, T. O. 1981. Tree roots—where they grow: implications and practical significance. New Horizons. Horticultural Research Institute, Washington, D.C.

REIGER, K. 1988. The Bag Way, Am. Nurseryman 168(10):117–119.

SACHS, R. M., and W. P. HACKET. 1972. Chemical inhibition of plant height. HortScience 7(5):440–447.

WATSON, G. W. 1986. Cultural Practices Can Influence Root Development for Better Transplanting Success. J. Environ. Hort. 4(1):32–34.

WEISER, C. J. 1970. Cold resistance and acclimation in woody plants. HortScience 5(5):403–410.

———. 1970. Cold resistance and injury in woody plants. Science 169:1269–1278.

WHITCOMB, C. E. 1985. Innovations and the Nursery Industry, J. Environ. Hort. 3(1):33–38.

ZIMMERMAN, R. H. 1972. Juvenility and flowering in woody plants. HortScience 7(5):447–455.

# Chapter 16
# Controlling Weeds, Insects, and Diseases

Weeds, insects, and diseases are the three most noxious, negative modifiers of plant growth in nurseries. They are common to all nurseries and cause a significant loss in either quantity of production or in plant quality, which, in turn, can result in a significant economic loss to a nursery. The negative aspects of these and other pests can best be minimized by an integrated crop production program that is directed toward quality plant production—the overall objective of the nursery. The program should be oriented primarily toward preventing pest problems from developing in the nursery. When they do develop, the program should be oriented to rapid eradication of the pest to minimize damage to valuable plants.

Many disease and pest problems can best be prevented by following cultural practices designed to produce healthy, vigorous plants. Plants that are properly spaced, pruned, fertilized, and watered are much less prone to pest problems than plants that are exposed to undesirable environmental conditions. Improper irrigation management, especially overwatering in the propagation or container production areas, predisposes plants to attacks by insects and to infection by disease organisms that are either spread by water or require warm, humid environments in which to develop.

## WEED CONTROL

The primary goal of a weed control program in a nursery is to provide optimum growth for nursery stock, while suppressing or eliminating weed competition for light, moisture, and nutrients. Weeds can restrict growth of trees and shrubs, provide a habitat for rodents, and act as host to many destructive insects and diseases. Effective weed control in nurseries requires timely and efficient use of biological, cultural, environmental, and chemical means. Since the development of selective herbicides in the late 1940s, many growers have depended solely on chemicals. This may be a mistake. Selective herbicides should be used with caution. Repeated use of one technique or chemical leads to development of tolerant weed growth or invasion and establishment of resistant weed species. Integration of several strategies can prevent these problems. Before starting a weed control program, analyze your situation and then determine the best course of action.

### Analyze the Situation

The nursery crop can be injured from various control methods. Vulnerability is highest at the seedling stage for the crop and weeds. Therefore, at that stage avoid any activity that would injure the nursery crop. On the other hand, follow practices that destroy weeds at the time of seed germination or kill them in the seedling stage. It is important to know at which stages of growth your crop is vulnerable to various weed control measures. Some plants, such as yew and arborvitae, are very sensitive to stem injury when young. They will often die if the stem is injured by hoeing or cultivating. Young plants with green stems are very susceptible to stem injury from contact herbicides, but are not affected by herbicides if the bark is brown and well developed.

Weed control measures in nurseries are influenced by the production method (Table 16–1). Plants in a broadcast seedbed cannot be cultivated, therefore fumigation is the best way to rid the soil of weed seeds prior to sowing seeds of trees and shrubs. In the production of liners (Fig. 16–1), where space is greater than in seedbeds but not as great as in production blocks, it is generally economically feasible to incorporate a preemergence herbicide prior to planting. However, on a relatively weed-free site, this process can be skipped and the plants can be cultivated, either by hand or treated with herbicide.

In extensive plantings on wide spacing (Fig. 16–2), the best weed control method is to apply a preemergence herbicide to weed-free soil and cultivate, or a combination of the two (herbicide in the rows and cultivate between the rows). If weeds are present, apply a postemergence herbicide. Another control method is to grow sod between the rows and apply an herbicide in the rows (Fig. 5–12). The sod allows access to the crops during wet periods, returns organic matter to the soil and provides erosion control. The sod should

**Table 16–1** Suggested Chemical Weed Control Programs for Nurseries

*A. Seedling and Liner Production*

Preplant
    Pasteurization: 160–180°F for 30 min. with portable steam generator
    Fumigation: Methyl Bromide, Dazomet, Metham-sodium
    Herbicide: Treflan
Postplant
    Spring and Summer: Dacthal, Pennant, Princep
    Fall: Kerb, Princep

*B. Container Production*

Preplant
    Pasteurization: 160–180°F for 30 min.
    Fumigation: Methyl Bromide treatment in bulk before filling containers
    Herbicide: Treflan
Postplant
    Spring and Summer: Dacthal, Devrinol, Gallery, OH-2, LassoII, Princep, Ronstar, Rout,
                   Southern Weedgrass Control, Surflan, XL
    Fall: Devrinol, Gallery, Princep
Slow-release formulations: Herbicides in granular or tablet formulation are easier to apply
    to container-grown nursery stock than are liquid formulations. For best results, use
    preemergence herbicides applied to a weed-free container medium and irrigate immediately
    following application.

*C. Field Production*

| *Weeds* | *Suggested Control* |
|---|---|
| Summer annual weeds: barnyard grass, crabgrass, fall panicum, foxtails, lambsquarters, pigweed, and purslane | Preemergence herbicides: Dacthal, Lasso, Princep, Ronstar, Surflan |
| Perennial weeds: bindweed, dandelion, dock, quackgrass, mugwort, and nutsedge | Fall application: Casoron, Kerb, Pennant Direct spray: Roundup, Amitrole |
| Winter annual weeds: annual bluegrass, chickweed, and pennycress | Herbicides: Betasan, Casoron, Devrinol, Princep |

*Source:* Adapted from Davidson (1984) and Smith (1992).

not be highly aggressive. Container production requires weed control both in the containers and in the container area. Weed growth in containers can be minimized by using a weed-free growing medium or by fumigating or pasteurizing the medium prior to planting. Control weeds in the container area by setting the containers on a soil-free surface such as crushed stone, black plastic, or a fabric weed barrier. Be sure to provide good drainage for this surface. If herbicides are applied by topical methods to container-grown plants, use granular formulations followed by irrigation to insure effective weed control. It is necessary to control weeds in the areas surrounding nursery production sites.

**Figure 16-1** Weed control in liner beds.

**Figure 16-2** Weed control at planting and during the growing season.

All too often these areas are neglected and weed seeds are blown into crop rows and containers.

A third consideration includes identification of the weed species, its vulnerability to control measures, and the source of the weed problem. Too often, weed control measures, especially herbicides, result in little or no weed control or disaster to the nursery crop. It is necessary to know the weed species to be controlled and the best means of controlling it without damaging the crop. Annual weeds are easily controlled at or soon after germination. Therefore, you should start the control early; a delay of a few days can negate the control. Selective herbicides are very specific as to the weeds they will or will not kill; preemergence herbicides are of little value if applied as a postemergence treatment. Cultivation is most effective when weed plants are small, and more difficult and often less effective on larger plants. Many perennial weeds, such as quackgrass and bermuda grass, are impossible to control by cultivation; in fact, they are propagated vegetatively and spread by cultivation. If you know the source of a weed problem, you can take measures to eliminate weeds from the source. Most weeds spread to the nursery site from nearby areas or through irrigation from ponds. By controlling them in these sites, you can avoid many weed problems. Some weeds spread within a nursery area by equipment contaminated with seeds. Other weeds can be introduced in soil, peatmoss, or plants from other sources. This problem, which is often overlooked, can become serious.

The fourth factor to consider is the effect of the production environment—soil type, moisture, temperature, and wind—on a weed control program. Many granular herbicides are most effective if they are cultivated into the soil or water-sealed into the soil or medium immediately following application. Sandy soils require less active ingredients per unit area than clay or organic soils. Do not cultivate when the ground is wet. Avoid applying herbicides when it is windy. Herbicide effectiveness is often reduced if the temperature is below 50°F or above 85°F. Liquid applications are best applied on a calm day when the temperature is between 65 and 75°F, and when the humidity is moderate to high.

### Biological, Cultural, Environmental, and Chemical Controls

The advantages and limitations of various weed control measures are the final consideration. Controls are biological, cultural, environmental, and chemical. Sometimes one control measure is adequate, while certain situations may require a combination of several controls to provide the best results.

Biological measures require the use of plants, people, or animals. Complementary grass aisle plantings between the rows can be advantageous, but if improperly managed, could directly compete with and inhibit the nursery crops. The integration of grass aisles and nursery plant rows can achieve effective weed control through competition and limited, selective application of herbicides. Hand weeding is very effective but is generally limited to small, intensive or high-value plantings since it is very costly. Geese are effective weed controllers, at least in nurseries, but they require proper management for optimum results and they are messy.

Cultural or mechanical weed control has been successful for centuries. Hoeing is effective but expensive and is generally limited to intensive nursery plantings. Mechanical means are used on extensive plantings but are also costly since they require power equipment and an operator. They can be cost-effective if they are properly timed. Cultivation is best when weeds are small, and the soil is not too wet. Mechanical methods should not be used on weed species that grow by rhizomes, such as quackgrass or bermuda grass, since sectioning the rhizome is a means of propagating and spreading the weed over wide areas. Mechanical cultivation can injure stems of trees and shrubs and result in death of plants if the operator is careless in using the hoe or operating certain types of equipment.

Weeds can be controlled environmentally by manipulating light and temperature. A weed barrier such as sheets of black plastic or woven plastic fabric placed over the soil surface restricts light and imposes a physical barrier to the germinating weed seedlings. High temperature obtained by controlled burning from various burning devices can be used to kill weeds and destroy weed seeds. It can be used effectively within and around the perimeter of nurseries, especially container production nurseries. Pasteurization of soil and potting media can also effectively reduce weed problems. Soil or media heated to 160°F for about 30 minutes will destroy most weed seeds. Pasteurized media are used primarily in the production of container-grown plants.

If used properly, herbicides can effectively control weeds in nurseries. If improperly used (e.g., the wrong chemical, repeated use of one chemical, errors in calculation or application, improper timing, drift, and carelessness) herbicides can produce devastating and costly results. Always read and follow label instructions. Many herbicide disasters could be avoided if label instructions are followed. Remember, it is the manufacturer who warrants the product. If the material is used contrary to label instructions, the warranty is null and void. As the name implies, herbicides are plant killers (*herb* means "plant" and *cide* means "killer"). Used properly, they are an excellent tool. Used improperly, they can seriously injure or kill economic plants as well as weeds. Some herbicides, like Paraquat, are toxic to animals and people, so they are available only for restricted use. In all cases, the objective of the weed control program will determine which chemical is best for effective, efficient control of weeds within minimum damage to the economic plants.

Although herbicides can be classified in many ways, three of the most practical are emergence, selectivity, and movement within the plant. Pre-emergence herbicides control weeds by destroying seedlings as they germinate. Most effective weed control with preemergence herbicides is obtained when the soil has been tilled and all weeds eliminated. Most preemergence chemicals will not kill seedlings or established weeds. Tilled soil allows for better herbicide penetration and distribution. When one-half in. of rainfall or irrigation follows within a few days after application of preemergence herbicides, most effective weed control is obtained. Application to moist soils is usually preferred to that of dry soils. Excessive moisture may reduce effectiveness of certain herbicides such as Treflan. Certain preemergence chemicals are affected by soil temperature. Products such as Casoron, Eptam, and Treflan must be soil incorporated at higher temperatures or volatilization can occur and effectiveness will be lost. Studies have shown that a considerable variation exists in effectiveness of preemergence herbicides with different soil types. Casoron, for example, is more effective in heavy, clay-type soils than in light, sandy soils, while Treflan controls weeds more efficiently in light or sandy soils. Organic matter in soil or in container mixes reacts with and absorbs herbicides. In general, the more organic matter the higher the herbicide rates required to control weeds. Dacthal is reduced in effectiveness by cultivation following treatment. Casoron, Devrinol, Pennant, Kerb, Princep, Ronstar, Surflan, and Treflan treated soil can be disturbed with shallow (1–1.5 in.) cultivation without reducing weed control. Cultivating deeper than 2 in. will reduce the effectiveness of all the herbicides. Table 16–2 lists preemergence herbicides used in nursery operations. Postemergence herbicides destroy weed growth after emergence. Postemergence chemicals are used for general weed clean-up around buildings, waterways, fence rows, and so forth. Used with extreme caution, these materials may be used in tree and shrub plantings. Avoid herbicide contact with foliage, trunks, or stems with green tissue as damage will result from each of these materials. Table 16–3 lists postemergence herbicides used in nursery operations. Selective herbicides kill only selected species of plants but not others. Nonselective herbicides are used to kill all species. Translocated or systemic herbicides move within the plant. Some are translocated following foliar application, such as Round-up, while others following soil application, like Princep. Nonsystemic or contact herbicides kill on contact and do not translocate, such as Paraquat.

The effectiveness of a chemical weed control is only as successful as the person responsible for selection, calculation, calibration, and application of herbicides. All herbicides will control weeds as specified on the label; therefore, it's up to the grower to follow the proper conditions necessary to achieve the desired results. Acceptable weed control can be achieved in field-grown nursery crops throughout the year with two or three applications of the appropriate herbicides. A late fall or winter preemergence herbicide treatment should be followed by a late spring or early summer application following the initial cultivation. The combination of autumn and spring treatments usually results in the most effective weed control program. Depending on the herbicide applied in summer, more than one application may be needed. If cover crops are to be grown in autumn, use a short residual herbicide such as Dacthal, Lasso, or Pennant rather than Princep or Ronstar combinations which may inhibit seed germination. Supplemental postemergence treatments may be necessary to control perennial weeds and those annuals not controlled with the preemergence herbicides. Table 16–1 gives suggested chemical weed control programs for nurseries.

A combination of Ronstar plus Devrinol may be safely used on many types of woody plants in containers. With widely spaced larger containers or small numbers of containers a broadcast treatment wastes a lot of herbicide that falls between the containers. One way to prevent this waste is to dilute the granular herbicides with sand and spread a measured amount evenly around the surface of each container. The granules can be thoroughly mixed with sand in a cement mixer in five gallon batches, for example, and then used as a preemergence treatment that will prevent most weed growth for 10 to 12 weeks.

### Application Equipment

Many types of sprayers are available for applying herbicides. You do not need expensive, high-gallonage, high-pressure spray equipment. A weed-control sprayer should have the following features:

1. A low-pressure pump that is easily replaced, not subject to damage by wettable powders, and a minimum capacity of 9 gal/minute

2. A solution agitator (i.e., stirrer) with either a mechanical or a bypass from the pump. If a power takeoff sprayer does not provide agitation, add a bypass to a galvanized tee between the pump and pressure gauge. To increase agitation in the tank, place an agitator nozzle on the end of the overflow hose. In this case, a separate valve on the bypass line will regulate pressure. If the pump does not have enough capacity for agitation under specific spraying conditions, provide it by using both the next lower tractor gear and nozzle tips with a smaller orifice.

3. It should have a 50 mesh screen for suction line and nozzles because wettable powders will not go through the 100 mesh screens, which are sometimes provided.

4. It should have a spray boom with adjustable nozzles for distance between nozzles on the boom and for height above the ground. This is especially important for band spraying.

5. A pressure gauge that will measure pressure accurately up to 100 pounds per square inch (psi).

6. It should have a nozzle that is equivalent to an 8004 Teejet. For most work, a wide-angle (73 or 80 degrees) flat fan nozzle is best because the boom can be held close to the ground to reduce drift. This is most important when it is windy.

**Table 16–2** Preemergence Herbicides Used in Nursery Operations

| Product | Uses, Cautions, and Limitations |
|---|---|
| Betason (Bensulide) | Controls annual grasses, especially crabgrass and annual bluegrass; irrigate after application; used primarily in flower and bulb plantings. |
| Casoron (Dichlobenil) | Controls annuals and perennials, especially mugwort, thistle, nutsedge, quackgrass, and bindweed; avoid use on fir, spruce, hemlock, certain Japanese holly, and viburnum; not as effective in fine, sandy soil; apply in fall or early winter; incorporate 2–3 in. if soil temperature is above 45°F. |
| Dacthal (DCPA) | Controls annual grasses and some broadleaf weeds, including dodder; irrigate following application to improve effectiveness; safe to use with most woody species and many herbaceous species. |
| Devrinol (Napropamide) | Controls annual grasses and broadleaf weeds, including chickweed, groundsel, lambsquarters, and redroot pigweed; registered for field-grown and container trees, shrubs, and ground covers; improve effectiveness with incorporation by tillage or water. |
| Pennant (Metolachlor) | Controls most annual grasses and yellow nutsedge; registered for field-grown and container trees, shrubs, and ground covers; improve effectiveness with incorporation by tillage or water; do not use on seedbeds, unrooted cuttings or on foliage that is wet or under covered polyhouses. |
| Derby (Metolachlor + Simazine) | Controls most annual grasses and broadleaf weeds plus yellow nutsedge; registered for container, field, and liner plantings. |
| Eptam (EPTC) | Controls annual weeds plus nutsedge, quackgrass, and mugwort; must be incorporated 2–3 in. for annual weed control and 6 in. by cross disking for perennial weed control. |
| Gallery (Isoxaben) | Controls broadleaf weeds such as bittercress, common groundsel, spurge, chickweed, and oxalis; more effective against broadleaf weeds but controls barnyard grass, annual bluegrass, crabgrass, and foxtail; can be used in containers, field stock, and ground covers. |
| Snapshot (Isoxaben + Oryzalin) | Controls annual grasses and broadleaf weeds, including chickweed, crabgrass, foxtail, groundsel, horseweed, lambsquarters, pigweed, purslane, ragweed, smartweed, spotted spurge, and velvetleaf. |
| Goal (Oxyfluorfen) | Controls barnyard grass, crabgrass, pigweed, lesser bittercress, lambsquarters, groundsel, chickweed, and purslane; use only for conifer seedbeds, transplants, and container stock. |
| OH-2 (Goal + Prowl) | |
| Rout (Goal + Surflan) | Controls lesser bittercress, chickweed, dandelion, groundsel, oxalis, and spurge, among others; do not apply in greenhouses or polyhouses or for 3–4 weeks following removal of poly; apply when foliage is dry; avoid treatment during a growth flush. |

| Kerb (Pronamide) | Controls annual and perennial grasses, chickweed, winter annuals, and curly dock; apply only in fall or winter for control primarily of established perennial grasses such as quackgrass; Kerb is a restricted use herbicide. |
| --- | --- |
| Lasso (Alachlor) | Controls most annual grasses plus carpetweed, pigweed, and purslane; reduces competition from seedling johnsongrass, yellow nutsedge, lambsquarters, nightshade, ragweed, and smartweed; irrigate after treatment to avoid crop injury; do not apply in polyhouses, on seed beds, or on uprooted cuttings; Lasso is a restricted use herbicide. |
| Princep (Simazine) | Controls annual grasses and broadleaf weeds for up to 3 months during the growing season; may injure birch, euonymus, deutzia, lilac, linden, privet, and spirea. |
| Ronstar (Oxadiazon) | Controls many annual grasses and broadleaf weeds, including lesser bittercress, common groundsel, galinsoga, smartweed, yellow woodsorrel, and barnyard grass; avoid application of 2% granular form to wet foliage to prevent phytotoxicity. |
| Southern Weedgrass Control or Prowl (Pendimethalin) | Controls six annual grassy weeds, including crabgrass, foxtail, goosegrass, barnyard grass, fall panicum, and annual bluegrass; annual broadleaf weeds include chickweed, henbit, oxalis, evening primrose, spurge, purslane, and knotweed. |
| Surflan (Oryzalin) | Controls annual grasses, chickweed, purslane, lambsquarters, and pigweed; labeled for trees, shrubs, evergreens, and ground covers; apply one-half in. of water to activate herbicide following application; tank mixes of Surflan and Roundup are registered as a combination product to undesirable vegetation; Surflan can also be mixed with Fusilade and Poast. |
| XL (Oryzalin + Benefin) | Controls barnyard grass, crabgrass, foxtails, goosegrass, johnsongrass (from seed), annual ryegrass, and annual bluegrass, as well as carpetweed, prostrate knotweed, common purslane, common chickweed, and henbit; labeled for container-grown stock. |
| Treflan (Trifluralin) | Controls annual grasses and some broadleaf weeds; incorporate 2–3 in. into the soil; best used as preplant treatment; one of the safest herbicides for use in nursery; do not apply 5% granular when the foliage is wet. |

*Source:* Adapted from Davidson (1984) and Smith (1992).

**Table 16–3** Postemergence Herbicides Used in Nursery Operations

| Product | Uses, Cautions, and Limitations |
|---|---|
| Acclaim (Fenoxaprop-ethyl) | Controls crabgrass species, barnyard grass, foxtail, and panicum species, as well as seedling johnsongrass. It will suppress the growth of common bermudagrass and johnsongrass from rhizomes. Acclaim is absorbed through the foliage, and injury is noticeable in 4–10 days, but control will take 12–21 days. A surfactant is advised. Optimum results occur when spray coverage is thorough and weeds are not under drought stress. |
| Amitrole (Amino triazole) | Applied to foliage of perennial broadleaf weeds and absorbed and translocated to the stems and roots. It is more effective against poison ivy than Roundup and very effective against mugwort. Commercial formulations of Amitrole are restricted use pesticides. If it should contact foliage of desired plants, leaves turn yellow, white and then brown. Use only as a spot treatment for perennial weeds in or near nursery crops. |
| Asulox (Asulam) | Controls annual grasses when applied as an over-the-top spray on juniper and taxus only. Apply to actively growing grasses between seedling and early seedhead formation for most effective control. Asulox is a systemic herbicide that requires 4–6 weeks for effective control. It is safe to replant in treated soil one month after treatment. |
| Basagran T/O (Bentazon) | Used as a directed spray for selective postemergence control of certain broadleaf weeds and sedges. Basagran T/O does not control grasses, but is effective on broadleaf species through contact action. Weeds should be small, actively growing and not under stress conditions. Weeds controlled include purslane, ragweed, smartweed, velvetleaf, Canada thistle, and yellow nutsedge. Oil additive improves effectiveness with some weeds. |
| 2,4-D and related compounds | The nonvolatile forms of 2, 4-D can be used among trees to control broadleaf weeds when there is no air movement. If grasses are also a problem, 2,4-D should not be used. |
| Fusilade 2000 or Ornamec (Fluazifop butyl) | A systemic herbicide that controls a wide range of annual and perennial grasses. For best control, treat grasses before they reach 8–10 in. in height. Over-the-top applications may be made to about 140 species of landscape plants. Approximately 40 species are labeled for directed spray applications. Read label for complete listing of tolerant plants. |
| Gramoxone Extra (Paraquat) | The commercial formulation is used for control of annual weeds and grasses and for top kill of perennial weeds and grasses around the base of trees. Avoid use on green-barked trees, including littleleaf linden. Repeat applications as necessary to control newly germinated seedlings and to control regrowth of perennials. A surfactant should be used. There is no soil residue. Use protective gloves while handling the concentrate to avoid contact with skin. Gramoxone Extra is a restricted use pesticide and replaces Gramoxone Super. |

| | |
|---|---|
| Poast (Sethoxydim) | Controls annual and perennial grasses but not sedges or broadleaf weeds when applied as an over-the-top spray. Foliage discoloration can be expected with some juniper selections. Read label for complete listing of tolerant plants. |
| Vantage (Sethoxydim) | Controls the same spectrum of grassy weeds as Poast as an over-the-top spray. Contains surfactant, so additives are unnecessary. Labeled for 315 species and cultivars of landscape crops, including trees, shrubs, vines, ground covers, annuals, and perennials. |
| RAD-E-CATE 25 or Phytar 560 (Cacodylic Acid) | Used to control annual and perennial weeds around trees and for general weed control in noncrop areas. A surfactant is not needed; it's inactivated on contact with the soil. If regrowth occurs, reapply as required. Do not spray on basal suckers. |
| Roundup (Glyphosphate) | Controls annual and perennial weeds when used before planting and in established fields of nursery stock. Nonionic surfactants such as Improve may be used to assist in wetting of foliage. Most effective control of perennial weeds is obtained when weeds are in flower bud or bloom stage at treatment. There is no soil residue; however, a waiting period of 3–7 days is necessary after treatment and before tillage to obtain maximum weed control. Highly recommended for use with rope wick applicators on labeled crops. Avoid contact with stems of green or thin-barked nursery crops; apply proper concentration to avoid rapid killing of weed stem, since transport to the roots is via phloem tissue; avoid multiple applications to the same crop to avoid possible injury; accumulation in nursery crops can cause chlorosis, dieback, witches-broom, and death. |

These materials must be used with considerable caution around valuable plants. Avoid chemical contact with green tissue, including the trunk of young trees and shrubs, basal shoots, and small branchlets on the trunk, since these are absorption sites for translocated herbicides.

*Source:* Adapted from Davidson (1984) and Smith (1992).

One of the most important factors in effective weed spraying is accurate calibration in determining the amount of spray material applied per acre. A range of 20–60 gal/acre, at a pressure of 20–60 lb/in.$^2$ is satisfactory. Adjust the boom height so that the spray overlaps about a third of the spray pattern. For overall spraying, using 80 degree nozzles, this places the nozzles about 18 to 20 in. apart on the boom and 18–20 in. from the spray surface. The following is a good way to calibrate a sprayer:

1. First check equipment for proper mounting, functioning of pump and nozzles.
2. Replace worn or defective equipment.
3. Use only bristle brushes and wooden matchsticks or tooth picks to clean out plugged nozzles.
4. Check the discharge of each nozzle for uniform pattern and quantity of discharge.
5. Thoroughly rinse and test equipment prior to calibrating the sprayer.
6. Fill the spray tank with water only.
7. Spray a measured area, in a field if possible, at a fixed tractor speed and pressure gauge setting. Be sure to allow for partial coverage if bands are used.
8. Measure the amount of water needed to refill the tank. Divide this amount by the fraction of an acre sprayed to get the gallons applied per acre.
9. Mix the amount of chemical desired per acre with water to give this much spray material. For example, if 10 gallons were applied on a quarter of an acre, the volume of spray material applied would be 40 gal/acre. If you change the tractor speed or gear, pressure setting, nozzle size, or number of nozzles, the amount of liquid applied per acre will be different, and recalibration will be necessary.

### Band Application in Row Crops

Since weeds in the crop row are usually the hardest to control, it may cost only 50% as much to spray herbicides in a band over the row rather than to cover the whole area. For band applications, adjust for the area actually sprayed and not for the total acres in the field. For example, suppose the recommendation for a chemical is 4 lb/acre, and 12 in. strips are sprayed over 36 in. rows. Only one-third of the ground area will be covered with spray material, so only one and one-third pounds of chemical (one-third of 4 lb) will be required per acre. Four pounds of chemical will then cover 3 acres of the crop. To adjust the sprayer for band application, place the boom so that there is one nozzle over each row, and plug the nozzles between rows. This is not always easy with standard booms, but you can buy adjustable booms, adapters, or use an offset 45 degree nozzle for use with taller plant materials.

### Cleaning Herbicide Sprayers

Keep weed control sprayers clean, especially if you use them to spray more than one crop or to apply fungicides and insecticides. Many nurseries will label a sprayer "for herbicide use only," to prevent plant injury from any herbicide residue. Do not use a sprayer to apply insecticides or fungicides if the sprayer has contained 2, 4-D type herbicides.

When cleaning, thoroughly rinse the whole sprayer with water, inside and out, including boom, hoses and nozzles, both before and after cleaning. Partially fill the sprayer with water before you add the cleaning agent. Keep the pump running so that the cleaning solution will circulate throughout the sprayer. Do not leave corrosive cleaning agents in the tank or spray system for more than 2 hours. When you are using only preemergence sprays, a good rinsing with water is enough. For other spraying purposes, remove weed killers from sprayers by adding 1 gal of household ammonia or 5 lb of sal soda to 100 gal of water. Allow this solution to stand in the sprayer for at least 2 hours. Drain it out through the boom and nozzles, and rinse the sprayer with water. Do not let spray solutions stand in the tank overnight. Do not allow solutions to run into streams or other water sources.

### Granular Spreaders

Granular herbicides are applied with some form of spreader, which must be calibrated for accurate application of herbicides. Some spreaders are adjustable for rate of delivery, others are not; it is best to utilize adjustable spreaders. After setting the delivery mode, fill the bin with a known weight of the herbicide and apply the material to a measured area, for example, 440 square feet (one-hundredth of an acre). Reweigh the remaining herbicide; the difference in weight times 100 will equal the rate being applied per acre. Adjust the delivery mode as needed to increase or decrease the rate, and recalibrate. Repeat as necessary until the proper rate of application is attained. For example, if you wish to apply Devrinol 2G at a rate of 5 lb/1000 sq. ft. (220 lb/acre) to a group of 1 gal container-grown junipers that occupy an area of 20,000 sq. ft., then you need to apply 100 lb of the product to the area. If the bin of spreader has a capacity of 25 lb, you will need to apply that amount to 5000 sq. ft. or two and one-half pounds to a 500 sq. ft. test application area. If the spreader is not delivering close to this rate, you will have to adjust the delivery mode.

## INSECT CONTROL

Control of pests in the nursery is unique in the business of agriculture. Because the product sold is a living plant (usually with accompanying soil), the chances of spreading parasites with plants are greater. Consequently, it becomes necessary for the nursery grower to keep nursery crops free of noxious insects, diseases, and weeds as much as possible. Many pest problems in the landscape encountered by homeowners and professional landscape managers are directly related to pests that accompanied nursery stock from a commercial nursery.

Another unique aspect of pest control in the nursery industry is the aid provided by the state department of agriculture in the identification of pests during the annual nursery inspection. Department of agriculture inspectors often diagnose pests and suggest control measures. The grower is informed of the problem and its solution so that control measures can be taken immediately. Should the grower not comply with suitable control measures, the inspector, as a last resort, can stop sales of the infested nursery stock (see Chapter 6).

Many growers recognize the gravity of pests infesting nursery stock and often apply insecticides and acaricides on a preventative schedule. Usually a mixture of insecticide/acaricide is applied on a 2 week or monthly basis during the growing season. Thus, the nursery grower is relatively assured of complete insect and mite control. Some growers depend on their own inspection of their nursery stock. This method saves time and money over the preventative method, but it is more risky if plants are not inspected on a regular schedule. Pest problems may escape notice until economic damage has occurred and the stock must be discarded or held until new foliage hides pest damage.

Nursery growers are constantly searching for ways to cut costs. Many grow varieties that are hardy and relatively pest free. This may seem like an easy way out, but the benefits for the consumer are more than imaginary. If the grower must constantly struggle to control a pest such as southern red mites on a variety like Heller holly, think what a problem that plant will be in the landscape for a homeowner or landscape manager. Unless they are given constant scrutiny for mites, chances are these plants will always have a chlorotic appearance and uneven growth. If the nursery grower grows varieties that the operation can maintain with ease, the consumer will start with a vigorous plant and will probably encounter fewer problems with maintenance.

When pest problems are encountered, the grower may call the county extension agent or the nursery plant inspector for control information. A grower may also consult with state extension service recommendations, which give information on insect, mite, and disease control, plant growth regulations, and weed control. Suggestions for pest control are also found in nursery association publications, which are available to members. Furthermore, nursery trade journals occasionally carry articles on pest control in the commercial nursery.

An often overlooked area in planning and operation of a nursery is development of an information center. This area should contain a library of standard reference books and other publications on nursery management, plant materials, fertilizers, equipment, and other subjects related to ornamental plants and nursery operations. A file should be developed of cooperative extension service bulletins that give information concerning nursery management in your growing area. Many nurseries are using computers for storage of up-to-date information on pest control chemicals which have EPA approval and rates to be used as well as for cultural, operational, and daily business uses. Catalogs and operational files should be kept of the equipment and materials used in the operation of a nursery. This will facilitate daily operations, servicing, and parts replacement of equipment as well as increase ease of obtaining frequently used materials such as pesticides, herbicides, fertilizers, containers, and potting media ingredients.

### Types of Insecticides

Information concerning the type of pest, its feeding habits, and its life cycle remains essential in determining the appropriate insecticide to use as well as the rate and method of application that will achieve satisfactory control. Since not all insects and mites are a threat to plants, a suspected pest will occasionally be recognized as a harmless or even a beneficial species. Consequently, the nursery information center should be geared to proper pest identification and responsible control measures.

Insect feeding habits determine, to some extent, the type of chemical control to be used. Pesticides can be classified as *stomach poisons, contact-residuals,* or *fumigants;* only the first two groups will be discussed. Fumigants must be used in enclosed areas and have very little application to the typical commercial nursery conditions.

Chewing insects, such as caterpillars, beetles, and grasshoppers, are the targets of stomach poisons. A diverse array of organic and inorganic chemicals make up this group. Stomach poisons must be ingested to kill pests. Since piercing-sucking pests (aphids, mites, leafhoppers, etc.) feed below leaf surfaces, they often avoid contact with stomach poisons. However, contact-residual chemicals, such as malathion, kill a wider range of pests. Such chemicals poison insects or mites that crawl on treated surfaces, eat treated leaves, or are sprayed directly.

The length of time a pesticide lasts depends to some extent on the chemical group to which it belongs. Materials like the plant-derived pesticide pyrethrin may last less than an hour, although similar synthetic pesticides are now being made that linger considerably longer. In general, an insecticide classified as a chlorinated hydrocarbon is long lasting. A good example is chlordane, which is applied to the soil for termite control. Such a treatment may be effective for several decades. The majority of pesticides recommended for insect and mite control on shrubs belong to the related organophosphate and carbamate groups. Less persistent than chlorinated hydrocarbons, most organophosphates and carbamates do not remain effective for more than 1–4 weeks. Many of the organophosphates and carbamates are systemic and may give 6 or more weeks of residual activity in treated plants.

Information on toxicity to man, formulations, chemical groups, and mode of action for most insecticides labeled for insect control on nursery crops is given in Table 16–4. This listing is not to be used as recommendations for control but as an aid to better understand the use and classification of pesticides. All pesticides must be used in accordance with the directions for use on the label. *When treating a specific plant or pest, refer to the label.* The pesticide trade names are listed in the first column in alphabetical order with the common name listed in parenthesis. In the second column, the LD-50 listed refers to the acute oral LD-50 of a rat. LD-50 indicates the amount of toxicant necessary to effect a 50% kill of the rats being treated. It is expressed in weight of the chemical per unit of body weight (mg/kg). The lower the LD-50 the more poisonous the chemical. The LD-50 is based on the pure active ingredient and not on the various formulations that contain the ingredient. Column three indicates the formulations available for use. Certain formulations are safer than others or more convenient to use, and these factors should be considered when selecting one of these products. The fourth column refers to the basic chemical structure of the active ingredient. If a certain pesticide is not giving effective control, a pesticide in a different class may give better results. Many growers continue using the same class of pesticide until it no longer seems effective and then switch to a different class. Others alternate classes with each application. Either method is acceptable as long as applications are thorough. The method used is usually a matter of the grower's preference. The mode of action in column five refers to how a pesticide actually kills a pest. Contact insecticides require contact with the insect to be effective. Direct spray on the pest or on the area frequented by the pest is necessary for the pesticide to be effective. Systemic pesticides are absorbed by the plants through the roots and leaf tissue and then ingested by the pest during feeding. Most systemic insecticides that are applied as sprays are also contact pesticides. Granular formulations such as Di-Syston are systemics designed to be applied to the soil surface but are not contact insecticides. Pertinent information about the pesticide is listed in column six.

### Factors Affecting Results of Sprays

A grower may take the time and trouble to spray plants only to be disappointed with the results. Although the chemical is usually blamed, this conclusion is rarely well founded. As a matter of fact, errors in pesticide application, such as improper storage, improper timing, and wrong concentration, most often account for apparent pesticide failure. The best and most expensive insecticide will produce poor results unless it is applied thoroughly and at the proper time. To be most effective, the pesticide must be applied when pests are present and vulnerable, and at proper rate in sufficient gallonage to permit thorough coverages of upper and lower surfaces of leaves and branches. However, even a well timed and thorough application is likely to be a failure if the correct pesticide is not used. Since few insecticides control all insects and mites, carefully check the label to make sure the chemical in hand is registered to control the problem pest.

Environmental conditions also affect the efficacy of a pesticide application. At temperatures below 50°F or above 95°F, insecticides may lose some of their activity. Therefore, applications other than dormant oils are usually not recommended in winter. Warm weather applications are best made in early morning or late evening when the wind is still and the temperature cool.

Nursery crops may be reinfested by a resurgence of the original pest population or by other flying insects. Even if a large percentage of pests in an infestation is killed, those remaining may rebuild the population to damaging levels. Such an occurrence is not unusual, since most insecticides applied to nursery crops last only 1–7 days. Therefore, recommendations often emphasize repeated applications at specific intervals to eliminate the pests.

*Resistance* is a general term which, in the broad sense, means insects that were previously killed by an insecticide have produced offspring that are not longer affected. To illustrate, let's suppose that an insecticide is applied and it kills 95% of the insects in a population, but there are 5% of the insects which received the same dosage but survived the treatment. This 5% is considered resistant to the insecticide. They live to produce another generation, and this generation, having had resistant parents, passes on to its offspring the resistance factor. Most likely there will be a greater number of new individuals carrying resistance to the insecticide compared to the first treated population. As repeated insecticide applications are made and more generations produced, it is only a matter of time before the majority of the insects in question will survive the insecticidal application. A possible explanation is that the insecticide has acted as a selecting agent, killing those members of the population which are susceptible to the chemical and leaving those which are resistant. Survivors breed and produce subsequent resistant generations. Resistance develops fastest in insects which have high rates of reproduction.

Last of all, improper pesticide storage is a possible contributor to pesticide inefficacy. Insecticides and miticides tend to degrade over a period of time once they have been opened. This problem may be common for the grower who purchases more pesticide than can be used in a single year or season. Moisture, air, light, and temperature extremes all adversely affect stored chemicals. Generally, pesticides should be stored in a dry, dark place where the temperature never falls below freezing or exceeds 100°F.

## DISEASE PREVENTION, MONITORING, AND CONTROL

A nursery grower should use an "umbrella" type concept that gathers all existing information on potential or existing disease problems to organize a coordinated effort against pathogens in all phases of the nursery operation.

**Table 16–4** Some Pesticides Labeled for Use on Insects and Related Pests of Trees and Shrubs

| Pesticide | $LD_{50}$ of Pure Active Ingredient | Formulations[a] | Classification | Mode of Action | Targets and Remarks |
|---|---|---|---|---|---|
| Acaraben (chlorobenzilate) | 960 | 25% WP, 45.5% EC | Chlorinated hydrocarbon | Contact | Mites |
| Avid (macrocyclic lactone glycoside) | 10 | .011% bait, .15% EC | Antibiotic | Stomach | Mites, leafminers, fireants |
| Azodrin (monocrotophos) | 8–23 | 55% EC | Organophosphate | Contact, systemic | Aphids, bugs, caterpillars, leafminers, mites, leafhoppers, sawflies, thrips |
| Cygon, De-Fend, Rebelate (dimethoate) | 320–380 | 23.4% EC | Organophosphate | Systemic | Aphids, lace bugs, thrips; will cause defoliation or deformation of Chinese hollies (*Ilex cornuta*); may damage 'President Clay' and 'Modesty' azaleas; phytotoxic to some trees; read label for details |
| _____ (diazinon) | 300–400 | 50% WP, 48% EC, 14.3% G | Organophosphate | Contact | Aphids, caterpillars, leafminers, thrips, whiteflies; may be effective as a soil drench to control certain pests |
| Dimecron (phosphamidon) | 20–22.4 | 75.5% EC | Organophosphate | Contact, systemic | Eastern tent caterpillars, webworms, mites, scales on deciduous fruit crops |
| Dipel, Biotrol (*Bacillus thuringiensis*) | >4000 | 1.5–3.2% WP | Bacterial | Stomach | Caterpillars |

| Name | LD50 | Formulation | Chemical class | Mode of action | Pests controlled |
|---|---|---|---|---|---|
| Di-Syston (disulfoton) | 2.6–12.5 | 15% G | Organophosphate | Systemic | Lace bugs, leafhoppers, scales, thrips, whiteflies; control may persist for 6–8 weeks from treatment |
| Dursban (chlorpyrifos) | 97–276 | 50% WP, 50% EC | Organophosphate | Contact | Borers, caterpillars, leafhoppers, mealybugs, mites, scales, spittlebugs, thrips, whiteflies |
| Dylox, Proxol (trichlorfon) | 450–630 | 41.2% EC, 80% WP | Organophosphate | Contact | Plantbugs, caterpillars, leafminers, webworms |
| NIA 1240, Vegfru-Rosmite (ethion) | 280 | 25% WP, 5% D, 46% EC + 82% EC, 5% G | Organophosphate | Contact | Scales, lace bugs, mites |
| Guthion (azinphos-methyl) | 13–16.4 | 35% WP, 22% EC | Organophosphate | Contact | Aphids, lace bugs, leafhoppers, scales, thrips |
| Imidan (phosmet) | 113 | 50% WP | Organophosphate | Contact | Leafhoppers, aphids, scales |
| Insecticidal Soap (potassium salt of fatty acids) | 16,900 | 51% active liquid, 1% liquid | Organic | Contact | Adelgids, aphids, lace bugs, mealy bugs, mites, plant bugs, psyllids, scales, thrips, whiteflies |
| Karathane (dinocap) | 980 | 25% WP, 48% EC | Nitro-phenoxy | Contact | Mites; will also control powdery mildew |
| Kelthane (dicofol) | 809 | 35% WP, 18.6% EC | Chlorinated hydrocarbon | Contact | Mites |
| (lindane) | 18–125 | 20% EC | Chlorinated hydrocarbon | Contact | Bark beetles, borers |
| (malathion) | 1375 | 57% EC | Organophosphate | Contact | Aphids, lace bugs, mealybugs, scales, thrips |
| Margosan-O (azadirachtin) | 5000 | 10% plant extract, 3% EC | Growth regulator | Stomach, contact | Larval growth, whiteflies, aphids, thrips, mealybugs, leafminers, gypsy moth |

*(continued)*

**Table 16–4** Some Pesticides Labeled for Use on Insects and Related Pests of Trees and Shrubs

| Pesticide | LD$_{50}$ of Pure Active Ingredient | Formulations[a] | Classification | Mode of Action | Targets and Remarks |
|---|---|---|---|---|---|
| Marlate (methoxychlor) | 6000 | 24.8% EC | Chlorinated hydrocarbon | Contact | Bark beetles, caterpillars, leafhoppers; long residual action |
| Morestan (oxythioquinox) | 2500–3000 | 50% EC | Miscellaneous quinoxaline | Contact | Mites; used as a prebloom spray on most deciduous fruits and in both prebloom and postbloom sprays on apples and pears |
| Oftanol (isofenphos) | 20 | 2 EC, 6 EC 5% G | Organophosphate | Contact | Japanese beetle, thrips, webworms, white grubs |
| Omite (propargite) | 2200 | 70% EC, 30% WP, 4% D | Phenoxysulfite | Contact | Mites; widely used on fruit trees; does not affect bees and is less harmful than many other acaricides to predatory mites; has residual killing action |
| Orthene (acephate) | 945 | 15.6% EC, 75% WP | Organophosphate | Contact, systemic | Aphids, caterpillars, lace bugs, leafhoppers, thrips, webworms; may be phytotoxic to young tender growth; moderate persistence with residual systemic activity of approximately 10–15 days |
| Pestroy (fenitrothion) | 250 | 4% EC, 8% EC, 40% WP, 3% G | Organophosphate | Stomach, contact | Aphids, leafhoppers, mites, whiteflies, scale, thrips, mealybugs, stem borers, spruce bud worms |

| Product (common name) | | Formulation | Chemical class | Action | Pests/Remarks |
|---|---|---|---|---|---|
| Plictran (cyhexatin) | 540 | 50% WP | Metallo-organic (tin base) | Systemic | Mites |
| Pounce (permethrin) | 430 | 1% EC, 2% EC, 3.2% EC, 4% EC, 25% WP, 1.5G | Synthetic pyrethroid | Stomach, contact | Leafminers, budworms, orangeworm, whiteflies |
| Sevin (carbaryl) | 500 | 50% WP | Carbamate | Stomach, contact | Chewing pests, thrips |
| Summer Oil (petroleum oils) | >4000 | 95% EC | Petroleum | Contact | Aphids, lace bugs, scales, mites |
| Talstar (bifenthrin) | 54.5 | 2% EC, 10% wp | Synthetic pyrethroid | Stomach, contact | Mites, aphids, leafhoppers, leaf rollers, budworm, whiteflies, thrips |
| Tedion (tetradifon) | 14,700 | Fumigant, 25% WP | Sulfonate | Contact | Effective in killing larval stages of mites |
| Temik (aldicarb) | 0.93 | 10% G | Carbamate | Systemic | Aphids; do not use with lime or other highly alkaline materials; *very dangerous*; Temik should not be mixed with other pesticides or fertilizers prior to use |
| Tempo (cyfluthrin) | 291 | 2% EC, 20% WP, 10% WP | Synthetic pyrethroid | Stomach, contact | Ants, cutworms, budworm, loopers |
| Thiodan (endosulfan) | 30–110 | 24.2% EC, 50% WP | Chlorinated hydrocarbon | Contact | Aphids, borers, mites, weevils, whiteflies |
| (toxaphene) | 69 | 20% D | Chlorinated hydrocarbon | Contact | Bagworms, fall armyworms, lace bugs, leafhoppers, earwigs |
| Trithion (carbophenothion) | 32.2 | 25% WP, 45% EC | Organophosphate | Contact, systemic | Aphids, mealybugs, mites, bagworms, potato leafhoppers, scales; long residual action |
| Turcam (bendiocarb) | 40 | 20% WP, 76% WP, 3–10% G, 1% D | Carbamate | Stomach, contact | Ants, borers, caterpillars |

[a]EC, Emulsifiable concentrate; WP, wettable powder; D, dust; G, granular.

*Source:* Adapted from Baker (1984) and Thomson (1992).

Usually this concept includes the following three courses of action: prevention activities that occur prior to disease incidence; monitoring early detection of diseases during the plant production phase; and control activities selected to reduce disease damage. Since most nurseries have distinct areas for stock plants, propagation, and production, the practices of prevention, monitoring, and control will be discussed for each area.


## DISEASE PREVENTION

### Stock Plant Area

Land for stock plant establishment should be cleared. All roots of hardwood species, especially native oaks, should be removed. Residual root debris in soil often serve as a food source for the shoestring and mushroom root rot fungi. If soil-borne diseases have been a problem in the past, such as bacterial crown gall and root knot nematode injury, apply a broad spectrum, preplant soil fumigant or nematicide. Field-grown stock blocks must allow adequate spacing between plants. This spacing will allow rapid drying of foliage, impede the spread of pathogens and other pests among plants, and facilitate better spray coverage of pesticides. Application of irrigation water should be so timed to consider the amount of natural rainfall. This will avoid saturated soils or droughty conditions that can stress root systems. Plant stress is one predisposing factor to root diseases. For woody ornamental species with persistent foliar disease problems, irrigation should occur between midmorning and early afternoon; always avoid wetting foliage prior to night hours. Daytime watering has been shown to aid in reducing foliar disease severity for certain species.

Certain safeguards must be taken to assure that those stock plants from which cuttings are taken remain healthy. Isolate all new stock plants to determine their health status prior to introduction into the existing nursery. Stock plants should be isolated from all possible sources of infection. Weedy and known disease areas should be avoided. Establish an independence between the production and merchandising part of the nursery and the maintenance of the stock blocks of plants. Stock blocks have been effective because of the ease and the low cost necessary to maintain such a small area. Practice regular spray schedules to control foliage, stem, or flower diseases. Drenching with soil fungicides is added insurance. Check with your state Cooperative Extension Service for specific chemical recommendations in your area.

### Propagation Area

Propagation cycles of a particular species should be timed to maximize the most rapid rooting for that species (additional information on plant propagation may be consulted in texts listed in Appendix B). This would limit exposure of cuttings to potential cutting or root rotting organisms. Water sources should always be checked for contamination by root rotting fungi. This should be the case when a root rot problem has been a persistent problem in a particular area for several years. Shallow water systems, such as ponds, rivers, creeks, canals, or shallow wells, should not be used for irrigation in propagation. In coastal areas where salt water intrusion is a problem, growers should not utilize a water source that is high or variable in soluble salts for propagation. High salts can stress root systems thereby predisposing young liners to root disease.

Success in propagation is often realized by observing reasonable sanitary procedures when collecting cuttings. Collect cuttings from tops of healthy plants. Top cuttings are usually free of soil-borne pathogens. Plants grown on above-ground level supports or trellises are generally free of soil pathogens. Avoid taking cuttings from plants at or near the soil level. Never use root divisions unless absolutely necessary. It is better to break rather than cut cuttings from stock plants. If knives or pruning shears are used to collect cuttings, have each worker use two separate pairs—one left soaking in disinfectant while the other is being used. As a suggestion, a household bleach, such as Clorox, solution (1 part bleach to 9 parts water) or 70% alcohol is effective. Bleach solutions should be changed every 30 min. since the disinfecting qualities diminish rapidly. Keep in mind that the bleach solution will cause rusting of ferrous metals. Therefore, thoroughly clean cutting blades twice daily. Frequent sharpening is also a must. Place cuttings on chemically disinfected surfaces of benches, flats, and baskets. A chlorine bleach solution is a good surface disinfectant. Mix up new solutions approximately every 30 minutes. Occasional use of copper naphthenate (2%) will disinfect wooden surfaces. Some growers spread unused newspaper or wrapping paper on disinfected work surfaces for added insurances. Never place cuttings on the ground. Never dip cuttings in water unless the water is pathogen free. This is a disadvantage of the liquid rooting hormone formulations. Some growers dip or soak cuttings in a fungicide suspension prior to sticking. Change the solution as often as is economically possible to maintain disinfecting concentrations.

Flats should be disinfected either after propagation or before reuse. Thoroughly remove rooting media adhering to the surfaces of flats or other containers with a brush before placing in a disinfectant (chlorine bleach or 2% copper naphthenate). Galvanized metal trays are preferred over wood because they are easier to clean and disinfect.

Never reuse propagating media. Media should be loose, porous, and well aerated. If propagation mixes contain soil, or if ground beds are used, pretreat before use with methyl bromide or heat. Media must be stored so that it does not become contaminated with disease causing organisms. Propagation media should be mixed on a clean concrete slab so that run-off water, such as rain or irrigation, will not introduce pathogens. Remember that a clean medium can become contaminated if carelessly handled or subjected to foot traffic.

Propagation areas should be kept clean. All benches must be free of infested media, leaves, and refuse. Use a household bleach or commercial disinfectant on all surfaces. Use wooden benches treated with copper naphthenate. A waiting period is necessary after treatment. Benches treated with most other disinfectants do not require a waiting period before use. All infested plant debris should be removed from the entire propagation area. Although this is sometimes tedious, it is very effective in reducing disease problems. Some growers provide their workers with carpenter aprons in which to place debris during daily activities to avoid dropping the plant debris on the ground. A covered garbage can should be placed at the end of each greenhouse for plant debris. Cans without lids have very little value in a sanitation program. Apply regular fungicide spray schedules to aid in the control of diseases which occur above ground. As added insurance against contamination, root media may be drenched immediately before or after sticking and at 4 week intervals with a fungicide combination developed to control the water molds, such as Rhizoctonia spp. and other fungi. Avoid unnecessary handling of clean media in the propagating containers or beds. Avoid dipping hands into media while conversing or checking moisture content. Use low water pressure when irrigating to avoid splashing. Prohibit anyone from walking over treated areas. Hose nozzles should be hung on conveniently located hooks, and not thrown carelessly on the ground. Workers' hands should be washed after working with raw contaminated media, soil, or unclean plants to avoid introduction of pathogens. Space cuttings properly when sticking. Poor air circulation contributes to an environment that favors diseases caused by Rhizoctonia spp. Avoid excessive overhead irrigation. Growers should regulate their misting schedule to allow no mist on plants 2 hr before sunset. On rainy, humid days, misting is terminated earlier in the day. Wet foliage and high-moisture regimes in rooting mixes provide a favorable environment for certain serious diseases. Remove any cuttings from containers or even whole flats of cuttings from the propagation area that exhibit disease symptoms; then treat the propagation area with a fungicide or disinfectant. Have a pathologist diagnose the problem so that appropriate action can be taken.

### Production Area

Woody species that are commonly affected by certain diseases can be grouped in adjacent areas within the nursery. This will allow for a greater ease in scouting and more rapid detection of diseases. Better pesticide control of diseases is usually the result. Examples of pathogens attacking several crops include *Entomosporium* leaf spots, *Cylindrocladium* aerial blights and powdery mildews. Consider blocking disease-prone plants together for day watering. Midmorning to early afternoon irrigation will minimize the actual hours the foliage remains wet. This practice reduces the potential for foliar diseases. Restrict nursery beds or block sizes to allow for a more efficient pesticide application with existing spray equipment. Block sizes should be based upon the spread of the mature plants, not newly planted liners. Spacing between plants on beds allows for better spray penetration of plants. This is not practical for 3 and 4 gal containers.

The basic concepts described previously in the propagation program are applicable in liner production. Liners should be grown above ground level to prevent contamination by soil-borne pathogens. Special attention should be given to irrigation frequencies and splashing. Keep hose nozzles off the ground and clean and disinfect benches prior to use. If you must purchase liners, it is important that you obtain high-quality, disease-free plants. Many growers in the past have purchased diseased liners, and unfortunately, this is a losing proposition because the disease probably cannot be cured. Plus, the diseased liners introduce pathogens into the nursery.

When developing a sanitation program for plants after potting, you should consider the following suggestions. In the preparation of a growing mix, use a cement slab of the proper elevation to prevent contamination by surface water run-off from surrounding areas. Mixing on the ground often leads to plant failure because of contamination by pathogens, insects, and weeds. Equipment should be assigned to this area. Ideally, it should not be moved off the slab. Avoid unnecessary foot traffic on the area. Consideration of slab size should also be made, because many slabs are too small. Determine components of the medium to be used: this determines drainage, aeration, and water-holding capacities. These factors influence root growth (good or bad). Too much or too little of the above media characteristics can provide those necessary environmental conditions within the mix for disease development. A well-aerated and well-drained mix is the most ideal. Plant no deeper in containers than the liners originally grew. You should store containers and media on a clean, nonsoil surface which is not subject to splashing water or run-off water. A large concrete pad is excellent for media preparation and storage. It is very important to prevent introduction of pathogens during storage and handling.

All sanitation program efforts made previously are wasted if plants are placed directly on the ground. Contaminated soil is often splashed into containers and this often leads to disease development. Growers should place containers on black plastic sheeting; prevent low spots by constructing beds as smoothly as possible (beds should be crowned by elevating the centers) (see Fig. 14–4); provide drainage ditches at bed edges; and compact the soil prior to spreading plastic sheeting to prevent settling of soil. Some growers are using gravel on top of the plastic sheeting. Beds constructed in this manner have been shown to reduce contamination by run-off water and to reduce splattering of soil. This approach aids in disease suppression; therefore, there is a corresponding reduction in plant disease losses. Increased cost initially is the main drawback for gravel beds. However, this is offset by increases in the number of saleable plants. There is also an increase in longevity of the container area which reduces the per-year labor and material expenditure.

A good grower frequently knocks plants out of the container to observe moisture and root condition. Diseases detected early can more easily be controlled. This practice can also reduce pathogen movement to large numbers of plants. Diseased plants should be removed from the growing area as soon as possible. The disposal area should be located well away from the growing area, storage area, potting area, and water source.

## DISEASE MONITORING

A systematic monitoring system by nursery personnel (disease scouts) aids in forecasting certain seasonal disease problems. The recognition of a particular production situation or practice that predisposes plants to disease would be recognized by the scouting activities and, thus, these problems could be corrected before disease becomes a serious problem. The scouting system is effective only when followed by rapid deployment of control practices. Therefore, a weak link between detection and disease control negates the usefulness of an entire disease control concept.

The production characteristics of an ornamental nursery are conducive to a disease epidemic if early stages of disease development are not detected. Therefore, more efficient and systematic disease monitoring practices should be incorporated into current growing activities by expanding the labor force or utilizing the existing one. The obvious gains from early disease detection include: reduction in plant loss; improvement in plant quality; reduction in production costs and delays; and increased profits.

### Stock Plant Area

This area should be routinely inspected every 2–4 weeks throughout the growing season. Two months prior to taking cuttings, this routine inspection should occur weekly. Inspect a minimum of 5% of the total plants in a block of one species and choose different plants each time. Begin inspection of plants from the windward side of a block and the side bordering an uncultivated area. Inspect the plants in a random fashion; check new and old growth, but concentrate predominantly on the new, more susceptible growth. Examine both leaf surfaces for disease symptoms. Observe leaves for a decrease in size, change in color or general loss in vigor. These symptoms could indicate lower stem or root problems. When common diseases are detected in a nursery, all susceptible plant species should be carefully monitored on a regular schedule. The incidences of diseases that are common to a number of woody ornamentals will depend upon a specific nursery's geographical location in the United States. Record where diseases occur and their precise location in stock blocks. This could help in the planning of future monitoring and control activities. Disease symptoms alone are often unreliable in a diagnosis; therefore, seek professional diagnostic services. Contact your local Agricultural Extension Service for instructions on the proper collection and submission of disease samples to a plant disease diagnostic laboratory.

### Propagation Area

Propagation beds should be routinely inspected on a 1–2 day interval while plants remain in this cycle. Be sure misting systems function properly; examine rooting media for water saturation. A too wet condition has been shown to predispose seedlings or cuttings to diseases. Examine seedlings or cuttings for damping-off disease. Damp-off appears as a small number of plants within a small area that have wilted or collapsed at the medium line. Propagation beds should be inspected for localized spots of root or cutting-end rot diseases. Foliage of cuttings will darken and drop from plants exhibiting obvious cutting-end discoloration or rot. Be aware of leaf diseases which often occur on foliage of cuttings. The propagation environment is ideal for disease spread. Collect and submit appropriate samples to the nearest diagnostic facility for an accurate diagnosis of any questionable disease problem.

### Production Area

Plants purchased from outside the nursery should be placed in a holding or quarantine area for at least 3 weeks. Make weekly inspections for insects and diseases so that problems can either be corrected or discarded. Production areas should be inspected every 10–14 days; this should involve a minimum of 5% of the total plants per bed. Select different plants for each subsequent inspection. Inspect both the windward side and any side bordering an uncultivated area; foliar pathogens can be expected to enter a production site from either area. Monitor randomly in blocks. Check both old and new growth for obvious disease symptoms. Be alert for root rot symptoms during monitoring. Roots of plants exhibiting decreased vigor, off color, smaller leaf size or wilt should be examined. Remove the container and examine the root system. Peripheral roots that are dark, discolored, and sluff easily to the touch indicate root problems. Lack of root penetration in the lower one-third of the growing media is another indication of root problems. A zone or band of off-color plants across a block may or may not be exhibiting wilt or dieback symptoms. The cause of such problems has been associated with overlapping irrigation patterns or two irrigation zones that fail to meet. The practice of resetting rooted cuttings or liners into containers located in the field where plants have failed to grow could be detrimental to the plant. Soil pathogens, if not responsible for the first plant's death, may exist in the plant residue in increased populations. When a particular disease is detected on several plant species, all other known susceptible species should be carefully examined.

Record all disease observations and associated production problems for future monitoring and control activities. When specific diseases cannot be accurately diagnosed on site, collect and submit appropriate samples to a plant disease diagnostic laboratory in your state.


## DISEASE CONTROL

Nurseries that have used disease control programs indicate that the difficulty lies in the control phase rather than in the disease detection components. Nurseries that use scouts obtain adequate disease detection, but translation into disease control activities is often lost or ignored. Growers understand the need for active control measures, but these actions are often given a low priority within the nursery as compared to the propagation, potting, irrigation, and sales. Developing specialization within existing nursery labor forces to control potential diseases can be beneficial in making management decisions. Individuals within the nursery could be given the responsibility for receiving disease monitoring reports on which disease control decisions are made. A group within the nursery could be responsible for all disease control activities including pesticide application. The departmentalization of a pest control group would help to develop a greater expertise in the selection and application of pesticides. Increased consistency in technology and safety as they relate to pesticide application would also result.

After the execution of certain control decisions and actions, an evaluation of such decisions would be beneficial. This would include success of disease control and the practicality of the precise actions taken as they relate to the accuracy of the monitoring system. Such evaluations should be based on visual observations, past records and effects of those control measures used previously. This type of assessment allows for a more positive approach to the preventive phase of disease control and may indicate the need for additional monitoring efforts.


### Stock Plant Area

Stock plants with localized disease problems can often be controlled easily and rapidly by selective pruning or handpicking of disease foliage. A thorough cleanup of all infected plants and uninfected plant debris should be included. Certain stock plants with severe disease problems, such as crown gall or mushroom root rot, should be rogued from the stock plant area. Control measures for foliar diseases should be initiated rapidly to insure that cuttings used in propagation are apparently free from disease. As stated previously, the propagation cycle creates a perfect environment for disease epidemics if pathogens are present in plant tissue. Obtain the most current and effective chemical control measures from the nearest Cooperative Extension Service office after making accurate diagnoses.

### Propagation Area

Areas of declining or dead plants with root diseases within propagation beds should be carefully removed, including rooting medium. Certain root-rotting fungi, such as *Sclerotium rolfsii* or *Rhizoctonia solani*, will produce an asexual, reproductive structure called a sclerotium. These structures are quite small and can be moved by various means from one site in the propagation bed to another. Extreme care should be taken when roguing individually infected plants. Where a root rot is the problem, apply an appropriate drench fungicide in the propagation bed. Drench the entire bed, not just the obvious diseased spots. Since some soil fungicides are specific for a particular organism, an accurate diagnosis is imperative. Root rot incidences should always be recorded and rooting media should never be reused. Severe root rot diseases of plants in propagation beds do not affect all plants; some will survive. It is always tempting to use these surviving plants which should be discarded. Since most growers will pot survivors, be sure to treat the potting mix with an appropriate fungicide as a protective measure. Monitor plants, plus repeat fungicide application at intervals described on the label. Rooting liners exhibiting foliar disease symptoms should be sprayed with an appropriate fungicide before introduction into the production area and continue on a regular basis. Consult your local county extension agent for specific recommendations.

### Production Area

All fungicide selection and application must be based on the latest and most accurate recommendations. Some diseases occurring on aerial portions of plants can be controlled by selective shearing or pruning of infected plant parts. Removal of severely blighted leaves will improve the efficacy of subsequent fungicide applications. Severely diseased plants should be rogued from the production site and appropriately discarded. Plants that must be rogued specifically are those with root rot, crown gall, and blight. This is especially important since chemical control for these diseases is unsatisfactory.

Disease control decisions directed toward root rot should consider several factors. If root rot diseases caused by *Phytophthora* and *Pythium* spp. are prevalent, disease development is favored by saturated soil moisture levels. Frequent and excessive irrigation will favor the continued reproduction and spread of these fungal pathogens. Therefore, proper water management must be recognized as an important facet of disease management. When root diseases exist, avoid water or fertility extremes. Both will place additional stress on an already weakened plant. Systemic fungicides are more effective than protectant fungicides. These compounds affect the target fungus in plant tissue. Drench fungicides applied to soil to control root rotting fungi should be deposited on and in the growing medium and not applied to foliage. If these products are applied through overhead irrigation, they should be washed off by additional water. Moisture content of the growing medium should be near container capacity when a fungicide drench is applied. Avoid applications to very dry mixes, because this can cause severe root damage.

For foliar situations, certain facets of the disease cycle should be reviewed prior to control activities. Most foliar fungal pathogens require long periods of leaf wetness if infection is to take place. This is one reason that late afternoon rainfall or irrigation is not good. When foliar disease severity is high, minimize the irrigation cycle. Application of fungicides or bactericides should not be expected to control a disease immediately. The variable length of time between penetration by a spore or bacterium and the appearance of the first recognizable symptom of disease, such as leaf spot, is the incubation period. This time may span days or weeks and will continue in spite of the application of a protectant fungicide with no kickback action onto the plant surface. This means that the disease can be expected to increase in incidence and severity until all incubation periods that began before pesticide applications become recognizable symptoms. Do not give up on the pesticide prematurely. Many diseases necessitate pesticide coverage on both leaf surfaces to be effective. Leaf underside coverage is particularly important with certain fungal pathogens like the *Cercospora spp.* on *ligustrum* and *pittosporum* that reproduce from the lower leaf surface. Irrigate plants prior to spraying to allow the longest contact of pesticide and foliage prior to the next watering.

### Types of Fungicides

Chemical control of most fungal diseases depends on the application of fungicides before the pathogen arrives. Fungicides used in this way are referred to as protectants (see Table 16–5). Most broad spectrum fungicides are of this type. Protectants prevent fungal spores from germinating or kill them as they germinate, prior to penetrating the plant surface. These fungicides are ineffective after infection occurs except to reduce new infections. A few fungicides destroy pathogenic fungi after infection has occurred. These fungicides are called eradicants or therapeutants. Their effectiveness is limited to a period of a few hours or days following infection. This postinfection control is referred to as kickback action. An exception is the eradication of powdery mildew with sulfur.

Most protectant fungicides are not absorbed by the plant and are not translocated within the plant. They form a protective barrier over the surface of the plant to prevent infection. Some redistribution of these fungicides may occur during rainy periods but the effectiveness of the fungicide is dependent on thorough coverage during application. They must be applied and dry on the plant before they are exposed to rain or overhead irrigation and they must be present on the plant surface when the pathogen arrives. Captan,

Mancozeb, Daconil 2787 and thiram are examples of nonsystemic protectant fungicides.

Recent technology has produced several fungicides that are absorbed and translocated within the plants. This type of fungicide is called a *systemic*. Even though systemics are translocated to new growth, they are essentially protectant fungicides. Most systemics cannot kill fungi which have established themselves inside a plant. Benomy, which is effective against a number of the Ascomycetes and Deuteromycetes, and Subdue, which is effective against members of the Phycomycetes, are examples of systemic fungicides. A number of the systemic fungicides also have kickback action. Strike, for example, is effective against the apple powdery mildew pathogen for up to 48 hr after infection.

Protective fungicides are washed from the sprayed plant surfaces over a period of several days by rain and overhead irrigation and new unsprayed growth may emerge from buds. Protective fungicides, therefore, need to be applied several times at appropriate intervals during the period when the pathogen is active and the host is susceptible. The grower should understand the action of a fungicide which is being applied to use it most effectively. Protectant fungicides are normally applied on 7–14 day intervals, but more frequent applications may be necessary in periods of heavy rains or frequent overhead irrigation. Systemic fungicides, on the other hand, are effective during wet or dry periods since they are translocated within the plant. Table 16–5 shows the action of some fungicides.

Portions of this chapter were adapted from extension publications listed in the references section. These references as well as the others contain much more additional information on controlling weeds, insects, and diseases in nursery operations. Since pesticide recommendations are fairly specific and their use regulated by law, it is suggested that nursery growers should regularly obtain current pesticide recommendations from their local county agricultural extension agent or from the state pesticide specialist, generally located at the various land grant universities.

## SUMMARY

Weeds, insects, and diseases are the three most noxious, negative modifiers of plant growth in nurseries. The negative aspects of these pests can be minimized by an integrated pest control program with a crop production system that is directed toward following optimum cultural practices to produce healthy, vigorous plants. Plants that are properly spaced, correctly pruned, fertilized, and watered are much less prone to pest problems than are plants that are exposed to undesirable environmental conditions.

**Table 16-5** Fungicide Disease Applications on Nursery Plants

| Fungicide Common Name[a] | Trade Name[b] | Anthracnose | Botrytis Blight | Damping-off and Root Rot (imperfect fungi) | Damping-off and Root rot (imperfect fungi) | Downy Mildew | Leaf and Twig Blight | Leaf Spot and Needlecast | Petal Blight | Powdery Mildew | Rust | Scab | Action[d] |
|---|---|---|---|---|---|---|---|---|---|---|---|---|---|
| Benomyl | Benomyl | x | x |  | x |  | x | x | x | x |  | x | S |
| Captan | Captan / Merpan / Orthocide | x | x |  | x |  | x | x | x |  |  | x | P,E |
| Chlorothalonil | Bravo / Daconil 2787 / Exotherm Termil | x | x |  | x | x | x | x | x | x | x | x | P |
| Copper Hydroxide | Kocide 101 | x | x |  |  | x | x | x | x |  |  | x | P |
| Copper Sulfate | Phyton 27 | x | x |  |  | x | x | x | x |  |  | x | P |
| Copper Sulfate + Lime | Bordo (Bordeaux Mix) | x | x |  |  | x | x | x | x |  | x | x | P |
| Cycloheximide | Actispray |  |  |  |  |  |  |  | x | x |  |  | P |
| Diclora, DCNA, | Allisan / Botran / Resisan |  | x |  | x |  | x |  | x |  |  |  | P |
| Dinocap | Dikar / Karathane |  |  |  |  |  |  |  |  | x | x | x | P |
| Dodemorph | Milban |  |  |  |  |  |  |  |  | x |  |  | P |
| Etridiazole (ethazol) | Terrazole / Truban |  |  | x |  |  |  |  |  |  |  |  | P |
| Fenarimol | Rubigan |  |  |  |  |  |  |  |  | x |  |  | S |
| Ferbam | Carbamate / Ferbam / Trifungol | x | x |  | x | x | x | x | x | x | x | x | P |
| Folpet | Folpet | x | x |  | x | x | x | x |  | x |  | x | P |

| Common name | Trade name[a] | | | | | | | Type[d] |
|---|---|---|---|---|---|---|---|---|
| Furalaxyl | Fongarid | | | | x | | | S,P |
| Iprodione | Chipco 26019 | x | x | | | | | P |
| Mancozeb | Dithane M-45 | x | x | | | x | x | P |
| | Dithane F-45 | | | | | x | | |
| | Dithane DF | | | | | | | |
| Mancozeb + thiophanate-methyl | Zyban | | x | | | x | | S |
| | Duosan | | | | | | | |
| Maneb | Dithane M-22 | x | x | | | x | x | P |
| Metalaxyl | Subdue | | x | | | | | S |
| PCNB | Terraclor | | | x | | x | | P |
| Phosetyl-AL | Chipco Aliette | | x | | | x | | S |
| Pipron | Piperalin | | | | x | | | P |
| Propamocarb | Banol | | x | | | | | P |
| Propiconazole | Banner | x | | | x | x | | S |
| Sulfur | Flotox | x | | | x | x | x | P |
| Thiophanate + ethazol | Banrot | x | x | | | x | | S |
| Thiophanate-methyl | Cleary's 3336 | x | x | | | x | | S |
| Thiram | AAtack | x | x | | | x | | P |
| | Arasan | | | | | | | |
| | Thiram 75 | | | | | | | |
| Triadimefon | Strike | x | | | x | x | | S |
| Triforine | Funginex | | | | x | x | | S,P,E |
| | Saprol | | | | | | | |
| Vinclozolin | Ornalin | x | x | | x | x | | P |
| | Ronilan | | | | | | | |
| Zineb | Dithane Z-78 | x | x | | x | x | | P |
| | Zineb 75 | | | | | | | |

[a]These are trade names of fungicides used in the nursery industry. Not all of these fungicides are labeled or recommended in all states. This list is not intended to be a complete list of all fungicides used in nurseries. There are numerous products which are combinations of two or more compounds; these are not included in this list.

[b]This list is for reference only and does not represent an endorsement or imply criticism of the products.

[c]Water mold, i.e., *Pythium*, *Phytophthora*, and imperfect fungi, i.e., *Rhizoctonia*, *Fusarium*.

[d]S = systemic, P = protectant, E = eradicant.

*Source:* Adapted from Jones (1982) and Powell (1990).

## REFERENCES

AHRENS, J. F. 1989. Taming container weeds. Am. Nurseryman 170(3):44–47.

AKERS, M. S., P. L. CARPENTER, and S. C. WELLER. 1984. Herbicide systems for nursery plantings. HortScience 19(4):502–504.

BAKER, J. R., ed. 1984. Insect and related pests of shrubs. N. C. Ag. Ext. Ser. Ag-189.

DAVIDSON, H. 1984. Weed control in nurseries and landscape areas. Michigan CES Bulletin E-1677.

DICKEY, R. D., E. W. McELWEE, C. A. CONOVER, and J. N. JOINER. 1978. Container growing of woody ornamental nursery plants in Florida. Florida AES Bulletin 793.

JONES, R. K., and R. C. LAMBE, eds. 1982. Diseases of woody ornamental plants and their control in nurseries. N. C. Ag. Ext. Ser. Ag-286.

KUHNS, L. J. 1982. How to control weeds—the basics and the herbicides. Am. Nurseryman 155(5):29–49.

KUHNS, L. J. 1982. How to control weeds—herbicide recommendations. Am. Nurseryman 155(5):50–61.

NIELSEN, D. G. 1989. Insect and mite control on woody ornamentals and herbaceous perennials. Ohio CES Bulletin 504.

MOORMAN, G. W. 1984. How nurserymen can plan effective disease control programs. Am. Nurseryman 160(4):66–71.

PETERSON, C., R. HEATLEY, G. ADAMS, D. SMITLEY, and D. ROBERTS. 1987. Diagnosing problems of ornamental landscape plants. Michigan CES Bulletin E-2024.

POWELL, C. C. 1990. Fungicides: an overview. Am. Nurseryman 171(6):61–70.

POWELL, C. C. 1988. Disease control in the landscape. Ohio CES Bulletin 614.

SKROCH, W. A. 1985. Basic principles of weed growth influence effective herbicide use. Am. Nurseryman 162(5):112–115.

SMITH, E. M. 1992. Chemical weed control in commercial nursery and landscape plantings. Ohio CES Bulletin MM297.

THOMSON, W. T. 1992–93. Agricultural chemicals book I, II, III, and IV. Thomson Publications, California.

URBANO, C. C. 1985. Some recommended herbicides and rates. Am. Nurseryman 161(8):87–88.

## SUGGESTED READING

ANONYMOUS. 1991. Turf and ornamental chemicals reference. Chemical and Pharmaceutical Press, New York.

ANONYMOUS. 1993. Crop protection chemicals reference. Chemical and Pharmaceutical Press, New York.

BOHMONT, B. L. 1983. The new pesticide user's guide. Reston Publishing Co., Inc., Virginia.

BUCHHOLTZ, K. P. Committee Chairman. 1981. Weeds of north central states. NCR Technical Committee NC-121. Bulletin 772.

DERR, J. F., and B. L. APPLETON. 1988. Herbicide injury to trees and shrubs: a pictorial guide to symptom diagnosis. Blue Crab Press, Virginia.

HUMBURG, N. E., Committee Chairman. 1989. Herbicide handbook of Weed Science Society of America. WSSA, Illinois.

KLINGMAN, G. C., F. M ASHTON, and L. J. NOORDHOFF. 1982. Weed science: principles and practices. Wiley-Interscience, New York.

JOHNSON, W. T., and H. H. Lyon. 1988. Insects that feed on trees and shrubs. Cornell University Press, New York.

MANION, P. D. 1991. Tree disease concepts. Prentice-Hall, Inc., New Jersey.

McGRATH, H., J. FELDMESSR, and L. D. YOUNG, eds. 1986. Guidelines for the control of plant diseases and nematodes. USDA Ag. Handbook 656.

MILLER, J. F., Committee, Chairman. Weeds of the southern United States. Georgia CES.

ORTON, D. A. 1989. Coincide: the Orton system of pest management. Plantsmen's Publications, Illinois.

RICE, R. P. 1992. Nursery and landscape weed control manual. Thomson Publications, California.

RIFFLE, J. W., and G. W. PETERSON. 1986. Diseases of trees in the Great Plains. USDA Forest Service, General Technical Report RM-129.

SCHUBERT, O. E. 1986. A compendium of chemical weed control research in ornamentals in the United States (1944–1985). Supplement to HortScience 21(2).

SCHWARTZ, P. H., and D. R. HAMEL, Eds. 1980. Guidelines for the control of insect and mite pests of foods, fibers, feeds, ornamentals, livestock, households, forests, and forest products. USDA Ag. Handbook 571.

SINCLAIR, W. A., H. H. LYON, and W. T. JOHNSON. 1987. Diseases of trees and shrubs. Cornell University Press, New York.

TATTAR, T. A. 1978. Diseases of shade trees. Academic Press, New York.

Chapter **17**

# Nursery Storage Facilities

Storage facilities are employed by nurserymen for many reasons, including temporary and winter storage of plants, seeds, equipment, and supplies. The greatest need is for the storage of plants.

The oldest and most basic reason for the storage of plants in controlled environments is to maintain viability and quality during the period after removal from their production sites until they are replanted either in the nursery or in the landscape. Once plants are dug in the field or taken from the container-growing area, they are removed from their primary source of water. If they are not properly cared for, they will dehydrate and die.

Controlled-environment storage is also used for the protection of tender or semitender plants that would be injured or killed if left exposed to the rigors of the winter climate. This is especially true for container-grown plants, which may be vulnerable to root injury if the temperature falls below the critical minimum for the species. Also, when the soil is frozen, many species are very vulnerable to desiccation, particularly during periods of high sunlight, wind, or both.

Storage facilities can also be used to precondition plants for flowering and transplanting. Many bulbs and plants, such as azaleas and hydrangeas, that are forced for special holidays, require a period of exposure to cold temperature before they will bloom; this can best be accomplished in controlled-temperature rooms. Cool temperatures obtained in storage buildings can be used to delay bud break and to hold back the growth of plants in early spring so that the spring planting season can be extended. Also, they can be used to condition the tender growth on landscape plants that are dug in full leaf during the growing season, assuring a greater success following transplanting. In addition to modifying the environment to affect a plant response, storage facilities are used to aid in the processing and marketing of plants. In many parts of the nation the spring digging season starts late, because of climatic conditions. It is often much too short to allow sufficient time to dig, process, and deliver plant material for spring sales. On the other hand, the fall season is generally mild, and there is sufficient time to dig and store plants. Many nurseries have constructed plant storage facilities so that plants can be dug in the fall, then placed into winter storage, where they are processed (graded, packaged into wholesale units, labeled) and maintained in good condition for many months until they are shipped in late winter or early spring.

Plant propagators use cold-temperature storage facilities to store seeds, cuttings, budwood, and scions. Since seed production is affected by a multitude of environmental, biological, and physiological factors, it is necessary to collect seed when it is available and to store it for use in years when there is little or no seed produced. For example, shortleaf pine (*Pinus echinata*), which is an important conifer for reforestation in the south, produces a good crop of seed about once in 10 years. Therefore, it is necessary to collect and store the seed for a decade or longer to ensure an adequate annual supply. Fortunately, seeds from most woody plants can be stored successfully for long periods of time. This topic is thoroughly discussed in USDA Agriculture Handbook 450, *Seeds of Woody Plants in the United States* (see Appendix B). Storing rooted cuttings in polyethylene bags under controlled low temperature allows the propagator to use high-cost greenhouse space more efficiently. It is possible to obtain two or three crops of cuttings from the same bench space that would normally be used to propagate and hold one batch of cuttings until the time of planting.

Plant storage is another tool by which the nursery manager can gain a degree of control over both the plants and various marketing problems. There are a number of different types of facilities in which plants can be stored; each has its advantages and disadvantages. The nurseryman should consider these carefully and then construct those that best fit his or her and the plants' needs.

## STORAGE FACILITIES

Use of *heeling-in grounds* is the oldest and simplest method of plant storage. It was used in ancient times and is still used extensively today. It is a method of temporary storage, providing minimal control of the environment, although sometimes plants are stored for many months. The plants are placed either on top of the ground or into a trench and the roots or rootballs are covered with a loose, damp medium. A mixture of peat and sawdust is often used to protect the roots of bare-root plants, since it is lightweight, retains moisture, and is easily worked about the roots. Year-old wood chips are used also for temporary storage of B&B plants where they are available. This method is used fairly extensively in nurseries, garden centers, and at landscape sites prior to planting (Fig. 17–1).

Dormant, bare-root, deciduous plants should be heeled-in with their stems oriented parallel to the noontime rays of the sun. This helps to minimize desiccation of the stems during storage. When plants are received in a dehydrated state, they will benefit by soaking in water for 2–3 hr prior to heeling-in or planting. The roots of plants should not be exposed to long periods of freezing temperatures, especially below 25°F, since roots are very vulnerable to low-temperature injury (Table 17–1). They should be mulched prior to the onset of freezing temperatures. Balled and burlapped (B&B) or containerized plants that are mulched after the soil balls have frozen are very prone to desiccation injury.

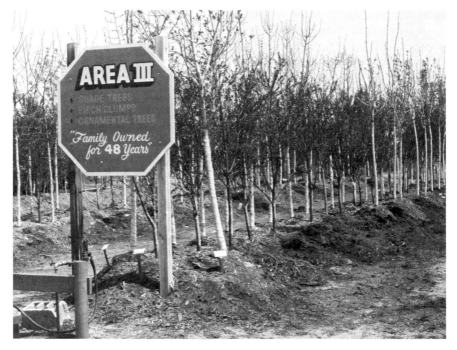

**Figure 17–1** Nursery stock in temporary heeling-in storage. (Courtesy Kluck Nursery.)

**Table 17-1**  Average Killing Temperatures[a,b] for Roots of Selected Species of Woody Ornamental Plants

| Botanical Name | Common Name | Killing Temperature °C | °F |
|---|---|---|---|
| *Magnolia soulangiana* | Saucer magnolia | −5.0 | 23 |
| *Magnolia stellata* | Star magnolia | −5.0 | 23 |
| *Cornus florida* | Flowering dogwood | −6.7 | 20 |
| *Daphne cneorum* | Garland flower | −6.7 | 20 |
| *Ilex crenata* 'Convexa' | Convex Japanese holly | −6.7 | 20 |
| *Ilex crenata* 'Hetzi' | Hetz Japanese holly | −6.7 | 20 |
| *Ilex opaca* | American holly | −6.7 | 20 |
| *Ilex crenata* 'Stokesii' | Stokes Japanese holly | −6.7 | 20 |
| *Pyracantha coccinea* | Fire thorn | −7.8 | 18 |
| *Cryptomeria japonica* | Japanese cedar | −8.9 | 16 |
| *Cotoneaster horizontalis* | Rock cotoneaster | −9.4 | 15 |
| *Viburnum carlesii* | Korean spice viburnum | −9.4 | 15 |
| *Cytisus praecox* | Warminster broom | −9.4 | 15 |
| *Buxus sempervirens* | Common boxwood | −9.4 | 15 |
| *Ilex glabra* | Inkberry | −9.4 | 15 |
| *Euonymus fortunei* 'Carrierei' | Carrier euonymus | −9.4 | 15 |
| *Euonymus fortunei* 'Argenteo-marginata' | Variegated euonymus | −9.4 | 15 |
| *Hederia helix* 'Baltica' | Baltic ivy | −9.4 | 15 |
| *Pachysandra terminalis* | Japanese pachysandra | −9.4 | 15 |
| *Vinca minor* | Common periwinkle | −9.4 | 15 |
| *Pieris japonica* 'Compacta' | Compact lily-of-the-valley bush | −9.4 | 15 |
| *Acer palmatum* 'Atropurpureum' | Bloodleaf Japanese maple | −10.0 | 14 |
| *Cotoneaster adpressa praecox* | Nan-Shan cotoneaster | −12.2 | 10 |
| *Taxus media* 'Nigra' | Black Anglojap yew | −12.2 | 10 |
| *Rhododendron* 'Gibraltar' | Gibraltar azalea | −12.2 | 10 |
| *Rhododendron* 'Hinodegiri' | Azalea hybrid | −12.2 | 10 |
| *Pieris japonica* | Lily-of-the-vally bush | −12.2 | 10 |
| *Leucothoe fontanesiana* | Drooping leucothoe | −15.0 | 5.0 |
| *Pieris floribunda* | Fetterbush | −15.0 | 5.0 |
| *Euonymus fortunei* 'Colorata' | Purple leaf wintercreeper | −15.0 | 5.0 |
| *Juniperus horizontalis* | Creeping juniper | −17.8 | 0.0 |
| *Juniperus horizontalis* 'Douglasii' | Waukegan juniper | −17.8 | 0.0 |
| *Rhododendron carolinianum* | Carolina rhododendron | −17.8 | 0.0 |
| *Rhododendron catawbiense* | Mountain rosebay | −17.8 | 0.0 |
| *Rhododendron* P. J. M. hybrids | P. J. M. rhododendron | −23.3 | −10 |
| *Potentilla fruticosa* | Shrubby cinquefoil | −23.3 | −10 |
| *Picea glauca* | White spruce | −23.3 | −10 |
| *Picea omorika* | Serbian spruce | −23.3 | −10 |

[a]Highest temperature that killed more than 50% of root system and reduced top growth.

[b]See Borland and Beattie in Suggested Readings for additional data.

*Source:* Adapted from Havis (1976).

*Cold frames*, of all types of construction, have been used for hundreds of years to modify the environment about young tender plants. In addition to their use as propagation structures, they can be used to overwinter plants. Although both shallow and deep-pit frames can be used as an overwintering structure, the deep pit provides the best protection. The environment is modified by the warmth of the soil and by the shadow cast by the south wall of the pit during the winter storage period. Therefore, the best orientation of the cold frames used for winter storage is in an east-west direction. To ensure successful storage, the plants must be fully dormant prior to sealing of the frame for the winter storage period. To ensure maintaining low storage temperature conditions within the cold frame, the sash may need to be shaded, and the structure or the plants within may need to be insulated. Bales of straw, a straw mulch, microfoam, or other appropriate materials can be used for this purpose.

*Microfoam tunnels* are the modern version of the cold frame and the heeling-in grounds. They are used to overwinter small container-grown plants, in situ. The dormant plants are laid on their sides, close together, in long narrow rows. The length and width of the rows are determined by the nurseryman, as are the size of the microfoam and white poly sheets (depending on winter temperature 1–3 layers of 0.63 cm [0.25 in.] thick microfoam is used). The microfoam is covered with 4 mil white copolymer (poly) and the edges covered with soil to seal the tunnels. In areas of the country where straw or hay is available nurserymen can use these materials to manufacture a straw-poly blanket (12 in. of straw or hay placed between two sheets of poly) to effectively protect container-grown plants against cold-temperature injury.

A suggested guideline as to when to cover in the fall and to uncover in spring is to use the F-dates (date of first frost in the fall and last frost in the spring). A time to cover in the fall might be F + 30 or F + 45, and to uncover in the spring might be F − 30 or F − 45. The exact dates will vary with the latitude of the nursery and with seasonal variation. When uncovering in the spring, be prepared to recover a time or two due to the return of freezing temperatures.

This method utilizes the moderating affects of soil heat to protect the covered plant from cold-temperature injury. In addition, the polyethylene cover protects the plants against desiccation injury. The ground temperature within the microfoam tunnel remains considerably warmer than the outside air temperature; some nurseries have reported ground temperature remaining in the low to mid-50s (°F) throughout the storage period.

A few precautions are necessary to ensure the success of this method: (1) All plants must be dormant prior to being covered; (2) the ground area must be well drained and free of organic debris; and (3) plants that are wet due to rain, snow, dew, or frost should not be covered, although the container medium should be well watered a day or two prior to covering.

The *shade house*, more commonly known as the lathhouse when lath construction is employed, modifies temperature, light intensity, and relative humidity. These, in turn, reduce the amount of transpiration that takes place from the plants stored within. Large groves of trees can serve the same purpose. The shade house is commonly utilized for the temporary storage of plant material during the shipping season and is often used in conjunction with the heeling-in grounds. Some nurseries utilize the shade house in the production of shade-tolerant species such as *Pachysandra* and *Vinca* and in the production of young evergreen transplants (e.g., *Taxus*).

Shadehouses are also used to precondition plants prior to planting them in low-light environments, such as are found in malls, atriums, and offices. A period of time, which varies with the age and species of the plant, allows the cells in the leaves to be modified to better accept the new lower levels of light and to some degree the change in the quality of the light.

When building lathhouses or constructing seed or transplant beds that will be protected with lath covers, it is best to construct them so that the lath strips are oriented in a vertical position on the south and west sides and in a north-south direction on the top. This orientation of the lath provides for a moving sun-shade pattern on a daily basis. During hot, dry periods this small difference can be critical, especially for young seedlings or recently transplanted plants. Structure orientation is less important when it is covered with shade cloth rather than with lath.

*Plastic houses*, although originally designed as a temporary structure for growing plants, are now used extensively for the winter storage of plants, especially for evergreens in northern areas. The houses are primarily of a quonset-type construction (Fig. 17–2) and covered with one or two layers of polyethylene. The double-layer, air-separated structure provides greater insulation due to the dead air space between the two layers of polyethylene. A small electric air blower positioned to blow air between the layers provides enough air pressure to keep the plastic layers separated, even on very large structures. The film used as the cover for plastic houses should be 4- to 6-mil polyethylene, to withstand the stress caused by winter storms. The film may be either clear or milky, depending upon the storage objective. The house should be constructed and the plastic installed in such a way as to form a relatively vaportight chamber to aid in maintaining a high relative humidity within the structure. Where clear plastic is utilized or where there is not a vapor seal, it will be necessary to shade or irrigate the plants occasionally in the late winter or early spring. It may also be necessary to ventilate to keep the temperature low to avoid rapid dehydration of plant tissue and prevent early breaking of dormancy. However, when houses are vented, they must be irrigated more frequently to replace the moisture lost during venting.

Polyhouses, constructed primarily for overwintering of evergreens in the most northern regions of the country, without the aid of irrigation, are best when they are designed with a low profile to reduce the heat-transfer area and

**Figure 17-2** Plastic storage house for overwintering evergreens. (Courtesy Conard-Pyle Co.)

to aid in retaining snow for insulation; oriented in a north-south direction to reduce solar heating, and covered with milky plastic to minimize penetration of the sun's rays. The combination of low profile, north-south orientation, and milky plastic aids in maintaining the desired environment for keeping stored evergreens in good condition through the winter period. However, plants stored in plastic houses can be induced into early growth by constructing them with a higher profile, orientating in an east-west direction, and covering with clear plastic. The plants must be irrigated periodically, since they will transpire more moisture under the warmer, low-humidity conditions. It will be necessary to ventilate the house on sunny days to minimize high interior temperatures, but venting should be avoided when soil balls are frozen.

The *common storage* is a building designed to take advantage of changes in air density and the insulating properties of soil. When air cools, it becomes heavy and flows like a fluid into areas of lower elevation forcing the lighter, warmer air up into the higher elevations. Early common storage buildings were constructed either below ground or in hillsides to gain these advantages. However, since the development of high-quality insulation materials, most common storage facilities are constructed totally above ground. By timely control of vents in the lower part of the walls and in the roof of the buildings, or by opening the drive-through doors at both ends of the building in the evening when the outside air temperature is lower than the interior temperature and closing them at sun-up, low temperatures can be maintained fairly successfully within the building during winter and early spring. However, common storage is not too effective in maintaining dormancy of plants in the late spring because of loss of cold-temperature control.

*Refrigerated storage* is an advanced model of insulated common storage. It is used to gain a greater degree of control over temperature and humidity to extend the storage period. The construction of a refrigerated storage is similar to that of an insulated common storage except that (1) the insulation is generally thicker, (2) the floor is of concrete and may be insulated, (3) refrigeration equipment is installed to control the temperature, and (4) humidification devices are used to control humidity.

There are many types of excellent insulating materials available, and since most of them have relatively low thermal conductivity, the choice of an insulator to use in the construction of a refrigerated storage will depend more on the total cost of construction and the cost of upkeep. The semirigid plastic or polystyrene foam types are easy to install and are relatively inexpensive. The thickness of insulation that is needed varies with the temperature differential between the outside and the interior of the storage and the relative cost of insulation versus the cost of refrigeration equipment and operating energy. For most nurseries in the northern part of the United States, the insulation equivalent of 4 in. of corkboard on the walls and 6 in. on the ceiling appears to be adequate. This is equal to a total resistance ($R_1$) value* of 20 for vermiculite-filled cinderblock walls and about 23 for the ceiling.

Whenever there are temperature differences on two sides of a wall, such as the walls of a storage facility, there will be movement of water vapor from the warm side to the cold side. When this takes place, the insulation becomes damp, thus reducing its effectiveness. A vapor barrier of material such as aluminum foil, polyethylene film, or asphalt-covered or impregnated materials should be installed to impede the flow of moisture into the insulation.

It is not advisable to place a vapor barrier on both sides of the insulation, since the moisture can become trapped within the insulation. The cool side should always remain unsealed to allow the insulation an opportunity to dry if it should become damp. The barrier should be placed on the high-vapor-pressure side, which is the interior side of the insulation for most nursery storage buildings during the winter months. Nursery storage buildings can be insulated with a moisture-resistant, rodent-proof insulation material that can be sprayed onto the interior walls and ceilings, thus avoiding the need to install a vapor barrier. A polyurethane, low-flame foam can be used for

---

*Calculated from values obtained from Heating, Ventilating, and Air Conditioning Guide, Amer. Assoc. Heat., Ref., and Air Conditioning Eng., N.Y., 1959.

insulation, but it is flammable and when burned produces a gas that is very toxic to human beings and animals. It should be used only when suitable thermal barriers are provided.

A method of construction that is used very successfully by some nurseries is to combine a clear-span roof with prefabricated FABCON walls (Fig. 17–3). The walls of the building are made of prestressed concrete with a sandwich of insulation in the middle. This gives an R factor of about 14. The clear-span roof system is available in various span lengths from a number of sources. The roof can be insulated with blown insulation, with the R factor adjusted to fit various climatic conditions. This type of construction produces a totally maintenance-free structure. The building is relatively easy to construct and to install refrigeration, humidification, and lighting.

In the storage pictured in Figure 17–3 the nursery installed an aggregate floor in place of a more expensive concrete floor. The aggregate floor buffers the temperature and the humidity and is seldom too wet or too dry. With proper construction forklifts and carts are operated without causing cracking of the surface. The clear-span design allows greater versatility in layout of storage bins.

**Figure 17–3** Fabcon precast concrete storage building with clear-span roof. (Courtesy Bailey Nurseries, Inc.)

Details on the construction and operation of nursery storages are contained in *Storage of Nursery Stock*, available from the American Association of Nurserymen, and USDA Agricultural Handbook 66, *The Commercial Storage of Fruits, Vegetables and Florist and Nursery Stocks*. For comparative cost data, see Beattie in suggested reading.

## ADDITIONAL FACILITIES

In addition to the previously discussed facilities used for the storage of plant material, the following facilities are used to prolong the storage life of various high-value horticultural products. They may at some time in the future be used more extensively for the storage of high-value nursery products. Therefore, a brief description of each is warranted.

The *jacketed system* of storage, originally designed for the storage of frozen foods, has been adapted for the storage of fresh fruit, vegetables, and nursery products. It is used fairly extensively by European nurserymen to provide better storage conditions and control pathogens such as botrytis. Bareroot nursery stock has been stored successfully up to 8 months with a good rate of survival following planting in the field. The system is designed to maintain a suitable low temperature (0°C/32°F), high relative humidity (95–98%), with a minimum amount of air movement. The jacket-cooled storage is a standard insulated refrigerated storage room with a built-in inner storage chamber constructed of asbestos plates which have high heat transmission. The inner storage room air is cooled by circulating cold air in the air space between the inner storage chamber (called the jacket) and the outer insulated storage room. This system prevents the plant material from being in direct contact with the cold, dry air from the evaporator. Also, the relative humidity within the storage room is not directly affected by the refrigeration equipment. The jacketed system prevents the condensation of water vapor in the insulation of the room and reduces frost formation on the refrigeration coils.

To assure high relative humidity within the jacketed chamber, the floor is wetted prior to loading, damp sphagnum moss is used on the roots of the plants, and the floor is dampened periodically, as needed, during the storage period.

Since the inner jacketed storage room temperature is dependent upon the air flowing outside the jacket, it is important that the outer chamber be controlled to within a half degree of the desired temperature with the aid of electronic thermostats. It is desirable that a number of sensors be employed and that they be aspirated.

A design that has proven practical and maintains a uniform temperature throughout the jacketed storage is one in which the rate of cool air flow in the side wall spaces between the jacket and outer storage wall is uniform all around the room. The air is blown into the ceiling space with fans and then flows by gravity down through the wall spaces and returns under the floor to the cooling coils. The volume of air flowing over the jacket should be sufficient to limit the temperature differential to 3°F (1.5°C) between the air entering and that leaving the jacket wall spaces. A vapor barrier is required to prevent the movement of moisture from the storage chamber into the jacket atmosphere. Details of design to meet the individual requirements can be obtained from the extension specialist in postharvest physiology, located at a land grant university, or from engineering firms familiar with the construction and operation of storage facilities.

The *filacell* is another method for maintaining a high relative humidity within a storage chamber at low temperature. A filacell is an efficient air washer that provides a high humidity at low temperatures with a high rate of air circulation. The filacell provides a massive wet-surface area within a small volume (2000 linear feet of nonfilament polypropylene per cubic foot of cell). It functions by chilled water moving down through the cell after being evenly sprayed, at low pressure (3–5 psi), over the upper surface as air moves upward through the cell. The temperature of the water controls the air temperature to within a variation of ½°C.

In practice, a bank of filacell units is supported over a large tank of water. The water temperature in the tank is controlled with refrigeration or heating units. The water is pumped to a spray nozzle located above the filacell. As the water moves downward in the cells, air is forced upward at a high velocity (600 ft³/min) producing a moisture-ladened air that both cools and humidifies the storage.

*Controlled atmosphere* (CA) *storage*, designed for the long-term storage of apples and pears, is not used for the storage of nursery stock, since the economic gain does not, at present, justify the investment in the construction of a gastight building. It decreases the rate of respiration, which is accomplished by increasing the level of carbon dioxide while decreasing the level of oxygen in the atmosphere. High concentrations of $CO_2$, 40% and greater, have been used to retard bud break and growth of dormant rose plants and herbaceous perennials. Use of this technique has been limited to small size containers. But it could be a useful technique to control bud break of dormant nursery stock.

*Hypobaric storage* or low-pressure storage (LPS) is a relatively new concept for the storage of perishable commodities. The idea originated in the late 1960s with S.P. Burg of Miami, Florida. The commodity to be stored is maintained in a refrigerated, vacuum chamber at a constant subatmospheric pressure. The chamber is ventilated with fresh, humid air by continuously evacuating the storage chamber with a vacuum pump. The optimum temperature, absolute pressure, and rate of air change vary with the commodity. LPS has been used successfully for the storage of a number of high-value flowers, fruits, and vegetables. Its economic feasibility for the storage of nursery products depends on the cost versus gain considerations compared to standard storage methods.

The selection and development of a plant storage facility must be related to the storage requirements and value of the plants to be stored, but must also meet the needs of management in attaining production and market objectives. It must be adjusted to the climate of the area where it is to be built and operated. Because construction of storage facilities represents a large capital investment, they should be carefully planned, constructed, and maintained. If properly managed, they are another tool that management can use to gain control over the environment, to provide quality plant material at the time the customer desires delivery, and to better program utilization of the labor force.

## FACTORS INVOLVED IN STORAGE OF NURSERY CROPS

Five important factors for the successful winter storage of nursery crops are physiological condition of the plants placed into storage, effective control of storage temperature, maintenance of a high relative humidity, air quality, and sanitation.

### Physiological Condition of Plants

Nursery stock intended for winter storage should be fully mature and dormant, free of insects, diseases, and mechanical injury. Deciduous species should be defoliated. Changing climatic conditions in the fall of the year, including short days and cold temperatures, initiate maturation of plant tissue to withstand the rigors of winter. These same conditions also aid in conditioning plants for winter storage. Mature plant tissue is less prone to injury due to cold temperature and desiccation than is immature tissue. Determinate species and plants that respond to short days appear to develop cold-temperature hardiness sooner than indeterminate species or plants that are not responsive to day length. Shoots and vegetative buds develop a greater tolerance to cold temperature than do roots or flower buds. Some species stored above ground in containers are more subject to root injury than are their shoots. Flower buds are often killed by exposure to specific low temperature, while the shoot buds remain fully viable.

Bare-root conifers, to be lifted in the fall for overwinter storage, should have completed their growth phase. The end of the root-growth period coincides with the time that soil temperature in the root zone declines to 50°F (10°C) and the white root tips are ½ in. or less in length. An examination of the root system can be a subjective guide to time of digging. Root systems of Norway spruce seedlings become inactive early in the fall and are sequentially followed by balsam fir, Douglas fir, white pine, and then red, Scots, and Austrian pine.

In addition to hardening of the roots of plants prior to harvesting, care must also be taken relative to handling of the plants during the digging and gathering operations prior to placing the plants in storage. To assure the best possible chance of having good plant survival during storage, the plants should be carefully lifted from the growing area with a minimum of injury to the plants. All too often, serious injuries are inflicted on plants during the harvesting operations. The five most common types of injuries associated with plant harvesting operations in nurseries, include abrasion of stems, breakage of branches, girdling of stems—especially at the root collar—breakage of roots, and worst of all, serious reduction of the functional root system. All of these injuries can be avoided by proper handling of the plants during the harvesting operation.

Dormant, mature plants should be placed in storage prior to onset of the adverse environmental conditions that prevail during winter. Nurserymen can speed up the process of maturation so that plant material programmed for winter storage can be begun earlier and the workload spread out over a longer time period. This can be accomplished to some degree by (1) withholding water in late summer, (2) withholding ammonium-nitrogen fertilizers in late summer, (3) root pruning in early fall, and (4) avoidance of top pruning after midsummer. Although it is not possible to control natural rainfall, irrigation practices can be terminated to aid in maturing plants. Plants in a healthy, vigorous condition will store better than unhealthy plants in a weaker condition. Therefore, plants should be maintained on a fertilizer program that results in good vigor. However, some plants appear to be less hardy when fertilized late in the growing season, with ammonium-nitrogen fertilizer.

Deciduous plants that fail to defoliate naturally, prior to digging for storage, can be aided in the process by employing one or more of the following practices: (1) hand stripping, (2) use of rubber-fingered mechanical beaters, (3) grazing activities of sheep, (4) sweating, and (5) by the use of chemical defoliants. Hand stripping, although used, is too expensive to employ when labor costs are high. Mechanical beaters or sheep can do considerable damage to the plants and should be used with care. However, all three methods have been or are used to defoliate nursery stock. The process of sweating is still used to remove remaining leaves prior to storing deciduous plants. It is time-consuming and, if not carefully done, can cause considerable injury to plants due to overheating.

Chemically induced defoliation, prior to digging for storage, is a potentially promising method of defoliation. Unfortunately, no single chemical has been found to be effective on a wide variety of plants. Research has demonstrated certain chemicals to be effective defoliants on some crops. Potassium iodide at a concentration of 0.2–0.3% was effective in causing defoliation (75–100%) in most cultivars of apple, cherry, peach, and apricots, although seedling fruit trees responded poorly. Bromodine was effective on a number of species. When applied at a concentration of 0.25% (200–300 gal/acre-in.), in two or three applications, at weekly intervals, leaf abscission (90–100%) was effected in cherry, pear, and peach. A 0.50% concentration was needed for similar results on apple and prune, and a 1% spray has effectively defoliated roses. Nacconol NR (0.5–4.0%) has been used to defoliate nursery stock in some nurseries. Ethrel (2-chloroethylphosphonic acid) applied at 2000 ppm in two or three weekly applications was effective in defoliating apples and Italian prune, whereas only 500–1000 ppm was needed to defoliate Mazzard cherry and Bartlett pear. However, a combination of ethephon (200–400 ppm) with a surfactant has caused injury to shoots of some cultivars of apple when used as a defoliant.

Nurserymen planning to use chemical defoliants should test the chemicals on a limited basis prior to extensive field application, since plant response is variable with species, cultivar, environment, and condition of the plant at time of treatment. Best response has been in late season, to hasten the natural abscission process. Legally, only chemicals registered as a chemical defoliant for nursery stock may be used.

After the plants have been dug, they must be transported to the storage building, graded, and placed into storage. Some plants, for example, roses, may be graded and bundled in the field and then transported to storage. However, most plants are dug and transported to a temporary storage until most of the digging has been completed. Following the rush of the digging season, the material is graded, pruned, tagged, bound, or packaged into wholesale units and placed in storage.

In most common storages, the plants are placed into ricks, whereas in refrigerated storages the practice is to use bins, pallets, or polylined boxes and stack them with the aid of forklift trucks. Snap-on frames, made of tubular steel, can be attached to pallets for storing container-sized material or B&B plants. Portable metal racks are used by some nurseries to good advantage. These freestanding, portable storage racks are available in a number of sizes and allow the storage manager greater flexibility in the utilization of the storage area than is permitted with stationary wooden structures. Also, the metal construction has a longer functional life than does wood. When possible, species that respond in a similar fashion should be stored together. Experience and good plant sense can be used as a guide in choosing the species that store well together. Superior storage life of nursery plants requires that only mature, quality plants be placed in storage.

### Temperature Control

Temperature has been defined as the degree of hotness or coldness measured on a definite scale and its degree determines the flow of heat. When a warm object is brought in contact with a cold object, the former is cooled while the latter is warmed. Thus, heat flows from the warm object to the cool object. If a layer of felt, rockwool, styrofoam, or a vacuum is placed between the two objects, the rate of change in temperature is much slower. It is this principle which is employed in the construction and operation of common and refrigerated storages.

Temperature plays an important part in all metabolic functions of plants. At high temperatures, photosynthesis, respiration, transpiration, and so on, go on at a rapid rate, whereas at a lower temperature the rate is much slower. The storage life of plants is prolonged by reducing respiration and transpiration to a low level by maintaining the plants at as low a temperature as possible without injury to the plants. Low ambient temperatures also reduce the incidence of infection by fungi.

In general, most deciduous, bare-root, plant material, when maintained at a temperature of 32–35°F, will remain dormant and free of mold. However, some will not and must be maintained at a colder temperature. It has been found, for example, that cherries, peaches, and lilac do best if maintained at a temperature of 33–35°F, whereas roses, herbaceous perennials, strawberry plants, and conifer seedlings do best if kept at a temperature below freezing in the vicinity of 28–30°F. Rooted cuttings store successfully at temperatures between 33 and 39°F.

Plant material in containers and B&B plants overwintered in plastic houses, which afford minimum control of temperature, are highly susceptible to root injury at temperatures below 24°F (Table 17–1). Therefore, measures must be taken to protect the roots of sensitive species from cold-temperature injury; this normally involves mulching.

The actual killing temperature will vary with the degree of plant dormancy at the time of exposure to the low-temperature stress. When plants are preconditioned for low-temperature storage and the temperature remains uniformly low prior to exposure to cold-temperature stress, the roots will generally survive provided that the temperature does not go below the average killing temperature for the species. However, if the low-temperature stress follows a period of fluctuating temperatures, especially temperatures that are conducive to growth, the roots could be injured at temperatures significantly higher than the average killing temperature. Also, the roots of newly rooted cuttings have a tendency to be less tolerant of cold-temperature stress than plants with a year or more of growth. To minimize root injury, plants should be stored at a temperature at least 3–5°F above the average killing temperature.

Best results in the storage of bare-root nursery stock are obtained if the temperature of the storage room is held fairly constant. Fluctuations of more than 3°F above or below the desired temperature are undesirable. An increase in temperature can result in decreasing storage life of the nursery stock, development of sprouts, and increased incidence of decay. A decrease in temperature by a few degrees can result in the formation of dew, and a large drop in temperature, below the critical temperature minimum, can result in freezing injury to the roots.

Large variations in storage room temperature can be avoided if the building is properly constructed, insulated, and provided with sufficient refrigeration equipment. Under these conditions, the temperature difference between the refrigerant and the ambient air of the storage room is kept relatively small (2–3°F). Temperature control is generally maintained better in large rooms than in small ones when both are filled to capacity. This is because the larger mass functions as a cold temperature "sink," moderating temperature changes.

Good-quality thermometers should be used to check temperatures of the storage room on a regular basis and to obtain data for the maintenance of continuous-temperature records. In many nursery storage rooms, thermometers are placed on a pole near a door at a height of 5½ ft as a matter of convenience. Temperatures should be taken at the floor, ceiling, and halfway levels, plus within bundles of nursery stock to determine if a uniform ambient temperature prevails throughout the room. By proper use of thermometers, it is possible to gain a high degree of temperature control, which in turn will increase the storage life and maintain the quality of the stored plants.

When placing the plant material into cold-temperature storage, it is desirable to remove the field heat of the plants and to obtain equilibrium between the product temperature and the ambient air of the storage as quickly as possible. This will reduce moisture loss, increase storage life, and maintain the quality of the product. Under most situations, plant material being placed into cold-temperature storage will be 20–40°F warmer than the air in the storage chamber. Under these conditions, the plant material loses moisture, which could result in desiccation of the plants. Plant material that is more than 10°F warmer than the storage air into which it will be placed should be precooled. This can be accomplished either by placing the plant material in a precooling room and circulating cold air (35–40°F), or by holding the material out of doors overnight (provided that the temperature does not go below the dew point or that which would injure the roots). Also, there should be a low probability of rain if the plant material is to be left out overnight. Wet plant material placed into storage increases the possibility of disease infection. Plant material harvested during periods when cold temperatures prevail can be placed directly into storage without precooling. Storage rooms should also be precooled to the desired temperature prior to loading with plant material. In some situations, particularly with common storage facilities, the storage room air can be cooled by opening the vents during cool night or evening periods and closing the vents during warm daytime periods.

Refrigeration needs for a nursery storage should be based on the storage temperature; the $R_1$ value of the insulation in the walls, ceiling, and floor of the structure; the anticipated heat leakage into the storage while it is being used during the warmest months; and the heat of respiration (HR) of the stored stock. An estimate for HR, based on information for bare-root, dormant rose bushes, is about 3000 Btu of heat by each ton of living plant material per day of storage at 32°–36°F.

A simple practice that can aid in reducing energy requirements in the operation of nursery storages is the planting of evergreen trees on the south and west sides of the structures to shield the walls from the direct rays of the sun. For small structures a hedge planting of arborvitae or a similar type of evergreen is satisfactory. For larger structures, a planting of pine or spruce trees is more appropriate.

### Humidity Control

Maintaining proper water-vapor levels within nursery storage facilities is an important factor in the successful storage of plant material. The moisture condition in the air of nursery storage rooms is generally described by relative humidity (RH). This is a ratio of the water vapor actually contained in the air to the amount that it would contain if the air were saturated at the observed temperature. Water vapor functions as a gas and exerts a pressure proportional to the amount present. For physiological purposes, the vapor pressure (VP) is expressed in millimeters of mercury (mm Hg). The moisture diffusion rate, all other factors being equal, is a function of the difference between the VP within the plant and the VP of the ambient atmosphere. This difference is known as vapor pressure deficit (VPD). The smaller the VPD, the slower the rate of moisture loss. For example, plant material in cold storage at 32°F with its intercellular spaces fully saturated has a VP of 4.5 mm Hg, whereas the storage atmosphere at a RH of 90% has a VP of 4.0 mm Hg, producing a VPD of 0.5 mm Hg (which is a small difference). With an increase in temperature to 41°F the VP of the plants (100% saturated) becomes a 6.5 mm Hg and the VP of the storage at 80% RH becomes 5.4 mm Hg, producing a VPD of 1.1 mm Hg, which is two times greater than the previous combination, resulting in a more rapid loss of moisture from the plant material.

Plants stored in plastic structures are subject to considerable variation in VP. If they are exposed to conditions that create a high VPD within the structure, they will desiccate. As previously stated, the orientation of the structure and the type of covering can seriously affect the VP conditions within the structure. When the sun's rays strike the structure in such a manner that they penetrate, they will warm the interior atmosphere, and if they strike the leaves the leaf temperature will be increased substantially. Under such conditions, a high VPD is produced, causing a rapid loss of moisture from the leaves. If the soil is frozen or if the plants are not watered, they will soon desiccate.

It is not uncommon for temperatures in clear plastic houses, oriented in an east-west direction, to reach 60–70°F, and leaf temperatures to attain levels of 100°F or more on clear, sunny days in winter when the outside air temperature may be in the low 30s (Fig. 17–4). If the inside air temperature were

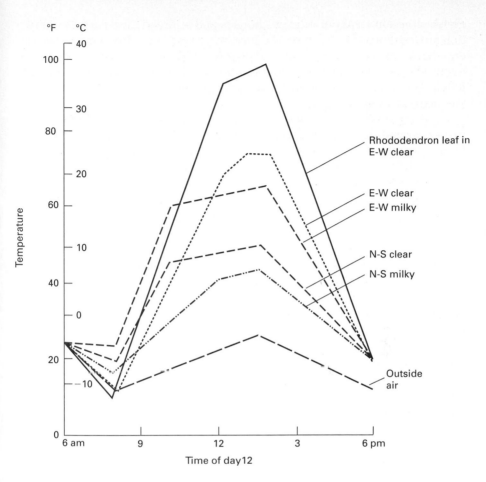

**Figure 17-4** Representative leaf and air temperatures occurring on a clear day in winter within plastic structures as affected by structure orientation and type of plastic covering. (From Davidson and Mecklenburg, 1974.)

68°F with a RH of 40% and the leaf temperature reached 104°F, the VPD would be 48.5.

|      | *Temp (°F)* | *RH* | *VP* |
| --- | --- | --- | --- |
| Leaf | 104 | 100 | 55.5 |
| Air | 68 | 40 | 7.0 |
| VPD |  |  | 48.5 |

Plants stored in clear polyethylene houses and oriented in an east-west direction are most prone to this type of injury, whereas plants stored in a house oriented in a north-south direction and covered with milky polyethylene will be exposed to a much lower VPD and generally will survive rather long periods of winter storage. The relationship between temperatures, RH, VP, and VPD is summarized in Appendix M.

Water vapor can be added to the storage atmosphere by various means. In refrigerated structures it is commonly added with the aid of humidifiers or by flooding the floor in concrete structures at periodic intervals. In common storages with dirt floors, it is maintained by placing damp shingletow* about the roots of the plants and wetting the floor periodically during the storage period. In plastic structures, it can be maintained at fairly high levels by using milky plastic as the outside cover, by spraying a latex paint onto clear plastic, by the use of shade cloth, or by adding water vapor to the enclosed atmosphere. Maintenance of a high RH in storage structures is directly related to maintaining the storage life and plant quality. Therefore, it should be checked periodically. This can be accomplished with the aid of a sling psychrometer, a hygrometer, or with electrical sensors. Instructions for use and calculation of RH are furnished with the psychrometer. The hygrometer and electrical sensors have direct readout of RH.

### Air Quality and Movement

Air quality and circulation are also important factors in maintaining the quality of plants in storage. The air must be fresh and free of pollutants that might cause problems to stored plants. The unsaturated hydrocarbons, ethylene and carbon monoxide, have been reported to adversely affect nursery plants in storage. Since fruit, particularly ripe or decaying fruit, generates ethylene, it should not be placed in the same storage with nursery plants.

Loading equipment operated within the storages should be powered either by batteries or propane, to avoid contamination of the air with carbon monoxide and ethylene. Gasoline-powered equipment should be used only in well-ventilated structures, although they can be equipped with a catalytic burner for use in closed structures. The burners are effective only on equipment that operates many hours at a time because they must be hot in order to function efficiently. They are of little value for equipment that is used for only a few minutes at a time.

Air in the storage area must circulate to maintain an even temperature throughout the structure. Good stacking and spatial arrangements within the storage are needed (Fig. 17–5). There should be air passages between the plant

---

*Fine, shred-like shavings produced as a by-product in the manufacture of cedar shingles.

**Figure 17-5** Bare-root plants in refrigerated storage. (Courtesy Bailey Nursery.)

material and the walls and ceiling, as well as between stacks, ricks, boxes, bins, or pallets. To assure even air distribution throughout the storage, a horizontal circulator fan should be installed in the ceiling of refrigerated storages and vertical circulator fans on the floor of common storage facilities. Horizontal air flow has also been found to be desirable in plastic over-wintering structures to maintain an even distribution of the heat, either natural or supplemental, throughout the structure. The slow horizontal air movement, within the structure, also minimizes potential disease problems. The air movement within the storage area should not be too rapid; a rate of approximately 50 linear feet per minute is usually sufficient.

## Sanitation

Good sanitation practices within the plant storage structure are essential to assure a high level of plant viability and quality at the time of take-out, following long periods of winter storage. These practices relate to three areas: the structure and related equipment, the plants, and the operators.

The storage structure should be thoroughly cleaned and inspected. It should be free of all forms of organic debris, with all unnecessary openings sealed, the vents should be screened to prevent the entrance of rodents, and the insulation should be inspected and repaired if necessary. All related storage equipment should also be cleaned and repaired as needed. If necessary, the interior of the structure should be painted. Finally, the structure and all related equipment should be either fumigated or sterilized, as appropriate.

Plant material going into long-term winter storage should be fully mature, dormant, and free of insects and diseases. In some situations it may be desirable to spray plants going into storage with a fungicide to minimize loss of quality due to diseases. At no time should fruit or vegetable products be stored in conjunction with valuable woody nursery products.

Finally, workers should enter the storage facility only to perform their duties associated with the operation of the facility. Their clothing, especially their footware, should be clean (free of decaying organic matter, which could be a source of infection). Workers should be instructed to keep the storage area clean and neat at all times and to report to their supervisor any signs of loss in plant quality or changes in the storage environment.

## PROBLEM AREAS

Five fairly common problems encountered in nursery storages are air pollution, desiccation, freezing, fungi, and rodents.

The *air pollutant* that has caused the most problems in nursery stock is ethylene. It is produced primarily by stored fruits, vegetables, bacteria, and fungi, but it is also produced by decaying plant material and certain woody plants, particularly arborvitae. Woody deciduous plants exposed to 1 ppm ethylene during storage may develop lesions on the stem, abscission, or death of buds and exhibit delayed bud break in the spring following planting. Broad-leaved evergreens may exhibit wilting or dropping of the leaves. Rose plants exposed to 10 ppm ethylene during storage are slow to initiate new growth following planting; flowering is delayed and total growth can be reduced. The ethylene problem can be avoided by storing only fully hardened, disease-free plants within the closed storage facility. Avoid storing fruit and plants in the same closed room. The room should also be maintained in a sanitary condition to avoid sources of ethylene production.

Ammonia gas, which can cause necrosis of foliage, is a potential problem for container plants stored in polyethylene structures. Therefore, ammonium-nitrogen fertilizers should not be used while the plants are enclosed in air-tight structures.

*Desiccation* of plants in storage can be minimized by maintaining a low temperature and a high relative humidity. Another method used to minimize the loss of moisture from dormant nursery stock, particularly rose plants, is to coat the canes with paraffin wax. The dormant tops are dipped in large baths containing paraffin wax at temperatures between 170 and 175°F. The solidified wax acts as a physical barrier, reducing both the loss of moisture and the rate of respiration. The net effect is the maintenance of quality plants that have a greater chance for survival after planting. Waxing is commonly done at the time of packaging, just prior to shipping to market. Root-wrapped plants displayed for sale are especially vulnerable to desiccation, owing to the high temperatures and relatively low humidities that commonly prevail in retail sales areas. Wax emulsions containing bentonite have been used successfully to spray wax onto dormant ornamental deciduous and evergreen trees and shrubs to protect them from desiccation. A solution should contain 13.8% solids, and the spray must be applied at temperatures above freezing, preferably above 60°F.

To reduce the loss of moisture from herbaceous plants or evergreen seedlings stored at temperatures close to or below freezing, the crates are lined with polyethylene, which functions as a vapor barrier and provides a confined atmosphere with a high RH. This method can also be used to protect small evergreens, especially broad-leaved evergreens, when stored in plastic houses. A thin sheet of plastic laid over the plants and sealed along the edges acts as an excellent vapor barrier, maintaining a high humidity about the plants. It should be used only during the midwinter storage period. The plants should be thoroughly watered prior to covering and checked periodically for dryness, fungi, and for the activities of rodents.

*Freezing of roots* is the most common form of cold-temperature injury to woody nursery stock during storage. Container-grown and B&B plants left unprotected above ground in cold climates will often sustain root injury due to freezing. Roots are much more sensitive to low-temperature injury than the crowns and should be properly protected. Plants in large containers or with large root balls may not have their roots completely killed, because of the insulation value of the soil. Plants that have suffered root injury normally appear healthy as long as they remain in a cool, humid environment. But when exposed to warmer, dryer conditions they express stress symptoms: evergreens fail to grow and soon desiccate; deciduous species may start to grow but new shoots wilt and the plant dies. Plants that sustain only partial root injury commonly display less vigor than plants without damaged roots.

In places where temperatures below 25°F (−4°C) are expected, it is necessary to protect the roots of sensitive species (Table 17–1) with a mulch such as wood chips, sawdust, or shredded expanded polystyrene. Another practice is to tip small-sized, container-grown plants on their sides, following a thorough watering, and cover the closely packed plants with a thermal blanket (e.g., microfoam). Microfoam is an excellent, lightweight, flexible insulator. Holly, boxwood, fire thorn, and other ornamental plants have been successfully overwintered under a blanket of microfoam. The micro-foam should be protected with a covering of polyethylene so that it does not become impregnated with water, which would reduce its thermal prop-erties. The blanket must be removed when ambient air temperature raises to 30°F (−1°C).

Freezing injury to the crowns of woody plants is not too common in well-operated storage facilities. Occasionally, plants stored in the vicinity of the evaporator in refrigerated storages may be frozen. Also, broad-leaved evergreens (e.g., *Rhododendron, Euonymus*, and boxwood) may be frozen while in winter storage in plastic houses. However, if the cold-temperature killing points were not reached, the plants would recover if left to thaw out gradually at temperatures slightly above freezing.

*Fungi* can be a serious problem in common and refrigerated storage if the room is not thoroughly cleaned prior to loading or if the plant material is not in a mature condition. Good sanitation must be practiced during the loading procedure and throughout the time the storage is in operation. Prior to loading the storage should be thoroughly cleaned. All sources of mold and disease infection should be removed and the walls, ceiling, floor, and storage bins disinfected. A solution of copper sulfate (1½–2 lb/100 gal water) is an effective and economical disinfectant for this purpose, although various commercial products can also be used. A good practice is to dust all plants with a fungicide just prior to ricking at the time the plants are graded, bundled, and labeled.

*Rodents* can cause considerable damage to plants in storage if proper precautions are not taken to exclude their entry or to kill or trap them if they gain entry or are accidentally enclosed within the structure. Mice cause the greatest damage by chewing the bark off plants. Rabbits and other rodents damage plants by cutting off branches and chewing the bark and foliage. The losses caused by rodents can be minimized by screening all vents and doors that must be open periodically for air exchange. Rodenticides and traps can be placed within the storage buildings. If rodenticides are used they should be put into specially marked safety containers.

Methylbromide, ¼ lb/1000 ft$^3$, is effective in killing mice that infest cold storage buildings. Carbon monoxide, 0.07% or more, for 3 hr at 32°F is also ef-fective but should only be used when no plants are in the storage. Consider-able caution must be exercised when using chemicals to avoid injury to human beings, domesticated animals, and wildlife.

## STORAGE OF CHEMICALS

Chemicals of all types, including fertilizers, insecticides, fungicides, herbicides, rodenticides, and growth regulators, should be stored with care. The materials are not only expensive and need to be protected from the elements to minimize loss and assure proper performance when used, but many of the chemicals are also poisonous.

A chemical storage facility should be (1) located away from areas frequented by people and animals; (2) constructed of fire-resistant materials and have a concrete floor; (3) maintained cool, dry, and well-ventilated; (4) posted as a pesticide storage area when used for pesticide storage; and (5) kept locked, with keys provided to a foreman.

And with the establishment of environmental regulations and the "right to know" law, it has become necessary for nurserymen in most states to obtain permits for the use and storage of hazardous chemicals, maintain up-to-date inventories of chemicals, provide protective clothing for employees who use toxic chemicals, and furnish employees with information pertaining to the proper use and handling of toxic substances. In areas where the potential for ground water contamination is high, regulation governing chemical storage may stipulate the requirement for double containment.

Where double containment is required, it can be accomplished by placing pesticide packages into plastic garbage cans or nursery containers without drainage holes for the first level of containment. The second level of containment can be attained by the construction of a retaining wall of appropriate size, within the pesticide storage that will provide a holding pit large enough in volume to contain the total contents of a major spill.

Pesticides and growth regulators should be stored in separate cabinets and appropriately labeled. Chemicals should be kept in their original containers at all times. Containers should be kept tightly closed to prevent volitilization of liquid formulations or the adsorption of moisture by certain fertilizers or wettable powders. If a leak or break is discovered in a container, the contents should be transferred to an identical container. A current inventory should be kept of all pesticides and growth regulators in the storage. Also, containers should be marked with the date of purchase, and identifying materials such as 2,4-D that require special handling can be color-coded. Consult the label for special storage conditions that may be required for a particular pesticide and for information on the proper disposal of empty containers.

## SUMMARY

Storage facilities are used by nurserymen to maintain postharvest quality of plants, for winter protection of cold-sensitive species, for the temporary storage of propagation material, to facilitate processing and marketing of nursery products, for the conditioning of plants, and for the storage of seeds, equipment, and supplies. A multiplicity of structures are used to modify the environment and gain control of temperature, humidity, air quality, and various biological organisms. By proper storage management, it is possible to maintain plant quality for extended periods of time following harvest, thus permitting extension of the market season and the radius of the market area. Proper use of storage facilities also ensures against the loss of tender plants due to desiccation or freezing injury and protects supplies and equipment from spoilage, deterioration, and theft.

## REFERENCES

ALDHOUS, J. R. 1964. Cold storage of forest nursery plants. J. For. 37:47–63.

ANONYMOUS. 1938. Does freezing injure planting stock? J. For. 36:1244–1245.

———. 1967. Is palletized storage feasible with general nursery stock? Am. Nurseryman 126(2):11.

BAILEY, V. K. 1969. Bare root storage of deciduous stock. Am. Nurseryman 130(5):15.

BRADLEY, K. 1959. Refrigerated storages. Am. Nurseryman 110(5):104.

CHADWICK, L. C., and R. HOUSTON. 1948. A preliminary report on the pre-storage defoliation of some trees and shrubs. Proc. Am. Hort. Soc. 51:659–667.

COOK, H. A. 1959. Plastic foam structure for low-cost storage. Am. Nurseryman 109(12).

CUNNINGHAM, J. L. and G. L. STABY. 1975. Ethylene and defoliation of ornamental lime plants in transit. HortScience 10(2):174.

CURTIS, O. F., JR., and D. R. RODNEY. 1952. Ethylene injury to nursery trees in cold storage. Proc. Am. Soc. Hort. Sci. 60:104–108.

DAVIDSON, H., and R. MECKLENBURG. 1974. Overwintering of evergreens in plastic structures. HortScience 9(5):479–480.

DEFFENBACHER, F. W., and E. WRIGHT. 1954. Refrigerated storage of conifer seedlings in the Pacific Northwest. J. For. 52:936–938.

DEWEY, D. H. 1982. Techniques for cold storage of plants, Voice MAN, November–December.

DILLEY, D. R. 1972. Hypobaric storage—a new concept for preservation of perishables. Ann. Rep. Mich. State Hort. Soc. 102:82–89.

DUFRESNE, P. 1970. General information on cold storage of nursery plants in jacket-cooled stores. Proc. Int. Plant Propag. Soc. 20:352.

DUNN, N. P. 1983. Mechanical lifting and cold storage of fruit trees and rootstocks. Proc. Int. Plant Propag. Soc. 33:282–285.

FLEMER, W., III. 1970. Cold storage in the nursery. Am. Nurseryman 131(9):7.

FLINT, H. L., and J. J. McGUIRE. 1962. Response of rooted cuttings of several woody ornamental species to overwinter storage. Proc. Am. Soc. Hort. Sci. 80:625.

FULLER, C. W. 1986. Horizontal air flow in winter storage houses. Proc. Inter. Plant Prop. Soc. 36:515–518.

GOUIN, F. R. 1973. Winter protection of container plants. Proc. Int. Plant Propag. Soc. 23:255.

HALL, C. W. 1965. Problems of humidity and moisture in agriculture. Humidity Moisture 2:87–94.

HARTMAN, H. T., and C. J. HANSEN. 1957. Effect of season of collecting, indolebutynic acid and pre-planting storage treatment on rooting of Marianna plum, peach and quince hardwood cuttings. Proc. Am. Hort. Soc. 71:57–66.

HAVIS, J. R. 1976. Root hardiness of woody ornamentals. HortScience 11(4):385–386.

HUNT, G. M. 1984. Microfoam use for winter protection—your fifth option. Proc. Int. Plant Propag. Soc. 34:418–421.

KRAHN, R., and DARBY. 1971. The "Filacell" system for refrigerated vegetable storage. Proc. Can. Soc. Hort. Sci. 10:24 (summary).

LARSEN, F. E. 1967. Five years results with pre-storage chemical defoliation of deciduous nursery stock. Proc. Int. Plant Propag. Soc. 17:157.

———. 1969. Pre-storage promotion of leaf abscission of deciduous nursery stock with bromodine. J. Am. Soc. Hort. Sci. 95:231.

———. 1969. Promotion of leaf abscission of deciduous tree fruit nursery stock with abscisic acid. HortScience 4(3):216–218.

———. 1971. Pre-storage promotion of leaf abscission of deciduous tree fruit nursery stock with bromodine-ethephon mixtures. HortScience 6(2):135–137.

———. 1973. Stimulation of leaf abscission of tree fruit nursery stock with ethephon-surfactant mixtures. J. Am. Soc. Hort. Sci. 98(1):34–36.

———. 1975. Chemical nursery stock defoliant needer. Am. Nurseryman 142(7):12.

LENTZ, C. P., and E. A. ROOKE. 1957. Use of the jacketed room system for cool storage. Food Technical 11(5):257–279.

———, L. VAN DEN BERGE, E. G. JORGENSEN, and R. SAWLER. 1971. The design and operation of a jacketed vegetable storage. Can. Inst. Food Technical J. 4(1):19–23.

LUMIS, G. P., and E. W. FRANKLIN. 1973. Winter studies show effective use. Am. Nurseryman 137(9):40–43.

LUTZ, J. M., and R. E. HARDENBURG. 1968. Commercial storage of fruits, vegetables and florist and nursery stocks. USDA Agric. Handb. 66.

McGUIRE, H. L., H. FLINT, and E. P. CHRISTOPHER. 1962. Cold storage of Christmas trees. Univ. R.I. Agric. Exp. Sta. Bull. 362.

MILLER, E. J., J. A. NEILSON, and S. L. BANDEMER. 1937. Wax emulsion for spraying nursery stock and other plant materials. Mich. Agric. Exp. Sta. Spec. Bull. 282.

NEILSON, J. A. 1930. Recent information on paraffining nursery stock. Natl. Nurseryman 38(47):5–12.

NYLAND, R. D. 1974. Fall lifting for overwinter cold storage of conifers. Appl. For. Res. Inst. State Univ. N.Y. Coll. Environ. Sci. For. Res. Rep. 22.

PELLETT, N. E., DIPPRE, and A. HAZELRIGG. 1985. Covering for overwintering container-grown plants in northern regions. J. Environ. Hort. 3(1):4–7

PETHERAM, H. D., and H. G. PORTERFIELD. 1941. Cold storage for deciduous planting stock. J. For. 39:336–338.

PRIDHAM, A. M. S. 1952. Preliminary report on defoliation of nursery stock by chemical means. Proc. Am. Soc. Hort. Sci. 59:475–478.

PRYOR, R. L., and R. N. STEWART. 1963. Storage of unrooted softwoody azalea cuttings. Proc. Am. Soc. Hort. Sci. 82:483.

SCHNIEDER, E. F. 1965. Survival of rooted cuttings of three woody plant species after low temperature storage. Proc. Am. Soc. Hort. Sci. 87:557.

SNYDER, W. E., and C. E. HESS. 1956. Low temperature storage of rooted cuttings of nursery crops. Proc. Am. Soc. Hort. Sci. 67:545–548.

TICKNOR, R. L. 1968. Defoliating roses with chemicals. Pacific Coast Nurseryman 17(11):21–22.

TOY, S. J., and J. P. MAHLSTEDE. 1960. Prolonging dormancy of nursery stock by increasing the concentration of carbon dioxide in the storage atmosphere. Proc. Am. Soc. Hort. Sci. 74:774–784.

——— , J. P. MAHLSTEDE, and F. G. SMITH. 1961. Some effects of coating the canes of dormant rose plants with melted paraffin wax. Proc. Am. Soc. Hort. Sci. 77:583.

UOTA, M., J. M. HARVEY, and R. W. LATEER. 1959. Commercial packaging and storing of bare root rose bushes. USDA Marketing Res. Rep. 308.

VANDERBROOK, C. 1956. The storage of rooted cuttings. Am. Nurseryman 103(9):10.

VERKADE, S. D., and G. E. FITZPATRICK. 1988. Cost-efficient methods for nursery compliance with environmental regulations for hazardous material storage. Proc. Inter. Plant Prop. Soc. 38:606–608.

WELLER, H. A. 1958. Propagation—dollars and sense. Proc. Int. Plant Propag. Soc. 8:54–58.

WORTHINGTON, T., and D. H. SCOTT. 1957. Strawberry plant storage using polyethylene liners. Am. Nurseryman 105(9):13.

ZELENKA, J. 1967. Overwintering evergreens under poly in northern climates. Proc. Int. Plant Propag. Soc. 17:351.

## SUGGESTED READING

BEATTIE, D. J. 1986. Principles, practices, and comparative costs of overwintering container-grown landscape plants. Southern Cooperative Series Bulletin 313.

BORLAND, J. 1988. Maping Flaws, (average low killing temperatures for plant parts). Am. Nurseryman 168(8):46–56.

DE HERTOGH, A., W CARLSON, L. AUNG, and A. F. G. SLOATWEG. Bulb forcers handbook. Netherlands Flower Bulb Institute, Inc., New York.

GAFFNEY, J. J. 1978. Humidity: basic principles and measurement techniques. HortScience 13(5):551–555.

GRIERSON, W., and W. F. WARDOWSKI. 1975. Humidity in horticulture. HortScience 10(4):356–360.

HEIDEN, R., and A. CAMERON. 1986. Handling bare-root perennials for optimum regrowth quality. Am. Nurseryman 163(7):75–88.

HOCKING, D., and R. D. NYLAND. 1971. Cold storage of coniferous seedlings, a review. App. For. Res. Inst., N.Y. State Univ. Coll. For. Syracuse Univ. AFRI Res. Rep. 6.

MAHLSTEDE, J. P., and W. E. FLETCHER. 1960. Storage of nursery stock. American Association of Nurserymen, Washington, D.C.

SMITH, E. M., ed. 1977. Proceedings of the Woody Ornamentals Winter Storage Symposium Coop. Ext. Serv. Ohio State Univ.

WRIGHT, R. D. 1985. Acclimation and winter protection of container-grown nursery crops. Proc. Inter. Plant Prop. Soc. 35:744–749.

# Chapter 18
# The Production and Use of Compost

The practice of composting is an accelerated version of the natural biological decomposition of organic matter occurring on the forest floor or wherever plant and animal debris accumulate and are kept aerated, moist, and reasonably warm. During composting, plant and animal waste products are reduced in volume by 40–75% and their physical and chemical structure as well as their aroma and color are lost creating a humus material. The organic humus-like material produced by the composting process is commonly called *compost*.

Composting is an ancient agricultural practice dating back to biblical times. The use of manures and other decomposing wastes to improve the productivity of both nursery field soils and potting mixes is a very old and well-documented practice with historic origins in both European and Asian nurseries. The use of manures and other organic wastes by nurseries, and most of agriculture in this country, continued until urbanization and the mechanization of agriculture reduced the ready supply of these materials for most nurseries. The plant nutrients provided by compost were replaced by the wide spread use of commercial fertilizers composed of more concentrated mineral sources of plant nutrients.

Composting urban wastes was essentially an historic art until Sir Albert Howard, a British agronomist in India, developed the *Indore Process* in 1931, named after the India state where it was developed. The Indore Process utilized a 5–6 ft high layered pile of leaves, night soil, wood ashes, animal manure, straw, and garbage and demonstrated that composting was a beneficial alternative for the disposal of organic wastes. The first windrow method for sewage-sludge composting, in the United States, was developed by the Los Angeles County Sanitation District in 1972 and the United States Department of Agriculture Research Station at Beltsville, Maryland in 1973.

A national concern for maintaining the quality of our environment has generated renewed interest in managing the composting process as an environmentally clean and inexpensive method for disposing of organic wastes. The first legal requirement for the composting of landscape wastes was established in September 1988 when the State of New Jersey banned leaves from all land-fill facilities. This action was quickly followed in the next three years by 10 other states. The decomposition of landscape wastes which make up 25–35% of urban waste, is a major factor in the settling of the land-fill after it is capped. The number of land-fill facilities in the United States dropped 28% from 1988 to 1991 making it essential that we conserve what land-fill space we have. By 1991 there were more than 2000 facilities in the United States composting yard waste and approximately one-third of them included grass clippings in their landscape waste composting operation. The procedures needed (particularly the requirements for proper curing) for the production of a consistent, high-quality horticultural compost are currently being defined.

Many nurserymen are becoming interested in the use of compost in both the container and field production of nursery stock for one or more of five reasons: (1) most composts have the physical characteristics of peat moss and can be an economical substitution for peat moss in container mixes; (2) most composts have a modest plant nutrient content, including minor elements; (3) properly cured compost has a beneficial microbial population which can be useful in the suppression of plant-root diseases; (4) it may be more economical to produce compost from plant debris generated by the nursery than to haul it to a land fill and pay a tipping fee for burial, and (5) the production and use of compost can enhance the public image of the nursery industry by converting waste products into very useful soil amendments.

A number of production nurseries have developed a composting facility to dispose of their own plant debris and to create compost from wastes generated by others for a tipping fee. Commercial composting of organic wastes can be an economical disposal system, but it has rarely been profitable without imposing a tipping fee paid by those generating the waste material. Facilities may also earn additional revenue by blending the cured compost with sand, bark, and other amendments, producing a variety of potting mixes and special soil mixes. The market potential for potting and soil mixes containing compost is very large. Approximately 12 million cubic yards of prepared organic soils and potting mixes were sold in the United States in 1991. A nurseryman considering the production of substantial quantities of compost from waste products brought to the site for a tipping fee should be aware that this type of activity may be considered a commercial operation which may lead to zoning problems.

## PLANNING A COMPOSTING FACILITY

A number of local governmental boards and committees as well as state agencies regulate the development and operation of composting facilities, particularly when nonagricultural off-site wastes are to be composted. The USDA Soil Conservation Service (SCS) can assist in the development of a site plan by providing drainage control and soil type information. The USDA Agricultural Stabilization and Conservation Service (ASCS) may be able to provide cost sharing support for the site modifications needed for the composting facility.

Compost site selection decisions should reflect the concerns of the public and involve local public officials. Frequently the successful development of a composting facility will require public educational programs on the advantages of composting for the entire local community. A number of environmental groups and the Cooperative Extension Service are currently involved in a variety of programs which can assist in gaining public and governmental approval for a local composting facility.

A number of issues must be considered in the development of a composting site plan: (1) the total composting, curing, and storage area required, (2) buffer zones, (3) environmental concerns, (4) soil drainage and surface runoff, (5) suitability of soil for the operation of equipment, and (6) availability of water, electricity, and fire protection.

Plans for the total area needed for composting, curing, and storage of compost should anticipate the additional time required at each stage in the composting process caused by excessive rain, seasonal fluctuations in the demand for finished product and the growth in availability of materials suitable for composting.

The need for adequate buffering zones for the composting site and the need for effective public education on the benefits of composting are frequently related and may be aggravated by poor site planning, problems with dust and noise generated by equipment, and inadequate odor control during the start up period. Table 18–1 indicates the buffering distances commonly recommended for composting facilities.

Composting systems vary in the need for expensive specialized equipment and also, therefore, in the volume of compost production required to justify the initial investment. Many landscape waste composting operations began with the least expensive composting system using equipment already available at the nursery. As the volume of composting grew, more expensive equipment was purchased and larger, more efficient composting systems were

**Table 18–1** Minimum Buffering Distances for Composting Facilities

| Sensitive area | Minimum Distance |
|---|---|
| Property line | 50–100 ft |
| Residence or place of business | 200–500 ft |
| Private well (potable water source) | 100–200 ft |
| Wetland or surface water | 100–200 ft |
| Subsurface drainage pipe or ditch Discharging to a natural water course | 25 ft |
| Water table (seasonal high) | 2–5 ft |
| Bedrock | 2–5 ft |

*Source:* On-Farm Composting Handbook

developed. Table 18–2 ranks composting systems based on increasing capital investment and, to some degree, the increasing volume of compost produced.

The decisions to develop a composting facility as well as planning the site involves a number of complex economic considerations. The specific composting area requirements, the unique nature of the site, the waste materials involved, and potential tipping fees and sales potential or value of the finished product must be part of the planning process. These considerations are beyond the scope of this chapter and are well documented in the *On-Farm Composting Handbook*—an essential reference for those planning a composting operation and facility.

## THE COMPOSTING OF LANDSCAPE WASTES

The generation of landscape wastes varies with the nature of plants in the landscape. Grass clippings and leaves can be composed without grinding. Landscape waste such as brush, logs, stumps, palm fronds, and potted plants are ground in a tub grinder, hammer mill, or shear grinder. The knives in brush chippers used by tree trimming companies are rapidly dulled when chipping dry wood and cannot be used to chip landscape waste. Tub grinders, hammer mills, and shear grinders reduce everything to splinters 2–4 in. long and 1/2 to 1 in. wide. Grinder hammers will be rapidly worn by landscape waste that has large quantities of abrasive sandy soil. Many landscape waste composting

**Table 18–2** Comparative Costs of Composting Systems

| Composting system |
|---|
| 1. The passive pile composting system |
| 2. The windrow composting system using a loader to turn and aerate the pile |
| 3. The windrow composting system using a specialized windrow turner |
| 4. The aerated static pile system |
| 5. The in-vessel composting systems |

*Source:* On-Farm Composting Handbook

facilities therefore load the grinder with a grapple hook or forked front end loader to remove as much of the soil as possible.

Biodegradable paper bags should be substituted for plastic trash bags for the collection of landscape wastes, because plastic bags will not decompose during the composting process and will be difficult to remove. Plastic bags filled with fresh grass clippings will also become anaerobic, producing very offensive odors within a day or two. Once a week, pick up of grass clippings in plastic bags will guarantee odor problems the moment the bags are opened at the composting site. More frequent pick up and the use of bags which allow air to penetrate into the bag will eliminate this problem.

Grinders can be purchased or a portable grinder can be contracted to periodically grind landscape wastes. Magnets attached to the grinder discharge conveyor remove metal, and water can be added at the discharge conveyer to reduce dust and to assist in getting the composting process started. Wood painted with paint that contains lead or has been treated with preservatives must be removed because it will introduce hazardous chemicals into the compost. Glass must also be removed.

Ground up landscape waste, including woody material, leaves, grass clippings, and the like are formed into elongated piles called windrows which are mixed or turned at least 4 times per year and possibly daily if the rate of decomposition warrants. Mixing also accelerates the composting process by blending and breaking up the composting materials. During the initial high temperature phase of composting, the windrows shrink in volume and are then combined to create larger curing windrows. The time required to complete the composting process depends primarily on the nature of the landscape waste and to a lesser degree on the size of the windrows, the frequency of turning, the moisture content and the local climate.

## FACTORS AFFECTING THE RATE OF COMPOSTING LANDSCAPE WASTES

***Microorganisms.*** Composting is carried out by a very diverse and highly interdependent population of microbes consisting primarily of bacteria, actinomycetes, and fungi. No single species of microbe dominates the composting process because the raw materials and conditions are constantly changing and are not uniform throughout the pile. Bacteria play a major role in the initial high temperature (160°F) phase of composting and may be responsible for the production of the organic chemicals during this phase which retard plant growth. During the second or curing phase when the pH, moisture content, and temperature of the compost drops, bacteria are followed by actinomycetes and fungi which break down the growth retarding chemicals. However, anaerobic conditions during the second phase of composting can result in the production of growth retarding chemicals. Bacteria are responsible for the initial breakdown of the easily decomposed organic materials followed by actinomycetes and fungi which are active in decomposing cellulose and other materials slower to break down.

There is little evidence for a substantial benefit from inoculating most common landscape waste materials with a specific composting microbial population before composting begins. Rapid composting however, may begin earlier with the addition of a small portion of rapidly decomposing compost. Composting waste materials which have been sterilized in their production, such as food processing wastes, benefit from inoculation with active compost. The succession of microbes as the waste materials are degraded creates a succession of population peaks. This complex and highly interrelated succession of microorganisms is controlled by temperature, moisture, aeration, and the availability of a specific substrate produced by the previous microbial population. It would be very difficult to manipulate this population by inoculation.

***Oxygen.*** Oxygen is essential to insure the development and growth of aerobic organisms which minimize the production of highly offensive odors. The oxygen concentration within the compost pile should be maintained at 5% or higher throughout the composting process and can be determined with a portable battery-powered oxygen meter. A ½ in. diameter tube is inserted into the compost pile and a sample of gas is removed from the pile and analyzed for oxygen. The aeration of rapidly composting piles can be achieved with fans which pull or push air through the pile or by mixing the pile with either a front end loader or with specially designed compost mixing equipment. A rise in the internal temperature of the compost pile above 140–150°F is frequently used to indicate when additional aeration is needed. On the other hand, excessive aeration on the other hand will reduce both temperature and moisture content, slowing the rate of composting. The lack of oxygen (anaerobic conditions), will result in the growth of anaerobic microbes which produce putrefactive odors and growth retarding chemicals. The cure for inadequate aeration is of course increased aeration which, unfortunately, will initially release great quantities of offensive odors. Proper aeration and the elimination of offensive odors are the prime concerns of compost facility managers, particularly those located in urban areas. Offensive odors have created a public outcry, shutting down multi-million dollar composting facilities.

***The Carbon:Nitrogen (C:N) Ratio.*** The C:N ratio of the materials to be composted will determine the potential maximum rate of decomposition. Composting will occur at C:N ratios of 20:1 to 60:1. A C:N ratio of 30:1 will result in the most rapid composting because microbes consume approximately 30 units of carbon for each unit of nitrogen consumed. Materials with very high C:N ratios (e.g., most bark and woody landscape debris) will decompose very slowly over many months requiring little, if any, attention to maintaining proper aeration. Waste products with C:N ratios lower than 30:1 (e.g., most manures and fresh grass clippings) will compost very rapidly requiring almost constant aeration to avoid the production of offensive odors. The carbon in

these waste products will be consumed before all of the nitrogen has been stabilized and the result is the loss of ammonia and the production of offensive
odors. Compost facility managers must determine the C:N ratio of each type
of organic waste they receive and use this information to develop a blend
(recipe) which will have the appropriate C:N ratio of 30:1 needed by microbes
(Table 18–3). The C:N ratio will help to predict the rate of composting and
therefore the relative need for aeration and the length of time needed to complete the composting process.

A recipe of waste products, producing a 30:1 C:N ratio, can be determined for organic wastes with C:N ratios above and below the ideal 30:1. The
calculations for the appropriate mixing recipe use the mathematical equation
for simultaneously solving 2 or more unknowns.

For example, two waste products are available. One, (WPA) with a carbon content of 14.5%, a moisture content of 25%, and a nitrogen content of
2.06%, and another waste product (WPB), with a carbon content of 20%, a
moisture content of 19% and a nitrogen content of 0.07%. The waste product
carbon and nitrogen contents must be based on (or converted to) a wet basis
(the state it will be in when you measure and mix it).

For the two recipe formulas I and II below;

$a$ = The weight of waste product A (WPA) needed

$b$ = The weight of waste product B (WPB) needed

$C\%$ = the carbon percentage in the waste products

$N\%$ = the nitrogen percentage in either waste products

$M\%$ = the moisture content of the waste products

Formula I: $a \times (C\% \text{ of WPA}) + b \times (C\% \text{ of WPB}) = C = 30$
Formula II: $a \times (N\% \text{ of WPA}) + b \times (N\% \text{ of WPB}) = N = 1$
Putting the percentages of nitrogen and carbon in the above example;

$$a \times (14.5\%) + b \times (20\%) = 30$$
$$a \times (2.06\%) + b \times (0.07\%) = 1$$

The standard procedure for solving $b$ is to divide each equation by its coefficient for $a$, eliminate $a$ by subtracting equation II from I, then solving for $b$,
then by substitution solve for $a$. The most convenient form of expression however, is a "determinant" constructed for each of two waste products and to
solve for $b$ as seen below:

$$b = \frac{(\text{WPAC\%}) \times N - (\text{WPAN\%}) \times (C)}{(\text{WPAC\%}) \times (\text{WPBN\%}) - (\text{WPBC\%}) \times (\text{WPAN\%})}$$

$$b = \frac{(14.5) \times (1) - (2.06) \times (30)}{(14.5) \times (0.07) - (20) \times (2.06)} = 1.18$$

**Table 18–3** Characteristics of common-waste products

| Waste product | Nitrogen % | C:N Ratio | Moisture % | Bulk Density |
|---|---|---|---|---|
| Cow manure | 1.7% | 18:1 | 67–87% | 1,215–1,674 lb |
| Laying hen manure | 6.3% | 15:1 | 62–75% | 1,377–1,620 lb |
| Broiler manure | 1.6–3.9% | 12–15:1 | 22–46% | 756–1,026 lb |
| Sheep manure | 1.3–3.9% | 13–20:1 | 60–75% | — |
| Pig manure | 3.8% | 9–19:1 | 65–91% | — |
| Horse manure | 2.3% | 22–50:1 | 59–79% | 1,215–1,620 lb |
| Turkey litter | 2.6% | 16:1 | 26% | 783 lb |
| Sewage sludge; | | | | |
| activated | 5.6% | 6:1 | — | — |
| digested | 1.9% | 16:1 | — | — |
| Blood | 10–14% | 3:1 | 10–78% | — |
| Animal tankage | — | 4.1:1 | — | — |
| Crab lobster waste | 4.6–8.2% | 4–5.4:1 | 35–61% | 240 lb |
| Mussel waste | 37% | 2.2:1 | 63% | — |
| Fish waste | 6.5–27% | 2.6–5:1 | 50–81% | — |
| Grass clippings | 2–6% | 9–25:1 | 82% | 3–800 lb |
| Leaves | 0.5–1.3% | 40–80:1 | — | — |
| Loose, dry | | | | 1–300 lb |
| Compacted, wet | | | | 4–500 lb |
| Shrub trimmings | 1.0% | 53:1 | 15% | 429 lb |
| Tree trimmings | 3.1% | 16:1 | 70% | 1,296 lb |
| Wood chips, | | | | |
| Hardwood | 0.006–0.11% | 451–819:1 | — | — |
| Softwood | 0.04–0.23% | 212–1313:1 | — | — |
| Lumbermill waste | 0.13% | 170:1 | — | — |
| Sawdust | 0.6–0.8% | 200–700:1 | 19–65% | 350–450 lb |
| Bark; | | | | |
| Hardwood | 0.10–0.41% | 116–436:1 | — | — |
| Softwood | 0.04–0.39% | 131–1,285:1 | — | — |
| Sea weed | 1.2–3.0% | 5–27:1 | — | — |
| Water hyacinth | — | 20–30:1 | 93% | 405 lb |
| Veg. wastes | 2.5–4% | 11–12:1 | — | — |
| Potato culls | — | 18:1 | 78% | 1,540 lb |
| Food waste-garbage | 1.9–2.9% | 14–16:1 | 69% | — |
| Fruit wastes | 0.9–2.6% | 20–49:1 | 62–88% | — |
| Tomato waste | 4.5% | 11:1 | 62% | — |
| Apple pomice | 1.1% | 48:1 | 88% | 1,559 lb |
| Corn cobs | 0.4–0.8% | 56–123:1 | 9–18% | — |
| Corn silage | 1.2–1.4% | 38–43:1 | 65–68% | — |
| Hay; | | | | |
| Legume | 1.8–3.6% | 15–19:1 | — | — |
| Non legume | 0.7–2.5% | 32:1 | — | — |
| Straw, wheat | 0.3–0.5% | 100–150:1 | — | — |
| Straw, oats | 1.1% | 48–98:1 | — | — |

*Source: The Art and Science of Composting 1991, Composting Fish By-Products: A Feasibility Study, 1988, and On-Farm Composting Handbook, Edited by Robert Rynk 1992 Northeast Regional Agricultural Engineering Service. Ithaca, N.Y.*

Substituting the value for $b$ in the original equation I:

$$\text{Equation I: } 14.5a + (20) \times (1.18) = 30$$
$$\text{Solving } 14.5a + 23.6 = 30$$
$$a = 30 - 23.6/14.5$$
$$= 0.44$$

the recipe, is therefore; 1.18 parts of waste product B to 0.44 parts of waste product A, or:

1.18 parts of WPA/0.44 parts of WPB

(or 2.68 parts of WPA to 1 part of WPB)

Similar calculations can be used to determine the moisture content of the final recipe. If the moisture content is below 50%, water can be added. If the final moisture content of the recipe is above 60% (lower if the waste products are not highly porous) then a drier or more porous waste product must be mixed in to bring the moisture content down. Now that the recipe has been established for the C:N ratio, the moisture content of the compost mix can be determined.

Moisture content = (1.18 lb of WPA × 25% moisture) + (0.44 lb of WPB × 19% moisture)/(1.18 lb + 0.44 lb) or 0.295 + 0.0836/1.62 = 23% which is too low for rapid composting and the moisture content should be increased by 25%; 25 lb (or 3 gal), of water per 100 lb of compost mix.

Recipes for combinations of three or more waste products can be calculated in groups of 2 waste products using the above formula and then combining them. Another solution is to solve 3 or more combinations of waste products in the above formula using trial and error, trying weights until the appropriate C:N ratio is achieved. A computer spread sheet can also be developed if calculations for three or more waste products are carried out frequently.

Seasonal variations in the availability of specific landscape or yard waste materials such as grass clippings (C:N ratio of 20:1) during the summer, and leaves and branches (C:N ratio of 60:1) in the fall make it difficult to create an appropriate C:N ratio throughout the year. One solution is to store surplus high C:N ratio materials until they are needed to blend with low C:N materials. Since high C:N materials compost very slowly, they can be stored with little risk of producing offensive odors and toxic fermentation products so long as they are well aerated. However, internal temperatures of large storage piles should be checked periodically to prevent the build up of very high temperatures which could result in spontaneous combustion. High C:N wastes should be stored where water may readily drain off and in windrows that are no more than 6 ft high and 12 ft wide. It would also help to keep the moisture content below 40%. If you suspect that the high C:N ratio waste material may have developed toxic substances during storage you should check its pH. If the pH is in the 1.8 to 2.5 range it should not be used.

Another solution is to use other local sources of organic wastes such as sawdust, wood shavings, or ground up waste paper with the appropriate C:N ratio to achieve a 30:1 C:N ratio in the final blend. Low C:N waste products such as animal manures, restaurant food scraps, and some food processing wastes are potential candidates to blend with high C:N landscape wastes. Grape pomace, a waste product from wine production, fish residues from fish processing plants, and cranberry pulp from juice plants have, for example, produced high-quality composts when appropriately blended with other materials.

Low C:N ratio wastes such as grass clippings can be blended into partially cured compost. Since grass clippings will decompose very rapidly, leaving little woody residue, they will not slow the curing process appreciably. They will have minimal impact on the need for greater aeration when mixed and diluted with large quantities of curing compost.

As the rate of decomposition slows and actinomycetes and fungi predominate, the compost pile will have temperatures approaching air temperatures. At this point the compost will have a C:N ratio ranging from 15:1 to 20:1. Mature or cured compost will continue to slowly decompose generating carbon dioxide until all that is left is water, carbon dioxide, and salt.

***Moisture.*** Moisture is essential for microbial growth and an efficient rate of decomposition. The ideal moisture content is a compromise between the need for sufficient moisture and the need for adequate aeration. Moisture contents below 40% (as a percentage of total weight) will substantially reduce the rate of decomposition. A moisture content substantially above 60% will restrict aeration which will result in both offensive odors and a reduced rate of decomposition. Highly porous waste products will compost best at moisture contents approaching 60% whereas waste products with fine particle and pore sizes must be maintained at moisture levels approaching 40%.

Frequent irrigation may be essential during high-temperature composting particularly during periods of limited rainfall. The high temperatures produced by microbes during the initial stages of composting, plus the substantial air movement needed to insure proper aeration, will rapidly drive off moisture.

***Temperature.*** Increasing composting temperatures will accelerate the rate of the composting process until temperatures of 150 to 160°F are obtained. Temperatures well above 150°F, fairly common in sewage sludge compost piles, will stop the composting process because most microbes are either killed or are dormant at very high temperatures. When temperatures have exceeded 150°F, increased aeration is needed to cool the compost. Rarely will cold weather stop the composting process during the initial stages of rapid composting. Even during very cold winter conditions, so long as all other growth factors are adequate, composting will proceed rapidly in the interior of the windrow because microbes generate substantial heat as they decompose organic waste and large piles tend to conserve heat. The most practical method for increasing the temperature of a compost pile is to make it wider and higher. Conversely, temperatures in the pile can be lowered by making the stack smaller, allowing the heat to easily dissipate.

High temperatures (140–150°F) during the composting process play a very important role in the pasteurization of all types of compost, by killing weed seed (145°F) and potential plant and animal disease organisms (131°F). Most composting regulations require that sewage sludge compost obtain a temperature of 131°F (or above) for 6–10 consecutive days if in a mechanical composter or aerated static pile. Fifteen consecutive days are required if composting in a windrow with at least five turnings of the windrow during the 15 days. The time requirement is imposed to insure that all of the compost is exposed to sufficiently high temperatures to insure removal of dangerous organisms. The pasteurization temperatures achieved during composting are similar to those used in the horticultural pasteurization of potting mixes. In the case of composting however, you do not have to burn fuel to heat the compost, the microorganisms provide the energy free of charge.

*pH.* The initial pH of most fresh organic wastes (pH of 5.5–9) appears to have little impact upon the array of microorganisms involved in the composting process. Usually the pH begins to drop to as low as 4.5–5.0 at the beginning of the composting process due to the production of organic acids. As the organic acids are consumed by other organisms the pH will usually approach neutrality.

Waste products with a high sugar content, such as fruit processing wastes, will produce large quantities of organic acids and may require liming to promote efficient composting. Adding lime to control pH should be avoided whenever possible since it will promote the production of ammonia and the loss of nitrogen from the compost. Gypsum (calcium sulfate) which has little effect on pH, has been reported to reduce odor production and help retain nitrogen during the composting process. This is particularly useful in composting high-nitrogen manures.

A more detailed discussion of various composting methods, management, site and environmental considerations, and production cost is available in the *On-Farm Composting Handbook*, 1992, edited by Robert Rynk.

## COMPOSTING SEWAGE SLUDGE

Most nurseries have not developed facilities for composting sewage sludge because of the regulations and permits needed, but may consider using large quantities of composted sewage sludge in both field and container production of nursery stock. State and federal regulations do not insure the production of a high-quality horticultural compost. It is important therefore that the user of compost be familiar with the production process in order to ensure getting the quality of compost needed for a specific horticultural application.

Sewage sludge composting facilities must meet more stringent facility design and operation regulations than landscape waste composting facilities. These regulations are enforced by federal, local, and/or state agencies. Regular reports must also be submitted documenting the quantity of sludge received and compost shipped, as well as the temperatures achieved during composting and an analysis of both endaphic (intestinal) disease organisms and heavy metals in the cured compost. These regulations are designed so that there will be no health hazard if the compost is applied to soils used for the production of food crops.

### How Sewage Sludge Is Processed

The basic process for composting sewage sludge begins with partially drying (belt pressing) the sludge, followed by the addition of sufficient saw dust and wood chips to produce a 30:1 C:N ratio. Large (2–3 in.) wood chips are added to increase pore space which is essential for adequate air movement and aerobic conditions during the composting process. Wood chips are mixed with the sewage sludge in ratios ranging from 4:1 to 1:1 on a loose volume basis depending on the type of composting facility being used. Composting facilities, ranging from simple aerated static piles to very mechanized silos, tubes, and tunnels are being used to compost sewage sludge. Different types of composting facilities and differences in operating procedures within the same facility will produce compost with different characteristics.

After the initial period of high temperature composting, (usually 30 days), the compost is dried to a moisture content of 45% or lower and the wood chips removed by screening. The wood chips may be sold as a dark colored mulch or mixed with fresh sludge and recycled through another high-temperature composting cycle. Large 2–3 in. wood chips may be recycled five or six times through the initial composting stage before they are consumed by microbes. Fine mesh screens (¼ in.) in either a rotary (trummel) or vibrating screener will remove more wood than either ½ or ⅝ in. screens and will reduce the subsequent curing time. Rotary or trummel screens will function with wetter compost than vibrating screens. Screened compost is then transferred to a curing pad so that it will not be contaminated with unpasteurized sewage sludge. Uncured compost is of limited horticultural value because it will frequently contain plant growth inhibiting substances.

Proper curing of sewage-sludge compost requires adequate moisture, aeration, and time. Depending on the effectiveness of the primary composting process, curing will usually require 2–9 months to produce a stable, cool, odor free, dry (20–30% moisture) compost.

## USE OF COMPOST IN THE NURSERY INDUSTRY

A review of the horticultural use of both landscape waste and sewage sludge compost is made particularly challenging by the variability in composts. Managing a compost facility with respect to quality can be viewed from two perspectives: (1) will the quality of the compost produced dictate its horticultural use, or (2) will the intended horticultural use dictate the management of the composting process? Many commercial compost facilities are managed as if they were a disposal facility rather than a production facility. The primary concern for these managers is to meet the state regulations for the sale of compost rather than to produce a specific more valuable high-quality horticultural compost. Composting regulations are aimed at protecting public safety and limiting potential environmental hazards rather than producing quality compost. Communication between the compost plant operator and those utilizing compost is crucial to ensure obtaining a consistently high-quality product. Adjusting cultural practices to compensate for a variable, low-quality compost reduces the value of the compost and prevents its use in many nursery applications.

The value of any type of compost for horticultural applications is primarily based on: (1) the availability of a consistent product, (2) freedom from offensive odors or hazardous chemicals, (3) freedom from materials that will prevent or retard plant growth, (4) stability and an active population of beneficial microorganisms, (5) a pH of 6–7 and particle size of less than ½ in., and (6) an acceptable level of soluble salts. Compost with growth inhibiting characteristics is limited to general field application for the addition of organic matter and the field must remain idle for some time before it can be used to produce a nursery crop. It is important that nurserymen be aware of the proper conditions needed to produce a high-quality compost whether they produce compost themselves or purchase compost produced by others.

Compost from the same facility may vary in nitrogen content from 1.23–2.42% and in pH from 5.6–8.11 depending on the composting and curing conditions. An analysis of 35 commercial sources of compost/fertilizers found a mean nitrogen content of 5.08% but a range of 0.09–11.53%. The mean pH was 6.12 but the range was from 3.9–8.0. The same wide range of content was found for phosphorous, potassium, and total salinity. Most states do not require compost producers to provide either nutritional, salinity, pH, or heavy metal content on the compost label. This information is essential for the efficient use of compost in the production of landscape plants.

## PUBLIC CONCERNS IN THE USE OF COMPOST

The most frequent public concerns in the use of compost focus on the potential presence of both human and plant pathogens in the compost. Completely pathogen free compost could be assured by sterilization at 212°F. This would be prohibitively expensive, create toxic chemicals in the compost as the result of heating, and would produce a sterile compost devoid of beneficial microorganisms which is one of its most unique and potentially valuable properties. Most endaphic human pathogens and plant pathogens are reduced to minimal levels by pasteurizing temperatures during the initial high-temperature composting stage, and beneficial microorganisms further reduce the population of pathogens during the curing stage.

An additional concern in using sewage sludge compost is the introduction of hazardous levels of heavy metals and pesticides into the soil and at some later point into human and animal food chains. Limits for heavy metal contamination by cadmium, chromium, copper, lead, mercury, nickel, and zinc in sewage sludge compost are established by each state and may vary depending on the intended use of the compost. Food crop production requires the use of compost containing the lowest heavy metal content. Compost with higher levels of heavy metals can be applied to areas which can be used for non food crop production. The heavy metal content of composts will vary dramatically depending on the heavy metal content of the sewage sludge being composted. Whenever possible it would be prudent to select compost with the lowest heavy metal content.

Analysis of landscape waste compost for pesticide content found minimal levels of pesticides, demonstrating the degradation of most of these materials during composting. The current replacement of slowly degradable (i.e., chlorinated) pesticides with more easily degradable organic pesticides has further reduced this hazard. Composting is not a method for the disposal of pesticides and if the materials used to produce compost have large quantities of pesticides, the compost will also have large quantities of pesticides.

No compost is completely free of odor even if produced in aerobic conditions. The goal in the management of a composting facility is to eliminate offensive odors during the composting process and to produce a finished compost which has the aroma of fresh soil. This aroma is characteristic of robust actinomycete growth, a microbe present in most soils and in well-cured compost.

## FIELD APPLICATION OF COMPOST

Compost is a relatively slow release, low analysis, balanced (with the typical exception of potassium) source of plant nutrients, including minor elements (see Table 18–4).

Composts will provide adequate levels of minor elements for excellent growth if applied at rates appropriate for their nitrogen content. (See Table 18–5.) Most landscape waste and sewage sludge composts will have 1–1.5% Nitrogen, 1.5–2% phosphorous, and less than 0.2% of potassium. Sewage sludge compost will usually contain 10% lime, range from 5.6–8.2 and will slowly

**Table 18–4** Mineral content of 35 commercial compost/fertilizers

| Mineral | Mean | Minimum | Maximum |
|---|---|---|---|
| Magnesium | 0.82% | 0.0% | 4.9% |
| Copper | 40.55 ppm | 0.8 ppm | 269 ppm |
| Manganese | 197 ppm | 3.0 ppm | 550.4 ppm |
| Iron | 2620 ppm | 73.6 ppm | 18056 ppm |
| Zinc | 287 ppm | 0.9 ppm | 1733 ppm |
| Chromium | 420 ppm | 1.9 ppm | 5585 ppm |
| Lead | 20.1 ppm | 4.4 ppm | 130 ppm |
| Cadmium | 1.8 ppm | 0.4 ppm | 11.0 ppm |
| Nickel | 12.4 ppm | 3.7 ppm | 25.3 ppm |

*Source:* Evaluation of Natural Amendments as Organic Substitutes for Conventional Fertilizers, Woods End Research Laboratory, Inc.

**Table 18–5** Recommended Rates for the Field Application of Compost

| Uses | Lb/1000 sq. ft. | Remarks |
|---|---|---|
| I Sod Production | | |
| Incorporated | 3–6000 lb | Incorporated into the top 4–6 in. of soil. |
| Unincorporated | 6–18,000 lb | Apply uniformly to surface, irrigate for germination and growth. |
| II Shrub and Tree Production | | |
| Establishment | 1900–7000 lb | Incorporate into the top 6–8 in. of soil. *Do not* use alkaline compost for plants requiring an acid–soil reaction. |
| Maintenance | 200–500 lb | Broadcast uniformly on the surface. |
| III Reclaiming Sub Soil | up to 9000 lb | Incorporate into the top 6 in. Check pH, add limestone or sulfur if needed. For each in. of additional incorporation beyond 6 in. add 1000 lb. |

1500 lb per 1000 sq. ft. equals ½ in. of compost per 1000 sq. ft. of area or 33 wet tons per acre (at 40% moisture and screened with a ½ in. mesh screen). One cubic yard of screened compost at a 40% moisture content will weigh approximately ½ ton and will cover 1000 sq. ft to a depth of ⅓ in.

*Source:* Use of Sewage Sludge Compost for Soil Improvement and Plant Growth. 1979. Science and Education Administration, ARM-NE-6, USDA Beltsville, Md.

increase the pH of soils. Based on its fertilizer value alone most compost cannot be transported substantial distances and remain competitive with high-analysis, slow-release commercial fertilizers.

The physical improvement to soils or potting mixes with the addition of either landscape waste compost or sewage sludge composts are increased cation-exchange capacity, and higher water-holding capacity when blended with sandy soils; and improved soil aggregation, friability and drainage when blended with clay soils. Compost has been successfully substituted for peat moss in many container medium based on its physical properties.

The most unique characteristic of compost is its biological component. A growing number of research reports indicate that use of compost (top dressing turf or incorporation in soil or potting mixes) suppresses the growth of harmful nematodes as well as bacterial and fungal plant diseases (including *Pythium spp., Rhyzoctonia solani, Fusarium oxysporum, Sclerolinia homoeocarpa, S. rolfsii, Phytophthora cinnamomi Typula incarnata, Laetisaria funciformus*). Well-cured compost has decomposed sufficiently so that pathogens can no longer colonize on plant tissue directly, and has a very robust and diverse microbial population. The natural fungicidal property of compost is thought to be both biological (through competition) and chemical in nature (through the production of inhibitors). There is good evidence that using compost as a soil fungicide enhances the effectiveness of biological insect control.

The beneficial microbes do not always become established during the curing process, and researchers at Ohio State University have patented a process for inoculating compost with beneficial disease-suppressing microflora. The beneficial microbes do not last forever. As the compost ages, the microbial population and the disease suppressing properties will diminish. A number of researchers are currently trying to develop quick and reliable methods for determining when the appropriate stage of curing has been reached to insure the production and delivery of consistently high-quality compost. The most reliable methods for determining when compost is properly cured are: (1) an oxygen concentration in the middle of the pile within 10–20% of air one week after turning, (2) a temperature which fluctuates with air temperature, (3) a lack of growth inhibiting properties and (4) an ability to generate less than 200 milligrams of carbon dioxide per kilogram of compost per hour.

Nearly all of the nitrogen in well-cured compost is in an organic form and must be mineralized to ammonia or nitrate to become available for plant growth. The rate of mineralization increases with increasing soil temperatures and increasing rates of rainfall and will range from complete mineralization within 2–3 months during the summer in central Florida to a slow mineralization rate of over 2–4 years in northern climates. The rate of mineralization of cured compost is much slower than that of uncured compost. From a plant production perspective, uncured compost is not a particularly valuable product. If uncured compost is available at a very reasonable price it may be worth finishing the curing process at the nursery before using it. Application of cured compost will have a dramatic impact on the physical properties of the soil, as mentioned earlier, particularly if the soil is depleted of organic matter as the result of soil erosion or production of nursery crops.

A potting mix containing well-cured compost will shrink 5–8% in volume in two years while peat moss and bark or wood chip potting mixes were found to shrink up to 20% in a 2 year period. This is an important consideration in the

2–3 year production of woody landscape plants and in the preparation of special soil mixes for ericaceous plants.

## USE OF COMPOST IN POTTING MIXES

Most sewage sludge and landscape waste composts are alkaline and must be amended with sulfur or an acidic potting amendment to lower the pH to 5.5–7.0. A complete laboratory nutrient analysis of the cured compost is needed to insure high quality plant production. Adjustments in the amounts of fertilizer added to the mix and in the subsequent fertilizer program are necessary with the incorporation of compost. Most recommendations indicate that no fertilizer should be added to a compost potting mix with the possible exception of potassium and that no fertilizer should be applied for 2–3 weeks.

Trials with sewage sludge and landscape waste compost produced excellent growth in Poinsettia, tomatoes, peppers, marigold, chrysanthemum, begonias, zinnia, geranium, Easter lilies, and petunias when cured compost was substituted for peat moss up to 20–30% of the total volume of the mix. Chrysanthemums however, grew well in potting mixes containing as much as 60% compost.

It is not uncommon to have a high initial salt content in a compost potting mix, particularly when using compost that is not completely cured. Leaching the compost potting mix during the first 1–2 days after planting will eliminate this problem, even when growing particularly salt sensitive seedlings. This is a common practice even though not every source of compost will have high salt levels. A 20–33% compost mix will usually provide all the trace elements required for the crop for at least 2 years.

The pH of 50 and 33% compost mixes can be lowered with the addition of granular sulfur (1½–2 lb/yard$^3$ for 50% compost mixes and 1–1½ lb/yard$^3$ for 33% compost mixes) in the production of azaleas, rhododendron, leucothoe, and andromeda. Sulfur lowers the pH faster in a potting mix with compost than in a potting mix without compost as the result of the increased microbial activity.

Wetting and vigorously mixing or grinding a compost-containing mix should be avoided. This results in further reduction of the size of the fine wood particles which will cause them to decompose, creating a potential competition for nutrients between the nursery crop and the composting microflora. The nursery crop will show signs of nutrient deficiencies even though adequate levels of nutrients were present before the vigorous mixing or grinding operation. Wetting agents have proved to be of limited value when applied to compost potting mixes.

## SUMMARY

Composting and the use of compost is an ancient agricultural practice which has become a modern method for the disposal of organic urban waste products. Understanding the proper management of the composting process and how compost can be most effectively used in the production of nursery crops can make it a very valuable resource. The production and use of compost is environmentally constructive. Nursery managers have the opportunity to take a leading role in maintaining the quality of our environment and improving the efficiency of their plant production systems.

## REFERENCES

BURGE, W. D., L. J. SIKORA, C. F. TESTER, S. B. HORNICK, G. E. WILSON, J. F. PARR, E. EPSTEIN, P. B. MARSH, R. L. CHANEY, and D. COLACICCO. Manual for composting sewage sludge, the Beltsville Aerated-Pile Method, Municipal Environmental Research Laboratory, Office of Research and Development, U.S. E.P.A., Cincinnati, Ohio.

J. GOLDSTEIN, editor, BioCycle, J. G. Press Inc., Emmaus, Pa.

HORNICK, S. B., J. J. MURRAY, R. L. CHANEY, L. J. SIKORA, S. F. PARR, W. D. BURGE, G. B. WILSON, and C. F. TESTER. 1979. Use of sewage sludge compost for soil improvement and plant growth. Science and Education Administration, ARM-NE-6, USDA, Beltsville, Md.

BRINTON, W. F., and M. D. SEEKIUS. 1988. Composting fish by-products: a feasibility study, time and tide research and development, mid-coast compost consortium, Woods End Research Laboratory, Mt. Vernon, Maine.

STAFF of BIOCYCLE. The Art and Science of Composting, Journal of Waste Recycling, J. B. Press Inc., Emmaus, Pa.

R. RYNK, ed. 1992. On-farm composting handbook. Northeast regional agricultural engineering service. Riley-Robb Hall Cooperative Extension, Ithaca, N.Y.

Appendix **A**

# Guide To Plant Locators

**All-Industry Horticultural Buyers Guide**
Branch-Smith Publishing
P.O. Box 1868
Fort Worth, TX 76101
800/433–5612

**Andersen Horticultural Library's Source List of Plants and Seeds**
Minnesota Landscape Arboretum
3675 Arboretum Drive
P.O. Box 39
Chanhassen, MN 55317
612/443–2440

**Buyer's Guide**
Rhode Island Nurserymen's Assn.
P.O. Box 99
Kingston, RI 02881
401/792–4528

**Combined Rose List**
A. Dobson, and P. Schneider
P.O. Box 16035
Rocky River, OH 52101
Sources for 7500 roses from 171 nurseries.

**Composite Stock List**
L. I. Nursery Growers List
P.O. Box 964
Riverhead, NY 11901

**Directory of Forest Tree Nurseries in the United States AAN**
1250 I Street, N.W., Suite 500
Washington, D.C.
202/789–2900
(#2–41350)

**Directory and Buyer's Guide**
Oregon Association of Nurserymen
2780 S.E. Harrison
Milwaukee,OR 97222
503/653–8733

**1992 National Daylily Locator**
Capability Books
2379 Highway 46
Deer Park, WI 54007
800/247–8154

**Flower Finder**
Inforpoint Software
P.O. Box 83DM
Arcola, MO 65603
407/424–3424
DOS-operated computer program
information on annuals and
perennials from seed.

**Fruit, Berry, and Nut Inventory**
Seed Saver Publications
Rt. 3, Box 239
Decorah, IO 52101
284 mail order nurseries.

**Gardening by Mail (a Source Book) 3rd Ed.**
Tusker Press
P.O. Box 1338
Sebastopol, CA 95473
707/829–9189

**Greenscope and Greenscan**
North Range, Inc.
P.O. Box 1188
Lumberton, NC 28359
Computerized nursery info
for NC, SC, TN, VA, GA,
LA, MS, and AL.

**Guide to Pennsylvania Nursery Stock**
PA Nurserymen's Assn.
1924 N. Second Street
Harrisburg, PA 17102
717/328–1673

**Handbook of Landscape Tree Cultivars**
East Prairie Publishing Co.
P.O. Box 174
Gladstone, IL 71437

**Fax Directory**
P.O. Box 1485
436 E. Fifth Avenue
Mount Dora, FL 32757
904/383–8811

**Hortus Opus**
B. Mendoza Gardens
18 E. 16th Street
New York, NY 10003
212/989–4253
Computerized plant index.

**Hortus Northwest**
P.O. Box 955
Canby, OR 97013
503/266–7968
Sources of native
Pacific-Northwest plants.

**Hortus Source List**
L. H. Baily Hortorium
462 Mann Library
Cornell University
Ithaca, NY 14853

**Landscape Materials Information Service**
P.O. Box 216
Callicoon, NY 12723
914/887–4401
Covers New England, NY,
NJ, PA, DE, MD, MI, IL,
KY, VA, and WV.

**Long Island Nursery Growers Guide**
P.O. Box 964
Riverhead, NY 11901

**North Carolina Grown Source Guide**
N.C.S.U. Arboretum
P.O. Box 7609
Raleigh, NC 27695–7609

**Nursery Exchange**
1010 Georgia Highway
Franklin, NC 28734
800/346–2874
704/524–9152
An electronic network of horticulturally related buyers and sellers.

**Nursery Source Manual**
Brooklyn Botanic Garden
1000 Washington Ave.
Brooklyn, NY 11225–1099

**Nursery Source for Native Plants**
New England Wildflower Society
Dept. NS Garden in the Woods
Hemenway Road
Farmington, MA 01701

**Nursery Stock Index**
Michigan Nursery and Landscape Assn.
819 N. Washington Ave., Suite 2
Lansing, MI 48906
517/487-1282

**Nursery Stock Survey**
Ohio Nurserymen's Assn.
2021 E. Dublin-Granville Rd.#1
Columbus, OH 43229–3530
614/431-2452

**Perennials—A Nursery Source Manual**
(Handbook #118)
Brooklyn Botanic Garden
1000 Washington Ave.
Brooklyn, NY 11225-1099

**PGA Brokers, Inc.**
P.O. Box 711
Marshfield, MA 02050
617/834-0001
Specialize in foliage and flowering plants.

**Plant-Line**
P.O. Box 8143
Holland, MI 49422
616/399-8830
An electronic horticultural service.

**Plantfinder**
Betrock Information Systems, Inc.
1601 North Palm Ave., Suite 303
Pembroke Pines, FL 33026
800/627-3819
305/438-2620
Monthly publication with 500 foliage and woody plant nurseries.

**Plant Locator**
Ornamental Growers Assn.
of Northern Illinois
P.O. Box 67
Batavia, IL 60510
708/879-0520

**Plantmaster**
P.O. Box 90525
Santa Barbara, CA 93190
805/964-7497
A professional plant data base referenced to color photographs.

**Plantsearch**
Bill Hutchenson
Betrock Publishing, Inc.
Betrock Information Systems, Inc.
1601 North Palm Ave. Suite 303
Pembroke Pines, FL 33026
A computerized locator, 10,000 plant listings.

**Plantsource**
PlantSource Magazine
606 110th NE, Suite 200
Bellvue, WA 98004

**Select A Plant**
Dennis Watson
Software Support Office
University of Florida
Gainesville, FL 32611
A landscape plant info and retrieval system.

**Sources of Native Seeds and Plants**
Soil and Water Conservation Society (SWES)
7515 NE Ankeny Rd.
Ankeny, IO 50021-9764

**Sources of Shade Trees in the United States**
OARDC, Mailing Room
1680 Madison Avenue
Wooster, OH 44691-4096
216/263-3775

**Suwannee Valley Florida**
Plant Locator Directory
Rt. 2, Box 2181
Live Oak, FL 32060
904/362-1725
Plants produced by 35 nurseries in Florida.

**Tampa Bay Wholesale Growers**
Plant Locator
6804-C Gunn Highway
Tampa, FL 33625
813/920-4393

**WSNLA Directory**
Washington State Nursery
and Landscape Association
Directory and Buyer's Guide
Furnishes information about
nursery and landscape
suppliers throughout the country.

**Wildland and Native Tree Foundation**
2402 Hoffman Dr. NE
Albuquerque, NM 87110
Source of custom collected seed from wild growing
    and native plants of the southwest.

**Wisconsin Wholesale Source Booklet**
WI Nurserymen's Assn.
9910 W. Layton Ave.,
Greenfield, WI 53228
414/529-4705

**Foreign Sources**

**Canadian**
The Canadian Plant Source Book
C. and P. Ashley
93 Fentimen Avenue
Ottawa, ONT K1S OT7
Canada

**Woody Plant Source List**
Canada Nursery Trades Association
Mississauga, ONT L4W 1R1
Canada
416/629-1367

**England**
**The Plant Finder**
The Hardy Plant Society
Worcester, WR2 4BR
England

**France**
Ou Trrouver La Plant
D. Perriere Hachette
79 Bd. St. Germain
Paris, France 75006

**Germany**
Pflantzen Einkaufsfuhrer
Verlog Eugen Ulmer
P.O. Box 70 05 61
D-7000 Stuttgart 70
Germany

**Switzerland**
Der Stauden Finder
Balz Schneider
Im Veltin 38
CH-8709 Meilen,
Switzerland

# Partial List of Books and Bulletins Pertaining to Areas of Nursery Management

**ARBORICULTURE**

*ARBORICULTURE.* 1992. 2nd. ed. Richard Harris. Prentice-Hall, Inc., Englewood Cliffs, N.J.

**COMPUTERS**

*COMPUTERS.* 1986. Special Issue. American Nurseryman. Vol. 164, No. 5. American Nurseryman, Chicago.

**CONTAINER GROWING**

*CONTAINER GROWING.* 1969. American Nurseryman, Chicago.

*CONTAINER GROWING OF WOODY ORNAMENTAL PLANTS IN FLORIDA.* 1978. Bulletin 793, Agricultural Experiment Station, University of Florida, Gainesville, Fla.

*PLANT PRODUCTION IN CONTAINERS.* 1989. C. E. Whitcomb. Lacebark Publications, Stillwater, Okla.

**GARDEN CENTER MANAGEMENT**

*CARE OF NURSERY STOCK IN RETAIL OUTLETS.* 1978. L. W. Kennedy and E. M. Smith. Bulletin 562. Cooperative Extension Service, Ohio State University, Columbus, Ohio.

*OPERATING A GARDEN CENTER*, 5th ed. 1957. J. J. Pinney. American Nurseryman Publishing Company, Chicago.

*PROFITABLE GARDEN CENTER MANAGEMENT.* 1982. L. Berninger. Reston Publishing Co., Inc., Reston, Va.

## NURSERY MANAGEMENT

*ENVIRONMENTAL PLANT PRODUCTION AND MARKETING.* 1974. T. Furuta. Cox Publishing Co., Arcadia, Calif.

*REWARDING CAREERS IN THE NURSERY INDUSTRY.* 1990. William Flemer, III. 1990. American Nursery Publishing Co.

*FOREST NURSERY MANUAL: PRODUCTION OF BAREROOT SEEDLINGS.* 1984. M. L. Duryea and T. D. Landis, eds. College of Forestry, Oregon State University, Corvallis, Oreg.

*NURSERY PRODUCTION.* 1989. C. W. Heuser, Jr. and R. F. Stinson. Pennsylvania State University, Pa.

*PRODUCTION OF LANDSCAPE PLANTS.* 1989. C. E. Whitcomb. Lacebark Publications, Stillwater, Okla.

## PEST CONTROL

*SCIENTIFIC GUIDE TO PEST CONTROL OPERATIONS.* 1978. P. Villard. Harvest Publishing Co., New York.

*TREE FRUIT AND ORNAMENTAL PESTICIDE GUIDE.* 1985. Thompson Publications, Fresno, Calif.

### Diseases

*DISEASES AND PESTS OF ORNAMENTAL PLANTS.* 1978. P. P. Pirone. John Wiley & Sons, Inc., New York.

*DISEASES OF FOREST AND SHADE TREES OF THE U.S.* 1971. USDA Agricultural Handbook 386. Superintendent of Documents, Washington, D.C.

*DISEASES OF TREES AND SHRUBS.* 1987. W. A. Sinclair, H. H. Lyon, and W. T. Johnson. Cornell University Press, New York.

*DISEASES OF SHADE TREES.* 1978. T. A. Tattar. Academic Press, Inc., New York.

*FOREST NURSERY DISEASES IN THE UNITED STATES.* USDA Agricultural Handbook 470, Superintendent of Documents, Washington, D.C.

### Insects

*A GUIDE TO INSECT INJURY OF CONIFERS IN THE LAKE STATES.* 1976. L. F. Wilson. USDA Agricultural Handbook 501. Superintendent of Documents, Washington, D.C.

*INSECTS AS PESTS.* 1973. H. S. Zinn and G. S. Fichter. Doubleday & Company, Inc., New York.

*INSECTS OF EASTERN PINES.* 1973. A. H. Rose and O. H. Lindquist. Canadian Forestry Service Publication 1313. Information Canada Center, Toronto, Ontario.

*INSECTS THAT FEED ON TREES AND SHRUBS*, an illustrated practical guide. 1988. W. T. Johnson and H. H. Lyon. Cornell University Press, Ithaca, N.Y.

### Weeds

*DIAGNOSIS AND PREVENTION OF HERBICIDE INJURY.* 1976. Michigan State University, East Lansing, Mich.

*HERBICIDE HANDBOOK.* 1989. Weed Science Society of America, Champaign, Ill.

*NEBRASKA WEEDS.* 1975. Nebraska Department of Agricultural, Lincoln, Neb.

*WEED SCIENCE: PRINCIPLES,* 2nd ed. 1983. W. P. Anderson. West Publishing Co., St. Paul, Minn.

*WEED SCIENCE, PRINCIPLES AND PRACTICES.* G. C. Klingman and F. Ashton. John Wiley & Sons, Inc., New York, N.Y.

## PLANT PROPAGATION

*GRAFTERS HANDBOOK.* R. J. Gardner. Am. Nurseryman, Chicago.

*NURSERY STOCK MANUAL.* 1975. J. G. D. Lamb, J. C. Kelly, and P. Bowbrick. Grower Books, London.

*PLANT PROPAGATION PRINCIPLES AND PRACTICES.* 1990. 5th ed. H. T. Hartmann, D. E. Kester, and F. T. Davies. Prentice Hall, Inc., Englewood Cliffs, N.J.

*PRACTICAL WOODY PLANT PROPAGATION FOR NURSERY GROWERS.* 1986. B. MacDonald. Timber Press, Portland, Oreg.

*PROCEEDINGS OF THE INTERNATIONAL PLANT PROPAGATORS' SOCIETY.* Center for Urban Horticulture, University of Washington, Seattle, Wa.

*THE REFERENCE MANUAL OF WOODY PLANT PROPAGATION.* 1987. M. A. Dirr and C. W. Heuser, Jr. Varsity Press, Inc., Athens, Ga.

*SEEDS OF WOODY PLANTS IN THE UNITED STATES.* 1974. C. S. Schopmeyer. USDA Agricultural Handbook 450. Superintendent of Documents, Washington, D.C.

## SOILS

*SOIL AND PLANT ANALYSIS LABORATORY REGISTRY FOR THE UNITED STATES AND CANADA.* 1992. Council on Soil Testing and Plant Analysis, Georgia University Station, Athens, Ga.

## OTHER PUBLICATIONS

*A TECHNICAL GLOSSARY OF HORTICULTURE AND LANDSCAPE TERMINOLOGY.* 1971. Horticultural Research Institute, Washington, D.C.

*TREE AND SHRUB TRANSPLANTING MANUAL.* 1981. E. B. Himelick. International Society of Arboriculture, Urbana, Ill.

# Appendix C
# Addresses of Nursery-Related Organizations*

All-America Rose Selections
P. O. Box 218
Shenandoah, IO 51601

American Association of Nurserymen
1250 I Street, NW, Suite 500
Washington, DC 20005

American Association of Nurserymen's
Group Insurance Trust
1250 I Street, NW, Suite 500
Washington, DC 20005

American Society of Agronomy
677 South Segor Road
Madison, WI 53711

Associated Landscape Contractors
of America
1750 Old Meadow Road
McLean, VA 22101

Garden Centers of America
1250 I Street, NW, Suite 500
Washington, DC 20005

Garden Council
500 North Michigan, Suite 1400
Chicago, IL 60611

Horticultural Research Institute, Inc.
1250 I Street, NW, Suite 500
Washington, DC 20005

The International Plant Propagator's
Society
Center for Urban Horticulture
University of Washington, GF-15
Seattle, WA 98195

International Society of Arboriculture
3 Lincoln Square, Box 71
Urbana, IL 61801

*Addresses subject to change.

Landscape Materials Information
Service
Callicoon, NY 12723

Mail-Order Association of
Nurserymen, Inc.
210 Cartwright Boulevard
Massapequa Park, NY 11762

National Arborist Association
3537 Stratford Road
Wantagh, NY 11793

National Association of Plant Patent
Owners
1250 I Street, NW, Suite 500
Washington, DC 20005

National Landscape Association
1250 I Street, NW, Suite 500
Washington, DC 20005

Nurserymen's Protective Association
c/o McGill & Son
Fairview, OR 97024

Perennial Plant Association
249 Howlett Hall
Ohio State University
2001 Fyffe Court
Columbus, OH 43210

Southern Nurserymen's Association
3813 Hillsboro Road
Nashville, TN 37215

Wholesale Nursery Growers
of America
1250 I Street, NW, Suite 500
Washington, DC 20005

# Appendix **D**
# Trade Journals*Related to the Nursery Industry

American Nurseryman
111 N. Canal Street
Suite 545
Chicago, IL 60606

Florist & Nursery Exchange
434 S. Wabash Avenue
Chicago, IL 60605

Garden Industry of America
Box 1092
Minneapolis, MN 55440

Grounds Maintenance
1014 Wyandotte Street
Kansas City, MO 64105

Home & Garden Supply Merchandisers
2501 Wayzata Boulevard
P.O. Box 67
Minneapolis, MN 55440

HortTechnology
American Society for
    Horticultural Science
113 South West St, Suite 400
Alexandria, VA 22314-2824

Journal of Arboriculture
International Society of Arboriculture
P.O. Box 908
Urbana, IL 61801

Journal of Environmental Horticulture
Horticulture Research Institute
1250 I Street, NW, Suite 500
Washington, DC 20005

Landscape Architecture
Schuster Building
1500 Bardstown Road
Louisville, KY 40205

*Addresses subject to change.

Landscape Design & Construction
2048 Cotner Avenue
Los Angeles, CA 90025

Landscape Industry
850 Elm Grove Road
Elm Grove, WI 53122

Lawn/Garden/Outdoor Living
1014 Wyandotte Street
Kansas City, MO 64105

Midwest Landscaping
1706 W. Chase Street
Chicago, IL 60626

Modern Garden Center
208 James Street
Barrington, IL 60010

Northwest Garden Supplier
311 Henry Building
Portland, OR 97204

Nursery Business
Brantwood Publications, Inc.
Northwood Plaza Station
Clearwater, FL 33519-0360

Nursery Manager
Branch-Smith Publishing
120 St. Louis Avenue
Fort Worth, TX 76104

Nursery Product News
9800 Detroit Avenue
Cleveland, OH 44102

Pacific Coast Nurserymen & Garden
    Center Dealer
832 S. Baldwin Avenue
Arcadia, CA 91007

Southern Florist & Nurserymen
P.O. Box 1868
Fort Worth, TX 76101

Turf-Grass Times
218 19th Avenue
North Jacksonville Beach, FL 32050

Weeds Trees and Turf
9800 Detroit Avenue
Cleveland, OH 44102

Western Landscaping News
1623 S. La Cienega Boulevard
Los Angeles, CA 90035

# Appendix E
# Approximate Metric Conversions

| Unit | To Metric | | | | From Metric | | |
|------|-----------|---|---|---|-------------|---|---|
| Length | inches | × | 2.5 | = centimeters | × | 0.4 | = inches |
| | feet | × | 30.5 | = centimeters | × | 0.033 | = feet |
| | yards | | 0.9 | = meters | × | 3.3 | = feet |
| | miles | × | 1.6 | = kilometers | × | 0.62 | = miles |
| Area | inches$^2$ | × | 6.5 | = centimeters$^2$ | × | 0.16 | = inches$^2$ |
| | feet$^2$ | × | 0.09 | = meters$^2$ | × | 11.1 | = feet |
| | yards$^2$ | × | 0.8 | = meters$^2$ | × | 1.1 | = yards$^2$ |
| | miles$^2$ | × | 2.8 | = kilometers$^2$ | × | 0.36 | = miles$^2$ |
| | acres | × | 0.4 | = hectares | × | 2.5 | = acres |
| Mass | ounces | × | 28.0 | = grams | × | 0.035 | = ounces |
| | pounds | × | 0.45 | = kilograms | × | 2.2 | = pounds |
| | tons (2000 lb) | × | 0.9 | = tonnes (1000kg) | × | 1.1 | = tons |
| Volume | teaspoons | × | 5 | = milliliters | × | 0.2 | = teaspoons |
| | tablespoons | × | 15 | = milliliters | × | 0.007 | = tablespoons |
| | fluid ounces | × | 30 | = milliliters | × | 0.03 | = fluid ounces |
| | cups | × | 0.25 | = liters | × | 4.17 | = cups |
| | pints | × | 0.47 | = liters | × | 2.1 | = pints |
| | quarts | × | 0.95 | = liters | × | 1.06 | = quarts |
| | gallons | × | 3.8 | = liters | × | 0.26 | = gallons |
| | feet$^3$ | × | 0.3 | = meters$^3$ | × | 35.0 | = feet$^3$ |
| | yards$^3$ | × | 0.76 | = meters$^3$ | × | 1.3 | = yards$^3$ |
| Temperature | (Fahrenheit − 32°) | × | 0.56 | = Celsius | × | 1.8 + 32° | = Fahrenheit |

# Rate per 1000 Ft² Nomograph

| Area | | Quantity of material | Rate Per 1,000 (sq. ft.) |
|---|---|---|---|
| sq. ft. | acres | | |

# Rate per Acre
# Nomograph

| Area | | Quantity of material | Rate Per acre |
|---|---|---|---|
| acres | sq. ft. | | |

Area

acres    sq. ft.

| | |
|---|---|
| 5 | 200,000 |
| 3 | |
| | 100,000 |
| 2 | |
| | 50,000 |
| 1 | |
| .8 | |
| .6 | |
| | 20,000 |
| .4 | |
| | 10,000 |
| | |
| | 5000 |
| .1 | |
| .06 | |
| | 2000 |
| .04 | |
| | 1000 |
| .02 | |
| | 500 |
| .01 | |

Quantity of material

4000
2000
1000
600
400
200
100
60
40
20
10
6
4
2
1
.6
.4
.2
.1
.06
.04
.02
.01

Rate Per acre

1000
800
600
400
200
100
80
60
40
20
10
8
6
4
2
1

# Fertilizer Proportioner
# Nomograph, 100 ppm*

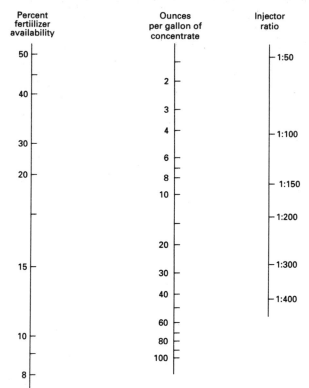

| Percent fertilizer availability | Ounces per gallon of concentrate | Injector ratio |
|---|---|---|
| 50 | | 1:50 |
| 40 | 2 | |
| | 3 | |
| 30 | 4 | 1:100 |
| | 6 | |
| 20 | 8 | 1:150 |
| | 10 | 1:200 |
| | 20 | |
| 15 | 30 | 1:300 |
| | 40 | 1:400 |
| | 60 | |
| 10 | 80 | |
| | 100 | |
| 8 | | |

*To obtain other ppm concentrations, multiply by appropriate factor. For example, to obtain 200 ppm, multiply ounces per gallon by 2.0; to obtain 50 ppm, multiply by 0.5.

# Appendix I
# Determining the Weight of B&B Plants

Nurserymen, landscape contractors, and arborists have need, periodically, to determine the weight of B&B trees. They need to estimate weight in order to determine what type of equipment will be necessary to move the plant or plants, estimate cost, and plan transportation routes in accordance with weight restrictions on some roads during the spring-thaw season in certain parts of the country. The weight of B&B plants is dependent upon a number of factors, including the size and species of the plants, the size and shape of the ball, and the soil type, including its moisture content.

The *weight of small plants*, whether they are B&B or in containers, can be readily determined by weighing plants in selected sizes and determining the total weight by multiplying the number of plants within a size class by the average weight of the class. When a group of selected small plants was subjected to a volume/weight analysis, the results indicated that the weight of B&B plants was directly related to the volume of soil, which was related to the type of root system; shallow-rooted plants weighed less than relatively deep-rooted plants. There was also a correlation between ball size and digging time (Table I-1).

*Determining the weight of larger plants* is a little more challenging, since the weight must be estimated without the use of scales. This can be done by either calculating the weight of the soil ball plus the weight of the tree or by abstracting the estimated weight from a weight table or graph. Various formulas have been suggested for calculating the weight of the soil ball, including:

1. $W = \frac{2}{3}(D^2 \times d) \times 110$ (dimensions in feet)
2. $W = \frac{2}{3}(D \times d) \times 0.075$ (dimensions in inches)
3. $W = \pi \dfrac{d}{3}(r_1^2 + r_1 r_2 + r_2^2) \times 110$ (dimensions in feet)

where

> $D$ = diameter of top of the ball
> $d$ = depth of the ball
> $r_1$ = radius of the top of the ball
> $r_2$ = radius of the base of the ball
> $\pi$ = 3.1417

For each formula, certain assumptions are made. In (1) and (2), it is assumed that the volume of the soil approximates two-thirds that of a cube-like block. In (1) and (3) it is assumed that the weight of an "average" cubic foot of soil is 110 lb; whereas formula (2) assumes that it is 0.075 lb/in.[3] (129.6 lb/ft³).

The weight of a tree can be determined by estimating the volume of the tree and multiplying by the average weight of a cubic foot of wood. The volume can be estimated by measuring the diameter (caliper) of the tree, determining the square-foot area (Appendix J), and this value multiplied by the effective height of the main stem or primary branches. (A subjective assessment must be made as to the effective height.)

The weight of a cubic foot of wood varies considerably from species to species. Wood in the red oak group averages 64 lb/ft³, whereas northern white cedar is a relatively light wood weighing 28 lb/ft³. However, on an average the wood of most trees used for landscape purposes weighs approximately 55 lb/ft³. Thus, a tree 10 in. in diameter, 1 ft above ground level, and 60 ft tall would have an estimated weight of 1800 lb (0.545 ft² × 60 ft × 55 lb/ft³). These calculations are based on the assumption that the total volume of the tree approximates the volume of a cylinder whose caliper and height can be measured.

If these assumptions are valid and since the *American Standards for Nursery Stock* recommends certain minimum depths for balls within a specific size class, it is possible to calculate the approximate weights for balls within these classes and to plot these data onto semilog paper (Appendix I), from which the weight can be read directly without further calculations. A second curve can be drawn depicting the combined weight of the tree and soil ball.

**TABLE I–2** Volume/Weight/Digging Time Relationship of Selected B&B Evergreen Shrubs

| | *Average Weight of B&B Plants (lb)* | *Average Ball Volume (ft³)* | *Proportionate Weight of Soil (%)* | *Average Time to B&B (min)* |
|---|---|---|---|---|
| Japanese holly, 18-24 in. crown, deep rooted | 52.8 | 0.63 | 90.6 | 10.1 |
| Pfitzer juniper, 18-24 in. crown, deep-rooted | 50.3 | 0.63 | 95.9 | 8.7 |
| Evergreen azalea, 18-in. crown, shallow-rooted | 22.1 | 0.45 | 90.1 | 5.2 |

*Source:* After Pease (1959).

# REFERENCES

AMERICAN ASSOCIATION OF NURSERYMEN. 1986. American standards for nursery Stock. AAN, Washington, D.C.

PEASE, R. W. 1959. The balled and burlapped pack for ornamental shrubs and trees. W. Va. Univ. Agric. Exp. Sta. Bull. 432, October.

PIRONE, P. P. 1978. Tree maintenance, 5th ed. John Wiley & Sons, Inc., New York.

TREE PRESERVATION BULL. 1, U.S. National Park Service.

FOREST PRODUCTS LABORATORY. 1940. Wood handbook. Superintendent of Documents, Washington, D.C.

# Appendix J
# Approximate Weight of B&B Plants

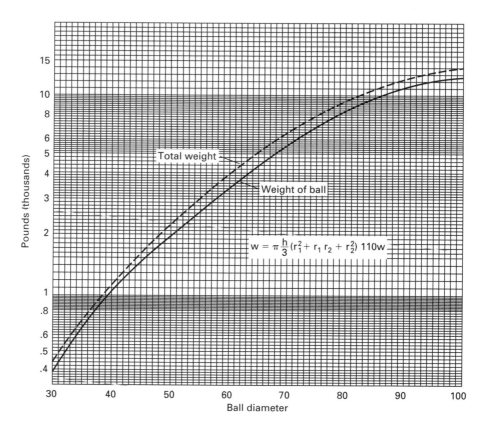

# Appendix **K**
# Area of Circles in Square Feet

Diameter in Inches and Half-Inches

$$A = \pi r^2 = \tfrac{1}{4}\pi d^2 = 0.7854 d^2$$

| Diameter | 0.0 | 0.5 |
|---|---|---|
| 1 | 0.006 | 0.012 |
| 2 | 0.022 | 0.034 |
| 3 | 0.049 | 0.067 |
| 4 | 0.087 | 0.111 |
| 5 | 0.136 | 0.165 |
| 6 | 0.196 | 0.230 |
| 7 | 0.267 | 0.307 |
| 8 | 0.349 | 0.394 |
| 9 | 0.442 | 0.492 |
| 10 | 0.545 | 0.601 |
| 11 | 0.660 | 0.721 |
| 12 | 0.785 | 0.852 |
| 13 | 0.922 | 0.994 |
| 14 | 1.069 | 1.147 |
| 15 | 1.227 | 1.310 |
| 16 | 1.396 | 1.485 |
| 17 | 1.576 | 1.670 |
| 18 | 1.767 | 1.867 |
| 19 | 1.969 | 2.074 |
| 20 | 2.181 | 2.292 |
| 21 | 2.405 | 2.521 |
| 22 | 2.640 | 2.761 |
| 23 | 2.885 | 3.012 |
| 24 | 3.142 | 3.275 |

# Appendix L
# Values for Selected Rates of i

Future Value $(1 + i)^n$ and Present Value $1/(1 + i)^n$

|      | 6.0% |        | 6.5% |        | 7.0% |        | 7.5% |        | 8.0% |        | 8.5% |        |
|------|------|--------|------|--------|------|--------|------|--------|------|--------|------|--------|
| Year | FV   | PV     | FV   | PV     | FV   | PV     | FV   | PV     | FV   | PV     | FV   | PV     |
| 0    | 1.0000 | 1.0000 | 1.0000 | 1.0000 | 1.0000 | 1.0000 | 1.0000 | 1.0000 | 1.0000 | 1.0000 | 1.0000 | 1.0000 |
| 1    | 1.0600 | 0.0434 | 1.0650 | 0.9390 | 1.0700 | 0.9346 | 1.0750 | 0.9302 | 1.0800 | 0.9259 | 1.0850 | 0.9216 |
| 2    | 1.1236 | 0.8900 | 1.1342 | 0.8817 | 1.1449 | 0.8734 | 1.1556 | 0.8653 | 1.1664 | 0.8573 | 1.1772 | 0.8484 |
| 3    | 1.1910 | 0.8396 | 1.2079 | 0.8278 | 1.2250 | 0.8163 | 1.2423 | 0.8050 | 1.2597 | 0.7938 | 1.2773 | 0.7829 |
| 4    | 1.2625 | 0.7921 | 1.2865 | 0.7732 | 1.3108 | 0.7629 | 1.3355 | 0.7488 | 1.3607 | 0.7350 | 1.3859 | 0.7216 |
| 5    | 1.3382 | 0.7473 | 1.3701 | 0.7299 | 1.4026 | 0.7130 | 1.4356 | 0.6966 | 1.4693 | 0.6806 | 1.5037 | 0.6650 |
| 6    | 1.4185 | 0.7050 | 1.4591 | 0.6853 | 1.5007 | 0.6663 | 1.5433 | 0.6480 | 1.5869 | 0.6302 | 1.6315 | 0.6129 |
| 7    | 1.5036 | 0.6651 | 1.5540 | 0.6435 | 1.6059 | 0.6227 | 1.6590 | 0.6928 | 1.7138 | 0.5853 | 1.7701 | 0.5649 |
| 8    | 1.5938 | 0.6274 | 1.6550 | 0.6042 | 1.7182 | 0.5820 | 1.7835 | 0.5607 | 1.8509 | 0.5427 | 1.9206 | 0.5207 |
| 9    | 1.6895 | 0.5919 | 1.7626 | 0.5674 | 1.8485 | 0.5439 | 1.9172 | 0.5216 | 1.9990 | 0.5002 | 2.0839 | 0.4799 |
| 10   | 1.7908 | 0.5584 | 1.8771 | 0.5327 | 1.9672 | 0.5083 | 2.0610 | 0.4852 | 2.1589 | 0.4632 | 2.2610 | 0.4423 |

# Appendix M

# Relationship between T, RH, VP, and VPD

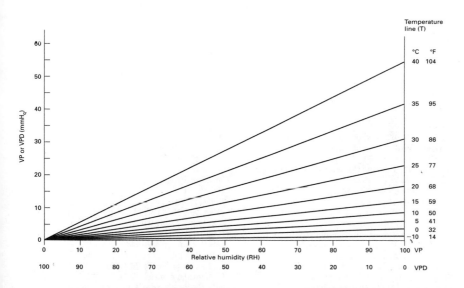

Relationship between temperature (T), relative humidity (RH), vapor pressure (VP), and vapor pressure deficit (VPD). To obtain VP at selected T, read RH scale from left to right. To obtain VPD at selected T, read RH scale from right to left.

# Index